CIVILIZED SHAMANS

Civilized Shamans

Buddhism in Tibetan Societies

Geoffrey Samuel

SMITHSONIAN INSTITUTION PRESS
WASHINGTON AND LONDON

To my mother, Gerty Samuel

Copy Editor: Robin A. Gould
Production Editor: Duke Johns
Designer: Kathleen Sims

Library of Congress Cataloging-in-Publication Data

Samuel, Geoffrey.
Civilized shamans : Buddhism in Tibetan societies / Geoffrey Samuel.
p. cm.
Includes bibliographical references and index.
ISBN 1-56098-231-4
1. Buddhism—China—Tibet. 2. Tibet (China)—Religion.
I. Title.
BQ7604.S26 1993
294.3'923'09515—dc20 92-12590

British Library Cataloguing-in-Publication Data is available

Manufactured in the United States of America
00 99 98 97 96 95 5 4 3 2

∞ The paper used in this publication meets the minimum requirements of the American National Standard for Performance of Paper for Printed Library Materials Z39.48-1984.

Contents

PART TWO

PART THREE

Preface

This book has been a long time in the writing. My initial fieldwork with Tibetans in India and Nepal took place in 1971–1972. The first version of the book was written during nine months I spent at the University of California in Berkeley in 1981–1982 as a research associate in the Department of Anthropology. In the subsequent years, the plan of the book has undergone several drastic changes, and three chapters that originally formed part of it have grown into a separate work on anthropological theory (*Mind, Body and Culture*, Cambridge University Press), which was published in 1990.

The nature of the project has also changed significantly over the years, in part because of the enormous growth in Tibetan studies since the mid–1970s. My primary objective throughout has been to present a coherent interpretation of Tibetan religion, but I have also tried to provide an overview of the present state of research, and a baseline from which other interpretations can begin. This survey aspect applies particularly to the overview of Tibetan societies in Part One, but I have tried throughout the book to give the reader an orientation towards the current literature. This has not been attempted since the surveys of Rolf Stein (*Tibetan Civilization*, 1972a), David Snellgrove and Hugh Richardson (*Cultural History of Tibet*, 1968) and Giuseppe Tucci (*Religions of Tibet*, 1980), books which were first published in 1962, 1968, and 1970 respectively, and were in any case not concerned with the anthropological literature, which hardly existed in those times. Work on Tibetan religion is scattered over several disciplines and languages, and it is not easy for a beginner in the field to appreciate how much has been done in how many areas, or for that matter to see the major gaps that still remain. I have no doubt that my efforts in this direction will rapidly become outdated, but I still hope that they will be of use for some time to come.

My own interpretation of Tibetan religion has also changed over the years, as I have learned more from the work of others and from my own research. Tibetan religion now appears both more original, and more an expression of universal human processes and abilities, than it did when I wrote my doctoral dissertation. I have tried in this book to suggest some of the ways in which the history of human thought in Tibet is of value to us all, and to sketch the specific forms that general human issues and conflicts took in Tibetan societies. Tibetanists may find some of the positions I have taken controversial, for example my comments on the defects of a Lhasa-centered view of Tibetan societies, or my general emphasis on the shamanic aspects of Tibetan Buddhism. I would be pleased if the book were to provoke some debate in areas that have been too prone, at times, to the respectful repetition of received wisdom. The rehearsing of taken for granted knowledge has little to do with genuine insight, whether we are talking about *saṃvṛti-* or *paramārthasatya*.

It remains to thank those who have assisted me, in many ways, during the writing of the book. They include Vincanne Adams, Michael Allen, Anak Dorje Namgyal, Michael Aris, Barbara Aziz, Yael Bentor, Ed Bernbaum, Ricardo Canzio, Krystyna Cech, Anne Chayet, Barry Clark, Barbara Cousins, Sophie Day, Elaine Dobson, Larry Epstein, Steve and Joan Goodman, Nelson Graburn, Toni Huber, Guan Jian, Marie-Anne Hockings, Bruce Kapferer, Ivan Karp, Linda Kemp, Per Kvaerne, Andrea Loseries, Dan Martin, Per Matthiesen, Bill Newell, Jamyang Norbu, Maria Phylactou, Françoise Pommaret, Santi Rozario, Ilana Silber, Martin Southwold, Elvira Sprogis, John Stephenson, David Templeman, Dwight Tkatschow, Linley Walker, Gehan Wijeyewardene, Chris Willcox, Jan Willis, Peter Wilson, Yang Enhong, and Zhang Liansheng. Others have doubtless been unintentionally omitted, but I am no less grateful to them.

My doctoral research in 1971–1972 was supported by a grant from the Social Science Research Council (U.K.). This book has also benefitted from recent field research on the Gesar epic and Eastern Tibetan society, which was made possible by an Australia Research Council award. I thank the authorities of the University of Newcastle, who allowed me research leave for this project, and also supported three overseas study leave periods and my attendance at the Csoma de Körös conference in Hungary in 1984 and the 5th IATS Seminar at Narita, Japan in 1989. The staff of the Auchmuty Library at the University of Newcastle also deserve much gratitude for their assistance, particularly with countless requests for obscure interlibrary loans.

Stanley Tambiah supervised the initial stages of my doctoral research, and his encouragement then and in more recent years has been deeply appreciated. The debt I owe to his own work on Buddhism in Thailand is evident throughout this book. Peter Wilson supervised the final writing of my dissertation. I thank him and hope that he enjoys my appropriation of some ideas from his *Crab Antics* (1973) in Chapter 11. I would like to thank Nelson Graburn, Marilyn Strathern, and the staff of the Berkeley and Manchester anthropology departments for their hospitality in 1981–1982, 1987, and 1990, Ariel Salleh for letting me live and work in her Glebe cottage, close to Sydney University and its library, during the summer of 1988–1989, and Maciej and Irina Ciolek for their friendship and encouragement during the many times that I have stayed with them in Canberra while consulting the Australian National University's Tibetan collection.

Janet Gyatso's comments on an early version of this book reoriented my thinking on the central issue of Tantra and shamanic insight and so contributed vitally to the final text. Detailed criticisms of later versions by Hamish Gregor, Lisse Stutchbury, and David Stott were of immense value, as were my discussions with Tashi Tsering of the Library of Tibetan Works and Archives. Robert Paul read the book for the Smithsonian and I would like to thank him here for his generous and helpful remarks. Many errors and misinterpretations undoubtedly remain, despite all the assistance and good advice I have received.

I also wish to acknowledge the many Tibetan lamas whose teachings have provided essential guidance and inspiration, among them the late Kalu Rimpoche, Matrul Rimpoche, and Chögyam Trungpa Rimpoche; Andzin Rimpoche, Ato Rimpoche, Chagdüd Rimpoche, Chime Rimpoche, Lama Karma Samten, Kunga Rimpoche, Namkha Drimed Rimpoche, Namkhai Norbu Rimpoche, Geshe Ngawang Dhargyey, Phende Rimpoche, Serkhung Rimpoche, Sogyal Rimpoche, Tara Tulku, Geshe Thubten Loden, Geshe Thubten Tshering, Tulku Jigme, and Yangtang Tulku.

The staff of the Smithsonian Institution Press, in particular Daniel Goodwin and Duke Johns, have coped gracefully and efficiently with the complexities of producing an overlong book by an often inaccessible author. Robin Gould, the book's manuscript editor, has done much to transform my unwieldy prose into readable English.

I have dedicated this book to my mother. As the Tibetans remind us, all sentient beings have been our mother at some point in beginningless time. I hope that the book will be of benefit to some of them.

Introduction

I

Introduction: Shamanic and Clerical Buddhism

This book is an account of the nature and evolution of religion in premodern Tibetan societies. The author is an anthropologist, and the approach is that of social and cultural anthropology, in a wide sense, although I have made extensive use of the work of historians of religion and of other specialists on Tibetan society, as well as of indigenous Tibetan scholarship. The plural usage, Tibetan *societies,* is intended both to stress the diversity of these societies, and to emphasize from the beginning that central Tibet, the Dalai Lama's government and the great monastic institutions around Lhasa, form only part of the context within which Tibetan Buddhism, and Tibetan religion as a whole, took shape and operated. Part One of the book (Chapters 3 to 8) consists of a survey of Tibetan societies and a critique of some aspects of the anthropological literature on these societies.

The term 'premodern' indicates, roughly speaking, the period to 1950, when the status of most Tibetan societies was changed drastically as a result of Chinese military intervention and occupation. Elements of the picture presented in this book still operate, both in Chinese-occupied regions of Tibetan population and among Tibetans living in India, Nepal, and Bhutan, but my primary intention is to describe Tibetan Buddhism as it developed until 1950.

The term 'religion' has been used in narrower and more extended senses; the sense intended here is a wide one. As an anthropologist, I assume that the history of 'religion' in Tibetan societies cannot be separated from the history of modes of consciousness or from the history of political and social structures within those societies. For Tibetans, the vocabulary and modes of thinking deriving from Indian Buddhism came to pervade many areas of experience that we do not necessarily think of as 'religious,' while the concepts of Tibetan folk religion, such as the maintenance of good luck and good fortune, continue to underlie virtually all facets of life. Understanding Buddhism in Tibetan societies means understanding the total picture within which Buddhism took shape. Among other things, this book is intended as a case study in the history of cultural patterns, a term which I use in this book as an equivalent to the 'modal states' of my previous book, *Mind, Body and Culture* (Samuel 1990, and see Chapter 19, below).

The history of cultural patterns within Tibetan societies has some unusual and characteristic features. The complex monastic, scriptural, and philosophical traditions of Buddhism link them to the centralized states of South and Southeast Asia. The limited presence of a state apparatus, however, suggests analogies with stateless societies such as those found among the 'tribal' populations of South and Southeast Asia or even in sub-Saharan Africa. The importance of what may be called a 'shamanic' mode of operating (see Samuel 1990:106–120) in Tibetan societies, which have highly developed and sophisticated techniques for the employment of nonordinary states of consciousness, points in the same direction.

As a consequence of these features, Tibetan societies, and especially their religious institutions, have presented considerable difficulties for conventional approaches in both anthropology and religious studies. Religion in Tibetan societies needs understanding in its own terms, and these are quite different from those of societies such as Burma, Thailand, or Sri Lanka where most early anthropological work on Buddhism was carried out. This point is developed at length in Chapter 2. Buddhism in Tibet may have the same ultimate aim as Buddhism in other Asian societies but it operates within a very different social context. Anthropologists are only beginning to arrive at an adequate picture of that social context, which is why Part One of this book provides a general picture of Tibetan societies in the premodern period. This picture emphasizes the diversity of those societies, a diversity that went along with the limited extent of state authority throughout the region.

In Parts Two and Three of the book, I present my analysis of Buddhism in Tibetan society. In Part Two, Tibetan Buddhism is described synchronically as it was in the premodern period and as it continues to be, to varying degrees, among Tibetan populations today. In Part Three, I look at Tibetan Buddhism diachronically, describing its evolution from the Buddhism of India and the indigenous spirit-cults of Tibet up until the first half of this century. In this account, I interweave the development of new modes of consciousness with the history of the social and political institutions that provided the context for their development and was in its turn directed by their development.

It will be apparent in the course of the book that I am sympathetic towards my subject. I am more inclined to view Tibetan Buddhism as one of the great spiritual and psychological achievements of humanity than as an ideological justification for the oppression of Tibetan serfs by their overlords. This is an anthropological study, however, rather than a work of advocacy. My intention is to present Tibetan religion as a whole, with its cultural, social, and religious background. Through the activities of refugee lamas, the methods and techniques of the Buddhism of Tibet are becoming part of the world's cultural heritage. That process can only be aided by a better understanding of the origins of those methods and techniques and the society within which they were developed.

BASIC CATEGORIES OF THE BOOK

Buddhism, as one of the world's major spiritual traditions, centers about the pursuit of Enlightenment or *bodhi*,[1] a goal of personal (and, for the Tibetans at least, collective) salvation that lies outside the compass of ordinary social life. I refer to this aspect of Tibetan religion in the book as the *Bodhi Orientation.* Much of the complexity of religion in Buddhist societies, as in other societies where such salvation-oriented religions prevail, derives from how people come to terms with conflicts, real or perceived, between the salvation orientation and the ordinary social life.

Such conflicts form a major theme, for example, of Max Weber's sociology of religion, and they have been a recurrent interest of anthropological studies of Theravāda Buddhist societies. More recently, Stan Mumford has used a framework derived from the work of Mikhail Bakhtin to discuss these issues for a society on the fringe of Tibetan settlement in Nepal; Mumford speaks of the growth of individual subjectivity and eventually of a sense of historical becoming that leads to the break-up of the 'ancient matrix' or shamanic world view (Mumford 1989:16ff). We can overstate the uniformity of the 'ancient matrix,' which corresponds closely to what I have elsewhere referred to as the shamanic mode of operation (Samuel 1990). The relationship between these phases is best understood as logical (and dialectical) rather than chronological; the 'ancient matrix' in Tibetan societies was constantly under attack, either overtly or implicitly, by Buddhism, but it continually reconstituted itself. Throughout Tibetan history, it provided a background against which Buddhism took shape and in terms of which it had to justify itself.

Salvation traditions such as Buddhism often originate in moments of antistructure and opposition to established power and hierarchy. Historically, however, they have rapidly been taken up and used by centralized states. Consequently, we are most familiar with Buddhism, as with Islam, Hinduism, or Christianity, as subordinate to, and closely integrated with the political order of the society in which it is found. This was not the case in premodern Tibet, and it is mainly for this reason, I believe, that the relationship between the Bodhi Orientation and the other components of Tibetan religion differs markedly from that characteristic of other Buddhist societies.

Briefly, in other Buddhist societies, the Bodhi Orientation has become subordinate in many ways to a second, explicitly ethical orientation. This orientation, the *Karma Orientation*, centers around the principle of karma, or of the linkage between an action and its result, which manifests in a subsequent life of the same individual. This karma-complex predated Buddhism and forms part of the philosophical background within which early Buddhism developed. The emphasis on morality and correct behavior, and the idea that the rich and powerful were well placed to secure a fortunate afterlife through generosity to the Buddhist clergy doubtless appealed strongly to rulers of Indic societies.

A third religious orientation, the *Pragmatic Orientation*, is concerned with this-worldly goals such as health and prosperity. Its relationship to Buddhism is complex and will be considered further in Chapter 2.

The 'ancient matrix' and its shamanic practices were generally less appealing to the rulers of Buddhist states than the karma-oriented aspects of Buddhism. Shamanic practitioners might offer the possibility of magical control over the problems of everyday life, but they also represented potential sites of rebellion against the order imposed by the state (see Chapter 2). They were generally tolerated in premodern Buddhist states, but they were kept firmly subordinate to state power, and were seen as inferior and marginal in relation to the Buddhism that reinforced that state power (see Samuel 1990:131–133). I refer to the Buddhism of such states in general as *clerical Buddhism*. Such state-sponsored clerical Buddhism was typical of Theravādin societies such as Sri Lanka, Burma, or Thailand in the precolonial period.

The general weakness or absence of state power in premodern Tibetan societies went along with a different situation. Clerical Buddhism was present, but it coexisted with and was in many ways subordinate to what I shall refer to as *shamanic Buddhism*. Within the Tibetan context, shamanic and clerical Buddhism refer to two modalities or orientations within the Buddhist and Bönpo[2] teachings, rituals, and practices of Tibet. Clerical Buddhism will be the more familiar modality to most readers, since it resembles more closely the monastic and scholarly Buddhism found in other Buddhist societies. Shamanic Buddhism is a more specifically Tibetan modality, although it has, as we shall see in Chapter 2, equivalents in Theravādin Buddhist societies such as Thailand, where it corresponds to the Buddhist expression of the marginalized 'ancient matrix.' The Tibetan version of shamanic Buddhism is, however, unlike that in Theravādin Buddhist societies, closely integrated with the goal of Enlightenment and the Bodhi Orientation. It is in no way a marginal phenomenon.

These two terms, shamanic Buddhism and clerical Buddhism, are a major subject of this book, since an exposition of their nature and of the relationship between them forms the basis of my analysis of Tibetan religion. They are, of course, no more than conceptual tools, but they have the advantage of a lesser weight of prior associations than other available conceptual tools, such as Sūtra, Tantra, Theravāda, Mahāyāna, or Bön. As a result, they help to provide a fresh look at the true nature of Tibetan religion.

I use the term 'shamanic' as a general term for a category of practices found in differing degrees in almost all human societies. This category of practices may be briefly described as *the regulation and transformation of human life and human society through the use (or purported use) of alternate states of consciousness by means of which specialist practitioners are held to communicate with a mode of reality alternative to, and more fundamental than, the world of everyday experience.*

The term 'shamanic' has been used in a variety of ways within the anthropological literature, of which this is only one. I have discussed my usage at length elsewhere and provided some theoretical justification for it (Samuel 1990:106–120, 144–147). Here I will simply note that (1) 'shamanic' in my usage is not restricted to the 'Siberian' shamanic complex, (2) it may involve any of a variety of specific vocabularies and techniques, including spirit-possession and spirit-mediumship as well as soul-flight, and (3) the term is in no way at all derogatory. In fact, I believe that the sophisticated body of shamanic practices within Tibetan Buddhism probably constitutes Tibet's most important single contribution to humanity (see Samuel 1989).

If we use the term 'shamanic' in this sense, Tibetan religion has two distinct, if overlapping, shamanic complexes: Tibetan folk religion (to adopt Tucci's term, 1980:163–211) and shamanic Buddhism. Few would dispute that many 'folk-religion' practices in Tibet, in particular the employment of spirit-mediums to communicate with local deities, may be described as 'shamanic' in my sense. By shamanic Buddhism I mean something rather different, which is certainly related to these folk-religion practices but is not a simple derivative of them and needs to be treated separately from them. My contention (which is not particularly original[3]) is that certain aspects of Vajrayāna (Tantric) Buddhism as practiced in Tibet may be described as shamanic, in that they are centered around communication with an alternative mode of reality (that of the Tantric deities) via the alternate states of consciousness of Tantric yoga. I shall argue that this communication forms the basis for much of the Tibetan lama's role in relation to Tibetan society.

This formulation reverses the usual Tibetan presentation of

Vajrayāna Buddhism. A Tibetan lama, asked to define the Vajrayāna, will normally describe it in terms of the Bodhi Orientation, as a technique for attaining Enlightenment or Buddhahood. The spiritual power generated by Vajrayāna practice and used for the benefit of the lama's lay following is a by-product. If lamas employ the power of Vajrayāna ritual for the welfare of their lay followers, this is held to be an expression of their compassion or their skillful means, a way of drawing their followers on towards the ultimate goal of liberation from suffering through the attainment of Buddhahood. At the same time, lamas are well aware that many of their followers are primarily concerned with the utilization of Vajrayāna power for this-worldly benefits or for securing a good rebirth in a future life rather than with the attainment of Buddhahood. Buddhahood as a goal is of immediate significance for a minority, although that minority is of vital importance to the system as a whole.

To put this in another way, the Vajrayāna's techniques for attaining Buddhahood function in practical terms as a means of training shamanic practitioners. Lamas in Tibet function as shamans, and they do so through the techniques and practices of Vajrayāna Buddhism. The specific form that Buddhism has taken in Tibet is bound up with this nexus between the pursuit of Enlightenment by a minority and the desire for shamanic services by the majority. This point will be elaborated on at length in later chapters.

Given all this, we can consider an initial formulation of the contrast between shamanic and clerical Buddhism:

Shamanic Buddhism works in terms of a relationship with an alternative mode of reality (defined by the divine forms of the Saṃbhogakāya and the Tantric *maṇḍala*). This alternative mode may be evoked through Vajrayāna (Tantric) ritual for the achievement of ultimate Enlightenment or Buddhahood, conceived of as a potentiality present within all individuals. It may also be evoked in order to bring about effects within this mode of reality, such as long life and health, protection from misfortune, or a suitable rebirth in one's next life.[4] The primary mode of activity of shamanic Buddhism is analogy and metaphor. Its typical figure is the Tantric lama, who undergoes a prolonged retreat in order to gain the shamanic power of the Vajrayāna, and subsequently utilizes that power on behalf of a lay population. The textual base of shamanic Buddhism is made up of the 'Old' and 'New' Tantric scriptures and commentaries and of the *terma* revelations of later Tibetan visionary-lamas.

Clerical Buddhism shares with shamanic Buddhism the goal of ultimate

Enlightenment. It dismisses activity within the cycle of rebirth as irrelevant, however, with the exception of the acquisition of merit through virtuous action, and the avoidance of nonvirtuous action. Its primary mode of activity is scholarship, philosophical analysis, and monastic discipline. Its typical figure is the scholar-monk studying texts or engaged in philosophical debate. Its textual base is made up of the Vinaya or monastic disciplinary code, the Sūtras of the Hinayāna and Mahāyāna, and the writings of Indian Buddhist philosophers and of their Tibetan followers.

These capsule summaries will be filled out as the argument proceeds. The contrast between shamanic and clerical aspects of Buddhism is a complex one, in part because the two are closely interwoven in practice. Virtually all Tibetan Buddhism, whether that of the Gelugpa scholar with his *geshé* diploma or that of the Nyingmapa yogin in his or her mountain hermitage, contains elements of both shamanic and clerical orientations. In addition, the subtle scholarship of the lamas has developed all sorts of ways of reconciling the two modalities, culminating in the two major syntheses whose development is described in the later chapters of Part Three: the Gelugpa synthesis originating in the work of Tsongk'apa (1357–1419) and the Rimed synthesis created by a group of nineteenth-century lamas in east Tibet.

The shamanic and clerical aspects are, nevertheless, rooted in fundamentally different orientations towards the world and towards human experience and behavior. Cross-culturally, one or the other orientation predominates in most human societies or social groups. By and large, small-scale preliterate societies had and have a dominantly shamanic orientation, while premodern states with developed literacy and centralized, bureaucratic government have been predominantly clerical with shamanic elements present in subordinate contexts (see Samuel 1990:93–133). Tibetan societies are unusual in that the shamanic complex has a strong and autonomous role within what is undoubtedly a literate and sophisticated culture.

A NOTE ON BÖN AND THE 'BÖN RELIGION'

Previous discussions of the shamanic aspects of Tibetan religion have often been confused by indiscriminate references to the so-called Bön religion.[5] The term Bön and its derivative Bönpo have been employed by many Tibetan and Western scholars to refer variously to all sorts of allegedly pre-Buddhist and non-Buddhist elements of Tibetan religion, often including the folk-religion cults of local deities mentioned above. Such usage conflates so many different things under the one label that serious analysis becomes impossible.

A major influence here has been Helmut Hoffmann's *Religions of Tibet*, first published in German in 1956 and subsequently translated into English in 1961 (Hoffmann 1979). Hoffmann reconstructs, on admittedly fragmentary evidence, a pre-Buddhist 'Old Bön Religion' (1979:13–27). This was a form of 'animism' (for example, 1979:21, 84) centered on a reverent and submissive attitude to the "powers and forces of [the] wild highland landscape whose divinities were reflected in the idea of numerous good and evil spirits the Tibetans thought to see all around them" (1979:17). The main practitioners of the 'Old Bön Religion,' the *shen*, were "[s]hamans. . . . very similar to their colleagues of north and central Asia" (1979:25). They practiced soul-flight in a state of trance,[6] and undertook elaborate funerary rituals for the Tibetan kings.

Subsequently, in Hoffmann's account, a deviant form of Buddhism, which he calls 'Padmaism' or 'the Padmaist religion,' was created under court patronage by a "strange holy man and sorcerer" from India named Padmasambhava (1979:47, 50–65). The 'old, primitive Bön religion and customs' survived among ordinary Tibetans but anti-Buddhist Tibetan nobles sponsored the creation of a new, 'Systematized Bön religion'. This Systematized Bön was a "syncretist system with a developed doctrine and a sacred literature," influenced by Buddhism, perhaps also by Persian and Manichaean teachings (1979:85). After the collapse of the Tibetan kingdom in the mid-ninth century, Buddhism (i.e., Padmaism), along with the new Systematized Bön, went into a period of degeneration and was largely absorbed by the old Bön religion. The religious revival of the eleventh and twelfth centuries, and the subsequent 'Reformation' initiated by Tsongk'apa, founder of the Gelugpa tradition, are explained by Hoffmann primarily as attempts to purge and purify Tibetan Buddhism and to return it to something like the Buddhism of the Theravādin countries (1979:121, 160, 166–167).

Given the limited sources available in 1956, Hoffmann's work was a praiseworthy attempt at understanding the historical evolution of Tibetan religion, and a notable advance on the crude caricatures of its best-known predecessor, L. Austine Waddell's *The Buddhism of Tibet*, *or Lamaism*, first published in 1894 (Waddell 1967). Hoffmann's work is misleading, however, in many respects. His 'Old Bön' is created from fragmentary evidence and dubious parallels with north and central Asia, and his 'Padmaism' is an ahistorical mélange of material from very different historical contexts. It is significant that while Hoffmann discusses Vajrayāna (Tantric Buddhism) at length, it has no real place in his explanatory scheme. Vajrayāna emerges in Hoffmann's writing as a compound of gnostic, magical, and erotic oddities to which the Tibetans are inexplicably attached despite the best efforts of their lamas to wean them away from it. Yet any real attempt to understand the religion of Tibet has to recognize that the Vajrayāna is at the center of Tibetan spiritual life.

Unfortunately, Hoffmann's work was adopted uncritically by several anthropologists (for example, Funke 1969), and his views have also been propagated in popular texts on the history of religion. To make matters worse, while Hoffmann carefully distinguishes between what he calls Old Bön and Systematized Bön,[7] following the contrast made by Tibetan scholars, many of those who have borrowed from him tend to collapse the two together, losing a vital distinction.

While there are some grounds for using the term Bön for the early religion of Tibet (see Chapter 23), there are few for applying it to the cults of local gods and spirits as they exist today, and I shall avoid using Bön to refer to this contemporary 'folk religion.' In this book, for all contexts after the ninth century A.D., Bön and Bönpo refer exclusively to the religious order of Bön[8] and its adherents. This order is similar in form and nature to the religious orders of Tibetan Buddhism, but claims to derive from the teachings of the pre-Buddhist master Shenrab Mibo rather than from the historical Buddha Śākyamuni. This modern Bön religion has shamanic and clerical aspects similar to those of modern Tibetan Buddhism and will be mentioned frequently in subsequent chapters.

Tibetan folk-religion, then, is 'shamanic,' in my sense, but it is to be distinguished from the shamanic aspects of Tibetan Buddhism (and also of the modern Bön religion, which is essentially, in this context, a variant of Buddhism). It is the interplay between the shamanic and clerical aspects of Buddhism (including Bön) that provides the interpretive framework of the present book. The remainder of this chapter is intended to give some substance to the two terms, shamanic Buddhism and clerical Buddhism, which will play an important part in the remainder of the book. A convenient approach to these two terms is a comparison of how the Bodhi Orientation, the explicit central goal of Tibetan Buddhism as of all Buddhism, appears within these two modalities.

Enlightenment *(bodhi)* or Buddhahood is variously defined in different schools of Buddhism but it is nevertheless accepted to be beyond verbal definition. It involves the transcendence of the normal condition of humanity (the cycle of rebirth or *saṃsāra*), thus reaching the state of freedom from suffering referred to as *nirvāṇa*, and the attainment of a condition beyond any mental or physical limitation, accompanied by omniscience and immense magical power.

This was the attainment of the historical Buddha Śākyamuni and it is the highest goal of all Buddhist practice. How does the path to Enlightenment appear within the shamanic and clerical modalities? The following examples will also introduce some of the principal concerns and modes of expression of Tibetan Buddhism.

A SHAMANIC APPROACH TO ENLIGHTENMENT: THE ASPIRATION OF KUNTU SANGPO

Here is a typically shamanic statement of how to go about the attainment of Enlightenment. This is the opening section of a short *terma* or 'discovered' text, the *Kunsang Mönlam* ('Prayer of Kuntu Sangpo' or 'Aspiration of Kuntu Sangpo'). Lamas who discover texts of this kind through visionary techniques are known as *tertön*. This text was found by one of the best known of all *tertön*, Göddemchen (1337–1409, see Schuh 1985:xxx–xxxviii).

> HO! The phenomenal world and all existence, *saṃsāra* and *nirvāṇa*,
> All has one foundation, but there are two paths and two results—
> Displays of both ignorance and Knowledge.
> Through Kuntu Sangpo's aspiration,
> In the Palace of the Primal Space of Emptiness
> Let all beings attain perfect consummation and Buddhahood.
>
> The universal foundation is unconditioned,
> Spontaneously arising, a vast immanent expanse, beyond expression,
> Where neither '*saṃsāra*' nor '*nirvāṇa*' exist.

> Knowledge of this reality is Buddhahood,
> While ignorant beings wander in *saṃsāra*.
> Let all sentient beings of the three realms
> Attain Knowledge of the nature of the ineffable foundation.
> (Dowman 1981:4)

The text is in the form of a 'prayer' or 'aspiration' by Kuntu Sangpo. Kuntu Sangpo (Samantabhadra in Sanskrit) is not a person but a Tantric deity. He is a symbolic representation of the underlying knowledge or *rigpa* "which is inseparable from the universal foundation, a plenum of all-pervasive, primal space" (Dowman 1981:2). He is termed the Primal Buddha[9] in the Nyingmapa tradition. As Keith Dowman explains (1982:2) in the introduction to this translation, 'prayer' here

> is to be understood as the deity's speech, a discursive *mantra*, resonating to inform the *saṃbhogakāya*[10] as an instructive vision of the deity, who in this case is Kuntu Sangpo. First Kuntu Sangpo. . . . expresses his vision of reality, and then he explains the meditation by which this vision is sustained. The means of realisation of Kuntu Sangpo's vision is passion, wherein lies Awareness in its five modes. Relaxation is the key to the meditation upon passion, and the goal is Buddhahood, or identity with Kuntu Sangpo himself.

In the subsequent sections of the text, the five modalities of passion are taken in turn, their origins in ignorance of the true nature of reality, their nature and their consequences are examined, and the practitioner advised not to suppress or indulge the passion but to release the inherent stress and allow the passion to dissolve into the universal foundation. Here for example is the section on desire:

> A dualising mind breeds doubt, hesitancy and insecurity,
> And with the development of subtle craving (in compensation),
> Overt compulsive karmic propensities gradually crystallise.
> Food, wealth and clothing, home and friends,
> The five stimuli of sensual pleasure, and loving companions—
> Obsessive desires beget torments of frustration;
> Compulsive desires are but worldly delusion,
> And the karma of an ego craving objects is never exhausted.
> When the fruit of craving ripens,

> Born as a hungry ghost tormented by frustrated desire,
> Oh, the misery of hunger and thirst!
> Through this my prayer, the Buddha's aspiration,
> All sentient beings possessed by compulsive craving,
> Neither setting aside and rejecting the pangs of frustrated desire
> Nor accepting and identifying with compulsive craving,
> Should release the stress inherent in dualistic perception
> So that Knowledge may resume its natural primacy—
> Let all beings attain All-discriminating Awareness.
> (Dowman 1981:6)

Here we can see what was meant above about *analogy* or *metaphor* being the primary mode of activity of shamanic Buddhism. Practitioners are intended to treat Kuntu Sangpo as an image of what they themselves can be. In reciting the prayer and in doing the meditation they are conceiving of themselves as Kuntu Sangpo, modeling themselves on Kuntu Sangpo, and through this analogical shift taking on his qualities. Kuntu Sangpo is a 'deity' or divine form of the *saṃbhogakāya.*[11] He represents a mode of reality that human beings (and other 'sentient beings' such as the gods, animals, hell-beings, and so forth) are all theoretically capable of entering, and within which the ordinary dualistic appearances that constitute them as human beings with a particular life-experience, gods, animals, and so on, are dissolved. As is generally true of Tantric deities, Kuntu Sangpo is best regarded not as some kind of external spirit-entity but as a mode of being that anyone is theoretically capable of actualizing.

An analogic shift of this kind, conceptualized as taking on the identity of one or another deity, is the central act of all Vajrayāna rituals. This is true whether the purpose of the ritual is, as here, the attainment of Buddhahood, or some other goal such as the destruction of demonic forces or the achievement of good health and long life. Saṃbhogakāya deities vary in type and complexity, and the more elaborate rituals may involve the visualization of a succession of divine maṇḍalas, each containing tens or hundreds of deities, the visualization of elaborate offerings, empowerments, and other manifestations, the chanting of complex liturgies with accompanying melodies and hand-gestures. In some cases, especially in the lower Tantra classes,[12] the deity is viewed outside the practitioner rather than directly identified with. Despite these variations, the essential process throughout is, as in this example, the shift into another mode of reality brought about through the use of the divine forms.

A CLERICAL APPROACH TO ENLIGHTENMENT: THE THREE MAIN POINTS OF THE PATH

Now let us counterpose a clerical account of how to go about the attainment of Enlightenment, written by a younger contemporary of Göddemchen. The 'Three Main Points of the Path' *(Lamtso Namsum)* is a short instructional text by the famous lama Tsongk'apa (1357–1419), already referred to as founder of the Gelugpa tradition.[13] After two introductory verses in which Tsongk'apa announces his intention of explaining the essential meaning of the Buddha's teaching to those who "are not tied to the pleasures of *saṃsāra* and wish to make full use of this human life" (i.e., for the attainment of Enlightenment), he presents the First Main Point of the Path, renunciation:

> Since those who have not achieved renunciation, and desire
> *Saṃsāra*'s joys, have no means to reach peace,
> And since too thirst for *saṃsāra* holds all beings
> Tied up firmly, then first seek renunciation.
>
> [1] Human birth is hard to find, and [2] this life may soon end;
> Thus train the mind, and turn from concern for this life.
> [3] On karma's certain action, and [4] on *saṃsāra*'s sufferings,
> Think always, and turn from concern for future lives.

The four topics, which I have numbered here, are a standard set of meditations found in all Tibetan traditions (see Chapter 11), intended to achieve the initial turning of the mind away from this-worldly concerns (1, 2) and from the inferior goal of seeking a comfortable future rebirth (3, 4).

> When you have trained thus, if longing never arises
> For *saṃsāra*'s highest joys for even a moment
> When day and night only a mind desiring of liberation appears,
> Then renunciation has arisen.

The next Main Point is the development of *bodhicitta*, the defining motivation of the *bodhisattva*. *Bodhicitta* is the desire to achieve Enlightenment in order to relieve all sentient beings[14] from their sufferings. For Tibetan Buddhists, Enlightenment can only be achieved through *bodhicitta;* the lesser motivation of a desire for one's own salvation from *saṃsāra* is insufficient.

> However renunciation, if it is not combined with
> Arousing *bodhicitta,* cannot yet become
> Through highest Enlightenment, the cause of perfect joy.
> So those with intelligence arouse *bodhicitta.*
>
> Carried away by the four mighty rivers,
> Held by the firm bonds of karma, so hard to reverse,
> Trapped in the iron net of ego-attachment,
> Covered all over in the black fog of ignorance,
>
> Born and born again endlessly into *saṃsāra*
> To suffer without break through its three sorrows;
> By thinking over [all beings,] our mothers' condition[15]
> As they turn through such a state, make the perfect mind arise.

The Third Main Point is insight *(prajñā)* and here Tsongk'apa outlines his characteristic philosophical position, adopted by the Gelugpa tradition which he founded. Its central feature is a particular interpretation of the unity of karma (causation) and *śūnyatā* (voidness, emptiness).

> But if without having the insight that sees into what is,
> You only practice renunciation and arousing *bodhicitta,*
> You cannot cut off the roots of *saṃsāra.*
> So work at the method of understanding dependent origination.
>
> Whoever sees all the dharmas of *saṃsāra* and *nirvāṇa*
> As never diverging from the sequence of causation,
> Whoever has destroyed completely all turning to objects of the mind,
> Is then on the path which delights the Buddhas.
>
> Your understandings of dependent origination in the world of
> appearance
> And of *śūnyatā* free from all assertions, these two,
> As long as they appear to be separate,
> You have still not understood the Sage's thought.

When at the same time, not having set them up separately,
Through that very seeing of dependent origination
All habitual views of objects as certainly known are destroyed
Then the study of views has been completed.

Further, if you know the way of arising as cause and effect
Of *śūnyatā,* which through the apparent destroys belief in existence
And through the void destroys belief in nonexistence,
No extreme view can deprive you of your insight.
(Tsongk'apa, *Lamtso Namsum;* my translation)

A final verse recommends that, after realizing the Three Points, the disciple should meditate in solitude.

The difference in approach from Göddemchen's text should be evident. In place of a direct entry into Kuntu Sangpo's mode of being, we are presented with a series of stages entirely within the conventional approach of Mahāyāna Buddhism. The disciple should first achieve Renunciation of *saṃsāra,* then arouse *bodhicitta,* the altruistic motivation of the *bodhisattva,*[16] and then achieve the correct philosophical viewpoint that defines Buddhahood. There is no suggestion here of meditation on Vajrayāna deities. Tsongk'apa was not opposed to the practice of Tantra, but he and his followers saw it as an advanced practice, to be undertaken only after extensive preliminary non-Tantric training on the lines suggested in this text. The Gelugpa order, in theory at least, has maintained this position.

The *Kunsang Mönlam* and *Lamtso Namsum* are both well-known texts of great authority within Tibetan Buddhism, widely respected across the whole range of traditions, and written within a few years of each other.[17] They nevertheless articulate quite different approaches to the fundamental issues of Buddhism.

In general, these texts are representative of the two traditions with which they are associated, in that the Nyingmapa tradition involves more emphasis on the shamanic approach and the Gelugpa on the clerical. The two other main Buddhist traditions, Kagyüdpa and Sakyapa, fall somewhere in between, while the Bönpo are similar to the Nyingmapa. We are speaking here, however, only of a difference in emphasis. It would not be difficult to find Nyingmapa texts with clerical features, or Gelugpa texts that are shamanic. We are only secondarily concerned here with an opposition between religious traditions or monastic orders. The two modalities go right through all of Tibetan Buddhist practice.

SHAMANIC BUDDHISM AND THE 'GREAT TIME' OF MYTH

One of the most important contrasts between clerical and shamanic Buddhism appears only tangentially in our example. Clerical Buddhism is scriptural, and it relates to the text as a source of rational argument. Shamanic or Tantric (Vajrayāna) Buddhism is oral, and it derives from a lineage of teachings that can be viewed as having originated in a 'primal time' or 'Great Time' of myth. Göddemchen's text, as I noted, is a *terma*. It is regarded not as a text composed by a human author but as a revelation from the primal time.

The texts of Tantra are primarily liturgical. They are specific means (Skt. *sādhanā*) of invoking the Saṃbhogakāya deities and they are subsidiary in importance to the experience, or rather the state of being, ideally brought about when the invocation succeeds.

The 'Great Time' of Tantric Buddhism is distinct from the ordinary time of everyday life. The beings, male and female, who populate it (Buddhas, *bodhisattva*, and other Tantric deities, along with great lamas of the past from Tibet, India, and elsewhere) might be described as 'culture heroes.' Through their activity in the 'Great Time,' they laid down the basic potentialities for human behavior in general and Buddhist practice and ritual in particular.

We will meet many such figures in the course of this book. One who plays a particularly important role is Chenresig (Skt. Avalokiteśvara), the great *bodhisattva* who fathered the Tibetan people, introduced agriculture, returned as several of the Tibetan emperors, and takes human form as the Dalai Lama and other high lamas. Another of comparable significance is Guru Rimpoch'e (Skt. Padmasambhava), the 'second Buddha' who tamed the local gods and spirits of Tibet and bound them to the service of the Buddhist teachings. Female figures include Drölma (Skt. Tārā), who is a kind of female counterpart to Chenresig and also has a significant role in Tibetan history, and Dorjé Neljorma (Skt. Vajrayoginī), an initiatory goddess who is intimately linked with the revelation of many Tantric lineages. Among the great lamas are figures such as Garab Dorjé, Longch'en Rabjampa, Marpa, Milarepa, Sakya Pandita, and Tsongk'apa, founders and codifiers of religious orders and central figures in the various Tantric lineages, and all directly invoked as Tantric deities in their own right.

This list includes a mixture of historical and partly historical characters (Milarepa, Tsongk'apa, Guru Rimpoch'e) along with beings who might be better described as deities or hypostatizations of human potentialities (Chenresig, Dorjé Neljorma). What all the members of the list have in common is that their power is thought to be still active and can be contacted and made use of by those with the appropriate skill. In certain contexts, such as the Refuge visualizations of the *guruyoga* practices, they are all imagined as arrayed in a vast assemblage, centered around the meditator's personal lama in transfigured form. Any of these culture-heroes may appear in visions, give teachings, and aid the practitioner to achieve this-worldly power and ultimate Enlightenment. The practitioner can also assume the identity of many of these figures directly in the course of Tantric practice. Thus within the 'shamanic Buddhist' perspective these culture-heroes appear as trans-historical sources of power and authority.

At the same time, Tibetans, particularly monastic scholars, are well aware of the historical nature of people such as Guru Rimpoch'e or Sakya Pandita. As this suggests, many of those whom I have described as shamanic culture-heroes can also be viewed in the perspective of clerical Buddhism, as human beings who lived at a specific time in the past and performed a series of actions recorded in the historical record.

In practice, the two perspectives constantly interpenetrate, and shamanic revelation is a central part of most Tibetan historical accounts. Even the great scholarly activity of lamas such as Sakya Pandita, Tsongk'apa, or Jamyang Ky'entsé Ongpo, shining examples of the rational and clerical aspect of Tibetan Buddhism, has its shamanic 'reading.' In the shamanic Buddhist perspective the scholarly work of these lamas is described in terms of these lamas having received revelations from, and having themselves been emanations of, the *bodhisattva* Mañjuśrī (Tib. Jampel Yang), whose specific field is scholarship. Iconographically they are depicted with the sword and book, the emblems of Mañjuśrī, as an indication of their identity with him.

The history of Buddhism in India may likewise be viewed by the Tibetans through this shamanic perspective. The work of men such as Nāgārjuna or Asaṅga, great scholars by any rationalist criteria, is described in terms of yogic and Tantric practice and of revelations from *nāga* and *bodhisattva* (see, for example, Obermiller 1932–1933). Similarly the Buddha Śākyamuni himself is seen less as a specific person who lived in northern India in the fifth to sixth centuries B.C. than as an earthly projection or emanation of the universal cosmic archetype of Enlightenment.

The vital point here is that a sufficiently powerful lama can always reestablish direct contact with these founding figures, who exist, rather like the Dreaming beings of the Australian Aborigines, on a different plane of reality that interpenetrates our ordinary reality. The lineage of the teachings is therefore in the shamanic Buddhist view not simply a heritage handed on from the distant past, it is something that is being constantly recreated and revalidated through the experience of contemporary lamas and yogic practitioners.

In this way the lamas, like the Siberian shamans or the 'diviners' or 'prophets' of sub-Saharan Africa, can realign human beings with their society and with the universe in which they lived by producing a new and contemporary reading of the tradition. Yet the lamas, unlike the shamans and diviners of tribal and preliterate societies, are not regarded as practicing their art only for this-worldly ends. The ultimate aim of Tantric practice is the same as that of all Buddhist practice, the achievement of the state of Enlightenment. This is the point of possible conflict between the individuating and ethicizing tendency of Buddhism and the 'ancient matrix' of the shamanic world view, with its emphasis on communal harmony (see Mumford 1989:16–23).

For the Tibetans, Tantric or Vajrayāna Buddhism is the preeminent way of achieving Enlightenment. It is universally accepted that while the Pāramitāyāna, the path of the Sūtras, leads to Enlightenment, it takes many thousands of lifetimes to reach the goal by this path alone. The Vajrayāna is the quick path, the immediate path, and if practiced intensively it can lead to Enlightenment within this present lifetime.

Consequently the upholders of the clerical strand in Tibetan Buddhism do not reject Tantra, and clerically oriented practitioners are themselves committed to Tantric Buddhism and reliant on its methods. At most the more clerical and academic of Tibetan practitioners, especially in the Gelugpa tradition, may cast doubt on the validity of those Tantric lineages that do not have a sufficiently respectable academic and textual tradition behind them. Even Tsong-k'apa, the prototypically academic and scholarly lama who founded the most 'clerical' of Tibetan Buddhist orders, the Gelugpa, was not, despite the suggestions of some earlier Western commentators, opposed to Tantra. He was deeply committed to Tantric practice, and his life was guided by a series of crucial revelations from various *bodhisattva* (see Thurman 1982, 1984, 1985, and Chapter 26).

THE TWO MAJOR SYNTHESES: GELUGPA AND RIMED

I noted above that there is a 'shamanic Buddhist' analysis of the clerical tradition, in terms of the activity of Jampel Yang and other Tantric deities. We might expect there to be a 'clerical Buddhist' interpretation of Tantra as well, in the sense of a philosophical analysis of what Tantra means and how it works. This is, in fact, the case. More precisely, there are several competing 'clerical' accounts of the meaning of Tantra, each with its own analysis of how Enlightenment is achieved through Tantric practice. I shall be giving some attention to these scholarly interpretations of Tantra, especially in the historical analysis in Part Three, because the arguments concerning them are often considerably more than narrow doctrinal disputes. Questions of the relationship between relative and transcendental 'truths,' of the reality of the world as ordinarily perceived, and of the preparations needed for proper Tantric practice, have had entirely real social and political implications within the Tibetan context.

Thus the shamanic approach has tended to go along with an emphasis on the validity of direct as opposed to gradual entry into the Enlightened state and on positive conceptions of the nature of Enlightenment *(tathāgatagarbha, shentong)*, while lamas more aligned with the clerical approach have emphasized gradual entry and a more negative, intellectually based conception of Enlightenment. The relationships here are not always straightforward, since the most influential lamas in Tibetan history all aimed at some kind of synthesis between the approaches, and the authority of Madhyamaka philosophy, with its basically negative conceptualizations, remained very great for all schools, but the significance of these linkages will emerge in the historical account of Part Three.

In particular, proponents of the clerical approach have insisted on the critical importance of adequate and extensive non-Tantric preparation for Tantric practice. Typically, this is taken furthest by the Gelugpa, the most 'clerical' of the four Buddhist orders, and the one most closely integrated with the structures of secular power. Such an insistence goes along with a relatively restricted role for Tantra, as something to be undertaken only by a small and thoroughly trained and vetted élite. This is particularly so for those who became lamas in the Gelugpa tradition.

Thus Buddhist history and practice in Tibet can be 'read' by the Tibetans themselves in terms of clerical Buddhism or of shamanic Buddhism.[18] This is not an either-or choice. For the Tibetans, the universe in which they live is seen as capable of multiple interpretations, which are not necessarily exclusive. Rationality is not, as it tends to be in contemporary Western society, the single dominant mode of legitimate discourse.

This was also true for the actors in the historical account of the evolution of Tibetan religion, which I shall present later in this book. Major figures such as Tsongk'apa or Longch'en Rabjampa might appear to be dominantly clerical or shamanic in their orientation but they generally operated in both modes, seeing them as complementary rather than opposed. Consequently it is not always easy, or even appropriate, for an external observer to assign specific events, people, or movements in Tibetan history exclusively to one category or the other. What took place was more in the nature of a series of syntheses between the two aspects. By the late nineteenth century there were two major competing syntheses, one advanced by the Gelugpa tradition and one, the so-called Rimed movement, which had developed among the other religious traditions.

As I suggested above, through most of Tibetan history the shamanic Buddhist orientation was dominant. Both Gelugpa and Rimed approaches retained this shamanic dominance, if with different degrees of emphasis. In terms of Buddhist practice, this corresponded to the dominance of the Vajrayāna over the Pāramitāyāna, of Tantra over Sūtra. In Part Two of this book (Chapters 9 to 18) we shall see how the dominance of 'shamanic Buddhism' worked out in terms of everyday religion in the early twentieth century. Part Three (Chapters 19 to 28) traces the evolution of the two major syntheses (Gelugpa and Rimed) from what seem to have been, in the early period, two relatively distinct traditions of clerical and shamanic Buddhism.

In Chapter 2, the remaining chapter of the Introduction, some of the issues relating to the social structure of Tibetan societies, which were sketched above, will be introduced in more detail through a comparison with the Theravādin Buddhist societies of Southeast Asia.

2

Tibetan and Theravādin Societies: A Comparison

I suggested in Chapter 1 that Tibetan Buddhism differed considerably from Buddhism in Theravādin societies. In this chapter, the two are compared in some detail, in order to specify the particular character of Buddhism in Tibet. My picture of Buddhism in Theravādin societies is based primarily on material from Thailand and Burma. A generally consistent anthropological account of religion in these two countries has emerged over the past couple of decades, despite differences in interpretation, from the work of Stanley Tambiah (1970, 1976, 1984), B. J. Terwiel (1975), Niels Mulder (1985), Gehan Wijeyewardene (1986), Melford Spiro (1967, 1971), E. Michael Mendelson (1975), and others. Much of this picture also applies to Sinhalese Buddhism as studied by Michael Ames (1964, 1966), Richard Gombrich (1971), Gananath Obeyesekere (1966, 1977), Bruce Kapferer (1983), Martin Southwold (1983) and others, although there are some substantial contrasts between Sri Lanka and the Southeast Asian societies, such as the influence of caste in Sinhalese society and the use of temporary monkhood as a *rite de passage* for young men in Thailand and Burma. We can, however, still put forward a number of general features as characteristic of Buddhist practice in all these Theravādin societies.

To begin with, in all of these societies the primary Buddhist role is that of the *bhikkhu*, the fully ordained Buddhist monk. In all of them, too, the Buddhist Saṃgha, which in Theravādin societies means the order of monks and (male or female) novices, is a centralized, state-sponsored and state-controlled organization. In each country there are large monasteries in the urban centers, often under royal or state sponsorship, which act as teaching (and certification) centers and which may be involved in important state ritual. Political rule is closely associated with Buddhism, both through the ideology of the *cakravartin* or *dharmarāja*, and through the significance of Buddhist sacred objects such as the Emerald Buddha in Thailand or the Tooth Relic in Sri Lanka as focal points of state power.

In recent years some of these urban monasteries have become centers for lay meditation practice, but traditionally meditation has been a monastic practice, carried out in hermitages and retreat centers well away from the city.

Aside from the large urban monasteries and the retreat centers, typical rural monasteries in Theravādin countries are situated within villages, and have a single *bhikkhu*, or perhaps two or three at most, in residence. These 'monks' have a distinctly clerical role towards the lay population. They recite scriptures, teach, and perform rituals mainly in the context of death or 'merit-making' ceremonies (which include the making of donations to monks and their temples).

'Merit' *(puṇya)* and demerit, good or bad karma, form the foundation of the Buddhist ethical code, which is justified by reference to the immutable laws of cause and effect. According to this law of karma, one's actions in this life, or more precisely one's intentional states, have effects in future lives, just as one's fortune in this life results from the karma of one's past actions. Tambiah has spelled out this 'dialectic of merit' for village society in northeast Thailand (1968, 1970). His demonstration would serve in its essentials for all Theravādin societies. It forms at least a first level of understanding of karma in Tibetan societies as well (see Chapter 11). This is what Melford Spiro referred to as *kammatic Buddhism* (a term derived from *kamma*, Pali for karma; Spiro 1971); I refer to it (see Chapter 1) as the *Karma Orientation.*[1]

The sphere of merit, death and rebirth, past and future lives, is conceptually differentiated in Theravādin as in Tibetan Buddhist thought from the ultimate Buddhist goal of Enlightenment (Buddhahood, *bodhi*). Enlightenment and *nirvāṇa* (Pali *nibbāna*) are regarded as being much the same thing in Theravādin thought, though not by Mahāyānists such as the Tibetans. Both are beyond the scope of the average villager or urban dweller, or even the majority of monks. Spiro referred to this as *nibbanic Buddhism;* I refer to it as the *Bodhi Orientation.*

A third sphere of religious activity is of much more salience for the majority of the population. This is concerned with attaining success and prosperity and avoiding misfortune in this life. These aims are achieved through interaction with the various worldly gods and spirits, an interaction mediated by a host of primarily nonmonastic specialists, spirit-mediums, astrologers, exorcists, priests of deity cults, and the like (for example, Spiro 1967, Mulder 1985). I refer to it as the *Pragmatic Orientation* (see Mandelbaum 1966[2]); in Spiro's terms it corresponds to what he calls 'supernaturalism,' and regards as a non-Buddhist religion (Spiro 1967), along with certain elements of Buddhism ('apotropaic Buddhism,' Spiro 1971).

We thus have three general spheres of religious activity in these societies:

1. The realm of this-worldly concerns, which in religious terms is the sphere of interaction with, and protection against, local gods and spirits, largely carried out by ritual practitioners who are not Buddhist monks (the *Pragmatic Orientation*);

2. The sphere of death and rebirth, past and future lives, dominated by the conceptual structure of karma and the 'ideology of merit,' and mediated by the Buddhist monks (the *Karma Orientation*);

3. The pursuit of Enlightenment or *nirvāṇa,* seen as escape from the cycle of rebirth *(saṃsāra).* This is, in practice, the preserve of a small number of 'religious virtuosi' (as Weber called them), and constitutes the *Bodhi Orientation.*

The relationship between these areas is the subject of some controversy in Theravādin Buddhist studies. Spiro, for example, has argued that the first sphere and the second and third constitute separate and largely distinct religions ('supernaturalism' and 'Buddhism'). It is evident that sphere 1 and 2 + 3 are oriented around different value-systems, but it seems to me to make more sense to consider the practices associated with these different orientations, as Tambiah does, as structurally related elements within a total field (Spiro 1967, 1971; Tambiah 1970, 1984:315).

Spiro argues that only a small number of individuals orient their lives around nibbanic Buddhism (=3) and that kammatic Buddhism (=2) is the norm for Theravādin Buddhist practitioners. This is doubtless true enough, but it is also true that, as Tambiah has shown, the small minority of people committed to the Bodhi Orientation are important for the system as a whole. This is not simply because they provide models or inspiration for the less religiously virtuosic remainder of the population, but because their attainments through Bodhi-oriented practice can be, and are, transferred into activity in the Pragmatic sphere (=1). As we shall see, this mutual involvement of spheres 1 and 3 is taken much further in Tibetan Buddhism.

THE SUCCESSFUL DOMESTICATION OF THE THERAVĀDIN SAṂGHA

Even in the Theravādin countries, many monks are involved in 'pragmatic religion' to a considerable degree as makers and empowerers of magical protective devices and occasionally as exorcists and the like. Such activity shades off into that of cult-groups that form around individual Buddhist monks or occasionally laymen to whom magical powers are attributed. These groups can have a strong 'millennial' character and even form the basis for political movements opposing the régime in power. Generally speaking, all of this activity, from empowering amulets to leading rebellions, can be considered Pragmatic in that it is concerned with the this-worldly benefit of those involved. All of it, too, is based on the premise that the spiritual power that is being turned to these Pragmatic ends is derived from Buddhist practice. Such power is more than the result of acquiring good karma; it arises out of the realm of Bodhi-oriented practice, Spiro's Nibbanic Buddhism.[3]

Ideologically, involvement with Pragmatic religion, let alone with millennial cult-groups, is defined by the authorities of Theravādin orthodoxy as marginal to the monk's role. It is associated less with the fully 'domesticated' monks of urban or village monasteries than with the ascetic meditators and hermits who live, in a sense, at the edges of orthodox Theravādin society. The role of these 'forest-saints' and of their followers is of particular interest when it comes to drawing a contrast with Buddhism in Tibet.

Tambiah, referring to the disciples of one such modern Theravādin saint in Thailand, Acharn Mun, makes a differentiation between 'rationalist' and 'tantric' approaches. The 'rationalists' are dedicated to the individual pursuit of *nirvāṇa,* while the 'tantrics' accept the pressure of their lay followers to convert the charisma of spiritual attainment into magical ritual action for this-worldly ends (Tambiah 1984:135ff). Here, the 'rationalists' represent the ideologically normative aspect from the point of view of 'domesticated,' State Buddhism, while the 'tantrics' correspond to the undomesticated or 'wild' orientation. To put this in slightly different terms, orthodoxy is happy with nibbanic Buddhism as long as it stays within 'rationalist' terms and does not move into the wider social arena.

'Tantric' here has to be taken metaphorically, since these monks (and occasionally laymen) are not Tantric in the Tibetan sense.[4] It is true however that in the explicitly Tantric context of Tibetan religion we will find that this kind of practice, oriented around the 'magical' pursuit of Pragmatic ends, is much more typical and central than in Theravādin societies. One of the main questions to be discussed in this book is why Tantric (Vajrayāna) Buddhism in Tibet should be associated with this kind of activity. The answer that I shall present is partly in terms of the internal procedures and techniques of Tantric Buddhism and partly in terms of the specific nature, in the historical period and in more recent times, of Tibetan society.

In the Theravādin countries, this 'magical' or 'shamanic' aspect of Buddhism forms a kind of fringe at the edge of orthodox Theravādin Buddhism. Cult-groups regularly form and grow in response to lay demand, but are as regularly suppressed and kept in their place by religious or secular authorities if and when they come to constitute a political problem.

In this respect, as in others, the rulers of Theravādin societies are typically concerned to keep the Saṃgha, the monastic community, in its place. The purification of the Saṃgha, which generally involves the reassertion of state control over the Saṃgha along with attempts at the removal or suppression of nonorthodox forms of Buddhism, has been a constant theme in these societies.

The concern of the State to control such forms of Buddhism can be explained by the ease with which 'charismatic' Buddhist miracle-workers can move into the political arena, become leaders of 'millennial' movements, and constitute real political threats. These millennial rebellions have been a regular feature of Theravādin societies for many centuries (Tambiah 1984, chapter 20). As the recent case of Suchart Kosonkitiwont in Thailand shows, such political challenges to the authority of the state are still possible today (Wijeyewardene 1986:23–25; Heinze 1988:263–278).

In the Theravādin context, millennial movements very rarely succeed in achieving political power. It is true, as Tambiah points out, that "millennial claims have always been part of the regular political process" in the "pulsating, galactic polities" of Southeast Asia. Military conquests or the establishment of new dynasties have regularly been justified in terms of the charismatic status of the ruler, seen in Buddhist terms. In such cases, however, we have a secular transfer of power legitimating itself in retrospect in Buddhist terms rather than the achievement of state control by a charismatic cult-leader.

The cult-movements themselves, as Tambiah notes, do not in general get to the point of an actual takeover of power:

> As esoteric cults built around individual masters, they have little staying power after the leader's death, though disciples may reproduce the cells, associations and networks established by the master. And when they boil up into militant revolts, they are unable to long withstand the organized force deployed by the established political authority. . . . Such bubbles form and burst typically in the territorial and social peripheries of established societies and polities, away from the capitals of their ruling political and ecclesiastical elites. In this sense, millennial Buddhism is the counterculture and counterstructure to organized and domesticated Buddhism. (Tambiah 1984:319–320)

THE FAILED DOMESTICATION OF THE TIBETAN SAṂGHA

Tambiah emphasizes that millennial Buddhism in the Southeast Asian context has to be seen "as part of a totality, in which 'established' Buddhism and polity constitute its dialectical, and frequently paramount, counterpart" (Tambiah 1984:320). When we turn to Tibet we find forms of Buddhism that resemble the 'millennial Buddhism' of the Thai and Burmese forest-saints, but which are part of a very different totality. Generally speaking, through most of the history of Buddhism in Tibet it has been 'millennial' Buddhism that has been paramount. The counterculture and counterstructure, which elsewhere might have become a 'domesticated' Buddhism, has established only a limited presence, primarily in the central agricultural areas.

The 'millennial'/'domesticated' terminology presents some difficulty in the Tibetan context. 'Domesticated' fits well enough, and corresponds closely to some indigenous Tibetan concepts (see Chapter 11). 'Millennial,' however, carries implications of a radical break with the established order that is not appropriate in a situation where 'undomesticated' Buddhism itself constitutes a large part of the established order. Neither are 'tantric' and 'rationalist' entirely satisfactory, since they may create a confusion between possible indigenous and anthropological senses of 'tantric.' The term 'tantric' in the Tibetan context is better reserved to the indigenous (emic) sense, that of being associated with a lineage of practice specifically defined as Tantra *(gyüd)* by the Tibetans. It is for this reason that I prefer to use the terms introduced in the previous chapter, shamanic Buddhism and clerical Buddhism.

Now let us look at the ways in which religion in Tibetan societies contrasts with the picture of Theravādin societies presented above. A first striking difference between Theravādin Buddhist societies and Tibetan societies is the question of religious leadership. The preeminent position, which in the Theravādin countries belongs to the *bhikkhu* or fully ordained monks, is taken by the lamas in Tibetan societies. The Tibetans have fully ordained monks or *gelong* (= Pali *bhikkhu*) and for them, as elsewhere in the Buddhist world, this is a key status in the monastic career; however, lamas are not necessarily monks or even members of religious communities. As a corollary, for Tibetans the monastic career itself is much less of a *sine qua non* for serious Buddhist practice than it is in Theravādin countries.

The defining feature of lamas in Tibetan thought is that they are teachers ('lama' is equivalent to the Sanskrit term *guru*), more specifically teachers of Tantric practice (*vajraguru*, *vajrācārya*, Tib. *dorjé lobpön*). To say that the lamas are by definition teachers of Tantric practice implies that they, too, are the most competent performers of Tantric practice. In Tibet, as in the Theravādin societies we have been considering, the relationship between human beings and their natural and social environment is conceived of in terms of a vocabulary of 'gods' or 'spirits' of various kinds with whom satisfactory relationships has to be maintained (Samuel 1990:79–133). For the Tibetans, as I have already suggested in Chapter 1, Tantra provides the primary body of religious techniques by which these local gods and spirits, and the general area of 'this-worldly' problems, are dealt with.

Thus it is to the lamas that the Tibetan lay and monastic population looks for the performance of these rituals, while the equivalent functions in Theravādin societies are carried out by practitioners who are not, or not necessarily, Buddhist monks or other representatives of specifically Buddhist power.[5] In this way the area of Pragmatic religion, which is only marginally within the Saṃgha's area of competence in Theravādin countries, is the direct concern of the Tibetan lamas.

Rather than these magical and shamanic operations forming an only partially acknowledged fringe to Buddhist practice, in Tibet they are an integral and fully recognized part of it. The lamas are not the only practitioners in this area but they are the most senior and powerful, and they direct and supervise other lesser types of practitioners (see Chapters 13 to 16).

What all this means in terms of the tripartite division, which I adopted above for the Theravādins, can now be spelled out explicitly. The corresponding spheres of religious activity for Tibetan Buddhism can be described as follows:

1. *Pragmatic.* The realm of this-worldly concerns, conceived of in terms of interactions with local gods and spirits, and carried out by a variety of ritual practitioners, foremost among them being the lamas, who employ the techniques of Tantric practice for this purpose;

2. *Karma-oriented.* The sphere of death and rebirth, past and future lives, again seen in terms of karma and the 'ideology of merit' and mediated by Buddhist monks and lamas. This is the primary realm of 'clerical Buddhism';

3. *Bodhi-oriented.* The pursuit of Enlightenment, here seen as having a strongly social or altruistic component, and carried out through Tantric practice.

There is some simplification here, since shamanic Buddhism is also involved in sphere 2 through the essentially Tantric process of *p'owa* or direct transference of consciousness at the time of death to a Pure Land such as Dewachen (Skt. Sukhāvatī). There are also nontantric methods involved in sphere 3, such as the so-called Sūtra Mahāmudrā system and the Dzogch'en practices. These complications however do nothing to weaken the central place in the system of shamanic Buddhism, which is dominant in spheres 1 and 3, and strongly present through the *p'owa* practices in sphere 2. Nor does it weaken the position of the lamas, who are also the prime authorities for Sūtra Mahāmudrā and Dzogch'en.

There are many ways of becoming a lama and many ways of pursuing the career of lama. I sketch some of these in Chapters 15 and 16. An important point is that there are only limited degrees of prescription and regulation in relation to the role of lama. Some lamas become lamas through formal and rational ('clerical') criteria, while others take less conventional routes to their position. Some are born into lama families, while others, the reincarnate[6] lamas or *trulku* are appointed by being recognized as the rebirth of a previous lama. Some men, and a few women, simply acquire a following as a result of their personal reputation for spiritual development, and so become lamas. Ascription of lama status may involve no more than the recognition of that person as a lama by a group of people. This fluidity has been part of Tibetan Buddhism from its early stages and it remains part of the contemporary situation. It is exemplified in Chapter 18 through accounts of the lives of eight modern lamas.

All this suggests that the Saṃgha in Tibetan societies is far less "domesticated," in Tambiah's phrase, than in contemporary Theravādin countries, or than it seems to have been in Theravādin societies in recent centuries. Instead of being a centralized organization of monks under state control, the Saṃgha consists of a number of autonomous religious orders, only partly composed of celibate monks, and based around various large teaching centers and their associated lamas. In place of the Theravādin monastery (*vihāra*, *wat*, etc.) we find the Tibetan *gompa*. This can be anything from a small village temple where local lay practitioners do occasional rituals to a sizeable monastic town containing temples, colleges, and residential halls for monks.[7]

Most of the larger *gompa* are centered around one or more series[8] of reincarnate lamas. Such a rebirth-series consists of a succession of lamas, each recognized as the rebirth of the previous member of the series. These rebirth-series have their own households or *labrang*, passed on from one rebirth to the next, and usually quite distinct from the *gompa's* own economy. Both the lama's household and the *gompa* can own property, and in Tibetan societies the ownership of property also generally implies the exercise of political power.

In the course of Tibetan history, hereditary lineages or, especially in the later period, rebirth-series of lamas often gained a degree of political control over large areas, either in association with local aristocratic leaders or on their own. This was so particularly in the central agricultural regions, where society had long been more stratified and contained more elements of state organization. The best-known example of such a regime was that of the Dalai Lamas from the seventeenth to twentieth centuries, with its capital at Lhasa, but there were many others of smaller scale or duration. The degree of control exercised by such régimes was limited in comparison with the 'galactic polities' of Southeast Asia, and many parts of Tibet were, in effect, outside any such centralized control.

In this respect I find descriptions of premodern Tibet as a centralized state under the rule of a theocratic government at Lhasa unconvincing.[9] The political system was far more complex than such a description would allow. Part One of this book (Chapters 3 to 8) attempts to present a more balanced picture. It is important to notice however that such political apparatus as was present was dominated, and indeed in large measure constituted, by the religious orders. This was the reverse of the situation in Theravādin countries. Attempts to 'domesticate' the Saṃgha occurred from time to time in Tibetan history, as will be seen from the historical account in Chapters 23 to 28, but they never had more than limited success.

SHAMANIC POWER AND THE STATE

The lack of success in domesticating the Saṃgha in Tibet is perhaps not surprising given the limited nature of centralized political control in Tibetan societies. This does not in itself, however, explain why the 'undomesticated' Saṃgha took the form it did, with strong leanings towards the shamanic and Tantric. Nevertheless, it seems to have been true within Tibetan societies that shamanic Buddhism was at its most effective in regions and at times where the social structure was relatively 'stateless.' Religious leadership within shamanic Buddhism had a free-floating and charismatic quality deriving from the personal power of a particular lama and readily transferable into the general political arena. Clerical Buddhism, by contrast, was a Buddhism of rules, regulations, and institutions. It was most at home in the context of a state with centralized government, or at least of a large monastic *gompa* with established property and political power continuing over many generations. What is it specifically about the two forms of Buddhism that explains their association with these contrasting social and political contexts?

Here I shall give only a brief answer, since at this stage I have introduced neither the descriptive material nor the analytic concepts necessary to understand these processes more fully. In brief, though, I see the difference as connected with the way in which Tantric practice legitimates an autonomous role for the practitioner.

The essential point is that, in shamanic Buddhism, a practitioner can relate directly to the sources of power and authority, by contacting the Tantric 'deities' and other central 'culture-heroes.' Once the practitioner becomes a lama, this direct contact with power legitimates a social role that can as easily extend into the political sphere as into the religious. In the clerical version, by contrast, the practitioner approaches authority much more gradually and indirectly, through the books and the established traditions of interpretation by which those books have to be read.

This is stated quite explicitly in relation to the classification of Tantric methods into four (for the Nyingmapa tradition, six) levels. A well-known tradition states that on the lowest level (Kriyā) the practitioner's relationship with the Tantric god or *yidam* (Skt. *iṣṭadevatā*) is as a servant to a lord, on the next level (Caryā) the relationship is that of friend to friend, while on the higher levels the relationship is no longer dualistic, and the practitioner becomes identical with the Tantric deity.[10]

The implications of 'becoming identical with a Tantric deity' will emerge in the course of Part Two. For the present, it is not difficult to appreciate that such a procedure places the source of authority firmly within the lama's own grasp, while always leaving open the possibility for someone else to acquire the status of lama and to become in turn the focus of popular esteem. Speaking in terms of ideal types, a purely shamanic lama has both far more authority than anyone in a purely clerical religious system (since he can, in effect, rewrite the rules) and far less security (since his position is always open to challenge by a more successful lama). To the extent that the position of the lama becomes 'clericalized,' this situation is modified: it is harder for a lama to introduce major changes or to challenge the structures of authority, but a formal organizational structure provides him with more security.

Certainly the Tibetan tradition is clear about the proper relationship between shamanic Buddhist lamas and secular rulers. The point is neatly made in the traditional descriptions of the first meeting between Guru Rimpoch'e, who is the prototype of the shamanic lama, and the revered Buddhist king Tr'isong Deutsen. Rather than the lama prostrating to the king, the king is forced by Guru Rimpoch'e's great power to prostrate to the lama (Douglas and Bays 1978, vol. 2, 376–383).

That this-worldly power is associated with the attainment of higher levels on the Buddhist spiritual path is implicit within the clerical version of Tibetan Buddhism and even, as Tambiah has demonstrated, within 'domesticated' Theravāda Buddhism (Tambiah 1984). All traditions of Buddhism recognize the magical powers involved in the attainment of Buddhahood. In practice, however, in the clerical and 'domesticated' varieties of Buddhism such attainment is seen at best as something that may happen in the distant future. In Tantra, by contrast, practitioners created the divine form to be attained directly through their imagination. This process was believed, once it had been mastered, to enable them to exercise in reality the powers associated with the divine forms they were assuming. This is part of what the Tibetans mean when they say that one of the characteristic features of Tantric techniques is that the 'result' becomes part of the 'path.'

Lay Tibetans are not necessarily knowledgeable about the detailed processes of Tantric meditation. Many have at least a superficial acquaintance with Tantric procedures, however, and stories like that of Guru Rimpoch'e and Tr'isong Deutsen, or of the epic hero Gesar, whose victories owe more to Tantric magical power than to force of arms (Samuel, in press b, in press c) are widely known. It is taken for granted that the power of lamas is comparable to, and in many cases greater than, that of secular rulers. As we shall see, lamas could, and did, use their charismatic power as the basis for the formation of secular regimes, with either themselves or a lay chieftain as ruler. The most successful of these visionary lamas, creators of new religious orders or founders of new political structures, were able to transform the shape of Tibetan religion and society through their activities. There are certainly figures in Thai or Burmese history who have attempted to occupy a similar role. In the end, however, as Tambiah notes (1984:319–320), none of them ever really succeeded.

The importance of the charismatic power of the lamas within Tibetan societies is linked to the weakness of centralized regimes in the Tibetan region, and Part One of the book, which begins with Chapter 3, examines this situation in detail. The lamas were only able to occupy their exceptional position, however, because of highly specialized training that prepared them for their combined shamanic and clerical role, and because of the total framework of thought, feeling, and action, which supported their role. These issues form the subject matter of Parts Two and Three of the book.

Part One

3

Tibetan Societies: Introduction and Central Tibet

I have suggested in the previous two chapters that the forms taken by Buddhism in Tibetan societies need to be understood in terms of the specific characteristics of those societies. In particular, the 'shamanic' aspects of Tibetan Buddhism only make sense in terms of the relatively 'stateless' nature of most Tibetan societies up to and into the 'premodern' period.

As I pointed out at the start of Chapter 1, the use of the plural form for 'societies' is deliberate. Premodern Tibet contained a greater variety of social and political formations than is often appreciated (Map 1).[1] Certainly, it makes little sense to think of Tibet as a strongly centralized state ruled by a theocratic government at Lhasa, although this caricature is still quite widely believed in, particularly among non-Tibetanists (see Chapter 8). The Dalai Lama's regime at Lhasa was only one, if in recent times the largest, of a variety of state formations within the Tibetan region.[2] This variety of political forms, and the general vulnerability and fragility of centralized power of any kind through most of Tibetan history, are vital elements for understanding the nature of Tibetan religion.

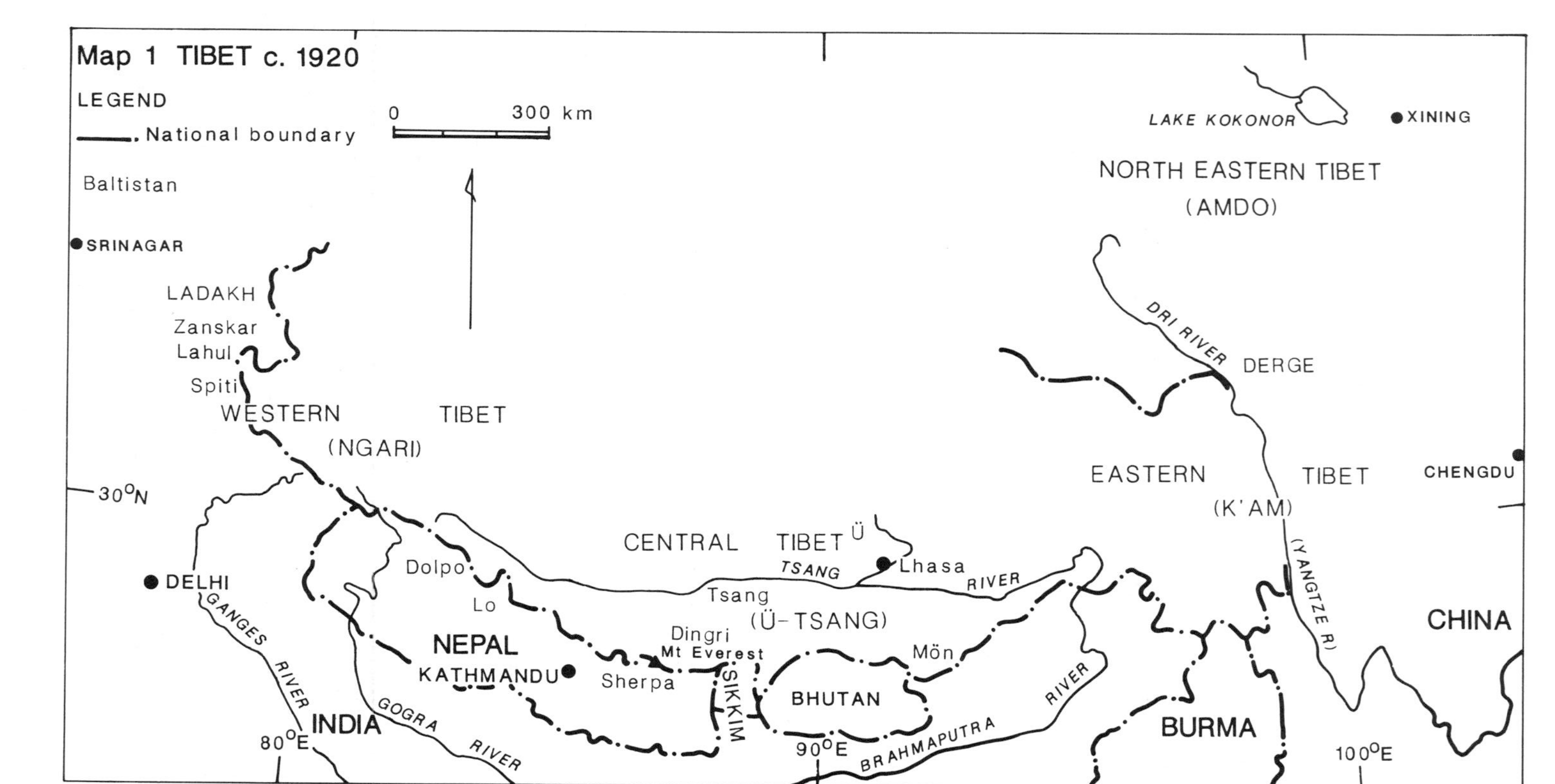
Map 1 TIBET c. 1920
LEGEND
National boundary
0
300 km
Baltistan
SRINAGAR
LADAKH
Zanskar
Lahul
Spiti
WESTERN
TIBET
(NGARI)
30°N
DELHI
GANGES
RIVER
80°E
INDIA
GOGRA
RIVER
Dolpo
Lo
NEPAL
KATHMANDU
Sherpa
Dingri
Mt Everest
SIKKIM
CENTRAL
TIBET
Ü
TSANG
Tsang
(Ü-TSANG)
Lhasa
RIVER
Mön
BHUTAN
90°E
BRAHMAPUTRA
RIVER
LAKE KOKONOR
XINING
NORTH EASTERN TIBET
(AMDO)
DRI RIVER
DERGE
EASTERN
TIBET
(K'AM)
CHENGDU
(YANGTZE R)
CHINA
BURMA
100°E

Chapters 3 to 6 present the major regions of Tibetan population. For each region, I shall describe the various political structures and give an outline of their history. In Chapter 7, I look at the kinds of local communities (agricultural, pastoral, and urban) that existed within these regions in the premodern period. Chapter 8 also presents some general conclusions about premodern Tibetan societies, conclusions that form the background for the discussion of Tibetan religion in Parts Two and Three of the book.

Tibetan societies and Tibetan religion have been in a process of continuous change for as far back as we can trace. There was no such thing as a 'static' society in Tibet in the premodern period, and the nineteenth and twentieth centuries were periods of particularly rapid change in many respects. Consequently, both in the survey we are now undertaking, and in the account of Tibetan religion in Part Two (Chapters 9 to 18), we are dealing with a social and religious field that was continually transforming. This process of transformation worked differently in the various regions, and social and religious forms belonging to the past in some areas were still recognizably present in others into the early twentieth century. In addition, any picture of Tibetan society or Tibetan religion has to depend on sources of information of varying quality and date for different aspects of the overall picture. We are much better informed, for example, about the social structure of Tibetan populations in northern Nepal, where there has been a substantial amount of modern anthropological research, than about populations in K'am or Amdo, where our main sources are reports by early travelers, the accounts of contemporary refugees, and such information as can be gathered from Tibetan literary sources.[3] It is still possible, however, to present an overall view of Tibetan societies as they were in recent times.

BASIC CONSTITUENTS OF THE TIBETAN ECONOMY

There were two primary modes of subsistence in premodern Tibet, pastoralism and agriculture. Most of the Tibetan population were agriculturalists *(shingpa)*. Some (called *samadrog*) maintained herds of animals alongside an agricultural base. The pastoralists proper *(drogpa)* were a substantial minority. They were found throughout the region. In some areas, such as the northern uplands (Changt'ang) or the south and west of Amdo, almost the entire population was (and still is) made up of pastoralists. The *drogpa* are distinctive in dialect, dress, and cultural style, although fully integrated into the general economic and cultural system of the Tibetan plateau (see Ekvall 1956).

Pastoralism in Tibet is based on cattle, including yaks and yak-cow hybrids, along with horses, sheep, and goats (see Downs and Ekvall 1965). Agriculture in the premodern period involved a variety of grains and vegetables, with the altitude-tolerant barley as the most widespread basic grain. In recent years the potato has become a major subsistence crop for some Tibetan communities in the Himalayas (for example, the Sherpas), but in the premodern period it had not yet had a substantial impact on most Tibetan populations.

Pastoralists and agriculturalists have always been mutually dependent. The staple food of Tibet, roasted barley-flour moistened with buttered tea, includes both pastoral and agricultural products. It also involves salt, which is produced in Tibet by the pastoralists and was in the premodern period one of the region's main exports to India, and tea, which was imported along long-distance trade routes by yak-caravans from China.

Travel through the Tibetan region in the premodern period was slow and arduous. Along with the Tibetan mode of subsistence, the sheer physical nature of the Tibetan landscape has had a strong influence on the nature of Tibetan polities. As is well known, the Tibetan population lives at among the highest altitudes of any human populations. The highest permanent Tibetan settlements are at around 4,000–4,500 meters, while the lower limit of the Tibetan cultural adaptation is at around 2,000–2,400 meters in the Nepal Himalaya and at similar altitudes in east and northeast Tibet. The high altitudes, the dramatic nature of the landforms, and the frequently treacherous climate made travel around Tibet slow, difficult, and often dangerous.

Tibetans nevertheless traveled extensively for purposes of trade and religion (the two were frequently combined). The importance of long-distance trade within the region in the premodern period was such that it should perhaps be counted as a mode of subsistence in its own right. The long-distance trading journeys in which many Tibetans were involved resulted in continuing contact among the various Tibetan populations, despite their being distributed over a vast area within which communications were more than ordinarily difficult.

These trading journeys also kept the Tibetans in close contact with the various other ethnic groups to their east, south, and west. Links among the far-flung populations of Tibet were also maintained, in the premodern period, by the extensive practice of pilgrimage and by the regular journeys of Tibetan monks from outlying regions to study in the large teaching *gompa* of central and eastern Tibet.

This is perhaps one reason for the marked contrast that exists between the relative cultural unity of the Tibetan plateau and the high degree of ethnic diversity found in the uplands of Yunnan, Burma, Laos, and Thailand to the south. Tibet was built on long-distance trade. At the same time, the existence of major long-distance trade routes created a differentiation between populations that were close to such routes and those that were not.

Agriculture in most of Tibet was (and still is) confined to river valleys. Many of these valleys are quite small, containing only a few villages each. Traveling from one valley to the next in the premodern period could involve an arduous traverse by foot or with pack-animals over high mountain passes where the traveller was exposed to the extremities of the Tibetan climate. In the more open pastoral regions, the threat of bandit attacks often made travel risky. In many parts of Tibet, travel was impossible during certain periods of the year and communities were isolated for the winter months.

Only along a few major rivers are there larger tracts of arable land, and these areas have consequently been of great importance in Tibetan history. Chief among them are the heartlands of the two central Tibetan provinces of Ü and Tsang, made up of the arable lands along the Tsang River and some of its major tributaries. Other major agricultural areas are along the lower parts of the four main river valleys of K'am, the eastern province of Tibet, and along the eastern borders of the northeastern region of Amdo. The major long-distance trade routes naturally tended to run between these more populous regions, where there were medium-sized towns such as Lhasa, Gyantsé, Shigatsé, Leh, Kangding, or Kandzé, with merchant and artisan communities, as well as local political authorities who could help ensure the security of traders.

The contrast between these relatively prosperous and productive agricultural areas, with direct access to long-distance trade routes, the more marginal agricultural areas away from the central regions, and those areas which support only pastoralism, is, as we will see, a basic factor within Tibetan society. Significant Tibetan political units have always been centered within major agricultural areas, which provide a tax base to support the state apparatus, while the marginal agricultural areas and the pastoral regions have never been more than partially incorporated into Tibetan states. However, shifts in the pattern of trade, as well as probable long-term shifts in the climate and ecology, have meant that areas that were at one time relatively central, such as the region south and west of Mount Kailash, later became much more marginal.

A NOTE ON TIBETAN POPULATION

There are no reliable population estimates for the premodern period, but the 1982 Chinese census figures give a detailed breakdown of the Tibetan population for that date. These figures are presented diagrammatically in a recent *Population Atlas of China* (Li Chengrui 1987:26, 33). Assuming that they are reliable,[4] we can estimate the present Tibetan population of central Tibet, i.e., the prefectures of Lhasa City, Xigazê (Shigatsé), Shannan (Lhok'a), and Nagqu (Nagch'u), as about 1.25 million (see Map 2). This corresponds to a considerably larger area than that of traditional central Tibet or Ü-Tsang.

We can estimate the Tibetan population of K'am, including the Qamdo (Ch'amdo) prefecture of the Tibet Autonomous Region, as about 1.53 million,[5] and of Amdo as about 1.05 million.[6] The areas of western Tibet within the Tibet Autonomous Region, administered as the prefecture of Ali (Ngari) have a Tibetan population of about 55,000. Altogether this makes a total of 3.87 million Tibetans living within the People's Republic of China, according to the 1982 census.

The Tibet Autonomous Region corresponds approximately to the premodern Tibetan state governed from Lhasa. Its Tibetan population, according to the 1982 census figures, is around 1.79 million. As can be seen, this is less than half of the total Tibetan population of the Chinese People's Republic, with the remainder living in traditionally Tibetan areas that have been incorporated into the provinces of Sichuan, Qinghai, Gansu, and Yunnan (the so-called Inner Tibet of the 1914 Simla Convention). This should be emphasized because sev-

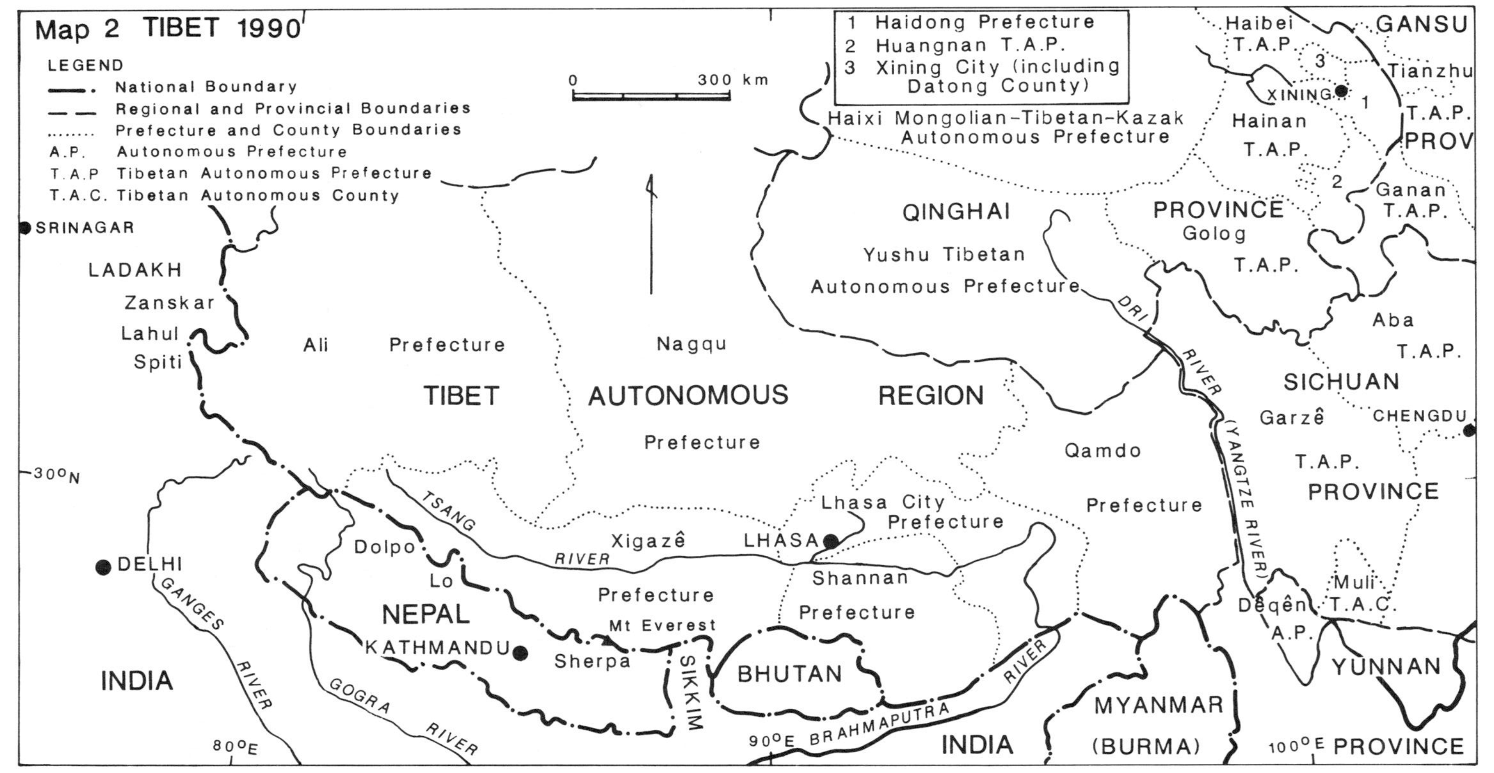
Map 2 TIBET 1990
LEGEND
National Boundary
Regional and Provincial Boundaries
Prefecture and County Boundaries
A.P. Autonomous Prefecture
T.A.P Tibetan Autonomous Prefecture
T.A.C. Tibetan Autonomous County
0 300 km
1 Haidong Prefecture
2 Huangnan T.A.P.
3 Xining City (including Datong County)
Haixi Mongolian-Tibetan-Kazak Autonomous Prefecture
Haibei T.A.P.
GANSU
Tianzhu T.A.P.
PROV
XINING
Hainan T.A.P.
Ganan T.A.P.
QINGHAI
PROVINCE
Golog T.A.P.
Yushu Tibetan Autonomous Prefecture
Aba T.A.P.
SICHUAN
CHENGDU
Garzê T.A.P.
PROVINCE
DRI RIVER (YANGTZE RIVER)
SRINAGAR
LADAKH
Zanskar
Lahul
Spiti
Ali Prefecture
Nagqu Prefecture
TIBET AUTONOMOUS REGION
Qamdo Prefecture
30°N
TSANG RIVER
Xigazê Prefecture
Lhasa City Prefecture
LHASA
Shannan Prefecture
Muli T.A.C.
Dêqên A.P.
YUNNAN
DELHI
Dolpo
Lo
NEPAL
KATHMANDU
Mt Everest
Sherpa
SIKKIM
BHUTAN
BRAHMAPUTRA RIVER
MYANMAR (BURMA)
INDIA
GANGES RIVER
GOGRA RIVER
INDIA
80°E
90°E
100°E
PROVINCE

eral authors (for example, Goldstein 1989) use 'Tibet' to refer to the premodern Lhasa state and its modern equivalent, the Tibet Autonomous Region.

It is difficult to judge how much these figures for central Tibet, K'am, and Amdo have been affected by the period of Chinese rule from 1950 onwards. Many people undoubtedly died either in combat with the Chinese, through ill-treatment in prisons and camps, or as a result of the widespread famines of the early 1960s consequent to Chinese agricultural 'reforms.' The Dalai Lama's Secretariat in India has published estimates that 1.28 million Tibetans died as a result of Chinese rule (*Tibetan Review*, March 1984, p. 7); 427,478 in central Tibet, 480,261 in K'am, and 299,648 in Amdo. The majority of these are listed as killed in fighting or as dying as a result of famine. There are also substantial numbers of deaths in prison, through torture and through execution, as well as 9,000 suicides. While there may be some exaggeration and duplication in these figures, they are, it is now clear, of the right order of magnitude.

The exodus of refugees in and after 1959 must also have had a substantial demographic impact, particularly on areas such as Dingri and Kyirong close to the Nepalese and Indian borders. The total number of refugees who left Tibet was around 70,000. Most of them settled in India and Nepal, where their population has since grown to around 100,000.

The culturally Tibetan component of the population of Bhutan was between 0.5 and 0.8 million in the 1960s (see Karan 1967). The various Tibetan-speaking regions of northern India (Sikkim, Lahul, Ladakh, etc.) and of Nepal would have added perhaps another 200,000 people to the total Tibetan population at that time. Because there are many partly Tibetanized 'tribal' populations along the edges of the Tibetan region, such as the Mon, Lepcha, Qiang, or Naxi, the question of exactly who is a Tibetan can be arbitrary.[7] A large part of the culturally Tibetan population of Bhutan, for example, speaks languages not mutually intelligible with Tibetan (see Aris 1979:xiv–xviii; Imaeda and Pommaret 1990). These figures, however, suggest a total Tibetan population in 1982, including the refugees, of around 4.7 to 5 million.

For a note on the monastic population of Tibet, which I believe has been substantially exaggerated, see Appendix 1.

CENTRAL TIBET: GENERAL DESCRIPTION

The remainder of this chapter is concerned with central Tibet (see Map 3) and with the Dalai Lama's government at Lhasa, which from 1642 to 1959 included all of this region as well as parts of western Tibet (Ngari) and K'am. The Lhasa government was known as the Ganden P'odrang ('Tuṣita Palace') or, less formally, as the Depa Shung ('[Central] Ruler's Government'). It was closely linked to the Gelugpa religious order of which the Dalai Lama, while not the titular head, is the most senior incarnate lama.[8] The three large Gelugpa *gompa* of Ganden, Drepung, and Sera, all close to Lhasa, have played an important role in the history of the Lhasa government.

At the center of the Lhasa state were the two provinces of Ü and Tsang, both containing wide and fertile agricultural valleys along the Tsang River (Brahmaputra) and its tributaries. The regions of Lhok'a, Lhodrag, and Dagpo to the south and Kongpo to the east, although distinguished by Tibetans from the two central provinces of Ü and Tsang, are culturally and historically closely linked to them and may be considered part of central Tibet. To the north lies the Changt'ang ('Northern Plain'), a vast area inhabited by pastoral nomads and without permanent settlements. The population of central Tibet in the 1982 census was around 1.25 million.

This was the most centralized region of Tibet in the premodern period. Its social structure, at least in the agricultural heartlands, was highly stratified, and characterized by large estates owned by aristocratic families, *gompa*, individual lamas, or the central government. Agricultural families were attached to the estates and were liable for extensive tax and corvée obligations in exchange for their right to work the land. This is what I refer to as the *centralized agricultural* pattern (see Chapter 7).

Ü had one large urban center at Lhasa, in the flat plain formed by the Kyid River, a northern tributary of the Tsang River. Lhasa was the capital of the Tibetan kings from the seventh to ninth centuries and it was the capital of the Dalai Lamas from the seventeenth century until 1959. At its center today there still lies the Jok'ang temple or Tsuglagk'ang, which houses the famous image of the Buddha Śākyamuni traditionally brought by the Chinese wife of a seventh-century Tibetan king, "without doubt the most sacred temple in Tibet"

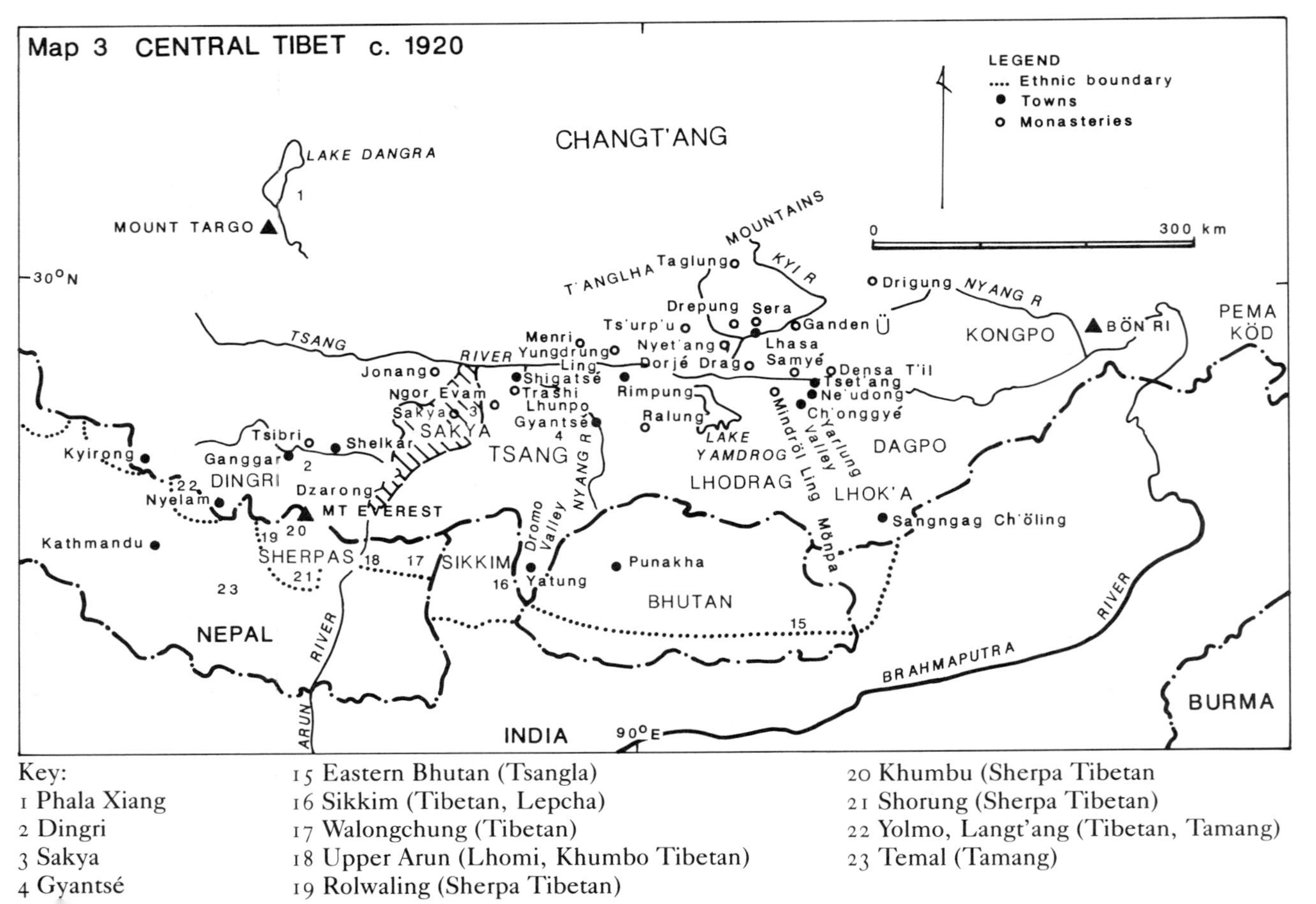

Key:
1 Phala Xiang
2 Dingri
3 Sakya
4 Gyantsé
15 Eastern Bhutan (Tsangla)
16 Sikkim (Tibetan, Lepcha)
17 Walongchung (Tibetan)
18 Upper Arun (Lhomi, Khumbo Tibetan)
19 Rolwaling (Sherpa Tibetan)
20 Khumbu (Sherpa Tibetan
21 Shorung (Sherpa Tibetan)
22 Yolmo, Langt'ang (Tibetan, Tamang)
23 Temal (Tamang)

(Batchelor 1987:79; Z. Taring 1980). The Bark'or or inner pilgrimage-circuit, with its hundreds of market-stalls, still runs around the Jo-k'ang, and around that are the surviving aristocratic residences and merchants' houses of old Lhasa (Z. Taring 1984). The population of Lhasa in the premodern period was around 20,000 to 30,000 people.[9] The Dalai Lama's principal residence, the Potala, still towers above the Lhasa plain at about 1.5 kilometers to the west of the city center, while his summer palace, the Norbu Lingka, lies another 2 kilometers to the west. The three great Gelugpa monastic centers of Ganden, Sera, and Drepung, the first of which was to be totally destroyed and the others seriously damaged in the course of the Cultural Revolution, all lay close to Lhasa. The other urban centers in Ü, such as the Neudong-Tset'ang area, all seem to have been much smaller than Lhasa.

Tsang in the modern period had two large urban centers at Shigatsé (the modern Chinese Xigazê) and Gyantsé, with populations of around 10,000 to 15,000 each. Shigatsé had been the capital of the Tsangpa kings who ruled central Tibet in the sixteenth and seventeenth centuries. The large Gelugpa *gompa* of Trashi Lhunpo, seat of the Panch'en Rimpoch'e from the seventeenth century onwards, was situated close to Shigatsé. There were smaller urban centers at Dingri, Nyelam, and Kyirong, along the trading route to Nepal and India.

Ü and Tsang also contained most of the original *gompa* of the other religious schools (Sakyapa, Nyingmapa, Kagyüdpa, Bönpo) although with the growth of Gelugpa power in central Tibet from the seventeenth century onwards, these *gompa* waned somewhat in importance in comparison with the large eastern Tibetan teaching *gompa* of the same schools.

CENTRAL TIBET: HISTORY AND PRESENT SITUATION

Ü, the more easterly of the two central provinces, has long been at the heart of Tibetan politics. It was the basis of the seventh- to ninth-century Tibetan empire. Its ruling dynasty originated in the Yarlung Valley on the south side of the Tsang River, the main river of central Tibet. Namri Lonts'en or Namri Songtsen, a local ruler from the Yarlung Valley, gained control of much of central Tibet in around A.D. 600 as the leader of an alliance of petty rulers (Kirkland 1982; Beckwith

1987a:13ff). His son, Songtsen Gampo (c. 618–649) completed the conquest of the adjoining non-Tibetan kingdom of Shangshung in what is now western Tibet.

This kingdom of Shangshung, again probably a confederation of local chieftains headed by the Ligmi dynasty, had ruled much of present-day western and central Tibet for some centuries. The Bön religion of the royal period (seventh to ninth centuries) is said to have come from Tagsig (Iran?) via Shangshung, and Shangshung is the probable source of other early components of Tibetan civilization (N. Norbu 1981, and see Chapter 23.)

Songtsen Gampo moved his capital to Lhasa and built a palace on the site where the Dalai Lama's palace, the Potala, would later stand. He also entered into an alliance with the Chinese and Nepalese courts. The later tradition associated him with the introduction of Buddhism to Tibet but it is clear both that there had been previous contacts with Buddhism and that the large-scale introduction of Buddhism did not take place until the late eighth century in the time of Tr'isong Deutsen. It was during the reign of Tr'isong Deutsen that Samyé, the first Tibetan monastic *gompa*, was built on the northern shore of the Tsang River.

While Ü was the original center of state power, the next large-scale regime in Tibet, the Sakya government installed with Mongol (Yuan) support in the late thirteenth century, was centered in Tsang at the monastic *gompa* of Sakya. After the collapse of the Sakya regime in the mid-fourteenth century, it was replaced by the P'agmodrupa dynasty, centered at Neudong in Ü. The next two central Tibetan states were centered in Tsang (at Rimpung and Shigatsé). Thus Tsang and Ü alternated as centers of power from the seventh century onwards, until the 5th Dalai Lama's Mongol supporters defeated and subsequently killed the last of the Tsangpa kings of Shigatsé. The 5th Dalai Lama moved the capital back to the old imperial capital of Lhasa but Shigatsé remained an important center of power, and the Panch'en Rimpoch'e, the reincarnate abbot of Trashi Lhunpo monastery outside Shigatsé, was the most senior reincarnate lama within the Gelugpa order after the Dalai Lama himself.

The Dalai Lama's regime was recognized by the Manchu (Qing) Emperors of China. While the Chinese government regarded the 5th Dalai Lama as a subordinate ruler, the Tibetans regarded the relationship as a reestablishment of the 'priest-patron' relationship that had existed between the Sakya lamas and the Mongol (Yuan) Emperors of China. The complex subsequent history of the Lhasa state will not be given here in any detail, although some aspects are summarized in Chapter 27 (see also Ahmad 1970; Dhondup 1984, 1986; Goldstein 1989; Petech 1973a; Richardson 1984; Shakabpa 1967). The 5th and 6th Dalai Lamas ruled through lay regents or *desid*. After the deposition of the 6th Dalai Lama by the Dzungars and the installation of the 7th with the support of a Manchu army (1720), this system was changed, and a cabinet or council of ministers *(kalön)*, was introduced. This council later became known as the *kashag* and continued to exist until 1959. From 1728 the Manchus stationed two officials (the Ambans) and a small garrison at Lhasa.

After 1728, effective power in Tibet was in the hands of one of the ministers, a Tsang noble named P'olhané, until his death in 1747. The 7th Dalai Lama took over as formal head of government in 1751 but died in 1757. The five following Dalai Lamas all died before or shortly after becoming old enough to rule. Consequently, while the Dalai Lama was the official head of state, the Lhasa government was headed by a regent *(desid)* for all but a few years between 1757 and 1895. The *desid* was usually a reincarnate lama from one of four *gompa* within Lhasa city. The 13th Dalai Lama was the first since 1757 to rule in his own right (Goldstein 1973).

In 1788–1792 a second Manchu army came to Tibet during the Gurkha-Tibetan war. The Qianlong emperor raised the status of the Ambans and introduced a system of control over the appointment of the Dalai Lama and other high reincarnate lamas (Lessing 1942:60–61; Shakabpa 1967:172); however, with the decline of the Manchu government in China in the nineteenth century the Ambans came to have little effective power at Lhasa.[10]

A British military expedition reached Lhasa in 1903–1904 and imposed a trade agreement on the Lhasa government. The Manchus responded with a new and more interventionist policy in 1905 (see Sperling 1976; Teichman 1922), culminating in the invasion of central Tibet by a Manchu army and the flight of the 13th Dalai Lama to India. After the Chinese revolution, the remaining Chinese troops were expelled from central Tibet, and the region, along with the portions of K'am west of the Yangtze, remained entirely independent of China, under the control of the 13th Dalai Lama and his successors, until 1950.

The period of rule of the 13th Dalai Lama is of particular significance. Much of our information about the Tibetan state dates from this period and subsequently; however, in evaluating this material, we need to be aware that the 13th Dalai Lama had embarked in the early 1920s on an ambitious and, in the short term at least, effective campaign to create a more centralized and powerful state (Burman 1976). A number of examples will demonstrate the nature of this campaign:

1. The Dalai Lama's government created the first Tibetan standing army, paid for by a tax on all estates within Tibet. This provoked a confrontation (see below) with the estate of the Panch'en Rimpoch'e, which was the most powerful single subunit within the Dalai Lama's realm. The Lhasa government won this confrontation, and the Panch'en Rimpoch'e fled to China in 1923 (Mehra 1976; Goldstein 1989);

2. The Dalai Lama's government sent several young men to British schools to receive a Western-style education, and also attempted to institute a Western-type school within Tibet (see Dhondup 1984, 1986:155–162);

3. In the religious sphere, the 13th Dalai Lama tightened up considerably the system of monastic degrees leading to senior administrative posts within the Gelugpa hierarchy. These posts were from now on only open to monks from the three major Gelugpa monastic centers near Lhasa, and not, for example, to monks from the Panch'en Rimpoch'e's monastic center at Trashi Lhunpo (Sherpa 1977);

4. Again in the religious sphere, the lama P'awongk'a Rimpoch'e, acting in association with the Dalai Lama, instituted a campaign to convert non-Gelugpa *gompa* in K'am to the Gelugpa school, by force where necessary (see, for example, Beyer 1973:239; Kapstein 1989:231 n. 40).

These innovations combined direct increases in state power (through the institution of a standing army), attempts at modernization (through Western education), and greater control over the *gompa*. The effects of these changes were in part lost during the two regencies following the 13th Dalai Lama's death in 1933, and the conservative influence on the Lhasa regime of the large Gelugpa monastic centers was reasserted. Much of our material on the Lhasa regime nevertheless reflects the exceptional strength of the Lhasa administration during this period.

In 1950–1951 the army of the People's Republic of China invaded Tibet and imposed the so-called 17-Point Agreement on the Tibetans (Richardson 1984:290–293). Resistance to Chinese rule began in K'am and Amdo, gradually spreading to central Tibet. In 1959 the 14th Dalai Lama, followed by about 70,000 refugees, fled to India, and the Tibetan government was dissolved. Central Tibet, along with western K'am and those parts of western Tibet under Chinese rule, now forms the Tibet Autonomous Region of the Chinese People's Republic.

Anthropological research within central Tibet has only been possible for Western scholars since the late 1980s, and under restricted circumstances. At the time of writing, the only published material is that from Melvyn Goldstein and Cynthia Beall's work with a pastoral population at Phala Xiang near Lake Dangra (Map 3, no. 1; Goldstein and Beall 1986, 1989, 1990; Goldstein 1987). Our information on agricultural communities is based on work with refugees. The principal studies of this kind are Barbara Aziz's on Dingri (no. 2; Aziz 1978), C. W. Cassinelli and Robert Ekvall's on Sakya (no. 3; Cassinelli and Ekvall 1969), and Melvyn Goldstein's and Eva Dargyay's work, both on villages near Gyantsé (no. 4; Goldstein 1968, 1971a, 1971b, 1971c, 1971d, 1986, 1988; Dargyay 1982).

THE LHASA GOVERNMENT AND THE *DZONG* SYSTEM

The Lhasa government incorporated substantial parts of K'am in the east and Ngari in the west as well as the whole of central Tibet. It was nevertheless based in central Tibet and governed from central Tibet and is therefore discussed in this chapter. There are accounts of the Lhasa government by several writers, among the more recent Ram Rahul (1969), Melvyn Goldstein (1968, 1971d, 1973, 1989), Martin Brauen (1974), and Franz Michael (1982). It was staffed by lay officials from families of aristocratic or *gerpa* status and by monk officials from the three great Gelugpa *gompa* near Lhasa. There was a college at Lhasa, maintained by the Finance Department, where the lay officials were trained (Rahul 1969:29–30; N. Thondup 1976). Officials were appointed to formal ranks, which ranged from seventh up to first rank, the highest being the rank of the four *kalön* or Cabinet ministers (three laymen and a monk in recent times). The entire bureaucracy was quite small. Brauen says that in the 1940s there were about 200 lay officials and 230 monk officials (1974:134), while Michael estimates 500–700 officials in all (1982:59). This included the local officials, known as *dzongpön* (Goldstein translates this as 'District Commissioner'), responsible for the local administrative centers or *dzong,* along with their subordinate stewards and clerks.[11]

The *dzong* were usually fortified buildings in high places. There were about 120 in recent times (Goldstein 1968; Brauen 1974:141). Each had one or two *dzongpön* appointed for a period of three years. These were generally laymen but in some cases one was a monk (Rahul 1969:40). They were of fourth or fifth rank depending on the importance of the *dzong,* the most important post being that of Chief Commissioner of Shigatsé. In some areas there was another official senior to the *dzongpön,* the regional governor or *chiky'ab.* There were six or seven of these, mainly in the outlying areas.[12]

Dzongpön could settle legal cases brought to them but their primary function was the collection of revenue on behalf of the Lhasa government. Most *dzongpön* made a handsome profit in the course of their three-year term. Rahul (1969:43) comments that:

> The amount of revenue due from each *dzong* was recorded in the Finance Department in Lhasa. . . . A *dzongpön* was in fact a contractor for this revenue and made what profit he could. His income, out of which he paid his revenue, consisted of dues from the people within his jurisdiction, proceeds of the fines imposed by him, large arrears of revenue he had diverted temporarily or otherwise to his own coffers, private trading in which he could compel traders to sell goods to him below market rates, and his own estate.

Rahul also notes that *dzongpön,* particularly those in charge of remote *dzong,* were virtually autonomous. They had hardly any relations with the Lhasa government beyond sending the annual revenue. Those nearer to Lhasa would be more careful and would refer serious cases to the Kashag (Rahul 1969:43–44).

We will find the *dzong* system in various forms in most other Tibetan polities, including the petty states of K'am (Chapter 4) and the monastic and later lay kingdom of Bhutan (Chapter 6). In these states succession to the position of some or all *dzongpön* became hereditary.

This does not seem to be the case with the Lhasa government *dzongpön*, who were in recent times regularly appointed for a limited term. I am unclear whether reappointment was common and unclear, too, whether officials were regularly sent to serve at *dzong* near to their own estates.[13]

As Goldstein has pointed out (1973), the system was, in recent times, slanted towards the interests of the powerful reincarnation-series who served as regents and of a small number of the high-status aristocratic *(gerpa)* families. Many of the remaining *gerpa* families provided lower-level officials and were not particularly wealthy or powerful in comparison to rich peasant families. It is unlikely that they were able to build up substantial alternative centers of power through their occupancy of *dzongpön* positions. Such alternative centers of power were constituted by large semiautonomous monastic estates such as Sakya and Trashi Lhunpo and occasionally by a few of the larger aristocratic estates, primarily those of *depön* and *yabshi* status.[14]

The position of the larger estates needs particular examination. We are best informed about one of the most important of these 'estates,' Sakya, though I will also look at two others, Trashi Lhunpo and Lhagyari.

SUBORDINATE UNITS WITHIN THE LHASA STATE: SAKYA, LHAGYARI, TRASHI LHUNPO

The Sakya estate was the lineal continuation of the Sakya government of Tibet during the Mongol (Yuan) period (thirteenth and fourteenth centuries). In the twentieth century it retained control over a large territory in the west of Tsang (marked on Map 3) as well as eight smaller territories in Tsang and two in K'am (see Cassinelli and Ekvall 1969:30–33 and Map 1). The head of the Sakya estate was the senior member of the same K'ön family who had been given authority over Tibet by the Mongols. He was known as the Sakya Tr'ich'en, and was also the hereditary abbot of the main Sakya monastery and the head of the Sakya religious order. The members of the K'ön family were believed to possess a particularly powerful body of ritual practices and the Sakya Tr'ich'en occasionally performed major rituals on behalf of the Lhasa government.[15] In recent times, the position of Sakya Tr'ich'en has alternated between two branches of the family.

Sakya (Map 3, no. 3) was studied by the political scientist C. W.

Cassinelli and the anthropologist Robert Ekvall. Their book, significantly titled *A Tibetan Principality*, was based on information from four refugees, three of them from the ruling family of Sakya (1969). *A Tibetan Principality* was the subject of an important critique by Melvyn Goldstein, who argued that it wrongly presented Sakya as an independent political entity (Goldstein 1971d). Two further valuable sources on Sakya in recent times are the autobiographical accounts by Dawa Norbu and Jamyang Sakya (D. Norbu 1974; Sakya and Emery 1990).

The relationship between Sakya and Lhasa was complex and I suspect that both Cassinelli and Ekvall (arguing for the autonomy of Sakya) and Goldstein (arguing for the superordinate status of Lhasa) tend to present it in inappropriately categorical terms. Both administrations, Sakya and Lhasa, were referred to in Tibetan by the same term, *shung*. Neither had "any polity-wide police network" (Goldstein 1971d:175) and both were oriented towards the collection of taxes rather than the day-to-day regulation of the lives of their subjects.

Goldstein's arguments for the superordinate status of the Lhasa administration (which he refers to as "the Tibetan central government") are as follows: (1) the Lhasa administration controlled and monopolized the army; (2) the Lhasa administration controlled a corvée transportation network throughout the entire region; (3) the Lhasa administration coined money, printed postage stamps, and controlled relations with foreign powers; (4) anyone could take a dispute to the Lhasa administration for adjudication, and its decision was authoritative; (5) the Lhasa administration could make rules that were binding on subordinate units such as Sakya, as with the tax imposed in the 1920s to support the new standing army; and (6) the Lhasa government had an office that would take over what Goldstein calls "runaway serfs."[16]

Goldstein's arguments are generally convincing, but it should be remembered that they refer to a period where the power of the Lhasa administration was at its height. 'Subordinate units' such as Sakya and Trashi Lhunpo had frequently negotiated on their own behalf with foreign powers in the past (item 3), while the "runaway serf" office (item 6) dated only from the early twentieth century. As for the power of taxation (item 5), the imposition of taxes on Trashi Lhunpo and Powo in the 1920s involved major conflicts, and, in the case of Powo, armed military intervention (see Chapter 4), before the tax was paid, an indication that the demand was regarded as unprecedented and unjustified. Looking at the period from 1642 to 1959 as a whole, we would doubtless find times when the Lhasa administration could intervene relatively effectively within the 'subordinate units' and other times when it had little option but to leave them to run their own affairs. These changes in the situation would not necessarily have been reflected by explicit changes in political vocabulary. As we will see again in relation to the Chinese power in eastern K'am (Chapter 4), formal titles, relationships of tribute, and the like could mask any of a variety of political realities. The parties concerned were often content to maintain a mutually acceptable fiction rather than forcing unnecessary confrontations.

On item 4, the question of taking disputes to Lhasa, Goldstein's example, the conflict over the succession to the throne of Sakya in 1950, is particularly interesting. In Cassinelli and Ekvall's account, the Lhasa administration's involvement in this episode appears as the last in a series of episodes of 'mediation' dating back to the early nineteenth century (1969:22–27). In the first case, a Lhasa aristocrat of the Rangchönba family, related to the Sakya ruling house, acted as mediator between the two branches of the family, setting up the original arrangement by which, whenever the ruler of Sakya died, he was to be succeeded by the eldest male member of the family, whichever branch he belonged to. Subsequently the regents for the 12th (in 1866), 13th (in 1887), and 14th Dalai Lamas (in 1935) were asked to intervene in disputes over the succession; in each case Sakya's status as a *shung* was recognized.

According to Goldstein, "Tibetan government officials," presumably meaning former officials of the Lhasa administration, described the intervention in 1950 as "adjudication" *(kached nang)* not "mediation" (*barshug;* 1971d:177–178). This could hardly be true of Rangchönba's intervention in the early nineteenth century, but the 1935 and 1950 episodes both seem to involve an acceptance of Lhasa's right to make the decision. Whether the 1866 and 1887 episodes should be regarded as 'mediation' or 'adjudication' is hard to say.

In fact, Cassinelli and Ekvall agree that Sakya recognized both the superordinate status of the Lhasa government and the Dalai Lama's claim to political control over the whole region. Their claims for the autonomy of Sakya are more to do with the lack of intervention from Lhasa in the operation of the Sakya administration:

> [Sakya] was part of a political system that included Lhasa and Shigatsé [i.e., Trashi Lhunpo], but this system was largely formal and had vir-

> tually nothing to do with the day-to-day business of governing the area of [Sakya] proper. In performing the essential governmental functions of collecting and allocating revenue, maintaining judicial processes, and selecting official personnel, the government of [Sakya] was answerable to no one. It was not linked with Lhasa as part of a federation or confederation, for there was no policy that applied to both Lhasa and [Sakya]; it was not part of an empire ruled by Lhasa, for the minor demands effectively made by Lhasa were too weak and infrequent to constitute an imperial relationship. The unity of western Tibet [i.e., Tsang] was cultural and religious; no one perceived a need for anything more than the most superficial political coordination. (Cassinelli and Ekvall 1969:44)

In a footnote, they add:

> It is not meaningful to speak of 'sovereignty' in the case of [Sakya]. 'Sovereignty' is either a concept of international law, which did not apply to these Tibetan governments, or suggests an absolute independence that no government possesses. (Cassinelli and Ekvall 1969: 44 n. 11)

Goldstein's material suggests that Lhasa's claims on Sakya in recent times went well beyond the "minor demands. . . . weak and infrequent" indicated by Cassinelli and Ekvall. To regard the relationship between Lhasa and Sakya as one of straightforward subordination is nevertheless too simple, and in Chapter 4 we will see that material on another small monastic state, Drayab, parallels Cassinelli and Ekvall's in several respects.[17]

Sakya was, in some respects, a special case, because of its former identity as the government of all Tibet. The administrators of Sakya were clearly very conscious of this status (for example, Cassinelli and Ekvall 1969:50); however, on closer examination, most of the 'subordinate units' of the Lhasa administration turn out to be special cases of one kind or another. The family of Lhagyari, for example, owned the small but wealthy estate of E-yul in Ü, claimed descent from the kings of the Yarlung dynasty, and had various privileges in relation to the Lhasa administration as a consequence (Karsten 1980; Yuthok 1990:35, 84–85). The head of the family (again known as *tr'ich'en*) was apparently not a tributary to the Lhasa government (Karsten 1980:165) and, although Lhagyari was one of the five *depön* families, its members did not serve as officials at Lhasa after 1642. In ceremonial matters, they ranked next to the Panch'en Rimpoch'e, who was the head of the Trashi Lhunpo estate.

Altogether, the region under the Lhasa administration was far less uniform in political structure than it might look at first sight. Numerous families and estates had special privileges of one kind or another, some areas (Changt'ang) had no *dzong*, in others (Ngari) the provincial governor had no control over the *dzong*, and so on. What has occasionally been presented (for example, Michael 1982) as a rational bureaucratic system consisted of a large number of special cases, with an underlying pattern of more or less formalized patron-client relations (see Goldstein 1973).

The Trashi Lhunpo estate was the most significant of all the subordinate units, and while we do not have the material for a comprehensive presentation of its position, it is worth discussing some aspects of this unit in detail. It was the largest subordinate unit within the Dalai Lama's state, and it had extensive holdings throughout Tsang, although I do not know of any detailed description of these holdings.[18] Michael comments that "[t]he organization of the Trashi Lhunpo *labrang* [estate] was indeed very similar to the Lhasa government" (1982:112). The Shigatsé aristocracy served as lay officials for the Trashi Lhunpo administration, just as their equivalents at Lhasa did for the Dalai Lama's administration, and "when the Trashi Lhunpo ecclesiastical and secular officials travelled to Lhasa, they were received and accorded honors in ceremony and seating arrangements that were equal to those reserved for the ministers of the *kashag* and the Dalai Lama's ecclesiastical agencies" (Michael 1982:112).

The monastery of Trashi Lhunpo was founded in 1447 by Gendün Drub (1391–1475), a personal disciple of Tsongk'apa and the originator of the Dalai Lama reincarnation-series (see Chapter 27; the title of Dalai Lama itself was first given to the third of the series). It was built close to the *dzong* of Samdruptsé (modern Shigatsé), which had just been seized by the Rimpungpa dynasty, still formally subordinate to the P'agmodrupa dynasty at Neudong but rapidly becoming the leading power in central Tibet (Wylie 1980a:322–333; Shakabpa 1967:86–87). It was thus closely associated with the Dalai Lamas, and was the principal residence of Gendün Drub and his successor the 2d Dalai Lama. The latter, however, moved to Drepung in 1494, apparently in response to the growing power of the Karmapa order in Tsang and to the threat posed by their Rimpungpa patrons, who had now taken control of Tsang (Wylie 1980a:328).[19]

The 1st Panch'en Rimpoch'e, Losang Chökyi Gyantsen (1567–1662), was tutor to the 4th and 5th Dalai Lamas and abbot of Trashi Lhunpo. He was given the title Panch'en (= *paṇḍita ch'enpo*, Great Scholar) by the 5th Dalai Lama and in 1665 the same Dalai Lama recognized his rebirth as the abbot of Trashi Lhunpo. This incarnation-line rapidly became the most important in the Gelugpa order after the Dalai Lama himself.

Shigatsé lost its leading position in central Tibetan politics with the rise to power of Lhasa but it remained an important place. The *gompa* of Trashi Lhunpo, with its large estates and the important Panch'en incarnation-line, represented an alternative focus of power to Lhasa. While the senior status of the Dalai Lama does not seem to have been overtly challenged, the series of previous rebirths identified for the Panch'en Rimpoch'e was traced back through K'edrubjé (1385–1438), who was an older and more senior disciple of Tsongk'a-pa's than the 1st Dalai Lama, Gendün Drub. There were indirect suggestions that the Panch'en's spiritual standing was in some respects higher than that of the Dalai Lama's (see Norbu and Ekvall 1969). Significantly, Trashi Lhunpo developed an independent foreign policy from Lhasa. The 3d Panch'en Rimpoch'e negotiated with George Bogle, emissary of the British Governor-General of Bengal, in 1774–1775, and the Manchu regime constantly attempted to play off one incarnation-line against the other, a strategy that was continued by the Chinese Nationalist and Communist governments in the twentieth century.

It is difficult to judge how far the two lamas themselves were caught up in the conflict. During the nineteenth century, all of the Dalai Lamas died young, so that power was in the hands of Regents for all but a few years. The position of Regent itself, significantly, was held by the Panch'en Rimpoch'e only for a few months (Mehra 1976:33 n. 63), otherwise it was monopolized by senior Gelugpa lamas from Lhasa and nearby. At any rate the relationship between Lhasa and Trashi Lhunpo deteriorated rapidly in the first decades of this century, following Trashi Lhunpo's ambivalent attitude to British and Chinese overtures during the Dalai Lama's flights to exile in 1904 and 1910. The Lhasa government asked Trashi Lhunpo in 1912 to contribute to the costs of the wars with China, but they paid only part of the amount requested.

Lhasa responded to the increase in tension by strengthening its administrative apparatus in Tsang. Shigatsé had previously been an ordinary *dzong*, with a fifth-rank lay official; it was now given a special status. A fourth-rank commissioner (immediately below the cabinet ministers) was appointed with responsibility for the whole province of Tsang (Goldstein 1968:37–38).[20] Lhasa had agreed in the past that peasants on Trashi Lhunpo estates were not liable to corvée duties to Lhasa, but they went back on this in 1917 and imposed corvée duties on Trashi Lhunpo peasants at Gyantsé, extending them to all of Tsang in 1923 and imposing a new annual tax on the Trashi Lhunpo estate. Trashi Lhunpo refused to pay any of the taxes, and the Panch'en Rimpoch'e fled to Mongolia in December 1923 and subsequently to China, apparently in the hope of forcing a negotiated settlement (Goldstein 1989:110–120). The Lhasa government responded by appointing an administrator to the Trashi Lhunpo estate. The issue was not resolved, and the Panch'en Rimpoch'e remained in China until his death in 1935. Meanwhile, the Lhasa regime was able to impose its new taxes on Trashi Lhunpo.

It is clear, as Goldstein comments, that "the fundamental issue was the extent of the authority of the central [i.e., Lhasa] government" (1989:120).[21] Lhasa's success (backed up by its new standing army) marked a further move towards a centralization, but the whole episode indicates that it would be mistaken to assume that Trashi Lhunpo had been 'traditionally' subject to Lhasa or that the Lhasa regime as a whole should be seen as a centralized state. The Lhasa regime generally had little interest in intervening at the local level, provided that the taxes came in regularly from the *dzong* offices. Indeed, its ability to intervene, even had it wanted to, was quite limited, especially before the 13th Dalai Lama's reforms.

TIBET AND THE GALACTIC POLITY

Much of the problem in conceptualizing the relationship between Lhasa and Sakya or Trashi Lhunpo, as Cassinelli and Ekvall rightly note, is the result of attempting to interpret Tibetan political structures in terms of Western political theory. There are perhaps more appropriate models than that of federation, confederation, or sovereignty for dealing with situations such as that of Sakya or Trashi Lhunpo. In particular, we might consider the 'galactic polity' model developed by Stanley Tambiah, primarily in relation to the Theravādin states of Southeast Asia (1976:102–131, 1985:252–286, and see Chapter 8). The galactic polity, with its *maṇḍala*-type structure based on an exemplary center, and regional administrations that replicated the structure of the center, bears some relationship to the Lhasa state (and also to the relationship between the Manchu regime in China and the various Tibetan polities). Regional administrations within the galactic polity drift historically between periods of attachment to one or another center and periods of autonomy. The galactic polity as a whole is weak at some stages, stronger at others. What is a center at one period (Sakya in the thirteenth–fourteenth centuries) may be a subordinate entity at another period (Sakya in the twentieth century) without undergoing a drastic change in identity.

The galactic polity "is a far cry from a bureaucratic hierarchy in the Weberian sense" (Tambiah 1985:266). Central rule is as much a matter of performance (as in the elaborate rituals of the Lhasa administration) as administration, and the primary focus of the whole enterprise is on the extraction of produce and the control of personnel. The control of labor power is as significant a theme in Tibet as in premodern Southeast Asia and for the same reason; in both cases population was low in relation to the available land. A constant theme in descriptions of Tibetan polities, both within and outside the area of the Lhasa administration, is control over people, not over land.

If we wish to see the Tibetan region as a galactic polity centered at Lhasa, that polity was undoubtedly a weak one, even at its strongest. Large parts of Tibet (primarily the pastoral areas and the less productive and more remote agricultural areas) were scarcely incorporated into the galactic polity in any real sense. In comparison with the traditional galactic polities of Thailand or Burma, the best analogy for such outlying parts of Tibet would have been not the fully developed subordinate polities such as Chiangmai (Lanna) or the larger Shan states, but the 'tribal' peoples of the hills such as the Kachin, Karen, and Chin. Such groups were only loosely associated with the galactic polity and lived much of the time under local chieftains and headmen in a relatively 'stateless' political system.

The analogy is not perfect. The geography and ecology are different, and there was a degree of cultural, linguistic, and religious unity throughout most of the Tibetan region, for all its diversity, which contrasts with the high degree of differentiation within the hill peoples of upland Southeast Asia. The picture of a region characterized by areas of greater and lesser centralization with fluctuating linkages between them is nevertheless closer to the reality of Tibet than that of a centralized bureaucratic state. We will return to these questions again in later chapters.

I have emphasized in this chapter the limitations to the power and authority of the Dalai Lama's government at Lhasa. The Lhasa regime was nevertheless the nearest to an effectively centralized state achieved by Tibetans in the premodern period. The relatively bureaucratic and hierarchical nature of the Gelugpa order, particularly after the 13th Dalai Lama's reforms, reflected its role as something resembling a state church. Elsewhere, as we shall see in the next two chapters, neither political nor religious forms were as structured or 'domesticated.'

4

Tibetan Societies: K'am (Eastern Tibet)

Chapter 3 examined central Tibet and the Dalai Lama's government. In this chapter we look at K'am, the eastern part of Tibet. K'am and Amdo,[1] the region to its north and the subject of Chapter 5, are the areas for which our information is weakest. The only real ethnographic research on these areas is the work of the former missionaries Robert Ekvall and Matthias Hermanns on Amdo nomadic pastoralists. The history of K'am and Amdo is also less accessible and more speculative, at present, than that of central Tibet. These areas were, however, visited extensively by Western travelers from the late nineteenth century onwards, and their writings provide a major source for reconstructing the complex social and political picture of east Tibet in the premodern period.

GENERAL DESCRIPTION

As Map 4 shows, K'am consists primarily of the four valleys of four great rivers, the Ngül River (Salween), Dza River (Mekong), Dri

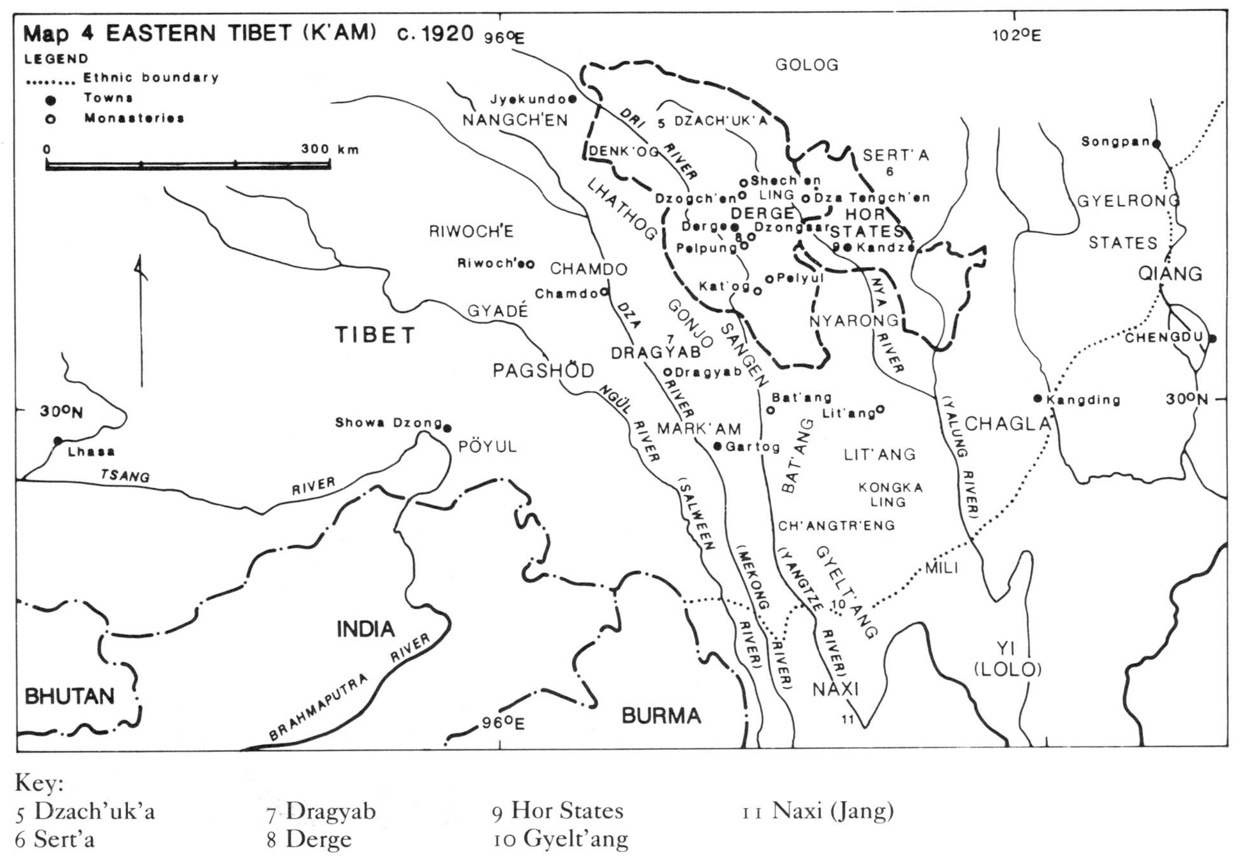

Key:

5 Dzach'uk'a
6 Sert'a
7 Dragyab
8 Derge
9 Hor States
10 Gyelt'ang
11 Naxi (Jang)

River (Yangtze), and Nya River (Yalung, a tributary of the Yangtze) along with their various tributaries, and the high pasture ground or *gang* between them. Traditionally it was described as consisting of six *gang* and four river valleys *(gangdrug rongshi)* although the names and locations of the six *gang* vary between lists (Wylie 1962:38–39, 97–98; Smith 1969a; Tshe-brtan Zhabs-drung 1986:2160).

The areas for cultivation are along the valley floors, the largest being in the Hor states (Trehor) around Kandzé, the present Chinese administrative center of Garzê (Teichman 1922:75–76). Towards the north the altitude rises, agriculture becomes impossible, and we reach the nomadic regions of Amdo. Towards the south the country becomes relatively lush, with vast forested areas, and Tibetan populations shade off into various partly Tibetanized hill peoples such as the Naxi (Nakhi, Moso), Yi (Lolo), and Lisu (see Gregory and Gregory 1923; Goullart 1957, 1959; Rock 1925, 1926, 1931; A. Jackson 1978, 1979; LeBar 1964). K'am is the most populous region of Tibet. In the 1982 census its population was around 1.53 million.

In K'am, as elsewhere in Tibet, trade routes were of vital importance to the economy and the social structure. Most towns of any size grew up at junctions of major trade routes. The biggest of these trading centers was Kangding, formerly called Tachienlu, which bordered on ethnic Chinese territory to the east. Kangding was formerly the capital of the Tibetan state of Chagla. Rockhill estimated its population in 1889 as 6,000 to 8,000 (Rockhill 1891:275). From 1927 to the 1950s, it was the administrative center for the Chinese province of Sikang, which theoretically included most of K'am; Goullart, who was there in the 1930s, gives its population then as about 40,000 (Goullart 1959:13). It was the major center for trading in tea, which was sold to Tibet in exchange mainly for wool, musk, or other pastoral products or bought with Indian rupees (see Rockhill 1975:277–284). There are numerous descriptions from the between-war period of this little town, in a narrow valley at the confluence of two rivers, with its tea-warehouses, its 'lamaseries,' its Tibetan and Chinese traders, and the missionaries who extended their hospitality to a constant stream of Western explorers en route to Tibet (see Duncan 1952:62–65; Goullart 1959:12–32; Migot 1957:79ff; Guibaut 1949:6ff).

At the other end of K'am was Jyekundo (modern Chinese Gyêgu). André Migot describes this small town in the 1940s (situated then as now within the Chinese province of Qinghai) as:

> easily the most important trading center in north-east Tibet. It derives this importance from the network of caravan routes which converge on it—from Sikang and Kangding in the south, from Lhasa in the west, from the Tsaidam and Mongolia in the north, and from the provincial capitals of Xining and Lanzhou in the north-east. Of these, the southerly routes carry by far the greatest volume of trade; traffic in the other directions is a trickle by comparison. (Migot 1957:166–167)

The big trading caravans between Jyekundo and Lhasa (two each year in each direction) brought back "cigarettes from India and high-quality cloth from Lhasa, finally travelling east into China with wool and hides from the rich breeding-grounds around Jyekundo" (Migot 1957:167).[2]

Another important center was Ch'amdo (modern Chinese Qamdo), site of an important early Gelugpa *gompa* and, from the 1920s to 1950s, the administrative center for that part of K'am that was within the Dalai Lama's government. Eric Teichman visited Ch'amdo in 1918 three weeks after its recapture from the Chinese who had destroyed the monastery in 1912–1913:

> Ch'amdo . . . consists of a few yamens and temples and a village of mud hovels built on a narrow spit of land between, and just above the confluence of, the Dza River and the Ngom River. The elevation is about 10,600 feet. On a sort of plateau immediately behind rise the gaunt ruins of the once great and splendid monastery, formerly the largest and wealthiest in K'am. The two valleys are so narrow as to permit of scarcely any cultivation. All around are bare and somewhat dreary-looking mountains. Though a miserable place in appearance, Ch'amdo ranks with Jyekundo as one of the most important centers of Eastern Tibet. It was formerly the capital of the lama-ruled Tibetan State of the same name, and was the residence of the lama ruler, locally known as the Tsangdrupa. The small Chinese commissariat official stationed here in those days with a few Chinese soldiers kept very much to himself and was careful not to interfere with the lama rulers. (Teichman 1922:114–115)

These towns and a number of other trading centers, such as Ba (Ba-t'ang), Lit'ang, and Kandzé, had sizeable communities of Han and Hui Chinese traders and of Tibetan and Chinese artisans, and small Chinese garrisons.[3] These Chinese garrisons in the premodern period consisted of only a few men each, and made no attempt to control the

Tibetan population. The people of K'am governed their own affairs under a variety of political arrangements, which we shall discuss shortly.

HISTORY AND PRESENT SITUATION

K'am was partly incorporated into the early Tibetan empire of the Yarlung dynasty, which collapsed around A.D. 842. Its history until the seventeenth century is still unclear, although then as later it was most likely a region of small states, pastoralist tribes and remote, self-governing villages. During the Sakya period (late thirteenth to mid-fourteenth centuries) there were large Sakya estates in Western K'am (Gonjo and Lingts'ang) but their administrators seem to have become independent rulers with a vague relationship to the Ming rulers of China after the collapse of the Yuan and Sakya regimes (Petech 1988).

We know very little about the internal dynamics of K'amba society in this period. Peter Kessler has suggested that an alliance of Tibetan tribes and non-Tibetan valley people or *rongpa* dominated by the iron-working nomadic Sumpa people was replaced around 1400 by another alliance centered about the large state of Lingts'ang. The dominance of Lingts'ang was in turn destroyed by the Gelugpa order's Mongol ally Gushri Khan in 1640 in the course of his conquest of K'am (Kessler 1984:53–68).

Since, as Kessler admits (1984:62), we know little at this stage about the Sumpa or Lingts'ang, his account is highly speculative. It is difficult to know whether Lingts'ang achieved anything like the extent he suggests (Kessler 1984:67). If so, it must have declined well before 1640, since it apparently played no significant role in Gushri Khan's campaigns in K'am; his principal opponent was the pro-Bön king of Beri (see Shakabpa 1967:105–107).[4] In later times Lingts'ang was a small state in northern K'am (see below) and its rulers claimed descent from the half-brother of the great K'amba epic hero King Gesar of Ling (Stein 1981; Pema Tsering 1982; Uray 1985). Gesar of Ling is of great importance in K'am mythology, where he appears as a founding ancestor of the people of K'am and as a culture-hero who defeated the demonic or non-Buddhist kings of the four directions and ruled over all of east Tibet.[5] The story is told in detail in the east

Tibetan versions of the Tibetan epic. Gesar is a culture-hero elsewhere in Tibet, however, including the far west, and his localization in Lingts'ang in K'am may be a secondary development.[6]

Whatever the situation prior to the 1640s there is no doubt that much of K'am was incorporated for a while into the Mongol-Tibetan regime of the 5th Dalai Lama and Gushri Khan. This was the period when most of the major Gelugpa *gompa* of K'am were founded, including those of the Hor states (Kessler 1984:182–185), Lit'ang, Ba (Bat'ang), and so forth.[7] In the early eighteenth century, after the Manchu government intervention in the crisis following the Dzungar invasion of Tibet and the death of the 6th Dalai Lama, the boundary between K'am and the Dalai Lama's realm was fixed. This boundary passed through a boundary pillar on the Bum La, a pass southwest of Ba, following a line somewhat to the west of the Dri River (the upper course of the Yangtse). According to Teichman, a British consular official who was responsible for negotiating the 1918 boundary agreement between China and Tibet, "[t]he country to the west of this point was handed over to the rule of the Dalai Lama under the suzerainty of the Manchu Emperor, while the Tibetan Chiefs of the States and tribes to the east of it were given seals as semi-independent feudatories of China" (Teichman 1922:2). By the mid-eighteenth century, as we saw in Chapter 3, Manchu 'suzerainty' over the Dalai Lama's government had become purely nominal. In the 1790s a second Manchu army came to central Tibet and expelled an invading Gurkha army. Manchu power over the Lhasa government was temporarily reasserted, and two official representatives or Ambans were again stationed at Lhasa. Their power soon became nominal, as it had been before.

It is more difficult to evaluate the degree of control exercised by the Chinese government on the 'semi-independent feudatories' of K'am during the eighteenth and nineteenth centuries. It was probably very limited, except along the eastern borders. By the 1860s, when Gompo Namgyel, one of the local chiefs of Nyarong in eastern K'am, gained control first over all of Nyarong and then much of the rest of K'am, there was no question of Manchu involvement. A Tibetan army from Lhasa eventually intervened, defeating and killing Gompo Namgyel in 1865 (T. Tsering 1985; Shakabpa 1967:187; Teichman 1922:5). Nyarong was formally taken over by the Lhasa government, apparently with Manchu approval, and Lhasa set up an office called the

Nyarong Chiky'ab (Teichman 1922:5–6). The rulers of Derge state and of the Hor states were restored to power by the Lhasa government.

Teichman, referring to this situation, writes:

> The Native States on the Sichuan border east of the old Sino-Tibetan frontier on the Bum La . . . sent periodical tribute missions to, and were under the nominal protection of, Chengdu and Peking. Some, such as the great Kingdom of Derge and the Five Hor states, had fallen under the influence of Lhasa, as related above; while others, such as the State of Chagla (Tachienlu), and the territories of Bat'ang and Lit'ang, remained, owing to their situation on the main road, more under Chinese influence. The powers of the small Chinese military officials and commissariat officers stationed at Tachienlu [Kangding], Lit'ang, Bat'ang and other centers on the main South Road, had, however, dwindled to vanishing point, while the soldiers of the frontier garrisons were often unarmed or existed only in the official imagination for pay roll purposes. (1922:8)

A similar picture is given by Susie Rijnhart, who traveled in this area in the 1890s:

> A colonel with a small number of soldiers is stationed at each post [on the road from Jyekundo to Kangding]. Though they have no authority over the Tibetan chiefs they report to Tachienlu [Kangding] on the condition of the country, so that should there be any difficulty brewing troops might be dispatched. . . . In the district governed by Sichuan the position of the Chinese officials is a very precarious one, and great tact must be used by them in dealing with the natives, who consider the Chinese as inferiors in courage and endurance. . . . (1901:358)

This situation remained little changed until 1904, when the Manchu government inaugurated a new and more interventionist policy in the wake of the 1903–1904 British expedition to central Tibet and the Anglo-Tibetan Convention that resulted from it. The new policy involved imposing a network of Chinese magistracies throughout eastern Tibet, and rapidly led to a general uprising among the Tibetan population of K'am. The Chinese, led by Ma Weiqi and later by the notorious Zhao Erfeng (known as 'Butcher Zhao'), destroyed several large *gompa,* including the great Gelugpa *gompa* of Ch'amdo, and killed several thousand monks and lay people. Chinese troops forcibly removed the governments of the various petty states of K'am, installing Chinese magistrates, and then invaded central Tibet, occupying Lhasa in 1910 (Shelton 1912; Teichman 1922:19–35; Dhondup 1986:24ff; Sperling 1976).

The fall of the Manchu government in China led to a general revolt against the Chinese in central Tibet and eastern Tibet and several further years of fighting between Chinese forces and local Tibetans. A central Tibetan army, under the leadership of the *kalön* Champa Tendar, was sent to K'am and had established control over a large part of it when the 1918 peace agreement was negotiated (with Teichman's assistance).

This agreement recognized Chinese sovereignty over the territories east of a border along the Dri River (Yangtze), including the Hor states and Nyarong, though with the exception of Derge and Pelyul. The Lhasa government retained rights over the *gompa* in the area under Chinese sovereignty. The agreement thus established the division between 'Outer Tibet' (the area under the Lhasa administration) and 'Inner Tibet' (consisting of the reestablished local states under Chinese rule), which had first been proposed in the abortive Simla Convention of 1914. The Lhasa government maintained a senior official stationed at Ch'amdo with responsibility for eastern Tibet, while in 1927 the Chinese organized the Tibetan areas east of the Dri River into the new province of Sikang with its administrative center at Tachienlu (renamed Kangding).

This was the formal situation until 1930–1933, when a conflict between Gelugpa and non-Gelugpa *gompa* in the Hor states led to further Tibetan-Chinese fighting and the Lhasa government's losing control over the remaining areas on the east side of the Dri River (Duncan 1952:139–158, 231). Descriptions by Western travelers during this period, however, suggest that, as in the nineteenth century, Chinese authority did not extend past the small garrisons on the two main roads from Kangding to Bat'ang and Jyekundo. According to Rock, writing in 1931, only nine of the thirty-one Chinese magistracies established by Zhao Erfeng were still held by the Chinese, "the remainder being ruled by Tibetan outlaws" (Rock 1931:14). Kongkaling and Ch'angtr'eng, always fairly wild areas, had previously been ruled by subchiefs under the prince of Lit'ang. After the removal of the subchiefs, the local Tibetans "attacked and murdered the Chinese garrison and seized rifles, pistols and artillery . . . the country became an armed bandit camp" (1931:14–17).

André Guibaut visited K'am a few years later, in 1936–1937 and 1940, and commented that:

> In point of fact the Chinese govern this province in a lax and easy-going fashion. The soldiers and civil servants, whose duty it is to control Sikang, are scanty in number. You meet a hundred or so of them on your journey along the large caravan roads, distributed among a small number of military outposts, entirely cut off one from the other. Thus, although it possesses a Chinese name, eastern Tibet has remained true to itself and, in spite of its situation on the map which places it within a day's march of its powerful neighbour, it does not differ in any profound sense from the other districts of Tibet. . . . (Guibaut 1949:14)

Migot, who traveled throughout K'am from 1947–1949, was in agreement with Guibaut:

> Chinese control is little more than nominal; I was often to have first-hand experience of its ineffectiveness. In order to govern a territory of this kind it is not enough to station, in isolated villages separated from each other by many days' journey, a few unimpressive officials and a handful of ragged soldiers. The Tibetans completely disregard the Chinese administration and obey only their own chiefs. One very simple fact illustrates the true status of Sikang's Chinese rulers: nobody in the province will accept Chinese currency, and the officials, unable to buy anything with their money, are forced to subsist by a process of barter. (Migot 1957:89)

One gets a similar impression of the ineffectualness of Chinese rule from Tibetan accounts of life in K'am in the first half of the twentieth century, in which the Chinese are notable by their absence. It was only in the 1950s that the new Communist regime began to impinge directly on the lives of Tibetans (see Trungpa 1971; Kalu 1985; J. Norbu 1986). In other words, K'am east of the Dri River was, during the premodern period, for all practical purposes independent of both the Lhasa government and the Chinese authorities.

Most of K'am was incorporated into the Chinese People's Republic in 1949–1950. Unlike central Tibet and the areas of K'am west of the Dri River (the present Qamdo prefecture), which retained a certain degree of political autonomy until 1959 under the Dalai Lama's government at Lhasa, the areas of K'am east of the Dri River were integrated directly into the administrative structure of the People's Republic. It was in these regions that fighting against the Chinese began in the mid–1950s, spreading to central Tibet in 1959, and culminating in the flight of the Dalai Lama and other Tibetan refugees and the end of the Lhasa government.

Since 1959, the Dri River has remained the boundary between what is now the Tibet Autonomous Region on the western side and the province of Sichuan on the eastern side (the separate Tibetan province of Sikang no longer exists). K'am is thus divided between six administrative divisions (see Map 2), Qamdo Prefecture (in the Tibet Autonomous Region), the Tibetan Autonomous Prefectures of Garzê and Aba (Sichuan), Dêqên (Yunnan) and Yushu (Qinghai), and the Tibetan Autonomous County of Mili in Sichuan.

INDIGENOUS STATES OF K'AM: INTRODUCTION

There is no detailed ethnography available for the K'am region.[8] Our knowledge of the region is based primarily on the reports of Western travelers and on accounts by refugees, and does not provide the basis for a detailed account of K'am social structure. There is some information on the political structure of the region, however, including a detailed survey by Eric Teichman, the consular official involved in the 1918 Chinese-Tibetan peace negotiations, and L. S. Dagyab's account of the political system of Dragyab (Dagyab 1980).

Teichman lists some twenty-six Tibetan 'states' under Chinese protection in the pre–1905 period. Some of these might be better described as stateless areas although all had some kind of formal head. To them may be added the nine or so partly Tibetanized states of Gyelrong and some states in western K'am, which were not of direct concern to Teichman, such as Powo. The largest of these states was the 'kingdom' of Derge, which was ruled by a hereditary king or *gyelpo*. Four other states in K'am had rulers called *gyelpo*. These were Chagla, Nangch'en, Lhat'og, and Lingts'ang, though the last two states were quite small. Most of the other twenty-one states also had lay rulers, generally referred to *depa* or *pönpo*, which are less specific titles than generic terms for lay rulers and administrators. Five had lama rulers (see also Carrasco 1959). Information about these states is summarized in the following pages. The modern Chinese counties often follow the old state boundaries, so their populations in the 1982 census (given from Li Chengrui 1987) are some guide to the current populations in these areas. The correspondence is far from exact, however, and the figures can be only a very rough guide to the population in the first half of the century.[9]

West of the Dri River (Yangtse)

These regions were generally accepted as being within the domain of the Dalai Lama's government before 1904, and they remained so from 1918 to 1959. After the Nyarong war in 1863–1865, these areas, along with those in the next section (Nyarong, Derge, and the Hor states), became the responsibility of the Nyarong Chiky'ab. From 1913 he was replaced by a provincial governor (Domé Chiky'ab, Dochi) at Ch'amdo with the rank of *kalön* or cabinet minister (Shakabpa 1967:250; Dhondup 1986:50–51, 58–59; Rahul 1969:39; Yuthok 1990:213–228).[10] Most of this region was administered by various traditional polities, although some parts of the region had been incorporated into the central Tibetan *dzong* system. In the northern part of the region there were two 'kingdoms' (Lhat'og and Gyadé) whose population was mostly pastoralist. In the center there were four monastic states (Ch'amdo, Riwoch'e, Pagshöd, Dragyab). Two southern areas, Mark'am and Gonjo, were administered by Lhasa, although not under the *dzong* system proper. Finally, the kingdom of Powo in the far south, which fought a war with the Lhasa government in the 1920s, needs treating as a special case.

Lhat'og was a small state of mostly pastoralist population, ruled by a *gyelpo* (Teichman 1922:156 n.2; Trungpa 1971:131–132). It apparently fell outside Lhasa's sphere of influence in the nineteenth century but was included within the Lhasa domain from 1918 onwards, being on the western side of the Dri River. It now forms part of Jomda County, which had a population of 52,506 in 1982, but most of this county formed part of the traditional state of Derge (see below).

Gyadé, also known as the country of the 'Thirty-Nine Tribes,' was in the basin of the upper Ngül River (the Salween). Like Lhat'og, its population was mainly pastoralist. It had traditionally fallen within the Lhasa domain, though as with other pastoralist areas it is likely to have been largely self-governing in practice. According to Rockhill, who traveled through the area in 1892, the people of Gyadé were on bad terms with the Gelugpa administration at Lhasa, in part because they were Bönpo rather than Buddhist, and they owed allegiance to the Lhasa *amban*, not to the Dalai Lama's government. He speaks of thirty-six local officials, called *depa*, appointed by the *amban* (Rockhill 1894:254, 260–261). Teichman describes the area as ruled by a lay *pönpo*. Gyadé would seem to correspond roughly to the modern Chinese counties of Dêngqên, Banbar, and Lhorong, with a total population in the 1982 census of 93,420, but parts of these counties may have fallen outside Gyadé.

Ch'amdo was a state in the Dza River (Mekong) basin; from 1917 onwards its capital became the center of the Dalai Lama's administration of K'am. The ruler of this state, a reincarnate lama known as the Phagpa Lha (Schwieger 1988:435 n. 4; Michael 1982:93), was the abbot of the large Gelugpa *gompa* at Ch'amdo, founded in 1437. The state was administered by a lama official known as the Tsangdrupa (Teichman 1922:114–115). The population of the modern county of Qamdo is 69,360.

Dragyab or Drayab (Map 4, no. 7) was another lama state in the Mekong basin headed by a Gelugpa reincarnate lama, the Dragyab Chamgön, whose monastery was founded in 1621. The state was established with the assistance of Gushri Khan in the course of his east Tibetan campaign of 1639–1641 (Schwieger 1988:436; Schwieger and Dagyab 1989). As at Ch'amdo, the administration was in the hands of a lama official, who was also the manager of the *labrang* (Teichman 1922:124ff; Michael 1982:91; Dagyab 1980). We have an account of the administration of Dragyab by the former Dragyab Chamgön (L. S. Dagyab), which gives a detailed listing of the administration at Dragyab, and some comments on the working of the government:

> The modern governmental structure of Dragyab goes back to the already-mentioned reorganization of government in 1806. While the Dragyab Chamgön was the nominal supreme head of the religious principality, the exercise of political power lay primarily in the hands of the *chidzöd* (General Treasurer), who was normally appointed by the Tibetan central government on the recommendation of the Dragyab

> Chamgön and generally governed for only three years. It should be emphasized that we are not concerned here with a Lhasa government official. Only monks were eligible for the position of *chidzöd.* He would make important decisions only after consultation with the Dragyab Chamgön. This aside, the practice of government involved close consultation with the *drönch'en* (Chancellor) and the *trungch'en* (General Secretary) whose ranks followed immediately after the *chidzöd* and who, in view of this practice of consultation, formed a kind of council of ministers along with the *chidzöd.* Interestingly, the group of these three government ministers was for this reason called *gyel lon sum,* in which *gyel(-po)* refers to the *chidzöd.* (Dagyab 1980:16; my translation)

According to Dagyab Rimpoche, the *chidzöd*'s office was under no obligation to consult the Lhasa government about its decisions (1980:16), though since the *chidzöd* was appointed by Lhasa, even if on the Chamgön's recommendation, there would seem to be some scope for intervention by Lhasa or, after 1918, by the *kalön* stationed in neighboring Ch'amdo. Michael mentions that there was a garrison of five hundred soldiers at Dragyab (1982:91). This would again refer to the post–1918 situation. The population of the modern county of Zhag'yab is 43,733.

Riwoch'e was another lama state in the Dza River (Mekong) Basin. This was one of the two main centers of the Taglung Kagyüdpa (Russell 1986), and the position of head of state alternated between the three principal reincarnation-lines of the large Taglung *gompa.*[11]

Pagshöd, although referred to as a 'state' by Teichman and others, was formally an unusually large estate attached to the Kundeling *gompa* at Lhasa. It is situated in the Ngül River (Salween) Basin below Gyadé. Kundeling appointed the administrator of Pagshöd, who was regularly given a *dzasa* title on his return to Lhasa.[12] The population figures given for the modern counties of Riwoqê and Baxoi are 27,546 and 28,986.

Further south were two areas more directly incorporated into the Lhasa administrative system. Mark'am was a province in the Dza River (Mekong) Basin, south of Dragyab.[13] It was administered by an official called the Mark'am T'eji appointed by Lhasa, and residing at Mark'am Gart'og. Lhasa rule over this area owed its origins to the campaigns of Gushri Khan (Sermé Ribur Tulku 1988:8–12; Teichman 1922:130, 195). Gonjo, further north, seems to have been administered by an official appointed by the Mark'am T'eji.[14] The population of Markam County in 1982 was 60,340 and that of Gonjo County was 35,914. Gonjo County, however, seems to be a larger area than traditional Gonjo, including parts of Sangen (see below) and perhaps also Derge.

The state of Powo or Pomé, ruled by a hereditary monarch known as the Kanam Depa or Kanam Gyelpo, was situated in the lower part of the region of Poyul, near the Tsang River (Brahmaputra) bend southwest of Pagshöd.[15] The Kanam Depa, like the Lhagyari family of E, claimed descent from the ancient Tibetan kings. In 1834, Powo was forced to pay taxes to Lhasa by a Lhasa army (Shakabpa 1967:175–176), but it seems to have been mostly independent of the Dalai Lama's government (Rgya-mtsho Don-drub 1989). A further confrontation with Lhasa in the 1920s over taxes led to a campaign against Powo and the deposition of the Kanam Depa in 1926 (see Shakabpa 1967:238, 265–266; Dhondup 1986:151–154; Rgya-mtsho Don-drub 1989). Subsequently "two district officers, with a small garrison" were stationed there (Shakabpa 1967:266); Michael speaks of three Lhasa government *dzong* within Poyul, also presumably referring to the post–1926 situation (1982:92). Poyul was a 'frontier region' with significant populations of the Mönpa and Lopa minorities (Rgya-mtsho Don-drub 1989:85–86). The present-day Bomi County has a population of 24,915, though it is unclear how similar its borders are to those of traditional Pomé.

Derge, Lingts'ang, the Hor States, and Nyarong

These areas, all in the northern and central parts of K'am, were independent of Lhasa before the Nyarong troubles in the 1860s, but became subject to the Dalai Lama's government from then until 1904. The Lhasa government retained some rights in these areas from 1918 to 1933, but lost them at that time, except for the section of Derge state to the west of the Dri River. It does not seem, however, that any of these regions were ever closely administered from Lhasa.

Derge (Map 4, no. 8) was a large state on both sides of the Dri (Yangtze) and Nya (Yalung) rivers. It was ruled by a hereditary *gyelpo* (Teichman 1922:157–159; Kolmaš 1968, 1988; Smith 1970; Trungpa 1971:106–107; Kessler 1983; and see below). The rulers of Derge claimed descent from the Gar family whose most famous member was chief minister to the central Tibetan king, Songtsen Gampo. In the early period, they seem to have been primarily a hereditary lama family. They became closely associated with the Sakyapa religious order from the thirteenth century onwards, and appear to have acted as the regional governors in K'am for the Sakyapa rulers of Tibet (Kolmaš 1968:30).

The Derge state first became a major power around 1700 as a result of the expansionist activities of the Derge rulers Champa P'unts'og (early seventeenth century) and Tenpa Ts'ering (1678–1738) (Kolmaš 1968:32–38). The *gyelpo* retained authority over the important Sakyapa *gompa* of Lhundrub Teng in the Derge capital. The eighteenth century was the height of Derge's power. The state came under Lhasa control in 1865, at the time of the Nyarong affair, but was protected from Gelugpa reprisals against its non-Gelugpa *gompa* by the political skills of its two leading lamas, Jamgön Kongtrul Lodrö T'ayé (1813–1899) and Jamyang Ky'entsé Ongpo (1820–1892), central figures of the Rimed movement (Smith 1970:33–34). After 1918 the parts of Derge state on the west bank of the Yangtse were incorporated into the Lhasa administrative structure under a lay *dzongpön*. The administrator of Denma *gompa* and the chief of the nomadic population around Kat'og *gompa* seem to have been incorporated separately into the Lhasa system (Michael 1982:91, 93).

Derge contained several important *gompa* apart from Lhundrup Teng. Among them was the main Karma Kagyüdpa *gompa* in K'am, Pelpung or Barbung. There were also the four main Nyingmapa *gompas* of K'am, Kat'og, Pelyul, Shech'en, and Dzogch'en, and the Sakyapa *gompa* of Dzongsar. All of these became active centers of the Rimed movement in the late nineteenth and early twentieth centuries (see Chapter 27).

The traditional state of Derge includes the counties of Sêrxü, Dêgê, and Baiyü (i.e., Pelyul), with a total population of 141,478, as well as parts of the modern Jomda and Gonjo counties. There are substantial nomadic populations in the northern part of Derge state. Namkhai Norbu, who visited the nomadic region of Dzach'uk'a (Map 4, no. 5) in 1951, has given a description of these people (Namkhai Norbu 1983, 1990a).

Lingts'ang was a small state in the upper Nya River (Yalung) area ruled by a *gyelpo*. Its population, mostly nomadic, was less than 1,000 families (Teichman 1922:79, 83; Duncan 1952:188 says 500). The precise status of this state after 1918 is unclear but it seems to have been more or less a dependency of Derge, within whose territory it lay.

The Hor states (Trehor or Hor Pönk'ag Nga; Map 4, no. 9) were five states with overlapping territories in the valley of Kandzé on the Upper Yalung east of Derge. The individual states were Drango, Dreo, K'angsar, Masur, and Peri. Each had a hereditary lay ruler or *pönpo* (Teichman 1922:71–72; Wylie 1962:104; Kessler 1984). The main population center was around Kandzé. The *pönpo* had authority over individual families rather than territorial units, so that families belonging to all five were distributed throughout the region. The Hor states were under the authority of the Nyarong Chiky'ab from 1862–1865 to 1905. The Lhasa government retained some rights in the area under the 1918 treaty, but lost them after the fighting of 1930–1933. The Hor states correspond roughly to the modern counties of Garzê (51,314) and Luhuo (33,869) along with part of Dawu (41,733).

The state of Nyarong occupied the valley of the Nya River (Yalung) below Kandzé. Before the ascendancy of Gompo Namgyel in the 1840s, there had been a number of local chieftains in Nyarong, and the region retained a 'tribal' structure in the twentieth century. According to Aten's (Rabten Dorje) autobiography (Jamyang Norbu 1986:14, 33, 48), referring to the 1920s, there were four 'tribes' in Nyarong (Nyatö, Nyamé, Khongshe, and Wulu), each with a 'chieftain' and each nominally consisting of a thousand families. The tribes were composed of ten to fifteen 'subtribes,' each of which had an 'Arrow Chief.' A 'tribal' structure is characteristic of pastoralist areas of Tibet. In Nyarong, which had a mixed agricultural-pastoral economy, it is more surprising. It may reflect the relatively recent 'Tibetanization' of this region (see below and Kessler 1984), although the *gompa* at Chandüd is one of the oldest Nyingmapa *gompa* in K'am. The population of Xinlong (Nyarong) County in 1982 was given as 37,415.

Other States East of the Dri River (and Nangch'en)

These areas were independent of Lhasa throughout the nineteenth century and twentieth centuries. The major states here were Chagla, Bat'ang, Lit'ang, Nangch'en, Mili, and the Gyelrong states. All except for Nangch'en are in the southern and eastern parts of K'am. There were also stateless areas such as Sangen in these parts of K'am.

Chagla was a large state in the west of K'am with its capital at the important trading center of Kangding (formerly Tachienlu). It had a hereditary ruler or *gyelpo*. Tachienlu has long been the center of Chinese power in the region. Rockhill, writing of his visit in 1889, comments:

> Tachienlu is the most westerly sub-prefecture . . . in the province of Sichuan, and is also the capital of the Tibetan prince, or king *(gyelpo)*, of Chagla. . . . An army commissary . . . administers this sub-prefecture, besides forwarding all the money, supplies, etc., necessary to the Chinese garrisons in Tibet. . . . Prior to 1700, Tachienlu and the country east of it for nearly a hundred miles was not occupied by the Chinese and was under the rule of the King of Chagla, but since that date this tract has been annexed to China, though the natives have been allowed to retain their tribal organization. The native prince still resides at Tachienlu, and is one of the most powerful chiefs of East Tibet, for among them he alone demands and obtains obedience from the lamas dwelling in his principality. He has the right to levy duties on all goods taken west of the city by Chinese or natives, and exercises exclusive control over all his people, native culprits arrested by the Chinese being turned over to him or his officers for punishment. (Rockhill 1891:274–276)

As mentioned earlier, Tachienlu (Kangding) was the capital for the Chinese administration of Sikang from 1927 until the 1950s. The state of Chagla would have included all of the modern county of Kangding (86,131), along with most of Danba (57,944) and perhaps also parts of Dawu (41,733) and Yajiang (34,512). Only about half of the population of Kangding in 1982 was Tibetan, and around two-thirds of that of Danba.

Ba (Bat'ang) was a large state adjoining the Dri River (Yangtze) ruled by a hereditary lay *depa* (Teichman 1922:136, 195); Rockhill speaks of two *depa*, both from the same family (1894:344–348). It had an important Gelugpa *gompa*. Jeffrey quotes J. H. Edgar's estimate of the population as "3,350 families or perhaps 20,000 individuals"; at least some of this was nomadic (1974:56; see Duncan 1952:86, 91–96). The population of Batang County today is 43,727.

Lit'ang was another large state between Chagla and Bat'ang, ruled by a hereditary lay *depa* and with another important Gelugpa *gompa*. At the time of Rockhill's visit (1892) there were two *depa*, one a layman and the second, his brother, a lama (Rockhill 1894:355–357). Jeffrey estimates the population as around 5,000, though this seems rather low (1974:62). The southern areas of Ch'angtr'eng and Kongkaling were wild and bandit-ridden. Lit'ang corresponds roughly to the modern county of Litang (40,767) along with Xiangcheng (Ch'angtr'eng, 22,725), Daocheng (23,075), and parts of Yajiang (34,512).

The kingdom of Nangch'en was in the upper Dza River (Mekong) area, to the west of the Dri River, but it fell within Xining's jurisdiction and thus, like other states considered here, was outside the control of the Lhasa government. It was ruled by a *gyelpo*, and its territory included the important trading center of Jyekundo (see above). The population of Nangch'en was mostly nomadic, although there was some agricultural country around Jyekundo and around the palace at Nangch'en. Teichman describes Nangch'en as consisting of some 10,000 families divided into twenty-five clans or tribes (Teichman 1922:108). According to Tashi Tsering, its structure was more complex than this, and traditionally consisted of four districts close to the capital under four officials known as *gyelts'ab* ('regent'), surrounded by a *nangdé* ('inner region') with thirty-three tribes and a *ch'idé* ('outer region') of thirty-five tribes. Of the *ch'idé* tribes, twenty-five (the Gapa or Gak'og) were administered from Jyekundo, and would seem to be the twenty-five clans mentioned by Teichman. From circa 1800 onwards, the senior official at Jyekundo, known as the Draur Beu, gained considerable autonomy from the Nangch'en king.[16] The territory of Nangch'en would correspond approximately to that of the modern counties of Yushu (Jyekundo, 54,463) and Nangqên (47,264).

Mili or Muli was a state on the borders of Yunnan, with an only partly Tibetanized population (see Rock 1925, 1931; Kessler 1982). The ruler of Mili was the Mili Chamgön, the incarnate lama who was head of the large Gelugpa *gompa*, and was always found in the ruling family or a closely related house.[17] In the 1982 census, the population of Muli County was given as 101,396. Tibetans made up around 30,000 of this; other major ethnic groups included Yi (around 27,000), Miao and Man (around 6,000 each), Naxi and Bai (around 3,000 each), and Lisu (about 2,000) (Li 1987:32–37, 194–206). The Yi (formerly known as Lolo), Naxi, and Bai (Minchia) are all Tibeto-Burman speaking groups (see LeBar et al. 1964).

The Gyelrong or Jyarong states were a group of small, partly Tibetanized states east and northeast of the Hor states. Lama Tsenpo lists eighteen of these in 1820, while noting that several no longer existed (Wylie 1962:102–103); Jeffrey, a missionary who worked in this area in the 1930s, lists six, Kroskyab (at the northwest end), Ziggag, Tambai, Chogtse, Wogzhi, and Wasze, the most easterly (Jeffrey 1974:47), mentioning that three others had disappeared (see also Kessler 1984, map 27). The population of the easternmost states is classified as Qiang today while that of the remaining states is regarded as Tibetan. The traditional boundaries of the Gyelrong states are unclear but they perhaps correspond to the modern counties of Jinchuan, Barkam, Xiaojin, Heishui, Lixian, Wenchuan, and Maowen. These counties had a total population of 463,293 in the 1982 census, of whom around 147,500 were classified as Tibetans (mainly in Jinchuan, Barkam, Xiaojin, and Heishui), and around 102,000 as Qiang (mainly in Lixian, Wenchuan, and Maowen). The remainder were Han Chinese.

Teichman also lists five small pastoralist states (Ge-she, Tongkor, Tzako, Yuko, Sert'a) to the east of the upper Nya River (Yalung), each with a lay ruler or *pönpo* (1922:3). The positions of most of these states are marked by Kessler (1984, map 27). The Sert'a are usually counted among the Golog (see Chapter 5); Namkhai Norbu has given some information on these people from his travels in the region in 1951 (Map 4, no. 6; Namkhai Norbu 1983, 1990a; see also Guibaut 1949). Some of the other states seem to have been part of the Gyelrong region. The Tibetan populations of these regions correspond to those of the modern counties of Sertar and Zamtang, with a total population of 58,891 in 1982, all but a few thousand being Tibetan.

Teichman's account gives the impression that the map of K'am could be split up relatively neatly into a series of petty states with clearly delineated boundaries, and this was true to some extent. At any given time, the large settled communities normally owed clear allegiance to one state or another through their local headmen and *pönpo*, and travelers along the main roads knew when they were passing from one domain to another. The more remote areas, however, particularly those inhabited mainly by pastoralists, were not necessarily integrated in any effective way into these petty states, whether or not there was some kind of *pönpo* with nominal allegiance to Lit'ang or Derge. We have already met this situation in the case of the 'wild bandit areas' of Ch'angtr'eng and Kongkaling. Another such area, the region of the Dri River Valley above Bat'ang, was simply known as Sangen ('badlands') and did not form part of any of the petty states, although Teichman mentions a *pönpo* recognized by the Sichuan authorities (1922:13, 142). Sangen corresponded to small parts of the modern counties of Gonjo and Baiyü, with a modern population of perhaps 10,000 to 15,000.

INDIGENOUS STATES OF K'AM: DISCUSSION

Altogether K'am provides a bewildering variety of Tibetan polities, and it must be admitted that we are not very well informed about many of these states. Some underlying patterns are, however, noticeable.

First, these states had a variety of leadership patterns: the above examples include hereditary lay princes, hereditary lamas, and reincarnate lamas, as well as officials appointed by the Lhasa administration. Many of the lay princes, however, were associated with powerful lamas and *gompa* (for example, Lit'ang and Ba).

Second, a particular 'state' might have subordinate status within a larger 'state.' Ch'amdo, Dragyab, Riwoch'e, and Mark'am were subordinate to the Lhasa administration; Gonjo was at one stage subordinate to Mark'am. Lit'ang included the subordinate units of Ch'angtr'eng and Kongkaling under lay sub-chiefs (Rock 1931). Most states of any size included subordinate centers of power, usually called, as in central Tibet, *dzong*. Derge, for example, had twenty-five *dzong*, while Gonjo had twelve *dzong* or *pön* (Teichman 1922:171, 176). The headmen of these districts were under varying degrees of control from the center; Teichman describes the hereditary headmen of the three largest districts in Derge state (Gaji, Adu, and Seshü) as "practically semi-independent chieftains" (1922:208). All of the Gonjo *pön* positions were hereditary, and in some cases one family had acquired control of more than one position.[18] We will come across this pattern again in other Tibetan states, such as Bhutan and Ladakh.

Third, there were situations, such as the five Hor states, where there were several local rulers of more or less equal status. The situation in Nyarong before Gompo Namgyel's rise to power was apparently similar (see T. Tsering 1985; J. Norbu 1986). The Hor states region contained, according to Teichman (1922:75),

> the largest tract of level cultivated land in the whole of eastern Tibet. . . . The Yalung River winds through the middle of it, and farms,

> hamlets, and monasteries are thickly dotted around. The inhabitants are prosperous and wealthy, being engaged in the lucrative Chinese-Tibetan tea trade, as well as in agriculture.

An interesting feature of the Hor states is that their territories were not strictly delimited from each other; "their jurisdictions were over families rather than lands" (Teichman 1922:76). Estates in central Tibet had a similar character in respect of both the noncontiguous nature of their territories and of jurisdiction being primarily over villages and households.

Looking back on Chapters 3 and 4, it is often hard to draw a rigid distinction between 'state' and 'estate.' The Hor states resembled central Tibetan estates in their lack of territorial boundaries, but unlike central Tibet they had no effective superordinate authority (except temporarily from 1865 to 1904, if the Nyarong Chiky'ab fulfilled that function). Were they 'states' or 'estates'? The main territory of Sakya was clearly delimited, and it had at least as much of a governmental apparatus as most of the 'states' of K'am. Should we term it an 'estate' or a 'state'? Entities such as the Trashi Lhunpo or Sakya 'estates' were in many ways comparable both to K'am 'states' such as Dragyab or Riwoch'e (which were subject to Lhasa control) and to those such as Derge or the Hor states (which were, 1865–1904 aside, not so subject). The 'state' of Pagshöd formed part of the Lhasa monastic estate of Kundeling. The Dalai Lama's government at Lhasa itself originated in a monastic estate and retained many features reflecting its origins.

Fourth, the degree of control exercised by these various polities over their populations clearly varied greatly. At one extreme were the settled village and urban populations in Derge or Kandzé. At the other extreme were 'wild' populations such as the people of Ch'angtr'eng (in Lit'ang state), the people of Sangen (Tibetan for 'badlands'), or the Lengkashi north of Bat'ang, whom Teichman describes as "turbulent and unruly" and "notorious" (1922:203 n. 1, 207), noting that they "have the advantage of living in a valley that is almost inaccessible to the Chinese" (see also Duncan 1952:164–172). Areas such as Nangch'en, with its mostly pastoralist population, or Nyarong, with its 'tribal' organization, also seem close to a 'stateless' political system. The people of K'am as a whole had a reputation for being independent, self-assertive, and aggressive when compared with the people of central Tibet.

Fifth, there was a tendency for non-Tibetan populations to be 'Tibetanized' and incorporated into Tibetan-style polities. The two most obvious examples are Mili, with its mostly Yi population, and the Gyelrong principalities, whose population is still largely Qiang. It may be that much of the present-day Tibetan population of K'am results from similar processes of Tibetanization since the seventh century or earlier.

In the extreme south of K'am, within Yunnan Province, various Naxi, Yi, and Lisu principalities were undergoing a similar process of Tibetanization in the early twentieth century. While some of this region is often considered as part of Tibet, most of the population is not really Tibetan. In 1982, Tibetans formed a majority in only one of the three counties of the Dêqên Tibetan Autonomous Prefecture (Dêqên, with 42,500 out of 52,757, the remainder being mostly Lisu with some Naxi, Pumi and Nu). Tibetans formed the largest ethnic group in Zhongdian County (around 45,000 out of 105,626, with large numbers of Naxi, Lisu, and Yi and some Bai). The 118,228 people of Weixi County seem to have been mostly Lisu and Naxi with some Tibetans, Bai, and Pumi. The Tibetan name for this region is Gyelt'ang (Map 4, no. 10; Corlin 1978, 1980), and it had close links in the premodern period with the Naxi people to the south (see Goullart 1957:239–243).

Lijiang Naxi autonomous county to the immediate south (population 291,940) contained the bulk of the Naxi population along with substantial numbers of Bai and Lisu and some Yi, Pumi, Miao, and Tibetans (Li 1987:32–39, 194–206). These ethnic classifications are not to be taken too seriously, since here as further south in Burma and Thailand ethnic identities are notoriously unstable and difficult to specify coherently (Leach 1970; Lehman 1967). The ethnic groups in these regions undoubtedly were adapting various features of Tibetan culture, however, including aspects of Tibetan Buddhism, as were peoples on the southern borders in Arunachal Pradesh and further west in Bhutan, Sikkim, and Nepal (see Chapter 6).

In the case of the Naxi, who are known as Jang in Tibetan, this process was undoubtedly of some antiquity (A. Jackson 1978, 1979). The kingdom of Jang (Map 4, no. 11), with its capital at the town of Lijiang (Sat'am in Tibetan), already had close links with the Karma

Kagyüdpa order in the early to mid-seventeenth century (Karma Thinley 1980:105–106) and the king of Jang sponsored the production of one of the first printed editions of the Tibetan Buddhist canon or Kanjur from 1609 onwards (Shastri 1987). Jang was first an enemy and then an ally of Gesar in the Tibetan epic, which can be read in part as an account of these processes of 'Tibetanization' of surrounding peoples (see Samuel, in press a). I shall discuss the question of Tibetanization further in Chapter 7. In the following chapter, we continue our survey with an examination of Amdo, the province to the north of K'am.

5

Tibetan Societies: Amdo (Northeastern Tibet)

The subject of this chapter is Amdo, the region to the north of K'am. Like K'am, much of the available information on Amdo society comes from travelers and explorers in the premodern period, although there is also some anthropological research on Amdo pastoralism by the former missionaries Robert Ekvall and Matthias Hermanns.

GENERAL DESCRIPTION

Amdo (Map 5) consists primarily of the areas around and to the north of the great lake of Ts'o Ngönpo ('Blue Lake'), better known in English by its Mongol name of Kokonor, along with the upper reaches of the Yellow River (Huang-Ho) or Ma River. Most of the Tibetans living in this region were nomadic pastoralists. In addition to Tibetan pastoralists, there were Mongol pastoralists, particularly to the north and west of Lake Kokonor, and groups such as the Sokpo Arik who, though of Mongolian origin, had been almost entirely Tibetanized (see Rock 1956:57).

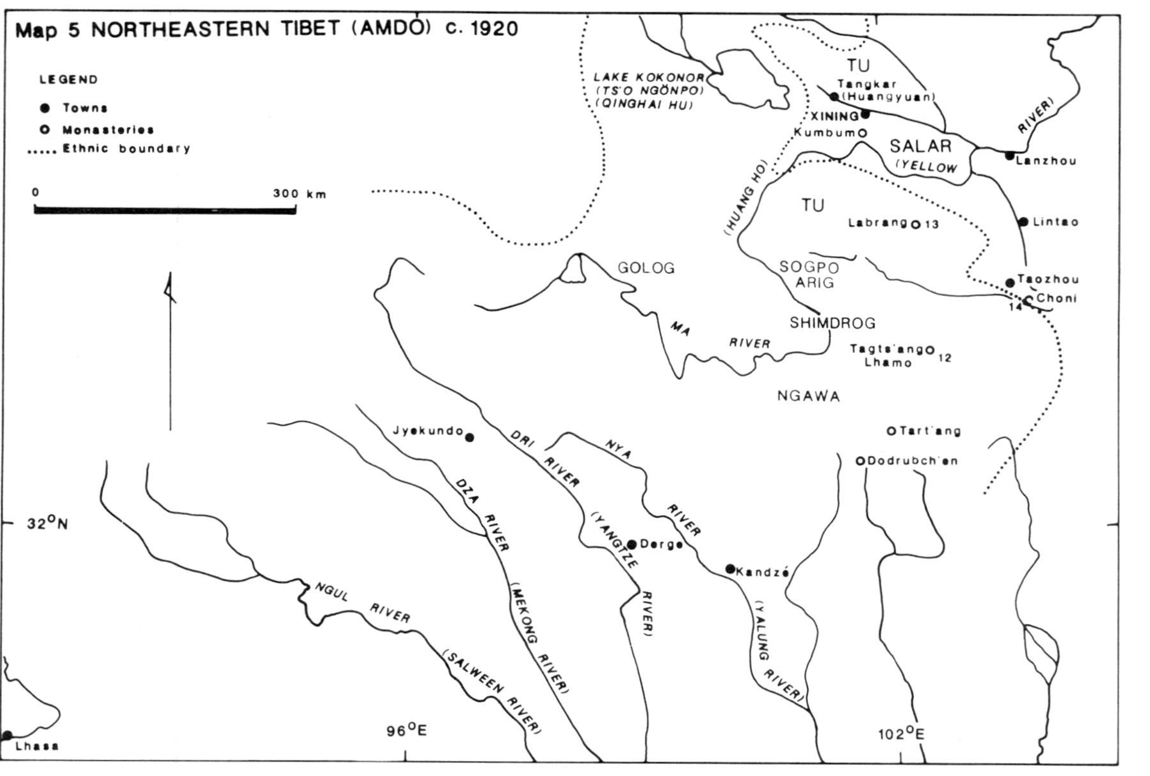

Key:
12 Tagts'ang Lhamo
13 Labrang
14 Choni

There were also substantial populations of settled Tibetan agriculturalists, particularly in areas towards the eastern edge of the Tibetan plateau. Many of these agriculturalist Tibetans were in close contact with a variety of other ethnic groups, including Hui or Chinese Muslims, Han Chinese, a Turkic people known as the Salar (Trippner 1964), and the partially Tibetanized population of the Tu (Monguor), who speak an Altaic language related to Mongolian (Schram 1954).[1] The Chinese, Salar, and Tu population was concentrated in the agricultural regions to the east and southeast of Lake Kokonor, where there was a series of towns serving as trading centers for the region. Many of these were walled and had Chinese garrisons.

The largest town in the region was Xining, then as now the main Chinese administrative center. The trading center of Tankar, from which caravans set off to central Tibet, was around 30 miles to the east (Rockhill 1891:109–115; Rijnhart 1901:133). Other urban centers included the old town of Taozhou (Teichman 1921:135–137; Rock 1956:25–26; Ekvall 1954a:74ff), and the combined monastic and trading centers at Choni (Rock 1928) and Labrang (Teichman 1921:138–145; Rock 1956:33–50; Yonten Gyatso 1988).

In the pastoralist areas there were trading posts with Chinese traders (mainly Chinese Muslims, i.e., Hui or Salar) attached to *gompa* in places such as Takts'ang Lhamo (Ekvall 1952, 1954a). Itinerant Chinese traders traveled throughout the region. There were also major long-distance trading routes which went through the area, such as that from central Tibet via Jyekundo in K'am to the Tankor-Xining area and on to China proper. Large caravans of hundreds of yaks traveled along these routes. At the turn of the century, the Lhasa government maintained a group of officials at Tankor to superintend these caravans (Rijnhart 1901:144ff).

Along the eastern edge of the pastoralist region, adjoining the Chinese plains, there were populations of agriculturalist Tibetans such as the T'ebo (see Ekvall 1939, 1952). These people, along with the similar communities of Sharwa and Sangskar in Sichuan to the immediate south,[2] were traditionally regarded as part of Amdo, but contrasted markedly with the dominant pastoralist culture to the west. Very little has so far been written about them, although a brief report on the Sharwa by Philippe Sagant and Samten Karmay (who was born in Sharwa country) indicates that they had a decentralized political system of "small autonomous federations" whose leaders were "neither hereditary chiefs, nor the representatives of centralized power, nor elected chiefs" (Blondeau 1985–1986:152; my translation). In other words, leadership was of a familiar 'big man' type, resembling that in parts of K'am and in northern Nepal (see Chapters 4 and 6). There was a linkage between the power of these local leaders and the cult of local gods (*shibdag;* Blondeau 1985–1986:152–154).

The small town of Songpan (present-day Jin'an) at the southern end of this region was another of the trading communities on the edge of the Tibetan plateau, exchanging Tibetan wool, medicinal herbs, and hides for Chinese tea (see Alley 1940).

HISTORY AND PRESENT SITUATION

In former times, Amdo was occupied by the ancient partly Tibetanized state of the Tangut (Kychanov 1978), Tibetan Minyag.[3] From the fourteenth century onwards, the region fell under the control of Mongol tribes, with a mixed Mongol and Tibetan pastoralist population. The city of Xining was established to serve as the administrative center of the Kokonor area at the beginning of the Manchu period, in the late seventeenth century (Rock 1956:3–4).

The large-scale conversion of Mongol tribes to Tibetan Buddhism of the Gelugpa school had begun in the previous century, and Mongol tribes from this region were active in central Tibetan politics (see Chapter 27). All this doubtless encouraged the Tibetanization of Mongol groups mentioned above.

Amdo contained many large *gompa* of the Gelugpa school, with close connections to the Lhasa government, and Lhasa must at times have had considerable influence in the region. The Lhasa government never had any direct control over Amdo, however, and Gelugpa *gompa* in the region were politically autonomous. They included a number of very large institutions, the most important being Kumbum and Labrang. Kumbum (Taer Si in Chinese) was a few miles to the southwest of Xining and marked the birthplace of Tsongk'apa, the founder of the Gelugpa tradition (Filchner 1933), while Labrang, in Eastern Amdo, was the seat of the important Jamyang Shepa incarnation series, and a major force in Amdo politics (Rock 1956; Y. Gyatso 1988). There were also large non-Gelugpa *gompa,* such as the Nyingmapa centers of Tart'ang and Dodrub Ch'en, both in the Golog region (Khandro 1988:98, 137–139, 151; T. Thondup 1984:115–124).

During the Manchu period the entire region was administered, at least formally, by the Chinese amban at Xining. In practice, the Tibetan pastoralists were mostly self-governing, although Rijnhart, speaking of the 1890s, commented that, in contrast to the region to the south (i.e., K'am) the Tibetans here "fear the Amban and the Chinese soldiers to a surprising extent: hence it is that the Amban's authority is unquestioned" (Rijnhart 1901:163).

The agricultural areas around Xining were, as mentioned above, settled mainly by Chinese Muslims (Hui and Salar). Both Hui and Salar populations were involved in a major rebellion in 1861–1874, during which the monastic center at Kumbum was sacked by Muslim troops. The situation was still restless at the turn of the century (Rijnhart 1901), with sporadic outbreaks of fighting between Muslim forces and Chinese government troops.

After the Chinese revolution, the Muslims became the dominant power in the area, and a Muslim general ruling from Xining was recognized as the local ruler by the Republican government in 1915. Fighting broke out in 1925 between Tibetan tribes west of Labrang *gompa* and the Muslims, and this eventually led to further reorganization in 1928, with the creation of the new province of Qinghai. Parts of Western Gansu Province were incorporated into the new province, but the Labrang area, which had previously been administered from Xining, was now transferred to Gansu (Rock 1956:3–4, 32). The Muslim general at Xining, Ma Bufeng, continued to be the dominant power in the region until 1949, and was largely independent of the Republican government.

In 1949 the entire region was incorporated into the Chinese People's Republic. The present administrative boundaries follow those set up in 1928. Most of Amdo continues to lie within Qinghai province, of which it forms the major part. Four of the six prefectures of Qinghai province are Tibetan autonomous prefectures (Hainan, Haibei, Huangnan, Golog) and a fifth, Haixi, is a Mongolian-Tibetan-Kazak Autonomous Prefecture. The sixth, Haidong, is about 15 percent Tibetan in population. There are also Mongolian, Hui, Tu, and Salar autonomous counties, two of them (Hanan Mongolian A. C. and Menyuan Hui A. C.) within Tibetan autonomous prefectures, indicating the ethnic complexity of the region. The Tibetan areas within Gansu form a Tibetan Autonomous Prefecture (Ganan) and a Tibetan Autonomous County (Tianzhu, in Wuwei Prefecture). The Tibetan population of Amdo in 1982 was around 1 million.[4]

PASTORALIST POLITICS

Our main source for the political structure of Amdo in the first half of this century is the American missionary, later anthropologist, Robert Ekvall, who lived at the monastic and trading center of Tagts'ang Lhamo (Map 5, no. 12) towards the eastern edge of Amdo nomadic country from 1930–1935 and 1939–1941 (Ekvall 1939, 1952, 1968, 1981). Another missionary-anthropologist, Matthias Hermanns, who spent many years in northeastern and eastern Amdo from 1935 onwards, also provides useful information (Hermanns 1949), as does the American explorer Joseph Rock (1956). The pastoralists of Dzach'uk'a and Sert'a described in Namkhai Norbu's study, in the border regions between K'am and Amdo, were probably not much different from the pastoralists of Amdo proper (N. Norbu 1983, 1990a).

Tibetans in the pastoralist areas of Amdo lived in *rukor*, encampments (Ekvall 1939:68; N. Norbu 1983:150), which were organized into *ts'o*, tribes; the term *gyüd* is also sometimes used.[5] The encampment usually had an informally recognized headman but leadership was exercised in practice by "the group of substantial middle-aged and elderly men" (Ekvall 1939:68). These were known as the *genpo* or elders.

The nomadic tribes around Tagts'ang Lhamo formed a loose confederacy known as the Shimdrog, and Ekvall's accounts would seem to refer mainly to the Shimdrog tribes and their neighbors. At the 'tribal' level, Ekvall discusses a variety of leadership structures. In some cases there was no chief, and decisions were taken by a council of tribal elders (again *genpo*). In other cases there was a hereditary chief or *gowa*.

> The power of the chief varies greatly, depending on the tradition of the tribe, the ability of his predecessors, and on his own gifts and resources. In some tribes the position of chief is little more than an

> empty title, the real power of control and administration being entirely in the hands of the *genpo*. At the other extreme are tribes in which the chief is all-powerful because he is the able scion of able forebears; the *genpo* is here nothing more than an advisory group, whose function is to nod assent to the orations of the chief. Yet even such autocratic control is sharply limited, not by any competing body of power, but by the individualism and hatred of arbitrary restraint which are very strong in the Tibetans. (Ekvall 1939:69)

Two tribes had intermediate divisions between the encampment and the tribes. These divisions, which had their own hereditary leaders, may have been separate tribes that had been absorbed into a single tribe. Other tribes were grouped into "confederations or associations," as with the Shimdrog. Three chiefs had acquired such great power and control "through the absorption of lesser tribes and the attracting of refugee groups by exercising patronage and diplomacy combined with military prowess" that they were referred to as *gyelpo* or 'king,' a title we have already met in K'am. Ekvall also mentions some tribes that are governed by the *gompa* with which they are associated; I discuss these later on.

Matthias Hermanns presents a similar picture, adding another possibility, that of the elected chief:

> There are tribes, especially the smaller ones, who have no chief and govern everything through the elders of the individual groups. Even this council of the elders is not formally elected, but recognized through their innate competence. Among other tribes, especially larger ones, these elders elect an outstanding person as their chief. There are also tribes in which the status of chief is inherited in a particular family, when there is a competent son; if this is not the case, someone else is chosen. Among others, this status is inherited in the family, because it is the richest and therefore the most respected. In a large confederation, which is divided into subtribes, the latter have sub-chiefs, with a general chief over them. These positions again can be elected or inherited. There is also a confederation of many tribes with a king at its head. This position is inherited. (1949:231; my translation)

Hermanns, like Ekvall, comments on how the authority of these rulers was dependent on the support of the tribal 'elders' and the population as a whole:

> The power of the chief depends entirely on the force, respect and the influence of the person in question. If these are not outstanding, he has only the title but no power, and power lies in the hands of the elders. However the autocratic power of a strong leader is also sharply bounded, limited and watched over with Argus eyes. This happens not through people who are appointed for this function but through the desire for freedom and the independence of the individual families. (1949:231; my translation)

Hermanns tells a story of a "rich and influential" chief (of the Dashi tribe, north of Lake Kokonor) who wanted to marry his son to the daughter of a fairly wealthy man of his tribe. He was unwilling to pay the substantial bridewealth that was arranged so sent his men who brought only a few gifts of little value and took the girl by force. The girl's father could not resist directly, but he moved his tent to a neighboring tribe. Once the news got around, the chief regretted his actions and sent the bridewealth along with some horses as compensation; the girl's father rejected them indignantly and remained in the neighboring tribe (Hermanns 1949:231–232).

All these tribes were involved in a system of fighting, 'feuding,' and negotiated settlement reminiscent of populations in the highlands of West Asia or the Balkans, or of African pastoralists such as the Nuer. I shall give some examples, taken from Ekvall's writings, in Chapter 7.

In a community organized in such a politically decentralized and nonhierarchical manner, any services required from the outside world, whether mediation in a dispute, military cooperation, storage of a nomadic group's property in a *gompa* through the summer, or whatever else, were negotiated for on a contractual basis. Real or fictive kinship links were used when appropriate to help set up the negotiations. Mutual aid networks within the community, and trading-friend networks beyond it also fit into this general picture (Ekvall 1939: 54–55, 1954a:77). The nomads paid no regular taxes to secular authorities. One could say, however, that they paid on a contractual basis for services that might otherwise be provided by a government. Ekvall comments that:

> If war is determined, levies on the economic resources are voted or decided upon by the *genpo* ['elders'] and the *gowa* ['chief']. If peace is made, all share in bearing the expenses of conference and treaty-

> making. The chief or leader derives no direct material benefit from his position except as position and influence give him unusual opportunity to amass wealth. There is no such thing as a standing army nor are there any paid public officials. Even the individuals required to handle affairs for the chief or ruler act as his personal retainers, and he may either pay them, or what is more likely, place in their way opportunities to profit in trade or war. (1939:70)

The *gompa* played a central role in *drogpa* life. The relationship between nomadic tribes and *gompa* was a close one, involving economic support of the *gompa* by the nomads and the performance of religious and other services by the *gompa* for the nomads. The religious services performed will be considered in later chapters. Nonreligious services included mediation in disputes (see Chapter 7), the storage and trading of nomadic produce, and protection in times of tribal conflict or external danger.

Some *gompa* had acquired political control over the tribes to which they attached themselves. Ekvall comments that:

> [i]n such a case the lamasery [i.e., *gompa*] functions toward the group in two ways. It has a general religious influence and taps the people for contributions and fees, in return for which it undertakes to neutralize the evil effects of all the malignant influences in the region, to maintain itself as a gathering-point offering constant religious opportunity to the religious-minded, and to celebrate for the benefit of all the inhabitants so linked to it the many religious festivals designated in the religious calendar. . . . Secondly, the lamasery, through its leaders acts as ruler for certain tribes. Lamasery rule tends to be autocratic, and, in general, the rôle played by the *genpo* in determining policy is a smaller one when the lamasery is the ruler than when a chief is the head of the tribe. (Ekvall 1939:69)

A few *gompa* had extended their power to some degree over whole groups of tribes, "ultimately either superseding the chiefs or reducing them to a very subordinate position." Many tribes and chiefs had, however, managed to resist "such ecclesiastical domination" (1939:69).

Ekvall does not indicate which *gompa* governed tribes or groups of tribes. His descriptions of Gurdu, one of two large Gelugpa monastic *gompa* at Tagts'ang Lhamo, suggest an incipient center of power; however, Ekvall describes the lamas of Gurdu as providing mediating rather than direct administrative services. The surrounding tribes, Shami, Samtsa, Rzakdumba, and the others, form part of a tribal confederacy (Shimdrog). Ekvall speaks of the *gompa* as belonging to the tribes, rather than the reverse (1954a:54).

Rock provides some details for the important Gelugpa monastic center of Labrang (Map 5, no. 13), which appears to have had a more direct administrative role in relation to the surrounding tribal population, and was probably one of the *gompa* Ekvall had in mind when speaking of *gompa* governing tribes (Choni may have been another, see Rock 1928). Rock discusses a system by which each of a group of Tibetan and Mongol tribes took it in turn to provide a year's food for the Labrang *gompa* (1956:38–39). Labrang also had officials who administered some of the surrounding tribes and villages, referring disputes they could not solve to the *gompa*'s judges (1956:34).

Labrang was a considerably larger and more powerful *gompa* than Gurdu. The *gompa* and the surrounding community were situated to the east of the Tibetan plateau proper and acted as a major trading and administrative center. Certainly one might expect to find a more 'centralized' and hierarchical style of politics in such a place. Our information is not really such as to allow any definite conclusions.

In Ekvall's *The Lama Knows*, a partly fictionalized account of Amdo politics in the 1920s and 1930s, he describes Labrang and Gurdu as building up alliances with the various nomadic tribes. One such alliance between Gurdu, the King of Ngawa, and the Tsharuma tribe came to dominate eastern Amdo politics for some years, while other tribes such as the Ngura and Sokpo Arik, allied to Labrang *gompa*, supported a rival claimant for the chief Gurdu incarnation (1981). Ekvall describes attempts by Gurdu to persuade Dragkar, a smaller monastic *gompa*, to shift its allegiance from Labrang (1981:36–37), and mentions how the Ngura tribe, who had rejected the authority of Labrang some thirty years before, were reconciled with Labrang (1981:30).

This kind of political style was less a question of permanent domination by the *gompa* over the nomadic population than a series of alliances between secular and religious centers of power for mutual support. As we shall see, it was very typical of central Tibetan politics too in an earlier period, although gradually shifting in the direction of greater centralization of power (see Chapters 23 to 27).

AGRICULTURAL COMMUNITIES

The agricultural communities of Amdo were mainly along the edges of the plateau and in the region around Lake Kokonor. Ekvall gives some information about them (Ekvall 1939), as do other travelers and missionaries, but there are no detailed descriptions of social or political structure. The villages had headmen and acknowledged the authority of local chiefs such as the prince of Choni (Map 5, no. 14; Teichman 1921; Rock 1928). Teichman's comment on the prince of Choni is worth noting, since it repeats some of the themes we have come across in K'am:

> Choni, the residence of a *tusi*, or native chief, ruling several Tibetan tribes in the neighbourhood, is a picturesque little place, a walled village built round the chief's residence on the banks of the Tao, and overlooked by a lamasery containing some 500 monks. . . . The Choni *tusi* is by far the most important native chief in Gansu and exercises jurisdiction over an extensive territory. Some of his tribes, especially those living to the south of the Min Shan, are turbulent and not easy to control. The chief is under the authority of the Governor [of Gansu Province] at Lanzhou, but unlike his colleagues in Sichuan west of Tachienlu [Kangding], he retains his power unimpaired over his Tibetans. On the east his jurisdiction is bounded by Chinese territory; on the west it fades away amongst the lawless nomads of the grasslands. His authority, like that of most native chiefs in China, extends rather over tribes and families than fixed territory, and its limits are therefore vague. (1921:134)

We note here once more the authority over people, rather than territory, and the lack of any real control over pastoral populations (the 'lawless nomads of the grasslands'). The comment about the native chiefs in Sichuan, incidentally, should be read in the light of the date of the book. Teichman had just been involved in negotiating the 1918 settlement by which these regions were allocated to China, and the ineffectiveness of Chinese control was yet to become apparent (see Chapter 4).

Historically, the agricultural regions of Amdo were areas of contact between Tibetans and a variety of other populations, Chinese (Han and Hui), Salar, Tu (Monguor) and, perhaps most important for

Tibetan Buddhism, Mongolians. The large Gelugpa monasteries, mostly in the agricultural regions (as with Labrang, Kumbum, and Choni) were major centers for the propagation of Buddhism among the Mongols, and many of the monks and lamas, including some of the most famous scholars, were from Mongol families. Perhaps by necessity in this complex multi-ethnic situation, even the Gelugpa scholars of Amdo were often more open-minded than their equivalents in central Tibet.[6]

If Amdo was a region of culture-contact, much the same was true, in various ways, of the remaining areas of Tibetan population examined in the next chapter. Here, however, the contact was not with Chinese and Mongolian populations, but with primarily people on the fringes of the Hindu civilization of South Asia and with the Muslims of Kashmir.

6

Tibetan Societies: Southern and Western Tibet

This chapter deals with the remaining areas of Tibetan population, lying along the course of the Himalayas to the south and west of central Tibet. Most anthropological research on Tibetan populations has been carried out in these areas (primarily from northern Nepal and Ladakh), and we are in many respects quite well informed about them. The accessibility of Ladakh and other Tibetan areas in India, and of Tibetan populations in Nepal, is itself a result of these populations having been incorporated into non-Tibetan polities. This, along with the geographically marginal position of these areas in relation to most of the Tibetan population, raises the question of how to integrate anthropological data on, for example, Ladakhi or Sherpa religion and society into an overall picture of Tibetan religion and society.

My own view is that the data from these regions is very important for an overall understanding of Tibet, but that it has to be interpreted in the light of the relationship between communities such as Ladakh or Khumbu and the wider Tibetan context. A major purpose of this chapter is therefore to provide the basis for understanding that relationship. These southern and western regions are also of interest, however, in other respects, for example as providing further examples of traditional Tibetan polities (particularly Bhutan and Ladakh).

GENERAL DESCRIPTION

The remaining areas of 'ethnic' Tibet lie for the most part outside the People's Republic of China and can be divided roughly into a southern group, consisting of Sikkim, Bhutan, with parts of eastern Nepal and the Indian state of Arunachal Pradesh (Map 6), and a western group consisting of parts of western Nepal, parts of the Tibet Autonomous Region, parts of the Indian state of Himachal Pradesh and part of Jammu and Kashmir (Map 7). With the exception of the independent state of Bhutan, these regions have been incorporated into the modern states of India and Nepal. Since the Tibetan populations within the People's Republic of China (PRC) were until recently inaccessible to anthropological research by non-Chinese, most modern research on Tibetan populations has been carried out, as mentioned above, within these southern and western areas. Nevertheless, the politically sensitive situation along the Chinese frontier has meant that not all have been accessible to Western researchers on a regular basis.

Most of these southern and western areas have at some time formed part of central and western Tibetan polities but by the premodern period they had, with a couple of exceptions, been politically independent of Tibet for some centuries.[1] By the twentieth century there were four culturally Tibetan states within southern and western Tibet: Bhutan, Sikkim, Mustang, and Ladakh, although Sikkim was a British protectorate, and Mustang and Ladakh were parts of the Kingdom of Nepal and the Indian princely state of Jammu and Kashmir respectively. The population outside these four states lived in communities that were effectively self-governing (stateless, in anthropological terms) with more or less nominal reference to the various non-Tibetan rulers of Nepal, Kulu, and Kashmir. These communities were mostly agricultural; there were few entirely pastoral Tibetan communities in India and Nepal although a mixed pastoral-agricultural adaptation was fairly common in high Himalayan valleys such as Khumbu in Nepal.

The following description of the history and present situation of the southern and western areas is divided into five parts corresponding to (1) Tibetan areas of Arunachal Pradesh and the southern border

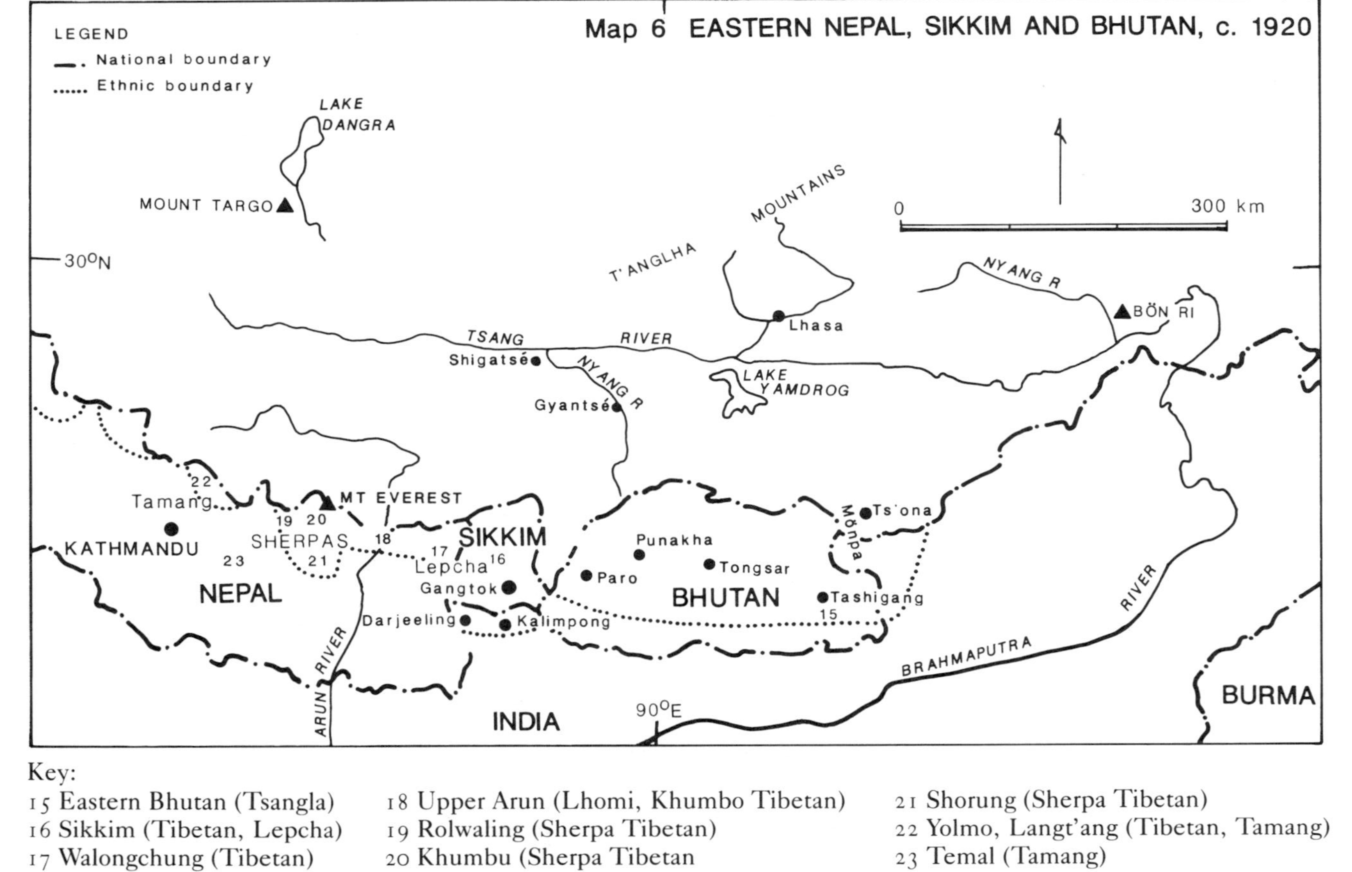

Key:

15 Eastern Bhutan (Tsangla)
16 Sikkim (Tibetan, Lepcha)
17 Walongchung (Tibetan)
18 Upper Arun (Lhomi, Khumbo Tibetan)
19 Rolwaling (Sherpa Tibetan)
20 Khumbu (Sherpa Tibetan
21 Shorung (Sherpa Tibetan)
22 Yolmo, Langt'ang (Tibetan, Tamang)
23 Temal (Tamang)

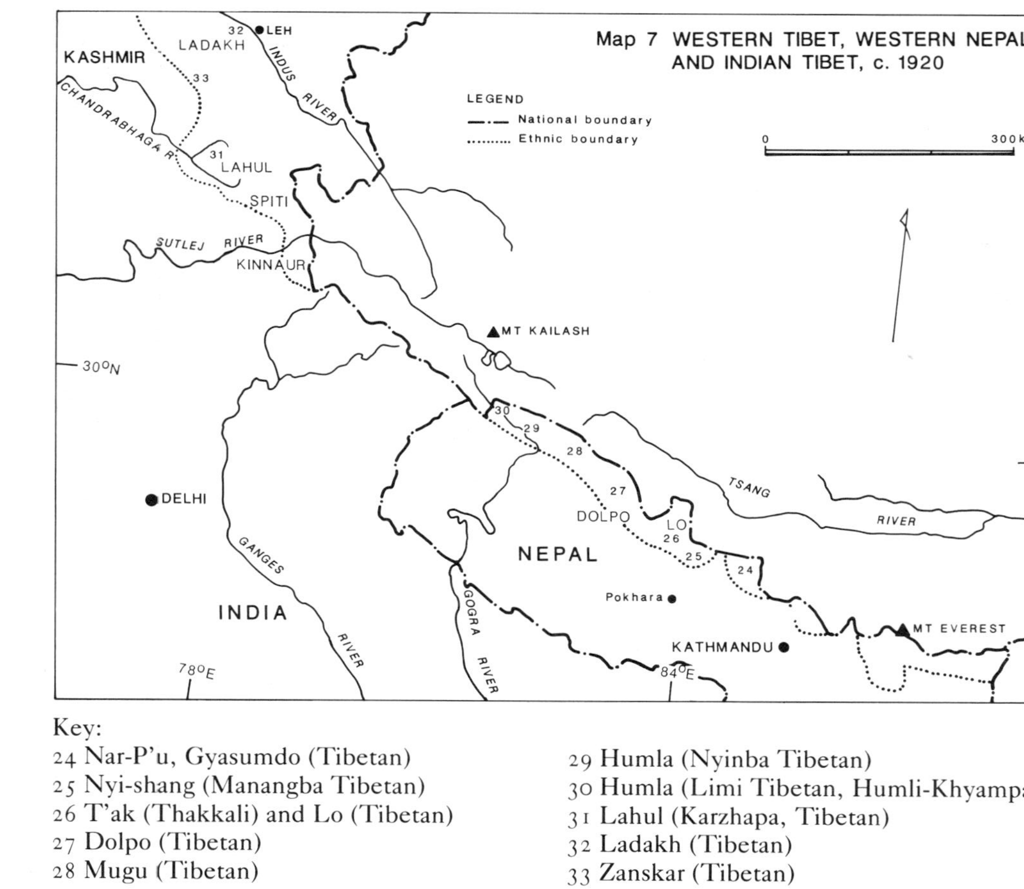

Map 7 WESTERN TIBET, WESTERN NEPAL AND INDIAN TIBET, c. 1920

Key:
24 Nar-P'u, Gyasumdo (Tibetan)
25 Nyi-shang (Manangba Tibetan)
26 T'ak (Thakkali) and Lo (Tibetan)
27 Dolpo (Tibetan)
28 Mugu (Tibetan)
29 Humla (Nyinba Tibetan)
30 Humla (Limi Tibetan, Humli-Khyampa)
31 Lahul (Karzhapa, Tibetan)
32 Ladakh (Tibetan)
33 Zanskar (Tibetan)

areas of the Tibet Autonomous Region (TAR); (2) Bhutan and Sikkim; (3) Tibetan areas of eastern Nepal; (4) Tibetan areas of western Nepal, and (5) Lahul, Spiti, Ladakh, and Zanskar.

ARUNACHAL PRADESH AND SOUTHERN BORDER OF THE TIBET AUTONOMOUS REGION

In Arunachal Pradesh, and further to the north and east along the southern fringes of the Tibet Autonomous Region of the PRC, we find a mixture of Tibetan-speaking peoples along with partially Tibetanized peoples who speak other Tibeto-Burman languages. These non-Tibetan groups live particularly in the lower valleys. The Tibetans traditionally referred to them as Mönpa and Lopa, although neither of these terms specified a single distinct ethnic group.

The Mönpa referred primarily, in modern times, to the people of the Tawang corridor immediately to the east of Bhutan, most of which now forms part of the Indian state of Arunachal Pradesh (the former North-East Frontier Agency or NEFA).[2] These people were distinctive from Tibetans but had been incorporated into the Tibetan cultural sphere. Aris, who visited the area in 1978–1979, divides these into three groups: a northern group whose language is similar to the people of the Bumt'ang province of central Bhutan; a central group indistinguishable from the Tsangla people of eastern Bhutan; and a southern group, also known as the Sherdukpen (1980; see also 1979:xv, 122). These languages are all Tibeto-Burman but none is mutually intelligible with central Tibetan.

The area, which had a series of petty kings from at least the twelfth century, was culturally linked with Tibet from then or earlier, and it came under Gelugpa influence in the sixteenth century. It was taken over by the Dalai Lama's government in 1680 after conflict between the Lhasa regime and the new Bhutanese state and a *dzong* was set up at Tawang, the site of a large Gelugpa *gompa*. It was the birthplace of the 6th Dalai Lama in 1683 (see Aris 1980, 1988).

Aris gives the text of the 5th Dalai Lama's decree in 1680, which refers to the setting up of the monk levy system and indicates the combined political and religious purposes of these Gelugpa *gompa:*

> In particular when the establishment of the authority of the Priest and Patron [i.e., the 5th Dalai Lama and the largely nominal Mongol 'King

> of Tibet'] was being introduced to Mön, in accordance with a command from here (it was declared that) military measures such as an invasion would not be required, and so . . . it became possible to establish authority by skillful means. (Within the region stretching) down from Nyingsang and up from the Indian border at Galing and from Ali, a binding oath was taken (which provided for the following) . . . : (1) the collection of monk levy to enable some communities to be founded, (2) the collection of an oblation of grain from every household which had been brought under authority, consisting of an offering of faith of just ten measures of grain every summer and autumn, (3) the petitioning of the sangha there for virtuous rites at birth and death lest these should be adulterated with evil; (4) permission to impose (requisitions for transport by) stages down from Ts'ona with ready compliance. Thus the gentle authority (was imposed) by means of the purest designs on the part of me and my monks. (Aris 1980: 15)

The area came under Indian control in 1944 and 1951 (Aris 1980:9). According to the 1971 census, there were 29,447 Mönpa in present-day Arunachal Pradesh. There are also Mönpa ('Menba') north of the border in the Tibet Autonomous Region; the 1982 census listed 6,248 Menba in Cona, Nyingchi, and Mêdog counties.

Lopa referred to the various 'tribal' peoples further to the east, such as the Aka and Dafla.[3] These peoples were technologically much simpler than the Tibetans and were only marginally Tibetanized. Most of the Lopa tribes, again, live in present-day Arunachal Pradesh (see Fürer-Haimendorf 1982). There are also some Lopa ('Luoba') populations in the People's Republic; the 1982 census listed 2,065 Luoba in Mainling and Mêdog counties of the Tibet Autonomous Region. Further to the east, in Zayü, there is another minority group, the Deng or Deang (12,297 in the 1982 census, see Wu 1989; Thar 1989:199–201).

BHUTAN AND SIKKIM

The states of Bhutan (Drugyül = 'country of the Drugpa') and Sikkim (Drenjong = 'valley of rice') were medium-sized Tibetan polities resembling those of K'am (Chapter 4). Both Bhutan and Sikkim had substantial populations of indigenous partly Tibetanized hill peoples as well as large numbers of nineteenth-century Nepali-speaking immigrants (who form the majority of the Sikkimese population today). In their premodern form they both originated in the seventeenth century, in reaction to the Gelugpa accession to power in central Tibet. They were both dominated by non-Gelugpa orders.

The history, politics, and geography of Bhutan have received some attention (see Karan 1967; Rahul 1971; Marks 1977a; Aris 1979; Frey 1983) but there has been no real anthropological research with the exception of Françoise Pommaret's work (1989a, 1989b) on the *delog* shamanic practitioners of the eastern region (Map 6, no. 15). Aris divides the Tibetanized population of Bhutan into three main components speaking mutually incomprehensible languages. These are (1) the Ngalong people of the six western valleys, whose speech and culture are closest to that of central Tibet, (2) a dialect group in the central Bhutanese valleys (Bumt'ang, etc.), which is close to that of the 'northern' Mönpa, and (3) the most numerous, the 'Tsangla'-speaking people of the eastern valleys. The national language, Dzongkha, was derived from the Ngalong dialects and, in written form, is close to standard literary Tibetan (Aris 1979:xiv–xvii).[4]

Tibetan Buddhist influences in Bhutan date from the time of the early kings of Tibet (seventh to ninth centuries). Two of the twelve temples traditionally built in the time of Songtsen Gampo (ruled c. 620–649) to suppress the indigenous powers of Tibet were in present-day Bhutan (Aris 1979:3–41).[5] Padmasambhava was held to have visited the Bhutanese region and meditated in various places, some of which are still important shrines (1979:142). Several important Tibetan lamas visited and taught in Bhutan including the Nyingmapa lama Longch'en Rabjampa (1308–1363, see Chapter 25) and several Kagyüdpa lamas including the 'crazy saint' Drugpa Kunleg (1455–1529, Chapter 26). Numerous *tertön* or visionary treasure-finders were active in the region from the eleventh to sixteenth centuries and most of the Bhutanese aristocracy in later times, including the present ruling family, claimed descent from the most famous of these, Pema Lingpa (1450–1521, see Aris 1979:160ff, 1988; Chapter 16). During this period most of Bhutan seems to have been included within the area of control of the P'agmodrupa and Rimpungpa rulers of central Tibet via their representative in southern Tibet, the Nangso ('prefect') of Lhok'a whose capital was at Lhalung (Aris 1988:69–71).

It was another Kagyüdpa lama, the first Shabdrung, Ngawang Namgyel (1594–1651), who established the independent Bhutanese state. He belonged to the hereditary lineage of the abbots of Ralung in central Tibet, the main Drugpa Kagyüdpa *gompa* at that time, and he was identified when a child as the rebirth of Pema Karpo (1527–1592), a great Drugpa scholar (see Chapter 26) and reincarnation of the Drugpa founder Tsangpa Gyaré (1161–1211; Smith 1968a; Aris 1979:205ff). He fled to Bhutan in 1616, however, after a dispute with the Tsangpa king of central Tibet, who favored a competing candidate to be Pema Karpo's rebirth and head of the Drugpa order. The Tsangpa king subsequently invaded Bhutan but the Tibetan army was defeated by Ngawang Namgyel's local allies. Ngawang Namgyel soon became the de facto ruler of Bhutan despite several attempts to dislodge him by the Gelugpa regime at Lhasa, which had taken over control of central Tibet from the Tsangpa kings in 1642. The country's Tibetan name, Drugyul (= land of the Drugpa) derives from the dominance there of Ngawang Namgyel's Drugpa order.

The Bhutanese state was theoretically headed in later times by Ngawang Namgyel's successors, known as the Shabdrung Rimpoch'e or (to Bhutan's Indian neighbors and the British) Dharma Rāja. In practice the state was ruled by a regent, the Drug Desid or Deb [= *depa*] Rāja:

> There appears to have been very little consistency in the manner of [the regent's] appointment, and generally speaking it was the strong man of the moment or his nominee who held office, defending it as best he could against the rivalry of the provincial governors. (Aris 1979:244)

The organization of the Bhutanese state had considerable formal resemblance to that of the Lhasa state, with an incarnate lama as head of state, a regent, a body of monk and lay officials and a system of around thirty *dzong* or regional headquarters. In practice, it worked quite differently. The regents were more often laymen than lamas, although they had to conform to semimonastic style as did all lay officials (Aris 1979:262, 1987). Perhaps because the Shabdrung had come to power with the assistance of the local aristocracy, not through the aid of an external Mongol ally, the aristocracy retained far more power than their equivalents in central Tibet. The major *dzong* were hereditary possessions and their rulers, especially the 'provincial governors' such as the Paro and Trongsar Ponlops, were often more powerful than the regent himself. It was one of these local rulers, the Trongsar Ponlop Orgyen Wangch'uk (1861–1926) who eventually overthrew the entire system and became the first hereditary *gyelpo* or *ch'ögyel* (= Skt. *dharmarāja*) of Bhutan in 1907 (see Aris 1979; Rahul 1971). No reincarnation was officially recognized after the death of the then Shabdrung, although at least two lamas have been unofficially recognized.

In Sikkim, the population, apart from recent Nepali immigrants, consisted of two components, one Tibetan (or 'Bhotia') and the other an 'indigenous' Tibeto-Burman-speaking and partly Tibetanized population, the Lepchas (Nakane 1966). The Sikkimese state traditionally owed its origin to a Nyingmapa lama, Lhatsün Kunsang Namgyel (b. 1595), who came there from southeast Tibet in the early seventeenth century. Along with two other lamas, Kunsang Namgyel installed the first Ch'ögyel or hereditary lay ruler in 1642 (Chakrabarty 1980). The ruling family of the Ch'ögyels was closely connected with the Tibetan nobility, and generally, unlike Bhutan, the Sikkimese state remained on good terms with Lhasa. Apart from Nakane's brief study, most anthropological work in Sikkim (Map 6, no. 16) has focused on the Lepchas (see Gorer 1939; Siiger 1967, 1976) who employed Tibetan-style lamas but also maintained an indigenous system of shamanic practitioners.

In 1835 the districts of Darjeeling and Kalimpong in southern Sikkim were annexed by the British, who imposed protectorate status on Sikkim some years later. When the British left India the state of Sikkim became an Indian protectorate. It was annexed by the Indian government in 1974 and incorporated as the twenty-second state of the Indian Union (see Rao 1978); the ruling family was removed from power.

Immediately to the south of Sikkim in West Bengal, the hill station of Darjeeling and the small market town of Kalimpong were, as mentioned, formerly part of Sikkim. Kalimpong was of considerable importance in earlier times as the southern terminus of the main trade route between India and central Tibet. Both Darjeeling and Kalimpong still have substantial Tibetan populations, and Darjeeling now also has a large community of Sherpas, culturally Tibetan people who have moved there from their homeland in northern Nepal (see below).

TIBETAN REGIONS OF EASTERN NEPAL

In Nepal itself, almost the entire far north of the country, from east to west, is occupied by culturally Tibetan ('Bhotia') populations, many of which have now been studied by anthropologists. Most of these Tibetan-speaking populations are small in size and, in the premodern period, remote of access both from Kathmandu and from central Tibet. All along the Himalayas these 'Bhotia' peoples traded salt and pastoral products from Tibet for grain and manufactured goods from India, so supplementing the marginal living that agriculture and pastoralism provided in the high Himalayan valleys. With the exception of Mustang in the extreme north of Nepal, which had a hereditary king or *gyelpo,* these communities were mostly self-governing with little reference to Nepalese or Tibetan authorities.

Some of these groups became quite wealthy through trading but, with the exception of the Sherpas who were able to substitute tourism for trade, many were badly hit by the near-cessation of Himalayan trade which has come about through Chinese government restrictions and through alternative sources of supply for salt (see Fürer-Haimendorf 1975). We will consider them in two groups, the people from north of Kathmandu east to the Sikkimese border, including the Sherpas (Map 6), and those in western Nepal (Map 7). The distinction is mainly for convenience, but there is something of a contrast between the eastern group of peoples, several of whom had active trading and cultural links to central Tibet (Dingri, Kydrong, etc.), and the western group, who were more traditional, more isolated, and aligned culturally more with western Tibet (Ngari).

Starting from the far east of Nepal, the substantial trading community of Walongchung in the upper valley of the Tamur River (Map 6, no. 17) and the Lhomi of the upper Arun River (Map 6, no. 18) have been described briefly by Fürer-Haimendorf (1975:106–131). Other studies include that of Heiko Schrader on Walongchung (1987), of Caroline Humphrey on the Lhomi (1985, 1987), and of Hildegard Diemberger and Christian Schicklgruber on the Khumbo, also in the upper Arun Valley (Diemberger and Schicklgruber 1984, 1988; Diemburger 1989; Schicklgruber 1989).

Next, we come to the various Sherpa groups of Rolwaling (Map 6, no. 19), Khumbu (no. 20), and Shorung or Solu (no. 21). The Sherpa are the most intensively studied by anthropologists of all Tibetan populations. They claim to have migrated from K'am several hundred years ago, apparently reaching their present location in the early sixteenth century (Oppitz 1974). They settled in the valleys of Khumbu, Shorung, and Rolwaling, south of Mount Everest, living through farming, some pastoralism, and trade. Oppitz estimated their population in 1965 as around 15,000 (1974:235).[6]

In the premodern period the Sherpas' relationship with the Nepalese government was restricted to the annual payment of tax via a Sherpa middleman or *pönpo*. Recently they have been much more fully incorporated into the Nepalese state. Almost all Sherpas are bilingual in Nepali and in the Sherpa dialect of Tibetan, and many have become prosperous through mountaineering and tourism, which have more than replaced the declining trade routes across the Himalayas as sources of income. Studies of Sherpa society and religion include the works of David Snellgrove (1957), Christoph von Fürer-Haimendorf (1964, 1984), Friedrich Funke (1969, 1978), Michael Oppitz (1968, 1974), Sherry Ortner (1970, 1973, 1978a, 1978b, 1978c, 1989a, 1989b), Robert Paul (1970, 1976, 1979, 1982a, 1982b, 1984, 1990), Kathryn March (1977, 1987), Alexander Macdonald (1980a, 1980b, 1981), Janice Sacherer (1974, 1977), and John Draper (in press) among others.

Finally, to the north of Kathmandu, we come to the Tibetans ('Lama people') of Yolmo ('Helambu') and Langt'ang (Clarke 1980a, 1980b; Map 6, no. 22). In this area Tibetans and Tamangs live close together, with the Yolmo Tibetans acting as Buddhist clergy to the local Tamang people. The Tamang themselves are an interesting case study in 'Tibetanization'; recent studies include David Holmberg's on the Tamang in this region (1983, 1984, 1989) and Brigitte Steinmann's on a Tamang population southeast of Kathmandu (Map 6, no. 23; Steinmann 1987, 1989). As with the Lepchas of Sikkim and many of the Tibetanized groups of K'am, the Tamang employ indigenous shamanic practitioners along with Tibetan-style lamas.

TIBETAN REGIONS OF WESTERN NEPAL

The various Tibetan populations in western Nepal have also received considerable attention from anthropologists in recent years. Going from east to west, we come first to the people of Tsum, Nub-ri, Nar-P'u, and Gyasumdo (Snellgrove 1961; Aris 1975). Nar-P'u (Map 7, no. 24) has been studied by Nareshwar Jang Gurung (1977) and Christoph von Fürer-Haimendorf (1983), while Gyasumdo (immediately to the south) was the subject of Stan Mumford's recent book on the encounter between Tibetan Buddhism and Gurung shamanism (1989). The Gurung and the Tamang are linguistically closely allied to the Tibetans and their indigenous shamanic practices may resemble pre-Buddhist religion in Tibet in some respects. Both have soul-concepts allied to the Tibetan *la* (see Chapters 10, 14), while the Gurung have songs (*pé*) narrating the origins of their rituals that seem to parallel old Tibetan practice (Strickland 1983; see Stein 1971).[7]

To the west of Gyasumdo are the people of Manang, also known as Nyi-shang (Map 7, no. 25; Snellgrove 1961; van Sprengen 1987).

The Thakkali people of T'ak (no. 26) in the upper Kali Gandaki valley are a partly Tibetanized and partly Sanskritized trading community that has been studied by Snellgrove (1961, 1979), Fürer-Haimendorf (1966b, 1975), Andrew Manzardo (1982), and Michael Vinding (1982). Charles Ramble has worked in the Bönpo community of Lubra, a little to the north of T'ak (1982, 1983, 1985) and the history of the small Tibetan kingdoms of Mustang (Lo) and Serib in the upper Kali Gandaki Valley has been studied by David Jackson (1976, 1978, 1984) and by Ramble and Vinding (1987).

The people of Dolpo (Map 7, no. 27) were described by Snellgrove (1961, 1967b), Fürer-Haimendorf (1975), and Corneille Jest (1974), whose detailed ethnography of the community of Tarap in southern Dolpo (1976) will be referred to in subsequent chapters.

On Mugu (no. 28), to the west of Dolpo, there are brief accounts by Fürer-Haimendorf (1975) and Clarke (1977). The Nyinba people (no. 29), further west again, are the subject of a series of studies by Nancy Levine (1976, 1981a, 1981b, 1981c, 1982, 1987, 1988). In Humla (no. 30), in the extreme northwest of Nepal, there are studies of the villagers of Limi by Melvyn Goldstein (1974, 1975, 1977a, 1977b, see also Fürer-Haimendorf 1975) and of an itinerant trader group, the Humli-Khyampa, by Hanna Rauber (1980, 1987a, 1987b).

WESTERN TIBET, LAHUL, SPITI, LADAKH, AND ZANSKAR

The remaining areas of traditional western Tibet (Tö Ngari) are Ali (Ngari) Prefecture[8] of the Tibet Autonomous Region in the People's Republic of China, and the various regions of so-called Indian Tibet in two Indian states, Himachal Pradesh (Lahul, Spiti, Kinnaur) and Jammu and Kashmir (Ladakh, Zanskar). These western regions were of considerable importance in Tibetan history, particularly in the earlier period. While the population of western Tibet was not originally Tibetan-speaking (the language of Shangshung seems to have been related to Kinnauri, and much of the Ladakhi population has been described as Dardic in origin), these populations were Tibetanized at an early stage and except for parts of Lahul and Kinnaur they all now speak dialects of standard Tibetan. After the collapse of the early Tibetan kingdom a series of dynasties claiming descent from the kings became local rulers in parts of western Tibet (see Petech 1977; D. Jackson 1976, 1984).

There are still substantial relics of this period and numerous old temples and meditation sites associated with the early translator Rinch'en Sangpo (958–1055), the Indian siddhas Padmasambhava and Nāropa and the thirteenth-century Drugpa lama Gödts'angpa (1189–1258). The population in western Tibet, however, seems to have been in decline for many centuries, and it is now the least populous of the major Tibetan regions. In the 1982 census, Ali Prefecture had the smallest population of any of the Tibetan prefectures in the People's Republic (49,448 people divided among seven large counties). It is inhabited almost entirely by pastoralists.

Lahul, Spiti, and Kinnaur all lie within the Indian state of Himachal Pradesh. Access to Spiti and Kinnaur has been restricted for foreign researchers, but I shall make some use in Chapter 17 of Elisabeth Stutchbury's work on Karsha in Lahul (Map 7, no. 31), an area which, after being a distant dependency at times of Ladakh and the various western Tibetan kingdoms, eventually became attached to the Hindu state of Kulu (Stutchbury 1986, in press; Datta 1970).

Ladakh (Map 7, no. 32) was a medium-sized Tibetan state, traditionally ruled by a *gyelpo* at Leh who claimed descent from the ancient Tibetan royal family. He was assisted by several semi-independent local rulers (Petech 1977, 1978; Marks 1977b; Rizvi 1983; Snellgrove and Skorupski 1979, 1980). After the rise of Gelugpa power in Tibet in the mid-seventeenth century, the Ladakhi state was in a weak intermediate position between the Lhasa regime to the east and the Mughal (later Sikh and Dogra) rulers to the west. Following the Dogra wars of 1834 to 1841 it became incorporated into British India and the power of the king of Ladakh and other local rulers was greatly reduced.

In contrast with the Tibetan areas of Himachal Pradesh, Ladakh, along with Zanskar to its south (Map 7, no. 33), has been open to researchers from the mid–1970s onwards and the Ladakhis have been more intensively studied by anthropologists than any other groups except perhaps the Sherpas (Brauen 1980a, 1980b, 1982; Dargyay 1985a, 1986, 1988; Dendaletche and Kaplanian 1985; Friedl 1983; Kantowsky and Sander 1983; Kaplanian 1981, 1985; Singh 1977; Dollfus 1989; see also Bray 1988). Much of this work is, however, still unpublished (see, for example, Day 1986, 1987, 1989; Grimshaw 1983; Marko 1985, in press; Phylactou 1989).[9]

Eastern Ladakh and Zanskar have remained Tibetan Buddhist but much of the Tibetan-speaking population of western Ladakh has been converted to Islam. Further west, in territory now administered by Pakistan, is the Tibetan-speaking region of Baltistan, but the population here has been entirely Islamicized and thus falls outside the general compass of this study. Ladakhi and Kashmiri Muslim or K'ach'e traders were significant in the context of the wool trade between Tibet and Kashmir, and a number of them settled in Lhasa, where there was a small Muslim community (Peter 1952).

CONCLUSION

With the exception of the refugee-based studies of Dingri and the Gyantsé region, and the scattered and variable work of missionary-anthropologists in Amdo, practically all significant anthropological research on Tibetan populations has been on the communities in Nepal and Ladakh discussed in this chapter. The question naturally arises of how representative this material might be of Tibetan society as a whole and (given that this is primarily a book on Tibetan religion) of Tibetan religion as a whole.

This is a difficult question to answer, in part because there are several different factors to take into account. Ethnic Tibet, despite the unifying effects of Buddhism, trade, and a common written language, has never been a particularly homogeneous region. The major provinces of K'am, Amdo, central Tibet, and western Tibet have different histories and have been shaped in many ways by those histories. It requires considerable effort for K'ambas, Amdowas, Lhasa people, and Ladakhis to understand each others' spoken languages. Within each of those regions, there are numerous communities with different dialects, social structures, kinship systems, and ritual practices. The area of folk-religious practices is probably particularly variable, but Tibetan communities generally seem to have welcomed diversity and accepted local variation as natural, and the difficulties of communication, along with the lack of any effective centralized state through most of Tibetan history, would have done nothing to reduce this diversity. From this point of view, no one part of Tibet is going to be representative or typical.

The Nepali and Ladakhi communities have however in common their marginal position in relation to the centers of Tibetan culture, religion, and political authority. Major transformations in Tibetan religion such as the nineteenth-century Rimed movement, impacted regions like Ladakh or northern Nepal only slowly and indirectly. In addition, many of these communities have formed parts, if poorly integrated parts, of South Asian social contexts, and this has doubtless had its effects. Aspects of Sherpa society such as the strong high-low dichotomy noted by several observers (Ortner 1978a, 1978b; Draper, in press) or the importance of *lu*-spirits, which echoes the Newari *nāga* cult (Singh Nepali 1965), may reflect their Nepali context. So may the systems of ranked groups of villages among the far western Nepalese groups and the Thakkali (Fürer-Haimendorf 1975). The relatively 'clericalized' position of the Ladakhi monks and lamas may reflect their 150 years of history within a Hindu state and within British and independent India. Thus the Ladakhi system by which the large *gompa* appoint individual monks to reside in village temples as a kind of village priest has not been reported from elsewhere in the Tibetan region (Dollfus 1989).

Thus, we cannot take these studies as typical of Tibet as a whole. However, it has to be recalled that *no* single region was typical of Tibet as a whole. Lhasa with its Newari, Kashmiri, and Hui Chinese traders, its rich aristocratic mansions, its great Gelugpa monasteries and the immediate presence of the Dalai Lama's government was not typical either, and the whole idea of locating a 'representative' Tibetan community is misconceived. What we need to do, rather, is to build up an overall picture of the various kinds of social, political, and religious contexts found in different regions of Tibet and of the ways in which they were linked together to form a diverse and perpetually changing totality.

From that point of view, our situation is not ideal, since our information on many parts of premodern Tibet will always be based on inadequate sources, but it is not hopeless either, since we do have an extensive body of material on a wide variety of Tibetan societies. That material is best interpreted, whether we are looking at social structure or at religion, in terms of a set of variations on some basic underlying principles. I shall try to illustrate this in the next chapter in terms of the structure of the various Tibetan communities, and this will also give us a basis for understanding the various roles played by Tibetan Buddhism within those communities.

7

Tibetan Communities

The material so far suggests that we can distinguish, in general terms, four kinds of Tibetan communities. I refer to these as centralized agricultural, remote agricultural, pastoral, and urban.

Centralized agricultural communities are agricultural communities in areas of relatively strong political centralization. Typical features (see below) are the fully developed estate system along with a household- rather than lineage-based kinship system. Examples are Barbara Aziz's material on Dingri (1978) and Melvyn Goldstein's on the Gyantsé region (1971a, 1971b, 1971c).

Remote agricultural communities are agricultural communities in areas of relatively weak political centralization. The estate system is absent or exists only in attenuated form, with limited tax obligations compared to the centralized communities. The kinship system usually stresses lineage (or quasi-lineage based on region of origin) rather than household. Examples are Corneille Jest's study of Tarap in Dolpo (1976); Nancy Levine's work on the Nyinba in northwest Nepal (1981a, 1981b, 1988); the Sherpas, as studied by Christoph von Fürer-Haimendorf (1964), and others.

All *pastoral communities*, whether or not formally linked to an estate, have considerable internal autonomy, and a lineage-based kinship system. Examples include the Amdo pastoralists as studied by Robert Ekvall (for example, 1968) and Matthias Hermanns (1949) and the pastoralists of central Tibet studied by Melvyn Goldstein and Cynthia Beall (1990).

Urban communities, all quite small in comparison to those found in the centralized states of East, Southeast, and South Asia, present certain special features. Their populations include merchants, aristocratic families, and artisans, and are often ethnically diverse. They are usually associated with important monastic *gompa*. The household-based kinship pattern predominates in these urban contexts, as with the centralized agricultural communities. Examples are Gang-gar (in Dingri, studied by Barbara Aziz, 1978), Lhasa, Gyantsé, and Kangding.

In this chapter I shall examine each kind of community in turn.

THE CENTRALIZED AGRICULTURAL PATTERN IN CENTRAL TIBET

The centralized agricultural pattern is found in regions of relatively strong political centralization. These are in general areas along the major rivers where there is enough land to generate a substantial agricultural surplus. In most cases, such areas are also close to the main long-distance trade routes. The key element in the centralized agricultural pattern is the estate system, by which peasant families have the hereditary right to cultivate land in exchange for the payment of tax and corvée labor to a particular estate.

This system appears to have been common to all the major agricultural areas of Tibet. In addition to the centralized areas within the Dalai Lama's state, it was found in east Tibetan states such as Derge and the Hor states, in Bhutan, and in the west Tibetan state of Ladakh. The most detailed accounts that we have are for central Tibet (more specifically Tsang). Our information on the estate system comes primarily from refugee sources; Melvyn Goldstein's writings on villagers near Gyantsé (1968, 1971a, 1971b, 1971c, 1971d; Map 3, no. 4), Eva Dargyay's book, also based on informants from near Gyantsé (1982), and Barbara Aziz's ethnography of Dingri (1978; Map 3, no. 2), a large trading community to the southwest of Tsang province. Cassinelli and Ekvall's analysis of the political system of Sakya (1969; Map 3, no. 3), based on refugee informants from Sakya ruling circles, is also of value, especially when supplemented with Dawa Norbu's autobiographical account of his childhood in Sakya (1974). It should be noted that all these areas (Dingri, Sakya, and Gyantsé) were near major administrative centers and on major trade routes. In other words, all were situated where the extractive ability of the Lhasa regime might be expected to be at its highest. All these accounts refer to the 1940s and 1950s. Along with the writings of Western visitors to central Tibet from 1904 onwards, and the studies of the central Tibetan political system by Ram Rahul (1969), Franz Michael (1982), and others, they provide a reasonably consistent account of the central Tibetan social and political system.

A major area of disagreement in the literature is over Goldstein's insistence that the situation of the Tibetan peasants can appropriately be referred to as 'serfdom.' The dispute refers more to nomenclature than to substance (see Michael 1986; Goldstein 1986, 1988; Miller 1987), but it has obvious political overtones, in view of Chinese attempts to display the Lhasa government as an oppressive and exploitative feudal system and so to legitimate their overthrow. I shall comment on it briefly below.

As Barbara Aziz has emphasized, the basic building-block of these central Tibetan village societies was the household (Aziz 1974, 1978: 117ff). All *drongpa* or full members of the village community belonged to a household within the village and bore its name. These full members are also referred to as *tr'elpa* ('taxpayers') with reference to their tax-paying status.[1] Households were named, status-ranked entities, with inherited property and economic obligations, passed on normally in the male line. Ideally they continued from generation to generation without subdivision, although in practice they did subdivide.

Tibetan villagers developed a series of strategies that were explicitly justified in terms of the preservation of the household. These strategies included polyandrous marriage, the sending of 'surplus' children to *gompas,* uxorilocal *(magpa)* marriage or adoption in cases where there was no male heir, and the retirement of parents to small adjacent houses so that their children could take over the household proper. Although households were ranked explicitly in contexts such as the seating at festivals, there were also many contexts in which the households making up the village were treated as equal. The sponsoring of the major agricultural festivals, for example, usually rotated from year to year through the households within a village.

The households in a village generally also all belonged to the same estate. Each household was allocated land by the estate, and had various tax and *corvée* obligations towards it. In addition, the village as a whole (that is, the body of full household members) had obligations which its members were collectively responsible for fulfilling (see Goldstein 1971a, 1971b, 1971c; Surkhang 1984).

Not all Tibetan villagers had the status of full household members. In particular there was a lower-status group called the *düdch'ung* (literally 'small smoke'). These were villagers who did not have permanent land rights and who lived as tenants on *drongpa* farms or as itinerant laborers. While they also had tax obligations to an estate, these were generally much less onerous than those of the *drongpa*. Aziz notes that while the *düdch'ung* were mostly poorer than the *drongpa* they had less obligations, and might be socially quite mobile. *Düdch'ung* and *drongpa*, along with the traders in the small towns of central Tibet and the *serky'im*, tax-paying farmers who were part-time religious specialists, made up the bulk of the central Tibetan population; around 90 percent in the Dingri area, by Aziz's estimate.[2]

The generic term for all these people was *miser*, which Aziz translates as 'commoner' and Goldstein as 'serf.' The issue, as already noted, is largely terminological, but the associations of 'serf' in English are such that it has unavoidable political overtones. Thus Goldstein characterizes 'serfdom' as "fundamentally an economic system in which elites hereditarily tie peasants to arable land to guarantee themselves a source of labor to work the land they control and thus produce their income" (Goldstein 1988:62).

No one in this dispute denies that the *miser* had inherited economic obligations to their estates—or, for that matter, that estate owners had duties towards their *miser*, including the provision of adequate land to live off and support in the case of famine. However Goldstein's rigid typologizing undoubtedly encourages the naive reader to see the central Tibetan estate system as the 'oppressive feudal system' regularly invoked by Chinese propaganda in the 1960s and 1970s, for all that he is careful to avoid the term 'feudal.'[3]

In particular, 'serf' suggests to the modern Western reader a situation of abject poverty. This was emphatically not the case. Many *miser* families, especially of the *drongpa* and other full tax-paying groups, were quite wealthy. Some were wealthier than many aristocratic families (Goldstein 1973). In the circumstances, it seems to be better to adopt a less loaded vocabulary, such as Aziz's term 'commoner.' Goldstein himself has noted that the chronic labor shortage in central Tibet and the possibilities of escaping to another estate or to an area outside the estate system acted as a strong brake on the potentially oppressive nature of the system.

As an example of a central Tibetan agricultural community, we can take Samada, a *shung-gyugpa* village (i.e., one owned directly by the Lhasa government and not by a monastic or aristocratic estate) near Gyantsé on the main trade route to India (Goldstein 1971a, 1971b, 1971c). Samada had a population of around 280 of whom 40 to 45 (eight households) were full taxpayers *(tr'elpa = drongpa)* and the remainder *düdch'ung* of the *mibog* or 'human-lease' variety (i.e., they were free to move between estates). The high proportion of *mibog düdch'ung* was typical of Lhasa government-owned villages (1971a:528). The total agricultural land owned by the village and distributed among the eight *drongpa* households was about 1,000 acres; their land holdings ranged from 30 to 300 acres with an average of about 100 acres (1971a:527). These are very substantial landholdings for peasant farmers, even given that the productivity of land in Tibet must have been relatively low. There was also some pastoral land.

The eight *drongpa* households "completely—and legally—monopolized all political authority and land in the village" (Goldstein 1971b:67). The *düdch'ung* worked on the fields allocated to the *drongpa* households either on a day-wage basis or, in most cases, leasing land annually for a certain amount of work on the owner's personal fields. As Goldstein notes, this was an open economic relationship and given the relative labor shortage "energetic and competent 'human-lease' serfs could economically do very well" (1971a:528). Elsewhere he gives examples of such *miser* gradually rising to wealthy *drongpa* status (1986:90–93).

The tax obligations on the *drongpa* households individually and as a whole were undoubtedly very substantial:

> [They] included taxes in kind (such as grain, money and animals) as well as very difficult and varied *corvée* services. One of the more difficult of these corvée taxes was the military tax. It required the village unit to provide 6¼ men to serve permanently as soldiers, and whereas these could be actual members of the taxpayer families, the usual practice was for the village as a whole to hire other ('human lease')

> serfs to serve in their place. The salaries they had to pay these hired soldiers were a substantial burden. Another, and probably the single most difficult obligation, was the corvée animal transport tax. This tax required the serfs to provide carrying and riding animals to persons and goods authorized by the central government on an open-ended basis. (Goldstein 1971a:527)

Tax and corvée obligations for the *drongpa* were duties on the household, which was a named corporate unit, not on the individual:

> *So long as their corvée labor obligations to the lord* were fulfilled, there were no restrictions on day-to-day movement or activity and a particular *miser* could leave his estate to do business, visit a relative, make offerings at a monastery, etc., without having to obtain any kind of permission from the lord or his steward . . . [L]ords were not interested in controlling *miser* or interfering in their lives as an end in itself. They were only interested in ensuring that *their own demesne land* and other resources were optimally utilized in production. (Goldstein 1986:94; his italics)

The *mibog* or 'human-lease' *düdch'ung* paid a single annual payment to their original estate-lords (not to the estates on which they were working) though they might be required to perform limited occasional corvée work on the lord's estate in addition or to supply a replacement to perform these services (1971a:526). The annual payment replaced the more substantial corvée services required of other (non-leased) *düdch'ung.*

The standard term for 'estate lord' was *pönpo* (Goldstein 1986:86), a term that Goldstein glosses as 'lord or ruler.' We have already met this term, *pönpo,* in a variety of contexts in Tibetan societies. Some of the semi-independent rulers of K'am were known by this title (see Chapter 4). However, we also saw it being used in K'am for subordinate officials within a Tibetan state. In central Tibet and elsewhere, the governor of a *dzong* is known as *dzongpön* (i.e., the *pönpo* of the *dzong,* see Chapter 3) while among the Sherpas *pönpo* refers to the person whose sole duty, in recent times at least, was to collect tax for the Nepalese monarch.[4]

Above the *miser* in status were the aristocrats or *gerpa* and the hereditary lama families or *ngagpa.* Both aristocratic and hereditary lama families were owners of estates, although the estate or *labrang* of a hereditary lama might be quite small and did not necessarily have attached *miser.* Below the *miser* were the *yawa*, a low-status group regarded as 'unclean' and making up around 9 percent of the population in the Dingri region. *Yawa* were found in most central Tibetan communities, at least among the agriculturalists. They probably formed around 5 to 10 percent of the population. They were looked down on by the majority, who avoided sharing drinking or eating utensils with them. Marriage with *yawa* was regarded as degrading to the non-*yawa* partner, who was himself or herself reduced to *yawa* status.

All these statuses, including those of *miser,* both taxpaying and *düdch'ung*, were inherited, although there was mobility between them, especially between the two *miser* categories. Only a small number of aristocratic families were of great antiquity. Over time, rich commoner families could attain aristocratic status through government favor or marriage into established noble families (Peter 1954:43). Dingri Tibetans, however, regarded aristocratic or hereditary lama status as reflecting an inherited attribute or *gyüd* (literally 'lineage'). The *yawa*'s low status also reflected an inherited *gyüd* (Aziz 1978:53–57).

Villages were of three kinds, those whose tax obligations were to aristocratic estates, those belonging to *labrang* or *gompa*, and those, such as Samada, belonging to the Lhasa government itself. Roughly a third of the central Tibetan estates were in each category. Aristocrats were government officials as well as estate-owners. Along with the large Gelugpa monastic centers around Lhasa, the aristocratic families provided the officials who staffed the bureaucracy of the Lhasa government, including the district heads or *dzongpön* who resided at the *dzong* or administrative centers throughout the area under the Lhasa government's control. Major *dzong* generally had two officials, a monk and a layman, a system that also applied to some senior ranks in the administration at Lhasa itself.

As we saw in Chapter 3, we should beware of oversystematizing this picture of the Lhasa regime, and also of overestimating the power of the government at Lhasa. Many of the larger estates in central Tibet, such as Trashi Lhunpo and Sakya, had considerable political and financial autonomy, as did the petty states of western K'am, which fell within Lhasa jurisdiction, such as Riwoch'e or Dragyab (see Chapter 4).

Both the central government and individual estates maintained law courts to which disputes might be brought. The estate lords and their officials had the right to arbitrate conflicts within the estate. Thus the large estate of Sakya, described by C. W. Cassinelli and Robert Ekvall again on the basis of refugee informants, had two 'Law Officials' or *tr'impön* at its capital town who arbitrated disputes unresolved by private mediation or by the local officials[5] in the various local communities attached to the estate. Cassinelli and Ekvall, however, emphasize in their study of Sakya that disputes were wherever possible settled by private mediators such as members of the disputants' families, friends, important local personages, or local officials of the Sakya administration (Cassinelli and Ekvall 1969).

Submission of a dispute to the law officials involved payments of fees and gifts, as well as the risk of the imposition of physical punishment and fines. Dawa Norbu's description of a dispute his own family was involved in at Sakya suggests the unpredictability and expense of such proceedings.

> The law officials were not supposed to accept bribes, though in actual practice bribes were the only way of achieving a result. Nearly every week Mother, with bribe in hand, had to go to each of the two officials. Mother recalls that one of the judges was 'an impartial holy man,' but that his colleague had a 'big stomach' for bribes. If she offered three balls of butter or a basin of sugar, this second judge would reply: 'I shall speed up your case, and the matter will soon be in black and white.' When she bribed him with a 100 *sang* note, he would solemnly intone: 'You need not worry too much, as the evidence is increasingly guaranteeing your victory.' He would then add: 'I am sure you will win the case, but it is a matter of time.' Indeed it was a matter of time. The officials would unnecessarily prolong a case until they were satisfied with the bribes received. (Dawa Norbu 1974:83–84)

It seems likely that Sakya villagers would settle their disputes outside the estate courts wherever possible! In the cases of homicide and some other offenses, such as theft of Sakya estate property, the law officials were automatically involved, and the chief administrator *(shabped)* of Sakya was responsible for ordering the arrest of those suspected.

The Lhasa government could also investigate cases of homicide in its own right, and its local officials would presumably have provided an alternative tribunal for litigants to approach. Neither the estates nor the Lhasa government maintained a standing army until the central government introduced one in the 1920s. Before then the Lhasa government could summon a levy of the population within its domain for military purposes, as presumably could the local estates. The estates and the Lhasa government had a number of police officers who could be used to arrest suspects in cases such as homicide (Cassinelli and Ekvall 1969:173).

Cassinelli and Ekvall also give some information about the choosing of village headmen within the Sakya domains. They were selected by the villagers through a process of consensus but the estate administration of Sakya could veto particular suggestions. Cassinelli and Ekvall's informants held that the headmen

> considered themselves primarily spokesmen for their people and secondarily officials of the [Sakya] government, and that the subjects saw them in the same light. . . . In choosing a Headman, the subjects of Sakya sought a man of prestige and character who could mediate their own differences and who would not be cowed by high governmental officials, noblemen and other powerful people. They sought protection from someone who was superior, but not too superior. (Cassinelli and Ekvall 1969:97–98)

Cassinelli and Ekvall's informants belonged to the Sakya ruling family, and may give an unduly rosy picture of the Sakya regime, just as they exaggerate its independence from the Lhasa government in some respects (see Chapter 4). Their statement however suggests, as does Dawa Norbu's account, that central Tibet had strong elements of what might be described as patron-client relationships within its formal bureaucratic structure. Tibetans tended to approach government in terms of patronage and influence rather than impartial bureaucratic decision-making. This was of course true of many traditional Asian states, but it is worth asserting against the tendency of accounts such as Cassinelli and Ekvall's or Franz Michael's (1982) to portray central Tibetan polities in terms of an idealized rational bureaucracy.

GANYÉ, TRADING FRIENDS AND OTHER HORIZONTAL LINKS

Most of the above has emphasized 'vertical' or hierarchical relationships whether bureaucratic or patron-client in nature. We also saw that there was a sense in which the Tibetan village, or at least its full tax-paying members *(drongpa = tr'elpa)* were equals. 'Horizontal' relationships were of great importance within Tibetan communities, including those of central Tibet, but they have received considerably less attention in the literature (for exceptions, see Miller 1956; Aziz 1978:186–197, 1981). Miller and Aziz both discuss the *ganyé* relationship. In Dingri this was a formal relationship between individuals such that each villager had several other villagers who were his or her *ganyé*. An individual's *ganyé* group had obligation to support that person in times of crisis, to act as a go-between on his or her behalf, to arbitrate in disputes in which their *ganyé* was involved, and to give him or her feedback on social behavior in general (Aziz 1978:189–197, 1981). As Sherry Ortner notes for the Sherpas, the establishment and maintenance of social relationships between Tibetan households was a matter of major importance and was often heavily ritualized (1978a:61–90, see also March 1987).

Other horizontal relationships included formalized friendship relationships and the permanent trading-partner relationships in distant places that were an essential component of the long trading journeys Tibetans undertook. In addition kinship relationships were important ways of establishing horizontal linkages when traveling. Tibetans in unfamiliar places would normally rely on any relatives in those parts as at least an initial resource. The fictive kinship relationships formed by mutual membership in a particular lama's following ('*vajra*-brothers and sisters,' technically those who have undergone a Tantric empowerment together) could also form the basis of important linkages in everyday life.

All these relationships help us to realize that even the relatively stratified society of central Tibet should not be seen simply in terms of relationships between Dalai Lama and estate lord or between estate lord and peasant (or 'serf'). Such relations were significant, but in terms of the daily texture of people's lives they were probably much less significant than horizontal relationships among friends, relatives, and neighbors. As Aziz comments, "The Dingri people seem to have little feeling towards their taxing authorities. They tolerate the visiting officials and they do what they must, hoping that contact can be kept minimal" (1978:201).

The one 'vertical' relationship that was highly salient in many villagers' lives was that with their personal lama or *tsawé lama*. This was entirely different in character from the impersonal attitude to the taxing authorities. The term literally translates as 'root lama,' but Aziz suggests that 'heart lama' would be more appropriate, as suggesting "the sense of endearment that is so important to the relationship" (1978:223). Devotion to one's *tsawé lama* is a central element in Tibetan religious life. In Part Two of this book we will look in more detail at the important links between lama and followers.

CENTRALIZED AGRICULTURAL COMMUNITIES OUTSIDE THE LHASA GOVERNMENT

We do not have much detailed material about centralized agricultural communities and the estate system in regions outside the Lhasa regime. Rinzin Thargyal's short account of Derge (1988) demonstrates some parallels with the central Tibetan system. Estates were held by hereditary nobles (presumably also by monasteries) and involved an obligation to bureaucratic service, as in central Tibet. Taxpayer households were liable to numerous taxes and to labor on the estate-owner's own fields, and they could not move to another estate without permission. There was apparently "more social mobility and latitude" in the system than in central Tibet (1988:394).

The estate system apparently existed in Ladakh until 1947 in much the same form that we have seen in Derge, with the role of the traditional Ladakhi aristocracy gradually being replaced by that of Muslim landowners. It seems, however, to have been more oppressive than in central Tibet, at least in recent times. How far this represents the legacy of a century of non-Tibetan (Dogra) rule is hard to evaluate. Most commoner households were heavily indebted and were forced to borrow grain each year and repay it with interest at the time of harvest. The system rapidly disappeared after 1947, in part through the arrival of the army and the influx of goods with its effect on local prices, but mainly as a result of deliberate government policy that placed a low ceiling on landholdings (the *gompa* were exempted after public protest) and abolished the traditional obligations involved with estate land (Kaplanian 1981:94–95; Dollfus 1989:67–69).

Pascale Dollfus's ethnography of the Ladakhi village of Hemis Shugpachen (1989) therefore describes a situation where the villagers own their own land rather than work on traditional estates. Her account shows many of the other features we found in central Tibet.

The population is stratified, here on a rather Indian model: there are four levels, royalty, aristocracy, commoners, and a low-status group that includes professional low-caste musicians *(mön)*, smiths *(gara)*, and itinerant minstrels *(beda)* (1989:33–47). There are also 'horizontal' linkages between households, here residential groups of ten households *(chutso)*, cooperative cult groups *(p'aspun)*, religious associations *(ch'ospun)*, and work groups (1989:159–193). As we shall see in the next section, however, both of these features can be found in less centralized parts of ethnic Tibet where the estate system was not traditionally in operation.

THE REMOTE AGRICULTURAL PATTERN IN NEPAL

The remote agricultural pattern is found in regions where there is little or no effective presence of any centralized political authority. These are usually areas of relatively low agricultural productivity, away from the major long-distance trade routes. Here the estate system as such is absent, although elements of it may exist in the form of limited tax or tribute obligations to a distant center of political authority. Our principal example will be Corneille Jest's ethnography of Tarap in Dolpo, which gives a detailed and exemplary account of one of these communities (Map 7, no. 27).

Tarap in the 1960s consisted of three small villages (Lang, Do, and Tok-khyu) with a total population of 464 people divided into 111 households. Jest does not give the size of landholdings, but they were clearly much smaller than the average 100-acre holdings of the *drongpa* (full taxpaying members) of Samada in central Tibet and were worked primarily by the owners of the land.

There was nothing corresponding to the basic differentiation among estate lords *(pönpo)*, *drongpa* villagers, and *düdch'ung* agricultural laborers that we saw in the centralized agricultural communities of central Tibet. There was nevertheless a marked degree of internal stratification in Tarap. Jest divides the households of Tarap into four groups (which he calls *strates*, 'strata'). The first two strata, *shimi* (63 households) and *ch'ogmi* (17 families) all belonged to named patrilineal descent groups or *rü* whose members were distributed throughout Dolpo though concentrated in certain villages (Jest 1976:241–246, 249). Stratum I consisted of local families and included the hereditary lamas and most of the lay religious practitioners (Chapters 15 to 17); Stratum II was made up of Dolpo families from outside the immediate locality. Stratum III was a group of eight smith households in Do village and Strata IV consisted of 16 low-status *bera* families.

> The men of Stratum I call them 'the men without lineage.' The *bera* are the marginal people of the community and their settlement according to tradition seems to have been relatively recent. Their houses, where they have them and own them, are built at the edges of the villages; their young people, after their marriage, often become, for lack of other resources, servants or *yogpo* in rich houses. (Jest 1976:248–249; my translation)

Seven more households, whose members originated from outside the Dolpo region (nomads, Thakali, etc.), were also marginal to the community.

There were village councils in Do and Tok-khyu consisting of all the men of the upper two strata. Each council had a *chiky'ab* or hereditary village headman and the posts of *tr'elpo* or tax collector and *trungyig* or secretary were taken in turn by members of the council. These councils met fairly often to regulate the times for farming and pastoral work, to allocate land to newcomers and to arbitrate in disputes including cases of divorce, inheritance, and theft (1976:277–279). Where unable to resolve a dispute, the council called in the hereditary lama of Tarap, Kagar Rimpoche (see also Chapter 17) or Nyima Tsering, the 'big man' of the Dolpo region (1976:279; for Nyima Tsering see also Snellgrove 1961).

Tarap was at one period subject to the king of Mustang, and later to the local chief of Kagbeni or Kag. Tarap households continued to pay a tax of one rupee a household to the king of Mustang until 1957 (Jest 1976:176). Around three generations ago, they came under the authority of Thakali chiefs. In the 1960s the Thakalis still acted as intermediaries with the government of Nepal for whom they collected taxes based on household size, the size of flocks, and the number of people in the household. Jest estimates that taxes amounted to about 8 percent of gross agricultural production (1976:174–176). Until 1959, when an electoral system was introduced, two other Thakalis had the office of *pönpo* or 'chief,' representing the Nepali government, and *tr'impön* or 'judge' (1976:285–286). In most respects, however, the community was self-governing.

The descriptions of Sherpa society by Fürer-Haimendorf and others and of populations in the far northwest of Nepal by Goldstein and Levine depict situations similar to Tarap in many respects. These communities were all internally stratified with the highest status belonging to members of the *rü* (patrilineal descent groups) who first settled in the area and the lowest to recent arrivals. There was often a specific low-status group comparable to the Tarap *bera* (e.g., the Sherpa *khamendeu*, Fürer-Haimendorf 1964, 1984). Tax obligations were paid through local intermediaries such as the Sherpa *pönpo* or *pembu* (Fürer-Haimendorf 1984:53–55) but these communities were essentially self-governing with local 'big men' taking a prominent role.

CONTRASTS BETWEEN CENTRALIZED AND REMOTE VILLAGES

There are evident contrasts between the centralized agricultural villages of central Tibet and these largely self-governing remote agricultural communities in Nepal. There are also points of similarity, especially if we compare the *drongpa* stratum (full tax-paying village members) in central Tibet with the full members of the village community (the *shimi* and *ch'ogmi* in Tarap, the *drongpa* among Levine's Nyinba, etc.). In both cases the household is the basic unit. The community is made up of separate households and there is considerable emphasis on maintaining the unity and continuity of households. Households are maintained as single units in Nepal, as they were in central Tibet, through strategies of polyandrous marriage, *magpa* marriage (where an only daughter marries uxorilocally and she and her husband take over her parents' household), monasticism, and the reversion of monks to lay life where they are needed to continue the household. The performance of ritual duties on behalf of the village rotates between full village-member households in the Nepali examples, as in Tibet. In both cases, it comprises an annual cycle of rituals concerning the local deities and the prosperity of the village's fields (see Chapters 9 and 10).

In both types of village, disputes are settled, where possible, by mediation within the community, occasionally formalized as in the case of the Tarap village councils. In the premodern period, serious problems might have gone to some external arbitrator such as the Thakali *trimpön* (Jest 1976:285) or simply remain unresolved, as often happened with the Sherpas in the premodern period (Ortner 1978a:26–27).[6]

The remote agricultural communities are less stratified than the central Tibetan examples, but the differences here can be exaggerated.[7] Hereditary lamas had high status, while the *bera, khamendeu,* etc., were endogamous groups regarded, like the central Tibetan *yawa,* as inferior and distinctive. Even those households who were full village members, while equal in many contexts, were meticulously ranked in order in others (such as seating at a festival or party, see Ortner 1978a).

The Tibetan aristocracy *(gerpa)* was absent in Nepal, except to the extent that figures such as the king of Mustang or the Kagbeni or Thakali notables could be said to represent the aristocratic role in relation to the people of Dolpo and nearby areas. The ubiquitous term *pönpo,* which we first met as referring to the estate lord in central Tibet, was applied by the people of Tarap to the Thakali who served as intermediary with the Nepal government. The Sherpas applied the same term (Sherpa *pembu*) to Sherpas who collected tax for the Nepali government, but did not necessarily have any political authority in consequence. It seems to have been true in central Tibet as well that the primary aspect of the role of both the estate *pönpo* and the government's *dzongpön* was the extraction of revenue (see Chapter 3).

One of the most striking differences, at any rate at first sight, relates to household status. In the literature on Tibetan societies in Nepal, difference in status according to membership of *rü,* a patrilineally defined group, is a pervasive theme (for example, Fürer-Haimendorf 1964 and Oppitz 1968 for the Sherpas, Levine 1981a for the Nyinba, Aris 1975:54–55, 69–74 on Kutang and Nub-ri, as well as Jest's Tarap material). In central Tibet, patrilineal descent has been discussed mainly in the context of the 300 or so aristocratic *(gerpa)* families (Bell 1928; Peter 1954; Goldstein 1973; Petech 1973b). It seems to have been unimportant in defining status among *miser;* Aziz states that status for Dingri *miser* was defined in terms of households not lineage (1974).

There are strong traces of patrilineal descent in Tibetan historical literature, where myths of six original ancestors, eighteen main lineages, and the like, are common (Smith 1969c; Karmay 1986). It is unlikely, in view of analogies elsewhere in the anthropological literature, that these ever formed a single, entirely consistent scheme. In fact, regional origin often became assimilated to the lineage model in earlier centuries (see Smith 1969c:14–15 n. 15), as seems to have occurred also with some of the Sherpa lineages (Oppitz 1968) and with other Tibetan groups in Nepal. Lineage in the form of the *ruspa* and *phaspun*[8] groups is still an important aspect of Ladakhi and Zanskari society (Brauen 1980a; Kaplanian 1981; Dargyay 1988; Dollfus 1989) and it clearly represents a significant mode of thought in Tibetan communities, often (as with Tarap, the Sherpas, Ladakh, and Zanskar) linked to the cult of a common 'folk-religion' deity.[9]

At the same time, as both Aziz (1974, 1978) and Brauen (1980a, 1980b) remark, 'lineage' *(rü, ruspa, gyüd)* was not a matter of a straightforward ideology of patrilineal descent. In practical terms the operative unit was a residential group of *households* and their members who had an associated status ranking and some degree of corporate identity for ritual and other purposes. The major difference from Aziz's Dingri material is that in Dingri status for the *drongpa* households was generally associated with the individual household, not with any kind of descent ideology.

All this helps to reduce the contrast between the central Tibetan pattern and those found in the southern and western areas. Aziz suggested some time ago that these areas may represent a transformation of the basic Tibetan pattern associated with their migration into Nepal (1974:35). Given the widespread occurrence of the lineage vocabulary in subsequent ethnography in Tibetan communities, it may make as much sense to regard the stateless pattern of village described for the Sherpas and elsewhere in Nepal as primary and the Dingri household-based pattern as secondary. There is little in the central Tibetan village pattern that is not in the Sherpa village, except for those features directly correlated to the estate system. The differences in status ranking can perhaps be explained by the effect of the estate system, with the major rank differentials associated with estate attachment and tax status overriding the lineage factor. It may also be significant that many of the people of Dingri were recent arrivals from elsewhere in Tibet (Aziz 1978:35–36). The lineage systems of the Tibetan populations in Nepal and elsewhere go back to about the early sixteenth century for the Sherpas and much longer for the people of Dolpo (Tarap) or Ladakh.

We should remember that our information on Tibetan villages is still quite limited. I have already pointed to the restricted size of our central Tibetan sample. The body of information from Nepal is more extensive but much of it may reflect recent changes. Nor can we be sure how far the people of Dolpo, the Sherpas, or the Nyinba resemble the much larger number of Tibetans in parts of K'am, in the agricultural areas of Amdo, or the less centralized regions of central Tibet who were partially or wholly outside the estate system.

Given these qualifications, I assume that many central features of Tibetan agricultural communities were similar throughout the range of Tibetan societies. The varying degree of centralization resulted in certain features being emphasized and others muted, but I do not see compelling evidence for more substantial differences between villages in centralized and remote areas. This basic similarity makes sense, since the degree of centralization has undoubtedly varied from time to time in different parts of Tibet. Communities that were at one time under the sway of a locally centered kingdom or a powerful local chieftain might find themselves 50 or 100 years later in a situation remote from any effective political authority. The Tibetan village needed to be able to adapt to these changes in its political environment, just as it had to deal with the changing seasons and the rigors of the Tibetan climate.

Remote agricultural communities, as we will see in Chapter 17, rarely had large *gompa* of celibate monks. They had neither the population nor the resources, and most religious services were provided by hereditary lamas and by part-time lay practitioners. There were, nevertheless, often a few monks in some small *gompa,* as in regions like Dolpo. The situation doubtless changed over time, in response to the general situation. We can contrast the Sherpas, where an economic upturn, and the influence of the new religious center of Dzarong not far to the north, led to the building of several new *gompa* for celibate monks and nuns in the course of the twentieth century (Ortner 1989a) with Limi, in the far west of Nepal, where several small Drigung Kagyüd *gompa* of originally celibate monks are now kept going by noncelibate part-time lay practitioners (Goldstein 1974, 1975). Dolpo, too, seems to have had a larger monastic establishment at some periods in the past than it does today (Snellgrove 1967b).

THE PASTORAL PATTERN IN AMDO AND CENTRAL TIBET

The pastoral pattern is most fully described in Ekvall's work on Amdo (Map 5, no. 12). The basics of the tribal organization in this region have already been discussed (Chapter 5). The household, which forms the basic building block of the agricultural communities, is here replaced by the 'tenthold' (Ekvall 1968). Tentholds are grouped into encampments, which are organized into tribes. Tribal affiliation appears to be normally on the basis of patrilineal descent. The relationships between tentholds and between tribes are best illustrated by looking at some material on dispute settlement among these groups, who were, as mentioned in Chapter 5, involved in a system of feuding similar to that analyzed by anthropologists in stateless populations in West Asia and sub-Saharan Africa.

Ekvall gives a variety of examples in the course of his autobiographical account *Tibetan Skylines* and the novel *Tents Against the Sky;* I summarize a few of them here.[10]

> Ekvall's Tibetan servant, Jarlo, meets a Tibetan girl who was on pilgrimage to Lhasa. He has an affair with her and arranges for her to join the encampment (i.e., 'tenthold') of Ekvall's friend Duggur, a rich nomad of the Samtsa tribe, where he has been watching Ekvall's herds during the winter. The girl has had several previous husbands and one of them, from one of the sedentary Tebu tribe, organizes a raiding party on Duggur's encampment. Duggur is ready for the raid and captures seven Tebu men with their horses and guns, sending one of the men back to inform the Tebus. The affair is mediated by the officials of Gurdu monastic *gompa* and compensation is arranged to be paid to Duggur. However one of the captured men, wounded in the fight, dies and the settlement falls through. (1952:45–78)

> Temchok Tsering, a wealthy man of 65 years from the Jangtsa Valley, who has himself acted as mediator in many disputes, kills his son-in-law in an argument. A large panel of mediators is appointed and a heavy payment for compensation is made. Despite the payment, Temchok is shot and killed while circumambulating a *gompa.* Subsequently the murderer and a group of companions raid Temchok's house, wreck it, and assault his widow. Temchok's son, who has been preparing for revenge with some friends, pursues them and kills seven of them. It is unlikely that this dispute would be settled. (1952: 183–207)

> Dorje Rinchen, of the Shami tribe, is a monk, but becomes involved with Lhamo Mtso, a girl of the Samtsa tribe, and leaves the monastic life. He kills a Samtsa man from a raiding party. The dispute is 'tied' by the head lama of the local monastic *gompa* but hostilities remain

> between the groups. Dorje Rinchen and Lhamo Tso settle down together among the Shami in Dorje's brother's tenthold. Subsequently a Samtsa man, the brother of the man who has been killed, is captured by the Shami, and a settlement is negotiated by a group of intermediaries. A new tenthold is set up for Dorje Rinchen and his wife in the Shami encampment. (1954a:44–118)

Elsewhere in Ekvall's writings, he mentions long-term relations of hostility between particular tribes: the tribal enemies of the Samtsa included the Rzakdumba and the Chakgama (1952:8, 121).

Conflicts among these groups were dealt with by mediation, since there was no supra-tribal authority capable of imposing any settlement. Ekvall discusses the process of mediation in several contexts (see also 1954b and 1964a:1140ff; the following comes from his ethnography *Fields on the Hoof:*

> In the interests of harmony the community, through its leaders and acceptable go-betweens, takes action: (a) to seal off reprisal and violence by securing a pause, or cooling-off period; (b) to mediate and secure agreement on the giving and accepting of indemnification as a substitute for reprisal; (c) to secure agreement on the amount of the indemnity; (d) to bind the parties to keeping whatever agreement is reached; and (e) to supervise and validate the payment of indemnity. (Ekvall 1968:77)

In the case of conflicts between communities, Ekvall lists potential mediators as chiefs, famous lamas, noted orators, and men of affairs. A group of mediators would have been assembled, and mediation could indeed be a lengthy affair, as these persons "are in no hurry to go home for they have oratorical reputations to maintain" (1968:79). Formal oratory among the Tibetan nomads was a sophisticated art, with special linguistic usages and extensive employment of proverbs. The importance of speech, formal oratory, and negotiation is a constant theme in Ekvall's writings (for example, 1952:15, 30, 43 and *passim*, 1964a:1140–1141, 1964b:100–102).

Were all pastoralist groups as stateless and self-governing as Ekvall's material suggests? Some of the limited central Tibetan material suggests otherwise. Melvyn Goldstein and Cynthia Beall have recently studied a contemporary nomadic group at Phala (Map 3, no. 1; Goldstein and Beall 1986, 1989, 1990; see also Cox 1987). This nomadic group had traditional links to the estate of Trashi Lhunpo:

> Before 1959 the nomads of Phala were subjects of Tibet's second greatest incarnation, the Panchen Lama, being part of one of his nomadic pastoral estates (fiefs) known as Lagyab Lhojang. Like peasants on agricultural estates, these nomads were hereditarily tied to their estate and did not have the right to take their herds and move to the estate of another lord. On the other hand, each household owned and managed its own animals and had rights vis-à-vis the lord. Not only were their tax obligations specified in written documents, but so long as they fulfilled these obligations, the Panchen Lama could neither evict them nor refuse them access to his pastures. Their economic obligation to the Panchen Lama consisted mainly of providing butter for the tea and votive lamps of Trashi Lhunpo, the Panchen Lama's huge monastery in Shigatsé, but they also provided such items as skins, ropes, wool, animals, and salt.
>
> The Panchen Lama was responsible for law and order in Lagyab Lhojang. He appointed local officials and functioned as an appellate court for disagreements over local-level decisions. His officials, together with the local nomad officials they appointed, conducted a triennial census of all adult livestock and allocated pastures (and taxes) to households on that basis. Each household had complete usufruct rights over its allocated pastures until the next census. (Goldstein and Beall 1989:621–622)

Dawa Norbu's description of a "roving religious mission" sent by the Sakya estate to collect donations from nomads in the Chang-t'ang (D. Norbu 1974:24–35) seems to present a looser relationship between estate and nomads. Norbu puts the emphasis on the nomads making offerings and receiving religious and medical services in response, though his account could perhaps be rephrased in terms of Sakya officials visiting their wealthy nomadic 'serfs.' The mission was certainly quite lucrative:

> Each contingent consisted of a contractor, four servants and a tantric practitioner (in this case my grandfather). . . . Getting such a contract was one of the surest ways of becoming rich, and consequently only the reputable *tr'elpa* families were granted the contracts. The lama of the mission was hired by the contractor and approved by the Sakya Lama. . . . Although each offering was recorded, together with the specific purpose for which it was offered, the monastery received very little out of the total donations and offerings. . . . Tradition decreed that the contractor, known honourably as treasurer, and the lama

> should take the biggest share of the donations. . . . The richest nomads were described as the owners of 'a million whites (sheep) and a thousand blacks (yaks).' Such men made the greatest contributions called 'a hundred offerings': a hundred sheep, about three yaks, and loads of butter and salt. The poorest possessed about a thousand sheep and eighty yaks. They offered about ten sheep and some butter. (Dawa Norbu 1974:24, 33–34)

Dawa Norbu's account of the political organization of the nomads, however, sounds not much different in practice from that described by Ekvall or Hermann for Amdo:

> [The nomads] lived and moved in small groups, each with its own elected leader, or *pön*. A number of groups within a large pastoral area formed a *garpa*. The central government appointed an administrator from among the nomads, a post that tended to become hereditary as the years passed. This tribal organization solved most of the problems. A governor, invariably an aristocrat from Lhasa, administered (or maladministered) the vast province of Western Tibet, including Chang-t'ang. A monk was appointed as his colleague. . . . The governor was there primarily to collect taxes of sheep, goats, yaks, salt and butter from the nomads. (Dawa Norbu 1974:26–27)

All in all, it seems that while some nomadic groups paid regular taxes (or made regular offerings) to a particular monastic estate, and perhaps submitted disputes to that estate for adjudication, all Tibetan pastoralists retained a high degree of autonomy.

The most 'independent' of all the eastern Tibetan nomads were the Golog or Ngolok, a group of pastoralist tribes on the southern border of Amdo notorious for their fierceness and hostility to travelers and people of other tribes (Rock 1956:123–129; Guibaut 1949; Wylie 1962:190). Rock quotes the following speech by a Golog:

> You cannot compare us Golog with other people. You obey the laws of strangers, the laws of the Dalai Lama, of China, and of any of your petty chiefs. You are afraid of everyone; to escape punishment you obey everyone. And the result is that you are afraid of everything. And not only you, but your fathers and grandfathers were the same. We Golog, on the other hand, have from time immemorial obeyed none but our own laws, none but our own convictions. A Golog is born with the knowledge of his freedom, and with his mother's milk imbibes

> some acquaintance with his laws. They have never been altered. Almost in his mother's womb he learns to handle arms. His forebears were warriors—were brave fearless men, even as we today are their worthy descendants. To the advice of a stranger we will not hearken, nor will we obey ought but the voice of our conscience with which each Golog enters the world. This is why we have ever been free as now, and are the slaves of none—neither Bogdokhan nor of the Dalai Lama. Our tribe is the most respected and mighty in Tibet, and we rightly look down with contempt on both Chinaman and Tibetan. (Rock 1956:127)

It would be nice to have this speech in the original Tibetan, but the general drift is entirely clear, particularly in relation to Golog political attitudes. While the Golog were extreme in their assertion of independence and self-reliance, the attitudes expressed here do not seem atypical for Tibetan nomads in general.

The Golog might be dismissive of the Dalai Lama and the Bogdokhan (the Jetsün Dampa Hot'ogtu, chief lama of Outer Mongolia), but they were nevertheless as interested in the spiritual power of the lamas as any other Tibetans. Michael tells the story of an early nineteenth-century Drigungpa lama traveling in Golog country and held up by one of the local men:

> The Golog asked impolitely, 'Who are you?' Choeden said, 'I am a student of Drigung Chamgon Padma Gyaltsen.' Thereupon the Golog said, 'I want a relic of this lama.' Choeden then gave the Golog a piece of his master's robe. The Golog said, 'I shall see whether it's a true relic or not.' He tied the piece of cloth to the neck of a dog, drew his gun, and shot. The dog's skin was undamaged. As a result, the Golog became filled with great faith and made many presents to Choeden, whose reputation spread widely. (Michael 1982:200 n. 8)

As we shall see in later chapters, this was not atypical of the religious attitudes ascribed to the nomads and other 'wild' populations of Tibet (see Dawa Norbu 1974:32; T. Tsering 1985:202–203 n. 31). The Golog region, like other pastoral areas, nevertheless supported several large *gompa* and provided many notable lamas.

THE URBAN PATTERN

Finally, we will look briefly at the urban communities of premodern Tibet. These varied from small communities such as Ganggar in Dingri, scarcely more than large villages, to genuine urban centers of 5,000 to 30,000 people such as Lhasa, Shigatsé, or Kangding.

Aziz's description of the town of Ganggar (Map 3, no. 2) gives us a picture of a small trading community. Ganggar, with 230 households, was the largest settlement in Dingri. The local *dzong* was some 60 km distant, at Shelkar, but a subordinate officer was assigned to Ganggar; Aziz comments that he had "such little work that he [was] mainly engaged in private business" (1978:15). Several trade routes meet at Dingri, but the most significant is that from central Nepal via Kodari and Nyelam, which continues to Lhasa (the same route as the modern Kathmandu-Lhasa highway). Others go to the Sherpa trading center of Khumbu, to Kyirong, and to western Tibet. There was a small military garrison stationed near the town. Aziz estimates that of the 2,000 or so people living in Ganggar, around 8 percent were Nepalese traders, around 40 percent tax-paying *(tr'elpa)* merchant families or *ts'ongpa,* around 40 percent *düdchung,* and around 10 percent *yawa.* There were a few individual aristocrats, though no permanent aristocratic households. The *ts'ongpa* were a varied group, some of them administrative officials for lay or monastic estates or for the army who are engaging in commerce in addition to their official duties ("government and business go together," the former Ganggar merchants say, 1978:74), others full-time traders. The Nepalese included four permanent Sherpa households and fourteen Kazara (Tibeto-Newar) families, as well as other transitory traders (Aziz 1978:68, 73–75).

People in the surrounding farming communities, according to Aziz, saw Ganggar as "a decadent community infested with thieves, suspect migrants of dubious origins, loose women following the single traders and—certainly not the least—cruel, greedy administrators" (1978:37). "Ganggar is the only place in Dingri with a jail," (1978:38), but the prevailing impression nonetheless is that the people of Ganggar are not that much different from the people of agricultural communities. Most of them, after all, came from other such communities themselves.

At the other extreme, Lhasa had, as we saw in Chapter 3, a population of 20,000 to 30,000 people, including substantial Kazara, Hui, Kashmiri, and other foreign communities, as well as the households of the Lhasa aristocracy and the offices of the Dalai Lama's government (see Z. J. Taring 1984), and a distinct urban lifestyle centered on the aristocratic and wealthy merchant households, described at length in accounts by European visitors such as those of Spencer Chapman

(1938) or Heinrich Harrer (1955) as well as in the memoirs of Lhasa aristocrats such as Rinchen Dolma Taring (R. D. Taring 1986) or Dorje Yudon Yuthok (Yuthok 1990). Lhasa had a city magistrate and a police force, as well as the elaborate court ritual surrounding the Dalai Lama, but it was hardly a large city compared to many of those in South or Southeast Asia.

Most urban centers of any size had large *gompa* nearby, which is not surprising, despite the emphasis in the Buddhist teachings on the desirability of siting monasteries in remote places. The towns were centers of taxation and of trade. With their wealthy merchants and administrators, they provided both the initial finance and incentive to build the *gompa*, and the continuing support that maintained its prosperity. At the same time, many sizeable *gompa* were distant from significant urban centers, so that the *gompa* never became totally dependent on urban tastes or on the requirements of government.[11]

Government and business go together, as we have already learned at Dingri. This was true also in the sense that government officials, aristocratic families, and wealthy merchant families in the urban centers had close links with each other, links that also included the lamas of major *gompa*. In fact, incarnate lamas were often members of prominent local families, while kinship links between aristocratic and rich merchant families were quite common. Business, politics, and kinship could thus be joined together in a single network of alliances. These linkages, important in central Tibet, were perhaps developed furthest in East Tibet, where no single center had the prestige or authority associated with Lhasa in central Tibet. The importance of these networks of kinship, religion, political alliance, and business interests in supporting and holding together the political and economic life of east Tibet is evident, although it has not yet been documented in any systematic way.

In the last chapter of Part One, I present some tentative conclusions about Tibetan social structure.

8

Some Conclusions

The purpose of Part One of this book, of which this is the last chapter, is to lay down the social background against which religion in Tibetan societies has to be understood. We can summarize the general picture that has appeared in the previous chapters under several headings: the Lhasa state and the diversity of Tibetan society; the question of 'Tibetanization'; and the underlying structural principles of Tibetan society.

THE LHASA STATE AND THE DIVERSITY OF TIBETAN SOCIETY

I have commented several times in the previous pages on the tendency in much of the literature on Tibetan society to see Tibet primarily in terms of a relatively strongly centralized state with its capital at Lhasa. This has had consequences both for how Tibetan politics is understood, as with Franz Michael's account (1982) of the Tibetan state as an ideal Weberian bureaucracy, and for how Tibetan religion is understood, as with the tendency to see the large Gelugpa monastic *gompa* near Lhasa as typical of Tibetan Buddhism, rather than representing one of several strands within it. In the above account, I have stressed that less than half the Tibetan population was incorporated in any sense within the Lhasa state, and that a considerable part of the population within the borders of the Lhasa state owed primary allegiance to local estate-holders (as with Sakya, Trashi Lhunpo, or Dragyab) or were remote from effective political authority.

The only period when all the Tibetan population appears to have been incorporated into a single 'state' was the heyday of the early kingdom (or empire, see Beckwith 1977, 1987a). Evidence for the structure of that state, which also included several areas of non-Tibetan population, is inconclusive, but it seems to have taken the form of a military alliance of several smaller states whose ruling families retained a powerful role in its leadership. Its collapse in A.D. 842 was followed by what Turrell Wylie (1963) has called the 'local hegemonic period' where local rulers, in some cases survivals of the old local ruling families or offshoots of the royal dynasty, had at most control over limited areas of Tibet. The Mongol conquest set up a central Tibetan state and there has been some state based in Ü or Tsang since that time (see Chapters 25 to 27); however, parts of K'am were only intermittently included within this central Tibetan state, and Ladakh, Bhutan, and other areas were independent of it.

We have seen a variety of different political forms in Chapters 3 to 5:

1. Two fairly large agriculturally based 'states' (population 0.8 to 1.5 million), one (Lhasa) ruled in the premodern period by a reincarnate lama and a council of ministers, the other (Bhutan) by a reincarnate lama and a lay regent until 1907 and later by a hereditary lay ruler, each having subordinate local rulers and an 'estate' system, and partially incorporated nomadic pastoralist tribes;

2. A variety of smaller agriculturally based 'states' (population 5,000 to 100,000), most headed by hereditary lay rulers (Derge, Powo, Sikkim, Ladakh) but some by hereditary lamas (Sakya, Mili) and some by reincarnate lamas (Ch'amdo, Dragyab); some of the smaller 'states' were included as subordinate units within other 'states,' particularly the Lhasa regime, and some were subordinate to, though in practice largely independent of, Chinese, Nepalese, or In-

dian regimes; these 'states' again might include 'estates,' subordinate rulers and pastoralist tribes;

3. Substantial agricultural populations on the edges of the various 'states' who are in effect self-governing, though they may be nominally attached to one 'state' or another (Dolpo to Mustang, the Sherpas to the Gurkha king of Nepal);

4. Nomadic pastoralist tribes, with a variety of leadership structures, some elected, some hereditary, and some joined together to form confederations or, in a few cases, quasi-'states' with a hereditary ruler (Ngawa); some are attached to religious and other estates, some are administered by those estates, others are independent.

I have left 'state' and 'estate' in quotation marks because the English terms suggest a clear distinction between the two which is scarcely present in Tibet, where the same term *(shung)* could refer to the Lhasa 'state' or the Sakya 'estate.' In general it may be noted that Tibetan political vocabulary has considerable fluidity: we have met key terms such as *pönpo*, *gyelpo*, and *depa* in a range of meanings over the last four chapters. *Pönpo* for example meant 'estate lord' in central Tibet, 'intermediary with government' in Nepal (Sherpas, Tarap) and 'local ruler' in K'am; the common element here seems to be the right to collect taxes.

We have met this kind of fluidity of terminology also in the term *gompa*, the most general Tibetan term for a religious community and a word of much wider application than the English 'monastery' or (say) the Thai *wat* (see Chapters 2, 17). We will meet it again in the case of that most significant Tibetan word 'lama' (see Chapters 12 to 14). This generalizing tendency has helped the Tibetan language and Tibetan cultural practices to cope with the enormous range of social, political, and religious institutions that have existed among Tibetan populations.[1]

The fluidity of Tibetan categories corresponds to a similar fluidity within social institutions. Our examination of the two types of agricultural communities (centralized and remote) suggested that they could be seen essentially as variants on a single basic type, adapting to the political situation within a specific context. Much the same is true of the pastoral type, which seems to encompass a variety of relationships to monastic estates and lay authorities with little real internal change.

It makes sense, perhaps, to think of the *degree* of centralization and of tax-indebtedness as a variable over space and time. Centralized regimes in Tibet rose and fell over the centuries and villages adapted to the overall political environment in which they found themselves at any given time.

The variety of political forms in the premodern period, along with the fragility and weakness of central government where it existed, is a key to the religious development of Tibet. Descriptions of Tibet as a centralized state ruled from Lhasa are still frequently encountered and they make it difficult to understand the evolution of Tibetan religious forms. While most recent authors have been fairly clear about the geographical and political limits of the Lhasa state, the role of areas such as K'am and Amdo within the total range of Tibetan societies has rarely been spelled out, with the exception of Carrasco's early and largely neglected survey (1959). Nor has the relationship between centralized and 'stateless' regions of Tibet been made explicit.

Yet without being clear about these factors, the weakness of the Tibetan state is inexplicable and its implications for Tibetan religion are obscured. In particular the dialectic between more and less 'domesticated' forms of Buddhism, culminating in the great syntheses of the Gelugpa school and the Rimed movement, makes little sense without this continuing contrast between more and less centralized areas. It is no accident that the Gelugpa order grew up in central Tibet and that Rimed originated in K'am and Amdo.

I suggested in Chapter 2 that had the population of Tibet been integrated into a state as effectively centralized as, for example, those of Thailand, Burma, Cambodia, or Sri Lanka over the last few centuries, Tantric Buddhism would never have developed and maintained its dominant role within Tibetan society. An effectively centralized state in Tibet would never have tolerated the kind of free-ranging and autonomous power that Tantric lamas and *gompa* exercised over the centuries. Indeed, as the historical account later in the book will demonstrate, state powers in Tibet generally did their best to 'domesticate' and restrict the lamas. That they failed was an indication precisely of the limits of state power within Tibet, and of the inaccuracy of the Lhasa-centric view of Tibet.

There are two major difficulties with the Lhasa-centric view. First, the Lhasa state itself has been misunderstood. Second, the Lhasa state has been taken as representative of Tibet as a whole, whereas, as we have seen, more than half the Tibetan population lived outside its boundaries. I shall take these two areas of difficulty in turn.

First, there are the misconceptions regarding the nature of the Lhasa state. These have a number of causes. Many of the best-known observations of Tibetan society were made by observers such as Sir Charles Bell (1924, 1928), Spencer Chapman (1938), Heinrich Harrer (1955) and others who were based in central Tibet during a period (1920–1940s) when the Lhasa regime was particularly strong and had begun to exercise an unprecedented degree of centralized control (see Chapters 3, 27). These observers spent most of their time in Lhasa and other heavily centralized areas in central Tibet, and the picture they give, though by and large accurate (and very valuable) at the level of description, is understandably skewed towards the Lhasa government, the great state monastic centers near Lhasa, and towards the government bureaucracy and its affairs.

In addition, there has doubtless been a desire to assert the power and independence of the Lhasa government in relation to the Chinese government as a way of reinforcing Tibetan claims to independence from China. It is unfortunately one of the realities of present-day international politics that claims to independence are afforded more recognition when stated in terms of the nineteenth-century European ideal of the nation-state under a nationally representative government. The relationship between Tibetans and Chinese can, however, scarcely be understood in terms of the relationships between two nation-states. If I point out that the Lhasa government in the premodern period was not such a state, I most emphatically do not imply that the Tibetan population was effectively incorporated within the Chinese Empire or that it should now be regarded as part of the Chinese state or Chinese people.

The centralized nation-state (one 'nationality' under a strong centralized government) is a recent development in Asia. Central Tibet was moving in this direction in the 1920s under the 13th Dalai Lama's administration, and there is no doubt that insofar as anyone has any plausible historical claim to constitute a 'Tibetan government' it is the legitimate successors of that administration, in other words the 14th Dalai Lama's administration in exile. We can scarcely understand the nature of Tibetan religion, however, let alone its historical development, without recognizing that most Tibetans, through most of Tibetan history, lived in communities that were not under the day-today control of any strong centralized government, whether that of Lhasa, some other Tibetan regime, or the Chinese.

It is not surprising that writers such as Bell, Chapman, or Harrer, none of them trained anthropologists, tended to take the Lhasa government at face value, since it is only in recent years that Asianists have begun to appreciate the relatively limited degree of centralized control found in many traditional Asian states. The model of 'Oriental Despotism' has, as Susanne Rudolph recently pointed out, distorted our perception of Asian polities in ways that are only now becoming evident.

Here the work of Stanley Tambiah on the 'galactic polity' in Thailand (1976, 1985:252–286), which I referred to in Chapter 3, and of various other authors writing on East, South, and Southeast Asia is leading to a rethinking of the nature of Asian state formations (see Rudolph 1987). Among other things this rethinking has involved understanding that the central governments of these states were far from having a monopoly of force within their territories and that these governments rarely exerted much detailed control over the daily life of the people they governed. There has also been a growing realization of the extent to which these states were symbolic and ritual entities as much as, or more than, structures of real political control.

Such a rethinking is due for Tibet as well. The Lhasa regime and other Tibetan polities were weak even in comparison with models such as Tambiah's 'galactic polity,' and both Tibetan and Chinese governments were particularly adept at maintaining the forms of sovereignty in situations where the substance of real political control was largely lacking. The payment of 'tribute,' for example, was often a convenient fiction for the maintenance of a trade relationship (for example, Wylie 1980b; Sperling 1980) and did not generally involve any real political subordination. In fact *all* Chinese relationships with foreign powers, including those with European powers, were formally conducted in terms of 'tribute' from lesser powers supposedly paying homage to the emperor (Fairbank and Têng 1941–1942).

We have seen that Chinese control over K'am was nominal during the late nineteenth and twentieth centuries (Chapter 4). We can imagine that Lhasa control over nominally subordinate polities such as Powo or Trashi Lhunpo was of much the same nature for long periods.[2]

The second problem about a Lhasa-centric emphasis, as mentioned before, is that most Tibetans lived outside central Tibet. The most populous areas of Tibet were K'am in the east and Amdo in the northeast. Substantial populations also lived within the boundaries of modern Nepal and India, including what is now the Indian state of Sikkim, and the independent Tibetan state of Bhutan.

The tendency to merge 'Tibet' as a whole into the central Tibetan state creates difficulties in several ways:

1. It privileges a single Tibetan state (containing well under half of the total Tibetan population), whereas there were several such states in the Tibetan region with significant structural variations between them;

2. It tends to reinforce the view of state power in the Tibetan region as an uncontroversial given, whereas state regimes, as indicated above, were fragile, weak, and limited in their control over the population they nominally controlled;

3. It privileges the relatively stratified and centralized regions of Tibetan society although many Tibetans, including such well-studied groups as the Sherpas and the Amdo pastoralists, lived in relatively egalitarian and stateless societies;

4. It privileges a region of Tibet that was relatively isolated from other linguistic and ethnic groups and so tends to portray Tibetan societies as existing in isolation, whereas many features of Tibetan societies can best be explained in terms of Tibetan contact with surrounding societies.

The first three points follow from what has been said already. The last point, that the Lhasa-centered perspective may involve seeing Tibet as unnecessarily isolated from its neighbors, raises two issues, the place of trade in Tibetan societies and the process of 'Tibetanization.' I shall say something about trade here and will discuss Tibetanization in the following section.

Tibetan societies must always have owed much of their significance and much of their viability to the trade routes to and from China, India, Nepal, Kashmir, and (in earlier times) Iran. Trading was an intrinsic part of the Tibetan ecological adaptation and it brought the Tibetans into constant contact with other surrounding populations.[3] Lhasa had substantial populations of Newaris, Kashmirs, and Chinese Muslims and the trading centers of K'am and Amdo had an equally heterogeneous character.

I have suggested elsewhere that the rise and fall of states in Tibet was probably closely linked to the prosperity or otherwise of the trade routes through the Tibetan region (Samuel 1982). The large religious orders were also heavily involved in trade and much of the spectacular expenditure on buildings, images, and ornaments for large *gompa* was financed in this way. Trade was also perhaps, as Caroline Humphrey has suggested (1987), an important metaphorical resource for Tibetans and one which was to some degree homologous with Buddhism as it developed in Tibet. Chinese society to the east of Tibet and Indian society to the south were both societies with a strong collective orientation. Tibet was much less so. Households and individuals, men and women, worked out their own destiny in their own way and made what they could out of the capital (real and metaphorical) that their karma had provided them with.

This gave Tibetan societies an enviable freedom and openness compared to, for example, those of China, Nepal, or India. One has only to look at the position of women in Tibet to see the difference from its neighbors (see Bell 1928:147–148; Migot 1957:84; Guibaut 1949:178–179; Rizvi 1983:118–119; Miller 1980 for some comparisons). However this freedom did not imply equality of opportunity, let alone of outcome, at the material or the spiritual level. Tibetan women were not equal to men in the opportunities available to them (see Levine 1981b; Aziz 1987, 1988; Klein 1987). Nor, of course, were aristocrats equal to *düdch'ung,* incarnate lamas to the 'ordinary' monks.

This is not to deny the key place of compassion *(karuṇā)* and of the altruistic motivation *(bodhicitta)* within Tibetan Buddhism, but it serves to place it in perspective. The individual may have been an illusion for the Tibetans as for other Buddhists, endowed with only a relative existence, but the image of the self-interested individual, searching for the best lama and the most effective teaching, gradually building up his or her resources for an attempt on the ultimate prize of Enlightenment, still says something about the specific character of Tibetan Buddhism.

THE QUESTION OF 'TIBETANIZATION'

In Chapter 4, I introduced the question of Tibetanization with reference to populations on the margins of the Tibetan cultural region such as the Qiang (in the Gyelrong states), the Naxi, and the Yi. It is possible that some features of K'am social organization, such as the 'tribal' structure of Nyarong, may reflect the fact that these areas had only undergone Tibetanization within the last millennium or so. There are certainly signs of such processes. Thus the Hor states of K'am were in the premodern period fully Tibetan in language and culture, but Hor is a Tibetan ethnonym referring to populations of Turkic origin, and indicates that the region may have been Turkic in population at some previous time. Kessler has suggested that most of K'am was originally not ethnically Tibetan (see Kessler 1984).

Similar processes of Tibetanization certainly occurred in Amdo to the north where Mongolian and Hor (Turkic?) populations had been absorbed and all along the Himalayas where a whole series of Tibeto-Burman-speaking populations in Poyul, in southern Lhok'a, in the Indian state of Arunachal Pradesh, and in Bhutan, Sikkim, and Nepal had become wholly or partly incorporated (see Chapter 6).

In the initial stages of this process of Tibetanization, these populations might have adopted Tibetan Buddhism or at least incorporated Tibetan-trained lamas along with local shamanic practitioners (as with the Tamang, Lepcha, Naxi, and the people of Mili). In the later stages, local languages might disappear in favor of Tibetan dialects, as with Shangshung in western Tibet and the Dardic populations in Ladakh. This took place in Amdo with the Hor and Sogpo Arig populations and perhaps also in K'am with the westernmost Gyelrong states.

Historically, this process goes back at least to the conquest of Shangshung (early seventh century) and should probably be considered as an integral part of the Tibetan cultural adaptation. Lamas from recently converted and fringe areas such as Gyelrong have played a key role in the development of Tibetan Buddhism over the centuries. The most spectacular conversion was that of the Mongols but, with the exception of small groups like the Sogpo Arig of Amdo, who were living in an otherwise Tibetan-speaking area, religious incorporation was not followed in this case by total cultural absorption. Mongol scholars studied in Tibetan *gompa* and wrote books in Tibetan and there was undoubtedly cultural influence (the Gesar epic was translated into Mongolian, for example), but Mongols remained culturally distinct. In some ways Buddhism always remained a foreign religion for the Mongols (see Heissig 1980).

This process of Tibetanization has been little studied so far (see

A. Jackson [1978] for the Naxi, Macdonald [1987b] for Nepal) although recent work on Tamang and Gurung populations in Nepal have indicated some of the complexities involved. The adoption of aspects of Tibetan Buddhist ritual and the presence of indigenous lama families within these populations does not necessarily mean that Buddhist ritual and the lamas are serving the same functions as in Tibetan society proper. Tamang lamas (Steinmann 1987, 1989; Holmberg 1989) seem almost exclusively concerned with pragmatic religion rather than the Karma Orientation and Bodhi Orientation outlined in Chapter 2. Mumford's stress on the dialogic nature of the encounter between Tibetan Buddhism and Gurung shamanism (Mumford 1989) is an important point, but it is also worth remembering that the encounter in these regions has been going on for many centuries, and that particular Gurung groups may have gone through several periods of greater and lesser incorporation into the Tibetan Buddhist cultural sphere. Much the same may be true of people such as the Naxi in Yunnan and the Qiang in Sichuan (Gyelrong). In other words, it is not clear whether in recent centuries the border of the Tibetan cultural adaptation was continuing to expand in these regions or simply moving slowly back and forth over the same territory.

In any case, these partly Tibetanized fringes helped Tibetan Buddhism to retain a missionary orientation within its own society. The lamas, as we will see in Chapter 11, were thought of as 'taming' the Tibetan population, just as they had tamed the wild gods of Tibet. 'Taming' involved the institutionalizing of the Karma and Bodhi Orientations within Tibetan communities, but it was never a once and for all process. Populations once 'tamed' could drift back towards pragmatic concerns and need to be reminded of the true meaning of the Dharma; Tibetan literature is full of restatements of simple moral principles for the lay population (Snellgrove 1967b; Kaschewsky 1973; Chokhorling 1978). In addition, there remained the 'wild' nomadic and bandit areas within the borders, including regions such as Gyadé where the Bönpo were still strong, and the constant challenge of the border region.

Such missionary activity could certainly be fueled by a genuine concern for the degraded condition of these 'untamed' populations, but it also had a clear material aspect. The lamas and *gompa* of different orders were in constant competition for lay support, and with the central areas largely divided into spheres of influence dominated by one or another major *gompa,* the margins provided scope for expansion and, at times, for the acquisition of politically and economically important lay supporters.

The activity of Sakyapa and Kagyüdpa lamas at the Mongol court in the thirteenth century, and the competition of Gelugpa and Kagyüdpa lamas for Mongol support in the seventeenth century, are perhaps the most dramatic examples of such processes. However there are many other examples, including the Karmapa suborder's links with the royal family of Naxi (see Chapter 4), and the gradual conversion of what is now Bhutan into a Drugpa monastic state. As the studies of Mumford (1989) and Ortner (1989a) remind us, these processes continued into modern times. It should not be at all surprising that in recent years many Tibetan lamas have responded to their vulnerable situation as refugees by looking to the potential of Europeans, Americans, and overseas Chinese as converts to Tibetan Buddhism and as patrons of its institutions.

UNDERLYING STRUCTURAL PRINCIPLES OF TIBETAN SOCIETIES

To conclude Part One, I shall mention a number of other structural principles of Tibetan societies that have emerged in the previous chapters and are of relevance in making sense of Tibetan religion.

The significance of *continuity* and of succession, whether conceived of primarily in *lineage* terms or in *household* terms, should be noted. I have stressed the fluidity and flexibility of Tibetan society. The converse to this fluidity is the importance that Tibetans attach to continuity. This emerges in lineage terms, for example, in the special status given to those households who can claim descent from the founding lineages of a Sherpa or Tarap village, or on a larger scale, in the high status of the few aristocratic families who can claim ancient descent (such as the Lhagyari family or the K'ön ruling family of Sakya). On the whole, however, the importance of lineage and of patrilineal descent is, as we have seen, relatively muted in Tibet. As Gananath Obeyesekere notes, this seems to be the case also in Therāvādin societies:

> On the institutional level Theravāda Buddhist societies, and some Mahāyāna ones (Tibet), are associated with the primacy of the nuclear

> family, as against the Hindu joint family, and, along with this, with the erosion of patripotestal authority and the religiously sanctioned role of the father. (Obeyesekere 1990:160)

The continuity and preservation of the *household* is, nevertheless, an important Tibetan value, whenever there is significant property to pass on to the subsequent generations. Rather than allow an existing household to be split up, Tibetans will go to considerable lengths to maintain continuity. We have already seen some of the mechanisms involved, which include polyandrous marriage (explicitly thought of as preventing division of property between brothers), the return of monks to lay life to take over the household of a deceased brother, and the marriage of only daughters to *magpa* husbands who take over the name and household of the girls' parents.

The emphasis on continuity is, as might be expected, evident in the realm of religion as well. In fact, religion could be considered the field *par excellence* of continuity within Tibetan society. All religious traditions place great importance on the lineage *(gyüd)* of the teachings and on valid transmission from one 'generation' to the next. The word *gyüd* refers to teaching-lineage as well as to genealogical lineage and inheritance, and it is closely related to the word for Tantra (also *gyüd,* with a slightly different spelling). Teaching-lineages may be very ancient, going back to the time of Guru Rimpoch'e (eighth century) or earlier, though they may also go back to more recent revelations by Tantric deities. Often there is a combination of the two, with an initial transmission that is revalidated through subsequent revelations. As we will see in Parts Two and Three, such revelations (*dagnang, gongter,* etc.) provide channels through which the ancient lineages of teaching can undergo modification for contemporary conditions. In this way, as pointed out in Chapter 2, religion in Tibet is not based only on linear descent from past masters but on a relationship (which can be thought of as perpendicular to linear historical time) to the timeless world of the Tantric deities.

The maintenance of the household is paralleled by the maintenance of the *gompa,* of ancient pilgrimage sites, and most directly by the *labrang,* the lama's household and personal property. The *labrang* may be passed down through genealogical descent, in the case of hereditary lamas, but it may also be passed down to appointed successors or through the successive members of an incarnation-series. The development and proliferation of the reincarnate lama system is itself a striking indication of the importance Tibetans have attached to continuity of institutions.[4] The reincarnate lama system is also, especially where it is explicitly combined with the concept of the emanation of a Tantric deity, a linkage to the underlying timeless level of reality symbolized by those deities (see Chapter 25). The 14th Dalai Lama is the present-day member of a series of rebirths stretching back through historical time to the 1st Dalai Lama and before him to the early Tibetan kings and the mythical monkey-ancestor of the Tibetan people. He is also, however, Chenresig (Avalokiteśvara), and as such he represents something which is beyond historical time.

A related issue to the question of continuity and succession is that of *protection* of the household. As we will see in the next chapter, the protection of the household is a major issue in Tibetan folk religion, and it is tied up with a system of folk-religion deities who have various roles in relation to the household, as well as with non-Buddhist rituals such as those of marriage, by which the household is constituted as a microcosm. The *gompa* and the religious order also have protectors *(ch'ökyong)*. Some of these (e.g., Pehar) are major Tibetan folk-religion deities who have been 'bound' by Padmasambhava or other great lamas to act as protectors of the Dharma. Others (e.g., Mahākāla) are deities of Indian origin who have been introduced to Tibet along with the various Tantric cults. The use of *maṇḍala* schemes in early *gompa* such as that at Samyé can also be seen as analogous to the creation of the household as a microcosm.[5]

A corollary to the weakness of Tibetan governmental structures is that it often makes more sense to see Tibetan structures of authority less in terms of a command structure in which all power derives from the ultimate power of the ruler, and more in terms of the negotiation of power between more or less equal partners. In the course of such negotiation, a conditional structure of government may be set up, but such structures always retain a tendency to fragment along the lines according to which they were initially constituted. This may well have been true of the early Tibetan empire, if the state of Songtsen Gampo and his successors is rightly interpreted as a ritual kingship accepted by several powerful regional ruling families. It was true in varying degrees of most successor states in the Tibetan region.

The early Tibetan alliances seem to have been between the ruling families of petty states, but in more recent times the partners to such alliances have been more varied, including not only local aristocratic families but also hereditary, appointed and incarnate lamas, and wealthy merchant families. As was noted in Chapter 7, it is primarily in the urban context that these various alliances are formed and maintained through complex political, economic, and kinship linkages. While the supremacy of the Dharma was everywhere recognized, these negotiations were, in many respects, negotiations between relative equals. The partners were frequently related by ties of kinship and marriage, and trade rarely seems to have been regarded by Tibetans as an inferior or lower-status occupation. In fact, the *labrang* of the lamas, and the aristocratic households, were often as extensively involved in trading as the merchants proper. I have suggested earlier in this chapter that Tibetan attitudes to trade have some similarities with Tibetan attitudes to religion.

In this connection, we can also recall the importance of *ganyé* groups and similar horizontal linkages in Tibetan communities, along with the principle of the equivalence of all full households within a single village, and of the election of village officials on a temporary basis (as in Tarap). Tibetans appear to treat social relationships in general as contractual or constitutional rather than as an expression of a divinely ordained hierarchy. Even Tibetan marriages, for all of the ritual creation of the new household as microcosm, are primarily civil contracts with clear expectations of mutual rights and obligations and carefully specified economic implications.

The emphasis on horizontal linkages, which has just been noted, goes along with a tendency in traditional Tibetan institutions to avoid giving all power to a single person. This phenomenon is most familiar in the form of the appointment of two persons, one lay and one monastic, to many *dzongpön* positions. It is not, however, simply a question of the relationship between lay and monastic power. It might be more accurate to see the lay-monastic relationship as a special case of the principle of division of responsibility. Thus, some *dzongpön* positions were occupied by two lay officials, and in Chapter 4 we saw that some east Tibetan states (Ba and Lit'ang) had two *depa* rather than one. A connection could perhaps be made to the concept of the polyandrous marriage, in which two or more men are seen as co-husbands of the wife and so, in a sense, simultaneous male heads of the household. In practice, one husband is the senior (the same seems to have been true of the Ba and Lit'ang *depa*), but the principle of mutual replaceability is clear.

The relationship between Dalai Lama and Panch'en Rimpoch'e also shows traces of this kind of division of responsibility. The Dalai Lama is unquestionably the senior partner, but elements of sharing of responsibility are clearly present. Such relationships were common in the major monastic orders and in large *gompa*. Two cases with some similarities to that of Dalai Lama and Panch'en Rimpoch'e are those of the two heads of the Karmapa order until the eighteenth century (Shamarpa and Shanagpa) and of the two heads of the Drigung Kagyüd order today (Drigung Ch'ets'ang and Ch'ungts'ang). In such cases, where the responsibility is shared between two incarnation-series, the two lamas are ideally of different ages, so that they can act alternately as each other's teacher, and one can act as head of the order during the infancy of the other. In practice, of course, this does not always work out.

The tendency to specify and distribute rights and responsibilities can also be seen in the context of the *gompa* or religious community. In a recent article, Ter Ellingson has studied the evolution of 'monastic constitutions' (*chayig*), and notes how these documents institutionalize extensive restraints against the abuse of power by those in high office. He points out that:

> the 'Lama' of monastic polity is a leader with specified and restricted powers, and . . . the community he leads is clearly governed by law rather than by personal caprice—a constitutional polity, in other words, rather than a 'feudal' or 'Lamaist' polity. (Ellingson 1990:217)

Later he suggests that the growth in size and complexity of Tibetan *gompa* led

> not to the widespread and apparently obvious solution of control by increasing concentration of authority to create a form of individual-centered despotism, whether 'Oriental' or 'Lamaistic,' but rather to increasingly explicit systems for deconcentration and distribution of authority among mutually counterbalancing, functionally-defined offices. (Ellingson 1990:218)

The emphasis on 'deconcentration and distribution of authority' that Ellingson notes for the Tibetan *gompa* is, I would suggest, true of

Tibetan societies more generally, and gives those societies, and the religious forms that developed within them, a very different character from the social and religious forms found in the centralized states of South, Southeast, and East Asia.

This concludes the survey of Tibetan societies comprising Part One of this book, in which we have sketched the social environment within which Tibetan religion has developed. In Part Two, we examine Tibetan religion itself.

Part Two

9

The Ritual Cosmos and Its Inhabitants

This is the first of a series of chapters that provide a description of Tibetan religion as it was in the premodern period. In Chapter 2, I described Tibetan religious activity in terms of three orientations, the Pragmatic, Karma, and Bodhi orientations. These orientations are not sharply divided from each other. The same people may be involved, and the same symbols may be interpreted differently in all three. Each orientation relates to a common perception of the nature of the universe, even though they may involve radically different attitudes towards that universe.

The universe that Tibetans perceive includes gods and demons, Enlightened beings and sacred sites, as well as human beings and their habitations. It is already pervaded, in other words, by the symbolic entities in terms of whom Tibetan religion is structured. This 'ritual cosmos' or 'sacred geography' is our starting point, since it forms the ground in relation to which all Tibetan religious orientations have to position themselves.

The Tibetans inherited several complex models of the universe from the Indian Buddhists, including the well-known scheme of Mount Meru, the four 'continents' and eight 'subcontinents.' Within this scheme, which was recapitulated millions of times daily in the *maṇḍala (mendel)* offerings of Tibetan monks and lay practitioners, and painted on thousands of *gompa* walls, the material world as the Tibetans knew it formed part of the Southern Continent of Dzambuling (Skt. Jambudvīpa). Dzambuling was one of the four main continents surrounding the great mountain of Meru, the axis of the universe, in the form of a *maṇḍala*. From the summit of Mount Meru upwards stretched the heavens of the higher gods. These became successively purer as one ascended through the gods of the desire-realm through those of the form-realm to the gods of the formless realm. Below Dzambuling were the hell-realms, subdivided into hot, cold, and accessory hells, and graded in terms of the intensity of punishment and the duration of stay.

This scheme was bound up with the equally familiar imagery of the Sipé K'orlo or 'Wheel of Life,' in which the various modes of rebirth (gods, demigods, human beings, animals, hungry ghosts, and hell-beings) were depicted as sectors of a wheel around which living beings revolved continually until they committed themselves to the Bodhi Orientation and began the process leading to escape from the cycle of *saṃsāra*.

These bodies of symbology will play some part in the following chapters, but I shall focus here on the actual environment within which the Tibetans lived, and which they conceived of, as we have seen, as part of the Southern Continent of Dzambuling.

The meanings attached to that environment incorporated both 'pre-Buddhist' and 'Buddhist' elements. There were mountains that were the homes of mountain gods, streams, and rivers where the *lu*-spirits dwelt, caves where holy lamas had meditated, marks that had been left in rocks by Guru Rimpoch'e or King Gesar, lakes whose patron spirits could aid lamas to divine the karmic currents or *tendrel*, hidden valleys that had been opened by seers of the past as retreat-places for spiritual practice or escape from political turmoil. This whole structure of meaning was maintained in order with the aid of symbolic devices distributed through the landscape and of religious specialists whose rituals constantly reactivated those devices.

These symbolic devices—temples, *gompa*, mountain-cairns

(laptsé), rock-carvings, *mani*-walls[1] inscribed with mantras, *ch'orten* (*stūpa*, reliquary-monuments) containing the remains of great lamas of the past—ranged from major places of pilgrimage like Kailash or Lhasa to minor reminders of Buddhist deities or mountain-gods. For people whose life was lived among them, they constantly recreated the structure of Tibetan religious meanings. Tibetan religion was literally grounded in such associations, which were evoked for Tibetan travelers when they climbed over high mountain passes whose summits were marked by cairns to the gods, prayer-flags, and *mani*-walls erected as a 'virtuous action' (see Chapter 11) by Buddhists of the past, when they walked around *ch'orten* or alongside rock-carvings of the goddess Tārā or the compassionate bodhisattva Avalokiteśvara, or when they visited the *gompa*, the monasteries, temples, and other religious centers, which until recently, were the most spectacular buildings in the Tibetan landscape, and which the Tibetans today are doing their best to rebuild after the devastation of the 1960s and 1970s.

Even in exile, the Tibetans have reconstituted this kind of sacred geography. Wherever Tibetans have lived for some years, the visitor will find that the landscape has been gradually sacralized and brought under control by a gossamer net of rock-carvings, small wayside shrines, prayer-flags *(lungta)*, *laptsé*, *mani*-wheels, and *ch'orten*, as well as through the *gompa* themselves, almost always the most conspicuous and elaborate buildings in any Tibetan settlement. In fact, despite the Western tendency to see Tibetan religion as dying or already dead, it is a living system among the refugees and among the Tibetan populations of Nepal and India, and has by no means disappeared within the regions of Tibet controlled by the PRC, and the following description will accordingly be couched, for the most part, in the present tense.

A common Tibetan expression for the universe is *nödchüd*, literally 'container-contents.' The world is seen as a vessel within which living beings *(semchen)* of various kinds are contained. The two, container and contents, are not really separable. Similarly, within the material universe, particular living beings have their own proper environments, which are to be appropriately maintained. This involves, as we will see, the ritual maintenance of human households, regular upkeep of the dwellings of the local gods (which are most often stone cairns, *laptsé*, high up in the mountains), and the construction and care of supports *(ten)* for the Tantric deities and divine aspects who guide the path to *bodhi*. This last term, *ten*, is a generic one, which includes images, religious books, shrines of all kinds, as well as the *ch'orten* (Skt. *stūpa*), part reliquaries for Buddhist saints and part universal reminders of the cult of Enlightenment (see Chapter 11).

Deward Walker has contrasted the kind of 'sacred geography' found in a stateless, preliterate society that has lived for centuries or millennia in the same environment with that of organized state religions (Walker 1987). His specific examples are Native American peoples of the Northern Rockies (Kootenai, Nez Perce, Northern Shoshone), which he opposed with the more complex Mesoamerican and Old World cultures, but his comments generalize well to Tibet and to the 'shamanic' and 'clerical' aspects of Tibetan Buddhism mentioned in Chapter 1.[2]

Walker suggests that in peoples without a centralized state a feeling of 'sacredness' within the landscape is assumed rather than imposed. Various places gradually come to act as foci of such sacredness, perhaps because of their aptness for processes of transition, their 'liminal' nature in Victor Turner's terms. For Tibet, we can think not only of the mountains and lakes associated with the folk-religion deities but also of the caves and other natural sites where great lamas such as Guru Rimpoch'e or Milarepa are believed to have meditated (see Dowman 1988; Aufschnaiter 1976).

In the more centralized, state-based form of social organization, meanings are imposed on the landscape through buildings. Pilgrimage centers and sacred cities with their associated clergy arise. Humans who live according to this pattern seek to transcend and transform the natural landscape, rather than to accept it and to live within it. In Tibet, this kind of approach is associated with the 'clerical' religious pattern. The great monastic pilgrimage centers of Lhasa or Kumbum represent the transcendence and transformation of the natural order, as do the figures with whom they were associated: the early kings and the great founders of monasteries such as Tsongk'apa and his disciples.

Tibetan societies, in other words, have elements of both approaches. The Tibetan landscape is not easily tamed or controlled, even with modern technology. Agricultural and pastoral life alike are difficult and laborious as well as being subject to violent and changeable weather. Much of the Tibetan population still lives in small communities in remote valleys. Arduous traverses over dangerous mountain passes may be needed to reach a neighboring valley, and communities can be totally isolated for months at a time during winter. Tibetans have always traveled extensively for trade, and also on pilgrimage, but long journeys were risky endeavors in the premodern period. In some regions the possibility of bandit attacks was added to the dangers of the physical environment.

Life in all societies, especially with premodern technology, has some element of risk and unpredictability, but it is understandable that the Tibetans are particularly concerned with such matters, and that a major focus of their concerns is the activities of the 'gods' *(lha)* associated with the natural environment. The gods of the high mountains in particular are capricious and dangerous figures, associated with wild and dangerous animals such as the argali, onager, and wild yak. These gods played a major role in Tibetan history as ancestors of ruling families. Originally opponents of Buddhism according to Tibetan religious history, they became half-willing protectors of the Buddhist teachings and clergy after their 'taming' and conversion by Guru Rimpoch'e (Padmasambhava). We will return to the 'taming' of the gods, and to the incomplete nature of the Tibetan domination of the environment, after a discussion of the gods themselves.

GODS AND SPIRITS

These gods and spirits of the Tibetan landscape (who are conceptualized as male or female) are not necessarily favorably inclined towards human beings. They can, however, be induced by ritual to be helpful and to prevent misfortune. This is a major function of Tibetan ritual, both 'folk religion' and Buddhist. Having caused offense to the gods is thought of as a kind of pollution, *drib*. *Drib* is the prime cause of misfortune in everyday life, and has to be remedied by appropriate ritual action to the gods. In addition, *drib* makes the individual vulnerable to attack by malevolent spirits of various kinds. Some degree of *drib* is almost unavoidable in everyday life and the attacks of offended deities and of malevolent spirits have to be ritually combatted on a regular basis.[3]

There are various classifications of the worldly gods and spirits, one of the best known being that of Eight Classes *(lhasin degyed)* found particularly in Nyingmapa texts. The members of the list vary slightly, but ten classes that are frequently included are listed and described by Philippe Cornu:

> The *lu* are aquatic deities. Of pre-Buddhist origin, they were very quickly assimilated to the Indian nāgas. They live underground, in springs, lakes and rivers. . . . [They] can be vindictive when their natural home is disturbed. The pollution of water, the construction of barrages and dykes, irrigation works, altering the course of rivers are acts that can lead to illness if not carried out at the astrologically correct time. The nāgas can take revenge by sending diseases such as leprosy to the responsible human beings.
>
> The *nyen* are spirits, generally badly intentioned, who live in the atmosphere or on the earth's surface, on plains and in forests. Many of them live in trees. One should be careful not to cut trees on certain days indicated in the astrological almanacs. The *nyen* cause many illnesses, and certain cancers are attributed to them. They are described as having an animal form, of bovine type, yellow or green in color.
>
> The *sadag* are the 'lords of the soil.' In general neutral, they can become irritated when one 'wounds' the soil, their domain, through work, excavation, or building . . .
>
> The *tsen* are red spirits who live in the rocks. They are all male, and are the spirits of past monks who have rejected their vows. *Tsen* who have been tamed by great practitioners often become protectors of temples, sanctuaries, and monasteries. One makes red offerings to them.
>
> The *gyelpo* or 'king-spirits' are said to be the spirits of evil kings or of high lamas who have failed their vows. They are white, often carry armor and are frequently local gods of great importance, as mountain deities.
>
> The *düd* are spirits who are openly malevolent. . . . These are beings who were violently opposed to the dharma in their past life. They create obstacles for the practice of yogis and they feed on human flesh. Their color is black.
>
> The *mamo* constitute a very numerous class of ferocious female deities. Although they preexisted Buddhism, they have been assimilated by it to the *mātrika*, a kind of sorceress of the charnel-grounds. These black goddesses personify natural forces that can be devastating when they are disturbed . . .
>
> The *sa*, called *graha* in Sanskrit, are malevolent planetary deities who cause illnesses such as epilepsy . . .
>
> The *nödjin*, assimilated to the *yakṣa* in Buddhism, are guardian deities of the natural riches of the soil. Vaiśravaṇa, the guardian king of

> the north, is their chief. He is a deity of prosperity. They are also associated with medicine: ten *yakṣa* generals made a vow before the Buddha of Medicine to protect all those who read his *sūtra* or his *mantra*.
>
> The *lha* proper, finally, are a class of white deities, well-disposed towards human beings. (Cornu 1990:226–229; my translation)

The main purpose of these classifications is to know which kind of deity is responsible for a particular misfortune, so that appropriate ritual counter-measures can be adopted. In the Eight Classes, local and regional gods such as the *nyen*, *sadak*, *tsen*, and *lha*, who may themselves be the objects of regular cult-offerings, primarily by lay people, are included along with spirits such as the *dü*, who are entirely malevolent. All, from the point of view of the lamas, are possible sources of affliction whom they may need to combat through Tantric ritual.

I shall discuss the local and regional gods in more detail in Chapter 10. They need to be distinguished conceptually from two other groups of entities, also referred to as *lha*, who are thought of as more elevated in nature. They are the 'gods' of the Buddhist heavens, and the Tantric 'gods' of Buddhist meditation. The gods of the Buddhist heavens (*jigtenlé depé lha*, 'gods that have gone from the world') are beings who form part of the system of rebirth (Skt. *saṃsāra*), described in more detail in the following chapter. Human beings may, theoretically at least, be reborn as these gods just as they may be reborn in hell, or as a hungry ghost or animal.

In Buddhist theory in Tibet, as in Theravādin societies such as Burma (Spiro 1967), the gods of the Buddhist heavens are fitted into the same system as the local deities, who are 'gods of this world' *(jigtenpé lha)* and can conceivably move up to the heavens through acquiring good karma over long periods (see Nebesky-Wojkowitz 1956:3–5; Chime 1981:30 on Pehar). Experientially, they are distinct. The heavenly deities have little or no place in lay people's folk-religion rituals, although some of them are important in monastic ritual as protectors of particular monasteries or religious orders, as are some of the major this-worldly deities.

Tantric deities (*saṃbhogakāya* forms), of whom the pre-eminent examples are the *yidam* or patron deities who are the central symbols of Tantric meditation, are a third group. At first sight, they seem entirely different in nature to the worldly and heavenly deities. *Yidam* are forms that the meditator learns to assume deliberately and consciously in ritual. Thus, treating the *yidam* as deities external to the individual is not entirely appropriate. The *yidam* are nevertheless not simply subjective fantasies, but are believed to correspond to real potentialities within human beings and within the universe as a whole. In Tantric ritual this is expressed in terms of the relationship between the *samayasattva* (*damts'ig sempa*, 'vowed being'), the divine form created through the practitioner's meditation, and the *jñānasattva* (*yeshé sempa* or just *yeshepa*, 'wisdom being'), the divine potentiality that is summoned through the ritual and merged with the *samayasattva*.

However, it would be wrong in Tibetan Buddhist thought to see the *yidam*, or Tantric deities in general, as unreal in comparison with the worldly deities or ordinary human existence. In an important sense, they are more rather than less real than reality as we ordinarily perceive it, since they correspond to underlying properties of the universe and of human nature rather than to the illusory realm of karmic appearance within which human beings, worldly deities, and heavenly gods alike have their existence. Thus, to see the world in terms of the *yidam* and their entourage is a form of 'pure vision' *(dagnang)*, by definition more true than the impure vision of everyday life.

One area where there is an interesting overlap between Tantric deities and worldly gods is that of protectors *(ch'ökyong, sungma)*. Protectors can be Tantric deities *(yeshepé ch'ökyong)* or worldly deities *(jigtenpé ch'ökyong)*; the contrast is between *yeshé* (Skt. *jñāna*), the wisdom of the Buddha, and *jigten*, ordinary worldly reality. To quote a contemporary Nyingmapa lama, Namk'a Drimed Rimpoch'e:

> The mind of *yeshepé ch'ökyong* never diverges from the Buddha's intention, they are emanated as fierce forms of the collectivity of the Buddhas. All the Gompo [forms of Mahākāla] and all the *ngag sungma* [mantra protectors] are of this kind. The *jigtenpé ch'ökyong* have made a decision to protect the Dharma of the Buddha, to help one who does virtue, to punish one who does misfortune. However their mental continuum [*gyüd*, Skt. *santāna*] is not the mind of the Buddha.[4]

The point here is that the *yeshepé ch'ökyong* are Tantric *(saṃbhogakāya)* deities, aspects of Buddhahood itself, whereas the *jigtenpé ch'ökyong* are ordinary worldly deities who have vowed to protect the Dharma (usually after being overcome by Guru Rimpoch'e or some other high lama). While both kinds of protectors are contacted in ritual, they are dealt with in different ways. The *yeshepé ch'ökyong* can be evoked directly by *mantra*, while the *jigtenpé ch'ökyong* are normally summoned by the lama after he has assumed the form of a Tantric deity. The worldly protectors are controlled through the power of the vows *(dam-ts'ig)*, which they have made to serve and protect the Dharma at the time that they were subdued by Guru Rimpoch'e, and through the secret name they yielded at the time of their submission. The Tantric gods operate on a different plane of reality (the *saṃbhogakāya*) to that of ordinary beings, worldly deities, and even to the heavenly gods (who are in fact not of great importance). They represent a source of transcendent power that can be tapped by the lamas in order to intervene in the ordinary world.

At the same time, Namk'a Rimpoch'e's explanation allows for a continuum within worldly gods, whose minds may be closer to or further away from the Buddha's intention. Some worldly gods, such as Genyen Ch'enpo Yedzu Lhadrag Karpo, the local deity of Drugu, near Chamdo, are referred to by names that indicate their commitment to the Buddhist path, in this case Genyen Chenpo = 'great *upāsaka* [lay follower]'.[5]

Tantric gods, in particular the *yidam*, are described in more detail in Chapters 12 and 13. Many of them are significant primarily to those who are involved in the appropriate ritual practices. Others, like Avalokiteśvara, are major foci of popular devotion. To the extent that Tantric deities may be considered to have autonomous existence, they are of a far more elevated nature than the other two classes of gods. Their intentions towards human beings are by definition wholly benign, though they may appear to manifest destructively. Except for deities such as Avalokiteśvara, Guru Rimpoch'e, and Tārā, who may be appealed to for assistance by anyone, Tantric deities are of direct concern only to those who were doing formal Tantric practice (which includes quite a few lay people). The power of the lamas rests in their ability to contact the Tantric deities.

RELATIONSHIPS AMONG LOCAL GODS, HEAVENLY GODS, AND TANTRIC GODS

The fact that the same term, *lha*, is used for all three categories, local deities, gods of the Buddhist heavens, and Tantric gods, suggests that despite the clear conceptual distinctions within Tantric practice, there is some scope for blurring the boundary among them, particularly in lay thought. One context where this can be seen is in the Gesar epic, where each song begins with a formula in which the singer invokes his or her patron deity. In some cases these are Tantric *yidam* such as Tārā or Guru Rimpoch'e, in others deities of the other two classes (Samuel, in press b).

Typically in the epic, the more spiritually developed characters, such as Gesar himself or his wife Drugmo, invoke Tantric deities. Lesser heroes may invoke the war gods of Ling, who belong to the local deities, while non-Buddhist kings are likely to invoke Śiva or other non-Buddhist gods who technically belong to the class of heavenly deities. Thus, the epic exemplifies the position normally taken by the lamas: one should ideally take refuge in the Three Jewels or Könch'og Sum, of whom the Tantric *yidam* are a manifestation, rather than in lesser deities. However, these 'lesser' deities are still sources of potential power who can usefully be contacted for assistance in this world, particularly for warlike purposes. We will see more of this attitude in the next chapter.

At any rate, local deities are appealed to for assistance by lay people both on a regular basis and in response to specific problems. In practice, the different techniques with which the various classes are approached helps keep them distinct, even for unsophisticated villagers or nomads. Asking a local deity for assistance and 'going for refuge' to the Buddhist deities are qualitatively different processes. To the extent that we can speak of a single Tibetan 'pantheon,' it therefore has several distinct components:

1. The Tantric *yidam*, protectors, and other accessory deities, who form a grouping of powerful symbolic entities, some of them important in popular religious observance, others restricted to the context of monastic and yogic practice;

2. The gods of the Buddhist heavens, who are of limited importance in most contexts, but include some protective deities of religious orders;[6]

3. The 'gods of this world,' local deities of mountains, lakes, and other geographical features. There are various groupings and classifications of these, and they merge downwards into the fourth category;

4. Malevolent spirits whose impact on human beings is entirely

harmful, along with malevolent human beings or former human beings who can be classed as witches, ghosts, etc.

The link between (3) and (4) is not always clear, but there is a widespread conception of a local deity having an entourage of lesser-level malevolent spirits. The god may keep his entourage under control or release them against human beings he or she wishes to punish.

The 'gods of this world' (3) are in an ambiguous situation. Their position varies between that of lower-level protectors of the Buddhist teachings (and as such assistants of the specifically Buddhist powers) and potentially dangerous and destructive elements who have to be kept in control precisely by use of the Buddhist powers. Consequently, while they are given offerings and their aid is requested both by laymen and in monastic ritual, the attitudes held towards them are decidedly mixed. The more elevated of these deities, however, may serve as protectors of specific regions and in this function be the focus of regional cults of some importance (see Chapter 10).

The above account is hardly very tidy. In some respects, however, even this is an oversystematization of the situation. The Tibetan pantheon is like the Tibetan political system in that it is an accumulation of special cases rather than a formal bureaucratic structure (see Chapter 3). The correspondence can be taken further, with the worldly deities being equivalent to secular authorities, local big men (Ortner 1978a), aristocrats, *pönpo*, *depa*, and *gyelpo*, to be feared and treated with respect, an unreliable source of protection in times of war and trouble, while the Buddhist Tantric deities stand for the power of the lamas, in theory at least of an altogether different and superior nature.

THE TAMING OF THE GODS AND SPIRITS OF TIBET

By now we can begin to see the structure of thought behind the idea mentioned earlier of the 'taming' of the gods and spirits of Tibet. The Tantric deities are more powerful than the worldly gods, and ideally speaking, they enable a competent lama to keep the worldly gods in order. In practice, their supremacy is less clear-cut, and lay people in particular are well advised to keep on good terms with the local deities.

Much of the mythological history of Tibet can be read in terms of the gradual taming of the environment and its forces, a process that reached its culmination in the activities of Guru Rimpoch'e, the divinized form of a historical Indian teacher who visited Tibet in the eighth century. The first stage in the process, according to the standard Buddhist histories, corresponds to a story first found in the twelfth-century text known as the *Mani Kabum* (Kapstein, in press). The *Mani Kabum* describes the fathering of the Tibetan people by an ancestral monkey, who was in fact a bodhisattva and an emanation of Avalokiteśvara. Later he was regarded as an early member of the rebirth-series of the Dalai Lamas. This divine emanation in monkey form consorted with a wild mountain-demoness or *sinmo,* herself an emanation of Tārā, to produce the first Tibetans. He then gave them the first grains to establish agriculture in the fertile valley of Yarlung in central Tibet. (As we will find in a later chapter, taming is closely associated with agriculture.)

The *Mani Kabum* is also an early source for a subsequent episode, held to have taken place in the time of King Songtsen Gampo (seventh century A.D.). At this time a second *sinmo,* whose body corresponded to the landscape of central Tibet, had to be 'nailed down' by a series of 12 temples forming three concentric squares around central Tibet before the famous Tsuglagk'ang (Jok'ang) Temple could be built in the new royal capital of Lhasa over the *sinmo*'s heart. This magical procedure was intended as "a grand design to secure the Tibetan Demoness for ever and simultaneously to convert the Tibetan people to Buddhism" (Dowman 1988:285; see Aris 1979:8–33; Gyatso 1987; Marko 1988).

The activity of Guru Rimpoch'e, the foremost of all Buddhist 'tamers' of the powers of the Tibetan environment, may be placed historically at the time of King Trisong Detsen (late eighth century). Guru Rimpoch'e is regarded today as a major Tantric deity. In the form of an Indian Tantric adept, he came to Tibet at the invitation of Trisong Detsen and forced the local spirits to accept the power of Buddhism. Guru Rimpoch'e's overcoming of the spirits is told in folk-epic style in several well-known texts, including the *Pema Kat'ang* (Douglas and Bays 1978; Blondeau 1980) and the *Lhadré Kat'ang* (Blondeau 1971). Guru Rimpoch'e is nevertheless an ambiguous figure in relation to state power, as we saw in Chapter 2, and he has strong associations with the shamanic side of Tibetan Buddhism. The characteristic sites associated with him, apart from the first Tibetan monastic *gompa* at Samyé, are small caves distributed in remote places throughout the Himalayas where he is held to have meditated and where his power can now be contacted (Dowman 1988; Macdonald 1986). Similar sites are associated with later figures of the shamanic tradition such as Milarepa (Aufschnaiter 1976; Huber 1989, in press) or Gödts'angpa (Stutchbury, in press).

So far I have been speaking of the Buddhists. The Bönpo, as might be expected, have an alternative but essentially similar series of myths, in which the initial taming of the gods and spirits of Tibet is attributed to the great Bönpo teacher Shenrab Mibo on the occasion of his visit to Tibet, which took place long before the time of Songtsen Gampo, Tr'isong Detsen, and Guru Rimpoch'e. To quote from a twentieth-century Bönpo history, the *Legshed Rimpoch'é Dzöd* of Shardza Rimpoch'e Trashi Gyentsen (1859–1935):

> When the Teacher [Shenrab] came to Tibet he imparted authority to invoke the gods, to exorcise demons, to expel the *yug* [a kind of demon], in the way I expounded above. (As a result) nowadays the gods and demons of Tibet listen to orders and carry out whatever task is entrusted to them. Since they long ago made vows under the powerful orders of the Teacher, now if a Bönpo makes offerings to the gods they give protection, if he strikes the demons they are subdued, and if he exorcizes them they depart. (Karmay 1972:30)

These myths, Buddhist and Bönpo, demonstrate the significance for premodern Tibetans of exerting symbolic control over the forces of the Tibetan landscape. At the same time, that symbolic control seems to have been more questionable and less conclusive than in neighboring premodern societies, such as the plains of northern India, or the highly populated regions of Southeast Asia. In such areas the dominance of the clerical regime was beyond any real contest. In Tibet it was, and is still, maintained through constant ritual performances in which Guru Rimpoch'e's initial 'taming' of the land and the deities are reenacted (see Chapter 14).

There are, in fact, stories explaining why the taming of the indigenous powers of Tibet was incomplete. The following explanation is by Namk'a Rimpoch'e, from whom I quoted before:

> Guru Rimpoch'e performed the *lhasin tamdrag* (ritual to subdue the gods and spirits) twice. Although Guru Rimpoch'e is himself Buddha, he was unable to perform the ritual three times, as he intended to, since King Trisong Detsen did not request him, partly through the king's neglect, and partly also through malicious gossip originating from the anti-Buddhist ministers, which placed the king and Guru Rimpoch'e in a difficult position.
>
> On another occasion, when Guru Rimpoch'e in the form of Garuḍa was subduing the *lu*-spirits, a disguised *lu* spirit assumed a helpless and distressed appearance, causing strong compassion in the mind of King Trisong Detsen, who was watching the ritual. The king asked Guru Rimpoch'e to leave the *lu* alone. Consequently, the ritual could not be performed. In this case, too, the king forgot to ask Guru Rimpoch'e to perform the ritual again. As a result, this *lu*, Lu Dugpachen, was able to cause great problems for Tibet in later years.
>
> On another occasion, Guru Rimpoch'e wanted to avert the future destruction of Buddhism at the time of King Langdarma, so he summoned a feeble, worn out, helpless ox and was about to bind it with mantras. The king saw this and felt compassion for the animal. Through the power of karma, the ox was able to escape. Later it was born as Langdarma and caused great harm to Buddhism.[7]

These stories have an interesting subtext concerning the relationship between the king, whose compassion is real but whose knowledge is limited, and Guru Rimpoch'e, who is aware of the need for destructive ritual in order to prevent future suffering. As we saw in Chapter 2, the king, although he is one of the prototypical figures of royal power in Tibet, is regularly portrayed as inferior in power and wisdom to Guru Rimpoch'e.

CONTRASTS WITH THERAVĀDIN SOCIETIES

Here we may return to the contrast between Tibet and Theravādin societies, introduced in Chapter 2. In Theravādin societies, as I noted previously, royal power takes precedence over the Buddhist hierarchy, and shamanic ritual is in a strictly subordinate place.

Tibetans and members of Theravādin societies are alike in having a variety of religious roles and functions, some 'Buddhist,' while others are associated with local gods and spirits. If, however, distinguishing between separate 'religions' ('Buddhism' and 'animism'), as in Melford Spiro's analysis of Burmese religion (Spiro 1967), is problematic in the Theravādin countries, it is even more difficult and questionable for Tibetan societies.

In Theravādin countries, the deity-cults coexist with Buddhism, and are very important to the population. They receive little explicit recognition from Buddhism, however, which, in theory at least, exists in a distinct and superior sphere. The religious specialists who deal with the local deities are distinct from the Buddhist clergy, and, unlike the latter, they are not normally celibate monks. These non-Buddhist practitioners include priests of local deities, spirit-mediums, and the like. Since the celibate monk has the highest religious status in Theravādin society, these other practitioners, however useful, are by definition lower in status.

Such priests and mediums of the local deities also exist in Tibetan societies, but they are much more closely linked to the specifically Buddhist practitioners, who are directly concerned with the local deities in their own ritual performances and religious careers. Spirit-mediums and other specifically folk-religion specialists act in practice as their assistants and subordinates, dealing with minor cases themselves and referring the more significant problems to the lamas.

As we have seen, the classic 'tamer' of local gods and spirits, Guru Rimpoch'e, was himself a form of Buddha, and a central representative of Buddhist Tantric power. Significantly, Guru Rimpoch'e, though not himself a monk at the time of his activity in Tibet, was closely connected with the inauguration of the first Tibetan monastic *gompa*, Samyé. The hill of Hepo, close by Samyé, was one of the major sites associated with his subduing of the gods and spirits of Tibet. In Tibet, the Tantric lama is superior to monks as well as to other ritual specialists.

The wider sphere of activity of Buddhism in Tibet can be connected with the explicit tendency of the lamas and other specialists to operate at several simultaneous levels of interpretation (the idea of *upāyakauśalya* or 'skillful means'). This provides a Buddhist justification for ritual performances that might be seen, in Theravādin or even Far Eastern Mahāyāna terms, as marginal to or outside the proper realm of Buddhist activity. Major Buddhist rituals such as life-empowerment rituals or *ts'ewang* are explained and interpreted in terms of all three of the orientations discussed in Chapter 2:

1. The Pragmatic Orientation, in terms of health and prosperity in one's present life (see Spiro's 'apotropaic' Buddhism);

2. The Karma Orientation, in relation to future lives (see Spiro's 'kammatic' Buddhism);

3. The Bodhi Orientation, corresponding to personal release from the cycle of rebirth ('nibbanic' Buddhism in Spiro's terms), and also to the altruistic motivation *(bodhicitta)* of the Mahāyāna Buddhist practitioner, a level not present in Spiro's scheme.

Consequently, it makes little sense, in many cases, to attribute any particular practice to one category or another. This is one reason why I speak of orientations of the practitioners rather than of types of practice. Most of those present at a particular life-empowerment ritual, the lay population in particular, may be involved primarily in terms of the Pragmatic Orientation, but the Karma Orientation is likely to be salient for many, and the Bodhi Orientation for at least a few. The form of the ritual itself encourages participants to be aware of different possible levels of motivation, since a *ts'ewang,* like other Tantric empowerments, will frequently include a summary of the entire range of Buddhist teachings as a preliminary component. The very openness of the system to multiple interpretation gives it a distinctive character from that of Theravādin Buddhism.

Within Theravādin societies, specific practices seem easier to characterize straightforwardly as part of one complex or another. Disagreement among anthropologists working in these societies (see Chapter 2) has focused mainly on the degree of connectedness between these complexes. Accounts such as Tambiah's (1970) replace Spiro's 'religions' with a more integrated field of relationships between types of specialists. Within such an integrated field, monks may play a role in practice as sources of protective power (Tambiah 1984); however, this is outside the proper sphere of monks in Theravādin society, and it is significant that Tambiah himself associates it with a 'Tantric' polarity within Thailand (see Chapter 2). While there are no doubt equivalents within Theravādin societies to the different orientations found in Tibetan Buddhism, the explicit multiple interpretation and level-shifting so characteristic of the Tibetan system are absent.

In Buddhist terminology, these differences can be associated with the different types of Buddhism in these societies: Mahāyāna and

Vajrayāna (Tantric) in Tibet, Theravādin in South and Southeast Asia. The doctrine of *upāyakauśalya*, skillful means of teaching, has been much more extensively developed by the Mahāyāna schools, so as to allow for a multiplicity of practices, rituals, and modes of presenting the Dharma (the Buddhist teachings) to coexist in a single society without their being seen as particularly inconsistent or contradictory. They are viewed instead as appropriate to different persons at different stages of practice. Tantra provided the ritual 'technology' by which the local deities were dealt with (Chapters 12 to 14) and thus linked together the Pragmatic and Bodhi orientations.

CONCLUSION

We have seen that there are a number of different possible attitudes that Tibetans could take towards their environment and the various beings believed to populate it. In broad terms these can be summarized in terms of the three orientations discussed above, Pragmatic, Bodhi, and Karma. We can summarize the implications of each orientation as follows:

Within the Pragmatic Orientation, this world is the environment within which human life takes place. This is not to say that, even for the Pragmatic Orientation, the world is assumed to be a simple given, in the form in which it appears to our senses. The senses are illusory and all appearances can be misleading. Nevertheless, the world is worth taking seriously. It offers possibilities for happiness and prosperity, and suffering and misfortune. Skillful management can, within limits, increase the former and reduce the latter.

Part of this management consists of dealing appropriately with the spirit world. Someone who is operating in terms of the Pragmatic Orientation sees the local deities and malevolent spirits as beings who have to be dealt with to ensure success within this world, just as powerful human beings or material forces have to be encountered and dealt with. Lay people make regular offerings to the local gods (see Chapter 10). Lay people rely on the regular rituals performed by lamas in the *gompa* and in the village, and on their own regular offerings to local gods, to maintain a workable relationship with these powers. Such a relationship should maintain a condition of good fortune *(lungta)* and auspiciousness *(trashi)* such that serious mishaps will be averted.

In cases of misfortune or danger, most people are likely to know a few mantras and prayers that can be used for assistance, such as the mantra of the goddess Tārā. If serious problems that may be attributable to local deities occur, however, lay people will need to consult a specialist, either a lama or some lesser specialist such as a spirit-medium, astrologer, or diviner. All this is the realm of 'folk religion,' and we will see more implications of this orientation in Chapter 10, where the folk-religion practices of the lay population are considered in detail.

The Karma Orientation treats attraction to the world as to be avoided at all costs. The world is significant primarily as a context within which virtuous action may be performed with the aim of improving one's chances for a future rebirth. Beyond that, the world is a series of signs, showing the validity of the law of karma. Sickness, old age, misfortune, and death, the differing abilities and fortunes of one's fellow human beings, should be seen as moral lessons through which one learns to turn one's attention away from attraction to the world. Involvement with the local deities is a waste of time, and a distraction from the performance of virtuous action, which can alone be of assistance at the time of death. The Karma Orientation will be further discussed in Chapter 11.

Finally, at the level of the Bodhi Orientation, several attitudes are possible and are found. The Bodhi Orientation implies, on the face of it, an even more radical rejection of the world than does the Karma Orientation, since one is here rejecting not only this life but all life within *saṃsāra*. However, for the Mahāyāna practitioner, *saṃsāra* and *nirvāṇa* are two sides of the same picture, and the ideal practitioner may remain within the world as an agent of the Buddha's compassionate activity.

Practitioners of the Bodhi Orientation operate primarily in terms of the Tantric deities. They hope through the practices of these deities to realize in themselves the Enlightened mind of the Buddha, of which the Tantric deities are aspects. As for the local gods and spirits, practitioners may deal with them in pragmatic terms, as obstacles and problems that may arise along the path to *bodhi*. In fact, those involved with the Bodhi Orientation may be particularly likely to run into problems with these entities, if they fail to take appropriate precautions, since spirits such as the *düd* are opposed to Buddhist practice and will do their best to block it. In addition, the Bodhi Orientation is the basis of the lamas' training, and lamas have to deal with worldly gods and spirits on a regular basis as part of their service to their lay clientele. Finally, there is the path of solitary yogic practitioners of the *chöd* practice, who visualize offering their body to the worldly deities and to the Tantric deities as a training in radical nonattachment.

We will see some of the implications of these various facets of the Bodhi Orientation in Chapters 12 to 14, on Tantra, and in Chapters 15 to 18, in which we look at the varieties of Tibetan religious practitioners, their communities and their careers.

10

The Folk Religion and the Pragmatic Orientation

Of the three orientations to Tibetan religious practice we have just discussed, the Pragmatic, Karma, and Bodhi Orientations, this chapter is mainly concerned with the first, the Pragmatic. In the Pragmatic Orientation, religious power is applied to deal with the contingencies of everyday life in the world. I referred to it in Chapter 2 as:

> the realm of this-worldly concerns, conceived of in terms of interactions with local gods and spirits, and carried out by a variety of ritual practitioners, foremost among them being the lamas, who employ the techniques of Tantric practice for this purpose.

In Chapter 9 we encountered the local gods and spirits. They form the basis of what Giuseppe Tucci has referred to as the 'folk religion' of Tibet (Tucci 1980:163–212) and Rolf Stein has called the 'nameless religion' (Stein 1972a:191ff). Neither label is ideal, though both avoid the multiple confusions involved in referring to this area, as some Tibetans and some Western scholars do, as Bön (see Chapter 1). Here I use Tucci's term 'folk religion,' which at least suggests the closeness of these concepts and practices to the lived experience of Tibetans.

THE HISTORY OF THE FOLK RELIGION

Tibetan history in general is obscure before the Tibetan empire of the seventh to ninth centuries. It seems likely that both the pastoral and agricultural modes of life go back at least several hundred years before that time. Certain religious practices are probably of similar antiquity, and have much in common with similar strata that can be identified in many societies in South, Southeast, and East Asia.[1] For comparative purposes the Tibeto-Burman peoples of the Himalayas, southwest China, and Southeast Asia are of particular relevance (Hitchcock and Jones 1976; LeBar et al. 1964).

The Tibetan practices included from early times a cult of local deities, communication with those deities by means of spirit-possession,[2] and concern with defence against malevolent and destructive spirits through the agency of the local deities. The most important deities were evidently from very early times the gods and goddesses of the mountains (see Spanien 1971b; Stein 1972a, 1985). Streams and lakes also had indwelling deities. Divination was important, as was the associated concept of good fortune or luck *(trashi).*

These folk-religion practices constituted what Bönpo scholars later referred to as the Bön of Cause *(gyui bön),* as distinct from the Bön of Effect or *drebui bön,* which consisted of the practices of the religious order of Bön, effectively a modified form of Buddhism. The Bön of Cause was classified in later times into twelve kinds of knowledge (see Karmay 1972:31 and n. 2). It also corresponds to the first four of the 'Nine Ways of Bön' in the classification of the *Sijid* (Snellgrove 1967a). These comprise (1) techniques of divination and medical diagnosis, (2) rituals for placating or overcoming local deities, (3) techniques for destroying enemies (i.e., sorcery), and (4) funerary rituals. Both Buddhist and Bönpo scholars agree that these practices were present in Tibet at the time of the early kings (Karmay 1972:31–34, 34 n. 1). As I have already said in Chapter 1, these techniques and rituals have no special relationship to contemporary Bön as distinct from contemporary Buddhism.

Practices of all these kinds continued into recent times, but they became integrated with later developments, forming the body of techniques and ideas constituting the folk religion of Tibet. The local gods nevertheless remained at the center of the folk religion and its practices, and we shall begin with them.

ATTITUDES TO THE LOCAL GODS

As illustrations of attitudes to the local gods in the premodern period, here are some short narratives about these deities. The first is a Gelugpa teaching story, retold here by Alex Berzin. It is intended to illustrate the moral that the true practitioner should not take refuge in local deities, but only in the Buddha and the Tantric deities:

> In the northern province of Tsang there was an earthly deity who was worshipped locally. Once, a man, who happened to have a goiter, had to camp overnight out on the open plain. Before going to sleep he took refuge in the local deity and asked him to protect his life during the night. The deity agreed and the man went to sleep. During the night the attendants and servants of the local deity . . . came by. Seeing the lone man sleeping, they said, 'Let's eat him!' The local deity, however, told them not to, because he had agreed to protect the man's life. He then suggested that they eat the man's goiter instead, because the man didn't really need it. . . . When the man awoke the next morning, he not only found himself safe, but also he discovered that his goiter was missing. Being very pleased, he returned to the village.
>
> Now it so happened that in this village there was another man who also had a goiter. Seeing the cured condition of the first man, he too decided to try the help of this local deity. He went out onto the open plain and, before retiring, he too took refuge in the local deity. That night the attendants and servants came again and once more asked the deity if they could eat this man. Once more the deity had to say no, because he had promised to protect his life; but again he suggested that they eat his goiter. 'Goiter again,' the attendants and servants said, 'why, that tastes terrible! In fact, we'll give him back the other man's goiter. We couldn't even finish it, it was so horrible.' And so when the second man awoke the next morning, he discovered that instead of having lost his goiter as he had hoped, he now had two. This goes to show that refuge in local earthly deities cannot be relied upon.[3]

In its original context in the Gelugpa Lamrim teachings, this story is taught in relation to the Refuge Teachings. The beginning practitioner is enjoined to reject any reliance on the worldly gods in favor of the Three Jewels of Buddhism. In practice, although it may be true that the local deities cannot be relied upon, few Tibetans will ignore them. The *Sijid*, the Bönpo text translated in part by David Snellgrove, is characteristically explicit on the subject, when discussing the need to propitiate the local gods before constructing a *maṇḍala:*

> Whichever *bön* way of the Nine Vehicles you practise,
> If you fail to give milk-offerings and pure sacrificial cakes to the powerful lords of this world,
> if you do not ask them (for a site for) your palace of the Blessed Ones,
> these powerful lords, the lords of the soil, the serpents and the furies [*sadag lu nyen*] are irascible, however much they may still protect the doctrine.
> However gentle their disposition, their lineage is still that of the titans [*lhamin*] . . .
> You must give pleasure to the powerful ones of the phenomenal world [*jigten*],
> and having made them happy, you can hold them to their former vows.[4]
> Ask them for a site for your worship and a place for you to stay, and hold them before witnesses to their oath to protect the doctrine.
> Afterwards you can make them attend to whatever you want,
> Thus happiness in phenomenal things depends on (the lords of) the soil.
> Fertile fields and good harvests,
> extent of royal power and spread of dominion,
> although some half (of such effects) is ordained by previous actions,
> the other half comes from the powerful lords of the soil. (Snellgrove 1967a:197–199).

As Snellgrove notes, this Bönpo text is only stating what all Tibetans believe, although the Buddhist texts generally avoid stating it outright, that it is necessary to keep on good terms with the local gods to secure good fortune in the world of everyday life (1967a:12–13).

A second narrative, from a book by Thubten Jigme Norbu (Tengtser Rimpoch'e), a Gelugpa incarnate lama from Amdo, and the elder brother of the Dalai Lama, gives a picture of the place of these deities in lay life. He is speaking of the cult of local gods in the village where he was born. The mountain of Kyeri was the seat of the deity of Tengtser village:

> It was towards Kyeri that our prayers were directed, because Kyeri was the throne of our protective deity and bore his name. . . . The temple which stood surrounded by shady trees on the outskirts of our village was dedicated to Kyeri out of a feeling of mingled love and gratitude. The temple precincts were quite roomy and offered plenty of space for the approximately one hundred and fifty inhabitants of our village, though the temple proper was quite small; and inside, because ours was not a rich village, it was a trifle austere. In the centre was a statue of our protective deity in the guise of a horseman. Like the other statues this equestrian one was made of clay . . .
>
> Behind the temple was a small eminence on which a stone altar had been erected, and here the inhabitants of Tengtser would burn incense in honor of our protective deity and to beg him to grant peace and prosperity to our village. Before going to the altar you first entered the temple and placed a few flowers to the effigies of the gods, or fixed a prayer-flag. There was no monastery in Tengtser and therefore there was no monk to look after the temple and supervise the ceremonies, and this was done by one of the men of the village who was appointed caretaker. (Norbu and Harrer 1960:51–52.)

The book from which this excerpt is taken presents a romanticized and euphemistic view of Tibetan religion, but Norbu's account is a straightforward description of the villagers' relationship to the local god, who is seen as a protector whose assistance is regularly requested.

A third narrative, by Anak Dorje Namgyel, a layman from an aristocratic family of Gonjo in K'am, gives a similar picture, but brings out the martial side of many of these local gods, which Norbu implies when he mentions that the god is portrayed as a horseman:

> In Gonjo, each of the *pön* families had its own *yüllha* or local god. The most important local god, however, was Dorjé Ngangk'ar, the regional deity of Gonjo. Gonpo Dorjé of the K'angsar *pön* family, who was born around 1900, was believed to be the son of Dorjé Ngangk'ar. During one of the Chinese-Tibetan wars earlier this century, Gonpo Dorjé led 221 men from Gonjo in an expedition against the Chinese who were in Derge state. The Tibetans were defeated and Gonpo Dorjé and his men were driven back against the western bank of the Dri River. However, a man dressed in white and riding a white horse appeared before Gonpo Dorjé in the river. Gonpo Dorjé jumped in the river, and told the other men to follow him without looking ahead. All but one crossed the river safely. That white rider was Dorjé Ngangk'ar.[5]

A fourth story, from a contemporary Nyingmapa lama, Namk'a Drimed Rimpoch'e, tells how a lama encountered Dorjé Dragtsen, the regional deity of Powo, while escaping from the Chinese in 1959:

> One night, when Lama A was staying in Pema Köd, he saw Dorjé Dragtsen in a dream. The god was in an angry mood and he gave the lama a red *torma,* saying that he would need it for a life-empowerment ritual. He also asked the lama to help him 'strengthen the local river.' Afterwards, one of the lama's monks asked him to write a prayer *(kulwa)* for Dorjé Dragtsen, and the lama understood the meaning of Dorjé Dragtsen's giving him the red *torma.*
>
> At that time the Chinese had already come to Doshangla in Pema Köd, on the other side of the river. Everyone was uncertain and tense. The lama did a *mo* and found that the Chinese wouldn't cross the river at that time. One day he fell ill and had another vision of Dorjé Dragtsen, who appeared as a red rider on a red horse and said that he was going to war, because the Chinese would not leave him in peace. Dorjé Dragtsen was followed by the *pat'ul* (heroes) of Ling, and the lama found himself going after them as they went off towards Doshangla to fight.
>
> Some days later they heard that Chinese reinforcements had come to Doshangla, but a Chinese officer had been killed and the soldiers went back. A Tibetan in Doshangla had dreamed that he should have no fear the next day but should go and shoot the Chinese officer. He killed the officer, and the same bullet rebounded and miraculously killed a second officer. Then the Chinese packed up and left. They didn't come back until the following year. The lama realized that Dorjé Dragtsen had known from the beginning that the Chinese were coming and had wanted to stop them at the river, but had needed his help in the form of the *kulwa.*[6]

As both the god's red color and his name indicates, Dorjé Dragtsen is one of the fierce *tsen* deities (see Chapter 9). A significant feature of this story is the reciprocity between god and lama. It is only through the help of Lama A's prayer that the god has the strength to inspire a man to attack the Chinese.

A last story, again from Anak Dorje Namgyel, relates an incident among the refugees involving Dorjé Ngangk'ar, the Gonjo deity we have already encountered:

> Lama B was rebuilding his *gompa* in North India when one day a man came to see him, wearing only a white shirt and trousers, and gave

> him a bundle of objects wrapped in white cloth. The lama asked who he was. 'I am from Gonjo,' the man said, 'I came to see you.' The lama knew all the people from Gonjo living there but didn't recognize him. He asked where he was staying. 'I have come from outside, but I am staying with a Gonjo family in the camp here. I have some old silver ornaments here to offer you. Please make a *dungma* (long trumpet) out of them, I love the sound of the *dungma*. In future I will come regularly and meet you again.' The lama was so busy that he didn't have time to receive the man properly or to offer him tea. Later he opened the bundle which did indeed contain many silver ornaments. However he forgot about the man's request, and used the ornaments for something else.
>
> About ten years later, Lama B had some dreams, and it turned out that the man had been the Gonjo regional deity Dorjé Ngangk'ar, and was angry with him. The lama made a few sets of beautiful *dungma* and *gyelling*, but he died some years after.[7]

These stories suggest something of the behavior expected of local gods. They are especially associated with war and violence. They may be benevolent but can easily be offended, and their anger can be dangerous. They may communicate through dreams and visions, particularly to lamas. As we will see, they may also communicate through spirit-possession mediums. We turn now to look at attitudes to them in ritual.

RITUALS OF THE LOCAL GODS

In lay ritual, these local Tibetan gods are treated with respect and deference. An important part of their cult is connected with the *laptsé* or *lhat'o*, stone cairns found in particular at the highest points of passes, but also at other places close to the abodes of these deities. Travelers across the passes carry stones up the ascent and throw them onto the cairn when they reach it, with a standard invocation, *"Kye kye so so . . . lha gyello lha gyello"* (the last phrase means 'the gods are victorious'). Stein links this invocation, with its opening war-cries, with the warlike nature of the gods and the idea of passing through a dangerous and strategic place (Stein 1972a:206).

Siegbert Hummel has suggested that the purpose of the cairns nevertheless has as much to do with restraining and imprisoning the deities as with worshipping them (Hummel 1960). He compares them with the thread-crosses or *dö* in which spirits are trapped by the lamas, and which are subsequently removed outside the village and destroyed (Nebesky-Wojkowitz 1956:369–397; Snellgrove 1961:139–140; Beyer 1973:318–359). The Buddhist symbols involved in the cairns (colored prayer-flags attached to poles projecting from the cairns, and the stones with inscribed mantras often added to the pile) are implicitly directed to this end. The cairns are called the castles of gods, but the gods are expected to stay there and give no trouble in return for being provided with a home and regular offerings.

The offerings take the form of the *sang* ritual, the basic component of lay worship of the local gods. The central feature of *sang* is the burning of incense, particularly juniper wood, accompanied often by the offering of prayer-flags (see Tucci 1980:199–201). The texts that are recited during the ritual invoke lists of regional and local deities. *Sang* is not merely a protective practice, but an auspicious ritual, whose performance may be hoped to create positive influences for the good fortune of the participants.

A few examples follow of the contexts in which *sang* is performed, mainly from Amdo and from Sherpa country in Nepal. For the first, we return to the autobiography of the Amdo lama T. J. Norbu. There was a *laptse,* which Norbu describes as "a heap of stones dedicated to the protective deity of the village," on a small hill near his Amdo village of Tengtser. "Here you offered up white quartz, coins, turquoises and corals, and prayed for rain, or for sun, or for a good harvest, or for protection from bad weather" (Norbu and Harrer 1960:53). Once a year the whole village went there along with monks from neighboring monasteries, burned incense, and erected prayer-flags. A few days earlier the villagers had gone on a three-day journey to the foot of the mountain to burn incense up at the ice-limit.

Though Norbu's account is not entirely clear, it seems that his family also burned incense daily to Kyeri in an earthenware vase in the center of the house's courtyard, after making the offerings and lighting the butter-lamps in the house chapel and in front of a Buddha image in his parents' bedroom (1960:31).[8] Here Kyeri was serving as the *p'olha* or protective deity of the household (see below).

Temples of local deities are reported from other regions, such as Lahul (Gill 1972:12–13). Among the Sherpas of Nepal, there are, as far as I know, no such temples. Each region of Sherpa country, however, has a regional deity, such as Khumbu Yüllha for the Khumbu region. Each is associated with a major mountain in that region. Lesser deities or *shibdag*, associated with other localities, are worshipped by particular clans (Fürer-Haimendorf 1964:21–22). There are three main occasions each year in Khumbu for the worship of clan deities. Christoph von Fürer-Haimendorf gives a description of one of these, the *yerch'ang* or 'summer beer' ritual performed in the high cattle pastures, and primarily concerned with the welfare of the herds (1964:208–210). It involves the burning of incense, the erection of prayer-flags, and the rededication of a number of yaks to Khumbu Yüllha and the clan deities. Kathryn March (for the Sherpas of Shorung or Solu, to the south) and Robert Ekvall (for Amdo pastoralists) also mention the practice of dedicating animals to the gods (Ekvall 1968:29–30; March 1977:95). In Khumbu villages, two other clan-deity rituals are performed as part of the annual cycle, and are the occasion for gatherings of clan members (Fürer-Haimendorf 1964:22).

March describes the ritual associated with high-altitude pastoralism among the Shorung Sherpa, which is basically similar to that in Khumbu. Incense and a short prayer are offered daily in the morning fire before cooking by those who are up in the pastures with the herds. A more substantial ritual is performed whenever the herd is moved to a new site, and this involves the offering of butter, milk, and incense. These offerings are to the two main Shorung regional deities, who are the *yüllha* of Numbur Mountain and the goddess of Womi Ts'o, to the goddesses of other nearby mountains, and to other local deities. A large ritual (*kang sung*)[9] is also performed annually in the village before the herds' departure for the highest pastures in late spring-early summer (March 1977, esp. 90–93).

Womi Ts'o itself is a high mountain lake and is the center of an annual festival attended not only by Sherpas but by Brahmin-Chetris, Tamangs, Rais, and Limbus. For the Sherpas this festival is concerned with the goddess of the lake and with the *yüllha* of the nearby mountain of Numbur (March 1977:93–94). Jest describes a similar annual pilgrimage to worship the local deity among the people of Tarap, in western Nepal (Jest 1974, 1976:300).

Such pilgrimages are a pan-Tibetan practice, merging into the specifically Buddhist pilgrimages to sites associated with Tantric deities and with great lamas of the past (Blondeau 1960; Nebesky-

Wojkowitz 1956:406; Jest 1976:353ff), such as the pilgrimage to Mount Kailash and Lake Manasarovar in western Tibet, which was and remains a sacred site for Hindus and Bönpo followers as well as for Buddhists (Govinda 1974; Johnson and Moran 1989).

All these are examples of ritual carried out primarily by lay people in non-Buddhist settings. In the ritual carried out by lamas and monks in the *gompa,* the attitude to the local gods is less unequivocally respectful. Snellgrove translates an invocation to an important deity of this class, T'anglha, as given in the Nyingmapa ritual text used in Sherpa country (from a *terma* cycle known as Tugjé Ch'enpo Drowa Kundröl). T'anglha, the 'God of the Plain,' is the god of a great mountain chain (Nyench'en T'anglha) north of Lhasa. Snellgrove comments on the way in which deities of this kind "are treated alternately to threats and offerings. In no way are they permitted to interfere with the Buddhist doctrine, to which they remain helplessly subject." Here is part of the invocation:

> Friend of us who now perform the ritual,
> The command to action has now been given,
> Subdue the raving fiends, cut down the hostile foe . . .
> It is time for action, O king of obstructive foes.
> Perform therefore your appointed task.
> You are the country-god of the four regions of Ü and Tsang.
> You are the god of Tr'isong Detsen, the Divine Son, the King who was Protector of the Doctrine.
> You are bound to the bond of your word by Padmasambhava of Urgyen.
> So hearken now to what is required of you . . .
> If you do not protect us living beings now in this last world-age,
> Will you not perhaps be mindful of these happenings:
> Firstly how Vajrapaṇi pressed the life from your heart on the way to the north,
> Secondly how Padma-Heruka forced you into subjection on Mt. Hepo by Samyé,
> Thirdly how Vajra-kumara, having collected together all gods and demons on the summit of the fair-formed king of mountains, forced them to take the vow.
> I now am Padmasambhava . . .
> O God of the Plain, we beg you to come.

> You yourself and your following of *nyen*
> We shall honor with the most splendid of excellent offerings . . .
> (Snellgrove 1957:239–242)

In this temple service the officiating monks take on the identity of Padmasambhava (Guru Rimpoch'e) who is treated here as a tantric deity. As Padmasambhava they are able to exert over the god the same power that Padmasambhava originally employed to overcome T'anglha and bind him to the service of the Buddhist religion.

LHA AND *LA*: CONNECTIONS BETWEEN 'GODS' AND HUMANS

March comments, in reference to the Womi Ts'o festival mentioned above, that on the occasion of a ritual in the 1970s the Sherpa participants "voiced great concern that the lake was so dried up: it was clearly shrunken to about one-third its normal size, a disturbing phenomenon to Sherpas who look to this lake especially, its fullness and purity, as a visible symbol of their own prosperity and health" (March 1977:94).

This lake, like other sacred lakes or mountains (Nebesky-Wojkowitz 1956:482) belongs to the category of places associated with the *la* or life-force of a region. This brings us to another major concept of the Tibetan folk religion, that of *la* (Tibetan spelling *bla*), which is, as we will see, connected in interesting ways with the cult of local deities (see also Chapter 14).

Individuals also possess *la,* and these commonly have their location in trees or animals, although this idea was, in premodern times, perhaps more common in folktales and in the Gesar epic than in present-day practice. The idea of the wandering of the *la* as a cause for illness or death has however remained significant, and rituals to recall the *la* are still carried out.

La is in no real sense a Buddhist concept. It corresponds to concepts such as the Northeast Thai *khwan* discussed by Stanley Tambiah, and is concerned, like the cult of the gods as a whole, with this-worldly good fortune, not with rebirth and salvation (Tambiah 1970; Heinze 1982).

As with many of the 'folk-religion' concepts, the ideas concerning the *la* cannot easily be expressed in a coherent and consistent form.

Ideas about *la* surface in a variety of contexts in ritual and in folk literature such as wedding songs and the epic, as well as in the rituals performed to call back the *la* of a person when it has wandered (Lessing 1951; Nebesky-Wojkowitz 1956:481–483; Tucci 1980:190–193; Karmay 1987; Mumford 1989:168ff). As we will see in Chapter 14, an important class of Tantric rituals, the *ts'ewang,* can be interpreted as concerned with the welfare of the *la.* The *la* is a spirit-essence or life-principle, residing in the body, and, particularly in the earlier period, it was seen as connected also with one or more external objects. Such external objects or resting-places of the *la* might be hills, lakes, or groves of trees. In some parts of Tibet it is customary to plant a tree at the birth of a child. This tree is the *lashing,* the tree of that child's *la.* According to Jäschke, the tree is a juniper, which is particularly associated with the local deities through its use in *sang* (Jäschke 1968:383). Duncan (1964:249) mentions the same concept for East Tibet, although there the tree is the *lashing* of a family, not of an individual.

The *la* can leave the body, weakening one's life and exposing one to harm. It can also be affected by damaging or destroying its external resting-place.

The concept of *la* has been commented on by Réné de Nebesky-Wojkowitz and also by Snellgrove. Both suggest that it is a pre-Buddhist idea (Nebesky-Wojkowitz 1956:481–483; Snellgrove 1961:143). Both Stein and Tucci argue that it is closely linked to the local gods in their role of personal protective deities or *gowé lha* (Stein 1972a:226–229; Tucci 1980:193). These *gowé lha* are a standard set of (usually) five gods who are 'born at the same time' as a child, in other words who become associated with the child at the time of birth. Lists of the *gowé lha,* as with everything to do with the 'folk religion,' are not standardized. One given by Nebesky-Wojkowitz lists them as *soglha* or 'god of life' with its seat in the heart, *p'olha* ('male god') in the right armpit, *molha* ('female god') in the left armpit, *drabla* ('enemy god') at the right shoulder, and *yüllha* ('god of the locality') at the crown of the head. Other lists substitute the *shanglha* ('god of the mother's brother') for either *yüllha* or *molha* (Nebesky-Wojkowitz 1956:264, 327–328).

Two of the *gowé lha* still have important roles in connection with the protection of the household in premodern times. These are the *p'olha* and the *molha,* which is more often referred to as *p'uglha.* They are the two most significant members of a series of gods associated with the household described in Tucci's account of the 'folk religion.' The *p'olha* ('male god') normally has a shrine on the roof where incense can be burned. This shrine *(p'olha k'ar)* is related to the *laptse* discussed above (Tucci 1980; see Stein 1972a:206). The *p'olha* is associated with the men of the family and with the external defence of the house.

The 'inner deity' of the house or *p'uglha*, also *k'yimlha* ('house deity') or *molha* (= 'female god'/'god of women') has a shrine inside the house in the central pillar. It is concerned with the well-being of the family and in particular of its female members. For the Sherpas, the *p'uglha* is normally a serpent-deity or *lu*.[10]

Barbara Aziz describes a ritual, the *lhadro*, which forms a regular part of marriage in the Dingri region. In the *lhadro* ritual the *p'uglha* of the girl's family is approached through a spirit-medium to give its permission for the girl to leave the household (Aziz 1978:253). Where the bride is going to live in an already existing household, the *p'uglha* of her new home also has to be taken into account. The illness of a bride in her new house is regularly attributed to the *p'uglha* not feeling well-inclined towards her, in which case it has to be won over by appropriate rituals (Tucci 1980:189).

Other deities watch over the hearth *(t'ablha)* and the storehouse *(bangdzöd lha)*. The hearth god can easily be upset by impurity, such as when a cooking-pot overflows, and *sang* may be performed in such a case to avoid trouble (Tucci 1980). Ekvall mentions these spirits in the context of a nomadic tent in his novel *Tents Against the Sky*, based on the author's long residence among Amdo nomads:

> Strange, jealous creatures, they swarm at the rising of the smoke in a new tent, and take proprietary though at times perverse interest in the new hearth. Because of their displeasure, children die or are born dead. Their spiteful blows bring blindness, strange swellings, and the swift rotting of anthrax, the 'earth poison.' What tent can hope for peace if the hearthstone spirits are angry? (Ekvall 1954a:117)

Later in the same novel the sickness of a child and other impending misfortunes are linked to the anger of the hearthstone spirits and of the serpent spirits (*lu*, 1954a:202).

The house among agricultural Tibetans (Corlin 1980 for Gyelt'ang in Yunnan; Dollfus 1989:129–146 for Ladakh) and the tent among nomads (Ekvall 1968:61–65; Faegre 1979) is conceived of as a microcosm. This idea is expressed in detail in the traditional songs and speeches associated with weddings (Tucci 1966; Aziz 1985). I am not sure how far it was still really a live idea in recent times, but it reinforces a view of the rituals for *p'olha* and for *p'uglha* as not simply rituals to external deities up on the mountains, but part of the ongoing process of keeping the proper balance of forces within the household.

The essential complement to the concept of the local deities is that of the malevolent spirits. These are a constant threat to life and property, and much ritual activity is directed to protection against them, both at the level of 'folk religion' and at that of formal monastic cult.[11] These spirits are countless in name and form, and the demarcation between them and the lower ranges of the gods is blurred. The formal classification of gods and spirits is mainly of concern to the monastic scholars and the lamas who have to deal with them through ritual. The primary concern of Tibetan lay people is with protection rather than detailed knowledge.

It is for purposes of protection that it is so important to keep on good terms with the local deities. If well inclined, the local deities could protect the individual, family, or village against the malevolent spirits. The gods, however, are also capable of unleashing the spirits on someone with whom they are displeased, either through directing the spirits, who form their retinue, or simply by withholding their protection. These spirits may be conceived of as symbolic representations of disorder and of lack of balance within individual or community (see Samuel 1990).

Fürer-Haimendorf, in his account of the Sherpas, distinguishes between malevolent spirits proper, *shrindi*, and two other classes of misfortune-causing entities, *norpa* or ghosts of "men guilty of great sins" and *pem* or witches (Fürer-Haimendorf 1964:251–256). Witches (who are always women) have also been discussed by Nancy Levine, Sophie Day, and others (Levine 1982; Ortner 1978a:79; Pallis 1974; and especially Day 1989:308–384). They are an issue of some concern in Tibetan communities, and witchcraft may be divined as the cause of misfortune. Death is a major time of crisis, both in terms of protection against the spirit of the dead person and also in that there is the risk of its becoming a malevolent ghost (see Tucci 1980). Funerary ritual, however, is nowadays, as in other Buddhist societies, the preserve of the Buddhist clergy, and is carried out by the lama or by monks (see Chapter 11).

The importance given to local deities seems to vary between communities and between individuals, though some of this may reflect the differing degrees of interest in these matters among Western observers. They were undoubtedly more important in the pre-Buddhist period, when they would have been the most powerful beings in the Tibetan scale of values. By premodern times, they had become in theory totally subject to the Tantric ritual power of the lamas. Deities such as Avalokiteśvara and Tārā, who are Tantric patron deities *(yidam)* and also major objects of popular devotion, are on an altogether higher level in the scheme of things. Yet the worldly gods are certainly thought of as capable of bringing both disease and prosperity, and for lay people in particular they remained forces to be reckoned with into the modern period. They are still communicated with regularly through the various forms of spirit-mediumship discussed later in this chapter.

In this way, despite their subordinate position in relation to Buddhism, the gods still play an important part in the whole system of ideas. The Buddhist teachings repeatedly describe them as foolish, vain, and untrustworthy, as not fit objects in whom to take refuge or seek protection, as involved only with the affairs of this world and not with salvation. Yet within the context of this life, as opposed to rebirth or Enlightenment, the gods can assist one or cause one harm, and relationships with them have to be negotiated properly. In Buddhist theory, all of these gods and goddesses were overcome by Padmasambhava, who bound them to serve as protectors of the Buddhist doctrine, and many of them are called on regularly in monastic worship, as in the invocation to T'anglha cited above, to perform their protective function.

The local gods, along with the malevolent spirits, and the whole complex of ideas about divination, spirit-mediums, and good and bad fortune, are an important part of the symbolic language through which the Tibetans deal with pragmatic, this-worldly concerns. They provide a critical set of symbolic associations through which the Tibetan landscape is perceived, a landscape that retained into modern times the dangers and threats to life and property with which these deities and spirits are so closely involved. While the lamas and the Buddhist Tantric deities represent a source of superior power to the local deities, that power does not perhaps have the direct and intimate relationship with the contingencies of ordinary life that the local deities themselves have. The ultimate source of the Tantric power of the lamas lies in a rejection of those contingencies, which become mere ciphers in a transfigured universe, aspects of the scenery in the Tantric paradise.

The attention that the local gods receive in domestic ritual, and the role they played in the causation of illness and misfortune, suggests the important function that they continue to fulfill for ordinary lay Tibetans. The 'pantheon' outlined in Chapter 9 is, characteristically for the Tibetans, less a rigid hierarchy than a series of intermeshing patron-client relationships. Thus, lay villagers negotiate from a position of relative weakness with the gods, through spirit-mediums and regular offerings, and at the same time seek the patronage of the Tantric lamas, who can negotiate from a far stronger position, to keep the gods in their place.[12]

OMENS AND DIVINATION

Another set of folk-religion beliefs and practices, which concern omens *(tendrel)* and divination *(mo)*, is closely related to the beliefs about worldly deities, and is certainly also of considerable antiquity. The connection between divination and the gods becomes explicit with the spirit-mediums, who are channels for communication between gods and humans, but in practice much divination of all kinds is concerned with staying on good terms with the folk-religion deities. Later, in Chapter 21, the relationship among gods, omens, and divination in early Tibetan religion will be examined. Here our interest is in how the beliefs and practices operate in the premodern period and, to a considerable degree, continue to operate today.

A concern with omens and divination is omnipresent in Tibet, as in many non-Western cultures. All things are interconnected. This is true in the specifically Buddhist sense of the connection of cause and effect through the karmic link or *tendrel* (Skt. *pratītyasamutpāda*) and in the more general sense of the mutual correspondence of apparently disparate phenomena within a single situation, such that the skillful observer can read in the signs, also referred to as *tendrel,* whether a particular action or undertaking would be successful. It is this second, wider sense that is more relevant here, but it should be remembered that for Tibetans it is reinforced and modified by the inevitability of good or bad outcomes through the impersonal accounting of karma.

The key question is whether a particular situation is auspicious, both in general and for a particular undertaking. This quality of auspiciousness, *trashi,* can be increased in various ways, and *sang,* the burning of incense and juniper at the start of many undertakings (and often of each day) has this function as well as the purpose of addressing the local deities. At the same time, there is a close conceptual connection between the situation being auspicious and the local deities being well-inclined. The point, indeed, is not so much that there are signs in nature through which the future can be predicted, as that all actions should accord with the nature of the total situation, and the signs act as indications of that situation.

We can perhaps understand this better through an analogy with the Western and traditional views of medicine. At a generalized level, modern Western ('allopathic') medicine identifies particular syndromes (diseases, malfunctions of various organs) within the total organism and deals with them individually through standardized techniques. The assumption of replicability, basic to the scientific method, encourages the Western doctor to see a problem as a repetition of some previous problem. It should always be possible to find the appropriate remedy for a specific problem, though in a particular situation one may have to deal with more than one at once, as well as with the side-effects of the remedies used.

By contrast, in most traditional Asian medical systems, including Tibetan medicine, which derives (via India) from the Greek medical tradition, the first priority is the restoration of balance and harmony within the organism as a whole. Individual symptoms are interpreted as a consequence of the organism being out of balance. Treatment therefore depends much more on the total situation than on the individual symptom.

Similarly, for the Tibetans, the performance of the actions specific to a particular undertaking, whether the undertaking is building a *stūpa,* erecting a prayer-flag, or setting out on a trading journey, are only part of the situation, and possibly not the most important part. One needs to know whether one's proposed action is harmonious with the total situation. Such knowledge is obtained through divination *(mo),* and, if the outcome is favorable, it is generally reinforced by the burning of juniper and other incense-herbs and the recitation of prayers designed to increase the general auspiciousness of the moment. The presentation of auspicious objects, such as bowls of yoghurt *(sho)* or greeting scarves *(kat'ag)* and the erection of 'prayer-flags' (*lungta*, the term also refers to the state of an individual's 'fortune,' see Karmay 1990; Calkowski 1990) also aid in this process of influencing the flow of reality in one's favor (N. Norbu 1966: Lichter and Epstein 1983; Chophel 1983:42; Kler 1957). If the outcome is definitely indicated as unfavorable, the undertaking will be delayed until a more auspicious time, or cancelled altogether.

Kurt Schwalbe's description of how he commissioned the building of a *ch'orten* (Skt. *stūpa*, a Buddhist reliquary and shrine) at the Sherpa monastery of Serlo provides a case study of how such processes work in practice (Schwalbe 1979). The first attempt at building the *ch'orten* came to grief through a series of bad omens. When Schwalbe and some Sherpas went to cut a tree for the 'tree of life' or central pillar of the *ch'orten*, they cut a tree of the wrong kind, it was crooked, and they hurt their backs carrying it back to the monastery (Schwalbe 1979:4–6). The attempt was abandoned, and only begun again on Schwalbe's next visit to Nepal.

On this second attempt, omens were again observed in cutting the tree, in preparing the earth, and in calling the workmen. The workmen were busy, wanted high pay, and raised other difficulties. This however was not taken as a sign to abandon the whole undertaking but rather as an indication that the monastery should use its own resources rather than hire outside labor. When Schwalbe handed over a Nepali thousand-rupee note as part of his donation, the image of a *stūpa* on the note was taken as a favorable omen. At later stages, the failure of the wood for the 'tree of life' to crack although it had been left too near the fire was taken as a good omen, though its being scorched was less favorable. The spontaneous formation of thirteen rings (corresponding to the thirteen powers of the Buddha) in the clay of the main body of the shrine was also a good omen (Schwalbe 1979:37–39).

At various stages in the erection of the *ch'orten*, juniper was burned, offerings were made to local deities, and the *Trashi Gyepa*, a prayer intended "to encourage the auspicious outcome of an undertaking," was repeatedly recited (Schwalbe 1979:9).[13] The 100,000-*line Prajñāpāramitā Sūtra*, an important canonical text, was also recited in order to create further auspicious influences (1979:27). Throughout there was a mixture of checks that the situation was not dangerously inauspicious combined with actions to increase auspicious influences.

In addition to the reading of signs *(tendrel),* such as those mentioned above there are many specific techniques for divination (Nebesky-Wojkowitz 1956; Ekvall 1963, 1964b; Chime 1981). Some of these, such as those which involve counting off beads on a rosary or finger-breadths on a boot-strap, can be performed by anyone. Others, such as the use of divining-arrows or divining-dice, are the preserve of specialists, who may be laymen or lamas. Divination is one of the most common activities performed by lamas for the laity, both in the kind of cases already mentioned and also in situations such as illness or the loss of property. Some lamas are believed to have clairvoyant powers and can divine without any specific divinatory apparatus or with the help of a mirror (a technique known as *tra*). There are also laymen who can exercise clairvoyance with the aid of a mirror or other technique. Fürer-Haimendorf discusses people of this kind among the Sherpa, where they are called *mindung* (Fürer-Haimendorf 1964: 262–263).

Astrology is also a highly developed tradition in Tibet as in other Asian societies (Cornu 1990). In Tibet it combines techniques from Indian (and thus ultimately from Greek) astrology with those from China. This is again expert knowledge, associated with the monastic context and the lamas, although it is also known to some laymen. The main concern is with determining whether a given day is auspicious for a particular undertaking. There is also a tradition of geomancy, or the siting of buildings to maximize favorable influences, related to the Chinese *fêng-shui* (Trungpa 1978:303–304; Chogay Trichen 1979).

The most spectacular and best-studied mode of Tibetan divination is through the use of spirit-mediums, or 'oracle-priests' as they are often called in the Tibetanist literature (*lhapa*, *pawo*, see Nebesky-Wojkowitz 1956:398–454; Fürer-Haimendorf 1964:254–262; Ekvall 1964b:273–274; Prince Peter 1978a, 1978b, 1979; Berglie 1976, 1980, 1982, 1983, 1989; Day 1989). Although the spirit-mediums are very much part of the folk-religion complex, and there is every reason to assume that they go back to pre-Buddhist times, they are well integrated into the Buddhist religious system, and a number of them reside in monastic *gompa* and are ordained monks.

These monastic 'oracle-priests,' called by more elevated terms such as *sungma* or *ch'ökyong*, are possessed by major protective deities of the monasteries (also referred to as *sungma* and *ch'ökyong*) such as Pehar or Dorjé Shugden and are consulted by monastic and state authorities on regular occasions. The best-known and most prestigious of them is the State Oracle of Nech'ung, formerly at the small Nyingmapa monastery of that name situated near the largest Gelugpa monastery, Drepung, and relocated after 1959 in Dharamsala where the Dalai Lama now resides. It was and is consulted by the Dalai Lama and his administration. The Nech'ung oracle and its involvement in Tibetan politics has been described by several authors. It is only one of a number of such monastic oracles, some of which were also consulted by the Lhasa government (see especially Nebesky-Wojkowitz 1956:444–454; Prince Peter 1978a; Chime 1981; Rock 1935; Dargyay 1985a).

As well as the monastic oracles there are lay spirit-mediums found in villages throughout the Tibetan region. These may be men or women, though most of those described in the literature have been men.[14] Typical terms for these practitioners are *lhapa*, *lhak'a*, and *pawo*. The most detailed description of them is given by Per-Arne Berglie, who also discusses their training at length. Berglie comments that "[t]heoretically the *pawo* is independent of the lama's authority. Nevertheless, all the *pawo* thought it necessary to have a lama's blessing for their work as a *pawo*" (Berglie 1976:93). Berglie also mentions the involvement of lamas in the training of mediums, as do other authors (Fürer-Haimendorf 1964:255–256).

The mediums studied by Berglie divined by vibrating rice on a drumhead (a common Tibetan technique) as well as through possession. When in the possessed state they also healed with the aid of healing animal spirits, sucking the illness out of the patient's body. In addition, they performed the *lak'ug* ceremony for recall of the wandering *la* or spirit-essence, which is normally performed by lamas.[15] The four *pawo* Berglie studied were possessed exclusively by mountain deities or *tsen* on the occasions he witnessed; they employed a common tripartite division of the local (folk-religion) deities: the *lha* above, the *tsen* in the middle, and the *lu* beneath.

Spirit-possession is of considerable interest because of the conceptual similarity with the system of incarnate lamas or *trulku*. Incarnate lamas are frequently 'emanations' of particular *bodhisattva* (Buddhist tantric deities) and as Barbara Aziz suggests they can be regarded as having been in a sense permanently possessed by those *bodhisattva*

(Aziz 1976a). Tantric ritual also involves what could be described as a temporary 'possession' by the Tantric deity, although in Tantric theory, as I have already mentioned, one would speak rather of the deliberate and conscious assumption of the nature of that deity.

In an interesting discussion of lamas, oracles, and witches in Ladakh, Sophie Day has recently argued that a single set of imagery centering on themes of taming, converting, civilizing, rendering productive, summed up in the Tibetan term *dulwa*, underlies this entire range of phenomena (Day 1986, 1989:419–420, 426, 430–431). The lamas' role in the major Tantric ritual dance-drama, the *ch'am*, is an acting-out of the power to tame and civilize disorderly and destructive aspects of reality. Becoming an oracle involves 'taming' the god, while the witch is a representative of the disordered and unbalanced forces that Tantric ritual has to overcome.

As we will see in Chapter 11, *dulwa* also refers to the 'taming' or 'converting' of human populations through the Buddhist teachings, and refers specifically to the code of discipline (Vinaya) for monks, novices, and lay followers. It may be true that the pursuit of the Buddhist Enlightenment has no necessary connection with the local deities, but the power of Tantra, the basic technique for achieving Enlightenment, is firmly grounded for Tibetans in the relationship of Tantric lamas to precisely these local deities. Further ramifications of this relationship will become clear as the Buddhist aspects of Tibetan religion are presented in subsequent chapters.

HOUSEHOLD AND FAMILY RITUAL: BIRTH RITUALS

Perhaps the most significant area for the 'pragmatic' aspects of Tibetan religion is that of household and family ritual. Unfortunately there has been little detailed ethnography on these topics as yet for Tibetan society. Some references were given earlier to the concept of house as microcosm as displayed in the wedding rituals (on which see also Aziz 1978:168–177, 252–253; Skorupski and Cech 1984). Thubten Sangay's descriptions of Tibetan traditions of childbirth and childcare and of death rituals (1984a, 1984b) also give some idea of the interweaving of specifically Buddhist and 'folk' rituals and of the importance of omens and auspiciousness in these two critical rites of passage.

The question of death rituals will be discussed further in Chapter

11 because of their close connection with karma and rebirth. A few examples from Thubten Sangay's material on birth and early childhood will, however, help to round out this chapter (see also Skorupski and Cech 1984; Aziz 1978:251–252; Yuthok 1990:171–175):

> If a child is destined to have a good life, the parents, especially the mother, will frequently have certain auspicious dreams in the latter part of the night. . . . Generally these auspicious dreams include those of picking and eating fruit, of certain auspicious objects such as a white conch shell [several more are listed]. . . . If the child is to have little good fortune in life, the parents will have inauspicious dreams. . . . Parents who have no son may ask a spiritual master [i.e., lama] to perform certain Tantric rituals using *maṇḍala* of deities, that can bring about the conception of a boy. If they ask for a special amulet to wear, they will be able to have a son . . . (Sangay 1984a:3–4)

Norbu Chophel notes, however, that Tibetans traditionally preferred their first child to be female, both to help the mother and "because it is believed that it will ensure her parents' long life" (Chophel 1983).

> During pregnancy, the mother should avoid eating food given by those who have not kept their moral obligations, nor should she be a guest of such people. She should not wear second-hand clothes. Her food should be neither very hot nor very cold, and strong liquors, large amounts of beer and hot, spicy and sour food should be avoided. . . . It is said that if once a month the expectant mother takes a little consecrated water blessed by a spiritual master, or if she regularly receives long-life initiations, or better still, if she can receive a high Tantric initiation, it will be conducive to the child's long life and fortune . . . (Sangay 1984a:4)

Mixed with these observances are others of a more physiological nature: the mother should take strong, nourishing food, do light housework, but avoid heavy work and frequent sexual relations, and so on. "If a traveller, even a monk or nun, arrives at a house close to the time of birth, harm caused by evil spirits may later come to pass" (1984a:7). Prayers or rituals are specified to deal with this eventuality. Two rituals for an easy birth, both involving the Tantric empowerment of a piece of butter, which is then given to the mother, are described (1984a:8).

The mother should greet the new-born child with auspicious words (1984a:8–9) and it should have the mantra-syllable *dhiḥ* or *hrīḥ* drawn on its tongue with saffron water before being first given its mother's milk (1984a:9).[16] A herbal mixture boiled in the milk of a white goat brought by a girl coming from a southern direction should be fed to the child so as to give it "wisdom, intelligence, a sweet voice and a clear memory" (1984a:9).

Purifying rituals follow the birth of the child (1984a:10, see also Chopel 1983:5), and a lama should be invited "on an auspicious day" to perform a Tantric ritual to strengthen the life of the child (Sangay 1984a:11). On a favorable day, prayer-flags should be flown from the roof and offerings made to the five personal deities *(gowé lha)* and the protectors, while household members and guests eat and drink to celebrate the birth (1984a:11). A lama may also be asked to name the child, though the parents often give the name themselves (see Chophel 1983:8–9).

The child's first outing should be on an auspicious day, and is accompanied by further ritual (Sangay 1984a:11, see also Chophel 1983:7). The outing should be to the holy places of the neighborhood and the parents' personal lamas. The child's first birthday is accompanied by more prayer-flags and offerings to deities and protectors, a visit to a lama, and another party for the household (Sangay 1984a:13). Care must be taken not to upset the child's protective deities, for example by walking over its clothes, although any offence can be remedied by a simple purification ceremony (Chophel 1983:9).

This kind of mixture of folk-religious observances (burning of incense to local gods and erecting of prayer-flags) and of rituals involving the lamas, with the underlying concerns with 'auspicious' timing and with avoiding offence to local deities, is very typical of the 'pragmatic' side of Tibetan religion. We note that the lamas may have been involved to a considerable degree, but that monks and the 'clerical' side of Tibetan religion in general are noticeably absent. (As I mentioned in Chapter 2, a lama may be a monk, but is not necessarily one, and most monks are not lamas.) As in other Buddhist societies, monks are more present in the context of death than of birth and their role in this context will be discussed in the following chapter. The general area of pragmatic religion, of everyday life, is dominated, as in these examples, by the folk-religion deities and the employment of the beneficial power of the lamas.

11

The Karma Orientation, Rebirth, and Tibetan Values

The second of the three orientations introduced in Chapters 1 and 2 was the Karma Orientation. I summarized this as:

> the sphere of death and rebirth, past and future lives, seen in terms of karma and the 'ideology of merit' and mediated by Buddhist monks and lamas. This is the primary realm of 'clerical Buddhism.'

Since karma is the basis of the major Buddhist moral system oriented around the concept of virtuous and nonvirtuous actions and their consequences, I shall also include some discussion of Tibetan value systems in this chapter.

KARMA AND REBIRTH: GENERAL

Karma and rebirth are commonplaces of Buddhist thought in all Buddhist societies, in origin doubtless part of the general Indian background against which early Buddhism developed (Keyes and Daniel

1983). They are familiar from anthropological studies of Theravādin Buddhist societies (Tambiah 1968; Spiro 1971). Karma, literally 'action,' implies the effect of actions in a past life on one's present existence, and (more especially) of one's present actions on future existences within a continuing cycle of rebirth *(saṃsāra).*

Rebirth and karma, and their associated moral system, are important in Tibetan life and in the Buddhist teachings of Tibet. The initial stages of the Buddhist teachings emphasize death and rebirth strongly as motivations to practice. A standard series of four meditations is universal among Tibetan Buddhist traditions (see Tsongk'apa's text in Chapter 1):

1. Human existence is precious. Being born as a properly endowed human being with the opportunity to practice the Buddhist teachings is a rare and valuable occasion within *saṃsāra.* We should take full advantage of it, or it is not likely to recur for many thousands of rebirths.

2. Human existence is impermanent. It may end at any time, so it is urgent to practice the teachings while we have the opportunity. Nothing else will help at the time of death.

3. The action of karma is inevitable. Our present actions will affect our future, so we must be aware of the need to perform virtuous actions and avoid nonvirtuous actions.

4. *Saṃsāra* as a whole is characterized by suffering. We should aim at liberation from it, and particularly we should aim to avoid the intense suffering of the three lower kinds of rebirth (hell-beings, *preta*-spirits, and animals).[1]

The Tibetans have the same basic set of ideas about possible rebirths as other Buddhist cultures. These ideas are based on the six kinds of rebirth or realms of existence: the three lower kinds, mentioned above, and the three upper kinds, human beings, *asura* (demi-gods), and *deva* (Tib. *lha,* gods), and are visually depicted in the well-known image of the Wheel of Life, generally displayed at *gompa* entrances. Major introductory teaching texts and systems of all Tibetan Buddhist traditions, such as the 'Jewel Ornament of Liberation' (*T'arpa Rinpoch'é Gyen* = Guenther 1970) by Gampopa, the 'Oral Instruction of Lama Samantabhadra' (*Kunsang Lamé Shellung,* Khetsun Sangbo 1982;

Bruyat 1987) by Dza Peltrul, the *lamdré* teachings of the Sakyapa (Ngorchen 1987) or the *lamrim* teachings of the Gelugpa (Berzin 1972; Mullin 1978; Wayman 1978; Driessens 1990) all go through the sufferings of these various modes of rebirth in detail, with heavy emphasis on the intense suffering of the three lower realms. Tibetans are exhorted to perform virtuous actions or *södnam* (Skt. *puṇya*) and to avoid nonvirtuous action or *digpa*.

This system provides the basis of Buddhist morality, and it is essentially common property between Buddhists in Tibet and Buddhists elsewhere. In Theravādin societies, it forms the basis of what Spiro has called Kammatic Buddhism (Spiro 1971).[2] Spiro's suggestion, however, that Kammatic Buddhism takes absolute precedence in Theravādin practice over Nibbanic Buddhism is problematic even in the Theravādin context, and a similar assertion in the Tibetan case would be even less plausible. To see why, we will stay for the moment with the Buddhist teachings and then move to the area of lay life.

In formal Buddhist terms, as in Theravāda Buddhism, the pursuit of a good rebirth is a secondary aim. The ideal is to renounce *saṃsāra* as a whole, including the supposed joys of the higher rebirths, through a realization that all rebirths within *saṃsāra* are characterized by suffering. For the Tibetans, this higher ideal is not the highest motivation to be aimed at, because (1) the Tibetans are Mahāyāna Buddhists rather than 'Hinayāna'; in addition, the whole question of karma is subtly undercut both by (2) Mahāyāna philosophy and (3) by Vajrayāna (Tantric) practice. Each of these issues is worth giving some attention to here, although they will be considered further in the historical chapters of Part Three.

'HINAYĀNA' VERSUS MAHĀYĀNA MOTIVATION

Tibetan Buddhism is Mahāyāna Buddhism. In comparison with the Theravāda tradition of Southeast Asia and Sri Lanka, it emphasizes the social aspect of Enlightenment. According to the Mahāyāna, the earlier ('Hinayāna') tradition taught liberation from *saṃsāra,* but this was only part of what was needed for the attainment of complete Enlightenment or Buddhahood. The other vital ingredient was the compassionate motivation of the bodhisattva. This motivational state, *bodhicitta* in Sanskrit (Tib. *changch'ub sem*) is a key element in Mahāyāna teaching. For the Tibetans, it is associated with a set of vows that were taken by Mahāyāna followers. These vows did not replace the *prātimokṣa* vows of Buddhist ordination instituted by the Buddha Śākyamuni, in which his followers were ordained as monks *(bhikṣu)*, novices *(śramaṇera)*, lay followers *(upāsaka)*, or their female equivalents, but they do in a certain sense take precedence over them.

The Mahāyāna dismissal of the non-Mahāyāna schools as a mere 'lesser vehicle' ('Hina-yāna') lacking the essential element of compassion has a large component of sectarian propaganda. There is no doubt that the social emotions of love, compassion, etc. (the four *brahmavihāra* meditations), were cultivated in early Buddhism, and that there has been a strong conception of social responsibility in Buddhism from early days (see Ling 1973). The Theravāda, the 'Hinayāna' school that predominates in Sri Lanka and Southeast Asia, continues this tradition. Monks are involved in society in all kinds of ways, as anthropologists studying these societies have observed (see Chapter 2). The Hinayāna-Mahāyāna distinction is important less as an ethnographic description of the differences between two schools of Buddhism than as a component of how Tibetan Buddhists understood what they were doing. In particular, it goes along with a subtle relativizing of the ideal of the monastic career and of monastic discipline as the key element of the path to Buddhahood.

The new Mahāyāna view of Buddhahood was propounded in the Mahāyāna Sūtras, texts claiming to represent the word of the historical Buddha that appeared from around the first century B.C. onwards. They were held to have been kept in hiding by the spirits and revealed only when humanity was 'ready' for this more advanced teaching (see Chapter 21). These sūtras formed the basis of Buddhism in the Far Eastern societies of China, Japan, Korea, and Vietnam, though subject to much later development under indigenous influences, as indeed occurred too with the Theravādin schools of Southeast Asia and Sri Lanka.

In the present context, one significance of the Mahāyāna is that it downplays the role of *bhikṣu* (fully ordained monk), which is central to the system of virtuous action in Theravāda countries today. The *bhikṣu* in Thailand or Burma are 'fields of merit,' and offerings made to them are the prime way to gain merit. Becoming a *bhikṣu* is itself the prime example of a virtuous action, performed normatively with the intention of making merit for one's parents. For the Theravādins, monastic ordination is a *sine qua non* for serious practice. In the Mahāyāna, the status of the lay practitioner is far higher than in the Theravāda, and the difference between *bhikṣu* and layman as far as the pursuit of Enlightenment is concerned becomes considerably less important. The monastic life is worthy of great respect, but it is by no means essential, except perhaps in the final rebirth in which the practitioner actually attains Buddhahood (see Harrison 1987).

Virtuous action as defined in Hinayāna terms, that is action which would lead to good karmic consequences, is still present in the Mahāyāna texts, but it is supplemented by the new idea of the six *pāramitā* ('Perfections') or qualities that need to be developed: *dāna* (generosity), *śīla* (discipline or morality), *kṣānti* (patience or endurance), *vīrya* (energy or perseverance), *dhyāna* (meditation, here meaning primarily the development of yogic 'trance-states' or *samādhi*), and *prajñā* (wisdom or insight into the true nature of reality). Thus, the old hierarchy of virtuous action, culminating in the supremely virtuous action of becoming a *bhikṣu,* and contrasted with the supremely nonvirtuous acts of killing a holy man, one's parents, and so on, was inevitably somewhat weakened.

THE IMPACT OF MAHĀYĀNA PHILOSOPHY

At the same time, the philosophy of the Mahāyāna, discussed in more detail in Chapter 21, also tends to relativize the moral absolutes of the law of karma. If the difference between *saṃsāra* and *nirvāṇa* is illusion, and will disappear at the level of ultimate truth *(paramārthasatya),* why should virtuous action be necessary at all?

Buddhist scholars developed a number of more or less satisfactory responses to this apparent dilemma: the accumulation of virtuous actions is necessary as a basis for the attainment of transcendent insight *(prajñā).* The difference between *saṃsāra* and *nirvāṇa* may be illusory, but this does not mean that the law of karma at the level of conventional truth *(saṃvṛtisatya)* is invalidated.[3] The dilemma remained, however, and the possibility of taking the antinomian option, in which conventional morality became a mere obstacle to be left behind by the advanced practitioner, never entirely vanished.

MAHĀYĀNA AND VAJRAYĀNA (TANTRIC) PRACTICE

Tibetan Buddhism is however not just Mahāyāna but Vajrayāna (Tantric), and this leads to a third way in which the moral absolutes of karma were weakened. The Tantras were a series of further 'revelations' that took place from (perhaps) the fourth century A.D. onwards, mainly in India (see Chapter 22). While they were eventually codified in texts, the direct transmission from guru to student remains a central part of these practices. A Tantra is defined, for the Tibetans, not by the text bearing its name but by the living tradition(s) of practice relating to the central deities and symbolic forms of that Tantra. The Tibetan word for Tantra *(gyüd),* like the Sanskrit, has the literal meaning of 'thread.' The metaphorical sense is of continuity through time. *Gyüd* is closely related to the word *gyüd* (with a slightly different spelling, *brgyud* rather than *rgyud*) meaning 'lineage' or 'descent group.'

The key aspect of Tantric practice is interaction with, and in later (more 'advanced') stages, self-identification with various visualized divine forms (Tantric deities). This is combined in the 'advanced' stages with practices involving the manipulation of subtle 'energy' within the body. These are similar to Hindu yogic practices and to some Daoist practices where the corresponding energy is referred to as *qi* (Samuel 1989).

For the non-Tantric Mahāyāna Buddhists, as for the modern Theravāda, Enlightenment seems to have been a distant goal, achieved at the end of a long sequence of lives. The Tantric methods of the Vajrayāna offer the possibility of a more rapid attainment, perhaps within this present lifetime. For the Tibetans, this is an often-repeated message; Tantra is much faster than other forms of practice, and the serious Tibetan practitioner will normally undertake Vajrayāna practice (or Dzogch'en, which involves Tantric preliminaries). Tantric practice, however, is 'difficult,' and is also 'dangerous,' especially if undertaken without proper preparation or without a competent guru.

This sets up a certain tension. On the one hand, Tantra is the supreme path, and everyone should ideally pursue it so as to attain Enlightenment as soon as possible and be able to relieve the sufferings of sentient beings. In addition, Tantra provides the techniques for performing the rituals essential for the well-being of Tibetan communities. On the other hand, serious Tantric practice is dangerous and demanding, an elect path that not everyone is qualified to undertake.

In practice, this leads to a situation in which many lay people and all monastic practitioners have some knowledge of Tantra, all *gompa* regularly perform large numbers of Tantric rituals, but a much smaller number of people actually undertake serious Tantric practice. Serious practice generally involves a minimum three-year retreat for the non-Gelugpa traditions and an equivalent level of commitment for the Gelugpas, who also insist on a very thorough non-Tantric training beforehand. Only those who have undergone such serious Tantric practice are likely to be referred to by Tibetans as lamas (see Chapter 15).

Entry into Tantric practice is by a series of rites of passage, the 'empowerments' or 'consecrations' *(wang,* Skt. *abhiṣeka)* in which the student is introduced to the Tantric deities and to the *maṇḍala* or divine palace within which they reside. The deities and the *maṇḍala* form a kind of cosmic diagram to which all aspects of the universe can be related. In the early days in India, these rituals would have created small cult-groups of practitioners attached to a single guru. In Tibet, where the guru has become the lama, they still have some of this character, but they are much more widely available, and both *gompa* members and lay people may have received numerous empowerments into different cycles of deities. As part of the empowerment, the student undertakes to observe a series of vows. These 'vows' associated with Tantric practice are additional to the two sets of 'vows' (Prātimokṣa, Bodhicitta) already mentioned.

Thus, while the Theravādin practitioner is presented with a simple unilinear sequence defined by 'taking Refuge' in the Buddha, Dharma, and Saṃgha,[4] followed by the progressive vows of ordination prescribed in the Vinaya code (lay follower, novice, fully ordained monk), the Tibetan situation is much more complex and varied. The Tibetans speak of three distinct sets of 'vows' or 'commitments' *(dompa,* Skt. *saṃvara),*[5] which follow the taking of Refuge,[6]

1. The Prātimokṣa *(sot'ar)* vows, associated with the various Vinaya grades common to Hinayāna, Mahāyāna, and Vajrayāna (Tantra);

2. The Bodhicitta *(changsem)* vows, which are the defining characteristic of the Mahāyāna practitioner and a prerequisite for Tantric practice;

3. The Tantric (*sang-ngag,* literally 'secret mantra') vows involved

in receiving a Tantric empowerment and thus being entitled to perform Tantric practice.

These three sets of vows are taken in sequence, and the practitioner is expected to take Refuge and to take Prātimokṣa and Bodhicitta vows before receiving a Tantric empowerment. The Prātimokṣa vows involved may simply be those of a lay follower or *genyen* (Skt. *upāsaka*). Many of those living a celibate life in monastic *gompa* only take the vows of novice or *gets'ul* (Skt. *śramaṇera*). Thus, being a fully ordained celibate monk or *gelong* (Skt. *bhikṣu*) is not regarded by the Tibetans as essential for serious Buddhist practice in the way that it has traditionally been regarded in other Buddhist countries.[7] Given the centrality of the monk in the scheme of karma, this again amounts to an implicit weakening of the role of karma in Tibetan Buddhist society.

What is more, the status of celibate monk makes it impossible to perform the sexual practices *(t'ablam)*, which are held to be essential for the attainment of enlightenment while still alive and in a material body.[8] The situation is stated rather bluntly but accurately in an episode from the *namt'ar* or hagiography of Yut'og the Elder, the late eighth-century founding figure of the Tibetan medical tradition. The opening sections of this biography deal with Yidtr'ogma, an incarnate *ḍākinī* and distant ancestress of Yut'og who acts as Tantric consort for a succession of Indian holy men. One of them, a *ṛṣi* named Bamiba, makes love to Yidtr'ogma after becoming intoxicated by the beer she gives him:

> When he was sober again he felt great regret at what he had done but it had happened. Then he thought: 'Yet I have not lost my wisdom and shall indeed increase my knowledge of the Mahāyāna view of the state of mind which recognizes the essence of all things. The vow and instruction of the Hinayāna is a possible, dispensable, and subsidiary cause of Buddhahood; but the certain and principal cause of Buddhahood is the Third Consecration [which involves sexual intercourse]. For the basis of the Third Consecration is the *t'ablam*, the method of uniting Emptiness and Bliss.' . . . He kept her for seven days as his consort for the growing of his Bliss of Emptiness. (Rechung 1973:156–157 = Yut'og Lhundrub Trashi, *Yut'og Namt'ar* 17–18)

Not all Tibetan traditions take as positive a view of the sexual practices as the *ṛṣi* Bamiba (or rather as Yut'og's biographer), but even the

Gelugpa, who are traditional upholders of the virtues of monastic celibacy, agree on the necessity of the Third Consecration for the achievement of Enlightenment during human life (Cozort 1986:92). The historical Buddha Śākyamuni himself was provided with a female consort, the celestial courtesan Tilottamā, by the gods for this purpose (see Lessing and Wayman 1968:36–37, 36 n. 23).

There is a built-in paradox to the role of the celibate monk in Tibetan society. The aim of being a monk is to make progress towards Enlightenment, and the status of monk is supposed to facilitate that progress, yet the most powerful and effective techniques for attaining Enlightenment are not fully available to those undertaking a celibate monastic career. The paradox is only partially resolved by treating the sexual practices as dispensable (since Enlightenment could still be achieved without them in the after-death state) or as only appropriate for those of high yogic attainment.

Another aspect of Vajrayāna practice also weakens the significance of karma and monasticism. Although in Theravāda practice there is an attempt to 'balance' nonvirtuous karma with virtuous karma, in Theravādin theory nonvirtuous karma cannot be wiped out; its consequences must be endured in some future life. Tantra however offers the possibility of wiping out and eliminating even the most terrible nonvirtuous karma, and obtaining Enlightenment, within a single life. This is the point of the well-known Tibetan *namt'ar* of Milarepa, the eleventh-century poet-saint, which has been translated into several Western languages (*Milé Namt'ar* = Bacot 1925; Evans-Wentz 1969: Lhalungpa 1979; see Chapters 24 and 27). Milarepa killed several people through destructive magic in the earlier part of his career. After meeting his lama, Marpa, and enduring many severe trials, he overcame all the nonvirtuous karma and attained Enlightenment.

Tantric methods of directing the path of the consciousness at the time of death, such as the *p'owa* practices, also allow for the possibility of evading the karmic consequences of one's actions (Evans-Wentz 1967:253–276; Guenther 1963:72–74, 197–201; Mullin 1987:173–191). *P'owa* is unlikely to bring Enlightenment at the time of death except in the case of a highly trained practitioner, but there is always the hope of attaining rebirth in Dewachen, (Skt. Sukhāvatī), the paradiselike pure realm of the Buddha Amitābha, which guarantees the subsequent attainment of Enlightenment without any subsequent rebirths in lower realms. *P'owa* is quite commonly taught to lay Tibetans with the intention that they will be able to practice it at the time of death (Brauen 1985).

In addition, a sufficiently powerful Tantric lama should be able to redirect the consciousness of the dying person through his own power. A story from the life of the notorious nineteenth-century K'amba warrior, Nyarong Gompo Namgyel (also known as Amgön, see Chapter 4), is worth recounting in this connection:

> Because of the immense sins he had committed in the course of his military adventures Amgön felt that he was sure to go to hell after his death. Therefore following the subjection of a place he would search out the most reverend and pious lamas of that district and ask them where he would be reborn. In most of these cases the terrified lama would at once tell him that he would be reborn in the highest of heavens. But conscious of his sins, he kept asking the same question wherever his campaigns took him. Once when he approached the 4th Dzogch'en Rimpoch'e and inquired about his next life, the Rimpoch'e replied that if he spoke the truth Amgön would be unhappy and punish him. When Amgön promised that he would not, the Rimpoch'e said that he would go straight to the deepest hell. At once Amgön took hold of him and said that he was the only lama who uttered the truth. Taking off the strings of *si* stones from his neck—some say that the gift was a wild yak's horn filled with gold dust—and offering them to the Rimpoch'e, Amgön adamantly requested that he be prevented from descending to hell when he died. Reluctantly the Rimpoch'e promised to save him for only one lifetime, and Amgön went away satisfied. (T. Tsering 1985:207–208)

KARMA IN TIBETAN LIFE

Amgön's story illustrates the salient place of karma and rebirth in Tibetan awareness. Life involves a constant accumulation of nonvirtuous action, even for those not involved in military campaigns and mass slaughter like the dreaded Nyarong leader. A sensible person makes efforts to accumulate merit in the hope of some kind of a balance. The main modes of virtuous action are similar to those practiced in Theravādin Buddhist societies. They include giving to *gompa,* lamas, and monks; building and repairing *gompa, ch'orten, mani*-walls, and other religious objects; becoming a monk oneself; sponsoring the recitation of the scriptures; sponsoring the printing of the scriptures; and observing the lay precepts permanently or temporarily. This last, which is observed in Tantric style under the patronage of the *yidam* Avalokiteśvara, forms the *nyungné* ritual frequently practiced by lay people in Tibetan Buddhist communities (for example, Fürer-Haimendorf 1964; Ortner 1978a; Dargyay 1982). Another highly meritorious practice is that of pilgrimage, mentioned in the previous chapter.

In addition, proper behavior to one's fellow humans and other living beings counted as virtuous action. Most anthropological observers of Tibetan society have commented on the importance of *södnam* (virtuous action) as a principle regulating people's behavior in these communities. This theme was first emphasized by Fürer-Haimendorf in his pioneering work on the Sherpas (1964) and has been reiterated by subsequent writers (Gombo 1985). As several recent authors, among them Barbara Aziz, Nancy Levine, David Lichter, and Lawrence Epstein have noted, there are possible areas of conflict between socially desirable action and karmically positive action, and these will require our attention below. First, however, we will take a more detailed look at the rituals surrounding death in Tibetan society, to see how karma and rebirth interweave in this critical context with other aspects of Tibetan thought.

DEATH AND REBIRTH

Death is the most critical point of the life-cycle for anxiety about possible rebirth, and it is not surprising that, in Tibetan as in Theravādin societies, this is the area *par excellence* for the monks and the Karma Orientation. Fürer-Haimendorf has discussed this topic in the context of the Sherpa, and there have been several contributions since from other writers (for example, Brauen and Kvaerne 1978b; Ramble 1982; Skorupski 1982; Loseries 1990). As I mentioned in the last chapter, the monks are certainly more salient here than in other major rites of passage such as birth and marriage. Death is, however, by no means entirely dominated by the monks.

The account below is a summary of another of Thubten Sangay's compilations (Sangay 1984b), which provides a survey of typical procedures. While somewhat normative in character, and referring primarily to agriculturalists in central Tibet, most of the description remains living practice in Tibetan communities (see, for example, Aziz 1978:253–254; Kaplanian 1981:257–262; Mumford 1989:195–224).

In reading this account it should be remembered that in Tibetan Buddhist theory, as in China and the Far East but unlike in the Theravādin view, rebirth is not instantaneous. It takes place after a period of up to 49 days in the 'intermediate state' or *bardo*. The idea of the 'intermediate state' is not particularly Tibetan; it was the common property of several Indian Buddhist philosophical schools, and was adopted by Chinese and Far Eastern Buddhists as well. The Tibetans have, however, developed the idea in considerable detail. The experiences undergone in the *bardo* are described in several groups of texts (Lauf 1977; Lati and Hopkins 1979; Mullin 1987; Orofino 1990). Among them are the texts which have become known in the West as the 'Tibetan Book of the Dead' *(Bardo T'ödröl)*. These are liturgical texts for a Tantric ritual whose purpose is to guide the consciousness of the deceased through the after-death period (Fremantle and Trungpa 1975). Tibetan death rituals thus work on the assumption that the 49 days following death are a period when the consciousness of the deceased may be wandering through the *bardo* state in need of ritual help from the living, above all to avoid rebirth in one of the three lower realms of the hells, *preta*, or animals.

A summary of Thubten Sangay's account of Tibetan death rituals follows:

The dying person is given specially blessed pills and relics to eat and drink, and urged to meditate on his personal *yidam* and lama. After death, the body is not handled by anyone until the consciousness transference *(p'owa)* has been performed by a lama. "Transferring the consciousness is a special tantric method to prevent the deceased from being reborn in *saṃsāra* and specifically to save him from being born in any of the three lower realms, by very powerfully lifting his consciousness to a pure realm" (Sangay 1984b:31).

Emergency prayers may be offered to great lamas along with "offering scarves, money, a prayer letter, and, if possible, a statue of Buddha Śākyamuni" (Sangay 1984b:32). Monks are invited to chant prayers, and to stay with the body continuously until it is carried away. These prayers are tantric, and include a daily purification ritual to purify the deceased of his bad deeds. An astrologer is employed to determine a suitable day for disposal of the body and to determine if any additional rituals are necessary. Where the deceased person has successfully practiced Tantric meditation at the time of death, certain signs indicate that the consciousness has left the body and that the body can be disposed of (1984b:32–33). Otherwise the astrologer has to make this decision.

The corpse is washed, tied into a crouching position, and wrapped. It is tied up partly as protection in case it becomes a 'walking corpse' or *rolang* (see Wylie 1964).

On the day before the disposal of the body, butter, offering scarves, and incense are offered by friends and relatives at local temples, and money and offerings are given for prayers to be carried out by as many lamas as are felt appropriate. A sword representing "the cutting of the continuum of future rebirths or the slaying of the Lord of Death" is prepared for offering in a shrine of the Guardians. On the day when the body is disposed of, the corpse is taken from the house to the disposal site at dawn, to the accompaniment of purifying incense. "A female member of the family stood by the door behind the corpse and performed the 'Retrieving of Good Fortune' ritual with a decorated arrow and an offering scarf. Some families, however, refrained from this ritual fearing it would impoverish the deceased in his next life" (Sangay 1984b:36).[9] "Some wealthy families" might invite monks from nearby monasteries to chant "for about half an hour." The body is then cut up and fed to the vultures. (In special cases bodies may be buried, thrown in rivers, or cremated.)

The house of the deceased is cleaned and purified with incense immediately after the corpse has left. Two or three monks are hired to recite the *Eight Thousand Verse Prajñāpāramitā Sūtra* in full. On the 7th, 14th, 21st, 28th, 35th, 42nd, and 49th days after the day of death, monks are hired to perform rituals for the good rebirth of the deceased. Offerings were made to *gompa*, temples, and monks. On the 28th and 49th days, alms are also given to beggars, and other virtuous actions performed. Offerings may also be made subsequently a year after the death and in subsequent years (Sangay 1984b:40).

In contrast with the birth rituals described in Chapter 10, the monks participate extensively in this series of rituals, both as receivers of donations and as performers of (mostly Tantric) rituals themselves. As in Theravāda societies, monks are appropriate means for generating merit. As specialists in death and rebirth, they are also suitable people to remain beside the body until it is taken off for disposal. The leading role is, nevertheless, taken by the lama who performs the initial transference of consciousness, not by the monks, and lamas feature primarily suitable recipients for donations and performers of additional rituals. In cases of epidemics, in East Tibet at least, it was the *chödpa*, lay Tantric yogic practitioners, rather than the monks, who were called on to deal with the dead bodies and to perform rituals to avert further spread of the disease (Tucci 1980:92; Namkhai Norbu 1986a).

Compared to the birth and wedding ceremonies, there is relatively little here that overtly relates to the Pragmatic Orientation, though we might note touches like the 'Retrieving of Good Fortune' carried out by a woman of the household as the corpse leaves. Nevertheless, consciousness transference is important not merely for the good of the deceased but to make sure that the living are not affected by a troublesome ghost (Fürer-Haimendorf 1964).

Here Stan Mumford's comparison between the death rituals performed in Gyasumdo by Gurung shamans and by Tibetan lamas is of considerable interest. Mumford points out that the Gurung shaman's ritual is also concerned with guiding the consciousness of the deceased in the after-death state, here to the land of the dead on top of a nearby mountain, but the destiny of the deceased, in this case, depends on the proper participation of his or her surviving relatives rather than on the state of consciousness of the person who has died. The focus is on "restoring harmony through reciprocal exchanges made in all three levels of the cosmos" (Mumford 1989:223). The Tibetan lama's ritual in Gyasumdo "initially draws a boundary around each merit-making and enlightenment career" (1989:224). As it continues, however, an "alternative discourse" emerges, drawing on the "older, shamanic layer." The offerings of the *chöd* and *ts'og* rituals and the subsequent distribution of the *ts'og* offerings to the entire neighbourhood recognizes the "invisible, uninvited demons who crash the party," reawakening the matrix of relationships within which social life takes place (1989:224).

In a sense, this is only to spell out the unstated shamanic implications of all Vajrayāna ritual, which depends for its efficacy on the resolution of the conflicts within human society, and between human society and its natural environment, as symbolized by the overcoming of demonic forces and the establishment of the Tantric *maṇḍala*. To the extent that a lama is involved, these implications are present, since they are an essential part of the role of the lama seen as a whole. The main emphasis in Sangay's description is, nevertheless, on trying to secure a good rebirth for the deceased, both through specifically Tantric ritual and through the accumulation of virtuous action of various kinds on the deceased's behalf (donations to *gompa*, alms to beggars, along with further procedures not mentioned here). Death is the central context of anxiety about rebirth in Tibetan life, and it is not surprising that it is dominated by the ideology of karma. In other contexts that ideology may be more contested.

KARMA AND OTHER VALUE SYSTEMS

I have already mentioned Christoph von Fürer-Haimendorf's early writings on the Sherpas, which provided the first anthropological study of a Tibetan value system (Fürer-Haimendorf 1962, 1964, 1967). Fürer-Haimendorf portrayed Sherpa society as pervaded by a single value system deriving from the Buddhist concept of merit or virtuous action *(södnam)*. Sherpa Tibetans, like Theravādin Buddhists, attempt to maintain a surplus of virtuous over nonvirtuous actions in order to achieve a happy rebirth in subsequent lives or at least to avoid an unfortunate one.

Subsequent analyses have shown that this picture is too simple. David Lichter and Laurence Epstein (1983) note that Tibetan belief in karma coexists, as we find in other Asian Buddhist societies, with the pursuit of worldly success and happiness, often by interaction with the local gods and spirits. We have already seen some of this in the previous chapter.

If Tibetans are concerned about their personal stock of *södnam* ('merit') they are also concerned about the state of their *lungta* or this-worldly good fortune. Much of the ritual carried out by lamas (and to a lesser degree monks) for the Tibetan laity is to do with good fortune and with protection from misfortune within one's present lifetime (see Chapter 14). According to Lichter and Epstein, most Tibetans try to achieve worldly success while maintaining a "slightly ironic detachment" from a happiness that they know they cannot ultimately hold on to (1983:257).

Other writers have noted that moral action for Tibetans is not simply a matter of virtuous action according to the laws of karma. Nancy Levine wrote in relation to the question of sexual morality among the Nyinba of northwestern Nepal:

> On the one hand, one can point to a set of unvarying moral precepts, fixed in Buddhist textual traditions to which all Nyinba overtly subscribe. On the other hand, there are also implicit values which are

> manifested in actual patterns of behaviour. . . . The various cultural messages encountered—from given moral precepts, implicit societal values, inner impulses and public valuation of conduct—may well prove contradictory. (Levine 1981c:122–123)

In another article in the same volume, Barbara Aziz (1981), referring to Dingri Tibetans in particular, explains how the *ganyé* system of jural friendship, essentially concerned with proper relations within the community, provides a parallel and occasionally conflicting moral system to that of karma and virtuous action. She cites examples in which behavior that might be thought 'virtuous action' on karmic grounds (such as donations to *gompa*) is regarded by fellow-villagers as against expected standards of communal behavior. A related theme is that of the *tr'amenma*, one of several kinds of witch in Tibetan folklore. The *tr'amenma* are "usually characterized by pious women who spend all their time in prayer and other religious activities, but whose thoughts turn evil and unconsciously harm other people" (Ardussi and Epstein 1978:329). The witch, here as in many cultures, pursues her own self-interest at the expense of other members of her community.

The Buddhist tradition itself in Tibet explicitly regards the fear of an unfortunate rebirth, and the desire for happiness in future lives, as the lowest level of motivation for a Buddhist practitioner. In the eleventh-century Indian teacher Atiśa's influential work, the *Bodhipathapradīpa,* later to become the basis of the Gelugpa *lamrim* scheme, this level of motivation is to be transcended by the desire for liberation from worldly existence, which is itself to be superseded by the bodhisattva's desire to attain Buddhahood in order to relieve the sufferings of other beings (for example, Wayman 1978; Sherburne 1983; Snellgrove 1987:481–484). A bodhisattva might act if necessary in ways contrary to the normal rules for virtuous action, while a fully Enlightened being is beyond the laws of karma.

Tibetan myth and folklore are full of tricksterlike figures, whose apparently immoral acts obey a higher morality. Among the best known are Drugpa Kunleg (see Chapter 26) and the epic hero Gesar of Ling, whose activities are frequently devious and treacherous according to the rules of ordinary morality, but always legitimated by a higher spiritual purpose (Samuel, in press d). Even Ak'u Tönpa, the well-known trickster-hero of bawdy and risqué folk stories, is occasionally claimed as a Buddhist saint (Dorje 1975).

All this points to the existence within Tibetan societies of a variety of explicit and implicit sets of values. It may be assumed, too, that individuals and social groups within premodern Tibetan societies varied in the importance they give to the different strands in their moral system. Monks at large Gelugpa monastic centers, such as Sera or Drepung, would have had different emphases from Golog pastoralists, and yogic practitioners in remote hermitages would not necessarily have had the same set of values as peasants on a large premodern central Tibetan estate or rich traders in Lhasa or Shigatsé.

REPUTATION AND RESPECTABILITY

This kind of coexistence within a single setting of hierarchical, linear value systems and more informal, egalitarian value systems has been noted in societies other than in Tibet, and it is worth looking at one such analysis for the light it might throw on the Tibetan situation. Some years ago, in an anthropological study of a small English-speaking Caribbean island, Providencia, Peter Wilson distinguished between two dimensions of the indigenous value system, which he termed *reputation* and *respectability.* Reputation is a complex of judgments deriving from face-to-face interaction and personal knowledge, while respectability is about conformity to a single set of values. Respectability originates in and reflects social stratification; in Wilson's words it "holds a society together around a stratified class structure with standards of moral worth and judgment emanating from the upper class or from overseas and imposed on the lower strata" (Wilson 1973:229).

In Providencia and the Caribbean generally, respectability derives from the teachings of church and school. This is a rational, clerical system, with its ultimate origin in white European colonial society. It is based on a single, uniform scale, and essentially depends on the individual's or family's efforts to behave in 'respectable' ways (for example, formal mutual entertaining). Such behavior is expensive, so respectability is also closely correlated with the income hierarchy of the island. Members of the population can easily rate each other as higher or lower on the linear scale of respectability.

Reputation has no such absolute scale of judgment: "Reputation is a standard of value that comes out of involvement with the world of relationships rather than the individualistic standards of respectability" (1973:227). Rather than being a total judgment of where the individual stood on a linear scale, people may have reputation in any of a range of fields, and these cannot be simply ranked against each other.

> [A person] may be a good singer, a poor fisherman, a mediocre stud, a kind father, and a silly drunkard. In each field he enjoys a degree of reputation for which there is no absolute standard, and as a whole person he is neither condemned nor elevated by any one status. There is no such thing as a perfect singer, the ultimate fisherman, the supreme stud, the ideal father, or the complete drunkard. Such status scales are relative to the given time and the actual performance of people in that time and place. (Wilson 1973:227–228)

Wilson's distinction is introduced in the specific context of the Caribbean, but it may be suggested that in general, effective rationalization and centralization of a society imply something like 'respectability.' The respectability value system is both unilinear and linked to the dominance of clerical religion (in Providencia the church, with its links to the colonial regime). Such a value system is of the essence of hierarchy. It is not surprising, for example, that Louis Dumont's classic study of hierarchical thought in India emphasizes a similar unilinear scale of values imposed by the upper classes and condemning the mass of the population to a permanently low status (Dumont 1970).

This suggests a relationship of respectability with clerical forms of religion and of reputation with shamanic forms. The situation in the Caribbean is rather similar to the 'encapsulation' of shamanic religion within contemporary Theravādin societies, where practitioners of a shamanic type persist but are subordinate to a basically 'clerical' regime (see Chapter 2, and Samuel 1990:131–133). Compared with contemporary village Thailand or Burma, the disintegration of shamanic religion has doubtless gone further in the Caribbean. There are nevertheless signs of its persistence in local versions of Christianity and surviving African-derived deity cults.

In Tibetan societies, into recent times, the shamanic mode retained much more autonomy, as we have seen, since the dominant religious system, Tantric Buddhism, itself gave a large place to the shamanic. Karma and virtuous action in the Theravādin societies form the basis of a code of 'respectability' analogous to that associated with the church in Providencia. In Tibetan societies, karma and virtuous action still represent a linear scale of this type. Since many of the most conspicuous forms of virtuous action (donations to lamas and *gompa*, the building of temples, the sending of a son to the *gompa* as a monk) demand substantial economic resources, there is a correlation in Tibet, as well, between virtue and wealth (see Mumford 1989:203–204).

This 'clerical' side of Tibetan Buddhism, however, is undercut in conceptual terms by the factors considered at the start of this chapter, and it coexists in practice with other equally strong, less linear and more reputationlike systems of values. We can see that the moral basis of a shamanic religion has to be closer to reputation than respectability. There is no standard way to be a shaman and there is no single way to be a Tibetan lama either. Each person occupies the role in a partly individual and idiosyncratic manner. The lamas are valued because of their power, more than because of their conformity to an abstract sense of values. Lay Tibetans too undoubtedly judge each other in terms of reputation-type criteria as well as on a respectability scale. Levine's and Aziz's articles both witness this conflict between reputation-type judgments and the linear scale of virtuous action according to the laws of karma.[10]

Wilson's work suggests a more abstract formulation of these conflicts, in terms of a linear scale derived from a universal clerical (or we could say 'rationalized') system, and a more amorphous and socially contextual recognition of people's personal qualities. These two aspects were both very much present in premodern Tibetan societies, as might be expected given their centralized and stateless poles. The Tibetans have their own ways of representing them, and we examine these in the remainder of this chapter.

CONTRASTS WITHIN TIBETAN VALUES: WILD AND TAME

In this context, a series of concepts concerned with 'wildness' and 'taming' (or 'domestication') is worth looking at in some detail. In Chapter 10, I mentioned Sophie Day's work on the concept of 'taming' in relation to Ladakhi religion (Day 1986, 1989). The tame implies the wild, while the polarities of 'wild' and 'tame' imply a third position, occupied by the process of 'taming' and the person of the 'tamer.'

To begin with, the wild/tame opposition is important in Tibetan animal nomenclature, with the wild yak or *drong,* wild sheep or argali *(nyen)* and wild ass or onager *(kyang)* all contrasting with 'tame' counterparts and all being of significance in relation to the cult of the Tibetan local deities. We may also note that the vulture or 'wild bird' *(chagöd)* plays a central role in the disposal of the dead in Tibet, and that the Tibetan for that strange creature the 'yeti' is literally 'wild man' *(migöd).*

Turning to 'wildness' in the human context, consider Robert Ekvall's comments on the usage of the term *go* ('wild,' 'untamed,' = central Tibetan *göd*) among Amdo nomads:

> *Wo go* (son untamed), warm with the affection of family, but often part of an encouraging war cry, concisely sums up the ideal man. In a Tibetan-Tibetan dictionary *go* is defined as 'not subdued' and 'like high pasturage not domesticated.' 'Son untamed' is the criterion by which men are judged to be able, dependable, undaunted, and fit to play any role—even the ultimate one when life and death are at issue. *Awo go chö* (Hail sons untamed you) is the universal compliment, the acknowledgement one offers, in good fellowship and admiration, to praise achievement, or in simple flattery. *Wo go ma* (son untamed female) also is the best way to thank a tentwife for a bowl of yoghurt, and in response she will probably give you a second helping along with the warmest of smiles. (Ekvall 1968:92–93)

The verbal form of *go,* as Ekvall points out, means 'to laugh.' This passage from Ekvall indicates that the quality of being 'wild' ('untamed,' 'tough') is particularly associated with nomadic pastoralists in Tibet, among whom it has a strong positive value. It seems less compatible with the settled life of agriculturalists in areas such as the great estates of central Tibet, or with celibate monks in a large monastery. Nevertheless, as many Western observers have noted, a certain degree of self-reliance was, and is, characteristic of Tibetan behavior in general (both male and female). Consider David Snellgrove's comment on the small Sherpa monastic *gompa* of Jiwong:

> Perhaps what is most impressive about these people is their strong sense of personal responsibility and their wide freedom of action. The monks are all there on their own responsibility, subject only to their obedience to an older monk, if they choose to ask him to be their mas-

> ter. They meet normally every morning, take tea together, intone prayers, and separate to go about their own affairs, namely attendance on their chosen divinity [*yidam*] in their own rooms, invocation and meditation, reading, copying and in some cases composing of texts, laughing and talking together, visiting relatives and acquaintances, either on family affairs or to perform ceremonies in private houses. (Snellgrove 1957:220)

Perhaps the acme of 'wildness,' at least as far as human beings are concerned, is represented by the Gologs of east Tibet, whom we have already met in Chapter 5. We might recall the Golog speech quoted in that chapter:

> To the advice of a stranger we will not hearken, nor will we obey ought but the voice of our conscience with which each Golog enters the world. This is why we have ever been free as now, and are the slaves of none—neither Bogdokhan nor of the Dalai Lama. Our tribe is the most respected and mighty in Tibet, and we rightly look down with contempt on both Chinaman and Tibetan. (Rock 1956:127)

The 'tame' polarity, however, also has its positive valuation within Tibetan society. The career of monk, even if very much a matter of personal responsibility, in many cases, is essentially about being 'tamed.' Here I refer to ordinary monks or *trapa,* not to the lamas. The monastic disciplinary code, the Vinaya, is in Tibetan Dulwa, from the verb *dulwa,* 'to tame.' The range of meanings given for this verb in Jäschke's dictionary is worth listing and makes a clear linkage between civilizing, the adoption of agriculture, and conversion to Buddhism:

> (1) to tame, to break in [of horses]; to subdue, conquer, vanquish [of enemies]; sometimes even to kill, to annihilate; (2) to till, to cultivate, waste land; to civilize, a nation, which with the Buddhist is the same as to convert, frq.; to educate, to discipline, to punish; *dulwé rigpa,* those fit for and predestinated for conversion; *dulcha,* id. frq.; also used substantively: *drowa ngé dulcha yin,* the beings are to be converted by me; *dag ky'edki dulcha shogchig* may we become your converts! (Jäschke 1968:278)

It may be recalled that in the Tibetan origin-myth of Avalokiteśvara's monkey-emanation (Chapter 9), the various kinds of grain are among the gifts of Avalokiteśvara to his as yet untamed monkey-descendants, the proto-Tibetans (for example, Wangyal 1973:59; on monkeys, see also Paul 1982b:216). Avalokiteśvara's function through history (culminating in his activity as the successive Dalai Lamas and other high lamas) is to tame the Tibetans, and this conversion from hunting and gathering to agriculture can be seen as the initial stage of the process.

Sophie Day points to the process of constant transformation and incorporation by which the wild gradually became the tamed: "Buddhas introduced religion or civilization *(ch'ö)* into the world, a process described in Tibetan by the word *dulwa. Dulwa* means to conquer, to convert, to educate, to civilize" (Day 1986).

It is easy to find correlates for 'tame' versus 'wild' at the social level (peasants on a large central Tibetan estate versus nomadic Golog pastoralists) and at the religious level (monks in a large central Tibetan monastery versus wandering Tantric yogins). As Day implies, however, the relationship between 'tame' and 'wild' is a dynamic process rather than a static opposition, and the key element here is the business of 'taming.'

Taming is the work of the lama. This is true in two senses. The lama tames demons and hostile forces, and he also tames his disciples.

The lama's role as tamer of local deities and malevolent spiritual forces is a central part of his relationship to the Tibetan lay population, and will be examined in more detail in Chapter 14. It is here that his shamanic power is exercised on behalf of society as a whole. The classic example is that of the prototypical Tantric guru, Padmasambhava (Guru Rimpoch'e) who, as mentioned in the previous chapter, performed the original taming of the deities of Tibet and bound them to the service of the Buddhist teachings. In the Tibetan conception, this act enabled both Buddhism and civilized life to be established within Tibet. Padmasambhava's binding of the demons is reenacted on a daily basis in the course of Tibetan Tantric ritual of the Nyingmapa tradition (see Snellgrove 1957:239–242).[11] The concept is by no means restricted to the Nyingmapa tradition, however, and 'Tamer of Foes, Protector against Hostile Forces' *(dradul nyenkyong)* is a common epithet of the Dalai Lama.

The lama also has a role as tamer in relation to his disciples. For a dramatic expression of this we can turn to a religious song or *gur* by the nineteenth-century Kagyüdpa lama Trashi Öser, included in the Rumtek edition of the *Kagyüd Gurts'o:*

> *Kyema!* My only protector, lord of wisdom, compassion, and power,
> Since your wisdom is limitless, please know my hidden mind.
> Since your compassion is impartial, please do not ignore me who is full of faults.
> Since your power is strong, please break this evil being quickly.
> If you spoil me, supreme *mahāsattva*,
> Even though you lead all beings to liberation,
> You will have to go to a lot of trouble just for me, this untamed one [*ma rung*];
> From the bottom of the deepest hell,
> It will certainly be difficult to get me out; so right now, do not let your compassion be small . . .
> My physical strength wanes and I am enslaved by myself.
> By your protection and discipline [*dulkyong*], please help me regain my health.
> If you give me a warrior's weapon, the sword of *prajñā*,
> I give my word that I will certainly use it; this is not the empty talk of a hypocritical man.
> I pledge myself now to act only in this way. (Trungpa 1980:94 = *Kagyüd Gurts'o*, ka)

The 'sword of *prajñā*' wielded by the bodhisattva Mañjuśrī is a common Mahāyāna Buddhist symbol, but the language here of fighting, of struggling to subdue oneself and of appealing to the lama to subdue one, is nevertheless very striking, and points to the intimate connection that existed between taming and Buddhism, and to the extent to which the Tibetans as a people remained 'untamed.'

The figure of the lama as tamer has a certain ambiguity, or rather has, in a sense, both tame and wild versions. As will be explained in more detail in Chapter 13, the lama or guru is conceived of as 'internal' as well as 'external' to the practitioner (Guenther 1977b). The external guru is ultimately only an aid to the practitioner's subduing of his or her own undisciplined thoughts and emotions. External and internal gurus, *sūtra* and *tantra* teachings, monastic vows and lay yogic practice, settled or wandering existence, all provide dimensions along which the taming process might vary, as we shall see in the following chapters.

Taming is nevertheless one of the central themes of Tibetan Buddhist practice. It is particularly evident in the rituals of devotion to the lama and in the *ngöndro* practices undertaken as a preliminary to Tantric meditation proper (see Chapters 12 and 13). Two other common ritual sequences that can be seen as concerned with 'taming' are the *tungshag* or ritual of the Buddhas of Confession (*Shedön Chetü* 415–425; Olschak and Wangyal 1987:136–143) and the Tantric purificatory practice of Vajrasattva (Dorjé Sempa), which forms a central part of *ngöndro* and an important introductory sequence in Tantric empowerments (Beyer 1973:27, 144, 194).

Before leaving the question of the tame and the wild, we might return briefly to the unfortunate *sinmo* (demoness) who was nailed down by Songtsen Gampo's temples in an early and symbolically rather brutal assault on the wild forces of central Tibet. That *sinmo,* as I noted in Chapter 9, had a predecessor in another *sinmo,* the demoness-mother of the Tibetan people, who forced Avalokiteśvara's monkey-bodhisattva emanation to abandon his meditation and father the first Tibetans with her. She and the monkey gave contrasting characters to the first Tibetans: "[F]rom their father they are hard-working, kind, and attracted to religious activity; from their mother they are quick-tempered, passionate, prone to jealousy, and fond of play and meat" (Wangyal 1973:59).

While the preference for the father's side is clear enough in the monastic chronicles, the myth could be read as implying that Tibet needs both the wild and the tame, both the celibate, restrained monk and the wild and potentially destructive energy. The *sinmo* was, after all, an emanation of Tārā, the Tantric goddess who is said to represent the activity of the Buddha to aid sentient beings, and whose mantra Tibetans will recite in times of danger. At any rate, both sides are still there, whether the Tibetans like it or not. For all of Songtsen Gampo's spectacular nailing down of the later *sinmo,* she managed to slip free quite quickly.[12] Tantra, with its emphasis on female symbolism and on the complementarity of the two polarities provided a context where a fair degree of wildness and energy could remain, or reappear, within Tibetan Buddhism. It is to Tantra that we turn in the next chapter.

12

Tantra and the Bodhi Orientation

Tantra is vital to Tibetan religion in two ways. As we saw in Chapter 11, it provides the techniques for attainment of the highest goal offered by Tibetan religion to its followers, that of Enlightenment. It is thus the foundation of what I have called the Bodhi Orientation. However, it also provides the basis for the lamas' control over worldly deities, for their ability to strengthen the life-force through the *ts'ewang* rituals, and for other ways in which the lamas operate as shamanic practitioners for their lay clientele. These matters relate to the Pragmatic Orientation. Most literature on Tantra concentrates either on its relationship to the Bodhi Orientation or (less frequently) on its Pragmatic usage. The linkage between the two has scarcely been discussed in the literature,[1] but it is very important for understanding how Tibetan religion works in practice, and how Tantra has come to be institutionalized within Tibetan society.

This chapter is mainly concerned with the Bodhi Orientation. After introducing some basic Tantric categories and ideas, I shall discuss the deity yoga practices and the 'subtle body' practices. Further aspects of Tantra will be dealt with in Chapters 13 and 14.

TANTRA: AN INTRODUCTION

Chapter 11 introduced the historical sequence of Hinayāna, Mahāyāna, and Vajrayāna (Tantra), the three components that make up the Buddhist teachings of Tibet. In Theravādin Buddhist countries such as Sri Lanka, Burma, and Thailand, only the first of these components is present today. Both the 'theory' of Buddhism (the body of philosophical ideas used to explain the nature of Enlightenment) and the 'practice' of Buddhism (the various meditation techniques used to attain the state of Enlightenment) are held to derive from a single body of scriptures, the Sūtras *(sutta)* of the Pali Canon, believed to have originated as teachings given by the historical Buddha Śākyamuni during his lifetime. The Vinaya or monastic rule also forms part of this Buddhist canon.

For the Tibetans, the situation is more involved. The Vinaya or body of monastic rules has much the same status as in Theravādin society, although the actual Vinaya used varies in minor details from the Theravādin Vinaya since it originates in a different 'Hinayāna' school, the Sarvāstivādins. The Tibetan canon (the Kangyur), however, is much larger than the Pali Canon. As well as the Hinayāna ('Lesser Vehicle') Sūtras corresponding to those of the Pali Canon, there are also the Mahāyāna ('Great Vehicle') Sūtras, which were believed to have been entrusted by Śākyamuni to various nonhuman guardians and revealed to human beings only several centuries later when appropriate human recipients became available, and the Tantras, which were revealed at subsequent times in a similar fashion. In addition, the Tibetans regard the Tengyur, a second collection consisting of writings of Indian Buddhist scholars and teachers, as also being highly authoritative.

The relationship between this large body of texts and the theory and practice of Tibetan religion is quite complex. The Mahāyāna Sūtras, many of which are philosophically far more complex than the Hinayāna texts, form the primary source for Buddhist theory or philosophy in Tibet along with the Indian commentarial literature, and texts such as the Five Treatises of Maitreya.[2] These texts emphasize the central importance of the altruistic motivation *(bodhicitta)*, the desire to achieve Enlightenment in order to relieve the sufferings of others. Acquiring this motivational state is for the Tibetans the defining characteristic of the Mahāyāna practitioner, in contradistinction to the

'Hinayāna' practitioner, who is regarded as being primarily interested in relieving his or her own suffering.[3]

Most Buddhist practice in Tibet, however, derives not from the Sūtras, whether Hinayāna or Māhayāna, but from the Tantras, from their Indian and Tibetan commentaries, and in particular from the oral transmissions of practice associated with them, and the countless later revelations that form part of that oral transmission. Tantra *(gyüd, sang-ngag)* in the Tibetan context is a general term for a large body of religious practices, also referred to as the Vajrayāna or 'Vajra vehicle' *(dorjé t'egpa)*. This term implies that the Tantras constitute a third major class of Buddhist teachings and practices alongside those of the Hinayāna and Mahāyāna, the Lesser and Great Vehicles, well known from other Buddhist societies. The Tibetans often contrast the teachings of the Sūtras as a whole (Sūtrayāna or Pāramitāyāna) with the Tantras (Vajrayāna). Both are important but in different ways.

As I have mentioned in Chapter 11 and will explain in greater detail in Chapter 22, Tantra in India developed in a context of small cult-groups each centered around a particular set of deities and practices. While the situation in Tibet differs in many ways from that of the original Indian Tantrics, the Tibetan Tantras retain features of this original context. Thus there are a large number of named individual Tantric traditions, corresponding to texts or groups of texts in the Kangyur and Tengyur, and evidently deriving from distinct original cult-groups. Of these, perhaps about twenty to thirty are still in widespread use. Each of these Tantras is a whole body of methods of ritual, practice and behavior according to one or more lineages of successive teachers (Indian gurus, Tibetan lamas), which go back through a sequence of named individuals to revelations from the Tantric form of the Buddha.[4] Further Tantric cycles originated in Tibet through revelations *(terma)* to Tibetan lamas (see Chapter 16).

In all cases, there is great emphasis on valid lineage. The identity between the Tibetan word for Tantra, *gyüd*, and that for lineage (spiritual or genealogical) has already been pointed out. The same word, *gyüd*, is also used to translate the Sanskrit term *saṃtāna*, 'karmic continuum,' the continuity of the activity of karma within human consciousness, another term that stresses continuity through time. While there are texts associated with each Tantric lineage, and these texts take up a large part of the Kangyur, each Tantra is defined essentially by the historical continuity of practice, and the literary expression is of secondary importance.[5] Tibetans practice Tantra when they have been given empowerment *(wang)*, textual transmission *(lung)*, formal teaching *(tr'id)*, and additional advice *(men-ngag)*[6] for a particular practice, and not simply through reading the books, which are in any case difficult to make much sense of without detailed oral explanation of the terms involved.

Each of the Tibetan religious orders and suborders has several associated Tantric lineages, along with the lineages for other non-Tantric practices, and these Tantric lineages form the core of both the rituals performed in the *gompa* and temples of that order and of the personal yogic practice of followers of the order.[7] Thus the Sakyapa specialize in the Hevajra Tantra, the Nyingmapa specialize in the various so-called Old Tantras and *terma* cycles, and the most important Kagyüdpa and Gelugpa tantras are Guhyasamāja, Cakrasaṃvara and Kālacakra.

Tantric practices are quite varied. Most, though not all, Tibetan ritual is Tantric in the sense of being connected with, and making sense in terms of, one or another Tantric lineage. For example, the common Tibetan recitation of the mantra *oṃ maṇi padme hūṃ* is an explicitly Tantric practice, with its major lineage going back to the revelation received by the lama T'angtong Gyelpo in the fifteenth century (see below). At the other extreme of complexity, the elaborate masked dances staged by most of the larger Tibetan *gompa* are equally derivative from one or another Tantric cycle. Tantra may be a matter of private meditation (yoga), aimed primarily at self-development, or of public ritual performance.

In all cases, however, the core of Tantric practice is the transformation of the practitioner and of the universe of which the practitioner is part. In the words of the *Sijid:*

> The notions of external and internal, of vessel [*nöd*] and essence [*chud*],
> of physical [= *saṃsāra*] and metaphysical [= *nirvāṇa*],
> are transformed from the nature of the Five Evils into the essence of
> Wisdom,
> and oneself is absorbed into the magical play.
> The whole phenomenal world, earth, stones, mountains, rocks,
> villages, shrines and dwellings,
> are transformed into the Body of Perfect Enjoyment [*saṃbhogakāya*].
> The outer vessel of the world is transformed into a temple
> and living beings who are the inner essence,

all those who draw breath,
are transformed into the form of gods and goddesses.
The forms of gods and goddesses who are the inner essence
become the Perfect Enjoyment of primeval *bön* itself,
the ocean realm of primeval buddhahood
and all characterizable phenomenal elements exist as a magic play.
(Snellgrove 1967a:173)

The *Sijid* is here dealing with the seventh Bön vehicle (see below), the Way of Pure Sound or Vehicle of the White A *(Akar t'egpa).* The description could, however, just as well apply to Buddhist Tantra, with the exception of the reference to '*bön* itself' *(bön-nyid),* where a Buddhist text would have *ch'önyid,* corresponding to Sanskrit *dharmatā.*

A term closely associated with the Buddhist Tantras is *vajra* (the Tibetan equivalent is *dorjé*). The *vajra* was by origin the thunderbolt-scepter of the Hindu god Viṣṇu, but for Tantric Buddhists it is a symbol of the strength, immovability, and transcendent nature of the state aimed at by the Tantras. The *vajra* is symbolized by an implement of the same name that is used in Tantric ritual. As mentioned above, the teaching of the Buddhist Tantras is often referred to as Vajrayāna, the *vajra*-vehicle, and contrasted with the Sūtrayāna or Pāramitāyāna, the vehicle of the Sūtras or vehicle of the Pāramitās. I suggested in Chapter 1 that these two contrasting 'vehicles' form the basis of the 'shamanic' and 'clerical' aspects of Tibetan Buddhism respectively.

CONFLICTS BETWEEN SŪTRA AND TANTRA

While Tibetan Buddhist scholars have put much work into reconciling these two traditions of teaching and practice, there is a sense in which they are opposed and are seen to be opposed. The point is made dramatically in an episode from the life of Nāropa by the fifteenth-century Tibetan yogin Lhatsün Rinch'en Namgyel. The subject of this largely apocryphal hagiography is the Indian guru Nāropa, teacher of the Tibetan Marpa, who was Milarepa's lama and so the founder of the important Kagyüdpa tradition. Nāropa is described as having been born in a royal family and renouncing married life to pursue a standard monastic career, rising to become a famous philosopher and abbot of the university of Nālandā, the most important Buddhist academic center of India. One day, as he sat in his study, his back to the sun, studying the Sūtrayāna treatises, a shadow fell across his books. Turning around he saw a hideously ugly old woman who asked what he was doing and whether he understood the books he was reading. The woman was a *ḍākinī,* a Tantric initiatory goddess, and she made him realize that, for all his study, he did not understand the inner meaning of the texts. Nāropa renounced his post at Nālandā and went off to find his Tantric guru, Tilopa, who inflicted a whole series of trials and severe ascetic practices on him before Nāropa came to realize the 'true meaning' of the texts (Guenther 1963:24ff = Rinchen Namgyel, *Naropé Namt'ar* 361ff).

Lhatsün Rinch'en Namgyel's narrative reflects the anticlerical attitudes of his own circle of fifteenth-century Tibetan yogins (see Chapter 26), but the rejection of clerical knowledge as simply knowledge of the words, where what really matters is internalizing and realizing the meaning of the words, is a classic Indian siddha argument that found many echoes in Tibet. For the Tibetans, as for the Tantric siddhas of India, the Sūtrayāna-based curriculum of the monastic colleges can give a mastery of philosophical concepts, but it cannot give the inner experience of Enlightenment. The inner experience is, with a few exceptions, the realm of Tantra.[8]

The story of Nāropa implies that the Vajrayāna is not regarded as involving a new or different conception of Buddhahood from the Pāramitāyāna. Nāropa's books contained the true meaning, if only he could attain the inner experience that would make their words become real. The difference between Vajrayāna and Pāramitāyāna is only in the methods employed.[9] The methods of the Vajrayāna are claimed by the Tibetans to be far more effective and more rapid than the ordinary Māhayāna practices of the Pāramitāyāna. They are also believed to be far more difficult and dangerous. Their propagation among human beings was justified by the darkness of the age in which they were revealed. For the Tibetans, it is these dangerous and advanced methods that are of primary importance, and in which the lamas are specialists.

SUBDIVISIONS OF THE TANTRAS: OLD AND NEW, *KAMA* AND *TERMA*

The Tibetan tradition contains two collections of Tantric lineages and texts, one initially transmitted to Tibet in the eighth and ninth centuries and continued by the Nyingmapa order, and another transmitted mainly in the eleventh and twelfth centuries to the lamas who founded what were to become the new orders of Kagyüdpa, Sakyapa, and eventually Gelugpa. These two sets of Tantric lineages are referred to as the Old *(nyingma)* Tantras and the New *(sarma)* Tantras.

The Old Tantras are so called because they are traced back to their introduction to Tibet in the time of the eighth-century Indian Tantric guru Padmasambhava (Guru Rimpoch'e). While Sanskrit originals for some of these texts are reported to have existed in earlier periods, none have survived to modern times, and the validity of these practices has occasionally been questioned by Gelugpa scholars on these grounds (Kapstein 1989). They are practiced by all Tibetan Buddhist religious orders (including the Gelugpa who adopted them at the time of the 5th Dalai Lama), but they are particularly a specialty of the 'oldest' group, the Nyingmapa (who are named after them). The Bönpo order, the technically non-Buddhist order that claims to originate in a separate revelation from that of the historical Buddha, has a series of non-Buddhist Tantras, claiming to be translations from the Shangshung language, but again without any extant originals.

The Old Tantras were regarded by Western scholars for many years as of dubious authenticity, because of the apparent lack of Sanskrit originals for the root texts of these Tantras, and the low regard in which they were held by some Gelugpa scholars. However, as Snellgrove has recently pointed out, the root texts are characteristically Indian in style, and there is no reason not to assume a genuine Indian origin for them (Snellgrove 1987:451–460). They presumably represent a separate and perhaps regionally distinct tradition of Tantric cult-groups within India from the tradition that led to the New Tantra lineages.[10]

In later years, the original Old Tantra material was supplemented by large quantities of further 'revealed' or *terma* material. This led to an important distinction within Old Tantra practice, between lineages going back to the original transmission of the Old Tantras to Tibet *(kama)*, and those deriving from later revelations *(terma)*. This *kama/terma* distinction is a speciality of the Nyingmapa orders, although *terma* (revealed texts) are again accepted by all traditions. The Bönpo have a similar distinction, though in their case virtually all their practices fall into the *terma* category.

Terma will be discussed in greater detail in Chapter 16. They are texts that, like the Mahāyāna Sūtras and the Indian Tantras, are held to have been revealed to Buddhist practitioners, either in material form or in some other way. Buddhist *terma* texts are all regarded as having been originally written by Guru Rimpoch'e or at his instigation, and the *tertön* or finders of Buddhist *terma* are all held to be rebirths of students of Guru Rimpoch'e. The Bönpo tradition have their own *terma* and *tertön*, which may have predated those in the Buddhist orders.[11]

As will become apparent in the historical chapters of Part Three, the concept of *terma* has allowed for a vital element of continuing revelation and change within Tibetan religion. While *terma* as such are primarily a feature of the Old Tantra lineages, direct revelations from deities, usually referred to as *dagnang* (literally 'pure vision'), occur frequently in both Old and New Tantra lineages.

CLASSIFICATION OF THE NEW AND OLD TANTRAS

The Tantras were not only differentiated in terms of their origins (Old and New, *kama* and *terma*) but also in terms of their type. The Tibetans were well aware that the Tantras contained a wide range of quite heterogeneous material. What was to become the standard Tibetan classification of the New Tantras developed in the thirteenth and fourteenth centuries, and was used in the definitive version of the Tibetan scriptural canon by its editor, the fourteenth-century scholar Putön Rinch'en Druppa. This scheme divides the New Tantras into four classes, Kriyā, Caryā, Yoga, and Anuttarayoga. The division is based on the kinds of practices that the Tantra in question is predominantly concerned with, in particular the relative importance of external ritual and of internal contemplation.[12]

The highest class is the Anuttarayoga ('supreme yoga') Tantra to which the Hevajra, Guhyasamāja, Cakrasaṃvara, and Kālacakra belong. Anuttarayoga Tantras include both the Developing and Completion Stages (discussed below). While the symbolism of deities in sexual embrace is occasionally found in the lower Tantras it is a pervasive feature of the Anuttarayoga Tantras. Male and female divine figures correspond to the two primary factors of *upāya* and *prajñā* (method and insight).

For the Tibetans, the lower three classes are significant primarily for purificatory practices to be undergone prior to Anuttarayoga practice, and as a general source for rituals concerned with the 'mundane siddhis,' with this-worldly purposes, such as the increase of wealth or the destruction of enemies. The Anuttarayoga Tantras are the preeminent sources of techniques for attaining Enlightenment.

The Old Tantra tradition (carried on by the Nyingmapa) adopted a ninefold classification into nine successive vehicles *(t'egpa,* Skt. *yāna).* In practice, it is not very different from the New Tantra's fourfold system. The first three classes refer to non-Tantric teachings. The fourth, fifth, and sixth correspond to Kriyā, Caryā, and Yoga, and classes seven to nine refer to three stages of what are in New Tantra terms Anuttarayoga Tantras. Other differences include the more explicitly progressive nature of this Nyingmapa scheme, which presupposes a linear development through the stages, and the identification of the last stage with the Dzogch'en teachings, a set of non-Tantric teachings that the Nyingmapa regard as more advanced than Tantra (for example, Guenther 1972:155–209; Trungpa 1972:67–71; N. Norbu 1986a:34–36, 1990b; Tucci 1980:76–81). The Dzogch'en teachings (see below, Chapters 24 to 27) were to become a vital part of the nineteenth-century Rimed movement.

The Bönpo also classify teachings into nine vehicles or *t'egpa,* with Dzogch'en as the ninth. There are at least two versions of the Bönpo classification, neither of them identical to the Nyingmapa system (Karmay 1988a:148, 174). Both are divided into four 'causal' vehicles and five 'result' vehicles. In the version given in the *Sijid* and presented in detail by Snellgrove, the four causal vehicles refer to essentially 'folk-religion' practices (see Chapter 10), while the remaining five are the teachings for the lay follower *(genyen),* the ordained monk *(trangsong,* corresponding to Buddhist *gelong),* two levels of Tantric practice, and Dzogch'en (Snellgrove 1967a; Reynolds 1988:3; for the Bönpo Dzogch'en tradition, see Kvaerne 1983; Karmay 1988a:201–205).

I have already mentioned, in Chapter 2, another way in which the classes of Tantra are traditionally distinguished. In Kriyā Tantra the relationship between the deity and the tantric practitioner or yogin is conceived of as a master-servant relationship. The basic pattern here is close to that of ordinary devotional Hindu or Buddhist practice. In Caryā Tantra, the yogin sees the deity as an equal. The results of the practice are not favors bestowed by master to servant, but assistance from a friend. In the higher classes there is no duality between yogin and deity, although it is only in the Anuttarayoga (and the three higher classes of the Nyingmapa system) that the nonduality is fully appreciated (see Longch'en Rabjampa, *Ngelso Korsum* = Guenther 1975b, vol. 1, 158).

This helps to explain why it was the Anuttarayoga Tantras that posed a real threat to the established patterns of society, possibly in India and certainly later in Tibet. The eroticism of their symbolic language, and the real or apparent flouting of conventional morality involved in their practices, were only superficial signs of the real problem, which is that the central goal of these practices involves a transcendence of the hierarchical order and rational dominance upon which a centralized state depends. This also goes some way to explain their appeal in India at a time when hierarchical politics could no longer guarantee a peaceful and civilized society, and the weakness of the conventional solutions was becoming apparent.

In fact, at least for the Tibetans of the New Tantra traditions, the three lower Tantra classes and the Anuttarayoga practices have different aims. The three lower classes are used primarily for various magical or 'provisional' aims, such as purification, preserving health, increasing wealth or prosperity, and guarding against dangerous influences, while the Anuttarayoga Tantra is the principal technique for attaining Enlightenment.

Namkhai Norbu has suggested that Tantric practice generally in Tibet has been strongly influenced by Yoga Tantra with its emphasis on purification and its precise and formal mode of practice (N. Norbu 1986a, vol. 2, 65; 1990b:112). The *sādhana* texts found in the Tenjur are very simple and concise compared to many of those in use today. Although internal contemplation is of primary importance in Anuttarayoga Tantra, in practice these Tantras, too, are usually performed today in a highly ritualized manner. At the same time, Anuttarayoga Tantra has affected the practice of the lower Tantras. Identification with the deity, originally restricted to Anuttarayoga Tantra and perhaps Yoga Tantra, is now a common feature of ritual sequences at all levels. The importance of Anuttarayoga Tantra is evident, and we will examine it in some detail below. First, however, we shall consider the 'deity yoga' practices common to all four New Tantra classes as well as to all the Old Tantras.

DEITY YOGA IN THE TANTRAS

The central practices of Tantra are known in Sanskrit as *sādhana* (Tib. *drubt'ab*), literally 'means for attainment.' They involve the evocation of a Tantric deity *(yidam)*, usually along with his or her entourage. It is through this evocation that the process of transformation referred to earlier is accomplished. To illustrate, here is a summary of a brief and famous practice of Avalokiteśvara (Chenresig), which derives from the visionary experiences of the fifteenth-century lama T'angtong Gyelpo:

1. *Refuge and Arousing of Bodhicitta*
One recites the standard verses of refuge in the Buddha, Dharma and Saṃgha, and of the arousing of *bodhicitta*, the motivation to attain Enlightenment for the sake of all beings.

2. *The Visualization of Avalokiteśvara*
One visualizes oneself as surrounded by innumerable beings, pervading all of space. Each has a white eight-petalled lotus above his or her head. On top of the lotus is a horizontal moon-disk, and above that is a white letter *hrīḥ*. The *hrīḥ* radiates light throughout the universe, representing the power and compassion of the Buddhas. (This and the subsequent visualizations are described in the verses that one recites along with the visualization.)

Then the *hrīḥ* transforms into the brilliant white form of Avalokiteśvara, smiling compassionately and emanating light rays of the five colors of the rainbow, which relieve the sufferings of the beings of the six realms of rebirth (gods, demigods, human beings, animals, *preta*, hell-beings).

Avalokiteśvara has four hands, two joined together in prayer at his chest, the other two holding a white lotus (left) and a crystal rosary (right). He is adorned with the silk garments and precious ornaments of a Bodhisattva, and has a deer skin across his chest (symbolizing his compassion). He wears a jewelled crown with a small figure of the Buddha Amitābha on it (the head of the Lotus family to which Avalokiteśvara belongs). Behind him is a white moon-disk. He embodies the essence of all the Buddhas.

3. *Homage and Recitation of Mantra*
Maintaining the previous visualization, one recites a short verse of homage to Avalokiteśvara several times, imagining that all other beings are joining in the recitation.

The deity is moved by the entreaty and rays of light emanate from his body, purifying all impure karmic appearances and confused ideas. The external world becomes the Sukhāvatī realm, and the body, speech, and mind of all living beings, become the body, speech, and mind of Avalokiteśvara. All sights, sounds, and thoughts become inseparable from emptiness. While maintaining this visualization, one recites the six-syllable mantra of Avalokiteśvara, *oṃ maṇi padme hūṃ* many times. This recitation of the mantra is the central part of the meditation.

4. *Dissolution into Emptiness*
Then one dissolves the entire visualization into emptiness, and rests in one's own nature, without conceptualization of any kind.

5. *Conclusion and Dedication of Merit*
Emerging from the state of absorption, one sees all of reality as the *maṇḍala* of Avalokiteśvara. Oneself and all other beings have the form of Avalokiteśvara, all sounds are the six syllables of the mantra, and all thoughts are an expression of Avalokiteśvara's compassion and wisdom. One recites the verse of dedication and sharing of the merit generated through the practice: "Through this merit may I quickly become Avalokiteśvara, and then establish all beings without exception onto that level" (Gyatso 1980c:16).[13]

This is a very short and basic Tantric *sādhana,* but it contains most of the essential components, including the opening Refuge and *bodhicitta* verses (section 1), the dissolution of ordinary reality into *śūnyatā* or 'emptiness' (section 3, 4) and the final 'dedication of merit'[14] (section 5). The recitation of the mantra, here the famous six syllables of Avalokiteśvara, *oṃ maṇi padme hūṃ,* is central to the whole process, since it is this mantra that evokes the real presence of Avalokiteśvara. Tantra is often referred to in Tibetan as *sang-ngag,* 'secret mantra.' In this particular case, as with a few other very important mantras, there is an extensive literature on the significance of the mantra and its six syllables. Each syllable corresponds to one of the six Perfections *(pāramitā)* and to rebirth in a pure realm in a particular direction in the *maṇḍala;* each syllable liberates beings from a particular defilement and from the negative rebirth associated with that defilement, and so on (see Karmapa n.d.; Govinda 1969). The associations of the mantra reinforce the idea of compassion for all sentient beings, which is the essence of Avalokiteśvara, who represents the Buddha's compassion for the sufferings of sentient beings.

Longer *sādhana* may include preparatory purifications of the environment and of the practitioner, and much more elaborate visualizations of the principal deity, which also incorporate visualizations of the surrounding deities of the *maṇḍala* (section 2). They typically have far more extensive sections of praise and homage, and may include long sequences of complex visualized transformations correlated with many different mantras (corresponding to sections 3 and 4). The principal deity may be visualized as above the meditator, as here, or in front of the meditator. In most of the 'higher' Tantras, especially those of the Anuttarayoga class (see below), however, meditators visualize themselves as being the principal deity, who may be male or female.

One element that is not explicitly included in the Avalokiteśvara practice, but which is particularly important when the meditator himself or herself becomes the deity, is the duality of *samayasattva* (Tib. *damts'ig sempa*) and *jñānasattva (yeshé sempa)*, already mentioned in Chapter 9. The *samayasattva* is the initial visualization, whose force is connected with the maintenance of the vow *(samaya)* taken before the guru. The *jñānasattva* is the deity as a real aspect of Buddhahood. The *jñānasattva* is visualized as merging into the *samayasattva*, where it is 'bound' by a series of mantra syllables.

Roger Jackson sums up the basic structure of the *sādhana* as follows:

> A *sādhana*, the context in which deity yoga usually is practiced, involves, at the very least, the following elements: (1) taking as one's spiritual refuge the Buddha, Dharma and Saṃgha; (2) generation of the altruistic intention to attain enlightenment or *bodhicitta;* (3) cultivation of immeasurable love, compassion, sympathetic joy, and equanimity toward other beings; (4) reduction of one's ordinary appearance to emptiness; (5) generation of oneself in the form of the deity, pure in body, speech, and mind; (6) absorption of the actual deity or gnosis being, *(jñānasattva)*, who is called from its abode, into the imagined deity or pledge being, *(samayasattva);* (7) initiation by the deities; (8) repetition of mantras that effect the welfare of sentient beings and symbolize the deity's speech; and (9) dissolution of the divine form into emptiness—from which one usually arises again as the deity, often in simpler form. (R. Jackson 1985:23)

Where the principal deity is surrounded by the other deities of the *maṇḍala*, the visualization can become quite complex. The basic structure of the *maṇḍala* assembly consists of the central deity surrounded by four or (especially for the Nyingmapa) eight other deities, who are conceived of as aspects of, or projections from, the central *yidam*. Each deity may have a consort, and there may be several circles of such deities, with attendant figures, adding up to several hundred deities, all of whom need to be visualized precisely. The imaginative control required can be considerable: "One is said to have accomplished the generation stage of the Kalacakra when one can visualize the entire *maṇḍala* in a drop the size of a mustard seed at the tip of one's nose, with such clarity that one can see the whites of the eyes of all 722 deities—and can maintain this visualization with uninterrupted one-pointed concentration for four hours" (R. Jackson 1985:32).

In other traditions, such as the Anuyoga practices of the Old Tantra, a less detailed visualization of the deities is required, and the emphasis is rather on developing a general feeling of being the deity. The basic principle remains the same, in that practitioners learn to replace their ordinary perception of the world, during, and to some extent also outside, practice sessions, with the vision of the world transfigured on the pattern of the *maṇḍala*.

To see the entire world around one as having the nature of the *maṇḍala* is a form of 'pure vision' or *dagnang* opposed to the impure vision of ordinary life. The *maṇḍala* vision is truer and more correct than the practitioner's normal perception of reality. Everything in the external universe can be seen as an aspect of the entities within the *maṇḍala*, and there are elaborate sets of correspondences between the deities of the *maṇḍala* and aspects of external and internal reality.

As we will see, the assumption of the role of principal deity as part of the deity-yoga process has a key role to play in the lama's performance of Pragmatic rituals within the *gompa* and for his lay clientele. Within the Bodhi Orientation, however, it is only part of the Tantric process. We now turn to look at the remaining part, the subtle body or *tsalung* practices, which are taught primarily within the highest New Tantra class (Anuttarayoga Tantra) and within its Old Tantra equivalents.

ANUTTARAYOGA TANTRA AND THE SUBTLE BODY PRACTICES

Anuttarayoga Tantra practice is divided into two conceptually distinct stages, the Development and Completion Stages *(utpattikrama, sampannakrama)*, although in an actual ritual sequence *(sādhana)* elements of both stages may be included. The Development Stage or *kyedrim* resembles the lower Tantra classes in that it involves the practitioners visualizing themselves as the deity within a *maṇḍala* or ordered arrangement of surrounding deities. It is the second or Completion Stage *(dzogrim)* that is unique to the Anuttarayoga Tantras.

This stage consists of a series of transformations or operations carried out with the so-called subtle or arcane body (the Buddhist term is illusory body, Tibetan *gyulü*). This 'body' is composed of *cakra* (Tib. *k'orlo*) or psychic centers, *nāḍī* (Tib. *tsa*) or channels, and flows of psychic energy or *prāṇa* (Tib. *lung*) along these channels. It is from *nāḍī* and *prāṇa* that the most frequent Tibetan term for these practices *(tsalung)* is derived.

The basic theory of the subtle body is common to Buddhist and Hindu yogic traditions, and similar concepts are well known from China and elsewhere (Samuel 1989). *Prāṇa* is also a central concept in indigenous medical theory in Tibet, like its equivalent *qi* in China (Epstein and Topgay 1982). Nevertheless, the subtle body has been one of the hardest concepts in Buddhist and Hindu thought for Westerners to appreciate, perhaps because it implies a lack of separation between 'body' and 'mind,' which Western science and medicine has had difficulty in accepting (see Samuel 1989). The Tibetans at times speak as if the *cakra* and *nāḍī* are really physically present in the body in the form they are described by tradition, and it is difficult to square such an internal anatomy more than approximately with that known to modern medicine. The system of *cakra* and *nāḍī* doubtless has some physical correlates but it is best understood as a kind of mental model of the human nervous system as seen from the inside. Such a model is not a straightforward description but a structuring; learning the map involves learning to make sense of one's nervous system in a particular way. Different Tantras in any case specify slightly different modes of visualizing the system, which would seem to remove any need to identify the *cakra* and *nāḍī* on a one-for-one basis with entities known to Western science.[15]

With the growing acceptance of Chinese medicine in the West, and especially the work on biofeedback experiments, which demonstrate the mind-body linkage in a form accessible to Western science, the subtle body is beginning to make more sense (Comfort 1979:27, 123). The subtle body theory provides a way of understanding and so making conscious use of the states of sleep and dreaming, another point of contact with shamanic traditions.

The process of death, and the events of the 'intermediate state' or *bardo*, are also interpreted in terms of transformations of the subtle body, and one of the primary experiences of the Completion Stage is precisely the deliberate undergoing of the subtle body processes associated with dying (Lati and Hopkins 1979). This leads to the cessation of dichotomizing (conceptualizing) thought, and the arising of the Clear Light.

Here we can see a sense in which the Tantras provide a sophisticated reworking of common shamanic procedures. I have suggested elsewhere that the training of the shaman involves the acquisition of control over a series of different potentialities or modes of operation within human existence. These modes are generally described in terms of a vocabulary of spirits but the spirits may be understood as symbols for different adjustments or tunings of the mind-body-environment system. If shamans are to operate with these modes, or deal with the spirits, they have to acquire some kind of further mode or state from which they can view them and balance them within themselves and their social context. In the process, they have to transcend or go beyond the normal experience of the world taken for granted within their social and cultural context. This, I have suggested, is the meaning of the symbolic death that forms such a common part of shamanic training and initiation (Samuel 1990: 108).

We can consider the three lower Tantra classes, culminating in the deity-yoga of the Anuttarayoga Tantra Development Stage, as equivalent to the gaining of control over the world of spirits. Here the 'spirits' are replaced by Tantric *yidam* who are clearly as much within as outside the practitioner. The *yidam* is sometimes identified with the energy distribution within the *cakra* and *nāḍī*.[16] In the Completion Stage, the practitioner undergoes a direct simulation of death by mimicking the subtle body processes associated with dying. The vision of the Clear Light to which this leads may be equated with the visionary state achieved by a successful shamanic initiation (Samuel 1990: 107–109).

Thus, if the lamas fulfill a quasi-shamanic role for their lay followers (see Aziz 1976a; Paul 1976; Stablein 1976b) they are prepared for doing so by a training whose central components are strongly reminiscent of a classical shamanic training. It is not surprising that the basic structure of the Tantric *maṇḍala* resembles quadripartite and other symmetrical patternings found in traditional shamanic cultures (see Wayman 1961; Samuel 1990:90).

It seems likely that early Tantric teachers had close links with surviving 'tribal' populations in India. Some of the major Tantric pilgrimage sites in India are still close to 'tribal' groupings. At one major site (Śrīparvata, nowadays known as Śrīśailam) the local tribal population retains a special association with the pilgrimage site (Ramesan 1962); in another (Kāmarūpa) there is a tradition that the priests of the temple were formerly of tribal origin (Desani 1973:13). My argument here is however not really about the possible origins of the Tantras, which have in any case undergone a long and complex series of historical transformations in their journey from any putative original tribal context. The historical origins of the Tantras are unlikely ever to become very clear. What is evident is that Tantra in Tibetan societies provide a functional equivalent to shamanic practice and operate through a vocabulary that may be considered as a more sophisticated and rationalized version of a typical shamanic vocabulary.

THE SUBTLE BODY AND THE TANTRIC USE OF SEXUALITY

The details of the manipulations carried out with the subtle body have been summarized by Giuseppe Tucci (1980:106–109) and described more fully elsewhere (for example, Beyer 1973:127–143; Lati and Hopkins 1979; see also Kvaerne 1975). Each of the Tantras has a different terminology for describing these processes. Later Tibetan authors such as Tsongk'apa developed synthetic schemes reconciling these terminologies. Perhaps the best-known series of Completion Stage practices is that known as the Six Teachings of Nāropa. This set of practices is held to have been taught by Nāropa to his Tibetan student Marpa and passed on through the latter's disciple Milarepa to the Kagyüdpa and Gelugpa traditions of Tibet. There are several English descriptions of these practices and one of the closely related Six Yogas of Niguma.[17]

The basic practice of the Completion Stage is the bringing together of the various psychic currents within the central channel of the subtle body, a process that is held to happen naturally at the time of death. The currents are then raised up the channel and through the successive *cakra.* In many traditions, including that of Nāropa, this process is conceptualized in terms of the awakening and raising of Caṇḍālī (Tibetan *tummo*), a female deity who corresponds to the female serpent-deity Kuṇḍalinī in the Hindu Tantric system.

Some attention has recently been given to the physiological correlates of the arousal and ascent of Kuṇḍalinī, and there is little doubt that the process is a real one, with measurable psychological effects (Sannella 1981). Caṇḍālī is associated with heat, and the practices associated with her are believed to create heat. This was doubtless an impressive attribute for premodern Tibetans, and the ability of the Tantric siddhas to endure the harsh weather of the high Himalayan valleys wearing only a single cotton cloth is an appropriate demonstration of their powers.

There are several well-known stories of this kind about Milarepa, who was the principal disciple of Marpa, Nāropa's Tibetan student (for example, in the *Milé Gurbum* of Tsangnyön Heruka = Chang 1977, vol. 1, 23–37). The *repa* tradition of cotton-wearing siddhas continues into modern times in the Kagyüdpa order, which Milarepa's disciples founded, as well as in allied orders such as the Nyingmapa. These Tibetan siddhas test their ability in creating heat by drying out wet blankets (David-Neel 1971; Khandro 1988:65, 171). Recent scientific studies have detected substantial rises in body temperature in *tummo* practitioners (Benson et al. 1982).

As such exercises may suggest, siddha practice requires a sound and healthy constitution, and the internal manipulations of the prāṇa-currents in *tsalung* practice are supplemented by external physical exercises *(tr'ulk'or),* which help to maintain the *nāḍī* and *cakra* in good order.

Caṇḍālī is only one of the numerous female deities in the Tantras. While Caṇḍālī herself is not strongly personified, other female deities such as the various forms of Vajrayoginī (Dorjé Naljorma) have a vital role as initiatory goddesses. The use of sexual and erotic language is characteristic of these texts. As already mentioned, the central deity (if male) represents *upāya* and his female consort *prajñā.* Their union is the nonduality of bliss and voidness *(śūnyatā),* while the internal processes of the Completion Stage parallel those of sexual intercourse.

Sexual union with an actual physical partner (who is referred to in the Sanskrit texts as a *karmamudrā,* literally 'action seal') is employed, on occasion, as part of the Completion Stage. A Kagyüdpa version of these practices is described briefly in the *Milé Gurbum* (394–399 = Chang 1977, vol. 2, 357–360) and in somewhat more detail in the *Nāropé Namt'ar* (420vi–424v = Guenther 1963:77–78). To be performed successfully the participants have to have acquired considerable control over the energy-flows within the subtle body. In Tibetan societies today the sexual yoga practices do not seem to be widely practiced, although they are still performed, and in Tantric theory have to be performed at least once if Buddhahood is to be attained in that lifetime.

Many Tantric yogins are monks and so restricted by their vows of celibacy. The strict observance of these vows implies foregoing the attainment of Enlightenment to a future life. At best it can be attained during the intermediate state after their death, as Tsongk'apa was believed to have done (see Chapter 15). In practice, a holy and respected teacher with a large following, whether monk or noncelibate yogin, is rarely described unambiguously as achieving Enlightenment, at least in recent centuries, since this would imply that a reincarnation cannot occur. As we will see in later chapters the finding of rebirths has become an essential part of the Tibetan Buddhist system.[18]

The role of sexuality in Buddhist Tantra is thus a complex one. Partly it is analogical; the male-female polarity stands for the unity that the Tantric yogin attempts to achieve, and so provides a convenient symbolic language to aid in achieving that union. Partly, the internal processes and the accompanying transformations in consciousness involved in ordinary sexual union are homologized with the transformations that the yogin undergoes. Ultimately, these are two different ways of saying the same thing; sexuality, real or imagined, is used in the construction of the special state of being at which Tantric practice aims. The sexuality of Tantra is not there for its own sake. It is a means to an end, although it is used because it is an appropriate means (see Guenther 1963, 1969, 1975a; Bharati 1976; Govinda 1977).

An important aspect of the Buddhist Tantric conceptualization of the subtle body processes, as mentioned in the next section, is the homology constructed between the concentrating of energy within the central *nāḍī* and the arousal and concentrating of *bodhicitta*, the basic Māhayāna motivation of the *bodhisattva*. This level of symbolism is in fact more pervasive and important than that of Caṇḍālī and similar figures. Here as elsewhere both the context within which Buddhist practice is done, and the structure, content, and symbolism of the practices themselves, constantly orients the practitioners towards the central Buddhist goal of Enlightenment, whatever the immediate aim of the specific practice being performed.

BODHICITTA AND THE ETHICAL DIMENSION OF BUDDHIST TANTRA

Enlightenment is the official *raison d'être* of Vajrayāna Buddhism, and is everywhere recognized as the central and ultimate goal. This was already true in the Indian texts, and indeed serves to distinguish Buddhist Tantra from Hindu Tantra. Its most central expression perhaps is the homology within Buddhist Tantric practice that is drawn between the arousing of *bodhicitta* and the internal process of Tantric yoga (Samuel 1989). *Bodhicitta,* mentioned earlier in this chapter, is the central Māhayāna motivation, the desire to achieve Enlightenment to save all 'sentient beings' from their sufferings. In the Completion Stage of the Anuttarayoga practices, the directing of energies into the central 'channel' of the body, which in Hindu Tantra was generally conceptualized as the ascent up the spinal column of Kuṇḍalinī, the coiled serpent at the base of the spine, is equated with the awakening and ascent of *bodhicitta.*

These Completion Stage yogas are among the most subtle and difficult of Tibetan Tantric practices; however, the emphasis on the Buddhist Enlightenment as the real goal of practice pervades all Tibetan Tantric practice. We have already seen that within the *sādhana* the actual deity yoga practices are premised upon the practitioner's dissolving himself or herself into 'emptiness' or *śūnyatā,* the basic Mahāyāna Buddhist assertion of the relativity of all apparent phenomena. Other components, such as the taking of Refuge and the meditation on the four brahmavihāra, are standard Buddhist practices common to all Theravādin and Māhayāna Buddhists. All *sādhana* include the defining act of Māhayāna Buddhism, the generation of *bodhicitta,* the altruistic motivation of the bodhisattva, and end with the dedication or distribution of the 'merit' attained through the practice, another standard Māhayāna practice reinforcing the practitioner's commitment towards bringing all beings to Enlightenment. The relative emphasis given to these elements varies between particular *sādhana,* but their constant repetition as part of virtually every Tibetan Tantric ritual sequence gives them a prominent position within the total body of Tantric practice.

The Bodhi Orientation thus provides Buddhist Tantra with an inbuilt ethical parameter, which is on the whole absent from Hindu Tantra. Hindu Tantric practice today, where it is not simply part of the ritual vocabulary of Brahmin priests, carried out within the general ethical context of Brahmin activity, frequently tends to the antinomian, to the rejection of conventional morality for the higher calling of the Tantric cult-group or individual *sadhu*. While there are occasional elements of this attitude in the Tibetan context, even the most outrageous of Tibetan holy men are interpreted as working within the ethical structure of Buddhism. I shall suggest in the historical chapters (Part Three) that this ethical aspect of Buddhism was significant for its relationship to temporal power within premodern Tibetan societies.

13

The Lama and the Tantric Deities

A central aspect of all Tantric practice, Hindu or Buddhist, is the key role of the guru. In Tibet, the place of the guru is taken by the lama. The word *lama* is the standard Tibetan translation for Sanskrit *guru*. As we will see in later chapters, the lama is more than is commonly understood by the guru. The lama's role in relation to Tantra and to the Tantric deities is, however, central to his activities, and is the subject of this chapter.

Before students can perform Tantric practice they have to receive the appropriate empowerments *(wang,* Skt. *abhiṣeka)* and be formally introduced or admitted to the *maṇḍala*. The empowerment ceremony itself has the general form of a *sādhana*, since the lama has to take on the role of the Tantric deity in order to empower the disciples so that they can subsequently perform the practice and themselves identify with the deity. The empowerment involves a series of formal 'consecrations' in which the lama's power and blessing, or *chinlab* (Skt. *adhiṣṭhāna*), is transferred to the student (see, for example, Dalai Lama and Hopkins 1985; Thondup 1986: 177–181; Muses 1961).[1]

The life of Tantric practitioners in Tibet involves a series of such empowerments, in each of which they acquire the ability to practice the *sādhana* of a particular deity or assemblage of deities. These empowerments are normally accompanied by the textual transmission *(lung)* of the *sādhana* and often also by a formal teaching or explanation *(tr'id)* of the practice, in which the *sādhana* text, which is usually in verse and often quite condensed, is explained in detail.

As mentioned above, practitioners do not necessarily perform all of the practices for which they have received empowerments on a regular basis, or at all. In some contexts, for example, that of a meditation retreat, an empowerment may in fact be conferred in order that a group of students can immediately commence to practice the appropriate *sādhana*. On other occasions, as discussed later in relation to the lama as performer of public rituals, this is not the case. Some empowerments carry the obligation to perform a short version of the *sādhana* daily, but most Tibetan religious practitioners, lay or monastic, acquire far more practices than they can perform on a regular basis. In addition, many of these practices are functionally equivalent to each other, even if they relate to different deities or different traditions.

Formally, though, the student who undergoes a series of these empowerments has been admitted into a series of practices of different Tantric deities, each with its own specific attributes and potentialities. All the Anuttarayoga Tantras (the highest of the four classes of the New Tantra classification) have the same purpose, Enlightenment, although different Tantras may be suited to different practitioners. The practices of the lower Tantras (Kriyā, Caryā, and Yoga) are often more specific and differentiated in their aims. Practices to develop compassion, to aid learning, to bring about prosperity, and to preserve health and life are all part of the Tibetan ritual vocabulary.

The lamas' central role in these empowerments, where they introduce the student to the deities of the *maṇḍala* and convey their blessing, is the paradigmatic situation for their central role in all Tantric practice, and indeed in Tibetan religion as a whole. This is true whether a particular lama's status is that of a recognized rebirth or *trulku*, hereditary or personally acquired, whether the lama is the head of a large monastic community or a householder with a primarily lay or noncelibate yogin following. The key component of the lama's identity is that he or she is believed to be a master of Tantric practice. The implications of this statement will now be considered.

The Tantras, as we saw in Chapter 12, are essentially lineages of practice. In the Indian context, Tantric practice had two aspects. The first aspect concerned the specifically Buddhist goal of Enlightenment. Here the lamas (or rather gurus) and their followers formed small cult-groups centered around the practice of Tantric rituals for the achievement of Enlightenment. The key elements here were the receiving of Tantric empowerments (Skt. *abhiṣeka*) from the guru, effectively a ritual of entry into the cult group, and the performance of personal Tantric practice *(sādhana)* in order to evoke the powers of a particular Tantric deity *(iṣṭadevatā* = Tib. *yidam)* and harness them towards the attainment of Enlightenment.

This aspect of Tantric practice survives in Tibetan societies both inside and outside the monasteries, although it has been modified in various ways. Thus, membership in a cult-group has become a much less salient feature, and empowerments are frequently conveyed, more or less explicitly, because of their general beneficial effect on the recipient's spiritual life rather than because he or she is actually going to perform the appropriate *sādhana* in the immediate future. One example of this was mentioned in Chapter 10, where expectant mothers are recommended to receive high Tantric initiations because of the possible beneficial effect on their babies.

The second aspect of Indian Tantric Buddhism is the performance of Tantric ritual for purposes other than the achievement of Enlightenment. Of course, the entire activity of a Buddhist Tantric guru is in theory concerned with helping others to attain Enlightenment. Rituals to attain wealth or long life, or to destroy opponents, contribute to these ends by providing the resources to practice the Dharma, removing obstacles to practice, or saving particularly obdurate enemies of the teachings from accumulating even more evil karma.

The distinction between the two objectives for ritual practice is nevertheless explicit. It is plain from the surviving Indian Tantric texts that Indian Tantric gurus had a large repertoire of rituals concerned with this-worldly welfare, attaining health and long life, destroying enemies and evil forces, and the like. These rituals also form an important part of Tibetan practice, where they are classified into four Indian-derived subdivisions: (1) calming or pacifying, (2) increasing (wealth, long life, etc.), (3) empowering, and (4) destroying or overcoming *(shi gyé wang drag)*. Rituals of this kind form the bulk of Tibetan lamas' ritual practice for their lay followers. Some of these rituals will be discussed in Chapter 14. In the remainder of this chapter, however, we will look further at the implications of lamas as the teacher of Tantric practice to their students.

THE NATURE OF THE TANTRIC DEITIES

As a preliminary, the question of the nature of the Tantric deities requires further discussion. I pointed out in Chapter 9 that the Tantric deities are not necessarily thought of as autonomous spirit-entities who are, as it were, out there somewhere. I suggested in Chapter 12 that Tantra belongs in its essentials to the 'shamanic' pattern. This implies that the symbolic entities of the shamanic pattern are less autonomous spirit-entities than symbolic devices to activate particular modes of being or particular ways of living (see Samuel 1990).

This has consequences for understanding what Tibetan Buddhist language is saying when it speaks, as it often does, of the activity of the Tantric deities within history. We have already come across examples of this in the case of Avalokiteśvara's early incarnations as the monkey-ancestor of the Tibetans and as King Songtsen Gampo. Avalokiteśvara is not a specific deity 'out there.' While he is more present in certain people, such as the Dalai Lama, the Gyalwa Karmapa, or the Gyalwang Drugch'en, all 'emanations' of Avalokiteśvara, than in others, he is present wherever his practice is done, and to the extent that it is done successfully. We can also say that to the extent that Avalokiteśvara's practice is properly performed, the universe becomes transformed for the performers into the pure vision of Amitābha's paradise, within which everyone partakes of the nature of Avalokiteśvara. Here the brief *sādhana* given in Chapter 12 can serve as a paradigm for the intended process.

If we regard Avalokiteśvara not as a deity but as a mode of feeling, cognition, and behavior, then to say that Avalokiteśvara is present whenever his practice is done is not some kind of a poetic statement but a simple description. Clearly, though, such an Avalokiteśvara has no specific external location or existence, for all that, he may be regarded as more strongly present in particular people or places or within particular rituals. To the extent that the Tantric deity Avalokiteśvara exists, he exists because he is brought into existence through the millions of Tibetans who do Avalokiteśvara practices, develop appropriate qualities, and thus, to a certain degree, 'become' Avalokiteśvara.

Avalokiteśvara, in other words, is best seen neither as a person nor as some kind of free-floating spirit entity. He is a potentiality that can be realized within the body and mind of a particular practitioner, and thus at the same time within the whole field of Tibetan Buddhist religious activity. To say that a specific person is an emanation of Avalokiteśvara implies that such a person epitomizes the qualities of Avalokiteśvara or, better, serves as a channel through which the mode of being symbolized by Avalokiteśvara can be active within society. Similarly for the many lamas who are regarded as emanations of Mañjuśrī, the bodhisattva of scholarship.

Of course, the nature of Tantric deities is not understood in the same way by all Tibetans, or even all lamas. However, the picture presented above is not simply a kind of Lamaist gloss on the more straightforward views of lay people. Even major deities such as Avalokiteśvara, Guru Rimpoch'e, or Tārā, who are well known to all lay people, are not treated as the objects of a devotional cult in the way that, for example, Kṛṣṇa or Śiva are in India. Even for lay people, the central aspect of the cult of Avalokiteśvara is the repetition of his mantra, not (for example) the making of offerings to his image, or the recitation of prayers to him to intervene in their lives. That repetition, undoubtedly the most common single religious act in Tibetan societies, is explained in terms of developing the compassionate qualities of Avalokiteśvara, directing that compassion towards the suffering beings of the six realms, not towards worshipping an external deity Avalokiteśvara.

In practice, it is scarcely possible to reduce Tibetan statements about the activities of Tantric deities to any consistent doctrine of divine intervention in human affairs. A good example is the relationship of the fourteenth-century lama Tsongk'apa, founder of the Gelugpa order, to Mañjuśrī, the *bodhisattva* of scholarship and transcendent insight (see Chapter 26). Tsongk'apa came to be regarded as an emanation of Mañjuśrī, and is depicted today with the sword and book of Mañjuśrī on lotuses on either side to symbolize his status. Several well-known texts by Tsongk'apa are however addressed to Mañjuśrī, and he is described in biographical accounts as having a series of crucial revelations from Mañjuśrī during his lifetime. These revelations formed the basis of the specific philosophical perspective of the Gelugpa school (for example, Kaschewsky 1971; Thurman 1982, 1984).

If Tsongk'apa was an emanation of Mañjuśrī, could he pray to

Mañjuśrī, have visions of Mañjuśrī, and receive teachings from Mañjuśrī? The contemporary Gelugpa lama Geshé Ngawang Dhargyey commented that Tsongk'apa's two leading disciples, K'edrubje and Gyalts'abje, saw him on one occasion in the form of Mañjuśrī. After Ts'ongk'apa's death, K'edrubje had a famous series of visions of Ts'ongk'apa, in one of which he appeared in the form of Mañjuśrī. However, the Geshé went on to explain, these two lamas were themselves emanations of other deities.[2] If they were themselves emanations of deities, we might imagine that they would have already been aware of Tsongk'apa's identity with Mañjuśrī before they 'saw' him as the deity.

The stories could be reconciled by assuming that Ts'ongk'apa, K'edrubje, and Gyalts'abje were in fact all deities and were consciously putting on a performance of having visions, seeing each other in divine form, and so on, for the benefit of their nondivine spectators. Such a line of argument is quite Tibetan. In the biography of a high incarnate lama the subject may be described in childhood as 'pretending to study' since such a highly developed being has no need of study, but acts as if he did so to inspire others to study. This is a mode of speaking, however, and too much emphasis should not be placed upon it. Tibetans are fully aware that their lamas are human beings as well as emanations and reincarnations.[3]

It is plain that Geshé Ngawang Dhargyey did not feel it necessary to present a single consistent story of the relationship between Ts'ongk'apa and the deity. This was certainly not a lack in logic, since like all Gelugpa *geshé* he had undergone a very extensive and rigorous training in logical reasoning. The point is rather that, at the ultimate level, all of these appearances are partial and delusory. The multiplicity of possible explanations, at different levels of truth or insight, is a characteristic feature of Tibetan Buddhism and it is nowhere more in evidence than in the complex question of the real nature of the lama, as we shall see below. Elements of several different theories of the nature and activity of Tantric deities can be found in Tibetan statements. They can be best treated not by trying to force them into a single consistent model but by understanding the contexts within which each of them is made.

In this particular case, it is mainly a consequence of attempting to tie down into ordinary language a mode of discourse whose real reference is to processes that transcend particular individuals. If Mañjuśrī is taken as a symbol for the mode of thinking, feeling, and acting represented by Buddhist philosophy of the Madhayamaka school, then it makes sense to say both that Ts'ongk'apa invoked Mañjuśrī and that, for his contemporaries and for later generations, he *was* Mañjuśrī.

The function of the Tantric deity is an issue of particular significance when we turn to the lama as teacher. The student is expected to see his or her personal lama as the Buddha. The lama as transmitter of the practices is explicitly to be seen as the Buddha's Tantric form of Vajradhara (Dorjé Ch'ang). To receive the full blessing and empowerment it is important that the student see the lama as the Tantric deity, who was in turn an emanation of Vajradhara, just as he or she has to visualize himself or herself as the Tantric deity. The Tibetans however take this line of reasoning well beyond the specific context of receiving a Tantric empowerment, which brings us to the topic of devotion to the guru in general, and the practice of guruyoga *(lamé naljor)* in particular.

GURU DEVOTION AND GURUYOGA

The importance of the guru (=lama) is emphasized over and over again in Tibetan Buddhist texts and oral instruction. A collection of Kadampa teachings includes the following anecdote about the Indian guru Atiśa, founder of the Kadampa order (predecessor of Tsongk'apa's Gelugpa order):

> When Atiśa arrived in Tibet, his three disciples Ku, Ngoke and Drom asked him, 'For attaining the high state of liberation and omniscience, which is more important, to follow the precept of the Lama or to follow the scriptures and commentaries?'
>
> Atiśa replied, 'The precept of the Lama is more important than scriptures and commentaries.'
>
> 'Why is that?' they asked.
>
> 'Even if you know that the primary characteristic of all phenomena is Voidness, and can recite the Tripitaka as well, you and the teaching will be completely separate if you do not apply the precept of the Lama at the time of practice.' (Wangyal 1973:121)

Thus the student has to see his or her lama as taking precedence over the teachings themselves. The student's attitude to the lama is a major topic of most Tibetan systematic presentations of the *sūtra* teachings, such as the Gelugpa *lamrim* literature. The qualities of the ideal teacher are extensively described in the texts (Obermiller 1932–1933, vol. 1, 62–76; Guenther 1970:33–34; Berzin 1972:30–32). A verse from the *Sūtrālaṃkara* gives the classical description of these qualities:

> Rely upon the spiritual friend [Skt. *kalyāṇamitra*, Tib. *geshé*] who is well-disciplined, self-controlled [in meditation] and able to calm [all passions], endowed with special knowledge, energetic [in teaching] and rich in [his knowledge of] the scriptures, having insight into *śūnyatā*, who is skillful in speech, compassionate in nature, and never tired or discouraged in teaching. (Obermiller 1932–1933, vol. 1, 63; Berzin 1972:30)[4]

A similar description is given in a Nyingmapa *terma* text from the seventeenth-century *Könch'ög Chindü* cycle discovered by Rigdzin Jat-s'ön Nyingpo (1585–1656):

> The qualities of an authentic Guru are many,
> But, in essence he should have mastered the Sutras and Tantras, together with their Pith-Instructions;
> He should have a thorough experience of the practice of meditation;
> he should be expert in the methods appropriate to the natures of others;
> he should have vast wisdom permeated by compassion;
> and with his great faith he should have perfected the supreme Dharma;
> If you rely on such a Guru he will, like the Precious Jewel,
> fulfil all your wishes and accomplish all your aspirations. (Anon 1989:15)

It is not enough for the lama to have the impressive lists of qualifications given in the texts. For a true lama-student relationship to be set up, it is held that there usually has to be present some connection between the two, as the karmic consequence of actions in a previous lifetime. Normally this results from one having helped or taught the other in a former life. To set up a valid relationship with a lama without any such basis is very difficult.

Conversely, once the relationship has been properly established, if the disciple fulfills all that is expected, he or she can be certain to meet the lama again in future lives. Thus the teacher-student relationship between the Panch'en Rimpoch'es and the Dalai Lamas, which goes back historically to the time of the 5th Dalai Lama, although for the Tibetans its origins were earlier again, is ideally renewed with each successive reincarnation of the two lamas, so that the 1st Panch'en taught the 5th Dalai, who taught the 2d Panch'en, who taught the 6th Dalai, and so on.[5] Such recurring teacher-student relationships are characteristic of other Tibetan religious orders, too.

Another well-known story recounts how when Marpa first went to India in the company of a friend, Nyö Lotsawa, he suggested that they both go to see Nāropa, the teacher who was to become Marpa's guru. Nyö wasn't interested. As far as he was concerned his own teacher was the only lama he needed. When Marpa met Nāropa, Nāropa asked after his friend, and seeing him by psychic power told Marpa that there was no karmic connection between Nyö and himself.[6]

The Gelugpa *lamrim* teachings expound at length how it is important to see all lamas, and in particular one's personal 'root lama' or *tsawé lama* as the Buddha, more specifically as the Buddha's Tantric form, Vajradhara. This applies especially to the lama who gives one Tantric teachings.

A second story relating to Nāropa and Marpa makes the point very graphically. I quote again from Lhatsün Rinch'en Namgyel's *Naropé Namt'ar:*

> Nearly two months later when he [Marpa] had received the symbolic initiations and instructions in the Oral Transmission, Nāropa appeared to him in the sky in the shape of the [Tantric] deity Hevajra with eight goddesses, and asked him whether he made obeisance to him or to the tutelary deity. Marpa answered, 'To the tutelary deity.' Nāropa said:
>
> There where there is no Guru
> Not even the name of Buddha is heard.
> The Buddhas of a thousand aeons
> Depend on the Guru for their appearance.
>
> 'The fact is that they are His manifestations.' The tutelary deity then disappeared in the Guru Nāropa who declared: 'Because of this your interpretation, your human line will not last long. Yet it is of an auspicious nature for sentient beings. Be happy that the line of the Dharma will continue as long as the Buddhist teaching lasts.'[7]

'Guru' here corresponds to 'lama' in the Tibetan text. Marpa's human line was indeed not to last long, and his teachings were carried on not by his son, who died while Marpa was still alive, but by his disciples, above all Milarepa.

This doctrine of the 'Vajradhara nature' of all lamas is summarized in a Gelugpa *lamrim* text by the First Panch'en Rimpoch'e (1569–1662):

> The Supremely Enlightened One has said in his precious Tantras and Sūtras that in this degenerate age the Lord Vajradhara manifests himself in the form of spiritual friends and acts for the good of sentient beings. Accordingly, our spiritual friends, apart from merely exhibiting different aspects of being, are the manifestations of the Lord Vajradhara in order to attract us who have the bad fortune of being unable to perceive Buddhahood directly. (Guenther 1977b:188–189)

Vajradhara (Dorjé Ch'ang in Tibetan) is sometimes used as a title after the name of incarnate lamas, as a reference to this 'Vajradhara doctrine' (Berzin 1972:10, n. 1).

The ideal attitude to the lama is thus one of warm positive affect, in fact of quasi-filial devotion. The guru-student relationship is frequently homologized with that of father and child, and seen as a kind of spiritual equivalent of the father-child relationship. As Barbara Aziz has pointed out, Tibetan lay people's attitude to their personal spiritual teachers does indeed often have this kind of positive feeling, both affectionate and devotional (Aziz 1978:223ff). Tibetans are encouraged to feel the link to the guru as much more real and immediate than the tie to the Buddha. Along with two or three major Tantric deities, Avalokiteśvara, Tārā, and Guru Rimpoch'e (who is himself, as his name suggests, a guru as much as a Tantric deity), the living lama is the chief object of devotion in Tibetan religious practice.

THE LAMA AS AN OBJECT OF *SĀDHANA*

The symbolic expression of this situation occurs in the *sādhana* or personal Tantric practice, where the Tantric deity may be explicitly homologized with the lama. Thus in a *sādhana* where the deity is visualized in front of or above the practitioner (i.e., rather than identical with the practitioner), this visualization may be combined with that of the root lama. The practitioner imagines that his or her personal lama, in the form of the Tantric deity, is at the center of the visualization. Such a combined lama-deity is generally evoked at the start of a *sādhana* as the center of an assembly of gods, Buddhas, *yidam,* past Indian gurus and Tibetan lamas, books of the Dharma, etc., representing the Three Jewels in whom the Refuge is taken. All of these are to be seen as emanations from or aspects of one's own personal lama. The practitioner has access to them only through his grace and kindness.

The actual refuge formulae used by the Tibetans are frequently much more complex than the simple thrice-repeated refuge in Buddha, Dharma, and Saṃgha of the Theravādin and Far Eastern schools of Buddhism, and they normally include specific reference to the lama. Thus in a typical *ngöndro* or Tantric preliminary text the student is instructed to recite the refuge verses in front of a 'Refuge Tree,' a vast visualized assembly of gods, lamas, and teachers, with the personal lama at the center in the form of Vajradhara, Guru Rimpoch'e, Ts'ongk'apa, or some other deity or lama:

> The Lama-Vajradhara is visualized on a throne above sun, moon and a lotus rising out of an ocean of ambrosia. Above him are the lamas of the Māhamudrā lineage, Tilopa, Nāropa, Marpa, and so on. All around him are the teachers of all schools of Buddhism of India and Tibet. In front are the tutelary deities of the Old and New Tantras. To the right are Śākyamuni and the Buddhas of the Three Times and Ten Directions. Behind are the 100,000-Verse Prajñāpāramitā Sūtra surrounded by all the books of the Dharma. To the left is Avalokiteśvara surrounded by all the Saṃgha. The hero-spirits *(pawo)* of Padmasambhava's paradise, the *ḍākinī,* the guardians of the Dharma and the gods of prosperity fill up the intermediate space. All look upon the meditator with pleasure. (K'amtrul Rimpoch'e, *Drugpé Ngöndro,* summarized from ff. 3b–4a)

Thus the visualization represents all these forms as being manifestations of the root lama *(tsawé lama)* himself, who is identical with Vajradhara (Dorjé Ch'ang).

It is in front of this visualization that the meditator takes Refuge and performs prostrations, visualizing that his or her father and mother and the six types of beings (gods, *asura* or demigods, humans, animals, *preta* or hungry ghosts, hell-beings) are also taking refuge and prostrating:

> (I along with) all sentient beings, my mothers (since all have at some time in beginningless *saṃsāra* been the meditator's mother) equal to the sky (in number) go for refuge to the Buddha-Dharmakāya of the Lama.
> (I along with) all sentient beings, my mothers, equal to the sky, go for refuge to the perfect Saṃbhogakāya of the Lama.
> (I along with) all sentient beings, my mothers, equal to the sky, go for refuge to the compassionate Nirmāṇakāya of the Lama.
> (I along with) all sentient beings, my mothers, equal to the sky, go for refuge to the precious Lama-Buddha. (*Drugpé Ngöndro*, f. 4a)

This is followed by an elaborate series of offerings to the visualized guru. As always in Tibetan practice, it should be noted that these sequences end with the visualization being dissolved back into the lama and the lama into the meditator: "The offering-field and the surrounding figures merge into the all-pervading lama. The lama radiates light and becomes one with me. The offerings, the offerer and the receiver of offerings are the same; I offer this offering of self-liberated great joy" (*Drugpé Ngöndro*, f. 13b).

Much of the personal ritual activity of Tibetan practitioners, particularly in the earlier stages of Tantric practice, consists of these elaborate *sādhana* directed to the lama. They seem to be a primarily Tibetan development, although there are some Indian precedents (see Klinger 1980).

THE LAMA AS A TRANSFORMATIONAL DEVICE

If the lama has to be seen as a Tantric deity, where does that leave the human beings who occupy the role of a lama? Certainly it gives them a very high status, but it also weakens in a sense the identification between them and the lama role. The ultimate lama is not physically identifiable with the human being who is giving the teachings.

In other words, seeing the lama as a Tantric deity implies, as with any Tantric deity, that the external status of the lama, and indeed the whole guru-disciple link, is only provisional in nature. It is part of the world of relative truth or conventional reality *(saṃvṛtisatya)*. At the ultimate level *(paramārthasatya)* there can be no separation between guru and disciple. The duality between them, like the other dichotomies of Tantric practice (wisdom and means, *samayasattva* and *jñānasattva*, etc.) is ultimately to be overcome and transcended (Guenther 1977b:178–195).

How much emphasis is placed on the devotion of one human being to another, how much on its ultimate transcendence, varies, as always within Tibetan Buddhism, between traditions and between contexts within a particular tradition.

The lama is a form of the Buddha, yet Buddhahood *(tathāgatagarbha)* is present in all men and women, indeed in all living things and all phenomena, as Gampopa, Milarepa's scholar-disciple, emphasizes in the first chapter of his *Jewel Ornament* (*Dagpö T'argyen*, Guenther 1970:2–3). All are manifestations of Buddhahood. Thus, when students regard their personal teacher as the Buddha, they are projecting onto someone outside themselves something which is essentially within themselves also (Guenther 1977b: 188). Through learning to perceive another being, the lama, in his true (i.e., Enlightened) nature, they may gradually come to realize this same true nature within everyone and especially within themselves. As part of that realization, the dichotomy between external lama and student, like other dichotomies, will fall away and be transcended.

At this point, the lama is no longer outside. He or she has become, as it were, the student's own better self. The lama in this sense is merely a symbolic device, used for the purpose of the transformation. This is the essence of the distinction between 'lama' *(guru)* and the ordinary terms for teacher *(gegen, lobpön)*, spiritual teacher *(geshé* = Skt. *kalyāṇamitra)* or Tantric teacher *(dorjé lobpön* = Skt. *vajrācarya)*, which refer unambiguously to the external teacher.

'Lama' is frequently used in this ordinary, external sense, in contexts where it may be substituted by one or other of these terms; however in the context of the union of lama and Tantric deity in a *sādhana* the term used is always 'lama' (= Skt. guru). In these *guruyoga* rituals, students visualize the lama outside themselves in the form of Vajradhara or another Tantric deity, and then visualize that the lama becomes one with them. These meditational procedures make little sense unless an underlying process of the kind described above, where the lama is ultimately a device for the student's self-transformation, is assumed. They are rituals in which the student attempts to perceive the Buddha-nature within through first visualizing it outside, a procedure which is indeed basic to all the Tantric rituals aimed at Enlightenment.

The lamas as real human beings, however, are also central actors within the Tibetan religious system, not only as teachers of Tantric practice to their students but as performers of rituals for the lay population. We have already seen a little of these activities in Chapter 10. We now turn to consider them in more detail.

14

Tantra and the Pragmatic Orientation

In Chapters 12 and 13, we viewed Tantra primarily in terms of the Bodhi Orientation. In this context, Tantra is the system of yogic processes that are held to lead to the central goal of Buddhism, the state of Buddhahood. The lama functions both as the student's actual personal Tantric teacher, and also as a kind of symbolic device leading to the attainment of Enlightenment. However, Tantra is also a vital part of the Pragmatic Orientation (see Chapters 9 and 10) where it provides the set of techniques through which lamas carry out rituals for the lay population. Many of these rituals have only a nominal connection with the cult of Enlightenment. Nevertheless the lama's role in relation to the Bodhi Orientation is still present, implicitly and often explicitly too, in the background.

Tantra links together these two apparently different contexts. As the teachers of the Tantric practices, the lamas are also the performers *par excellence* of Tantric ritual, and Tantric ritual provides the magical technology through which the people of Tibet attempt to exert control over the circumstances of their lives and deaths. Consequently, lamas

(Tantric gurus) are the most appropriate and valued performers of these rituals.

This does not mean that all significant rituals are performed by lamas, even when domestic rituals carried out by members of the household are left out of account. The lama is the preferred performer for major rituals, but there are many rituals carried out by less important practitioners. A distinction can be made here between those areas where the celibate-monk pattern dominates and those where lay ritual specialists (*serky'im*, etc.) are more important (see Chapter 17). In both cases, however, a small number of high-status lamas, whether hereditary, reincarnate *(trulku)*, or appointed, are responsible for certain major rituals.

The ritual practice of the lamas includes many different kinds of rituals. Despite an enormous variety in terms of form and degree of elaboration, the basic structure of almost all of them is the same, in that it involves the lama performing a *sādhana* in which he takes on the identity of a major Tantric deity and then employs the powers of that deity for the desired ends. I shall examine two types of major ritual in some detail, the life-empowerment ceremony or *ts'ewang*, and the ritual dances *(ch'am)*. In the conclusion to the chapter, I shall also discuss some rituals relating to the *la* or life-essence.

The *ch'am* or ritual dances are in essence an elaborate version of regular temple rituals in which Tantric power is summoned and directed to the destruction of malevolent spirits. Both *ts'ewang* and *ch'am* are performed annually as part of the ritual cycle in many areas, and the performance is attended by the local lay population, one of the few occasions where Tantric rituals are performed for a mass lay audience.

MASS EMPOWERMENTS AND LIFE EMPOWERMENT RITUALS *(TS'EWANG)*

Tantric meditation, as I pointed out in Chapters 12 and 13, requires the lama to first give an empowerment or initiation *(wang, wangkur)* into the particular Tantric cycle concerned. While rituals of this kind are primarily designed for those who are intending to perform the meditation subsequently, they are frequently attended by large numbers of lay followers. Such attendance is meritorious in itself, and is believed to plant karmic 'seeds' that may ripen in a future life when the practice can be actually undertaken. It is also, however, felt to confer power or blessing, *chinlab*, on the assembled congregation.

Thus, when Serkong Rimpoch'e, a respected Gelugpa lama and assistant tutor to the Dalai Lama, gave the empowerment of Hayagrīva to a group of monks from one of the colleges of Sera monastic *gompa* during my stay in Dalhousie in 1971, several hundred lay Tibetans also attended. It was rumored that the empowerment carried protection against the cholera then prevalent in north India. On several recent occasions when His Holiness the 14th Dalai Lama has given large-scale empowerments of the Kālacakra Tantra, a practice popularized in the 1920s by the then Panch'en Rimpoch'e, up to 100,000 Tibetans and other Buddhists are reported to have attended.

Clearly, all of these individuals are unlikely to become serious practitioners of the complex and difficult Kālacakra yogic practices, at any rate in their present lives. They would be unable to do this anyway without further detailed instruction, and, in fact, the Kālacakra empowerment as given on these large-scale occasions only empowers those in attendance to do part of the Kālacakra Development Stage *(kyedrim)* practices (see Dalai Lama and Hopkins 1985; Dhargyey 1985; Sopa et al. 1985). Such empowerments are often seen as 'sowing seeds' within the karmic continuum *(saṃtāna)* of those who come that will 'ripen' in a future lifetime when they will actually have the opportunity to pursue the practice in full.[1] Attendance at such an occasion is certainly a meritorious act in karmic terms. Many people, however, attend because of the incidental blessing *(chinlab)* involved. In other words, attendance gives access to some of the power that the lama channels.

Lamas have been known to dismiss the desires of their lay followers for empowerments (and teachings in general) as a nuisance and as a distraction from the lama's own serious spiritual pursuits (see Snellgrove 1967b, vol. 1, 111–113). In practice, however, they are frequently asked to perform such empowerments, and they regularly consent to do so. A special class of rituals, the life-empowerment or life-consecration rituals *(ts'ewang)*, is specifically devoted to the general conferral of blessings and empowerment to the recipient with the aim of conferring good health and long life, and these will now be considered in a little more detail.

Ts'ewang are often given at the end of a series of standard Tantric empowerments, to preserve the health of the students for future practice. They are also, more significantly in the present context, regularly given as part of major seasonal festivals in Tibetan communities. Here they act as a general conferral of benefits on the lay people who attend (see Snellgrove 1961; Paul 1979).

Descriptions of these *ts'ewang* rituals are available in a variety of sources (see in particular Beyer 1973:375–398; Snellgrove 1961). These empowerments use the standard methods of Buddhist Tantric practice. The officiating lama transforms himself into the appropriate Tantric deity and then transfers his power into consecrated pills and liquids that the members of the congregation eat and drink. In the context of a meditation retreat, these practices focus on the teaching of a specific *sādhana* for one of the long-life deities, such as White Tārā or Amitāyus,[2] but in contexts such as the annual fifth-month ceremony at Shey in Dolpo, described by Snellgrove (1961:141–145) the emphasis is much more on the immediate transfer of blessing.

Ironically, probably the best-known *ts'ewang* in the anthropological literature, that performed as part of the Mani Rimdu festival at Tengboche and at other Sherpa monasteries (Fürer-Haimendorf 1964; Jerstad 1969), is not, from the lamas' point of view, a *ts'ewang* at all, but a *torma*-empowerment. The empowerment of pills is the central part of the Mani Rimdu ceremony, and in fact gives the ceremony its name (= '*mani*-pill practice'); however, the two most senior lamas involved with performing these rituals in Sherpa country at present (see Chapter 17), Tr'ulshig Rimpoch'e and Tengboche Rimpoch'e, both maintain that the ritual is not a *ts'ewang*.[3] The deity involved, a special form of Avalokiteśvara known as Pema Garwang ('Lotus Lord of the Dance'), is not specifically associated with long life, and the empowered pills are intended to bring about spiritual effects primarily and long life and health only secondarily. The emphasis on the curative powers of the pills is what comes through in Fürer-Haimendorf's ethnography and other popular accounts, however (see Kite and Childs 1988:24: Zangbu and Klatzel 1988:36–38), and it is not surprising if lay Sherpas regularly refer to the ritual as a *ts'ewang* (see also Draper in press).

The giving of consecrated liquids and foods suggested a similarity with the Christian Eucharist to early observers, and L. Austine Waddell argued that the *ts'ewang* probably originated in Nestorian Christianity (Waddell 1967:444–448). The likeness is, however, more apparent than real. The consecration of liquids is a regular component of all Tibetan Tantric empowerments, and the empowerment of medicinal pills is also a standard ritual procedure (Dhonden 1986:214–218). The eating of food consecrated through having been offered to the gods is standard procedure in Indian religion, while the Tantric priests *(pedanda)* of Bali empower water through rituals very similar in form to those of Tibetan lamas, if simpler in detail. The Balinese *pedanda* takes on the identity either of Śiva (for a Hindu priest) or of a Buddhist Tantric deity (for a Buddhist; Korn 1960; Hooykaas 1966, 1973a, 1973b).

Several different Tantric deities are associated with and employed in these rituals. In Snellgrove's Nyingmapa ritual the central figure is Amitāyus, the principal long-life deity. Amitāyus is a form of Amitābha, and so is closely related to Guru Rimpoch'e, the central figure in most Nyingmapa Tantric lineages, who is regarded as an emanation of Amitābha. Beyer's description is centered around the goddess White Tārā, another important long-life deity who is herself considered an emanation of Amitāyus.

Human life is important, in Buddhist theory, because it is the essential basis for the attainment of Buddhahood, and this motivation is emphasized in *ts'ewang* rituals. One should wish to gain long life and health so as to be able to practice the teachings with the proper Mahāyāna motivation of desiring to gain Enlightenment so as to relieve the sufferings of others. The basic idea behind the ritual, however, is that the lama uses his Tantric powers to confer long life and health upon those receiving the empowerment. As with many other Tibetan rituals the process may be interpreted at any of a number of levels, and the participants are free to take the ritual at whichever level they wish.

In the *ts'ewang* ritual described by Beyer, the officiating lama first prepares himself in private. After the usual preliminaries of going for Refuge and arousing the *bodhicitta* motivation within himself, he assumes the identity of White Tārā, and makes offerings and recites praises to her (that is, to the goddess in his own person). Then he generates the goddess outside himself in a *torma* or offering cake. All these stages, and those that follow, involve appropriate mantras, *mudrā* (hand-gestures), and recitations.

The assembled followers then visualize the lama, who has now entered the room where the empowerment is to take place, as White Tārā. They perform the rice-*maṇḍala (mendel)* offering to him as a 'fee' for the life-empowerment, requesting that he perform the ceremony.[4] They are told to visualize the *torma* as well as the lama in the form of White Tārā, surrounded by lamas, Buddhas, Tantric deities and so on, and to imagine themselves as in her divine mansion. Next they repeat the refuge and *bodhicitta* verses and visualize that they themselves have the form of White Tārā.

The scattered life-essence is recalled into the form of White Tārā, and then radiated in the form of a 'stream of nectar' into the bodies of the congregation. Similar streams of nectar restore their degenerated life, renew their weakened strength and merit, and repair their broken vows and pledges. All this forms a preparation for their own assumption of the identity of White Tārā, which is the center of the ritual.

This involves visualizing the deity over their heads, and all the other deities as merging into her, and then imagining a second form of Tārā as separating off from her form and merging into them. At this point the *torma* is placed on the head of each of the recipients of the empowerment. The lama recites a prayer to the lamas of his own lineage, requesting each to join in the empowerment, and visualizes the deity dissolving into each of the participants.

Finally the lama empowers the 'nectar of life,' made from milk mixed with sugar, and the 'pills of life,' made from herbs and potions, mixed with the relics of departed lamas, and gives them to the congregation. The ceremony ends with verses of good fortune for the increasing of life, and with the disciples offering up another rice-*maṇḍala* in thanksgiving for the empowerment (Beyer 1973:373–398).

In the Nyingmapa ritual described by Snellgrove, more of the emphasis seems to be on the actual empowerment of the objects. These are water, spirit, and pellets of cooked flour, which correspond respectively to the empowerment of body, speech and mind. Snellgrove comments that the "conventional consecrations" that precede the distribution of the life-giving substance were of "little interest" to the villagers in Dolpo (where he witnessed the ritual) and that the Buddhist technical terms involved were "all but meaningless" to them (Snellgrove 1961:142–143). Beyer also observes that the congregation cannot be expected to have any skill in carrying out the visualizations or in performing the re-creation of reality that goes along with them. It is essentially upon the attainments of the lama conducting the ceremony that its success depends (Beyer 1973:398, 389–390).

Snellgrove suggests that the 'life' *(lats'é)* being restored is closely related to the *la* or life-essence discussed in Chapter 10 and to concepts such as the Gurung *pla* (Mumford 1989), Tamang *bla* (Holmberg

1989:154), or, from a Theravādin Buddhist society, the Northeast Thai *khwan* (Tambiah 1970:57–79: Heinze 1982). As we see in the following quotation from the ritual text used at Shey, the *lats'é* may have "wandered, strayed or disappeared" like any of these other wandering life-essences. The ritual draws it back and strengthens it:

> O you whose supernal life [*lats'é*] has wandered, strayed or disappeared! The pure essence of the four elements of earth and water, fire and air, the happiness and splendour of living things who dwell in the threefold expanse of the threefold world, the whole essence derived from the compassionate grace of the ocean of buddhas of past, present and future, all this is compounded as nectar in the form of light rays of various colours. It seeps through the pores of your bodies and vanishes into the centre of the heart, which is identical with the syllable *hrīḥ*, the pure force of Wisdom itself; thus the well-being of your supernal life will be restored and you will gain the perfection of deathlessness. Passing into the living items *(ts'edzé)* that lie before us, they become the great adamantine essence. Even thus must we concentrate our thought! (Snellgrove 1961:143–144)

There are similarities between the *ts'ewang* and the Northeast Thai soul-strengthening *(sukhwan)* ritual, though the differences are also illustrative. The Northeast Thai ritual involves the invoking of the *thewada* (i.e., *deva*, here the gods of the heavens rather than local gods and spirits) who are asked to assist in summoning the *khwan* into a ritual structure called the *phakhwan*. The *khwan* is then transferred to the person or people for whom the ritual is being performed, and 'tied' into the body with a white cord. The ritual's purpose is to create happiness, good fortune, and prosperity, and it is performed at life-crises such as pregnancy, marriage, ordination as a monk, or reintegration into society after a long journey, a period in prison, or recovery from an illness. The ritual is performed by a lay elder, one of whose names *(pahm* = Skt. *brahman)* derives from the Hindu Brahman priest, but while the elder is likely to have been a Buddhist monk, like all respected senior village men, this is relevant primarily in that it will have provided him with the literacy needed to read the chants (see Tambiah 1968:107–112).

A closer analogy in Thai society is the sacralizing of amulets by particularly holy monks, as described in Tambiah's *Buddhist Saints of the Forest*. This is precisely the kind of activity that Tambiah was led to describe as 'tantric' in that book (see Chapter 2). In Tibetan societies, there is no doubt that the lama's ritual is intended to have a pragmatic function, or at least is taken by the lay people for whom it is performed as primarily pragmatic in orientation.

The life-giving power of the lama is transmitted on other occasions beside these major life-empowerment rituals. Lay Tibetans visiting a lama may request or be given pills empowered in previous rituals, amulets, small clay images, relics, and other consecrated objects, which conveyed something of the lama's power and blessing. These may be carried around in the *gau*, the metal amulet-case that many Tibetans wear and which can, as Ekvall observes, be taken off and used as a miniature shrine to which circumambulation and prostration may be performed (Ekvall 1964b).

Many of the amulets and devices contained within the *gau* are concerned with what is in a sense the converse of the lama's ability to strengthen the life-essence of his followers. They are protective devices against the various hostile and malevolent spirits that have already been described (in Chapter 9) as present throughout the environment in the folk-religion view of the world. For the lama's power can also be turned to protective use, and if necessary to destruction.

THE LAMA AND MALEVOLENT SPIRITS

In the major rituals concerned with defense against these spirits, the lama's destructive power comes to the fore. There are several modes of operation against these evil forces (Tucci 1980:171ff; Cantwell 1985). In the mode I shall discuss here they are destroyed in the form of an effigy. This effigy or *lingam* is made out of dough, or occasionally wax or paper. The evil spirits are made to enter it, and are then magically destroyed within it. The dead bodies of the malevolent spirits are offered to the deities of the *maṇḍala*,[5] while their consciousness is sent to rebirth in the heaven of Guru Rimpoch'e.

This whole process forms a climactic sequence in, for example, the *ts'og* (literally 'multitudes') ritual discussed by Beyer, versions of which are performed frequently by all *gompa* communities (Beyer 1973:312–318). Beyer's ritual falls into two parts. In the first, ordinary *torma* (offering-cakes) are offered to the deities of the *maṇḍala*. In the second, the 'bodies' of the destroyed spirits in the *lingam* are offered to the deities. In this particular version of the ritual, the *lingam* is visualized as superimposed upon another set of *torma* rather than represented directly.

The creation of the *maṇḍala* of deities, and the offering to it of the destroyed spirits, forms the basic structure of the ritual dances or *ch'am* as well, and we now turn to these most spectacular ritual performances of the large Tibetan monastic *gompa*. These dances are performed once or twice annually by most major monasteries of all the religious orders, although they are generally based on Old Tantra (Nyingmapa) texts, and have been described many times.[6] Ritual dances are occasionally performed by lay practitioners, but the large-scale performances are all monastic.

The principal dancers in the *ch'am* represent the central figures of the *maṇḍala*, such as the eight manifestations of Guru Rimpoch'e, or the set of eight Dragshed deities, who are also characteristically Nyingmapa.

A large number of additional dances may represent various local deities, *ḍākinī*, or short comic interludes, but are secondary to the main theme.[7] The officiant dances in the form of a black-hat priest or *shanag*, although, as Stein notes, the principal lama, rather than actually dancing this role, normally performs the ceremony in duplicate, parallel to its enactment in the dance (Stein 1972a:190). Local deities are frequently included as protectors, although they are secondary to the various Indian-derived guardians such as the various forms of Gompo (Mahākāla). In the Thami and Chiwong *ch'am*, Sharlung Genyen Chenpo, the local protective deity of Dzarong *gompa*, from which the dance tradition derives, is represented in the dances (Kohn 1988:304–308). In the Tengboche *ch'am*, he has been replaced by Surra Rakye, the protector of the nearby hidden valley of K'embalung (Kohn 1988:307; Zangbu and Klatzel 1988:39–40; Kite and Childs 1988:38).

Often the black-hat priest is identified, at least in popular interpretations, with Pelgyi Dorjé, the Buddhist monk in disguise who killed Langdarma, the ninth-century persecutor of Buddhism and last king of the early Tibetan state, giving the dance an additional level of meaning as a commemoration of this act.[8]

In an article on *ch'am* some years ago, P. H. Pott outlined a third and more sophisticated level of interpretation (Pott 1965). The gradual domination of the groups of dancers by the central performer, in preparation for the destruction of the malevolent spirits in the *lingam*, represents the progressive bringing under control of different aspects of the personality on the path to Enlightenment, while the destruction of the *lingam* itself is the destruction of the ego. This is equivalent to viewing the demons and evil spirits as obstacles to one's own attainment of Enlightenment, which is ultimately how they have to be viewed, since they, like everything else, have no real external existence.

Like many aspects of Tibetan religion, the dances can be taken at a variety of levels. Pott's interpretation may be over-sophisticated for many of the lay Tibetans who watch these dances, but experienced Tantric yogins would find such a mode of approach obvious enough. The late K'amtr'ul Rimpoch'e of Trashi Jong, a Drugpa Kagyüdpa lama who was himself a noted ritual dancer, proposed a similar interpretation in a guide for Western viewers of the dances:

> What is characteristic of esoteric methods [i.e., Tantra] is that while these things which should be abandoned (the emotions of cupidity, malevolence and bewilderment, the five poisons, i.e., pride, lust, anger, jealousy and ignorance) are to be regarded as inimical to spiritual development, they are in their ultimate nature identical with the five forms of transcending awareness. In practice these worldly emotions can be used as devices in realizing the Ultimate.
>
> In the dances you will see, you will find deities, gods and goddesses, peaceful and wrathful. These represent both vicious emotions that run rampant in one's psyche and the manifold illusions of Ultimate Awareness. The adornments and gestures represent the qualities that we normally (but incorrectly) attribute to our illusions. Try to see all as projections of your own psyche. (Khamtrul n.d.:2)

CONCLUSION

The two major types of ritual considered above demonstrate two principal modes of functioning of the lama in relation to the laity, both of them concerned primarily with the Pragmatic Orientation. In the *wang* and *ts'ewang*, positive spiritual energy *(chinlab)* is conveyed from the lamas to their followers. In the *ts'og* and *ch'am*, malevolent demonic forces are suppressed through the power of the Buddha and the Tantric deities.

Despite their foundations in the Buddhist Tantras and the Bodhi Orientation, these rituals are similar in basic concept to rituals carried out by non-Buddhist shamanic practitioners in many Asian societies. We have already noticed that the *ch'am* deals with the local deities and spirits by incorporating the more important ones as protectors and destroying the remainder through the power of Tantric ritual, while the *ts'ewang* strengthens the same life-force (*la* and its equivalents) with which many Himalayan and Southeast Asian religions are concerned. In another set of rituals dealing with the *la*, the *lak'ug*, *lalu*, and similar rituals designed to draw back the *la* into the body, the similarity to non-Buddhist rituals is quite striking. These rituals are performed by lamas in response to specific cases of illness, just as they would be performed by non-Buddhist shamanic practitioners (Tucci 1980:190–192; Mumford 1989:168–179; Karmay 1987). In Mumford's study of the Gurung, we can see the Gurung shaman and the Tibetan lama in competition for the same ritual ground.

The *lalu* ritual described by Mumford involves the 'luring' back of the soul and also the offering of a ransom-substitute or *lu* to the demon who has taken it. Mumford notes that the *lalu* as performed in Gyasumdo is more generalized and stereotyped than the equivalent ritual of the Gurung shaman, and has lost the latter ritual's detailed grounding in the social relationships of the village and the geography of its environment. The same might be said of the two rituals of this type, one Buddhist and one Bönpo, discussed by Samten Karmay (1987). The summoning of the *la* is nevertheless a ritual that could be performed by a shaman; as we noted in Chapter 10, the *lak'ug* ritual, which has the same function, is actually performed by some Tibetan *pawo* spirit-mediums. The lama may claim superiority on the grounds that his ritual draws its power from the Tantric *yidam* rather than from the local deities, but the job being performed is essentially the same as that carried out by the *pawo* or by the Gurung shaman with the aid of the local deities. The *ts'ewang* is another matter, and can only be performed by a lama, since the whole point is the strengthening of the life-energy by the lama transformed as a Tantric long-life *yidam* such as Amitāyus or White Tārā, although even there the Northeast Thai *pahm* brings about similar ends by invoking the *thewada*.

Through all these pragmatically oriented rituals, the lama turns his spiritual powers to the this-worldly benefit of his followers, even while what he does can be interpreted in a more sophisticated manner as relating to the path to Enlightenment. The lama in these rituals can be seen as obtaining for his followers precisely that worldly happiness which, as they progress along the path, they are taught to regard as deceptive and worthless.

As always, the paradox can be resolved in Buddhist terms through the doctrine of *upāyakauśalya* or 'skillful means.' Life and good health are a necessary basis for practicing the teachings at all, and people attending the ritual for Pragmatic purposes are nevertheless exposed to the teachings and to the transformative effect of the ritual itself, and may be drawn onwards into the Bodhi Orientation as a consequence.

To see the rituals purely in terms of a this-worldly versus otherworldly contrast is itself, perhaps, too 'clerical' an approach. The rituals need to be considered within the 'shamanic' world-view, which was sketched in Chapters 9 and 10. The participants do not necessarily expect any specific this-worldly benefits from participation at the rituals. What is at issue is more the restoration of a general state of well-being, harmony, and balance in the order of the universe. In bringing this about, the lama is performing an essentially shamanic role, while the state of harmony and balance involved, as K'amtrul Rimpoch'e's comments remind us, is also open to interpretation in terms of the general Buddhist goal of Enlightenment.

15

Lamas, Monks, and Yogins

Chapters 9 to 14 have introduced three areas of Tibetan religion, the folk religion, Sūtra, and Tantra, and shown how they correspond to the Pragmatic, Karma, and Bodhi orientations. We can summarize this as follows: Pragmatic concerns are dealt with by folk-religion practitioners, using techniques of spirit-mediumship and other forms of divination along with various kinds of rituals. They are also a primary area of concern of the lamas (Chapters 10 and 14). The Sūtra teachings provide the basis for Buddhist ethics and morality, and are particularly prominent in the context of death, where the monks who are most closely associated with them play an important part. The Karma-oriented Buddhist ethical system is, however, only part of the Tibetan value-system, which can be seen overall as containing both 'tame' and 'wild' modes or polarities (Chapter 11). Tantra is the basis for the 'cult of Enlightenment,' but it also provides the set of techniques by which lamas operate in the pragmatic sphere and through which they are involved at the time of death (Chapters 12 to 14).

In this chapter and Chapter 16 we look at the various kinds of practitioners who operate within these different spheres. After the survey of Tibetan societies in Chapters 2 to 8, it should come as no surprise to find that Tibetan religious practitioners are characterized by variety and fluidity of roles. There was relatively little centralized control over the religious system in premodern times. The Lhasa government in theory reserved the power to recognize reincarnate lamas (see below) within its realm, but its ability to enforce its recognition was limited. At least one senior Kagyüdpa lama, the Shamarpa incarnation, continued to have recognized rebirths despite a ban from Lhasa in the late eighteenth century.[1] It was not until the time of the 13th Dalai Lama (in the 1920s) that centralized control was imposed over even the monastic degrees granted by the large Gelugpa monastic centers affiliated with the Lhasa government.

This lack of centralization went along with a situation in which the roles undertaken by lamas were, and still are today, strongly dependent on their individual personalities and abilities. While the status of ordained celibate monk is clear enough, that of lama has a multitude of variations: lamas may be monks, unmarried lay yogis, or married householders; they may be heads of *gompa* or solitary hermits; they may be great scholars or unlettered practitioners. They may also be either male or female, although the vast majority are men. There are as many ways of being a lama as there are lamas. This chapter discusses the five religious orders and examines the statuses of lama, monk, and lay yogic practitioner. Chapter 16 discusses some of the less conventional and more shamanic forms of Tibetan religious practitioner, in particular the *tertön* or visionary.

THE FIVE RELIGIOUS ORDERS

The five religious orders (Nyingmapa, Kagyüdpa, Sakyapa, Gelugpa, and Bönpo) have already been mentioned on numerous occasions, and their individual histories will be traced in the historical chapters of Part Three. At this point in the book, however, it may be useful to present a brief synoptic view of these orders and the differences between them, since Tibetan religious practitioners are generally affiliated with one or another of these orders.[2] The orders differ along several dimensions, including (a) the importance of monasticism, particularly celibate monasticism (see below); (b) the place of the Old Tantras, and of Tantric practice in general; and (c) what might be called a greater or lesser commitment to hierarchy and structure.[3] These differences can also be correlated with a more 'shamanic' or more 'clerical' emphasis, and with differing political roles.

Of the five orders, the Gelugpa order,[4] founded by Tsongk'apa (or rather by his disciples) in the early fifteenth century, is the most centralized, hierarchical, and 'clerical.' It is closely connected to an earlier order known as the Kadampa, founded by the Indian teacher Atiśa and his Tibetan disciple and patron Dromtön in the eleventh century. The largest Tibetan monastic *gompa* belong to the Gelugpa order and celibate monasticism is most emphasized in this tradition. The Gelugpa became politically dominant in central Tibet in the seventeenth century, and their leading lamas include the Dalai and Panch'en Lamas. The Lhasa administration was closely linked with the large Gelugpa monastic centers around Lhasa (Sera, Ganden, Drepung, see Chapter 16).

Historically (see Chapter 27), the growth of the Gelugpa marked a reassertion of the importance of celibate monasticism, which they integrated with the study of a philosophical curriculum based primarily on the Mahāyāna Sūtras and their Indian commentaries. Serious Tantric practice in the Gelugpa order is reserved to more advanced stages, typically after twenty years or more of scholastic study, and, in theory at least, is carried out only by celibate practitioners who have taken full *gelong* vows.

The Gelugpa eventually became the largest Buddhist order in Tibet. Through the institution of the Dalai Lamas, they were, from 1642 onwards, the rulers of central Tibet (see Chapter 27). The Gelugpa, however, never have rejected Tantra, and their insistence on celibacy does not involve a denial of the necessity of the sexual practices for complete Enlightenment (see Chapter 11). Their objections are rather of a practical nature, that Tantric practices need to be restricted and closely supervised (and in the case of the literal performance of the sexual practices, avoided) in order to maintain the correct discipline and motivation in the student (see the story cited below regarding Tsongk'apa's refusal to perform these practices).

The other major orders (Sakyapa, Nyingmapa, Kagyüdpa, Bönpo) each consist of a group of independent suborders sharing a common set of teaching lineages. Like the Gelugpa, they have monastic traditions, and their large teaching *gompa*, all with a substantial complement of monks, were the central institutions of these orders within premodern Tibet. Unlike the Gelugpa, however, these orders also maintained active traditions of lay yogic practice.

The most 'shamanic' and least centralized and hierarchical of these orders are the Nyingmapa and Bönpo. The Nyingmapa go back to the early phases of Buddhism in Tibet (seventh to tenth centuries). The pattern of small hereditary noncelibate religious centers established in the tenth to twelfth centuries remained a common one among the Nyingmapa, although several large Nyingmapa monastic *gompa* with reincarnate lamas developed in later years, mainly in K'am.

The Bönpo order, like the Nyingmapa, goes back to a group of hereditary lineages of Tantric ritual practitioners in the tenth to twelfth centuries. This order is a special case in that it claims to derive not from the teachings of the historical Buddha but from that of a prior teacher named Shenrab ('Supreme *shen*-priest'). Although technically non-Buddhist, it can be regarded in most respects as a fifth Buddhist order. It is particularly close in its practices to the Nyingmapa, with whom it shares the important Dzogch'en tradition of non-Tantric meditation.

The other two major orders or groups of orders, Kagyüdpa and Sakyapa, are somewhat intermediate in terms of hierarchy, centralization, and 'clericalization' between the Nyingmapa-Bönpo and Gelugpa extremes. The Sakyapa and Kagyüdpa both go back to the Indian teachers of New Tantra lineages in the tenth and eleventh centuries and their early Tibetan disciples. These two orders were founded by Tibetan practitioners who transmitted the yogic practices from specific Indian siddhas (Virūpa and Nāropa, respectively). These central New Tantra lineages are only part of the teachings now owned and passed on by these orders, having been supplemented by other practices derived from Indian or Tibetan lineages, including the various 'discovered' *(terma)* lineages (see Chapters 12 and 16). The Sakyapa founders were hereditary Nyingmapa practitioners and the Sakyapas continue to practice several of the Old Tantras.

Both the Sakyapas and the Kagyüdpas played important political roles in Tibetan societies. The Sakyapa were rulers of Tibet during the Mongol period, and two Kagyüdpa suborders had major political power, the Karmapas as the allies of the Tsangpa rulers in the late sixteenth and early seventeenth centuries, and the Drugpas in Bhutan from the seventeenth to twentieth centuries.

Sakyapa, Kagyüdpa, Nyingmapa, and to a lesser extent Bönpo all participated in the nineteenth-century Rimed or 'nonsectarian' movement (see Chapter 27) and their modern forms have been significantly shaped by Rimed. As a consequence, there were basically two groups of orders by the mid-twentieth century, the Gelugpa on the one hand (subdivided into the affiliates of the major teaching centers, Ganden, Sera, Drepung, and Tashi Lhunpo, and their various subdivisions) and the Rimed orders (Sakyapa, Kagyüdpa, and Nyingmapa) on the other. The Bönpo were divided into a 'modernist' faction ('New Bön' or *bön sar*), centered in east Tibet, who were closely aligned with Rimed, and a 'traditionalist' faction ('Old Bön,' *bön nying*), mainly in central Tibet, although relations between the two groups were and remain close.[5]

This coming together of the non-Gelugpa orders was, as we shall see in the historical chapters (24 to 27), the culmination of a process that went back several centuries. These orders had in common the existence of a lay yogic tradition and an interest in the Old Tantras and the *terma* lineages. Both Sakyapa and Kagyüdpa, while based on the New Tantras, had become deeply involved with the Old Tantra tradition. There was therefore already considerable overlap between the practices of the three non-Gelugpa Buddhist orders, whether formally Old Tantra or New Tantra. Since Dzogch'en played a central part in the Rimed synthesis, and provided a unifying perspective beyond the specific Tantric lineages and deities, Rimed also offered a place for the Bönpo order, which had had its own Dzogch'en tradition.

By the mid-twentieth century, the effects of Rimed were still spreading through the non-Gelugpa orders but most leading lamas, especially in the east, were already a product of Rimed teaching centers such as Shech'en or Pelpung as much as of their own specific orders or suborders. We will see some examples in Chapter 18. There seems every reason to suppose that this process will continue and be strengthened in the years to come, especially since the non-Gelugpa orders in exile have fewer lamas and *gompa* than the Gelugpa, so that many of their smaller lineages and suborders are scarcely viable as independent traditions.

CELIBACY AND MONASTICISM

The issue of celibacy and of celibate monasticism is, as we have seen, one of the points of contrast between the various Tibetan religious orders, with the Gelugpa requiring it and other orders regarding it as one of several alternatives. The question of celibacy in Tibetan Buddhism requires some explicit consideration because of its implications for Tibetan religious practitioners.

Celibacy has been one of the more confusing aspects of Tibetan Buddhism for Western observers, particularly for those used to Buddhism in the Theravāda countries, where celibate monasticism is normally regarded as essential (Chapter 2). Thus, many early accounts of Tibet refer to the presence of 'married monks' or 'married clergy.' If we use the generic Tibetan term *ch'öpa* below for religious practitioners, the situation is less confusing. *Ch'öpa* can be lay or have taken vows of celibacy. Lay *ch'öpa* can and do marry and have sexual relations.

To describe such married *ch'öpa* as 'monks' or 'nuns' is a misunderstanding. The Tibetans have male and female practitioners who have taken vows of celibacy *(trapa, ani)* in large numbers, and such people might reasonably be called 'monks' and 'nuns.' These practitioners cannot marry and should not have sexual relations, at any rate without formally returning their vows. It is true, however, that the place of celibacy and monasticism in Tibetan practice is different from that in Theravādin Buddhism, or in the Buddhism of the Far Eastern countries (China, Japan, Korea, Vietnam). To understand this situation, we need to return to the two important distinctions, between Hinayāna and Mahāyāna and between Mahāyāna and Vajrayāna (Tantra), introduced in Chapter 11. As was pointed out there and in Chapter 12, these distinctions between the Buddhism of Tibet and the Buddhism of the Theravādin countries have significant consequences for the nature of Buddhist practice.

For the Tibetans, as for other Buddhists, celibacy and withdrawal from lay life are traditionally regarded as necessary, or at least highly desirable, for non-Tantric Buddhist practice,[6] after the practitioner has progressed beyond the elementary moral training of the taking of refuge, the five precepts, and the avoidance of nonvirtuous actions. Neither celibacy nor withdrawal from lay life, however, are necessarily required for the practice of Vajrayāna or Tantric Buddhism in Tibetan societies. In fact, celibacy may be inappropriate past a certain point in an individual's spiritual career, since the literal performance of Tantric sexual practices is incompatible with the strict observance of celibacy.[7]

As mentioned in Chapters 11 and 12, these practices involve the use of (actual or visualized) sexual intercourse as a meditative technique, in conjunction with the yogic processes relating to 'energy flows' within the body. They may be performed by visualization (using an imagined consort or *jñānamudrā*, 'wisdom seal') rather than by using an actual physical sexual partner (*karmamudrā*, literally 'action seal'), and this mode of practice was much more common in premodern Tibet than their literal physical performance. Practice with an actual physical partner, however, was believed to be more efficacious than practice with a visualized partner, and it was in no way improper if those involved had not taken vows of celibacy. Practice with an actual partner enables Enlightenment to be achieved in this lifetime, whereas with an imagined partner it can be achieved at best in the intermediate state *(bardo)* following death.

Even the Gelugpa, who place most emphasis on celibate monasticism, do not contest the validity of these practices. Thus Daniel Cozort summarizes the account of the eminent contemporary Gelugpa teacher Jampel Shenp'en (the present Ganden Tr'ipa, Abbot of Ganden) as follows: "Śākyamuni Buddha, in his last lifetime prior to enlightenment, used an Action Seal [an actual physical consort], but it is said that although Tsongk'apa also became a Buddha, he did not use an Action Seal, becoming enlightened in the intermediate state instead. Tsongk'apa did this because he feared his followers would imitate him without being properly prepared, thus hampering instead of enhancing their practices" (Cozort 1986:92; see also R. Jackson 1985:30).

As is well known, Hindu Tantra in India, at any rate of the 'left hand' *(vamamarga)* variety, uses related sexual techniques. The Tibetan practices, however, do not have the aura of dubious morality and social unacceptability that is today often associated with their Hindu equivalents. They are essentially a private matter between the partners involved and their guru. Even in the not infrequent cases where the male partner is a *trulku* (reincarnate lama) and might technically be a celibate monk, there may be some gossip but there is usually no serious public disapproval.[8]

All this can doubtless be connected with the more relaxed and permissive attitudes towards sexuality of all kinds, including pre- and extramarital relationships, characteristic of Tibetan societies in comparison with Hindu society with its strong emphasis on female virginity and chastity. It can also be associated with the importance of 'reputation' as well as 'respectability' value-systems in Tibetan societies (see Chapter 11) and with the general acceptance of a multiplicity of paths (the concept of *upāyakauśalya*, skillful means appropriate to the particular practitioner). For the most part, Tibetans are more interested in whether lamas have ability or power rather than in whether they are celibate, provided that their motivation (i.e., *bodhicitta*) is not suspect.

It is therefore both possible and appropriate for a Tibetan to be an advanced practitioner while not being celibate, although it is taken for granted that for such a person sexuality has a different meaning than it has for ordinary people. In fact, since mastery of the sexual yogic techniques implies a high degree of control over Tantric ritual, someone who is known to be adept at these practices will usually be regarded as a highly valued ritual performer. Such lay practitioners can build up a considerable reputation for sanctity and spiritual attainment among local people, who will consult them for spiritual and practical advice, or ask them to perform rituals.

The general term for Tantric practitioners *(neljorpa,* fem. *neljorma)* is used by the Tibetans to translate the Sanskrit *yogin*, *yoginī*, i.e., practitioner of yoga (Tib. *neljor*), and I shall use 'yogin' or 'yogic practitioner' as a translation in this book. Female practitioners have a necessary part in these traditions both as teachers and as female partners to male yogins (Allione 1984; Dowman 1984). The Indian masters of these practices were also known as siddhas or mahāsiddhas, but the Tibetan equivalents to these terms *(drubt'ob, drubch'en)* are rarely applied to living people except perhaps as a title of respect for lamas known for their Tantric practice. The term *neljorpa/ma* does not necessarily imply that any particular *neljorpa/ma* performs the sexual practices, and many such practitioners are in fact celibate. The *neljorpa/ma* role, however, is distinct from that of a monk, in that these people have not necessarily taken vows of celibacy and as a whole are practicing a tradition incompatible with celibacy.

The busy life of a large monastic *gompa* is, in any case, not thought of as conducive to serious yogic practice, and yogins and yoginīs are found in small communities, sometimes attached to nearby (normally non-Gelugpa) monasteries, whose lamas provide them with instruction. Other yogins and yoginīs wander from center to center, sometimes meditating in the caves high in the mountains where famous yogins of the past such as Milarepa performed their yogic practice.

Milarepa, the great Tibetan lama, yogin, and poet of the eleventh century, is the best known and the prototype of the nonmonastic yogic tradition (Chapter 24). Other important early figures include the Indian teacher known in Tibet as P'adampa Sangyé (Kaschewsky 1973; Aziz 1980), his Tibetan female associate Machig Labdrön (Allione 1984:141–204), and several Nyingmapa figures, above all Guru Rimpoch'e (Padmasambhava) and his disciples, as well as the various *tertön* or finders of revealed treasures (see Chapter 16). There are some distinct teaching lineages practiced by these yogis, such as the *chöd* traditions (Tucci 1980:87–93; Gyatso 1985) but much of their practice is similar to that of celibate monks. The development of the yogic practices will be considered further in Part Three (Chapters 19 to 27).

As suggested in Chapter 11, the importance of yogic practice in Tibet implies a relative depreciation of the monastic status. A common view is that once control over the *tsalung* (internal psychic currents, see Chapter 12) has been attained, vows have no meaning. In the non-Gelugpa orders, the primary qualification for acting as a lama is to have undertaken at least one long retreat (normally three years, three months, and three days) during which it is assumed that one will have gained control over *tsalung* and so become a competent ritual performer.[9] Consequently, a 'serious' Tibetan practitioner is as or more likely to be a lay yogin (or yoginī, if female) than a celibate monastic. Nor are lamas necessarily monks.

The issue of celibacy also, of course, has implications in relation to inheritance, and these will be discussed later in this chapter.

VARIETIES OF BUDDHIST PRACTITIONER

We are now ready to look at the different types of Buddhist religious practitioner *(ch'öpa)* within Tibetan societies. *Ch'öpa* in Tibetan societies belong to one or another of the several main religious orders or groups of independent suborders (Gelugpa, Kagyüdpa, etc.) mentioned above, although it is not unusual for them to receive teaching from lamas of several orders. Each suborder had one or more large central teaching centers in the premodern period, along with smaller *gompa* scattered throughout the country. Monks and noncelibate *ch'öpa* went to these large teaching centers from the entire Tibetan region for training in ritual practice, meditation, and Buddhist philosophy. While many of these large teaching centers were destroyed during the Cultural Revolution period, and all were brought to a standstill, communities from most of the major teaching centers were reconstituted in exile and are now gradually rebuilding their *gompa* in Chinese-controlled Tibet.

A minority of the people who undertake such studies become qualified teachers and ritual practitioners, able to conduct major Tantric ritual performances. These are the lamas. In many cases, these exceptional individuals are identified at an early age as rebirths of recently deceased lamas, and after training they take over the previous lama's monastic establishment. These are the so-called reincarnate lamas *(trulku)*. Other lamas come from hereditary lineages of lamas *(dunggyüd)*, and may inherit the management of a family *gompa*, lay or monastic. Yet other lamas have no specific post to succeed to, and become teachers at an established religious center, or gradually gather a following and begin a new religious community. Examples of some of these possibilities will be considered in Chapter 18.

All of these lamas act as performers of Tantric rituals for the lay public (see Chapter 14). Most are also the focus of a group of followers or disciples, including celibate monks, noncelibate yogis, or ordinary laymen, who themselves learn to perform Tantric ritual on a lesser scale. As I emphasize throughout this book, the variety of possible roles and careers is itself a significant characteristic of Tibetan societies as opposed to the situation elsewhere in the Buddhist world.

The roles available for religious practitioners within Tibetan Buddhism differ from the corresponding roles in other Buddhist societies, and they have not always been presented adequately in previous writings about Tibet. Early authorities such as L. Austine Waddell (Waddell 1967), with their references to 'Lamaism,' 'lamaseries,' and the like managed to cause a considerable degree of confusion between 'lamas' and 'monks,' as well as creating the mistaken impression that Tibetan 'monks' were married. Nonspecialist accounts of Tibet still often repeat such misconceptions.

As is now clear, only a small proportion of religious practitioners in Tibetan societies are properly referred to as 'lamas,' but this small number of people (a few thousand) plays a very important part in the system. The lamas are a group within a larger class of Buddhist religious practitioners. This larger group includes both 'monks,' in the sense of celibate *ch'öpa* living in communal residences, and noncelibate *ch'öpa* of various kinds. Lamas may be of either kind. We now turn to look at the lamas in a little more detail.

THE MEANINGS OF 'LAMA'

We have already seen that the term 'lama' in Tibetan usage has come to have a wider meaning than that of *guru* or religious teacher. In everyday usage, lama has developed a number of overlapping areas of meaning:

(1) 'Lama,' like guru, means 'personal religious teacher.' The term 'root lama' *(tsawé lama)* refers to an individual's principal personal religious teacher. The *tsawé lama* is, in many ways, the focus of an individual's personal spiritual practice. At the same time, it is explicit within the tradition that even the *tsawé lama* is only an aid on the path; the ultimate source of the teaching is beyond any dichotomy between teacher and student, Buddha and ordinary human being (see Chapter 13).

While any teacher of religious knowledge (beginning with the person from whom one learned the alphabet) may be referred to as a lama in the sense of religious teacher, the paradigmatic case is the teacher of Tantric practice, the central Tibetan Buddhist technique for the attainment of Enlightenment. The important role of the lama in the context of Tantric practice has already been explored at some length in Chapters 12 and 13.

(2) 'Lama' by extension can mean the head of a *gompa;* not necessarily the administrative head (*k'enpo,* 'abbot'), but the principal 'teacher' around whom the gompa is organized. Large *gompa* often have several such lamas in this sense. One consequence of the system of inheritance by reincarnation is that it involves a substantial period in which the principal lama (usually the reincarnation of the *gompa*'s founder) is too young to act as head of the *gompa.* Other senior lamas necessarily have to take over during this period. A very large *gompa* in premodern Tibet, with numerous subunits, might have had twenty or more reincarnate and other senior lamas, each with an attached *labrang* (household, religious corporation) economically distinct from the *gompa* proper.

(3) 'Lama,' again by extension from (1), can also mean someone who is a properly qualified performer of Tantric ritual. It is this mean-

ing that allows one to speak of married lay Tantric practitioners as 'lamas,' and in the Sherpa case, even of a 'lama clan' of hereditary practitioners of this kind. As stated earlier, someone who has performed a three-year retreat is commonly referred to as 'lama.'

There are several further ramifications of the concept of 'lama.' Thus 'lamas,' as heads of *gompa,* may also become important political leaders by virtue of their position. The Dalai Lama, Panch'en Rimpoch'e, Shabdrung Rimpoch'e (former head lama of Bhutan), Jetsün Dampa Hot'ogt'u and Changkya Hot'ogt'u (head lamas of Outer and Inner Mongolia) are preeminent examples, but many Tibetan lamas had significant political roles, both in their own right as heads of estates and as officials in larger Tibetan polities, as we saw in Chapters 3 to 6 (see Carrasco 1959; Rahul 1971; Aris 1979).

In addition, there is the question of 'incarnate lamas' *(trulku),* which needs separate treatment.

TRULKU AND THE TRIKĀYA CONCEPT

Many important lamas, particularly those who are heads of large *gompa* or major *labrang* within *gompa,* or who are of major political significance, are *trulku,* a concept most often, if slightly misleadingly, rendered in English as 'incarnate' or 'reincarnate' lama. To be referred to as a *trulku* implies either that the individual is an 'emanation' of one or more specific Tantric deities or, more commonly, that he is a rebirth *(yangsid)* of a previous lama, whose office and status he has inherited. Frequently both meanings are combined.

The concept of recognized rebirth *(yangsid)* is fairly straightforward, if unusual to Westerners, but that of emanation is more complex, and requires some discussion at this point, because of its bearing on the whole idea of the lama. We have already seen that disciples are taught to regard their lamas as Vajradhara, the Tantric form of the Buddha, and that the lama as an object of *sādhana* is visualized in the form of Vajradhara or another Tantric deity (chapter 13). This status of the lama as Tantric deity is both generic (all lamas are Vajradhara) and situational (disciples regard their individual root lamas as Tantric deities). The *trulku* concept goes beyond this to imply that some lamas are more specifically and permanently emanations of particular Tantric deities, most commonly Avalokiteśvara, Mañjuśrī, or Vajrapāṇi.

We have already seen something of what Avalokiteśvara, the embodiment of compassion, represents in Tibetan thought. Mañjuśrī (Jampel Yang) represents insight *(prajña)* into the nondichotomizing nature of reality, and he is the patron of the academic tradition in Tibet, while Vajrapāṇi (Ch'agna Dorjé) is a fierce emanation of the Buddha and represents powerful and, if necessary, destructive action. A whole series of important Tibetan figures were regarded as emanations of Mañjuśrī, Avalokiteśvara, or Vajrapāṇi, and several will be discussed in Chapters 25 to 27. By identifying these lamas in this way, the Tibetans were not just involved in boosting the prestige of religious figures. They were also defining what kind of activity those figures were engaged in, and attempting to strengthen that particular mode of activity within Tibetan society.

In other words, the bodhisattvas, buddhas, and goddesses, like the spiritual entities of West African religions, can be understood as symbolic markers for different patterns within Tibetan culture ('modal states' in the language of Samuel 1990; see also Chapter 19). They were not simply beings existing outside humanity, but forces that were active within human life. The rituals of Avalokiteśvara, like the rituals of African shamanic societies such as the Ndembu or the Yoruba, were deliberate attempts to invoke and direct these forces (Samuel 1990).

The nearest to a systematic framework for describing these relationships in Tibetan Buddhist thought was an adaptation of the Trikāya or 'three bodies' theory. This theory seems to have first developed among the later Hinayāna schools, and it was extensively developed by the Indian Mahāyāna (Conze 1962:172–173, 232–233). The doctrine of the Trikāya was an attempt to define the nature of Buddhahood and the various aspects of its manifestation.

In this scheme Buddhahood was described in terms of three *kāya* or 'bodies' (the term might better be translated as 'planes of existence'):

(1) The *dharmakāya* (Tibetan *ch'öku*), which is the true nature of the Buddha, beyond any specific manifestation, sometimes symbolized by Vajradhara or (in the Nyingma tradition) Samantabhadra (Kuntu Sangpo).

(2) The *saṃbhogakāya* (Tibetan *longchödku*), corresponding to the forms of the celestial Buddhas and Bodhisattvas such as Amitābha,[10] Avalokiteśvara, and Mañjuśrī, which are meditated on in Tantric prac-

tice, and which can be perceived directly only by those who have reached a specific level of attainment;

(3) The *nirmāṇakāya* (Tibetan *trulku*), the material form in which the Buddha appears to ordinary human beings. The historical Buddha, Śākyamuni, was such a *trulku*.

The precise usage of these terms varied somewhat from tradition to tradition, and they are sometimes subdivided further to make four or five *kāya*, but the above is the basic structure.[11] We can take the *dharmakāya* as corresponding to the perception of reality, beyond time, space, and all dichotomies, of the 'shamanic vision,' and the *saṃbhogakāya* forms as constituting a personified vocabulary of cultural patterns (Chapter 19, and Samuel 1990) of the type commonly found in shamanic societies, which the apprentice shaman had to master as a prelude to confronting the *dharmakāya* realm of potentiality from which they emerge.

The idea of lamas as *trulku* in the sense of the Trikāya doctrine probably developed over several centuries, and will be examined in some detail in Chapter 25. When Tibetans use the term *trulku* to refer to a lama, the meaning can doubtless vary over a range from deeply significant to merely conventional. The term is used regularly to refer to *yangsid* lamas, in part perhaps because recognition as a *yangsid* carries the implication that the lama has acquired control over the intermediate state *(bardo)* and so has access to the *saṃbhogakāya* level. *Trulku* nevertheless remains the term for *nirmāṇakāya*, the physical presence of Buddhahood, as well as the ordinary word for a lama who is a recognized rebirth.

TRULKU, RIMPOCH'E, AND THE QUESTION OF SUCCESSION

There are several thousand of these reincarnate *(yangsid)* lamas or *trulku* today, and they had a dominant position in the premodern Tibetan religious system. High-status reincarnate lamas are often found in the families of hereditary lamas or in families where other reincarnates have already been identified. Thus the present (14th) Dalai Lama's elder brother (Thubten Jigme Norbu, Tagtser Rimpoch'e) had already been identified as a *trulku* some years before the Dalai Lama was identified, and a younger brother was later identified as a *trulku*.

Trulku are also commonly found in aristocratic families,[12] and one often finds a complex interweaving of reincarnation and hereditary *ngagpa* (lama) and *gerpa* (aristocratic) status. The genealogies of the various Ky'entse and Kongtrul rebirths in east Tibet include numerous examples (see Smith 1970).

Not all *gompa* and *labrang* heads are chosen through the finding of 'reincarnations.' Hereditary succession was at one time the most common procedure and it is still quite frequent, as for example with the head abbot of Sakya (Sakya Tr'ich'en, Sakya Tr'idzin), who is nevertheless also a *trulku* in the sense that it is held that all eligible male members of the K'ön family are emanations of a Tantric deity (normally Mañjuśrī).[13] Other head lamas are chosen by a process of examination and selection, as with the Ganden Tr'ipa, who is abbot of Ganden monastery and titular head of the Gelugpa order, and the other head lamas and college heads of Sera, Ganden, and Drepung and the two Gelugpa Tantric Colleges at Lhasa (Sherpa et al. 1977).

The question of inheritance has implications for the issue considered earlier of monastic celibacy. It is possible to combine monastic celibacy and the hereditary principle by having the succession go from a celibate monk to his noncelibate brother or brother's son. This happened, for example, in the early years of the ruling K'ön dynasty of Sakya, and also with the lama-prince rulers of Derge state in K'am; however, no major *gompa* have maintained this mode of succession over more than a few generations. A wealthy *labrang* may be able to afford several wives for its sons and so produce large families, as happened at times at Sakya, but demographic factors may still lead to a lack of male heirs, especially if the expectation is that most of the males become celibate monks.

Conversely, one common explanation for having a noncelibate head lama, as with Sakya in recent centuries, is that it enables the *dunggyüd* (hereditary lama lineage) to be continued. *Dunggyüd* here refers not merely to genealogical descent but also to the valued spiritual properties inherent in the lineage (Aziz 1978), which would be lost if the family died out. A large family also allows for the multiple alliances through marriage that are characteristic of high-status Tibetan lama families.

Succession by reincarnation *(yangsid, trulku)* can also be combined with hereditary succession. Some *gompa* have both hereditary and *trulku* lineages, and it is reasonably common for *trulku* themselves to marry and have children. In addition, since *trulku* are commonly from high-status lama or aristocratic families, there may be extensive property interests involved in such decisions, quite apart from the personal preferences of the lama concerned.

The title Rimpoch'e, literally 'very precious,' is used in reference and address after the names of any of these lamas and of other lamas of recognized high status. It does not necessarily imply 'reincarnate lama' *(trulku)* status. Both 'lama' and Rimpoch'e are somewhat elastic terms in that, while there are some people whose lama status is, as it were, beyond any argument, such as the Dalai Lama and other senior *trulku* of the various orders, there are others who may be referred to by some people (such as personal students) as lama or Rimpoch'e but would not be so referred to by the population as a whole. The terms, in other words, refer to a relationship rather than an office.

To a certain extent the same elasticity applies to *trulku* (in the sense of recognized rebirth). The *trulku* or *yangsid* status of major reincarnations is not in doubt. It is certified by the head lamas of the religious order in question and, in the premodern period, was generally confirmed also by the Lhasa administration, in areas where it had authority. Less important lamas may be recognized locally as *trulku* of a recently deceased local lama without wider recognition being obtained. Disputes over the recognition of *trulku* are not uncommon, and Tibetans are well aware of the possibility of fraud. In the premodern period, wealthy estates were frequently at issue in such cases and for a family to have its child recognized as a major *trulku* made a dramatic difference to the family's status and resources. Melvyn Goldstein quotes a Lhasa street-song ridiculing a Lhasa aristocratic lady who hoped that her unborn child would be the next Dalai Lama and allegedly burned incense under her dress so as to "sanctify her genitals for the 'emanation' of the Dalai Lama":

> The sun, which is the happiness of the world,
> has risen in Takpo.
> Her excellency, Mrs. Doring's
> ass, has become black with soot. (Goldstein 1982:64)

The reality of *trulku* and the validity of the *trulku* system as a whole, however, is rarely questioned. The critical comments of the fifteenth-century yogin Tsangnyön Heruka, quoted in Chapter 26, are exceptional in this respect, and even they do not amount to an outright denial of the concept.

MONKS AND NUNS

'Monk' and 'nun' are, of course, European terms with a primary reference to Christian monasticism, and they are not exactly equivalent to any Tibetan (or other Buddhist) term. As a consequence, their usage by Western authors in relation to Tibetan male and female celibate *ch'öpa* has not always been consistent.

Thus 'monk' is sometimes used to translate Tibetan *gelong* (= Sanskrit *bhikṣu*, Pali *bhikku*) or its Bönpo equivalent *trangsong*. A *gelong* is a man who has undergone the full monastic ordination, with the complete set of Prātimokṣa vows given in the Buddhist Vinaya texts.

Only a minority of the celibate inmates of Tibetan monastic *gompa* are fully ordained *gelong*. Most have undertaken one of the two lesser sets of vows, *genyen* (Sanskrit *upāsaka*) or *gets'ul* (Sanskrit *śrāmaṉera*).[14] Members of all these categories are bound by vows of celibacy, and normally live in a monastic community apart from lay society. The term 'monk' and its equivalents in other European languages are frequently used by Western authors to mean this more inclusive group.

The general Tibetan term for all three categories of male monastic inmates *(upāsaka, śrāmaṉera, bhikṣu)* is *trapa*.[15] Its literal meaning is 'scholar' or 'student' (*trats'ang* = 'college'). Another term, *rabchung*, literally 'renunciate' (of secular life), can be used in the same sense. This usage derives from *rabchung* as a term for the *genyen* ordination when that is taken, as it often is in Tibet, as the first stage of a monastic career. Consequently, all *trapa* have normally also taken *rabchung*. The usage of 'monk' to refer to anyone who has taken *rabchung* is reasonable enough, since in most contexts the precise ordination status of an individual is not significant, but it can cause some confusion when comparisons are made with Theravādin or Far Eastern Buddhist monasticism.

Most *trapa* expect eventually to undertake the full vows of a *gelong (bhikṣu)*, but they may not do this until well advanced in their monastic careers. At the same time, a substantial complement of fully ordained *gelong* is an indication of a well-disciplined *gompa* whose inmates are seriously dedicated to the religious life. The Gelugpa place particular emphasis on this, as they do generally on issues of monastic discipline and the desirability of withdrawal from secular life.

Ordained women practitioners (generically referred to as *ani* or *chomo*) can only undertake equivalents to the first two of the three monastic grades *(genyenma, gets'ulma)*. The *bhikṣunī* or *gelongma* ordination lineage is generally regarded as having died out in Tibet, as it did long ago in the Theravāda countries.[16] Female religious practitioners, however, always seem to have been fewer in number than monks in Tibet. In general they are also lower in status, as seems to be the rule in most Buddhist societies (Aziz 1976b; Fürer-Haimendorf 1976; Willis 1984; Tsomo 1987).

The three grades mentioned (five, with the two grades for women) do not exhaust the distinctions among monastic inmates. There are various administrative offices concerned with the running of the community, particularly in the larger *gompa*, as well as posts concerned with the ritual and teaching side of the establishment. In addition, some Tibetan monastic *gompa*, particularly in the Gelugpa order, award academic 'degrees' after extended study and examination. The best known of these degrees is the title of *geshé*, which was awarded at various levels to graduates of the three very large Gelugpa 'monastic universities' near Lhasa (Sera, Ganden, Drepung) and of some other large Gelugpa monastic centers.[17]

In many of the larger *gompa* in premodern Tibet there was also a special group of monks who were noted for their physical strength and who formed a kind of monastic militia, helping to keep order within the *gompa*, employed on missions outside, and occasionally involved in fighting with other *gompa*. The *dabdob* of Sera Monastery, near Lhasa, probably the most extreme development of this monastic role, have been described by Melvyn Goldstein (1964), and the autobiography of one of these monks has been edited by Hugh Richardson (1986). In the Amdo monastic *gompa* described by Ekvall, a group of ex-monks or *wanlog* living on the monastery premises carried out some of these functions (Ekvall 1960, also 1952, 1954a for examples).

The most important distinction within a monastic community is between the ordinary inmates *(trapa)* and the lama or lamas. Here 'lama' has the sense both of spiritual director of the community and of charismatic personality about whom it is centered. The lama's household *(labrang)* in a *gompa* of any size, is separately administered from the monastic community proper, and often has considerable property and other wealth attached to it.

Lamas, it should now be clear, may or may not be celibate monks. In the Gelugpa order, they have to be, but in the other religious orders (Nyingmapa, Sakyapa, Kagyüdpa, Bönpo) this is not necessarily so, even for a lama who is acting (like the Sakya Tr'ich'en) as the head of a community of celibate monks. As already mentioned, only a few celibate monks are referred to as 'lamas.' Most celibate monks have a relatively subordinate status within the system.

NONCELIBATE *CH'ÖPA:* LAMAS, YOGINS, AND LAY PRACTITIONERS

Lamas outside the Gelugpa order, as we have seen, are not necessarily celibate. Neither are their followers. Thus the non-Gelugpa orders have a series of further roles for noncelibate religious *ch'öpa.* It is these *ch'öpa* that were sometimes described as 'married monks' by earlier Western observers and their presence interpreted as evidence of depravity, laxity, and the generally degenerate state of Buddhism in Tibet (see Waddell [1894] 1967:193; or even Tucci 1956:53 commenting on the married *ch'öpa* of Ralung). Similar comments have been made about the married Buddhist priests of Bali and the Kathmandu Valley *(pedanda, vajrācarya).* For the Tibetans, however, noncelibate practice is not necessarily an inferior and degenerate alternative to real Buddhism. Noncelibate *ch'öpa,* like celibate *ch'öpa,* are judged on their individual merits, and many lamas of recognized high status are noncelibate. A competent noncelibate yogi, particularly a hermit or a wandering *chöd* practitioner, is likely to be regarded as having more ritual 'power' than an average monk.

Noncelibate lamas have already been discussed. They include many heads of highly reputable and prestigious monastic *gompa.* The best known of these was the Sakya Tr'ich'en, the hereditary head of the main Sakyapa order and of the large and important Sakya estate (Chogay Trichen 1983; Amipa 1976; see Chapter 3). The Sakya Tr'ich'en's family, like the princes of Derge in K'am, who were also originally a hereditary lama lineage (Kolmaš 1968, 1988; see Chapter 4), claim aristocratic descent apart from their religious role, and were undoubtedly of very high status in premodern Tibet.

There are many more modest lineages of hereditary lamas, such as the *ngagpa* families described by Aziz for Dingri (Aziz 1978:53–54, 220–221). Even in these cases, being born into a *ngagpa* family carries the implication of inherited spiritual power. Aziz notes that the Dingri *ngagpa* were equal in social status to local *gerpa* or aristocratic families. Individuals who are not from *ngagpa* lineages might become lamas of this kind through their own abilities. We will see an example of this in Chapter 18 (the lama Changch'ub Dorjé of Nyarong).

Of a less elevated status again are the so-called village lamas or *serky'im* discussed by Barbara Aziz for Dingri and common in many parts of Tibet (Aziz 1978:76–94; see Chapter 17). These are lay people who traditionally received some religious training and acted as performers of ritual. In Dingri, these 'village lamas' were distinct from hereditary lamas of the *ngagpa* type. As Aziz's informants put it, anyone can become a *serky'im;* it is only a matter of training. These people are perhaps comparable to the village exorcists, weather-makers, and other minor religious experts also found throughout Tibet, and about whom we know very little at present.

The noncelibate yogins who live in retreat communities or who travel around Tibet and the Himalayas between various hermitages and other meditation places also have a significant role as religious practitioners for local populations. From their point of view, their religious practice provides a way of supporting themselves on their travels, while for the lay communities these people are particularly effective sources of spiritual power.

It is mostly among the various kinds of noncelibate *ch'öpa* that we find the most overt expressions of the 'wild' and shamanic side of Tibetan Buddhism. These lamas, the *tertön* and the 'crazy lamas' or *lama nyönpa,* are the subject of Chapter 16, along with the shamanic practitioners of the folk religion.

16

Folk Shamans, *Tertön*, and Crazy Siddhas

Chapter 15 presented the overall range of Tibetan Buddhist practitioners. These include celibate monastics similar to the *bhikkhu* in Theravādin Buddhist countries, but they also include a range of lay Buddhist practitioners who are much less characteristic of Theravādin Buddhism, along with the lama who, as an autonomous religious leader and performer of Tantric rituals, has no real parallel within established Theravādin society.

I argued in Chapter 2 that such 'shamanic' styles of Buddhist practice have historically been marginalized in Theravādin societies and, to the extent that they survived at all, were subordinated to what I have referred to as 'clerical' Buddhism. I also suggested that this subordination took place because centralized state power in these societies was able to bring it about. All this suggests that a more detailed look at the wilder and more shamanic end of the Tibetan spectrum would be worthwhile. This is the function of the present chapter. We will be paying particular attention to the *tertön* or visionary lamas who have played a large, if often neglected, part in Tibetan religious history, and to the 'crazy siddhas' who provide a clear indication of the tolerance of the Tibetan religious environment towards unconventional modes of Buddhist practice.

While the *tertön* and crazy siddhas are undoubtedly Buddhist religious practitioners, they are, of all the Buddhist religious personnel, the closest to the folk religion of Tibet, and the visionary activities of the *tertön* in particular bear some resemblance of the practices of Tibetan folk shamanic practitioners. There are several kinds of folk shamanic practitioners, and I have already briefly discussed two types, the spirit-mediums and the oracle priests, in Chapter 10. It will be useful here to describe them somewhat more systematically and to present material on two other types of practitioner not yet considered, the past-life revenants *(delog)* and the visionary Gesar bard *(babdrung).*

SPIRIT-MEDIUMS, ORACLE PRIESTS, REVENANTS, AND VISIONARY BARDS

Spirit-mediums have already been discussed briefly in Chapter 10. They are found throughout Tibetan village or nomadic communities. They include both men and women, and are known by a variety of names, such as *lhapa, lhak'a* ('god person,' 'god mouth'), *pawo* ('hero,' with reference to the 'heroes,' *vīra*, of Tantric practice), *k'androma ('ḍākinī').* They are channels through which the local deities can be contacted, generally to discover the causes of illness and misfortune. The idiom is primarily that of 'spirit-mediumship,' common to much of South, Southeast and East Asian society, involving the ordinary conscious personality of the 'medium' being temporarily replaced by that of the local deity (see Nebesky-Wojkowitz 1956; Kalsang and Sagaster 1971; Paul 1976; Peter 1978a, 1978b, 1979; Day 1989). In some cases, as with Berglie's material from a Changt'ang pastoralist background, the *pawo* takes a more active role, closer to the soul-flight or spirit-journey idiom of some Siberian and Nepalese shamans (Berglie 1976, 1980, 1982, 1983).[1]

People generally become *lhapa, pawo,* and so on, through a classic shamanic initiation process, in which they fall seriously ill, undergo a series of visions, and discover through the diagnosis of a lama or an experienced spirit-medium that they must take on the career of a spirit-medium. Frequently, however, such people belong to families with a long history of spirit-mediumship, and once the *lhapa* or *pawo* have been diagnosed they are taken in hand by an experienced spirit-medium for training (Berglie 1976; Schenk 1990).

These practitioners are not particularly Buddhist, and would not normally be referred to as *ch'öpa* ('Dharma people'). They are simply a means of communication with local spirits. Thus Robert Paul reports a southern Sherpa community using non-Tibetan spirit-mediums from the Hindu cultural region *(jhāṅkri)* when Sherpa Tibetan practitioners were not available (Paul 1976). Tibetan spirit-mediums, however, are usually under some degree of supervision from local lamas (see Fürer-Haimendorf 1964; Berglie 1976).

Gompa also employ spirit-mediums of this kind, which I refer to, following earlier Western writers, as oracle-priests (Peter 1978a, 1978b, 1979; Nebesky-Wojkowitz 1956; Rock 1935; Brauen 1980b; Dargyay 1985a; Tewari 1987). Some of the largest monastic *gompa* in premodern Tibet, along with the Lhasa government itself, had permanent oracle-priests. The Tibetan terms for these are *sungma* and *ch'ökyong*, 'guardian,' 'protector of the Dharma,' and actually refer not to the human medium but to the possessing deity. The Nech'ung oracle-priest, employed by the Lhasa government, played a significant role in Tibetan politics in recent times.

Alongside the spirit-mediums there are specialists in other modes of divination, including clairvoyants (Fürer-Haimendorf's *mindung*) who operate through mirror-gazing and similar techniques. As mentioned in Chapter 10, lamas are also frequently asked to perform divination *(mo)* in cases of difficulty, and one of the techniques they use *(tra)* also involves viewing signs in a mirror or other reflective surface.

Revenants *(delog)* and visionary bards *(babdrung)* have similarities to the spirit-mediums proper. In particular, people take on the role of *delog* and *babdrung* as a result of the same kind of classic shamanic initiatory experience that characterizes entry to the career of *lhapa* or *pawo*. The *delog* ('gone-returned') is a person who is believed to have died and then returned from the dead. The *delog* is sent back to the living with a mission to inform people of the sufferings that await them in the hell-realms if they do not reform their lives. The *delog*'s message is thus closely linked to the Karma Orientation, although the *delog* themselves belong on the shamanic side of Tibetan religion, where this orientation is generally muted. Because of the *delog*'s connection with the Buddhist teachings, they are generally considered, unlike the spirit-mediums proper, to be a kind of *ch'öpa*.

There are literary accounts of several famous *delog*, and most research on the *delog* has emphasized this literary material (Epstein 1982, 1990b; Pommaret 1989a). Recently, however, Françoise Pommaret visited and described two contemporary *delog* in eastern Bhutan (Pommaret 1989a, 1989b). Unlike the 'classic' *delog* of the literary accounts, these practitioners (both women) have regular seances and are consulted by fellow-villagers for advice. During the seances they visit the hell-realms and report back on their experiences.

The Gesar epic is very widely known among all Tibetan populations, and is particularly prevalent in K'am and Amdo. It is performed both by amateurs and by professional bards (Stein 1959a; Samuel, in press a, in press b, in press d). Often it is read from manuscripts or blockprinted texts, or performed from memory without any implication of visionary techniques. There are, however, visionary bards *(babdrung)*, usually illiterate and of nomadic background, who sing versions of the epic that derive from their own visionary experiences (Yang 1989, 1990). Often, as with spirit-mediums, the profession is passed from parent to child, but, as with both spirit-mediums and *delog*, there is a version of the classic shamanic initiatory experience, in which the future *babdrung* falls ill, has visions, and is diagnosed (usually by a lama) as being a *babdrung*.

Attitudes to the Gesar epic vary considerably among Tibetan lamas and monks. Many Gelugpa disapprove of the epic, while Kagyüdpa and Nyingmapa lamas generally favor it and see it as an expression of the activity of Guru Rimpoch'e and as a vehicle for Buddhist teachings, especially of the Dzogch'en school. Consequently, the question of whether *babdrung* should be regarded as *ch'öpa* will be answered differently by those who favor and those who oppose the epic. The *babdrung* themselves, however, generally emphasize the connection of the epic with *ch'ö* (Dharma) and so see themselves as a kind of *ch'öpa*.[2]

One of the intriguing features of the Gesar epic is the way in which it constitutes an area of overlap between folk religion and more explicitly Buddhist concerns. In particular, many new Gesar episodes have been written by Nyingmapa and Kagyüdpa lamas, among them the late K'amtr'ul Rimpoch'e of Trashi Jong (see Chapter 14) and the late Kalu Rimpoch'e (see Chapter 18). In these cases, the idiom used to describe the writing down of the text is not that of *babdrung,* but is closer to that of *gongter,* a variety of *terma* (see below). A lama typically has one or a series of visionary experiences that awaken memories of a past life in which he was one of Gesar's followers. These memories then form the basis for the composition (Samuel, in press b). *Gongter,* and in some respects all *terma,* are similarly grounded in memories of a past life in which the *tertön* was a disciple of Guru Rimpoch'e.

The spirit-mediums, *delog,* and *babdrung* all bear witness to an extensive variety in Tibet of what I have referred to elsewhere as shamanic mechanisms (Samuel 1990). The boundary between the practices we have considered so far and the specifically Buddhist visionary processes of *terma* and *dagnang* is not a rigid one. Nevertheless, the *tertön* or finders of *terma,* to whom I now turn, differ from spirit-mediums, *delog,* and *babdrung* in that they are unquestionably Buddhist practitioners *(ch'öpa),* if normally noncelibate and often eccentric and controversial in their behavior. *Terma* discoveries and *dagnang* revelations provide the key to the ability of Tibetan Buddhism to adapt and transform to its changing social and political context throughout the centuries.

TERTÖN: FINDERS OF HIDDEN TREASURES

The *tertön* are finders of hidden treasures *(terma),* which are sacred objects of various kinds, especially texts believed to date from the time of Padmasambhava. In Chapter 12, I referred to *terma* as sources of teaching lineages within the Old Tantra traditions. In fact, while *tertön* and *terma* are a Nyingmapa specialty, they are found in all traditions, even the Gelugpa (Dargyay 1981). Thus the great Gelugpa scholar T'ukwan Ch'ökyi Nyima (1737–1802) correctly pointed out in relation to an attack on the validity of Nyingmapa texts, including *terma,* by another Gelugpa scholar (and his own teacher) Sumpa K'enpo (1704–1787).

> It is a bit coarse to declare that all treasure-doctrines [*terma*] were perpetrated by frauds. Not only the Nyingmapa, but all the Indian and Tibetan schools have them. . . . Even among our own virtuous sect

> [the Gelugpa], Gyüdch'en Sangyé Gyats'o revealed some rites of Dharmarāja, which had been concealed as treasures in the shrine of the protectors of Segyüd by Dulnagpa Palden Sangpo; and even the all-knowing Jamyang Shedpa [founder of Labrang *gompa*] seems to have intended to acquire the prophetic declaration and treasure-sacraments of Machig in accord with a prophecy from a treasure. . . . Thus, there would seem to be no purpose (in asserting) that all treasure-doctrines are Nyingmapa doctrines, or that all revealers of treasure-doctrines are deceitful frauds. (Kapstein 1989:241–242)

As Kapstein rightly points out, the Gelugpa lamas who attacked Nyingmapa *terma* and Tantra revelations were not engaged in modern text-historical criticism. Their purpose was to defend their own canon of texts, and they had no interest in applying the critical method that they used on Nyingmapa texts to the texts of their own tradition. At the same time, there were Gelugpa scholars of equally high status who were prepared, like T'ukwan Ch'ökyi Nyima, to defend the validity of the non-Gelugpa traditions.

Tulku Thondup, in a study based on a text about *terma* by the 3d Dodrub Ch'en Rimpoch'e, gives the names of 278 *tertön* from the eleventh to twentieth centuries (T. Thondup 1986:189–201). It is clear that this is far from a complete list, although it includes most of the major figures. Most of the leading Rimed lamas of the nineteenth and early twentieth centuries, such as Ju Mip'am, Jamgön Kongtrul, Ch'oggyur Lingpa, and Adzom Drugpa, are included in Tulku Thondup's list (Chapter 27). There are also many *tertön* among contemporary Rimed lamas.

Thondup subdivides the *tertön,* following Dodrub Ch'en's account (on which see also Gyatso 1986), into 'earth' *tertön,* who discovered actual material *terma* or 'treasures,' and a smaller number of 'mind' and 'pure vision' *tertön,* who found their treasures within their own consciousness or through visions. As mentioned above, *tertön* do not only discover texts and teachings. They find material objects such as images (Thondup includes photographs of some of these) and they also find 'hidden valleys' or *beyul* suitable for retreat (Aris 1975; Reinhard 1978; Bernbaum 1980; Diemberger 1990) or for escape from dangerous political situations. Several Himalayan states and communities, including Sikkim, the Sherpa settlements in Nepal, and Pema Köd in southeast K'am are said to have originated in this way through the leadership of *tertön* (see Brauen 1985; Bernbaum 1980; Martin 1985; Zangbu and Klatzel 1988:10).

Span Hanna has recently given a personal description of the discovery of two objects in a hill in K'am by a contemporary Bönpo female *tertön* or *k'androma* (= Skt. *ḍākinī*), K'andro K'achi Wangmo. These events took place in September 1986. K'andro K'achi Wangmo, along with her brother, who is a reincarnate lama named Mangyal Lhasey Trulku, led a group of Tibetans on a pilgrimage around the hill of Bönri near Nyingchi on the Lhasa-Sichuan road. Hanna and two other Westerners were able to join them. After some days of traveling, K'andro located the hiding place and removed two objects, a small figurine of Amitāyus and a nine-pointed *vajra*. Mangyal Lhasey Trulku told the group that the objects had been manifested in order to 'encourage faith in the Dharma' (Hanna, in press).

The *tertön* seem to represent the 'wildest' and most 'shamanic' end of Tibetan Buddhist practice. Most of them are male but very few are monks. According to Tulku Thondup, most *tertön* do Tantric practice with a female consort, and the presence of the right consort is part of the circumstances (*tendrel*, see Chapter 10) which enable the discovery of the *terma* (Thondup 1986:82–83). The typically shamanic theme of auspiciousness and of the appropriateness of circumstances is prominent in the historical *terma*. On the occasion referred to above, Mangyel Lhasey Trulku noted that "the auspiciousness of the occasion had only been 'middling' " and that consequently other *terma* concealed at the spot could not be revealed at that time (Hanna, in press).

Tertön are not necessarily unconventional in their behavior, but unusual or bizarre activity is a frequent part of the *tertön* role. The 3d Dodrub Ch'en (who was a *tertön* himself) comments that *tertön* should not be judged by their behavior:

> Among the false *tertön* there are many who are harmonious with people, who seem to have disciplined conduct, and are fortunate and charismatic. At the same time, among the authentic *tertön* there are many who are loose in speech and behaviour and who, without the least hesitation, get involved in many activities that people will condemn. In that way the *tertön* take many grave obstructions of the doctrine on themselves in the form of infamy and ill repute and they use them for the practice of taking every experience in the great equal taste.[3] (Thondup 1986:157)

'False *tertön*' are mentioned in this passage, and it is clear that the authenticity of a *terma* is not necessarily taken for granted even among the Nyingmapas. *Tertön*, genuine or otherwise, are likely to behave eccentrically and may run into considerable resistance. We may wonder how a *tertön* comes to be accepted and how a particular revelation becomes regarded as genuine. A recent study of the life of the famous *tertön* Pema Lingpa (1450–1521) by Michael Aris suggests the kind of opposition which claims to be a *tertön* might arouse (Aris 1988). The following account is summarized from Aris (1988:15–106).

Pema Lingpa

Pema Lingpa was born in 1450 to a family of hereditary Nyingmapa lamas in the valley of Bumt'ang in present-day Bhutan. He later claimed to have a series of previous rebirths including the eighth-century Pema Sel, a daughter of King Tr'isong Detsen and disciple of Guru Rimpoch'e, and also the famous fourteenth-century Nyingmapa scholar Longch'en Rabjampa. His mother came from a pastoralist family and her father, Pema Lingpa's grandfather, was a blacksmith and artisan, who brought the child up at a small *gompa*, which he patronized so as to leave the mother free to look after a younger child. From his grandfather he learnt the crafts of metalworking. He also studied woodwork and weaving. These crafts were, Aris suggests, to come in useful later in life in fabricating the *terma* he discovered. He received no formal religious training at all, but by observing a monk and a Bön priest learned how to perform some rituals. He also received the authorization for all the teachings discovered by the *tertön* Dorjé Lingpa (1346–1405) from his father-in-law, a local lama.

His grandfather died in 1473, entrusting him and a nun with the care of the *gompa*. Two years later he had a series of dreams, trances, and visions, culminating in the discovery of his first *terma*, a chest containing a text in *ḍākinī*-script, the *Longsel Sangwa Nyingchüd*, in a rock by a river. He transcribed this into Tibetan and, after a series of visions, which gave him further instruction, bestowed the initiation for it in public.

His next treasure was discovered in the same place shortly afterwards. A large crowd was in attendance and the discovery "seems to have been aimed specifically at convincing the people of the truth of his former exploit" (Aris 1988:41). As on the previous occasion, he dived naked into the river to find the entrance of the rock, this time bearing a lighted butter lamp. He extracted an image of the Buddha and a "sealed skull filled with miraculous substances" (1988:41).

Over the next ten years he discovered many more texts, mostly of a ritual nature, and objects. In the earlier years he was frequently accused of fraud, but by his later years his claims had become widely accepted, and he acquired lay patrons and disciples. He had a number of female consorts and several children, dying in 1521. According to Aris, practically all of the Bhutanese nobility today, including the royal family, claim descent from him (1988:15). A series of incarnations of Pema Lingpa was discovered, with their seat at the monastery of Lhalung in Tibet, where his chief lay patron, the *nangso* or prefect of Lhodrag, had lived. His ritual texts spread rapidly throughout the Tibetan cultural region and became the basis of monastic ritual in the Drugpa Kagyüdpa monasteries of Bhutan. Further sequences of incarnations originated with his son, also at Lhalung, and his grandson, at Gangteng in western Bhutan.

Pema Lingpa was one of the most controversial of *tertön* (see Martin 1985), although his claims were eventually widely accepted. His autobiography is full of denunciations of those without faith in his revelations (Aris 1988:52–53), attacks from more scholarly lamas (Aris 1988:47–48, 64ff), and even accusations of ritual murder (1988:68). Many of Pema Lingpa's revealed texts contained passages praising local chieftains and high officials who might offer patronage and support (1988:71–72).

Aris's conclusion is that he was an outright fraud even if he and his fellows "did no harm to anyone" and "made a lasting contribution to the cultural and spiritual life of their regions" (1988:5). Pema Lingpa is perhaps a poor case on which to argue the authenticity of *terma* revelations, but Aris's judgment of fraud may go too far. Pema Lingpa probably used his skills as an artisan to dress up and stage-manage the production of his revealed texts, but his numerous trances and visions, with their traditional shamanic language (1988:53ff) seem to have been real enough.

Being a professional *tertön* must have involved a constant pressure to produce material revelations and we may accept that Pema Lingpa, like many shamans in preliterate cultures, developed a repertoire of tricks and devices to maintain his audience's credibility. Such devices to impress the shaman's clientele do not imply that the revealed texts are also the product of conscious fraud. Earth *terma* texts are expected to be in a coded or symbolic script that has to be 'translated' into the form in which they are eventually transmitted and propagated. In the process, a text of one or two pages of indecipherable symbols may become several hundred pages of Tibetan text. There is plenty of room here for the kind of visionary processes found in many other cultures (Samuel 1990) and which probably also underlay the production of the Mahāyāna Sūtras and many other religious scriptures.

In the last analysis, the question of how far particular *tertön* are acting in good faith is less important than whether their revelations are accepted and what the implications are for the ongoing processes of Tibetan religious life of their acceptance or rejection. We should remember also that accusations of fraud within Tibetan society, such as those of Pema Lingpa's contemporaries, or of Sumpa K'enpo, have a different implication from similar statements by Western scholars. The former move within a complex field of religious and political activity, within which the possibility of 'genuine' spirit-revelations is taken for granted. Unlike the judgments of Western scholars, they do not imply a reduction of shamanic process to empiricist rationality. Guru Rimpoch'e and his constantly reincarnating disciples do not fit comfortably into a linear historical sequence, but there is no reason why they should. They are not part of a world based on such sequences.[4]

It is interesting to contrast the highly individualistic career of Pema Lingpa with that of an important seventeenth-century *tertön* Mingyur Dorjé, discoverer of the *Namch'ö* teachings ('Sky Dharma,' see Khandro 1988:35–52; Muses 1961; Schwieger 1978:39–40). Here we can see the other side of the *terma* process: the adoption of the new teachings within the context of an organized community of practitioners. The following account of Mingyur Dorjé's life is mainly summarized from Tsering Lama's book on the Pelyül tradition (Khandro 1988:45–52).

Mingyur Dorjé

Mingyur Dorjé was born in K'am in 1645 from a family claiming descent from the ancient kings of Tibet. As soon as he could speak, he said that he was a lama from the K'am *gompa* of Kat'og, giving detailed descriptions of the *gompa* as he remembered it. One day he had a vision of Guru Loden Ch'ogsed, one of the eight forms of Guru Rimpoch'e, and understood how to read and write. At the age of seven, in a pure vision, many *ḍākinī* told him of the importance of relying on a guru. Instantaneously he had a vision of the great scholar and siddha Karma Ch'agmed Rimpoch'e, who was in solitary retreat.

At the age of ten he finally met Karma Ch'agmed, who examined him and "found that he possessed all of the signs and marks of an unmistakable manifestation of Padmasambhava [Guru Rimpoch'e]." He gave him teachings and meditation instructions, and many signs indicated "the strength of his innate realization."

In his eleventh year he entered into retreat with Karma Ch'agmed. During the retreat he received continuous visions of Tantric deities, who gave him empowerments and transmissions of teachings. These empowerments and transmissions were written down and collected in the thirteen volumes of the *Namch'ö* teachings. Then Mingyur Dorjé practiced and realized[5] each of these teachings, and predicted that Karma Ch'agmed and two other lamas would be their principal 'dharma keepers.' In a vision he saw gods, demons, and local spirits rejoicing at the appearance of the teachings and promising to protect them. During the next twelve years he gave many transmissions of these teachings to famous lamas and local notables, including the Vidyādhara Kunsang Sherab, who was to become the first head of the great Nyingmapa *gompa* of Pelyül in K'am, and the local king. At the age of 19, Mingyur Dorjé was invited to Kat'og *gompa*, and went to live there. He died in 1668, at the age of 23. He was cremated amid miraculous signs and his remains placed in numerous golden *stūpa* built and offered by the great lamas from the surrounding regions.

In some ways Mingyur Dorjé was an atypical *tertön*. He was very young when he received his principal visions, and he was only 23 at his death. We would need detailed knowledge of the *Namch'ö* teachings and of the subtleties of seventeenth-century K'am politics to attempt a thorough analysis of the reasons for his success, but certain factors in Mingyur Dorjé's life are surely significant. In particular, Karma Ch'agmed (1613–1678), his guru, was both a lama of considerable reputation in his own right, and was closely involved with the founding of Pelyül *gompa*. Kunsang Sherab (1636–1699), the first head of Pelyül, was a disciple of Karma Chagmed and had received teachings from Mingyur Dorjé, and Pelyül was to become the major center for the transmission of the *Namch'ö* teachings and one of the four main Nyingmapa centers in east Tibet.

One might look for similar 'fortunate circumstances' in the cases of other successful *tertön*. The role of the prefect of Lhodrag and other major lay patrons in the case of Pema Lingpa come to mind. For the Tibetans, such circumstances would be expected as a sign that the conditions are auspicious for the spread of those particular teachings. The emphasis on auspicious circumstances that we find in relation to *terma* (see Thondup 1986; Aris 1988; Khandro 1988, *passim*), and in fact with the Nyingmapa generally, again suggests the connection with folk religion and with the shamanic side of Tibetan society (see Chapter 10).

TERMA AND *DAGNANG*

Western comments on *terma* have mostly focused on the earth *terma*, material objects discovered in rock faces, temple columns, etc., often before a large audience. In these cases, the possibility of fraud in the form of the manufacture of 'discovered' artifacts or texts is most salient. Many *terma* are, however, *gongter*, where the discovered text is not an external object but buried within the consciousness of the *tertön*. The discovery of *gongter* is not necessarily a spectacular or dramatic affair, as the discovery of earth *terma* tends to be. Their significance would seem to be less that of 'encouraging faith in the dharma,' or, for that matter, in the particular *tertön*, and more that of providing a mechanism for the introduction of new material, whether primarily philosophical, literary, prophetic, or (most often) ritual into an otherwise closed corpus of traditional practices. The same is, in fact, often true of those earth *terma* that are textual in nature. Their real significance is as a mechanism for cultural change.

A major *terma* cycle such as the *Namch'ö* or the *Könch'og Chindü* will contain empowerment rituals, *ngondrö* practices, historical and philosophical texts, and large numbers of individual *sādhana* relating to the different Old Tantra vehicles and dealing with various kinds of ritual action *(shi gyé wang drag)*. If a *terma* cycle of this kind becomes popular, it will become the subject of commentarial literature and may be extended by subsidiary *terma* of later *tertön*. The resulting corpus may be comparable in size and content to the texts associated with an individual Tantric lineage, and as with a Tantric lineage, such a *terma* cycle constitutes a complete path to Enlightenment in its own right, as well as providing a large range of rituals directed to the Pragmatic Orientation. The symbolic material of such a cycle (Tantric deities, *maṇḍala*, etc.) may be taken directly from that of earlier *terma* cycles or of *kama* lineages but there is also scope for change and innovation, such as the incorporation of new forms of deities or the increased importance attached to previously minor figures.

The importance of such cycles within Tibetan Buddhism is considerable, since they provide a large part of the basic corpus of rituals used in Nyingmapa and Bönpo *gompa* and were adopted in varying degrees by *gompa* of the other orders. Another way in which *terma* have interacted significantly with Tibetan society is by introducing new historical texts supporting the claims of one group or another (see the *Mani Kabum*, Chapter 25), texts that may provide the basis for later political and ideological developments. *Terma* also provide scope for philosophical innovation. The development of the Dzogch'en tradition, some of which is traced in the historical chapters of Part Three, largely took place through successive generations of *terma* revelations.

Terma were primarily, although not entirely, a Nyingmapa specialty, connected as they were with the activity of Guru Rimpoch'e and with the Old Tantra lineages. The concept of *dagnang* ('pure vision') is used to refer to visionary encounters with Tantric deities, and is not restricted to Guru Rimpoch'e and his manifestations. It was therefore able to serve some of the same functions within the New Tantra lineages.[6] While *dagnang* probably did not allow for as great a degree of innovation as *terma* in terms of symbolic material, it could nevertheless generate new rituals, new iconographic forms of deities, and new philosophical insights, as with the Mañjuśrī revelations that played an important part in Tsongk'apa's development of what became the Gelugpa philosophical position.

We will see more of the role of *terma* discoveries and *dagnang* revelations in the course of Part Three. In the remainder of this chapter, I shall look briefly at the question of eccentric behavior, which has already been alluded to as part of the *tertön* role. In fact, while many *tertön* acted eccentrically, by no means all of the 'crazy siddhas' and other religious eccentrics were *tertön*, and these figures require examination in their own right.

SAINTLY MADMEN, 'CRAZY SIDDHAS,' AND *TULSHUG CHÖDPA*

As John Ardussi and Lawrence Epstein noted in 1978, the idea of the 'saintly madman' is a well-established stereotype in Tibet:

> One of the most fascinating characters that runs through the oral and literary traditions of Tibet is a tricksterlike figure that is perpetually

> engaged in one sort of perverse activity or another—drinking to excess, fornicating, thieving, defying authority, playing magical tricks. . . . When Tibetans are questioned about the motivation and meanings of these figures, they almost invariably say that they behave the way they do because they are really Buddhas. (Ardussi and Epstein 1978:327)

Apart from lamas such as Drugnyön (Drugpa Kunleg) and Tsangnyön, who are explicitly referred to as 'crazy' *(nyönpa)*, similar stories are also told about the behavior of well-known figures such as Milarepa and T'angtong Gyelpo. Ardussi and Epstein summarize the "principal attributes of the saintly madman" as follows:

> a. A generalized rejection of customary behaviour which society-at-large, and the monastic establishment in particular, regard as appropriate for the religious man . . .
>
> b. An inclination towards bizarre modes of dress . . .
>
> c. A disregard for the niceties of interpersonal behaviour, particularly with regard to social status, modes of address, deferential behaviour and so on . . .
>
> d. A professed disdain for scholasticism, the study of religion through books alone . . .
>
> e. The use of popular poetical forms, mimes, songs, epic tales, and so forth, during the course of their preaching . . .
>
> f. The use of obscenity and vulgar parlance. (Ardussi and Epstein 1978:332–333)

To these we could add two further features that emerge from the descriptions of these lamas: they have great insight, and so are capable of seeing through other people's behavior and motivations; and they have great attainment, which is demonstrated by their magical power.

As Ardussi and Epstein note, these saintly madmen consciously echo the crazy behavior of some of the Tantric siddhas of India. Ardussi and Epstein's examples are from Tibetan history, and several of them (in particular Milarepa, T'angtong Gyelpo, Tsangnyön and Drugpa Kunleg) will feature in the historical narrative of Part Three. Such figures are, however, not confined to past centuries. The 'crazy siddha' *(drubnyön)* has remained a recognizable figure in Tibetan religious life into modern times. Often rough and crude in their behavior, with no respect for conventional social standards, these lamas are nevertheless respected for their attainment and their magical power. Namk'a Drimed Rimpoch'e described two of these *drubnyön* in passing in the course of a conversation:

> The son of the lama at [*gompa* C] is still in Tibet. He is a *drubnyön*. There are stories about his doing miraculous feats like finding water-*terma*. He also has a lot of magical ability *(nüpa)* and is very good at curing sick people. His character and habits are quite rough *(tsidpo)*. Many people from his area have requested him to rebuild the *gompa*, but he refused to do it, saying 'There used to be a *gompa* but it was all destroyed. What is the use?' He refused to claim or take care of the *gompa* . . .
>
> [Lama D] was also a *drubnyön*. He could tie needles and swords into knots without any hesitation. He was very good at curing illnesses and afflictions by malevolent spirits *(dön geg)*. He was also very good at curing diseases of animals. His character was very rough.[7]

Tying a sword into a knot is a characteristic feat of a *drubnyön*. Ardussi and Epstein tell a story of Drugpa Kunleg in which he performs a similar feat (1978:334).

In his book *The Crystal and the Way of Light*, Namkhai Norbu Rimpoch'e describes an eccentric lama whom he encountered in his youth in K'am (Norbu 1986b:68–72). This man had been a Sakyapa *trapa*, but had been expelled from his *gompa* after breaking his vows of celibacy. He went into retreat in a small hut on the mountainside near his native village, but after some years:

> he suddenly seemed to go crazy. One day while he was doing his practice he began to throw all of his books out of the window; then he burned them, smashed up all his statues, turned everything upside down, and partly destroyed his retreat house. People began to call him 'The Lunatic.' Then he disappeared, and no one saw him for three years. At the end of that time somebody came across him quite by chance. He was living in a very remote spot, right at the top of the mountain. Everybody wondered how he had managed to survive and get enough to eat up there all that time, because nothing grew there and nobody normally ever went there. So people began to take an interest in him and to visit him. Although he refused to communicate with them, the way that he lived convinced people that he wasn't

crazy. Instead of calling him 'The Lunatic,' they began to speak of him as a realized being, a saint. (Norbu 1986b:69)

Norbu's uncle, who was the abbot of a Sakyapa *gompa*, went to see him one day with a group of people, including Norbu. After a brief and eccentric encounter, the lama ordered them to go in a particular direction. After several hours' walking, they found a hunter who had broken his foot and was unable to walk. Some of the party carried him back to his family. The others went back to the lama, but he simply told them to go away (1986b:71–72).

Elsewhere, Namkhai Norbu has referred to another 'rough lama,' a man in Derge state whose knowledge of the Dharma was restricted to the single mantra syllable *hūṃ*. This man had learned to chant his single *hūṃ* with such power that he was regularly invited to participate in major rituals at the Derge court.[8]

Another fairly recent figure who exemplifies many *drubnyön* characteristics was the 2d Ch'ogling Rimpoch'e of the Neten line, Ngedön Drubpé Dorjé (c. 1871–c. 1917), one of the two recognized reincarnations of Ch'oggyur Lingpa, a famous nineteenth-century *tertön* (see Chapter 27) who had himself been known for his magical power and unconventional behavior. The following excerpts are taken from a short account of this lama's life by Orgyen Tobgyal Rinpoche:

he was, from an early age, very wonderful, displaying many miracles. He refused to listen to anyone, so no one could give him orders. Sometimes he hung his clothes on the rays of the sun. When his tutor taught him reading, he would neither learn nor study, only play. . . . When [he] was older, he learned reading even without being taught . . .

Neten Ch'ogling's conduct was extremely crude, like that of an Indian mahāsiddha. He drank a lot of wine and took lots of snuff. When people came to see him he would send for women and wine. Having higher perceptions, he could immediately reveal his visitors' thoughts, and he would expose any hidden faults right away. When great lamas or dignitaries came to visit him, the servant boys would be ordered to come in naked while bringing tea and in addition to fart loudly . . .

He had many amazing disciples and he also displayed many miracles. One day while performing a tantric dance, lightning struck his head, but, though the stones beneath his feet shattered, he neither flinched nor interrupted the ritual.

> Neten Ch'ogling enjoyed playing dangerous games. In the area [of his *gompa*] was a big river. One day he wanted to cross the stream in a boat. Once in the boat he took the oars, and midstream threw them both overboard. As the current swept the boat downstream, all his attendants were frightened and closed their eyes while Ch'ogling simply roared with laughter. . . . Finally the boat approached rapids. Just before entering them, Ch'ogling touched a big rock with his hand and said to Genyen Borang, a *nāga* living in the river, 'It's enough now!' The boat immediately began moving upstream, his hand leaving a deep imprint on the rock. Though no one can reach it, the mark can be seen through binoculars. (Tobgyal 1988:49–51)

The description of Neten Ch'ogling's death is also striking for its reversal of the accepted norms for a high lama: "[T]onight I'm going to die. My body shall not remain in the meditation posture; bind a rope tightly around its neck, put it in a sack and take it directly to Neten Monastery. My *trulku* will be immediately reborn in Derge" (Tobgyal 1988:52).

As these examples indicate, the *drubnyön* role was not an uncommon one in premodern Tibetan society. Some of these *drubnyön* were uneducated, and evidently none had much regard for the clerical and philosophical Buddhism of the *gompa*. Some of them, however, came from respectable lama families (as with the two *drubnyön* mentioned by Namk'a Rimpoch'e), or were reincarnate lamas, as with the Neten Ch'ogling, who was the reincarnation of an important *tertön* lama and took over his predecessor's *gompa*. Other *drubnyön* commenced a celibate monastic career and later broke away, as with the ex-Sakyapa monk described by Namkhai Norbu Rimpoch'e.

Naturally, not every crazy person in premodern Tibet was regarded as a saintly madman. There are, as Ardussi and Epstein point out, several other indigenous classifications for what Western medicine might regard as psychiatric illness, none of which carry any implication of saintliness (1978:329–331; see also Epstein and Topgay 1982). The deliberate rejection of conventional behavior could nevertheless, for the Tibetans, be part of a recognizable form of spiritual path.

The reference to "the practice of taking every experience in the great equal taste" *(ronyom ch'enpö tulshug chödpa),* at the end of the quote from Dodrub Ch'en Rimpoch'e earlier in this chapter, incorporates a standard term for this kind of yogic practice, in which obedience to conventional social dictates is rejected as an obstacle to the yogin's spiritual progress. *Ronyom ch'enpo*, the "great equal taste," is recognized Buddhist terminology for regarding all phenomena as alike and rejecting conventional responses of like and dislike, good and bad. The term *tulshug chödpa* refers to various kinds of yogic practice, including the internal *tsalung* practices of Anuttarayoga Tantra, but it can also be used to refer specifically to the path of rejection of conventional behavior. The aim of *tulshug chödpa* is to go beyond the needs for ordinary social restraints, so that the practitioner acts out of the necessity of the situation itself.

A well-known modern example of such *tulshug chödpa* was K'enpo Gangshar, who was one of the teachers of the Karma Kagyüdpa lama Trungpa Rimpoch'e (Chapter 18). The title K'enpo in this case refers to a Kagyüdpa monastic degree similar to the Gelugpa *geshé* title. K'enpo Gangshar was a highly trained scholar and a famous teacher. In his earlier years he was also a fully ordained *gelong* and observed monastic discipline faultlessly. Later, he was 'awakened' and adopted the *tulshug chödpa* style. He took a female consort, renounced his vows, and became famous for his eccentric behavior. He was said, like Neten Ch'ogling, to be able to tell people's inner thoughts immediately by just looking at them, and all his words were an expression of his enlightened state. Many of those who knew him regarded him as a truly liberated being, although others found his actions embarrassing and disturbing. He died in the 1960s, on his way, according to one story, to Beijing, having announced that he was going to teach the Dharma to Mao Zedong.[9]

Tibetan societies in premodern times had many of these various kinds of unorthodox Buddhist practitioners. The variety of political systems and the lack of any effective centralized government made it relatively easy for them to survive, and Tibetan lay people were prepared to tolerate and support holy men and women despite their occasionally bizarre behavior. The *tertön* were not necessarily as rough or eccentric in their outward behavior as some of these *drubnyön* and *tulshug chödpa* practitioners, although, as Dodrub Ch'en indicates, some of them certainly adopted such behavior. The *tertön*, however, generally were given space to develop and flourish by the tolerance of Tibetan societies towards this wide range of assorted shamanic practitioners, the spirit-mediums, revenants, and inspired bards, the wandering *chöd* practitioners, solitary hermits, and eccentric lamas. Doubtless, many *tertön* remained in obscurity, their revelations dismissed as fraudulent or accepted only by a few local villagers, but enough were taken up and their *terma* propagated to create a vital mechanism for innovation within Tibetan religion.

Theravādin societies such as Thailand or Sri Lanka also had eccentrics and marginal holy men and women, and some of them also attained a degree of fame and respect. While it is difficult to demonstrate this conclusively, it seems likely that Tibet provided far greater scope for such people. It certainly seems true that, as Tambiah notes, religious leaders in the Theravādin countries who were perceived as a threat to the state were effectively dealt with and removed (Tambiah 1984). The converse to this tolerance of diversity in Tibet was that Tibetan Buddhism had abundant scope for movement and change in comparison with Buddhism in the Theravādin societies to the south. While the Theravādin societies developed a purist approach to Buddhism, claiming strict adherence to the original teachings of the historical Buddha, the Tibetans grounded their religion not so much in the teachings of the historical Śākyamuni but in the continuing process of revelation from a shamanic realm inhabited by beings beyond the constraints of historical time such as Vajradhara, Avalokiteśvara, and Guru Rimpoch'e.

This concludes our survey in Chapters 15 and 16 of the types of Tibetan religious practitioner. In Chapter 17, we look at the types of religious community *(gompa)* within which they operated, and the relationships between these *gompa* and the societies of which they formed a part.

17

Tibetan Religious Communities *(Gompa)*

It is commonplace to think of premodern Tibet as a land of monasteries, and it certainly contained some very large monastic establishments. Celibate monasticism in traditional Tibetan societies was nevertheless neither as uniform nor as extensive as is often supposed. In Appendix 1, I discuss the proportion of the population in premodern Tibet that was involved in celibate monasticism. Estimates such as 25 percent to 33 percent of the male population appear to be greatly exaggerated. A more plausible estimate would be about 10 percent to 12 percent in the central agricultural areas, along with a much smaller number of women. In some areas it was higher, but in others it was considerably lower; however, many laymen and laywomen were involved in religious practice either as full-time or part-time residents of religious communities or as regular participants in ritual at local religious centers.

As has been already pointed out, the term *gompa* is one of those generic terms common in the Tibetan language. It groups together institutions that are in many respects very different. As one might expect, also, the various kinds of society within Tibet have their own characteristic kinds of *gompa.* We will look at three major patterns corresponding to the *Centralized Agricultural, Remote Agricultural,* and *Pastoral* areas (see Chapter 7), with examples of each type.

Examples of the centralized agricultural pattern include Dingri, Sakya, and Ladakh. We will also look more briefly at the Lhasa region and at two parts of K'am. In all these areas, we find medium and large monastic *gompa* with upwards of fifty and often several hundred celibate *ch'öpa* (*tr'apa,* monks). Such *gompa* generally have at least one reincarnate lama *(trulku),* usually the reincarnation of the founder, and sometimes several. Occasionally, in the non-Gelugpa orders, the head lama may be hereditary rather than reincarnate. These lamas are distinct from the *k'enpo,* the administrative head of the community, who is usually elected or selected in some manner from the community.

In these areas, we also find smaller *ani gompa* for female religious practitioners *(ani),* often close to the villages, since *ani* are expected to keep up close links with their natal households and may live there and assist with household work for part of the time.

It is in these centralized agricultural regions that the very large monastic *gompa,* which acted as teaching centers for the various orders and suborders, are mostly located. The largest, Sera and Drepung, both near Lhasa and belonging to the Gelugpa order, had over 10,000 *trapa* each before 1959.

While the existence of medium- to large-size monastic *gompa* is a typical feature of the centralized agricultural pattern, it does not exclude other types of Buddhist practice. There are usually some hereditary lamas with their own family *gompa.* There may also be small to medium-size communities of lay *ch'öpa,* either householders who practice part-time, or full-time noncelibate yogins. Such communities may or may not focus on a hereditary or reincarnate lama.

In the remote agricultural pattern, found in the less centralized agricultural areas, we find these communities and practitioners also exist but without the large monastic *gompa.* There are still *trapa,* but they are few in number and represent an exceptional rather than a regular choice of life for the local population. Our examples of this pattern are two contrasting Tibetan-speaking areas of northern Nepal, Dolpo, and the Khumbu-Shorung region, and a third area, Lahul, now part of India.

In several such areas, there has been a growth of small- to medium-size non-Gelugpa monastic *gompa* in recent years. This may be attributed to a variety of causes: the impact of the Rimed movement (see Chapter 27), the economic surplus produced by new crops such as the potato (Fürer-Haimendorf 1964), or in recent years through tourism, the activities of refugee lamas and *trapa* who have settled in these regions since 1959.

A third pattern is found in the pastoral regions. No detailed studies are available of religious communities in these parts but a general impression may be derived from the works of Ekvall and Rock on Amdo (Ekvall 1952, 1954a, 1964b, 1981; Rock 1928, 1956), Namkhai Norbu on the K'am-Amdo border region (Namkhai Norbu 1983, 1990a), and from scattered comments in the literature (Teichman [1922] on K'am, Dawa Norbu [1974] on the nomads of the Chang-t'ang). The pattern here is of medium to large monastic *gompa*, often on the edges of the nomadic country proper. They are associated with trading and market centers and have political and economic functions in relation to the nearby pastoral nomadic tribes. These large *gompa* may be supplemented by smaller 'tent-monasteries' among the nomads themselves (N. Norbu 1983, 1990a).

We examined the various political arrangements in Amdo in Chapter 5. The major *gompa* in the eastern areas of Amdo studied by Ekvall and Rock were Gelugpa. This reflects factors other than the religious preferences of the nomads themselves. Many of the *trapa* at Kumbum, Labrang, and Choni were Mongolian, and these large monastic centers received substantial patronage in the past from Mongol patrons and from the Manchu imperial dynasty. Several authors mention that pastoralists prefer the more shamanic and 'magical' aspects of Tibetan Buddhism (Teichman 1922; D. Norbu 1974; and see Chapter 8). A preference for the non-Gelugpa traditions would go along with this (see N. Norbu 1983:77) and there were several large Nyingmapa *gompa* in southern Amdo and Golog country (see Paltul n.d.) including Tart'ang, which is reputed to have had around 2,000 *trapa*, making it perhaps the largest of all Nyingmapa monasteries (Khandro 1988; Thondup 1987), and Dodrub Ch'en, a major center for the Longch'en Nyingt'ig teachings (Thondup 1984, 1987, and Chapter 27).

The centralized agricultural, remote agricultural, and pastoral patterns did not exist in isolation from each other. Students from outlying areas, where the remote agricultural or pastoral patterns prevail, regularly traveled to areas where there are large monastic training centers, and might remain there as *trapa* for many years. *Trapa* trained at these centers would go to settle in more remote areas and perhaps stimulate the growth of monastic life there for a few decades or more permanently. The major pilgrimage centers, which include holy mountains such as Mount Kailash, caves associated with Guru Rimpoch'e, and small hermitages where famous past lamas had practiced, as well as the major monastic centers, acted as foci attracting pilgrims and permanent settlers from all over the Tibetan region.

The destruction of the major monastic teaching centers after 1959 brought this pattern of interaction to a temporary end, although it also led to many senior lamas settling as refugees in formerly remote areas and revitalizing the religious life there.[1] In more recent years, much of this pattern has been reconstituted around refugee *gompa* and around pilgrimage centers in India and the border regions such as Bodhnath in Nepal, Bodhgaya and Sarnath in India, and the Dalai Lama's residence at Dharamsala in India. The major refugee *gompa,* constructed by refugees from the big central and eastern Tibetan teaching *gompa,* have taken over the role of teaching centers for remote areas in India and Nepal, for the refugee communities and, increasingly, for areas within the PRC where religious life is being reconstructed.

While destruction and change on this scale is a new phenomenon within Tibetan society, the premodern position was not static, and changes in the relative importance of different regions happened at various times throughout history, as a result of shifts in the economic importance of different regions, and of the destruction of *gompa* in a particular region through war or their closure by hostile political authorities. The *gompa* within Tibetan societies form a dynamic and shifting pattern, not a static network, and in Chapters 23 to 27 we will examine some of the historical background to these processes of change.

In this chapter, we now examine examples of each of the patterns identified in more detail, beginning with the centralized agricultural pattern.

THE CENTRALIZED AGRICULTURAL PATTERN

In this pattern, found in the larger, more productive and more centralized agricultural areas of Tibet, we find medium to large monastic *gompa* with substantial communities of *trapa,* along with smaller *ani gompa* and various nonmonastic types of *ch'öpa.*

The Dingri Region: State Gompa *and Popular* Gompa

The major trading center of Dingri, studied from refugee accounts by Barbara Aziz, was a large and populous community on the major trade route from Lhasa to Kathmandu (Aziz 1978). The area was under the control of the Lhasa administration until 1959. It had been depopulated during the Nepal-Tibet wars during the eighteenth and nineteenth centuries, and much of the Dingri community in the 1950s was made up of recent immigrants. Aziz estimates the population of Dingri at 12,000 people, of whom 2,000 lived in the urban trading center of Gang-gar, and the rest in the surrounding rural area.

During the time of the 5th Dalai Lama (seventeenth century), Shelkar Ch'ödé, a small *gompa* on the hill at Shelkar, was taken over by the Gelugpa and developed into a large monastic *gompa.* The main administrative center for the Lhasa regime, Shelkar *dzong,* adjoined the monastery. In the 1950s the *gompa* of Shelkar Ch'ödé had about 300 *trapa,* many of them recruited from Dingri households under the 'monk levy' system, by which a village was obliged to provide one or more *trapa* to a particular monastery (Aziz 1978:233). It also had extensive estates in the region. Two other more distant Gelugpa *gompa* also imposed monk levies on Dingri villagers.

The *gompa* at Shelkar did not perform religious services for Dingri households, although it did hold a big annual festival with performances of ritual dances (*ch'am,* see Chapter 14). According to Aziz, Dingri people attended the festival but said they went only for the market; they resented both the monk levy and the other economic obligations towards the *gompa* (1978:237). The prevailing pattern of religious practice in Dingri until the twentieth century was that of part-time lay *ch'öpa* or *serky'im.* Aziz estimates that there were about 850 active *serky'im* in the region, living in 27 village communities. These communities, inhabited entirely by *serky'im,* were called by the familiar term *gompa.* The *serky'im* of each village performed ritual services for a small group of neighboring villages.

There were also a number of hereditary lamas *(ngagpa).* These men and their families were accorded high social status and were believed to possess inherited religious power, but they were not attached to large monastic communities. There were small communities of yogins associated with the two major pilgrimage sites at Tsibri and Langkor.

Large-scale celibate monasticism (apart from the Shelkar *gompa*) seems to have been a recent development, deriving from the activities of three charismatic lamas and from the economic growth of the region in the first half of the twentieth century. The first lama, Ngawang Tenzin Norbu (also known as Dzatrul Rimpoch'e,[2] c. 1866–1940; Aziz 1978:209–211), founded (or perhaps rebuilt?) the Nyingmapa monastic *gompa* of Dzarong in the hills south of Dingri in 1902.[3] By the 1950s, Dzarong had some 500 *trapa* and *ani* in thirteen communities *(gompa)*, four of them small female *gompa* close to the villages so that the *ani* could remain near their natal households. The founder had been succeeded as abbot by a lama, the 11th Tr'ulshig Rimpoch'e[4] (b. 1921, see Kohn 1988:xi; Aziz 1978:211–214), who was the recognized reincarnation of Ngawang Tenzin Norbu's own teacher. The religious practice of Dzarong was derived from that of the central Tibetan Nyingmapa teaching center of Mindröl Ling, where Tr'ulshig Rimpoch'e and other Dzarong lamas went for training.

The Dzarong lama also visited the Sherpa region across the main Himalayan range to the south. He was instrumental in the building of several small celibate or partially celibate monastic *gompa* there. These *gompa* derived their religious practice from Dzarong and Mindröl Ling (Aziz 1978:209–215). It is from Dzarong that Sherpa monasteries derived their ritual dance *(ch'am)* tradition, linked to the Mani Rimdu festival (Fürer-Haimendorf 1964; Jerstad 1969; Fantin 1976; Kohn 1988; see Chapter 14); *ch'am* was performed regularly at Dzarong.

A third lama, Tsibri Tr'ipön Pema Ch'ögyel (1878?–1958 or 1959) founded a group of small communities belonging to the Drugpa Kagyüdpa tradition near the pilgrimage site of Tsibri (Aziz 1978:215–217). This lama was born in Ladakh but had gone to east Tibet at the age of 18 to study with the famous Rimed teacher Śākya Śrī (1853–1919), a Drugpa-married lama from Tsari in southwest K'am.[5]

The Dzarong and Tsibri lamas acted as personal religious teachers, *tsawé lama* or 'heart lamas' to use Aziz's translation, for many of the Dingri villagers. Aziz describes seven other Dingri lamas who headed small monastic *gompa* or had a following of lay *ch'öpa*. Three of these were hereditary *ngagpa* lamas, respected in the community but active in recent times more as performers of ritual than as personal religious teachers. She estimates the total number of celibate religious practitioners in the region as about 900 (it is not clear how this is divided among *trapa* and *ani*).

Sakya: A Religious Estate

In the same general area of southwest Tibet was the large monastic estate of Sakya, discussed at some length in Chapter 3. By contrast with Dingri, this was a region dominated by monastic *gompa* of a single order, the Sakyapa. Cassinelli and Ekvall's study of Sakya gives us a glimpse of the social structure of religious life in an area of large state-supported *gompa* of celibate monks.

The *gompa* of Sakya were supported by the Sakya estate administration, which owned a number of small estates around Tibet as well as the principal estate surrounding the town of Sakya itself in west-central Tibet. This estate covered some 2,100 square miles and had a population, according to Cassinelli and Ekvall, of around 16,000, of whom 7,000 lived in the town of Sakya and the remainder in the surrounding rural areas. There were two large monastic *gompa* in the town of Sakya itself, both dating back to the period of Sakya power over Tibet, with 300 and 200 *trapa* respectively. In the surrounding region there was another large *gompa*, Ch'ök'or Lhunpo, with 200 *trapa*, and 13 smaller *gompa* with from 4 to 50 *trapa* each. Some of these were communities of retired *trapa* from the urban *gompa* (Cassinelli and Ekvall 1969:33, 259, 289–301, 311, 400–404). Altogether Cassinelli and Ekvall estimate that there were 985 *trapa*, of whom around 230 came from outside the main Sakya estate. There were also about 250 *ani* but these spent much of their time working outside the *ani gompa* in their family households.

All these *gompa* belonged to the Sakyapa order. There were some followers of other religious orders, including the Bönpo, and there were several Nyingmapa hereditary lama households *(ngagpa)*, but apparently no *gompa* belonging to other orders. Cassinelli and Ekvall do not give much information about the provision of religious services by the Sakyapa *gompa* or by hereditary lama households. Dawa Norbu's *Red Star over Tibet*, an autobiographical account of life in Sakya, which is a valuable complement to the Cassinelli and Ekvall study, discusses his mother's father, a (presumably Nyingmapa) hereditary lama who was employed as the head lama of one of the Sakya government's annual fund-collecting missions among the nomads of the Changt'ang (D. Norbu 1974:23ff, see Chapter 7 and below). Norbu also mentions consulting a lama, Zongchung Rimpoch'e, about his father's illness (1974:41), but it is not clear if this was Sakyapa or Nyingmapa.

Norbu also describes the monastic festivals of Sakya, which as usual included performances of *ch'am* and served as occasion for popular celebrations and village fairs (1974:38–41).

Ladakh: Tibetan Kingdom within an Indian State

In the far west of Tibet, the region of Ladakh, now part of India, also had a mixture of *gompa* of different traditions, mainly belonging to the Gelugpa and to two Kagyüdpa suborders, the Drigungpa and Drugpa. The *gompa* of Ladakh have been extensively studied in recent years (Singh 1977; Snellgrove and Skorupski 1979, 1980; Brauen 1980b; Grimshaw 1983).

Again, the reasons for the precise mixture of monastic orders can be found in the history of the region (Petech 1977, 1978; Snellgrove and Skorupski 1979; Schuh 1983; N. Tsering 1979, 1985). Ladakh as a separate polity dates back to the establishment of the Ladakhi kingdom, one of the successor states to the old Tibetan empire, around A.D. 950. Lamayuru is said to be the oldest *gompa* in Ladakh, and traditionally dates from the time of Nāropa (late tenth century?). There are several other old *gompa* that date back to the eleventh century and seem to have been initially Kadampa centers: Alchi, Spituk, and perhaps also Likir.

The Ladakhi kings patronized the Drigung Kagyüdpa from 1215 onwards, and Lamayuru became their main center. In the fifteenth century the rulers of Ladakh came under Gelugpa influence. The old *gompa* at Alchi, Spituk, and Likir were rebuilt as Gelugpa centers, and a new *gompa* was built at Tiktse.

A second Drigungpa *gompa*, Phiyang, dates from a Drigungpa revival in the early sixteenth century. There followed a period of Drugpa Kagyüdpa influence associated with the lama Tagts'ang Repa, who was a close associate of one of the most famous Ladakhi kings, Senge Namgyel (ruled 1616–1642). The *gompa* of Hemis was founded on the site of a hermitage associated with the early Drugpa master Gödts'angpa. This *gompa* became the Drugpa center in Ladakh and remained closely linked to the royal family. Its head lama was a reincarnation of Tagts'ang Repa, and in recent years it has also been the residence of the head lama of the Tibetan branch of the Drugpa suborder (the Gyalwang Drugch'en). Other Drugpa *gompa* were founded at this time at Shey, Stagna, and Chemre.

A war between the Ladakhi kingdom and the new central Tibetan regime of the 5th Dalai Lama broke out in 1679. The causes were complex but reflected, in part, the poor relations between the Gelugpa and the Drugpa Kagyüdpa who were now the dominant order in Bhutan. The Ladakhi king was forced to buy help from the Moghul governor of Kashmir. The treaty with the Moghuls and the subsequent treaty with Lhasa involved the loss of more than half of Ladakh's territory and the end of Ladakh's role as a significant Himalayan power (see Petech 1977:70–80). Subsequently, the Dalai Lama's regent at Lhasa attempted to impose a hierarchical structure on the monasteries of Ladakh in which both the Gelugpa *gompa*, organized under the leadership of Tiktse *gompa*, and the non-Gelugpa *gompa* were to come under control from Drepung, the large Gelugpa *gompa* near Lhasa. The integration of the non-Gelugpa *gompa* never took place and Ladakh, after the Dogra conquest of 1834, became absorbed into the Hindu state of Jammu and Kashmir, ending any possibility of intervention by Lhasa. Tiktse retained authority over most of the other Gelugpa *gompa* and became in the nineteenth century the seat of the Bakula Rimpoch'e, now the principal Gelugpa incarnate lama in Ladakh.

Another Gelugpa *gompa*, Ridzong, was founded in 1829. There is a small Sakyapa *gompa* in Ladakh at Matro and a small Nyingmapa *gompa* at Tragt'ok, both dating back to before the war with Tibet, but neither of these orders have ever had significant political influence in Ladakh.

The sixteenth-century king Trashi Namgyel laid down a rule that every family of more than one male child had to give up one to become a *trapa* (Petech 1977:168). Rules and practices of this kind existed in several parts of Tibet, as did tax obligations by which villages are required to supply a certain number of *trapa*. As we saw, the Gelugpa *gompa* in Dingri, Shelkar Ch'ödé, was supplied with *trapa* in this way (Aziz 1978). While it seems unlikely that many regions of Tibet reached a level of one *trapa* per family (see Appendix 1), celibate monasticism became firmly established in Ladakh, and Ladakh today has monastic *gompa* belonging to all four Buddhist orders (and two of the Kagyüdpa suborders), as well as a number of village temples.

None of the Ladakhi *gompa* are very large compared with the largest monastic *gompa* in central or east Tibet. Singh gives figures of 500 'lamas' (presumably *trapa*) 'attached to' Hemis and Likir, 300 for Tiktse, Chemre, and Stakna, and lower numbers for the others. These figures however include *trapa* (and perhaps noncelibate *ch'öpa* in the case of the non-Gelugpa *gompa*) at smaller *gompa* throughout Ladakh and Zanskar who are affiliated with these places. The actual numbers of *trapa* in residence at the main Ladakhi *gompa* nowadays are much smaller than this. Two recent guidebooks estimate the number of *trapa* at Likir as 100 (Hirschberg 1980:163; Schuttler 1980:104). There are also some small *ani gompa* or *chomoling* in Ladakh (for example, near Hemis Shukpachen; Phylactou 1989:42).

As in Dingri and Sakya, the main *gompa* in Ladakh put on annual performances of *ch'am*. That at Hemis has become particularly famous outside Ladakh because it takes place in summer and so has often been seen by visitors (Rizvi 1983:175; for a description see Helffer 1980). Others take place around New Year, including those at Spituk (Marko, in press), Matro, Stok, Leh, T'iktse, and Phiyang (Brauen 1980b:117). These are separate from the cycle of village and lineage rituals focusing on the local gods (Brauen 1980b; Dollfus 1989).

Ladakhi *trapa* however spent a considerable amount of their time performing rituals for local villagers. Goldstein and Tsarong studied a small Drigung 'branch monastery' (perhaps Phiyang) in 1981. This *gompa* had 34 'full-time permanent' *trapa*. Goldstein and Tsarong noted that two *trapa* whose activities they studied in detail performed rituals for villagers on over half the days of the year (1985:24). Villagers also frequently commissioned rituals to be performed at the monastery.

The extensive involvement of *trapa* in performing rituals for laymen in Ladakh may explain the apparent absence of hereditary lamas as significant ritual performers. While not often described at length in the literature (see below) they nevertheless seem to be important performers of ritual for lay people in most Tibetan communities. There is little or no mention of them for Ladakh, where all the *gompa* appear to have been integrated into a series of hierarchical structures as branches of the various major monasteries of central Ladakh (see

Singh 1977). This may be connected with the system, reported as far as I know only from Ladakh, by which the major *gompa* appointed resident *trapa* for two or three years at a time to look after village temples and provide ritual services for the local lay population.

Thus the village of Hemis Shugpachen in Ladakh has four village temples *(lhak'ang)*, three of them affiliated to Chemre, Rizong, and Likir. Caretaker *trapa* from those *gompa* reside in the village for a two- or three-year period. The caretaker is joined by other *trapa* from the parent *gompa* on the occasion of major rituals. The fourth temple was built some fifty years ago by the villagers to hold a set of the Kangyur (Tibetan Buddhist scriptures) and is not affiliated to any outside *gompa* (Phylactou 1989:40–44; see also Dollfuss 1989). The village's strongest connection is with the nearby *gompa* of Ridzong, which has a residence *(labrang)* and a granary within the village for the "collection and distribution of tithes and loans" (Phylactou 1989:44).

All this suggests a more 'clericalized' situation for Ladakh than elsewhere in the Tibetan region. If this is true, it is probably to be explained in terms of the incorporation of Ladakh in the Hindu state of Jammu and Kashmir and subsequently in British and independent India.

Dingri, Sakya, and Ladakh are the only centralized agricultural areas for which I have relatively complete information about the major *gompa*.[6] Less complete data is available for some other regions and it is worth looking briefly at the situation in premodern times in the area around Lhasa itself and in two regions of K'am.

The Lhasa Region: Center of the Gelugpa State

The region around Lhasa was understandably Gelugpa territory, dominated as it was by the Potala, palace of the Dalai Lama, and with the two largest Gelugpa *gompa*, Sera and Drepung, within a few hours' walk of the city. The third major Gelugpa teaching center, Ganden, which is also the seat of the formal head of the Gelugpa order, was a couple of days' journey to the east. The Jok'ang, the central temple in Lhasa itself, was under Gelugpa control, as was the Ramoch'e temple, which, like the Jok'ang, dated from the early royal period. Most of the other *gompa* in Lhasa were Gelugpa. They included the two Gelugpa Tantric Colleges, Gyütöd Trats'ang and Gyümed Trats'ang, as well as the *gompa* of Ts'emön Ling, Tengyé Ling, Meru

Sarpa, and Shidé Trats'ang at the Ramoch'e temple (Batchelor 1987; Dowman 1988).

The only non-Gelugpa *gompa* in the immediate vicinity of Lhasa seems to have been Nech'ung, the small Nyingmapa *gompa* close to Drepung, which was the seat of the Lhasa Government's principal oracle. A number of important *gompa* of other orders were however within two or three days' travel from Lhasa. These included Ts'urp'u, Drigung, and Taglung, which were the head *gompa* of three Kagyüdpa suborders (Karmapa, Drigungpa, and Taglungpa) and the important Drugpa Kagyüd center of Dech'en Ch'ök'or. There was also Nalendra, which was an important Sakya center, and the two main Nyingmapa teaching centers in central Tibet, Dorje Drag and Mindröl Ling. These central Tibetan *gompa*, all of them dating back to the period before Gelugpa supremacy, had waned somewhat in importance in comparison with the newer and larger east Tibetan teaching *gompa* but were still the seats of lamas of great authority and prestige.

Figures for the size of these communities in premodern times are hard to come by, except for the major Gelugpa centers of Ganden, Sera, and Drepung. These were traditionally supposed to have 3,300, 5,500, and 7,700 *trapa* each. In recent times the numbers were considerably larger, approaching 5,000, 11,000 and 15,000 respectively (Chang and Shefts 1964:119–124). Each was divided into two or three colleges or *trats'ang* and had several hostels or *k'angts'en*, each taking students from a different part of Tibet (see Lodro 1974; Rato 1977; Sherpa et al. 1977; Rabten 1980). The two Tantric Colleges in Lhasa, whose members were *geshé* graduates from Ganden, Sera, or Drepung, were restricted to 500 *geshé* each.

Dergé and the Rimed Gompa

Dergé in K'am (see Chapter 4) was the third largest independent Tibetan polity (after the Dalai Lama's government and the Drugpa monastic state of Bhutan). Its ruling family were originally hereditary lamas of the Nyingmapa tradition (see Kolmaš 1968:27). In the thirteenth century they adopted the teachings and practices of the Sakyapa order. They gradually gained considerable secular power and founded a large monastery of the Sakyapa tradition, Lhundrub Teng, also known as Dergé Gonch'en, the 'great *gompa* of Dergé,' at what was to become the capital of the state of Dergé (late fifteenth century? Kolmaš 1968:31).

The real power of Dergé dates from the seventeenth century and reached its height in the eighteenth and nineteenth centuries. During this period the head lama of the monastery continued to belong to the family of the kings of Dergé. As might be expected, several other Sakyapa monasteries grew up within Dergé state (see Teichman 1922; Kessler 1984, map 27). This official connection with the Sakyapa did not, however, prevent the Dergé rulers from tolerating and patronizing the other traditions. The old Nyingmapa center of Kat'og was refounded in 1656, and the three other major Nyingmapa monastic centers in K'am, Pelyül (1665, see Khandro 1988), Dzogch'en (1685), and Shech'en (1734) were all within the territory of Dergé, as was the major Karma Kagyüd center in K'am, Pelpung or Barbung (founded 1727, see Chang 1961; Trungpa 1971:101ff). There were no Gelugpa *gompa* in central Dergé, but there were several in the north of the state. One of the main remaining Bönpo centers, Dza Tengch'en, was also in Dergé territory.

This nonsectarian orientation climaxed in the mid-nineteenth century, when Dergé was the location for the growth of the Rimed movement, a nonsectarian synthesis of all Tibetan Buddhist traditions that grew up primarily among the three non-Gelugpa Buddhist orders (see Chapter 27 and Smith 1970). Pelpung, Dzogch'en, Shech'en, the Sakyapa *gompa* of Dzongsar, and other *gompa* in Dergé state were among the main Rimed centers. From here the movement spread to central Tibet and to regions such as Dingri, where it was represented by lamas such as Tr'ulshig Rimpoch'e and Tr'ipön Pema Ch'ögyel, and beyond.

These monasteries were not as large as the largest Gelugpa centers in central or eastern Tibet. Eric Teichman, who visited the area in 1918, gives figures of 400, 400, 1,000, and 300 *trapa* for Kat'og, Pelyül, Dzogch'en, and Shech'en (1922:231, 237) while Lama Paltul, referring to the 1950s, gives 800, 600, 850, and 200 respectively (n.d.:121, 79). The Kagyüdpa teaching centers of eastern Tibet were on a similar scale. Each of these *gompa* had several incarnate lamas.

Peter Kessler has compiled available information about the *gompa* in Dergé (1983); he lists 18 Nyingmapa *gompa,* 7 Kagyüdpa *gompa,* 23 Sakyapa *gompa,* 11 Gelugpa *gompa,* and three Bönpo *gompa.* Kessler gives figures for the sizes of most of the *gompa*, but the reliability is probably low. For what they are worth, they amount to about 2,700 in the Nyingmapa *gompa*, about 465 Kagyüdpa, 2,600 Sakyapa, 1,200 Gelugpa, and 270 Bönpo, making a total of around 7,235 *trapa*.

The Hor States: Gelugpa Gompa *outside the Gelugpa State*

The Hor states or Trehor (see Chapter 4) was a complex polity whose territory was divided among five ruling families. This, in contrast to Dergé, had been a Gelugpa stronghold since the conquest of the region by the Gelugpa order's Mongol ally Gushri Khan in 1641 (see Kessler 1984:176–186).[7] Most of the large Gelugpa *gompa* in the Hor states, such as Gönsar, Dza Samdrub, Dargyé, Peri, Dranggo and the two monasteries at the main town, Kandzé, were founded at that time, their purpose doubtless as much political as religious. Kessler lists 25 Gelugpa *gompa* in all,[8] with a total of around 8,200 *trapa*, though, as with Dergé, most of the numbers seem little more than guesses (1984:182–185). Teichman's figures for some of the same *gompa* are considerably lower (for example, 1,500 for the two Kandzé *gompa* rather than 3,000; 100 rather than 700 for Samdrub *gompa*). There were monasteries of the Nyingmapa, Kagyüdpa, and Sakyapa orders in the Hor states (Kessler lists three, five, and six, respectively, with roughly 200, 200, and 800 *trapa* in total per order), but with the possible exception of the Sakyapa *gompa* of Nyarag at Kandzé, with 500 *trapa*,[9] they were much smaller than the Gelugpa *gompa* (Kessler 1984:176–181). Many of the leading Gelugpa lamas in recent years have come from the Hor states (Dhargyey 1978:1–2; Rabten 1980:3–11, 75ff) and from other Gelugpa areas in K'am.

THE REMOTE AGRICULTURAL PATTERN

This second pattern is typical of more remote, less productive, and less centralized agricultural areas. In these areas, there are sometimes small communities of *trapa* and *ani* but there are rarely monastic *gompa* of any size. The leading religious practitioners are hereditary or (less often) reincarnate lamas, often of the Nyingmapa order. Communities of part-time *ch'öpa* who are noncelibate and do agricultural work as well as their religious duties are also common.

Hereditary lamas and lay *ch'öpa* also exist in the centralized agricultural areas, but they have rarely been given much attention in descriptions of such regions, authors preferring to focus on the more conspicuous and spectacular monastic communities. Aziz is unusual in describing both hereditary lamas and lay *ch'öpa* at some length in her account of Dingri (1978:76ff, 220ff). Cassinelli and Ekvall mention them briefly in relation to Sakya, and they undoubtedly formed part of the religious life of the other areas we have considered as well, with the possible exception of Ladakh.

Hereditary lamas are far more prominent in the literature on remote agricultural areas since they and the small communities of married *ch'öpa*, *trapa*, and *ani* are the main actors on the religious scene in these regions. I look at three areas of this kind. Two of them, Dolpo and the Khumbu-Shorung region, are in Nepal, and a third, Lahul, is in India (Himachal Pradesh).

Dolpo: Remote Himalayan Valleys

Dolpo consists of a series of valleys in northern Nepal (see Chapter 6). This area has been populated by Tibetans since at least the thirteenth and fourteenth centuries. By the mid-twentieth century, it had become, as Fürer-Haimendorf (1975:137–138) notes, something of a backwater, off the main trading routes and poor by Tibetan standards. While the king of the tiny state of Mustang in northern Nepal was occasionally acknowledged as having some authority over Dolpo, and in more recent times Thakali intermediaries have collected taxes on behalf of the Nepalese government (Fürer-Haimendorf 1975:147; Jest 1976), the people of Dolpo were in practice autonomous until very recent times: "Dolpo never belonged to any kind of feudal system. The villages, often by their very remoteness from one another, have remained responsible for their own affairs" (Snellgrove 1967b:14). Dolpo has been described in some detail by Snellgrove (1961, 1967b) and Christoph von Fürer-Haimendorf (1975). Corneille Jest has given a detailed ethnography of the valley of Tarap (1976; see also Jest 1974, 1978, 1985; Chapter 8).

The religious communities of Dolpo are Bönpo, Karma Kagyüdpa, and Ngorpa (a Sakyapa suborder) in origin. Several of them include some *trapa* but most consist only of lay *ch'öpa*. These may live at the *gompa* permanently, for part of the year only, or simply come along for ritual performances. The oldest community is the Bönpo *gompa* of Samling, founded in the thirteenth century. Snellgrove spent some time here in 1956. At that time the *gompa*'s inhabitants were a lama and two *trapa*. "The others were part-time practisers, assembling for the performance of ceremonies at any time when they were available, and remaining in residence for longer periods during the winter months, when their fields and their animals no longer demanded attention" (Snellgrove 1961:118). Other Bön centers are at Barlé (1961:41), Ringmo (1961:61), Pungmo (1961:66), Shipch'ok (1961:157, see also Jest 1976), and Ts'arka (1961:159). In the 1950s, these were all similar to Samling in composition, with a hereditary lama and a group of mostly noncelibate lay *ch'öpa*.

The Buddhist *gompa* had the same pattern. The main ones are Yets'er (Snellgrove 1961:85ff, 1967b:59ff), a Sakyapa foundation from the late sixteenth century,[10] and Shey, a Karma Kagyüd *gompa* dating from around 1700, whose abbot, the reincarnation of the founder, was in 1956 the only generally recognized reincarnate lama in Dolpo (1961:73ff, 134ff; see 1967b:11 for date). Both of these have small communities of mostly married *ch'öpa* resident during at least part of the year. These *gompa*, like most Tibetan *gompa* outside a few of the large state-sponsored institutions, consist of a few central buildings surrounded by separate houses that belong not to the *gompa* but to particular families from local villages whose members use them when they are resident at the *gompa*. The communities can thus easily accommodate celibate or noncelibate *ch'öpa* or a mixture of the two.

Snellgrove describes about a dozen other small Buddhist *gompa* throughout Dolpo. Most of these have a hereditary lama and some lay *ch'öpa*. Jest describes the resident hereditary lama of Kunsang Ch'öling in the valley of Tarap, Kagar Rimpoch'e, and his community in some detail (Jest 1976:220–221, 305ff; the Lama Kyap in Snellgrove 1961:154ff and 1967b:44ff is the same person).

Although many of these *gompa* were Sakyapa or Kagyüdpa in origin, the rituals practiced in the 1950s were mostly Nyingmapa. Snellgrove suggests that the revival of Buddhism in Dolpo in recent years has been primarily Nyingmapa. The leading figure in this revival was a lama from central Tibet, Shang Rimpoch'e, who was active in Dolpo, the upper Kali Gandaki and Nye-shang from the 1940s onwards, and was responsible for the building or restoration of a whole series of temples in the region. Shang Rimpoch'e died in 1958 and his mummified body was placed in the new *gompa* at Dragyam (Snellgrove

1967b:65; see also Jest 1976:308–309, 1985:140ff). A reincarnation was found by Kagar Rimpoch'e and installed at Dragyam in 1965.

The annual festivals centered around *ch'am* performances at the Dingri, Sakya, and Ladakh *gompa* took place in Dolpo, too, on a smaller scale, and with lay *ch'öpa* rather than monastic performers. Snellgrove provides descriptions of these festivals at Shey (1961:134ff) and Yets'er (1967b:59ff). Both festivals included *ch'am* and *ts'ewang;* the Shey festival was the occasion of the *ts'ewang* referred to in Chapter 14 (1961:134ff). Jest describes a similar festival in Tarap (1976: 336–341).

The Sherpas: Nyingmapa Revitalization

The Sherpas of Khumbu and Shorung (Solo) are probably the best studied of all Tibetan groups as far as modern ethnography is concerned. Extensive information about Sherpa religious communities can be found in the work of Snellgrove, Fürer-Haimendorf, Funke, Alexander Macdonald, and others, and a recent book by Sherry Ortner, *High Religion,* deals specifically with the cultural processes underlying the foundation of temples and monastic *gompa* in Sherpa country (Ortner 1989a).

The Sherpa communities were founded more recently than the villages of Dolpo. They traditionally originated in an immigration from K'am some four centuries ago (Oppitz 1968). They were, in recent times, also unlike Dolpo in their relative prosperity and their exposure to modernizing and Westernizing influences. The Sherpa communities were nevertheless, like those of Dolpo, largely self-governing until the 1950s. Ortner has observed that the lack of formal judicial mechanisms was such that even homicide could be punished only by ostracizing offenders until they left the region (Ortner 1978a:26–27).

In recent years Sherpa participation in foreign mountaineering expeditions, and the development of the route to Everest as a major tourist attraction, have both brought the Sherpas to the notice of foreigners and exposed the Sherpas themselves to extensive modernizing, 'Nepalizing,' and Westernizing influences. As Fürer-Haimendorf notes, almost all Sherpas by the early 1970s spoke some Nepali as well as their own Tibetan dialect whereas few people in Dolpo knew any language but their own (1975:137).

Another factor in Sherpa religion in this century has been its relative closeness to the thriving Nyingmapa monastic *gompa* at Dzarong (founded 1902) in the Dingri region to the north of the Himalayas. Given all this, we can expect both similarities and contrasts between the religious life of Dolpo and of Sherpa country. In comparison with the areas considered under the centralized agricultural pattern, however, the religious life of Dolpo and of the Sherpas were relatively alike. In both areas there were lay *ch'öpa,* hereditary lamas, small numbers of *trapa* and *ani,* and a recent Rimed-linked movement of religious revitalization. The main difference is the growth of several somewhat larger communities of *trapa* and *ani* among the Sherpas, no doubt a consequence of the greater wealth of the area and of its close connection with Dzarong. Some downgrading of the role of noncelibate *ch'öpa* has accompanied this growth of celibate monasticism.

The older pattern in Sherpa country was one of hereditary noncelibate Nyingmapa-style *ch'öpa,* who belonged to a single lineage or group of lineages (the 'Lama' or Serwa clan), and most closely resembled the *serkhy'im* of the Dolpo region. Fürer-Haimendorf refers to the men of this clan as 'village lamas' and discusses them at some length (1964). Some were ex-*trapa* but almost all eventually married (1964:163). Many of them undertook prolonged retreat or *ts'am,* ideally for the standard period of three years, three months, three days, and Fürer-Haimendorf comments that this was regarded as a necessary preparation for "conducting independently rites for which great spiritual powers are required, such as the rite of 'Life-Consecration' known as Tshe-wong [i.e., *ts'ewang*]" (1964:163). Fürer-Haimendorf also gives an interesting list of the rituals performed by one village lama, "popular and well-situated but only moderately learned" during five months in 1957. These included death and funeral rituals, rituals to earn merit for a dead person, and *kurim* rituals on the occasion of illness or for the general welfare of an individual or family (1964:163–166). This lama also took part in the *yer-chang,* a folk-religion-style ritual held in the high pastures and consisting of offerings to the local deities (see Chapter 10).

Some of these 'village lamas' were attached to specific village temples *(gompa).* Other *gompa* were owned by a single hereditary lama as in Dolpo. In Khumbu the oldest *gompa* were associated with the semimythical figure of Lama Sangwa Dorjé and his two brothers (sixteenth or seventeenth century).[11] Sangwa Dorjé's principal religious tradition seems to have been the Changter or 'Northern Treasure' discovered in the fourteenth century by Göddemchen; the 'Aspiration of Kuntu Sangpo' in Chapter 1 came from this collection of *terma*.

Sangwa Dorjé is credited with various miraculous feats, and with the foundation of Pangboche *gompa*. He died in the Dingri region, near the future monastery of Dzarong. Ngawang Tenzin Norbu, the founder of Dzarong, was held to be his fifth reincarnation. Sangwa Dorjé's two brothers (though there is dispute about whether they really were his brothers) established *gompa* at Thami and Rimijung. The 'brothers' seem to have been political rivals, and Ortner treats this as the initial instance of a repeating Sherpa 'cultural schema' involving rivalry between brothers (Ortner 1989a:67–70). A fourth *gompa*, Zhung (Junbesi) in Shorung, was founded by a 'friend' or 'disciple' of Sangwa Dorjé (1989a:62–65), and a fifth was founded at Khumjung in the early nineteenth century. None of these were celibate *gompa*, though there is some suggestion that there may have been *trapa* at Pangboche at one time (1989a:48).

The first celibate *gompa* was founded in 1916 by a local hereditary lama, Lama Gulu, with encouragement from the lama of Dzarong. This was to become the *gompa* of Tengboche, famous in later years for its monastic dances *(ch'am)* in the Dzarong tradition and its spectacular position on the route to the Everest base-camp. Ortner emphasizes the role taken in the foundation of Tengboche by Karma, the senior of the three lay sponsors, and eldest son of a Shorung *pembu* (i.e., *pönpo*, here meaning one of the Sherpas who acted as tax-collectors on behalf of the Nepalese government).

An *ani gompa* was established nearby at Devuche in 1925. After Lama Gulu's death in 1933, a reincarnation was found and taken to Dzarong for training. He is the present incarnate lama of Tengboche. In 1957 there were 32 *trapa* at Tengboche and 20 *ani* at Devuche (Fürer-Haimendorf 1964:136–138). Five of the *trapa* had taken the full *gelong* vows. The number of *trapa* at Tengboche fell to 14 by 1971 but had risen again to 30 by 1983, with another 15 boys attending the *gompa*'s boarding school (Fürer-Haimendorf 1984:91–92).

Around the same time as the founding of Tengboche, moves began to convert Thami to a celibate *gompa*. The *gompa* was moved to a larger site in 1920 and performances of *ch'am* began with encouragement from Dzarong, although the changes (and the *ch'am*) came to a temporary halt when the abbot and most of the *trapa* moved to the new *gompa* of Chiwong in Shorung in 1923. Eventually, movement towards a celibate *gompa* resumed. Since the death of the hereditary lama in 1958, the community has been a community of celibate *trapa* under the leadership of his reincarnation, and most of the remaining married *ch'öpa* have moved out to nearby villages (Ortner 1989a:188–191). Much the same happened at Kyerok *gompa*, which had also been a community of married *ch'öpa* (Fürer-Haimendorf 1984:93–94).

Similar developments had been taking place further south in Shorung, where the prevailing pattern had again been of small *gompa* with hereditary lamas and attached lay *ch'öpa* (see Funke 1969:88–92). The monastic *gompa* of Chiwong (or Jiwong), was founded in 1923 (see Snellgrove 1957:217ff; Ortner 1989a:140–142); the lay sponsor, Sangyé, was the younger brother and rival of Karma, chief sponsor at Tengboche (so supplying Ortner with the other main instance of her 'cultural schema'). Other monastic gompas were founded in 1946 at Trakshindo (the founder was a *trapa* from Tengboche, Fürer-Haimendorf 1964:135) and in 1958 at Serlo (Funke 1969:89; Macdonald 1980a, 1980b, 1981). This move towards celibate monasticism (see table in Funke 1969:93) was further strengthened when Tr'ulshig Rimpoch'e, the former head lama of Dzarong, settled in Shorung after 1959, along with many refugees from the Dingri region. T'ubten Ch'öling, the new *gompa* built for Tr'ulshig Rimpoch'e in the late 1960s is now much the largest *gompa* in the entire region, with over a hundred *trapa*. Barbara Aziz's account of life in this monastic *gompa* gives a good impression of the close relationship it rapidly developed with the surrounding Sherpa and refugee population (Aziz 1977).

In Sherpa country we can thus see a move from the older pattern of hereditary lamas and lay *ch'öpa* to a new pattern of Nyingmapa celibate monasticism, coinciding with the greater economic prosperity of the community and, as with Dolpo, a period of revitalization deriving here from Dzarong and ultimately from the Rimed movement. It is interesting that in neither area has there been significant support for the Gelugpa tradition.[12]

Lahul: Kagyüdpa Revitalization

Lahul, a region of Tibetan population that became incorporated into Kulu state around 1700 and is now part of the Indian state of Himachal Pradesh, is another example of the remote agricultural pattern. The traditional Tibetan name of Lahul is Karsha, although this is now used mainly for the region around Kardang in the Bhaga River Valley. As in Dingri and in Sherpa country, the pattern in Lahul up to the early twentieth century was of hereditary lamas and married *ch'öpa*. Lahul has very old Buddhist associations with Guru Rimpoch'e and with the important early Drugpa Kagyüdpa lama Gödts'angpa, whom we have already come across in nearby Ladakh. Its affiliations remained with the Drugpa Kagyüdpa order, which had, as we have seen, several medium-size *gompa* not far away in Ladakh.

We have some information about Lahul in the nineteenth century from A. F. P. Harcourt, assistant commissioner of Kulu ([1870] 1972). At that time the region, with a population of some 6,300, had "perhaps 8 small monasteries" (1972:65). Some of these may have been simply isolated temples. Others seem to have been small communities of lay *ch'öpa* attached to hereditary lamas, since Harcourt quotes Lyall as finding that there were "only 7 real lamas [sic] who have no other occupation." By 'real lamas' Lyall and Harcourt may have meant hereditary *ngagpa* lamas or celibate *trapa*. According to Lyall no less than 1,100 of the *zemindars* (i.e., small peasant proprietors) "are also lamas, who marry and cultivate land, and have very little of the monk about them." They could all however both read and write. There were also 71 nuns "who could both read and write" (Harcourt 1972:66).

The contrast between Lahul and the neighboring region of Spiti is intriguing.[13] The total population of Spiti according to the 1878 census was only 2,272.[14] Nevertheless, it had five medium-size *gompa*. Four of these contained celibate *trapa*. These were the three Gelugpa *gompa* of Tap'o, Kyi, and Drangk'ar, and the Sakyapa *gompa* of Tanggyüd at Hikim. There was also a Nyingmapa or Drugpa Kagyüd *gompa* of married *ch'öpa* at Peen. According to accounts by Indian writers from the 1950s and 1960s, the situation was more or less the same at that time, with Peen remaining a community of married *ch'öpa*.[15]

According to Harcourt, the four celibate *gompa* contained 282 *trapa* in the 1860s, which would represent about 25 percent of the male population, an exceptionally high proportion (see Appendix 1). Harcourt along with later writers notes that in Spiti the eldest son took over his father's land and all younger sons went into 'monasteries.' However these *trapa* resided in their monasteries only during the winter. During the rest of the year they were frequently in their village communities helping with farming and trading. If all this is true, the high proportion of *trapa* in Spiti was part of a local adaptation to severe environmental pressure. It may be, however, that the relatively large size of the celibate *gompa* in this apparently remote area can be attributed to the deliberate Gelugpa policy of maintaining large *gompa* in strategic positions, as with Shelkar Ch'ödé at Dingri (see above) and the Gelugpa *gompa* in Mön (see Chapter 6 and Aris 1980). There was a significant trade route going through Spiti to Lahul and Kulu.

Lahul, at any rate, was an example of the remote agricultural pattern. Like Dolpo and the Sherpa region, it went through a period of revitalization early this century, in this case associated with Drugpa Kagyüdpa teachers of Rimed background. Elisabeth Stutchbury's work on the *gompa* of Kardang in Lahul (1986, in press) gives a rather different picture of this process than Ortner's book on the Sherpa monasteries. While Ortner concentrates on the political motivations of the lay sponsors (though see Ortner 1989a:168–192), Stutchbury emphasizes the spiritual concerns of the *ch'öpa*.

Kardang *gompa* was founded in around 1912 by Norbu Rimpoch'e, a Lahuli disciple of the Drugpa married lama Śākya Śrī (1853–1919). We have already met Śākya Śrī as the teacher of Pema Ch'ögyel of Tsibri in the Dingri region. Kardang *gompa* is closely linked to the neighboring village, and most of the families in the village also have houses at the *gompa* where those members live who are undertaking a religious life. The *gompa* had 17 small houses and 34 members in 1983, half male and half female. Most had taken *gets'ul* (or *gets'ulma*) vows and were therefore celibate. Kardang was the largest *gompa* in Lahul in 1983, but the pattern of a mixed *ch'öpa* community of men and women, only some of whom have taken vows of celibacy, and all of whom have close ties to nearby villages, was typical of Lahuli *gompa*.

Several small groups of Lahuli people have carried out three-year retreats on the 'Six Teachings of Nāropa' in recent years, either in Lahul itself or at the Drugpa *gompa* in nearby Manali. This Manali *gompa* was founded by the refugee lama Ap'o Rimpoch'e, a grandson of Śākya Śrī who resided at Kardang for some years before moving to Manali. Ap'o Rimpoch'e died in 1974, but the small Manali *gompa* has remained the main teaching center for the Drugpas of Lahul, under the direction of Gegen Ky'entsé, a disciple of Tr'ipön Pema Ch'ögyel.

The village has an annual cycle of rituals that does not involve the *gompa* but there is also a major Guru Rimpoch'e ritual performed by several village households just before the onset of winter involving a *wang* given by the presiding lama. Stutchbury comments that:

> It is as if the villagers wish to activate the special blessings and transformative power of the Vajra Guru before the *ch'öpa* retire for the winter to meditation and yogic practices in the *gompa*, situated above their village, and the villagers themselves embark on a few months of village festivities, *ch'ang* drinking and other social activities after the six strenuous months of summer. (Stutchbury 1986:211–212)

In Stutchbury's picture, the *gompa* is an extension of the village community. The group of people residing in the *gompa* is in a constant state of flux, as people move back and forth between *gompa* and village. Men or women do not necessarily go to the *gompa* with the intention of immediately taking on a celibate monastic career. They may spend several periods of time at the *gompa* over some years, gradually taking the various sets of vows as they become more committed to the life of a *ch'öpa*. She contrasts this with the situation of a boy or young man conscripted to a central Tibetan *gompa* (like Shelkar Ch'ödé in Dingri) through the monk levy system, who had much less choice about his religious career. Even in the more centralized areas, men and women often actively choose to become *ch'öpa* or *trapa*, as careers such as those of Geshé Rabten and Ayu Khandro, recounted in Chapter 18, demonstrate.

THE PASTORAL PATTERN

As I indicated at the beginning of this chapter, the pastoral areas need to be considered separately from the agricultural areas. There are no really adequate ethnographic accounts of religion in pastoral areas. Our main case study is of the monastic and trading center of Tagts'ang Lhamo, described in some detail in Robert Ekvall's various writings on Amdo.

Tagts'ang Lhamo: The Gelugpas in Eastern Amdo

Ekvall and his family spent several years at the monastic center and trading post of Tagts'ang Lhamo towards the eastern edge of the pastoralist regions of Amdo. His specifically anthropological work on religion is often general and uninformative in nature (Ekvall 1960, 1964b) but his autobiographical account (1952) and his two novels (1954a, 1981) help to round out the picture (see Chapter 5).

The settlement of Tagts'ang Lhamo is situated near a large cave that contains a famous shrine of the goddess Palden Lhamo. There are two large *gompa,* Gurdu and Sechu, on opposite sides of a valley, with trading posts attached to each. The surrounding country was occupied by the Shimdrog confederacy of nomadic pastoralist tribes. We have already examined the political and economic relationships linking these and other Amdo *gompa* to the pastoralist tribes (Chapters 5 and 8). *Gompa* mediated disputes, provided storage for pastoral produce, and provided a location for trading. It is clear from Ekvall's writings that the two *gompa* were closely integrated with the surrounding tribes through the ritual services they performed as well as through the political and economic services they provided.

Ekvall gives no direct information about the religious affiliation of Gurdu and Sechu. They were in fact both Gelugpa. Gurdu or Kirti *gompa* (its full name was Ganden Trashi Ky'il) was founded in 1748 by the 5th Kirti Rimpoch'e, Lobsang Tenpé Gyants'en (1712–1771). The Kirti Rimpoch'es were a *tulku* lineage that went back to one of Tsongk'apa's disciples. They had previously resided in Gyelrong; Gurdu eventually became their main seat. Sechu or Sertr'i (also called Ganden Shedrub Ling) was founded in the same year as Gurdu by Tr'ich'en Gyantsen Sengge (1678–1756), a former abbot of Ganden in central Tibet.[16] According to Kirti Tsenshab Rimpoch'e, who was abbot of Gurdu for some years in the early 1950s, the two *gompa,* at that time, had around 700 and 500 *trapa,* respectively. Both had three colleges, *ts'ennyid* (philosophy or dialectics), *gyüdpa* (Tantra), and *dük'or* (Kālacakra Tantra and astrology). The two *ts'ennyid* colleges were based on different traditions; that at Gurdu used the texts from Losel Ling college at Drepung, whereas that at Sechu used the texts from Gomang college (by Jamyang Shedpa, who was also the founder of the famous Amdo *gompa* of Labrang).

According to Ekvall, each monastery had several lamas (see 1954a:39). Both they and the ordinary *trapa* were consulted to perform rituals, give advice or do divinations *(mo)* on behalf of the nomads. Both *gompa* put on an annual festival, centered around a performance of *ch'am,* which was followed, at Gurdu at any rate, by the typically

Gelugpa Festival of the Butter Images (1952:79ff, 1954a:30ff; see T. J. Norbu 1982).

In fact, although Ekvall's later work emphasizes the nomadic *(drogpa)* context of Tagts'ang Lhamo, the settlement was situated in the border area between pastoralists and the agricultural people of the valleys *(rongpa)*, and there were both *rongpa* and *drogpa* in the nearby area. Again according to Kirti Tsenshab Rimpoch'e, most *trapa* at both *gompa* were from farming communities, although there were some *drogpa* monks at each.

Other Examples of Pastoral Areas

Brief descriptions of interactions with pastoralist populations occur throughout the literature on Tibet and it is worth citing a few of these to illustrate the situation elsewhere. The Sakya missions to the Changt'ang nomads (see Chapter 7) represented a different kind of relation between nomadic tribes and monastic *gompa* to that in north-eastern Amdo, where it was more the practice for the nomads to come to the *gompa* when they required rituals, divinations, or other religious services. The Sakya missions included a tantric lama as well as a collector of 'taxes' (or donations, see Chapter 7 and D. Norbu 1974:24). Norbu's grandfather acted as lama on one of these missions, performing rituals to avert snowfalls and avalanches, treating diseases of human beings and animals, performing *sang* and *ts'ewang* rituals, and exorcising evil spirits (1974:30–32). Norbu mentions the nomads' preference for Tantric ritual and yogic powers (see Chapter 5).

Another facet of the pastoralist-*gompa* relationship can be seen from the autobiography of the Gelugpa incarnate lama Rato Khyongla, whose *gompa* was in Dragyab in central K'am (see Chapter 18). Rato Khyongla gives a brief description of the relationship between his *labrang* (i.e., the lama's personal household within the monastery) and the four nomad families who looked after the *labrang*'s 400 yaks and dris (female yaks) along with their own herds. Rato Khyongla describes a visit he paid to the nomads after returning from his studies in central Tibet:

> I formally entered each of the four tents, to greet individually the members of each family. They asked me to perform an incense ceremony [*sang*, see Chapter 10], and so together up the hill we climbed

> to a highland tract above the tents, where they built a fire of fragrant juniper boughs while I read the appropriate prayer. I had brought along some consecrated pills called *chinten,* which we now dissolved in water. When everyone had tasted this drink the herders set out some in buckets for their yaks. (Rato 1977:177)

Rato Khyongla's description of the consecrated pills, although not specific to the pastoral context, is worth quoting, since these and similar consecrated objects, believed to transfer some of the power of Tantric Buddhism from the lama to the laity, were a staple of Tibetan Buddhism. We have already met these pills in the context of the *ts'ewang* ritual in Chapter 14:

> Such pills, of barley flour mixed with medicinal herbs and the ground-up relics of saints, fragments of their garments, holy objects, and consecrated by a special Tantric ceremony were popular throughout Tibet. It was thought that if eaten just before death they would help one to a better rebirth. I had therefore brought from Lhasa a good number, many of which had been given me by the Dalai Lama himself, and there was a large stock kept in the *labrang* as well, with records of their sources and the particles they contained. I was told that some held relics even of Milarepa and Marpa. Anyone asking at the *labrang* for such pills would be given them in an envelope bearing a wood-block stamp testifying to their contents and their source. (Rato 1977:177)

As I mentioned at the start of this chapter, Ekvall's material on the predominantly Gelugpa monasteries of eastern Amdo may give a misleading picture of pastoralist religion. Nyingmapa and other non-Gelugpa practice was also prominent, and nomadic peoples such as the Golog provided many of the leading lamas of the Rimed movement in the late nineteenth and early twentieth centuries. They were traditionally more interested in yogic powers than in scholarship. Further research on religion in the pastoral areas would be welcome and it is to be hoped that the rather sketchy picture I have drawn here will be filled in by research in pastoral areas within the People's Republic of China over the next few years.

What we may note in conclusion though is the *continuity* between the three religious patterns described in this chapter for the centralized agricultural, remote agricultural, and pastoral areas. The same multifaceted and polyvalent institution, the *gompa*, can, as I have noted several times already, be any of a variety of things: a remote hermitage, the residence of a hereditary lama, a community of non-celibate *ch'öpa*, or a monastery of celibate *trapa*. In premodern Tibet, it could even be the seat of government for a large region. *Gompa* can also be a mixture of two or more of these functions, and can gradually change over time from one to another.

The *gompa* is an adaptable and flexible institution, like many of the basic building-blocks of Tibetan society, such as the household or such political roles or role-labels as *pönpo* or *depa*. A group of Tibetans moving from, say, Lahul through central Tibet to the nomadic tribes of Amdo would encounter people physically quite different from themselves, speaking dialects they could hardly understand, landscapes and vegetation very different from those they were familiar with, but the political and religious structures of the lands through which they traveled would be built up of familiar and universal elements.

We will find this same combination of diverse possibilities within a common vocabulary in Chapter 18 when we look at the lives of some modern lamas and discuss the trajectories those lives have taken through the space mapped out in this and the previous chapters.

18

Some Recent Lamas

We have come across a variety of contrasts within the Tibetan religious system in the previous chapters: Sūtra and Tantric practices; Pragmatic, Karma, and Bodhi orientations; celibate and lay practitioners; tame and wild value systems; centralized agricultural, remote agricultural, and pastoral patterns. Beneath all of these, I suggested in Chapter 1, we can distinguish the underlying contrast between what I have called the shamanic and clerical aspects of Tibetan religion.

In this chapter we examine the lives of some recent lamas to see how the clerical and shamanic aspects manifest in practice. The oldest of these lamas was born in the mid-nineteenth century and the youngest, Trungpa Trulku, in 1939. The accounts are mostly taken from published autobiographies or from biographies by the lamas' disciples and so tend to emphasize events in the subject's spiritual life rather than the progress of his or her career in the Tibetan religious system. They nevertheless contain much of interest. We begin with some lamas from the most clerical end of Tibetan religion: the *geshé* of the Gelugpa order.

CLERICAL LAMAS: SOME GELUGPA *GESHÉ*

If the Gelugpa are the most clerical of Tibetan Buddhist orders then the *geshé,* the product of the lengthy philosophical and scholastic training system at the great Gelugpa monastic centers, were the most clerical people in the Gelugpa system. There is nevertheless, as we will see, more than one way of being a *geshé.* My first example is a contemporary lama, Geshé Rabten, who has given a particularly detailed account of his upbringing in eastern Tibet and his training at Sera in *The Life and Teachings of Geshé Rabten.*

Geshé Rabten

Geshé Rabten, who came from K'am like most of the lamas in this chapter, was an 'ordinary *trapa*' rather than a *trulku* (reincarnate lama). He commenced his studies and his monastic career at the relatively late age of 17. His life illustrates how such a *trapa* can work his way gradually through the Gelugpa monastic system. It also illustrates the obstacles he might have to overcome. Geshé Rabten was obviously dedicated to pursuing a monastic career. He entered the monastic life against his parents' wishes and with little support from them. His life at Sera was materially very difficult for the first few years and it was only later when he became tutor to a young reincarnate lama that he could be sure of enough to eat.

The following account is summarized from Rabten (1980) and a Rikon Institute leaflet:

Geshé Rabten was born around 1920 in a fairly well-off agricultural family in a village in the Hor states (Trehor) region of K'am, about 50 miles southwest of the large Gelugpa monastery of Dargyé. He was the second of four children. His mother died when the children were quite young. The third child, a girl, became a nun, while the youngest son eventually entered Sera *gompa* near Lhasa.

The eldest son, Rabten's elder brother, was originally going to be a *trapa,* and went to study with an uncle, who was already a *trapa,* for some years in a mountain retreat. Rabten's father became too old to run the farm, so Rabten's brother returned to take over the household, married and had three children.

Rabten decided at the age of about 17 to become a monk at Dargyé. To do so, he would have to study for some years in one of the three major Gelugpa teaching centers near Lhasa, so he asked his father's permission to go there, with the intention of returning to Dargyé after his studies. His father refused, since he wanted him to stay at home, and the journey to Lhasa was long and dangerous. Two years later, he decided to leave without his father's permission, with the aid of a wealthy relative who was traveling to Lhasa. His father discovered his departure, but agreed to let him go and gave him some food and money.

Rabten went to Sera *gompa*, where he was taken care of by a *trapa* in the Trehor hostel, a friend of his uncle's. He was assigned to a teacher, *geshé* Jampa K'edrub, in Sera Ché College, and after a couple of months took the *gets'ul* ordination. He continued his studies, undergoing considerable poverty and deprivation.

Six years later he returned to Trehor in order to visit *geshé* Jampa K'edrub, who had gone back to K'am and become the abbot of Dargyé monastery. After an arduous journey, Rabten met the *geshé*, who told him that he should have remained at Sera, and sent him back to complete his studies. His uncle, the *trapa*, assisted him, but advised him not to tell his father, who would not want him to go.

Back at Sera, he was chosen to be the tutor to a young *trulku* (reincarnate lama), Gonsar Rimpoch'e, and a religious assistant to another *trulku*, so he was now materially much better off. After another 10 years, he entered the Karam (or lower *geshé* grade) class, and after graduating from this was admitted to the highest *(geshé lharampa)* class. By now he had taken *gelong* vows. During these years, he also took numerous tantric initiations and practiced meditation whenever possible.

He would normally have remained in this class for nine years, but in 1959, after two years, he left for India. He continued studying in the refugee monastery at Buxaduar, and was examined for and awarded the *geshé lharampa* title in 1963, at the age of 43. After becoming a *geshé* he joined Namgyel Trats'ang (the Dalai Lama's palace *gompa*) and became one of the Dalai Lama's religious assistants. He continued to tutor Gonsar Rimpoch'e and other Tibetan disciples.

In 1969 the Dalai Lama asked him to begin teaching Western students, and he acquired many of these during the remaining years of his life. After two visits to Europe, he was appointed the abbot of the Tibetan Monastic Institute at Rikon in Switzerland in 1977. Apart from Geshé Rabten, there were five Tibetan *trapa* from the Gelugpa and Sakyapa orders at the institute. The curriculum was based on that at Sera. Geshé Rabten died in 1986.[1]

These are the bare bones of Geshé Rabten's story. In the actual narrative, the opposition of his father to his entering the monastic career, the difficulty of his early years at Sera and particularly his devotion to *geshé* Jampa K'edrub, his *tsawé lama*, are strongly expressed. Geshé

Rabten also gives a detailed account of his philosophical studies at Sera. He mentions Tantric practice several times in his account (Rabten 1980:52–53, 64, 78) but the emphasis is more on the Sūtra teachings, which formed the basis of the Sera curriculum (the 'Five Treatises' by Indian scholars[2] and the commentaries on these works by Tsongk'apa and his successors).

In his own teaching, too, Geshé Rabten emphasized the clerical side of the Buddhist tradition. The curriculum at Rikon was based on that at Sera, and the second half of his autobiography, which consists of Tibetan Buddhist teachings, is primarily a presentation of the Sūtra path along traditional Gelugpa *lamrim* lines, although it also includes the Tantric preliminary practices of meditation on Vajrasattva and *guruyoga* (1980:137–142, 144–145).

Rato Khyongla

Geshé Rabten was an ordinary *trapa* at Sera, and lived in considerable poverty until, nearly 30 years old, he became the tutor of a *trulku*. There were many *trulku* at Sera, Ganden, and Drepung, since most Gelugpa *trulku* were trained at one or another of the three main *gompa*. An autobiography by Rato Khyongla Nawang Losang[3] *(My Life and Lives)*, makes an interesting contrast to Geshé Rabten's narrative. The following account is summarized from Rato Khyongla's autobiography (Rato 1977):

Rato Khyongla was born in 1923 in a prosperous agricultural family in the small village of Ophor, some five days' travel south of Chamdo, in the state of Dragyab in K'am. His paternal grandfather's brother was a senior official in the Dragyab government, and the family had become wealthy through trading journeys to China and India. At the age of five, he was identified through divination and oracles as the rebirth of the 9th Khyongla *trulku*. He was taken to the *labrang* or lama's household at Kat'og *gompa*, a monastery a few hours away from Ophor, which had been founded by the 2d Khyongla.[4] At the age of eight, he began training with *geshé* Ts'ering Ch'öp'el who had studied for 20 years at Sera. The following year he was ordained as *genyen* by Dragyab Rimpoch'e at the *gompa* in the nearby town of Yendum.

At the age of 13, he was sent to central Tibet and was enrolled as a member of Ratöd monastery, a short distance southwest of Lhasa. This *gompa* had a *k'angts'an* or hostel for students from Dragyab, as did Ganden and Drepung, and his predecessor, the 9th Khyongla, had studied there. He lived at Ratöd for 11 years in a three-room apartment with a young *trapa* as attendant.

He was ordained as *gets'ul* by Tagtrag Rimpoch'e and studied the Sūtra curriculum at Ratöd. He also attended classes at Drepung, Sera, and other *gompa* around Lhasa.

At 20 he was ordained as *gelong* by P'awongk'a Rimpoch'e. He took the *geshé lharampa* degree in 1947 at the age of 23. He then went on to study Tantra at Gyüdtöd Trats'ang, one of the two Gelugpa Tantric colleges in Lhasa. At 25 he took a year off, traveling around Tibet and to Bhutan. Later, he visited India and Nepal, where he had been invited by some Nepalese Buddhists to help found a monastery. He continued his studies at Gyüdtöd Trats'ang and after a short visit back to K'am was appointed head of a new school opened by the Chinese in Gyantsé in central Tibet.

He left Tibet in 1959, and was a member of the committee set up by the Dalai Lama to write textbooks for the Tibetan refugee school system. In 1962 he went to Leiden, where he was employed for four years cataloging the Tibetan material in the Rijksmuseum voor Volkenkonde. He subsequently settled in New York, where he renounced his monastic vows and got work first as a Tibetan language teacher and later as a stockroom clerk. Subsequently he was one of the founders of the Tibet Center in New York.

Rato Khyongla took his *geshé lharampa* degree at 23; Geshé Rabten, who began his formal studies four years later, took his at 43. In fact, Rato could have taken his degree even earlier than this; he comments:

> I was to be the first monk of my class to take the *lharampa* examination because, as an incarnation, I had the privilege of being advanced rapidly in my studies. Incarnations gained their degrees normally in six or seven years, but because of [his teacher] Könch'og's advice I had prolonged my studies to eleven. Regular monks, on the other hand, were chosen for the examination by their abbots mainly by seniority, and some had to wait as many as twenty years for their degree—but, as a result of this, they were frequently better educated than incarnations. However, there were never in Tibet any barriers, such as social standing, lack of property, or nationality, to keep a monk from progressing in his scholarship. All that was required were personal ability and arduous study to bring one to the top. Indeed, only a few incarnations ever rose to become the abbots of Drepung, Sera, Ganden, or the Gyüdpa [Tantric] colleges: most of the great leaders were from the regular ranks. (Rato 1977:115)

As Rato later mentions, at Gyüdtöd Trats'ang they made a point of treating the *trulku* just like everybody else. This was hardly the general rule in Tibet. In fact, despite Rato's comments, many of the abbots of Ganden (the titular heads of the Gelugpa order) and occupants of other senior Gelugpa positions in recent years were *trulku*.

Rato's life is interesting both for the contrast between the progress of a *trulku* and an ordinary *trapa* through the system, and for its indications of the kinds of opportunities and choices that were available to a medium-level *trulku*. For example, after gaining his *geshé lharampa* degree he considered returning to his monastery in K'am and studying Tantra privately rather than continuing his Tantric studies at Gyüdtöd Trats'ang. He quotes his teacher's comments when he suggested this:

> 'Yes,' he replied thoughtfully, 'in theory that would be possible. Many before you have done so. But such a course would take you much longer than a season of work at Gyüdtöd and finally not be as thorough. Furthermore, people are going to respect you more if you have a Gyüdtöd degree, and that for a teacher is important. . . . But finally,' he conceded, 'this will have to be your own decision. Some, after gaining their *geshé* degree, return directly to their own monasteries and either teach or devote themselves there to meditation. Others, retiring to hermitages, concentrate exclusively on religious practice. Many return to their homes to work and teach among the people. The majority, however, would choose to go on to higher Buddhist studies, and what that means is intensive study of the Tantras.' (Rato 1977:124)

Ling Rinpoch'e

The Gelugpa *geshé* are at the most clerical end of Tibetan religion. The extensive philosophical study and the elaborate system of degrees and examinations are reminiscent of the universities of medieval Europe, and indeed go back to the strikingly similar Buddhist universities of sixth- to twelfth- century India, although the system as we see it now was centralized considerably by the 13th Dalai Lama (see Chapter 27). These highly clerical lamas are nevertheless all Tantric practitioners as well, at least to some degree. Indeed the most senior personnel in the system had to undergo extensive Tantric training, even after the 13th Dalai Lama's reforms. These most senior Gelugpa positions were appointed from among those who had served as *gekö* (Proctor) and subsequently as *lama umdzed* (Master of Discipline) and *k'enpo* (Abbot) of one of the two Tantric colleges in Lhasa. These last two posts were only open to holders of *geshé lharampa* first class degrees. From here appointment to the headship of one of the Ganden colleges and to the position of abbot of Ganden and titular head of the Gelugpa order followed by strict succession.[5] We can see how this worked out in practice in the life of Ling Rimpoch'e, who at his death was both Abbot of Ganden *(Ganden Tr'ipa)* and Senior Tutor to His Holiness the Dalai Lama. The following account is summarized from an autobiography by Ling Rimpoch'e himself (Ling 1983) and an obituary by Sherpa Rimpoch'e (Sherpa 1984).

Ling Rimpoch'e was born in 1903 at Yabp'u, a sacred site near to Lhasa, which is associated with the deity Cakrasamvara. He was recognized at an early age as the rebirth of the 5th Ling Rinpoch'e,[6] who had been tutor to the 13th Dalai Lama. He was taken to Lhasa and enthroned in the usual manner.

At the age of ten he was enrolled in Losel Ling College at Drepung, and the following year received *genyen* and *gets'ul* ordination from the 13th Dalai Lama. At the age of 20 he took *gelong* vows, again from the 13th Dalai Lama, and the following year, despite his youth, was permitted to take the *geshé lharampa* examination, in which he was awarded second place.

At this point he entered Gyüdtöd Trats'ang. At the age of 24 he became *gekö* of Gyüdtöd Trats'ang, and in 1933 was one of the lamas in charge of the funeral rites for the 13th Dalai Lama. In 1936, at the age of 34, he was appointed the head lama of Gyüdtöd Trats'ang, and soon afterwards was appointed one of the assistant tutors to the 14th Dalai Lama. In 1941 he was appointed Junior Tutor, and in 1953 Senior Tutor. In 1949 he was also appointed Sharpa Ch'öjé, the second post in precedence in the Gelugpa order. He was abbot and preceptor when the 14th Dalai Lama took *gelong* vows in 1954, visiting China with him shortly afterwards. He also accompanied the 14th Dalai Lama to India in 1956, and accompanied him on his flight to India in 1959.

After the death of the Abbot of Ganden in Lhasa, Ling Rimpoch'e was appointed to this post, the highest in the Gelugpa order. He was enthroned in 1965 at Bodhgaya in India, also becoming abbot of the Gelugpa *gompa* at Bodhgaya. In 1968 he visited Switzerland along with Tr'ichang Rimpoch'e, the Dalai Lama's Junior Tutor, for the consecration of the Rikon Institute. He visited Europe again in 1972, and North America in 1980. In 1972 he paid his first visit to the three major Gelugpa *gompa* (Ganden, Sera, Drepung), which had been reformed in South India, and was enthroned as abbot by the monks of Ganden. He died in 1983, remaining in absorption in the state of clear light for twelve days. His rebirth was subsequently found.

Ling Rimpoch'e seems not to have been greatly oriented towards Tantric practice before he entered Gyüdtöd. In his autobiography, he mentions only a couple of initiations received during his childhood, in marked contrast to, for example, the wealth of Tantric empowerments listed for the early years of the Dalai Lama's Junior Tutor, Tr'ichang Rimpoch'e (Dzemay Rinpoche 1982:9–15). By the time he left Gyüdtöd, however, and was appointed Assistant Tutor to the 14th Dalai Lama, he had spent fourteen years studying Tantra and would have been deeply steeped in Tantric procedures. The description of his death implies that he had attained advanced mastery of these processes, as would be expected of a lama of the stature of the Ganden Tr'ipa. It was normal for a Ganden Tr'ipa, if not already a *trulku* as in Ling Rimpoch'e's case, to initiate a series of reincarnations, which again implied to Tibetans that he could maintain control of consciousness during the intermediate state and rebirth periods.

Tromo Geshé Rimpoch'e

The life of a fourth Gelugpa *geshé*, Tromo Geshé Rimpoch'e, illustrates another set of possibilities. Here we have an example of an 'ordinary' monk who followed his scholastic studies with a prolonged retreat as a hermit, founded his own monastery and initiated an reincarnation series. Tromo Geshé Rimpoch'e subsequently became the teacher of the Austrian lama Anagarika Govinda, and it is from Govinda's autobiography *The Way of the White Clouds* that I summarize the following account (Govinda 1974:7–11, 116–22):

Ngawang Kelsang was born in around 1865. He studied as an ordinary monk without *trulku* status at one of the great Gelugpa *gompa* in the vicinity of Lhasa, eventually acquiring a *geshé* degree, indicating mastery of the traditional Indian-derived philosophical curriculum. Rather than pursuing a monastic career, he withdrew for 12 years into solitary meditation, living as a hermit in various retreats and caves in southern Tibet and performing *chöd* practice.[7]

After some 12 years he was discovered by villagers who lived in the nearby valley of Tromo. They persuaded him to settle in Dungkar *gompa*, a small *gompa* nearby. Dungkar *gompa* rapidly grew into a major center of study and worship, and Ngawang Kelsang acquired a following in many areas of Tibet. He was particularly concerned with developing the cult of Maitreya, and encouraged the building of temples to him in many places. During a visit to the Guru Rimpoch'e pilgrimage site of Ch'orten Nyima he and his followers saw a vision of various buddhas and bodhisattvas, which was taken as an indication of his high spiritual attainment. Now known as Tromo Geshé Rimpoch'e, he decided to travel throughout the Himalayas, teaching not only to Tibetans but to people of other nations. He also went on a number of pilgrimages to India.

Tromo Geshé died at Dungkar *gompa* in 1937, after predicting his return. He died in meditation posture, and the body remained unchanged and erect for several weeks, showing no signs of decay. Eventually it was preserved and placed in a memorial stupa. His rebirth was found in the family of a Sikkimese nobleman three or four years later, after consultations of the monastery's own oracle priest and the Lhasa Government's oracle at Nech'ung. The child was taken to Dungkar after satisfying the usual tests, and at the age of 7 sent to Sera to begin studies for his *geshé* degree.

Here we can see a lama who after his initial scholarly training moved right into the shamanic end of Tibetan Buddhist practice, living as a solitary hermit and *chöd* practitioner, before being adopted by local villagers and installed in a monastery. As the attendance of Tr'ichang Rimpoch'e (Dzemay 1982:21) and other high lamas at his death indicates, he had become fully accepted into the Gelugpa system.[8]

Thus, the Gelugpa order, for all of its clerical emphasis, offered a range of possibilities involving different mixes of clerical and shamanic Buddhism. All senior Gelugpa lamas had a thorough training in both aspects.

When we turn to the lamas of the other three orders, more specifically of the Rimed movement, we find a similar range of variation. If we can say that the Rimed lamas are more shamanic and the Gelugpa are more clerical this is more a comment on the overall range than on any particular individuals. The Rimed movement also produced great scholars and the Gelugpa included famous Tantric meditators. The difference is real, however, and it is particularly noticeable in the case of those Rimed lamas who had little or no formal academic training.

SHAMANIC LAMAS: PRODUCTS OF THE RIMED MOVEMENT

Ch'ögyam Trungpa Tulku

My first Rimed example, however, is of a Kagyüdpa *trulku* lama who received an academic training comparable to that of the two Gelugpa *trulku* we have considered, Rato Khyongla and Ling Rimpoch'e. There are, however, significant contrasts between the career of Ch'ögyam Trungpa, the 11th Trungpa Tulku of Surmang, and that of my Gelugpa examples. This account is taken mainly from his autobiography *Born in Tibet* (Trungpa 1971).

Ch'ögyam Trungpa was born in 1940 in the pastoralist community of Geje on the high plateau country of Nangch'en, in the northwest of K'am. His father owned a little land locally, but had left Ch'ögyam's mother shortly before his birth, and he was brought up by his mother and her second husband. Various signs accompanied his birth. A few months later a visiting Gelugpa lama asked that the child should be given to his monastery, Trashi Lhap'ug, where Ch'ögyam's mother's uncle was a monk.

Before this could happen, however, he was identified as the rebirth of the 10th Trungpa *Trulku*, abbot of the Surmang group of *gompa*,[9] by a search mission following a prophecy of the 16th Gyalwa Karmapa, who was visiting Pelpung *gompa* in K'am at the time. The child was taken to Düdtsi T'il, one of the two main Surmang monasteries, where he was to live for the next few years. Here he passed the test of being able to recognize the monks he knew and objects he had possessed in his previous life. A month later he visited Namgyel Tsé, the other main Surmang monastery, where he was given the *genyen* vows by Gyalwa Karmapa and enthroned as the new *trulku*. He seems to have been only a year or so old at the time. His mother came along to stay at Düdtsi T'il until he was five.

At five he began study with a tutor, moving shortly after to a retreat center some way from Düdtsi T'il where there was less distraction. At eight he was ordained as a *gets'ul* by Jamgön Kongtrul of Pelpung, one of the rebirths of the famous Rimed lama Jamgön Kongtrul (1813–1899, see Smith 1970). The Jamgön Kongtrul reincarnations of Pelpung and Shech'en had been students of the 10th Trungpa *Trulku* and were teachers of the 11th, and the second, the Shech'en reincarnation, was Trungpa's principal meditation teacher. Another of his gurus, Dilgo Ky'entse Rimpoch'e, was one of the rebirths of another principal Rimed lama Jamyang Ky'entse Ongpo (see Chapter 27).[10]

At the age of 11, Trungpa was moved to another retreat center where he began the Tantric preliminary practices or *ngöndro*. The whole area had now been taken over by the Chinese, but the two Surmang *gompa* were still undisturbed. Shortly after Trungpa went on a tour to Lhat'og and then to Shech'en, where he wanted to study with Jamgön Kongtrul. He studied academic subjects as well as meditation at the seminary at Shech'en but soon had to return to Surmang, where one of the senior lamas had died. After a visit to Drölma Lhak'ang in Pagshöd and to the major Karmapa *gompa* of

Karma Geru nearby, he studied ritual dance *(ch'am)* for some months before returning to Shech'en for further study. He also visited Dzongsar Ky'entsé Ch'ökyi Lodrö, another reincarnation of Jamyang Ky'entsé Ongpo, at the Sakyapa *gompa* of Dzongsar. In 1957 his principal tutor at Shech'en, K'enpo Gangshar, came to teach at Surmang, and many students came to study with him there.

In the main part of K'am (in Sichuan province) the resistance movement against the Chinese regime had begun to grow and many refugees were leaving for central Tibet. Several important *gompa* including Pelpung and Dzongsar were destroyed and their *trapa* arrested or killed. Trungpa passed the examination for the *kyorpön* and *k'enpo* degrees (roughly equivalent to the Gelugpa *geshé* degree) and he was ordained as a *gelong* by Rölpé Dorjé Rimpoch'e, the regent abbot of Düdtsi T'il. In 1959 open fighting against the Chinese began in the Surmang region. Namgyal Tsé was destroyed and many *trapa* were killed or captured. Düdtsi T'il was looted. Trungpa escaped to India.

Subsequently Trungpa studied at Oxford and in 1967 founded one of the first Tibetan meditation centers in the West, Samyê-Ling, in Scotland. He was severely injured in a car crash in 1969. In 1970 he renounced his vows and married, subsequently moving to the United States and Canada where he founded a series of Tibetan meditation centers, the main ones being in Vermont, Colorado, and Nova Scotia.

Trungpa Tulku died early in 1987 and was cremated at his center in Vermont. The ceremony was conducted by his former teacher Dilgo Ky'entse and attended by many senior Rimed lamas. Following his death, Trungpa's Buddhist organization, Vajradhatu, was headed by an American disciple, Ösel Tendzin (Thomas Rich), who himself died in 1991. Trungpa's son, Sawang Ösel Rangdröl, was then appointed the head of Vajradhatu by Jamgön Kongtr'ul Rimpoch'e with the concurrence of Dilgo Ky'entse Rimpoch'e and the Karma Kagyüdpa hierarchy in India. Trungpa's son was to be trained in Nepal and Bhutan by Dilgo Ky'entse Rimpoch'e.[11]

As in the case of Rato Khyongla's autobiography, this lama's early life is full of the names of great and famous lamas, but, whereas for Rato Khyongla these were Gelugpa lamas such as P'awongk'a Rimpoch'e or Tagtrag Rimpoch'e, we here find senior Rimed lamas such as the two Ky'entse reincarnations, Dilgo Ky'entse and Dzongsar Ky'entse, and the two Kongtrul reincarnations of Pelpung and Shech'en.

Although Trungpa was a Karma Kagyüdpa *trulku*, his teachers included lamas from the Nyingmapa and Sakyapa orders. Shech'en, where he studied for some time was, as we saw in Chapter 17, a Nyingmapa center. This is entirely typical for a Rimed lama of Trungpa's generation. The differences between the non-Gelugpa orders were essentially differences of practice, and students went to the most famous and reputed teachers regardless of formal affiliation.

The Gelugpa hardly figure in Trungpa's autobiography, with the exception of the early request for him to become a monk at a Gelugpa *gompa*, and the Dalai Lama's visit to east Tibet in 1956. Trungpa mentions visiting a Gelugpa *gompa* on one occasion (1971:125–126) just as Rabten mentions visiting a Nyingmapa *gompa* (Rabten 1980:63). There was no objection to such visits, and Trungpa mentions that he was interested in finding out something about the Gelugpa. In addition high lamas from one tradition might occasionally be asked to give initiations or teachings to the members of the other. We will come across an example of this in the next case study. With few exceptions, however, Gelugpa lamas trained at Gelugpa centers and Rimed lamas trained at Rimed centers, and contact between them was limited.

The Tantric initiations and texts that Trungpa mentions also include typical Rimed texts such as the Rinch'en Terdzöd, the great compilation of Tantric practices of *terma* origin made under the auspices of the nineteenth-century Rimed lamas. Trungpa received the empowerment for this vast cycle of Tantric teachings from Jamgön Kongtrul of Shech'en (Trungpa 1971:73–74) and subsequently gave the empowerment himself on two occasions (1971:83–84, 138–142).

Tantric practice was a more central component of Trungpa's training from an early age than it would have been for the Gelugpa lamas we have considered, but for him as for the Gelugpa there was a mix of Tantric and academic study. Trungpa, as we saw, took an academic degree similar to the Gelugpa *geshé* degree although, as with the Gelugpa *trulku*, his studies were briefer than those of an ordinary monk such as Geshé Rabten and were interrupted by official duties such as visits to his monastery or the giving of Tantric empowerments.

The shamanic side of Trungpa's life came out more in his later activities in the West. As with most Rimed lamas, visions played an important part in Trungpa's life. An example is the experience at Tagts'ang in Bhutan in 1968, which he briefly mentions in the 1971 'Epilogue' to *Born in Tibet* (1971:252). This vision became the basis of a meditational practice taught to his Western students in the early 1970s, 'The Sadhana of the Embodiment of All the Siddhas.'

K'enpo Gangshar, who became Trungpa Rimpoch'e's root guru, was a highly unconventional lama (see Chapter 16), and Trungpa followed in his footsteps. Trungpa often spoke in favor of the 'crazy wisdom' of the *siddha* tradition, and he was evidently deeply influenced by K'enpo Gangshar's adoption of *siddha* behavior.

Trungpa taught standard Tantric practices to his Western students, taking his students through *shiné* (Skt. *śamatha*) meditation, Vajrayoginī and Cakrasaṃvara practice. His activities went well beyond those of a traditional teacher of Buddhist philosophy and meditation, however. Trungpa associated with Allen Ginsberg and other well-known American poets and himself wrote poetry in English (see Trungpa 1972). Nāropa Institute, the college he founded at Boulder, Colorado, offered courses not only in Buddhist philosophy but in painting, dance, theatre, psychotherapy, physics, and creative writing.

In his later years he also became interested in Japanese culture and introduced a new non-Buddhist 'Shambhala training,' based on the symbolism of Tibetan folk religion. His students paraded in quasi-military 'field uniforms,' chanted invocations to Tibetan folk-religion deities and studied Japanese calligraphy and martial arts. Trungpa was said to have indulged heavily in alcohol and other drugs, and to have had numerous sexual affairs. The bizarre events at Nāropa Institute caused the occasional scandal in the American press, and considerable confusion in the Western Buddhist community.

Trungpa's bizarre behavior should be seen in the context of what was an unprecedented position for a Tibetan lama. He was one of the first lamas to teach in the West and, being remarkably successful at communicating with Westerners, he rapidly acquired a large following. By the 1970s, he was in charge of the largest Buddhist organization in North America, with several thousand devoted followers, many of them attracted by his unconventionality and prepared to encourage it further. There were few guidelines for Trungpa to follow. What is nevertheless striking is the extent to which he was simply, as he said, following in the footsteps of the 'crazy siddha' *(drubnyön)* tradition, and particularly of his own root guru, K'enpo Gangshar.

K'enpo Gangshar's students in Tibet would have read their lama's eccentricities in terms of the Tibetan cultural background, where such behavior marks an occasional and expected departure from a deeply ingrained pattern of respect for traditional knowledge, and is in any case justified as an expression of the Buddha's wisdom and compassion. Trungpa's Western students brought a different set of expectations, and it is understandable that they were confused at times by his teaching as well as stimulated by his undoubted ability to reach the minds and hearts of his Western disciples. Yet many of his disciples went on to study with other, more conventional, Tibetan lamas, and Trungpa himself retained the respect of other senior Rimed lamas, as their attendance at his cremation and their subsequent involvement with Vajradhatu indicated.

Other *trulku* from a similar Rimed background, such as Tarthang Tulku (of the Nyingma Institute in Berkeley, California), Sogyal Rimpoch'e (whose organization, Rigpa, is now centered in London) or Namkhai Norbu Rimpoch'e (who settled in Italy), have not been as outrageously unconventional as Trungpa, but they have shared his willingness to make original and creative adaptations of their Tibetan training. Tarthang Tulku's system of meditation on "Time, Space, and Knowledge," again originating in a personal vision, is a case in point (Tarthang 1977a).

None of the Gelugpa lamas in the West have, to my knowledge, moved anywhere like as far from the basic training they received in Tibet, although there is certainly a range of variation from, say, lamas such as Geshé Ngawang Dhargyey (see Dhargyey 1978, 1985; Berzin 1972) at the traditional end to the late Lama T'ubten Yeshé, founder of the F.P.M.T. centers, at the other. Nevertheless, not all Rimed lamas have chosen such unconventional paths. My next example, Kalu Rimpoch'e, an older lama from a similar if less exalted background, was throughout his career a teacher of the traditional Kagyüdpa yogic practices, despite acquiring an extensive following among Western Buddhists towards the end of his life.

Kalu Rimpoch'e

Kalu Rimpoch'e was known primarily as a Tantric teacher, and had a substantial following among both Tibetans and Westerners. He came, like Trungpa, from a monastic background in the Karma Kagyüdpa tradition. The following account is taken mainly from Kalu Rimpoch'e's own autobiography (Kalu 1985) and a short account by Dezhung Rimpoch'e (1977).

Kalu Rimpoch'e was born in Trehor in 1906 not far from the Gelugpa *gompa* of Dargyé (see Geshé Rabten, above). His father was a married reincarnate lama, Ratak Trulku, whose family claimed descent from the family of the 1st Karmapa. The 5th Dzogch'en Rimpoch'e felt that the child was a *trulku* and requested his father to allow him to be brought up at Dzogch'en *gompa*. His father refused, wishing to bring the child up himself. Later, Kalu Rimpoch'e was recognized by several lamas as the activity reincarnation of the great Rimed lama Jamgön Kongtrul.[12]

At the age of 13 he was ordained by the 11th Situ Rimpoch'e of the Karma Kagyüdpa *gompa* of Pelpung. Three years later he began a three year, three month, three day retreat at the retreat center near Pelpung. His root lama was Norbu Dun-kun Drubpa and he also studied with Situ Rimpoch'e and other great lamas, receiving the transmission of the Karma Kagyüd and Shangpa Kagyüd teachings.[13] After completing the retreat he went to Bengen *gompa* in Trehor, his birthplace.

For thirteen years, from the age of 25 onwards, he did yogic practice in many uninhabited meditation spots, completing the Tantric practices of *kyedrim* and *dzogrim*. His level of accomplishment became widely known, and Situ Rimpoch'e appointed him director of the retreat center at Pelpung where he taught for many years. Kalu rebuilt the Pelpung retreat center and traveled throughout Hor raising money for a fund to maintain the monks in retreat there. He also constructed many *maṇi*-stones, *stūpas*, and other religious objects. On a journey to central Tibet he restored various Shangpa sites and taught the Six Doctrines of Niguma from the Shangpa tradition to many Gelugpa lamas.

In 1955 he left K'am, where the political situation had deteriorated seriously, and moved to the head Karmapa *gompa* of Ts'urp'u in central Tibet. A year later, he was asked by the 16th Gyalwa Karmapa to take charge of a *gompa* in Bhutan where he built two more retreat centers and a large *stūpa*. In 1962 he moved to India, settling at Sonada near Darjeeling in West Bengal. He subsequently established Buddhist centers teaching traditional Tantric practice in India, France, the USA, Canada, and elsewhere. Kalu Rimpoch'e died at Sonada in 1989.

Kalu Rimpoch'e's informal recognition as a rebirth of Jamgön Kongtrul did not involve the assumption of headship of a *gompa*, and the Rimpoch'e attached to his name indicates the high regard in which he was held rather than any formal *trulku* status. His career is thus in some ways more like those of the 'ordinary monks,' Geshé Rabten or Tromo Geshé Rimpoch'e, than those of the various *trulku* we have considered, although he was the son of a *trulku* and was clearly destined by his father for a religious life from early on (see Kalu 1985:30–33).

Kalu Rimpoch'e's life was more exclusively oriented towards yogic practice than that of any of the other lamas we have considered so far.[14] Kalu Rimpoch'e was a monk, however, not a lay yogin, and most of his career took place in the celibate *gompa* setting of Pelpung. This combination of celibacy and yoga was a feature of the lives of many Rimed teachers, whether ordinary monks or *trulku*, although it was by no means universal. In Chapter 17 we came across another example, the Nyingmapa lama Tr'ulshig Rimpoch'e, a celibate monk, formerly abbot of Dzarong and now the abbot of a *gompa* in Sherpa country, but there were also famous lamas such as Ch'oggyur Lingpa and Śakya Śrī (see Chapter 17) who were not celibate practitioners.

Kalu Rimpoch'e's centers in the West give a traditional presentation of the Tantric teachings and yogic practice according to the Karma and Shangpa Kagyüd lineages. He was the first lama to take a group of Western students through the traditional three year, three month, three day retreat, in France in 1976–1980 (Kalu 1985:48).

My last two examples take us outside the context of celibate monasticism altogether. We will consider two Rimed practitioners who remained, formally at least, lay people: Ayu K'andro and Changch'ub Dorjé. These lamas, one female and one male, were both students of a famous K'ampa lama and *tertön* of the late nineteenth century, Nyagla Pema Duddul, and they were both teachers of the contemporary lama and scholar, Namkhai Norbu Rimpoch'e, whose accounts of their lives I summarize here. These lamas belong to an older generation than Kalu Rimpoch'e: Ayu K'andro met some of the actual founders of the Rimed movement.

Ayu K'andro

Ayu K'andro is the only woman among the eight lamas discussed in this chapter. Female teachers were not unknown in Tibet, although there were always fewer of them than male lamas. Another recent example, Jetsün Lochen Rimpoch'e, beginning like Ayu K'andro as a wandering yoginī, became abbess of a community of more than three hundred female practitioners at the *gompa* of Shugseb in central Tibet (Dowman 1988:143).[15] The background of female teachers is usually yogic rather than academic, which doubtless reflects both the acknowledged role for women in Tantric practice and the difficulty for women of undertaking academic and philosophical study.[16] There were no female equivalents of Drepung or Sera. This account is summarized from Namkhai Norbu's short biography in Tsultrim Allione's *Women of Wisdom* (1984:236).

Ayu K'andro was born in 1839 in the village of Dzongsa in Tagzig in K'am and named Dech'en K'andro by a local yogin, Togden Rangrig. Her family had once been wealthy, but was of middling status at the time of her birth. She was the youngest child of three sons and four daughters. The sons were all traders and the daughters did nomad's work, looking after animals.

Dech'en K'andro's aunt was a yogic practitioner, living in a cave near the Togden, and the girl went to stay with her aunt from the age of 7 to 18. A disciple of the Togden taught her to read and write. At the age of 14, she went with her aunt and the Togden to attend a consecration performed by three of the leading Rimed lamas, Jamyang Ky'entse Ongpo, Jamgön Kongtrul, and Ch'oggyur Lingpa. The two women received many teachings, and on the way back Ayu K'andro also visited Situ Rimpoch'e. Subsequently, she began doing the Longch'en Nyingt'ig preliminary practices. Later Jamyang Ky'entse Ongpo initiated her and her aunt into a White Tārā practice he had received as a *gongter*.

When she was 19, she married a man from a wealthy family at her parents' insistence. Her husband was kind and generous, but she became ill because her desire to lead a spiritual life was being blocked. After three years, her husband agreed that they should separate so that she could go into retreat. When she was 27, the Togden, who had been her principal teacher, died at the age of 77, exhibiting various miraculous signs. During the cremation her aunt also died. Ayu K'andro did a three-year retreat in her aunt's cave, assisted by the Togden's disciples.

At the age of 30 she began to travel around practicing *chöd* along with two of the Togden's disciples. She visited Adzom Gar, the center of the teacher Adzom Drugpa, and stayed there for the visit and teachings of Nyagla Pema Duddul. She continued to travel, visiting the *gompa* of Dzogch'en, Shech'en, and Dzongsar, and Derge Gonch'en, and going to stay for some time with Nyagla Pema Duddul. He sent her and a female friend off to travel around Tibet doing *chöd* practice in cemeteries and sacred places and prophesied that they would meet two yogins who would be important for them at Ts'aba and Lhok'a. They traveled to central and western Tibet and Nepal, meeting the prophesied yogins and developing their practice.

In 1881 she returned to her home country. Her former husband, who had remarried, built a hut for her and in 1885 after another visit to the lamas

Adzom Drugpa, Jamgön Kongtrul, and Jamyang Ky'entse Ongpo she began a seven-year retreat. With one brief interruption in 1890, she remained there for the rest of her life, dying in 1953 at the age of 115.

The story of the enforced marriage is a characteristic problem for female practitioners[17] but, this aside, Ayu K'andro's life was similar to that of many male yogins. When Namkhai Norbu visited her in 1951, she was still living in her tiny stone hut with two assistants, an old man and an old nun, both yogic practitioners themselves (Allione 1984:236).

Changch'ub Dorjé

We have less information about Changch'ub Dorjé's life than on Ayu K'andro's. His life is nevertheless of considerable interest as showing how a lay *ch'öpa* can establish a reputation as a teacher and gather a community of lay followers around him. The following is summarized mainly from material in Namkhai Norbu's *The Crystal and the Way of Light* (1986b:107, 131–135, 156–157; also see Norbu 1988).

Changch'ub Dorjé originally came from the Nyarong region in southeastern K'am. He was born in the mid-nineteenth century and studied with Adzom Drugpa, Nyagla Pema Duddul, and the Bönpo teacher Shardza Rimpoch'e. Changch'ub Dorjé headed a community called Nyagla Gar in a remote valley in Gonjo to the east of Dergé. According to local legend, he met his future wife in Gonjo while on his way to Lhasa on pilgrimage. He met her again on the way back.[18] They settled down together in Gonjo in 1895, and the community gradually grew up as people came to live around him and study with him.

Nyagla Gar was a self-supporting community consisting entirely of lay practitioners, yogins, and yoginīs.[19] Changchub Dorjé was widely known as a physician and consulted by people from far around, although he had never actually studied medicine, his medical knowledge having arisen as a by-product of his meditational accomplishment.

Free soup and simple food were provided daily at Nyagla Gar for those without resources and paid for by other members of the community who could afford to do so. Everyone who lived at the community participated in working in the fields, collecting herbs, and preparing medicines.

When the Chinese Communists arrived in the area they left the community alone since it already fitted their definition of an agricultural commune. Later, however, Changch'ub Dorjé was arrested and tortured. He died in 1981 shortly after his release. His daughter died in a Chinese prison camp, exhibiting the signs of achieving the Rainbow Body *(jalü)*, a mark of high meditational attainment.[20] Two of Changch'ub Dorjé's sons were killed by the Chinese, but a third, Sé K'awang, is the present head of the community.

Nyagla Gar continues to exist under the direction of Changch'ub Dorjé's surviving descendants. We have met similar small communities in Dolpo and Sherpa country, again built around a particular lama. In Nepal, they have often been regarded by Western writers, even those as well informed as Snellgrove (1961, 1967a), as marginal or decadent survivals of an older tradition. It is interesting to see that such communities formed part of the religion of twentieth-century K'am along with celibate monasticism, and that the young Namkhai Norbu Rimpoch'e was advised to visit Ayu K'andro and receive the Vajrayoginī initiation from her by his own tutor at one of the Sakya colleges of K'am (Allione 1984:236; N. Norbu 1986b:155–156).

This might be less likely to happen in the Gelugpa tradition, but it continued a long-standing respect for the lay yogic tradition on the part of celibate monastic lamas of the non-Gelugpa orders. For these lamas, meditational attainment counted for as much or more than scholarly learning, and spirituality was not restricted to celibate practitioners. Namkhai Norbu makes the point clearly in a few verses from his Tibetan poem, "The Little Song of 'Do as You Please'." This was written in answer to a Western critic who belonged to a Gelugpa center and asked how Norbu could practice and be a teacher when he lived like a lay person.

> The incomparable father, Ever Good [Samantabhadra],
> The Lord, Knowledge holder, Changch'ub Dorjé,
> Who resides in the dimension of the essential sphere at the center of his son's heart, my heart,
> Inseparable from it in any moment.
>
> This is the sum of the practice of the Teaching, and that's enough to give me complete satisfaction.
> I don't aspire to false religious practice.
>
> As for this title of so called reincarnation,
> If it's useful I adopt it for beneficial activities.

> When it's not useful for that, I just stay natural in my own way.
> You who desire a rank in a hierarchy, do as you please . . .
>
> As for this consort, the so-called fruit of previous *karma*,
> If she has good motivation, I instruct her in the teachings as far as I can,
> If not, I do anything I can to make her happy.
> You who are taken up with attachment and aversion, do as you please . . .
>
> The ineffable way of being of the *Prajñā Pāramitā*
> And the experience of direct understanding, I have joined together, within myself.
> To the intellectual path of study, I don't aspire.
> You who claim to be great scholars, do as you please.
>
> In the natural condition, the space which does not fall into limits of measurement or even the concept of direction,
> Whatever presents itself there, I enjoy as an ornament.
> I don't make any effort to create or reject anything.
> You who take up preferences, do as you please.
> (Namkhai Norbu 1986c:11, 15, 17, 21)

Namkhai Norbu's view here, as we shall see in later chapters, is in line with the views of lay yogic practitioners from the Indian siddhas and Milarepa through to the 'crazy yogins' of the fifteenth century and their nineteenth-century successors such as the Rimed lama Dza Peltrul Rimpoch'e. This is the voice of the shamanic side of Tibetan Buddhism and it runs throughout its history to the present day.

Part Three

19

From Structure to Process

Chapters 9 to 18 have presented an essentially synchronic view of Tibetan religion as it was in the premodern period and, to a large extent, remains today. The idea of the contrasting shamanic and clerical aspects of Buddhism underlies these descriptive chapters. We have seen how these shamanic and clerical modalities interact with the various other dimensions of Tibetan religion: celibate and lay, *sūtra* and Tantra, folk religion and Buddhist. We have also seen how they interact with the contrasting social forms outlined in Part One of the book: the agricultural communities, with greater and lesser degrees of centralization, and the pastoralists *(drogpa).* The relationships here are complex. The lives of the eight lamas in Chapter 18 were individual paths traced through the many possibilities and options offered by premodern Tibetan Buddhism, but they also demonstrated how those options have been structured in recent times by the two major syntheses of Gelugpa and Rimed and their differing relationships to the various political regimes that existed in premodern Tibetan societies.

I have already provided some historical background to the political forms of premodern Tibet in the regional summaries of Part One, and have referred in Chapters 3 and 8 to the significance of the Lhasa regime's moves towards greater centralization in the early twentieth century. Parts One and Two have nevertheless been essentially synchronic. The structure they depict contained internal contrasts and conflicting forces, but I have not attempted to set them into motion. Part Three, which is historical, is meant to demonstrate how these religious and political forms came into existence in the course of Asian history. Before commencing to trace this development with the origins of Indian Buddhism (Chapter 20), I shall discuss some of the theoretical issues raised by my description.

Shamanic and clerical modalities may well correspond to fundamental dimensions of human society (see Chapter 1, and Samuel 1990), but shamanic and clerical Buddhism are labels for social phenomena that arose as part of specific historical sequences. The significance of Tibet as an anthropological case study, and as part of the cultural heritage of humanity, lies in the unusual path that Tibetan society took. Shamanic procedures in other complex literate cultures became subordinated to state power and were marginalized in relation to clerical religions and governments (see Samuel 1990:121ff). In Tibet, this did not take place. The nearest parallel to the Tibetan situation seems to be provided by some Islamic societies, such as the Cyrenaican Bedouin, Morocco during the 'maraboutic period,' or Swat (Samuel 1982), but even in these cases shamanic procedures rarely obtained the dominance they acquired within Tibet, and the political supremacy of shamanic leadership was mostly short-lived.

These unusual situations are associated with some specific social, ecological, and political factors. Tibet and the Islamic societies I have mentioned shared low population densities, difficulties in communication, and a heavy dependence on long-distance trade, all factors that probably inhibited the development and maintenance of effective centralized regimes (Samuel 1982). These material factors are significant, but they hardly constitute a full explanation of why particular forms of religion developed in these societies, why they were maintained, and how they transformed in time into other religious forms.

Religious forms are not simple derivatives of their social and economic contexts. They are themselves an active part of those contexts. The development of Buddhism in Tibet cannot be reduced to the development of Tibetan social formations, because those formations were enabled by or inhibited by the specific forms that Buddhism took. Understanding the history of Buddhism in Tibet involves understanding the nature of social processes in human society in general, and we are some way from a satisfactory general explanation of such processes.

Perhaps the most powerful theoretical approach to be applied to these large-scale social processes within Asian religions was that of Max Weber. Weber wrote on Buddhism, including the Buddhism of Tibet, and, considering the primitive state of the data with which he worked, what he had to say was remarkably insightful (1967:282–290). My reference here, however, is more to Weber's general sociological approach. Weber's work assumes that a straightforward distinction can be made between social reality and how human beings understand that reality; in other words, he believed in a value-free social science (Samuel 1990:17–19). That belief is harder to sustain today, after all that has happened both in our understanding of science and our understanding of culture. Consequently, while echoes of a Weberian sociology occasionally emerge in this work, its fundamental assumptions are not Weberian.

Thus, the shamanic-clerical distinction bears some resemblance to Weber's opposition between charismatic and bureaucratic authority; however, both the general categories shamanic and clerical, and their particular forms in the Tibetan context, shamanic Buddhism and clerical Buddhism, refer to considerably more than a contrast in modes of authority within religious organizations. Ideas or cultural practices are more deeply constitutive of social reality than a purely Weberian sociology can allow. Religious forms create and shape the reality within which those who accept it live, and shamanic religion in particular involves the continuing transformation of such realities. If we do not take these transformations seriously, we will be unable to understand shamanic religion (and Weber is perhaps at his weakest in dealing with such religious forms, see Weber 1966; Tambiah 1984:329). If we dismiss the ability of shamanic religion to reconstitute the world for its followers, we also miss a basic key to the understanding of how societies transform.

I have developed these themes at length elsewhere. They raise significant and complex issues in the philosophy of social science and in the understanding of human culture, but those issues are not central to the present book, and I refer anyone interested in these aspects of the position presented here to my book *Mind, Body and Culture* (Samuel 1990).

What is significant in the present context is that each religious form needs to be seen as part of a total social whole if it is to be fully understood. Tambiah has referred to this method of exposition as 'totalization.' In relation to his analysis of the galactic polity, he comments:

> I have tried to show that the geometry of the galactic polity is manifest as a recurring design at various levels that [a hypothetical analyst might label] cosmological, territorial, administrative, politico-economic, but of which the accurate exegesis is that this recurring design is the reflection of the multifaceted polyvalence built into the dominant indigenous concepts, and of the traditional idea of a simultaneous convergence of phenomena in a mandala pattern. A corollary of this demonstration is that the cultural model and the pragmatic parameters are in concordance and buttress one another, and cannot be disaggregated. (Tambiah 1985:280)

In following the development of Tibetan religion and Tibetan societies, we are following the growth, mutual competition, and decline of a series of such totalities. In *Mind, Body and Culture,* I refer to these totalities as 'modal states.' Here, so as to make my account more comprehensible to readers less oriented towards questions of anthropological theory, I have chosen to use a more familiar term, 'cultural patterns.' I should make it clear, however, that the term 'cultural pattern' here has a specific sense, which goes considerably beyond that familiar from, for example, Ruth Benedict's classic *Patterns of Culture* (Benedict 1935).

The concept of cultural patterns, as used in this book, provides a way of tracing transformations in society and culture without implying a one-sided reductionism either to purely materialistic factors or to factors operating purely at the level of consciousness. The cultural pattern refers to the patterning of the field of relationships within human society, and between that society and its natural environment. The patterns manifest in human beings as culturally acquired ways of operating with the mind-body totality. Each of us acquires a repertoire of such patterns, and they define the contexts within which we think, feel, and behave.

A social group can also be characterized, at a particular point in space and time, in terms of a repertoire of patterns, in other words, in terms of the range and kind of patterns operative within it. Social change involves change in the cultural patterns, and it is not assumed that this change is always driven either by changes at the material level or by changes at the level of consciousness. The two always go along with each other. They can be described as having a dialectic relationship with each other, but this is already to reify the distinction between them to an inappropriate degree.

It is important to understand that we are not speaking here of bounded cultures dominated by a single cultural pattern. Any social context contains a variety or *repertoire* of such patterns, and given individuals also characteristically have a repertoire of patterns that form the basis of their thoughts, feelings, and actions. At times of rapid social change, such repertoires may be heterogeneous in nature and individuals may feel consciously torn between different possibilities for living (involving 'traditional' or 'modern' modes of family structure, for example, or conventional and millenarian religious forms). At other times, the repertoire may involve less obvious internal contrast. There is always both contrast and change, however, within the repertoire of patterns, both for individuals and for societies.

Consequently, I feel that a complete understanding, for instance, of the growth of celibate monasticism among the Sherpas would involve more than demonstrating the recurrence of a single 'cultural schema,' however pervasive, throughout Sherpa history (Ortner 1989a, see Chapter 17 above). What we should be looking for is the decline of one cultural schema and the growth of another, or perhaps a shift in the consequences of a single cultural schema given transformations in other factors within the society.[1]

The historical account in Chapters 20 to 28 is concerned with large-scale processes throughout Tibetan society as a whole, and it is rarely possible to do more than suggest some of the underlying shifts in cultural patterns. Several of these suggestions are little more than a spelling out of the implications of the work of other scholars. Tibetanists will recognize, for example, that my basic orientation towards the Nyingmapa-Rimed developments and much else is greatly indebted to the work of E. Gene Smith (1969b, 1970a, etc.). Other suggestions are perhaps more original. If the proposals have value, it ought to be possible to demonstrate both the patterns and their historical development in more detail in specific studies of particular periods, regions, and bodies of material.

The concept of cultural patterns (or modal states, in the language of Samuel 1990) also provides the basis for a model of how shamanic processes work. Such processes can be interpreted as operating with the balance of cultural patterns within individuals and societies. They are generally carried out with the aid of symbolic representations of cultural patterns. These symbolic representations may take various forms, which are usually interpreted in Western terms as vocabularies of gods, spirits, witchcraft, sorcery, ancestor-shades, or other 'supernatural' entities. In the Tibetan context, the local gods, the *la* spirit-force, and Tantric deities can all be interpreted in these terms.

The shaman's symbolic vocabulary is typically treated as deriving from some other realm of reality more fundamental than ordinary, everyday reality. Shamans are held to communicate with this realm through alternate states of consciousness, and their access to it justifies and authenticates their pronouncements. It will be recalled that shamanism was defined in Chapter 1 as *the regulation and transformation of human life and human society through the use (or purported use) of alternate states of consciousness by means of which specialist practitioners are held to communicate with a mode of reality alternative to, and more fundamental than, the world of everyday experience.* This definition is consistent with, and derives from, the analysis of shamanic processes suggested here (see Samuel 1990).

Shamanic processes are most common and most fully developed in nonliterate and stateless societies. Effective state power tends to control and limit them, because they represent an alternative source of power and authority. This underlies the contrast between Buddhism in Theravādin societies and in Tibetan societies traced in Chapter 2.

Cultural patterns may be in varying degrees *egocentric* (focused on the satisfaction of goals defined at the level of the individual) or *sociocentric* (focused on goals of the social group). 'Altruistic' behavior is motivated by sociocentric cultural patterns. Each pattern implies an ethics, an emotional vocabulary, a set of goals and a framework for rational thought. Shamanic techniques are essentially concerned with manipulating a subset of the cultural patterns in symbolic form, and particularly with maintaining a balance of patterns within the individual and society, which is adequately weighted towards the sociocentric. To perform these tasks the shaman needs to be able to enter a *visionary state* within which the cultural patterns can be seen and operated in a symbolic manner. The shaman can also act as a source of innovation by introducing new combinations or variations of cultural patterns.

Such procedures may be contrasted with the *rationalized* procedures typical of, for example, clerical Buddhism or modern Western societies, where there is a universal rationality and an accompanying linear ethical code deriving from an officially endorsed cultural pattern.

Major world religions such as Buddhism, Islam, and Christianity frequently derive their initial impetus from a 'shamanic'-style revelation. The initial stages of many such religions have a 'millenarian' character, and can be seen as a response to a period of radical social change. Buddhism seems to have originated in this way in the sixth century B.C. as a response to the collapse of tribal society and to the initial growth of large centralized states in North India. We can see early Buddhism as an attempt to create a framework that could reconcile the literate, rationalized, hierarchical society that was coming into being with the human values of the older, shamanic form of society. In its subsequent development in India, Buddhism increasingly took on the role of a clerical religion within the new 'rationalized' states; however, the shamanic dimension never altogether disappeared, and at times regained major significance. The Buddhism that the Tibetans received from the Indians preserved these complementary aspects, and developed them into a uniquely Tibetan synthesis.

In Chapters 20 to 27, I shall follow the convention of listing and numbering the principal 'cultural patterns' to be discussed within each chapter at the beginning of the chapter. It should always be remembered that these patterns refer to structurings of mind and body as well as patternings of relationships among human beings and between human beings and their environment (Samuel 1990). In cases where a particular social role (for example, folk shamanic practitioner, I3) is used to label a pattern, it should be noted that each pattern implies not only that specific role but the other social roles that accompany it. Thus, the folk shamanic practitioner pattern (I3) implies not only the role and modes of behavior, thought, and feeling of the practitioners themselves, but also those of their clients and patients.

As I have pointed out elsewhere (Samuel 1990:78), the delimitation of these patterns depends on the level of analysis. In this book, we are dealing throughout at a general level. This is particularly true of the earlier chapters, where patterns referred to by a single label (such as I5a) cover many centuries and considerable internal development.

In the lists of cultural patterns, I indicates India, T refers to Tibet. Numbers indicate main patterns (e.g., I5); letters indicate subdivisions (e.g., I5a). The antecedent patterns to a given pattern are indicated, where appropriate, after each pattern (<I1 should be read as 'derives in part from I1'). The implication is that the specified antecedent pattern provided much of the material for the later pattern. In some cases, more than one antecedent pattern can be seen as contributing to a particular pattern.

20

India: Buddhist Beginnings

In this chapter, I shall examine some components of early Buddhism, as one of the starting points for the historical analysis of Tibetan religion. This chapter, the following two chapters on India (Chapters 21 and 22) and that on early Tibet (Chapter 23), are necessarily sketchy in comparison with those dealing with more recent Tibetan history. I am not an expert on early Indian history,[1] Indian Buddhism,[2] or on the early Tibetan material,[3] and the available material on these subjects is, in any case, limited and contradictory in comparison to that available for the later periods of Tibetan history. For example, the dates of perhaps the most important single figure in Buddhist history after the Buddha himself, the great philosopher Nāgārjuna, are uncertain to within a couple of centuries (Ruegg 1981:4 and n. 11).

My chapters on India and early Tibet therefore do not claim to present an exhaustive and final analysis. Their aim is to give a plausible sketch of the context within which there came into being the various components that developed into premodern Tibetan religion.

TABLE 1.
Cultural Patterns in Chapter 20

Early Indian States, Seventh to Fourth Centuries B.C.

I1 'Tribal' shamanic practitioners
I2 Vedic Brahman priests
I3 Folk shamanic practitioners
I4 Wandering ascetics
I5 Urban monastics; Buddhist and Jain
  I5a Buddhist monastic
I6 Philosophy
  I6a Buddhist
    I6a1 Abhidharma

EARLY BUDDHISM: HISTORICAL CONTEXT

The Harappan societies of the Indus Valley were centralized states with at least some use of literacy for purposes of trade and administration. With their collapse, generally dated at around 1700–1500 B.C., both literacy and large-scale centralized polities seem to have disappeared from the Indian subcontinent. They did not become effectively reestablished until about the seventh century B.C., a development that was probably connected with the revival of trade with the Middle East (Diringer 1965). By this time, much of north India was dominated by populations speaking Aryan languages, but the historical events underlying their arrival are by no means clear.[4] The relationships between 'Aryan' and non-'Aryan' elements during this period are obscure, as are the processes leading to the establishment of distinctive 'tribal' populations in the hills and more remote areas. These 'tribal' peoples were the ancestors of contemporary 'tribal' (i.e., not caste Hindu) societies such as the Gonds or Santals. The tribal peoples are of some significance for the development of Tantra, since they seem to have acted in later centuries as a reservoir of shamanic techniques (I1 in Table 1) to be drawn upon by Tantric practitioners.

Religion during this stateless period can probably be regarded as 'shamanic' in the sense referred to in Chapter 19. Its relationship to the later Vedic literature is doubtless complex, but it seems reasonable to assume that shamanic practitioners transmitted in oral form a body of rituals that was later to become the Vedas. The *ṛṣi* or sages who appear in the Upaniṣads, in the Mahābhārata, and other Hindu religious texts, are likely to represent such nonliterate shamans as viewed by the later Indian tradition. Their version of shamanic procedures was the basis of what later became yoga (part of patterns I4 and I5 in Table 1).

The development of centralized polities in north India is conventionally described in two stages, the growth of small 'republics,' whose elected rulers governed with the aid of a council of elders, and their amalgamation into larger centralized states whose rulers were hereditary and had a greater degree of independent power. By the time of the Buddha Śākyamuni (500 B.C.), the larger states were already emerging in the Ganges Valley. His own home state, Śākya, in what are now the foothills of southern Nepal, was still a 'republic' of the older kind, administered by an elected rāja and council of elders (Warder 1970; Ling 1973:51, 89).

The Buddha, like his near-contemporary the Jain founder Mahāvīra, lived during this period of transition between nonliterate,[5] politically small-scale societies and literate, centralized, states. The religions that Śākyamuni and Mahāvīra founded (forming part of the new cultural patterns labelled I5 in Table 1) were part of a transformation between a 'shamanic' and locally based religious pattern and a full-scale 'clerical' religion, as were other monastic and clerical developments within the total Indian religious scene. In this transformation, the locally grounded cultural patterns of small-scale societies were replaced by the more universalizing modes of thought, feeling and action characteristic of the larger-scale contexts within which social life now took place (see Samuel 1990).

As this process got under way, the characteristic Indian relationship between urban and folk religious variants, analyzed by Singer and others in terms of the Great and Little Tradition model, began to take shape.[6] Several new cultural patterns emerged, and would seem to have separated out from the shamanic complex of Vedic society.[7] These included the patterns centered around the religious practice of Brahmin priests (I2 in Table 1), that of folk shamanic practice at the village level (I3), and that of the wandering ascetics (I4).

The Brahmins took on a clerical role, closely linked to the new hierarchical power-structure. Village shamanic practice (I3) lost much of its previous autonomy with incorporation into a centralized state (see Samuel 1990:131–133), and this transition was possibly linked to a movement from an active soul-journey vocabulary to the more passive spirit-possession vocabulary typical of modern Indian shamanic practitioners outside the tribal areas. Only the wandering ascetics (I4) maintained the shamanic ideal of a source of power outside the established social order that could be contacted by visionary processes, and they were a major source for the new Buddhist pattern (I5a). When Prince Siddhārtha, later to become the historical Buddha Śākyamuni, left the Śākya capital to practice meditation with wandering ascetics in the forest, he was moving back into a mode of thinking and behaving that was closer to that of the shaman than to the centralized state. The magical abilities Siddhārtha attained at his Enlightenment under the *bodhi*-tree, and his power over the local spirits and demons, reflected and continued the shamanic approach to reality.

The Buddha's main supporters, however, were to be the rulers and merchants of the large new states in the Ganges Plain to the south of the Śākya republic, and the new Buddhist and Jain monastic pattern (I5) was distinct from that of the wandering rural ascetics (I4). Buddhism's greatest early patron, 250 years later, was Aṣoka, ruler over the largest centralized state the Indian subcontinent had yet known. Buddhism was to be, in India at least, a religion closely associated with the centralized state, and with the commercial classes of the cities. The resolution of this apparent paradox can be seen through a study of the relationship between early Buddhism and the shamanic tradition as we know it elsewhere. The Buddha's teachings were an adaptation of the shamanic training for the new urban social context. This helps also to explain the combination of 'mystical' techniques and of social concern that is so striking in those teachings.[8]

Early Buddhism had two components, a series of moral teachings for the general population, centered around the doctrine of karma, and a system of training for the minority that was in effect a reformulated version of the shamanic training. The goal of this training was the attainment of the state of *arhat* (equivalent to entry into Skt. *nirvāṇa*, Pali *nibbāna*). The *arhat* is held to have achieved the insight into the nature of human existence that was originally reached by the historical Buddha at his attainment of Enlightenment (Skt. and Pali *bodhi*) under the *bodhi*-tree at Bodhgaya.

Central to the Buddhist goal of Enlightenment is the achievement of impartiality towards the concerns of ordinary human society and towards the phenomenal world. The Four Noble Truths, the paradigmatic statement of the original Buddhist insight, states this clearly. Involvement with the ongoing process *(saṃsāra)* of life in the world in any form brings suffering, and it is only by a systematic rejection and reversal of one's clinging to that process that relief from suffering may be attained.

I have argued that such a rejection of involvement with the everyday concerns of a culture (with the 'ordinary' cultural patterns, or modal states in the modal-state language of Samuel 1990) is an essential part of the shamanic training. Shamans have to be able to 'go beyond' these patterns and attain a degree of impartiality to them in order to carry out their mediatory and manipulatory function in relation to the patterns (see Samuel 1990:107–108). The Buddhist Enlightenment was believed to confer the ability to perceive the karmic connections behind everyday reality and to act appropriately so as to teach each individual being. As Mircea Eliade, among others, has suggested, there is a close likeness between such yogic techniques, which were common to Buddhism and other Indian traditions, and the techniques of shamanism (Eliade 1958, 1970).

The Brahmanic scriptures, the Vedas, had not been written down in Śākyamuni's time, nor were Śākyamuni's own words to be committed to writing for several centuries to come. The Buddha's teachings were codified in the Sūtras, texts that narrate Śākyamuni's instructions to his disciples on various specified occasions. They were initially transmitted orally, as also was the Vinaya, the set of rules for the Buddhist community of monks, nuns, and lay followers.

For the Theravādin school of Buddhism, which in modern times has been the prevailing school in Sri Lanka and most of Southeast Asia (Thailand, Laos, Burma, Cambodia), these early Sūtras form the only authentic teaching of the Buddha.[9] For the Tibetans and other Mahāyāna Buddhists, the early Sūtras represent the first of several (usually three) 'turnings of the wheel of the Dharma.' They are held to be the teachings suited to the Buddha's early human disciples, whereas the later Sūtras, claimed to have been taught by the Buddha to gods and other nonhuman audiences, were preserved until the appropriate time for their revelation to human beings came about several centuries later.

Both Theravādins and Tibetans are in agreement that the 'Hinayāna' Sūtras, those existing, if in variant recensions, in both the Pali

Canon and the Tibetan and Far Eastern traditions, represent Buddhism as it was understood in the first few centuries after the Buddha's death. For the Tibetans, this 'first turning of the wheel' nevertheless represented only part of the teaching of the Buddha, and was to be supplemented by the revealing of the Mahāyāna and Vajrayāna teachings. If we leave aside the issue of the historicity of the gods and *nāga* who are said to have passed down the Mahāyāna Sūtras, and regard them as part of the universal language of shamanic insight, then we can understand the Tibetans to be saying that the later Sūtras and also the Tantras were part of an ongoing process in which the insight of early Buddhism was constantly reformulated and re-created. For the Tibetans, the term 'Buddha' or *sanggyé* referred less to a historical personage who lived in north India at a specific time than to a universal principle or possibility of human existence, the Dharmakāya or *ch'öku*, which could manifest appropriately anywhere in time and space.

Western perspectives on the authenticity of the various stages of Buddhist revelation have tended to remain closer to the Theravādin position than to that of the Tibetans. In other words, most authors who have gone beyond treating Buddhist teachings as simple mystification or ideological camouflage have assumed that the various stages of Buddhism represent a series of radically different historical phases, each having greater or lesser claim to authenticity. Within this perspective, the 'Hinayāna' Sūtras are thought of as representing a reasonably close approximation to the words of the historical Buddha Śākyamuni, while the later texts, Mahāyāna Sūtras and Tantras, are more distant and less authentic.

In one sense, the question of 'authenticity' goes beyond the realm of anthropology, the academic discipline within which this book is located. It is important here, however, to maintain a middle road between a naive acceptance of the Buddhist texts at face value and an equally naive cynicism that would treat their contents as bearing no relationship to genuine experiential data. The latter position would lead to some kind of materialist reduction, while the whole point of the approach taken here is to treat consciousness and material reality as co-equal components of the developmental process.

The position suggested here represents such a middle road, and its key element is the assumption that the Buddhist teachings initially represented the old shamanic training reformulated for a large-scale, literate society, and that later phases consist of further reformulations of the same underlying approach in terms of the specific social and historical contexts of the visionaries and scholars of those periods. Naturally, the Buddhist teachings of each period were also shaped by the specific personalities, interests, and social context of those who propounded them. If, however, the central assumption here is correct, then we would expect that the formulations of later periods, where they do not simply reflect the political interests of pro-Buddhist rulers, should continue to be shaped by the same shamanic orientation. This orientation (see Chapter 19) may be described as involving the attainment of contact with a realm of symbolic entities beyond ordinary reality, and the eventual transcendence of that realm.

This perspective seems to me to have much to recommend it, since it avoids the question of authenticity, which is, as stated above, a religious question rather than an anthropological one, without supposing that later Buddhism consists simply of a mass of forgeries by various self-interested clerics. It also provides a starting point for analyzing the contents of successive stages of Indian and Tibetan Buddhist thought. As Martin Southwold pointed out recently, we have little idea in any case what the historical Śākyamuni actually said (Southwold 1983). Even the 'earliest' Sūtras have undergone a great deal of clerical reformulation in the Pali, Sanskrit, Tibetan, and Chinese recensions in which they now survive.

The development of Buddhism in India and Tibet was a complex process involving numerous social groups with their contrasting interests and cultural patterns. While this process cannot be reduced to a simple formula, an underlying tension can be sensed throughout this long historical process, and for me this tension provides much of the interest in Buddhist history as well as accounting for the dynamic behind the continuous innovation of the later Indian and Tibetan tradition. The tension is between the visionary and yogic side of Buddhism, with its recurrent struggle to recreate and maintain the shamanic vision, and the clerical and scholarly side, with its orientation towards the development of the Buddhist community as part of a wider hierarchical social order.

The visionary side ultimately has no allegiance to any political order, being part of the 'nomad thought,' in the phrase of Gilles Deleuze (1985), by which humanity has constantly attempted to dissolve and weaken the always solidifying hierarchical structures of the state. The clerical side is the voice of realism, which accepts and works within the structures of state power. It is hardly surprising that the most promising environment for nomad thought and shamanic vision would be Tibet, with its large nomadic population and general absence of effective state power. This is to anticipate the chapters that follow, however. In the next section, we turn to examine the early stages of Buddhism in India in more detail.

EARLY BUDDHISM: MORALITY AND YOGA

The early Sūtras exist in the version transmitted by the Theravādins (the 'Pali Canon') and also in separate versions preserved in Sanskrit and in translation in Nepal, Tibet, and China. It is, as already noted, unclear how close these texts are to the Buddha's actual teachings. The written versions cannot reliably be traced back beyond the time of Aṣoka (around 250 B.C.) and by this period the process of scholastic and literary reworking was certainly well under way (Bareau 1955).

The teachings of these early Sūtras tend to be formulaic or analogical in expression, rather than having the form of a developed philosophical system of a rational kind. The Buddha counseled withdrawal from the concerns of everyday life. In the case of his male and female lay followers *(upāsaka, upāsīkā)* this withdrawal was necessarily limited, but for the two grades of male celibate practitioners *(sramaṇera, bhikṣu)* and their female equivalents it was more extensive. Along with this withdrawal went the general moral teachings summed up in the lay precepts, the monastic rules and the Eightfold Path.

The other major component of early Buddhism was the practice of 'meditation' or yoga. The term *yoga* was not much used by the early Buddhists, although it was to become common in the Tantric period. It is a convenient term, however, for the large variety of techniques practiced by Buddhists, Hindus, and Jains. The techniques of yoga can be characterized, in a preliminary way, as exercises for the training of the mind and body as a totality.

A number of yogic techniques have been popularized in the West in modern times, among them the primarily physical exercises of Haṭha Yoga and the mantra-practice of Transcendental Meditation. Yoga, however, does not refer to any single technique but to a wide variety of, at first sight, quite diverse methods. There are numerous yoga practices ranging from the simple to the extremely complex, and practiced by Hindus, Buddhists, and Jains. Similar practices can also be found in Islam among the Ṣūfīs of India and elsewhere, as well as in other religious traditions.

Yoga in the early Buddhist Sūtras has two primary aspects, 'concentration' *(samādhi)* and 'mindfulness' *(smṛti)*. This pair of terms corresponds to the last two members of the Eightfold Path, which is undoubtedly a very early formulation.

I suggested in Chapter 19 that shamanism can be described as a set of techniques for operating with the cultural patterns within a given social group (see Samuel 1990). These patterns are ways of organizing the relationships among individuals, and between individuals and their natural and social environment, internalized as learned structurings of mind and body within particular individuals. In these terms we can see concentration or *samādhi* as the deliberate stabilization of a single pattern out of the fluctuating repertoire of patterns between which human consciousness typically moves. These patterns (the modal states of Samuel 1990) are not located simply within the 'society' or the individual, but in the interaction between individual and surroundings. Withdrawal from sensory awareness, with its continual distractions, is therefore a prerequisite for such an attempt to induce and maintain a particular pattern. The quiet, restrained lifestyle of the Buddhist monk, and the practice of meditating in solitary places, contribute to achieving success.

A variety of meditative objects can act as supports for this procedure. They include material objects of various shapes and colors, the process of breathing, and also the four 'immeasurable' states of compassion, love, sympathetic joy, and equanimity. The Buddhist yogin gradually attains the ability to induce these intensive, 'one-pointed' states at will and to hold them as long as desired. The tradition lists a series of eight progressive stages of this process (the eight 'trances' or *dhyāna*). These are held to correspond to the state of being of various classes of deities in the heavenly realms that the Buddhists took over from general Indian cosmology.

Mindfulness or *smṛti* is the complement to *samādhi*. If *samādhi* involves the reduction of sensory awareness, *smṛti* involves its cultivation. Mindfulness is total awareness of the immediate situation. This is, however, a detached, noninvolved awareness, free from desire or aversion. Desire and aversion are two of the three roots of *saṃsāra*, the repetitive and unsatisfactory experience of everyday life from which the Buddhist attempts to escape. The third root is ignorance, above all ignorance of the illusory nature of the self. The aim of *smṛti* is the cultivation of an awareness that goes beyond any specific cultural pattern and is totally and immediately responsive to the situation. Such an awareness would be by definition centered on the total situation rather than the demands of the individual self. It would, in other words, represent what I referred to in Chapter 19 as a 'sociocentric' rather than an 'egocentric' pattern. As I pointed out in Chapter 19, sociocentric patterns are central to the shamanic mode of functioning (see also Samuel 1990:98–103).

The self-concept *(ātman)* is seen in Buddhism as being a major obstacle to such awareness, and the achievement of *smṛti* implies the disappearance of the self-concept. The individual becomes a totally responsive mirror to experience, with no substance of its own. Any substantial self-image would involve a limitation on the ability to respond, because it requires that the response be such as to maintain that self-image.

Early Buddhism used two other terms, *śamatha* and *vipaśyanā*, which were more or less equivalent in their implications to *smṛti* and *samādhi*.[10] *Śamatha* techniques were concerned with the development of the states of single-pointed concentration, while *vipaśyanā* techniques were concerned with the development of insight into the true nature of reality. Early Buddhists defined this true nature of reality in terms of the absence of the self-concept. This was the famous doctrine of *anātman* (Skt.) or *anattā* (Pali), the distinguishing mark of Buddhism according to both Indian Buddhists and non-Buddhists.

While Buddhist sociocentric patterns were constructed around a denial of the ordinary self, the corresponding Hindu language was of unity between the self and some wider principle (Brahman). For non-Buddhist Indians in the period when Buddhism was an active part of Indian religious life (roughly to the thirteenth century A.D.), Buddhism was preeminently the doctrine that denied the self, though in practice, as we will see in later chapters, more positive phraseologies have also been of significance in Buddhist thought.[11] The Buddhists themselves, while explicitly rejecting the idea of a permanent and eternal self, saw their position as a Middle Way between the 'eternalist' doctrines of Hindu theism, and the 'nihilist' doctrines of Indian materialists, such as the Cārvākas.

Śamatha practice was (and is still) regarded as a preliminary to *vipaśyanā* practice rather than as an end in itself. *Śamatha* corresponds to the shaman's ability to master and control a single 'visionary' state (see Chapter 19, and Samuel 1990:107–109). This equivalence is confirmed by the various 'magical' powers associated with mastery of the stages of *samādhi*. With the exception, however, of the four 'immeasurable' states (compassion, love, sympathetic joy, and equanimity), there is no sign here of the explicit repertoire of cultural patterns employed by the shaman. These early Buddhist 'shamans' were not concerned with controlling the social world around them except through generalized positive social emotions. In this they contrasted with their later Tantric counterparts in India and Tibet.

Vipaśyanā corresponds, in shamanic terms, to entry into the realm of possibility from which the shaman selects or creates the cultural pattern (or subpattern of an overall cultural pattern) appropriate to a given situation. The Buddhist practitioner, like the shaman, has to undergo severe trials to attain this ability, and the death of self involved in the Buddhist attainment can be compared with the ritual death and rebirth involved in many forms of shamanic training.[12]

This shamanic interpretation of the death of self in Buddhism was, incidentally, to be taken up explicitly in the famous Tibetan practice of *chöd* (see Chapter 24). Here the yogin undergoes a characteristically shamanic experience of death and dismemberment which is explicitly conceived of as an exercise in giving up the self-concept. *Chöd* takes place under the auspices of a goddess who is a deified form of the discriminating insight *(prajñā)* aimed at by the *vipaśyanā* practitioner (see Tucci 1980:87–92; Gyatso 1985).

A familiar classification of the Buddhist teachings sets the moral teachings of Buddhism alongside the two forms of meditation to reach a threefold division: *śīla*, *samādhi* (= *śamatha*) and *prajñā* (= *vipaśyanā*). For the rulers of the new centralized states of north India, it was doubtless *śīla*, morality, which was of most concern, and we turn now to examine the moral teachings of Buddhism and the doctrine of karma in the context of the political developments of this period.

MORALITY AND THE TRANSITION TO A RATIONALIZED SOCIETY

In shamanic society, morality is implicit in the various subpatterns that make up the overall cultural pattern. Each of these defines a morality appropriate to particular situations (see Wagner 1978; Samuel 1990). The shaman fine-tunes the system, by prescribing more or less of a particular pattern and where necessary modifying a state or creating a new one. Neither Śākyamuni, the founder of Buddhism, nor the other Indian religious teachers of his time could hope to reconstitute this system for society as a whole. It was lost forever in India with the growth of literate rationality and the hierarchical legal and administrative procedures of a centralized state. The order of society was now a historical creation, not a projection into human terms of an order within the universe.

The Sūtras explicitly describe hierarchical government as humanly instituted through the election of the first king. Their approach to morality and ethics is based on the doctrine of karma. Karma was a commonplace of the various Indian philosophical schools of this period, and by no means a specifically Buddhist development. The term *karma* literally means 'action.' The law of karma is the principle by which each action has its consequence at a later time in the present or (in most cases) a future life.

Karma in Indian society can act as an ideology to explain and justify social inequality. The lower castes have been born as such as a proper and impartial consequence for their actions in a previous life. While this kind of thought is present in Buddhist societies, and karma is often used as an explanation of the apparent differences of ability between people, the emphasis in Buddhist thought has always tended to be in the opposite direction. Karma acts as the foundation for ethics and morality. One should avoid morally bad actions because of their unpleasant consequences in a future life, and cultivate morally good actions that will both help to ensure a good rebirth and provide a sound foundation for eventual escape from the cycle of rebirth (see Tambiah 1968, 1970; Spiro 1971).

There is an apparent contradiction between the doctrine of karma and the central insight of the Buddhist Enlightenment. That insight, we have seen, involves a going beyond the desires, hatreds, and motivations of the everyday world. How can it be reconciled with a teaching in which certain actions are proper and to be cultivated, and others are not?

The Buddhist answer to this paradox has remained essentially the same since the days of the early Sūtras. Ordinary men and women are caught up in the realm of *saṃsāra*, of everyday life. This is a dreary round of perpetual rebirth in one or another of several different states. These are traditionally six in number; hell-beings, *preta* or hungry ghosts, animals, human beings, *asura* or demi-gods, gods. Karma refers to rebirth within *saṃsāra*. Those who accumulate good karma will be reborn in a higher and more pleasant state, while those who accumulate bad karma sow the seeds that will ripen (in the Buddhist image) as rebirth in the hells or as a hungry ghost or animal.

The central insight of Buddhism is equivalent to escape from this whole cycle of karma and rebirth. It is described as entry into *nirvāṇa*, the opposite term to *saṃsāra*. Enlightened beings act without accumulating karma; their actions sow no seeds for a future rebirth. Enlightened beings are thus, in a sense, beyond morality, but the antinomian implications of this assertion are countered by the idea that such beings will naturally and spontaneously act according to the highest possible morality, by doing whatever is conducive to the release from suffering and progress towards enlightenment of other 'sentient beings.'

There are themes here that are to return over and over in the subsequent history of Buddhism. Early Buddhism, once it became institutionalized within Indian society, implied a division between serious practitioners, by definition monastic, and a lay following who provided them with support. The goal of shamanic insight, rephrased as the Buddhist Enlightenment, was a goal for a small minority of what Weber used to call "religious virtuosi," while the teachings for the rest of the population were of a straightforward moral kind (for example, Weber 1966:162–163). Buddhism took this elitism over from the shamans. It was softened by the idea of the progress to Enlightenment as taking place over many lives, so that one's accumulation of good karma might permit the attainment of Enlightenment in a future life, if not in this life. The division between virtuosi and lay followers, however, remained characteristic of Buddhist societies in practice.

Another continuing theme concerned the relationship between the continual process of rebirth and the doctrine of absence of self. If there was no self, what was reborn? This became a topic of controversy between some of the early Buddhist schools, although in practice most schools had little difficulty in arriving at a more or less consistent explanation. The beginnings can be seen here, as in the distinction between elite and lay follower, of a tendency that was to become more and more significant in later times. This is the development of the Buddhist teachings into different categories, the superficial and the more subtle, appropriate for different categories of hearers. One of the qualities of a Buddha, an Enlightened Being, is said to be the ability to give the appropriate teaching to his listeners, and if necessary to teach at several different levels of understanding at the same time. This is the 'skillful means' or 'skill in techniques' *(upāyakauśalya)* of a Buddha (see D. and A. Matsunaga 1974; Pye 1978; Samuel 1975:56–58, 71ff).

It was doubtless the morality of early Buddhism, with its strong social and interpersonal orientation, that proved attractive to the rulers of the large and culturally diverse populations of the growing centralized states of north India. The Buddhist philosophy of restraint and of the gradual accumulation of merit went well, too, with the growing mercantile populations of these states. The climax of this development was reached when the Emperor Aṣoka, ruler of the largest centralized state in the Indian subcontinent to that time, stretching from Afghanistan to Bengal and the Deccan, adopted Buddhism as a state religion. Many of the inscriptions in which Aṣoka enjoined the practice of Buddhism have survived, and there is no doubt that Buddhism was established by that time as a major force in Indian society. The conversion of the kingdom of Sri Lanka to Buddhism is also traditionally said to have taken place in Aṣoka's time.

The early Buddhist schools developed alongside the various Hindu and Jain philosophical schools, and for the population of the villages and the countryside there was probably never a sharp distinction between these Hindu and non-Hindu traditions. Buddhists, like Hindus and Jains, accepted the cults of local gods, while denying them more than a conditional utility. The only ultimate refuge could be in the Three Jewels *(triratna)* of Buddhism: the Buddha, his teachings (the Dharma), and the community he founded (the Saṃgha).

While early Buddhism had, as suggested above, the potential to develop antinomian and antihierarchical forms, there is little sign of its having done so until a much later period. The goal of the early Buddhists was the attainment of the state of *arhat.* The *arhat,* like the Buddha himself, attained *nirvāṇa,* extinction of the self-concept and escape from *saṃsāra,* but his attainment was already considered less than the Buddha's own supreme Enlightenment. While the Buddha has the full complement of magical powers of the traditional shaman, these are much less emphasized in the case of the *arhat.*

There could be only one actual Buddha in this world at a given time, and a long period elapsed between successive Buddhas. The next Buddha, Maitreya, was very far in the future. His coming would follow many thousands of years of gradual decline and deterioration in the Buddhist teachings (the Dharma) and in human affairs generally. This is the Buddhist version of the common Indian idea of recurrent cycles of growth and decay in human affairs and in the universe as a whole, in which linear, diachronic time is, as it were, embedded in a larger static (synchronic) context.

According to later Theravādin tradition, it was only for a few generations after the Buddha's own lifetime that even the state of *arhat* could be achieved. With the progressive decay of the teachings and of social conditions generally, even the lower grades of attainment ('never-returner,' 'once-returner,' 'stream-winner') became harder and harder for human beings to reach, although it is occasionally held that one or another exceptionally saintly modern Buddhist may have attained to these levels.

All this is part of what Melford Spiro, studying a Theravādin community in contemporary Burma, has called the shift from 'Nibbanic' Buddhism to 'Kammatic' Buddhism (Spiro 1971). In the terms of this book, this is a shift from the Bodhi Orientation to the Karma Orientation. 'Nibbanic' Buddhism, the Theravādin version of the Bodhi Orientation, is concerned with the attainment of *nirvāṇa* (Pali *nibbāna*), the goal of the Buddhist yogic practices referred to above. 'Kammatic' Buddhism (from Pali *kamma*, karma), the Theravādin version of the Karma Orientation, involves the performance of meritorious actions in the hope of a good rebirth, since actions (karma) in this life, along with their accompanying volitional states, determine the nature of one's future life.

'Kammatic' Buddhism is not really, as Spiro tends to imply, a later adaptation of Buddhism in which the original goals were entirely lost sight of. The two orientations are already present at very early times, and as Spiro's own ethnography indicates, contemporary Buddhists are quite capable of seeing them as complementary and interrelated (Spiro 1971). There is little doubt, however, that *nirvāṇa* came to seem a distant goal in the later Theravādin tradition, especially for lay followers of Buddhism. Tibetans, by contrast, came to believe that the goal of Enlightenment was attainable by human beings within a single lifetime through the techniques of the Vajrayāna, and the Bodhi

Orientation became a central preoccupation for many thousands of Tibetans.

THE PHILOSOPHY OF EARLY BUDDHISM (16A1)

If early Buddhism was a reformulation of the shamanic insight, in a language relevant to the new situation, then the philosophy of early Buddhism should represent an attempt at a rational framework consistent with that insight. In fact, the early Sūtras do not present a complete philosophical system. They provide fragments of several different conceptual frameworks, not necessarily compatible with each other. Each is held to be the teaching appropriate to the Buddha's audience at that time, so that the contradictions present no particular problem for Buddhist followers. The need for a more systematic philosophical presentation seems to have been felt from early on. In the centuries immediately following the Buddha's death the hints and fragments in the Sūtras were developed into a coherent philosophy. It is this philosophy, the Abhidharma (I6a1), which we now examine (see Conze 1962; Guenther 1974a).

With the development of the Abhidharma, the tension between rationalizing (clerical) and shamanic aspects of Buddhism first comes to the fore. The Abhidharma, with its systematic analysis of reality into long lists of possible constituents, is a classical expression of an early literate culture (see Goody 1977). Each of the various Buddhist schools developed its own, slightly different version of it.

The Abhidharma can be seen as primarily an aid to meditation and so to the entry to quasi-shamanic states; however, it also marks the beginning of a long and distinguished tradition of Buddhist philosophical thought, appropriate to the developing literate and commercial society that patronized the new Buddhist intellectuals. We will trace the complex relationship between rational and shamanic aspects of Buddhism through many centuries of Indian and Tibetan history, until we reach the symbiosis between clerical and shamanic forms of Buddhism already described for premodern Tibet in Chapters 1 and 2 and in Part Two.

One of the most important schemes given in the Sūtras is that of the five *skandha*, 'heaps' or 'accumulations,' which formed the basis of the early Buddhist analysis of the self. The five *skandha* are a set of categories into which all that might correspond to a self can, in theory, be exhaustively divided, so demonstrating the illusory nature of the apparent self. The Abhidharma philosophy is an elaboration of this scheme.

The first *skandha*, *rūpa* or form, corresponds to the basis for the process of perception, the 'givenness' of the material world insofar as that is assumed in early Buddhism. The second, *vedanā* or sensations, corresponds to the input of the senses (which include the mind itself as a source of sensory data) prior to interpretation. The process of interpretation is described by the third and fourth *skandha*, *saṃjñā* and *saṃskāra*, translatable as 'concepts' and 'volitions,' while the entire process was reflected and perceived through the fifth *skandha*, *vijñāna* or consciousness. It was within this fifth *skandha* that the 'seeds' created by the volitions were laid down as *vāsanā*, 'impressions' or 'propensities'—the literal meaning is closest to 'perfumings'—which would bear fruit in future lives, since *vijñāna* alone continued from one rebirth to the next. *Vijñāna* (Tibetan *namshé*) is the nearest thing within this system of ideas to a reincarnating entity or self, but since the content of *vijñāna* is continually changing and has no permanent essence, it is quite different from a reincarnating soul or spirit.

In the Abhidharma philosophy, each *skandha* consists of a succession of point-moments (*dharma*, one of the many meanings of a central Buddhist and Hindu term) of shape, color, various kinds of sensation, volition, conceptualization, and so forth. Each school has a slightly different list of these *dharma*. Progress towards Enlightenment consists in some of these factors (the virtuous dharmas) coming to dominate, while the others (nonvirtuous and neutral) gradually vanish. This process is brought about by the triple practice of *śīla*, *samādhi*, and *prajñā*, 'morality,' 'meditation,' and 'insight.' Here *samādhi* and *prajñā* correspond to the two modes of meditation, *śamatha* and *vipaśyanā*, considered earlier. The attainment of the full Enlightenment of a Buddha through this process is thought of as taking an extremely long time, many millions of successive rebirths of the individual.

The Theravādin version of the Abhidharma continues to be studied in Sri Lanka and Southeast Asia, where that school is dominant. A slightly different version of the Abhidharma, that of the Sarvāstivādin and Sautrāntika schools, was transmitted to Tibet, where it became part of the academic curriculum of the Tibetan *gompa* (see Guenther 1972; Sopa and Hopkins 1976; Lati 1980).

The Abhidharma regards the *dharma* or point-moments, which are its basic components, as really existing, although the precise manner of that existence was disputed among the early schools. There are indications, however, that the Buddha himself attempted to convey a more subtle insight into the relational nature of things in his early teachings. This can be found in the famous formula of *pratītyasamutpāda*, 'dependent origination' or (as translated by the great modern Buddhist scholar Edward Conze) 'conditioned co-production,' which was traditionally regarded as an especially profound formulation of the Buddha's central insight:

> Once when the Lord was staying among the Kurus, the venerable Ānanda approached him and said: 'It is wonderful, Lord, that while [*pratītyasamutpāda*] is so deep and looks so deep, to me it seems perfectly clear.'
>
> 'Do not speak like that, Ānanda. For this [*pratītyasamutpāda*] is deep and looks deep too. It is from not awakening to this [teaching], Ānanda, from not penetrating it, that this generation, become tangled like a ball of thread, covered as with blight, twisted up like a grass-rope, cannot overpass the sorrowful state, the bad bourn, the abyss, the circling on *(saṃsāra).*' (*Dīghanikāya* II, 55; Conze 1964:69–70)

Pratītyasamutpāda literally means the arising in mutual causation or mutual conditioning. It is traditionally summed up in the twelve *nidāna* or causal links:

> Conditioned by ignorance are the karma-formations; conditioned by the karma-formations is consciousness; conditioned by consciousness is mind-and-body; conditioned by mind-and-body are the six sense-fields; conditioned by the six sense-fields is impression; conditioned by impression is feeling; conditioned by feeling is craving; conditioned by craving is grasping; conditioned by grasping is becoming; conditioned by becoming is birth; conditioned by birth there come into being ageing and dying, grief, sorrow, suffering, lamentation and despair. Thus is the origin of this whole mass of suffering.
>
> But from the stopping of ignorance is the stopping of the karma-formations; from the stopping of the karma-formations is the stopping of consciousness; from the stopping of consciousness is the stopping of mind-and-body; from the stopping of mind-and-body is the stopping

> of the six sense-fields; from the stopping of the six sense-fields is the stopping of impression; from the stopping of impression is the stopping of feeling; from the stopping of feeling is the stopping of craving; from the stopping of craving is the stopping of grasping; from the stopping of grasping is the stopping of becoming; from the stopping of becoming is the stopping of birth; from the stopping of birth, ageing and dying, grief, sorrow, suffering, lamentation and despair are stopped. Thus is the stopping of this whole mass of suffering. (*Vinayapiṭaka* I, 1; Conze 1964:66–67)

Both the doctrine of *pratītyasamutpāda* itself and the twelve links received a wide range of interpretations in the course of Buddhist history, and they will recur in subsequent chapters. Here I will point out that while it is possible to interpret the twelve links of the causal nexus as spreading over two or more human life times (in which case the birth is the birth of a human being), it is equally possible to take them more metaphorically as a series of factors arising at one time in a single situation. This interpretation was advanced in the Abhidharma text of the Vaibhāṣika (Sarvāstivādin) school and so included in the *Abhidharmakośa*, the authoritative presentation of the Abhidharma for the Tibetans (Wayman 1971, 1980a).

In either case, *pratītyasamutpāda* can be taken as an assertion of the relational nature of existence, of all things being part of a generalized nexus of mutual causation. As such it points towards a less mechanical outlook than the Abhidharma philosophy with its really existent point-moments, and to the possibility of a theory more compatible with the shamanic insight. This possibility was to be taken up by the next major school of Buddhist philosophy, the Madhyamaka school founded by Nāgārjuna. This was the first of the Mahāyāna schools (see Chapter 21).

The corollary to either of the two interpretations of *pratītyasamutpāda* in the early schools is the same. It is ignorance, *avidyā*, which allows the volitions to arise and create karma. If we can perceive the true nature of things as without self, attachment to and repulsion from them will vanish, and our actions will no longer be accompanied by the karma-forming volitions. Thus the 'ball of thread,' the 'twisted grass-rope,' will become unravelled.

For the early schools, ignorance continued to be defined as belief in the reality of the self-concept, while the perceived world was regarded as in some sense real. Subject and object imply each other, however, and the counterpart of the illusory nature of the self is the illusory nature of what the self perceives, in other words of the ordinary world of *saṃsāra*. This was perhaps part of what the Buddha meant when he insisted that *pratītyasamutpāda* not only seemed deep, but was deep. At any rate, it was the foundation of the next major development in Buddhist thought. As we will see, the teaching of *pratītyasamutpāda* was to remain a constant source of reflection and innovation for later Buddhist schools.

CULTURAL PATTERNS

What we have seen in this chapter is an initial situation characterized (as far as the religious field is concerned) by 'tribal' and folk shamanic practice (I1, I3) and Vedic Brahman priesthood (I2), and the gradual birth and growth of several new patterns, forest asceticism (I4), urban monasticism (I5), and scholastic philosophy (I6). These developments formed the context for the initial growth of Buddhism (I5a, I6a1) but are themselves part of a wider social context that was briefly sketched in the chapter and could be described in terms of numerous additional cultural patterns, which are here omitted for simplicity.

Part of the point of this formulation is to emphasize that the development of Buddhism needs to be understood, in India as in Tibet, not through a simple genealogy of isolated cultural patterns (Therāvāda leads to Mahāyāna, which leads to Vajrayāna, etc.), but as part of a complex overall picture. A series of new phenomena (cultural patterns) crystallize, as it were, out of a supersaturated solution. We need to understand the nature of the liquid as well as that of the seed (e.g., a particular historical figure) around which the crystallization takes place.

While I speak here for simplicity of 'cultural patterns,' the concept intended is similar to that of the 'modal state' in my book *Mind, Body and Culture*. These are, in other words, patternings of the bodymind totality, operating at both social and individual levels, and transformed and transforming through the onward life of society. Thus, the urban monastic pattern (I5) corresponds to a complex assemblage of behaviors, modes of thinking, and modes of feeling of monastics, their patrons, neighbors, and of the whole society of which they are part.

This pattern gradually becomes established (crystallizes) in the practices of a particular population, as one of a number of such assemblages that in varying proportions make up the changing behavioral, emotional, and intellectual vocabulary of that population over time. Readers who wish to pick up on the theoretical argument hinted at here and in the subsequent chapter summaries are referred to *Mind, Body and Culture* (Samuel 1990).

21

India: Mahāyāna Schools

The period from the first century B.C. to the fourth century A.D., that of the origin and growth of the Mahāyāna schools, was a time of general prosperity in north Indian society. There was a gradual development of long-distance trade both throughout India itself and beyond to Southeast Asia, China, and the West, along with the emergence of a prosperous mercantile class. The growth of Mahāyāna Buddhism (I7, see Table 3) and of the related philosophical schools (I6a2,3, see Table 3) was only part of the general growth of a sophisticated, literate Indian culture. Few of the various rulers of India during this period seem to have been personally committed to the Buddhist teachings in the manner of the Emperor Aṣoka, but many of them supported the Buddhist community along with the other religious communities in their territories. This was a period of peaceful coexistence between the Buddhists and the various Hindu and other religious and philosophical tendencies of the time.

The openness and tolerance of Indian society during this time is also shown by the relatively high status of women. India was doubtless

TABLE 2.
Cultural Patterns in Chapter 21

Mature Indian States, Third Century B.C. to Fourth Century A.D.

I1 'Tribal' shamanic practitioners
I2 Vedic Brahman priests
I3 Folk shamanic practitioners
I4 Wandering ascetics
I5 Urban monastics; Buddhist and Jain
  I5a Buddhist monastic
I6 Philosophy
  I6a Buddhist
    I6a1 Abhidharma
    I6a2 Madhyamaka
    I6a3 Yogācāra, Tathāgatagarbha
I7 Mahāyāna religious traditions
    I7a Devotional tendencies
    I7b Ritual and magical tendencies
    I7c Yogic tendencie
I8 Bhakti (Hindu devotional) movement

a patriarchal and male-dominated society, but the near-total exclusion of women from public life was a later development. While the Brahmanical law codes originated at this time, their effective use as a support for a rigid, hierarchical society lay some centuries ahead. The caste system at this period was also more fluid and open than it was later to become.

The large centralized states and the extensive mercantile communities of this period provided an ideal environment for the growth of philosophy and for the development of complex systems of rational thought. It is in this context that the Mahāyāna philosophical schools (I6a2,3) arose, in particular the first of them, the Madhyamaka school originated by Nāgārjuna. The Mahāyāna ('great vehicle,' by distinction to the 'lesser vehicle,' Hinayāna, of the early schools), however, was by no means either purely rational or exclusively concerned with philosophy. It is best to distinguish between Mahāyāna as a religious form (I7) and the philosophical schools developed by Mahāyāna Buddhist scholars (I6), while bearing in mind that philosophy for Mahāyāna Buddhists was always intended as an aid to the Buddhist path rather than as an end in itself.[1]

Our main evidence for Mahāyāna religious practice is a series of texts that began to appear in around the first century B.C., along with the commentarial literature that grew up around them. The texts themselves are referred to as Sūtras, and like the original Sūtras they claim to represent the teachings of the historical Buddha Śākyamuni. The Mahāyāna Sūtras are often much longer than the early Sūtras had been, and they include extensive passages of philosophical material, which were to provide the basis for the various Mahāyāna philosophical schools.

The Mahāyāna Sūtras also included passages that provided the foundation for a theistic and devotional interpretation of Buddhism, centered around the cult of deified Buddhas and Bodhisattvas (I7a). Here they paralleled a similar devotional *(bhakti)* movement within Hindu thought (I8), focused on the deities Śiva and Viṣṇu and especially on Kṛṣṇa and Rāma, earthly avatars of Viṣṇu (I7b; Zaehner 1977; Zvelebil 1977).

DEVOTIONAL RELIGION AND THE CENTRALIZED STATE (17A)

In these developments, we can see a parallel to the general political and social transformations of the period, which had their inevitable concomitants in terms of the general patterns of consciousness of the population. The emergence of these devotional cults centered on single supreme deities is another aspect of the breakdown of the old shamanic order, and is closely related to the development of centralized states with supreme rulers. Here, a process whose initial stages we saw in the time of the historical Buddha reached completion.

The growth of devotional forms within Buddhism and Hinduism indicates how far the old shamanic world-view had been left behind. In a world where the order of things is laid down by a supreme deity in heaven and an absolute ruler on earth, the only cultural pattern to be encouraged is that of willing obedience to His (very rarely Her) will. Ethics and rationality derive from this essentially hierarchical pattern. The shaman's ability to play with and manipulate the possibilities of relationships is no longer welcome.

It cannot be denied that monotheism has its temptations. It is not simply the weight of established political power that has made it so widespread and attractive a solution to the dilemmas of humanity. Do as we say, the monotheistic religions suggest, and everything will be all right. In a world that no longer afforded the security of the established patterns of shamanic religion, nor the freedom of the shamanic approach to construct one's individual solution on the basis of those patterns, submission to the new supreme deities offered an answer. It was no longer necessary to comprehend the new and changing world, only to obey God's Commandments and Caesar's in their respective spheres.

At the same time, monotheism retained the possibility of a more radical and 'shamanic' interpretation, in which any individual could become identified with the supreme deity. This identification provided a symbolic equivalent to the shaman's entry into the realm of spiritual agencies. In India, such tendencies seem, for the most part, to have been tolerated, provided that they did not constitute any political threat. Elsewhere, as the history of Christian and Islamic mysticism records, they were often brutally suppressed.

The moral order of these new centralized states, with their monotheistic cults, reflected the move away from the situation-bound morality of the older shamanic order. The growth of trade and of a uniform currency went along with the growth of a sense of rational self-interest as the appropriate attitude in all spheres of life. This at any rate is what we find in much of the literature of the period, especially the various texts on *kāma* and *artha*, where it is taken for granted that interpersonal relationships are to be manipulated and exploited for individual ends (Archer 1966).

It is difficult to judge how successful the Buddhist devotional cults were on their Indian homeland in comparison with the Hindu *bhakti* movement, although all the literary activity and the surviving statues and inscriptions must witness a movement of considerable scale. In China and the Far East, where Buddhism was rapidly spreading by this period, the Mahāyāna Sūtras were to provide the foundation for lay Buddhism until modern times. The so-called Pure Land school of Buddhism, centered around the worship of the Buddha Amitābha with the aim of attaining rebirth in his western paradise or 'pure land,' Sukhāvatī, was the most significant of these developments. These texts were also to come to Tibet, where devotion to certain

Buddhas and bodhisattvas, such as Avalokiteśvara, Tārā, and Mañjuśrī, was to become an important part of lay and monastic religion. They did not, however, form the basis of a separate devotional school of Buddhism within Tibetan societies in the way that they did in the Far East.

UPĀYA AND PRAJÑĀ: DUALITY AND SYNTHESIS

The new Sūtras also introduced a whole range of 'magical' ritual practices in which ritual formulae *(dhāraṇī, mantra)* were used for protective and other purposes (I7b). Here they were taking much further practices of which the roots can already be found in the early Sūtras, in the magical and protective use of the Buddha's words. Another major component of the new Sūtras is a whole range of new and complex meditational techniques that prefigure the later development of the Buddhist Tantras (I7c).

Some of the shorter Mahāyāna Sūtras concentrate on one or another of these elements, but in the longer works all of these different kinds of material can frequently be found. In fact, it is not as easy to distinguish between them as might at first sight appear. The language of the Sūtras, and the practices and teachings within them, can often be interpreted at more than one level, so that figures like Avalokiteśvara or Amitābha, rather than 'deities' external to the individual, may also be states to be developed within the individual. This enabled the theistic and devotional language of the Sūtras to maintain the possibility of a 'deeper' interpretation more compatible with the central goal of Buddhism.

The quality of *upāyakauśalya,* of skillful means, by which the historical Buddha was able to suit his teaching to any given audience, and if necessary speak so as to be understood differently by his various hearers in accordance with their needs has already been referred to. The Mahāyāna Sūtras took the idea of means *(upāya)* much further, making it into a central aspect of Buddhism. The early Sūtras were now explained as manifestations of *upāya,* so accounting for differences between the teachings within them and those of the new Sūtras. These early texts were of 'indirect meaning' *(neyārtha);* they did not represent the ultimate insight of the Buddha, because it was inappropriate for him to have taught that ultimate meaning to his disciples at that time.

The Mahāyāna Sūtras themselves might be of 'direct' *(nītārtha)* or 'indirect' meaning (see Murti 1970:53, 254–255). The concept of *upāya* opened up the possibility of a series of interpretations of any text, from the superficial to the progressively more subtle. The philosophical passages of these texts often imply positions of considerable sophistication and complexity. One can see the beginnings of a situation like that in Chinese Buddhism in modern times, where the Pure Land teachings are thought of as suitable for the average lay person, while the more advanced meditational and philosophical teachings are reserved for a monastic elite (Blofeld 1972).

Thus the Mahāyāna argument was that the old teachings had been appropriate for their period, but that it was now time for new and more subtle ideas and methods to be introduced. Certainly the Mahāyāna Sūtras were a response to a new situation. Indian society had changed very considerably in the five centuries or so after the Buddha's death. If it is correct to identify those changes as implying a much greater dominance of rational, dichotomizing thought and the collapse of the old shamanic moral order in the direction of a manipulative, commercially oriented morality built around a stronger sense of self, then the Mahāyāna prescription was an understandable one. It had two major components: the idea of the bodhisattva and the concept of *śūnyatā* or 'voidness.' We have already seen something of the later importance of these concepts for the Tibetans in Chapters 11 and 12.

In the Mahāyāna, bodhisattvas are heroic beings who work over countless successive lives to attain the Buddhist Enlightenment, not for their own personal benefit but to rescue other living beings from their sufferings in the everyday world of *saṃsāra*. The Buddha Śākyamuni had been such a bodhisattva before his attainment of Enlightenment, and the well-known Jātaka stories, common to all Buddhist schools, recount the stories of some of his lives as a bodhisattva (Cowell 1952). Avalokiteśvara, Mañjuśrī, and various other bodhisattva figure in the Mahāyāna Sūtras as celestial beings who can be appealed to or invoked in misfortune or danger.

The concept of bodhisattva has another side, too. What defines a bodhisattva is the possession of a specific motivational state, technically called *bodhicitta*, 'enlightenment mind.' This state is defined in terms of the desire to attain Enlightenment in order to relieve the sufferings of all living beings. In the Mahāyāna teachings, the creation of this state within oneself is a necessary stage on the path to Enlightenment. The old *arhat* ideal, or to use the more common Mahāyāna expression, the 'vehicle' of the *śrāvaka* and *pratyekabuddha,* now dropped out. Since the teachings leading to the status of *arhat* did not emphasize the altruistic motivation of the bodhisattva, they could only be indirect and incomplete teachings. The development of *bodhicitta* within oneself became a central practice for Indian Mahāyāna Buddhists and subsequently for Tibetans also. As we saw in Chapters 12 to 14, it remains a basic element of almost all Tibetan Buddhist ritual sequences.[2]

The teachings on the bodhisattva's path or career were a central part of the Mahāyāna, and complemented the more philosophical aspects to which we will shortly turn. In fact, they included them, since the bodhisattva's career is traditionally described in terms of the developing to transcendence of the six *pāramitā* or 'perfections,' of which the sixth is *prajñāpāramitā,* the 'Perfection of Prajñā.' *Prajñā* is sometimes translated as 'wisdom,' but something like 'critical insight into reality' might be closer. The term refers to a dynamic process rather than to its result.

The other five *pāramitā* are giving, moral discipline, patience, energy, and *samādhi.* The classic presentation of the six *pāramitā* scheme for the Tibetans is a famous treatise by the early eighth-century Indian scholar Śāntideva, the *Bodhicaryāvatāra* (Matics 1970: Kelsang Gyatso 1980), but the scheme was widely used by both Indians and Tibetans (Gampopa's *Dagpo T'argyen* = Guenther 1970).

With the growth of the bodhisattva ideal, the magical and shamanistic powers of the Buddha began to return to the center of attention. They are part of the Buddha's *upāya,* his skill in means, and they are the necessary complement to his *prajñā,* his insight into the true nature of reality.

This complementarity of *upāya* and *prajñā,* later to occupy a central role in the Tantras, is a continuation and extension of the complementarity of *śamatha* and *vipaśyanā* practices (see Chapter 20). Just as *śamatha* practice with its cultivation of the *samādhi* states was closely associated with the acquisition of shamanic powers, the bodhisattva was now expected to gain a variety of such magical powers as part of his acquisition of *upāya.* In the Mahāyāna Sūtras hundreds of new *samādhi* states were introduced, and their cultivation evidently became an important part of Buddhist practice (Beyer 1974:116–124).

Upāya and *bodhicitta,* skillful means and the altruistic impulse, are closely related concepts in the Mahāyāna. They are complementary to *prajñā*, 'wisdom' or 'insight' into the true nature of reality. The dialectical relationship between *upāya* and *prajñā* was to be a central theme in later developments, particularly in the Tantras and in Tibet. We can see here a new synthesis emerging between the shamanic and rationalizing tendencies in Buddhism. *Upāya* stands for the shaman's powers to manipulate the various aspects of the cultural pattern, now supported and driven by the universal love of the bodhisattva. *Prajñā* is the rationalizing insight into the constructed nature of all cultural patterns that was to balance those powers by training the bodhisattva out of the illusion of self and hence out of all egotistic motivation. Here we can see the common structure of ideas that underlay the developing roles of Buddhist ritual practitioner and lay patron in the Mahāyāna.

As I have argued elsewhere, a characteristic feature of shamanic procedures is the ability to enter a visionary state that transcends and encompasses some or all of the 'ordinary' modal states corresponding to the cultural pattern of everyday life (Chapter 19; Samuel 1990: 107–109). The shaman cannot have too personal an interest in the cultural pattern. He or she has to be able to see it from the 'outside,' and this involves going beyond any personal sense of self. Whether a particular shaman is able to achieve such a state or not is actually not so much the point at issue. What is important is that people see the shaman as representing a kind of nonpartisan compassion.

The duality of *upāya* and *prajñā* is one of the key Buddhist expressions of this central issue. The insight into selflessness provided by *prajñā* is the foundation of the Buddhist version of the shamanic vision. At the same time, the bodhisattva's motivation to serve and rescue all beings is the emotional drive behind the intellectual vision of *prajñā*. Ultimately, the two are held to achieve synthesis in a single state, Enlightenment. The specific techniques by which this might be achieved, and the development of some kind of systematic scheme of training for, in effect, Buddhist shamans, were to become a key issue in Tibet.

The Mahāyāna Sūtras, as mentioned, claim to be the Buddha's own word. They were held to have been entrusted to *nāga* (serpent-spirits of the waters) and to other deities during the lifetime of Śākyamuni to await the appropriate time for their revelation to human beings. We can assume that these and similar statements were in a sense shorthand for the 'shamanic' processes by which these texts were in fact generated. The Mahāyāna Sūtras contain many descriptions of visionary techniques and states *(samādhi),* and their originators undoubtedly practiced such visionary procedures. The core of many of the texts was surely revealed through such techniques, and we have no reason to assume that those who wrote them down did not believe that they were transcribing the genuine words of the Buddha. The repetitive and unsystematic nature of some of the Sūtras certainly supports an origin in shamanic visionary processes, although the texts were undoubtedly subjected to later 'literary' reworking, often existing in several different versions.

THE PHILOSOPHY OF THE MAHĀYĀNA: MADHYAMAKA (16A2)

It was on the basis of a group of the Mahāyāna Sūtras, the Prajñāpāramitā Sūtras, that the great Buddhist philosopher Nāgārjuna created the Madhyamaka philosophy (I6a2) at some time between the later part of the first century and the third century A.D.[3] Prajñāpāramitā is often translated 'Perfection of Wisdom.' More precisely it means the 'going beyond,' the 'transcending' of *prajñā. Prajñā,* conventionally translated 'wisdom,' might, as I stated above, be rendered as something like 'critical insight into reality.' It corresponds to the use of the cognitive or rational faculty as an instrument to Enlightenment. The sword of *prajñā* held by the celestial bodhisattva Mañjuśrī, patron of scholarship and intellectual activity, cuts through the illusion of dualistic, conceptual thinking.

The Madhyamaka philosophy of Nāgārjuna and his followers is indeed an attempt to express the central insight of the Buddhist Enlightenment through a universalizing application of reason. It is also a culmination of the extensive philosophical developments both within and outside Buddhism over the previous centuries, and it bespeaks the dominance of literate, rationalized thinking in India at that time. It is a sustained attempt to use that mode of thinking against itself.

At the same time, the origins of the Madhyamaka in the visionary and shamanic context of the Mahāyāna Sūtras is worth remembering, and Nāgārjuna himself, according to the traditional accounts, was strongly associated with this side of the Buddhist tradition (Dutt 1962:278–280). It was believed that the Prajñāpāramitā Sūtras had been revealed to him personally by the *nāga* spirits, and his name alludes to his relationship with these spirits. He is still known in modern Indian folk literature as the author of alchemical and erotic *(kāmaśāstra)* treatises, and the Tibetan sources also describe him as an alchemist and magician. Much of the Nāgārjuna legend is doubtless apocryphal, and some of it may reflect the use of his name by later Tantric teachers. The basic story, however, was already recorded by Xuanzang who visited India in the early seventh century.

For all of the magical and shamanic ambience surrounding Nāgārjuna, his philosophical writings, like those of his followers, are entirely logical and rational in their mode of discourse. Nāgārjuna's most important text, the *Mūlamādhyamakakārikā* or 'Root Verses of the Madhyamaka,' takes the fundamental terms of Indian philosophy and the Abhidharma in 27 short verse chapters. In a highly aphoristic style, Nāgārjuna examines each term in turn, demonstrating that it is incapable of yielding a consistent meaning. Once rational thought has been demonstrated to lead to a series of dead ends, the way is open for the attainment of direct insight into the nature of reality.

Here are the first seven verses of the first chapter, in which Nāgārjuna argues against the concept of causality. The whole chapter, which is preceded by two introductory verses of homage to the Buddha as the teacher of dependent origination *(pratītyasamutpāda)*, is only fourteen verses long:

1. Never are any existing things found to originate
   From themselves, from something else, from both, or from no cause.

2. There are four conditioning causes:
   A cause *(hetu)*, objects of sensations, 'immediately preceding condition,' and of course the predominant influence—there is no fifth.

3. Certainly there is no self-existence *(svabhāva)* of existing things in conditioning causes, etc.;
   And if no self-existence exists, neither does 'other-existence' *(parabhāva)*.

4. The efficient cause *(kriyā)* does not exist possessing a conditioning cause,
   Nor does the efficient cause exist without possessing a conditioning cause.

Conditioning causes are not without efficient causes,
Nor are there [conditioning causes] which possess efficient causes.

5. Certainly those things are called 'conditioning causes' whereby something originates after having come upon them;
As long as something has not originated, why are they not so long '*non*-conditioning causes'?

6. There can be a conditioning cause neither of a non-real thing nor of a real thing.
Of what non-real thing is there a conditioning cause? And if it is [already] real, what use is a cause?

7. If an element *(dharma)* occurs which is neither real nor non-real nor both real-and-non-real,
How can there be a cause which is effective in this situation?
(*Mūlamādhyamakakārikā*, chapter 1, vv. 1–7; Streng 1967:183)[4]

Nāgārjuna's position can be summed up as follows. Any assertions we choose to make about the true nature of reality can be shown through strict logical argument to be inconsistent. This is the famous doctrine of *śūnyatā*, 'emptiness.' Reality is *śūnya*, 'void' or 'empty,' in that no assertions can validly be made about it. It is not made of eternally existing substances of any kind. Equally, however, it is inconsistent to say that nothing truly exists. Thus 'emptiness' does not imply non-existence, only the impossibility of consistent rational knowledge, since such knowledge is based upon a dichotomizing process which cannot ultimately be justified.

Madhyamaka, literally 'the middle way,' claims to avoid both extremes, of eternalism and nihilism, and to make no assertions about what really is, although as is clear from the above excerpt Nāgārjuna does assume the validity of logic. *Nirvāṇa* for the Madhyamaka Buddhist is not a definite 'thing' to be attained, but an alternative way of seeing and experiencing the world and so of acting within it. Once the deceptive nature of conceptual thinking is fully realized, the cessation of conceptualization will of itself transform *saṃsāra* into *nirvāṇa* and bring about the attainment of Enlightenment.

Madhyamaka, despite its rationalist orientation, always retained a close connection to the central motivation of Buddhism. In Robert Thurman's words:

> It is all too often forgotten by students of the central way [Madhyamaka], with their rigorous philosophical attention to metaphysical and epistemological questions, that, as Nāgārjuna says, 'emptiness is essentially compassion' *(śūnyatākaruṇāgarbhaṃ)*. . . Nāgārjuna's fundamental central way work is called *Wisdom* [i.e. *Prajñā-nāma-mūlamadhyamakakārikā*], and so he confines himself therein to the pathways of critical reason. At no moment, however, is he, or should the student be, unaware that wisdom is but the doorway for the energy of compassion. The razor-sharp sword of critical wisdom cuts through the fetters of conceptual excuses that obstruct the open dynamic flow of compassion, full sensitivity to the sufferings of other beings who are the fabric of relativity [*pratītyasamutpāda*], and overflowing love that radiates happiness to them, once all self-concern has melted in the bliss of self-fulfillment in the great emptiness of selflessness. Wisdom smashes the hard atoms of intrinsic identities; compassion is the all-powerful energy released to reshape relativity into the gentle jewelline forms of pure lands of bliss. (Thurman 1984:171)

Nāgārjuna's 'root verses' were the subject of extensive commentaries, of which the best known are those of Buddhapālita (late fifth? to early sixth century) and Candrakīrti (early seventh century) (Ruegg 1981). This combination of a short verse 'root text,' suitable for memorizing, and a detailed prose commentary was incidentally to become a standard literary form in later Indian Buddhist writing and then in Tibet, with the same author often writing both the verse text and the extended commentary. The basic framework of Madhyamaka remained central to all later Buddhist philosophy. Philosophical activity continued, however, right up to the final destruction of the Buddhist academic centers with the Muslim invasions of the late twelfth century (Warder 1970; Ruegg 1981). Transplanted into Tibet, it continued there until modern times.

THE YOGĀCĀRA PHILOSOPHERS AND THE TATHĀGATAGARBHA DOCTRINE (16A3)

The next major school of Buddhist philosophy, the Yogācāra school (I6a3), originated by Asaṅga and his followers from the late fourth century onwards (Conze 1962; Warder 1970; Willis 1979), contrasts in certain respects with the Madhyamaka. As the name Yogācāra suggests, this school, really a set of related approaches rather than a single, clearly defined position, was explicitly connected with the practice of yoga. Asaṅga himself, in Tibetan legend, meditated for twelve years on the future Buddha Maitreya before Maitreya appeared to him and revealed an important series of texts known as the 'Five Teachings of Maitreya.'

The Yogācāra also relied on further Mahāyāna Sūtras that had appeared at or since Nāgārjuna's time. These Sūtras are referred to by the Tibetans as the 'third turning of the wheel of the Dharma,' while the Prajñāpāramitā constituted the 'second turning' (Obermiller 1932–1933:, vol. 2, 73–100; Lessing and Wayman 1968:43ff).

This does not imply that the Yogācāra teachings were held to supersede the Madhyamaka. In fact, Tibetan scholars (though not necessarily Tibetan yogins) have generally taken the reverse position, and regarded the Yogācāra teachings as a step on the way to the 'higher' and more subtle Madhyamaka position. Thus the later academic tradition in Tibet studied a series of five basic philosophical positions, made up of two 'Hinayāna' positions, the Yogācāra (Cittamātra), and two Madhayamaka schools, as well as considering a number of subsidiary positions within the Yogācāra (see Guenther 1972; Sopa and Hopkins 1976).

The Madhyamaka philosophy offered the nearest approach that could be managed in words to a view of reality as totally relational and interdependent. It is by no means easy, however, to understand the relationship between our ordinary view of the world and the reality which the Madhyamaka describes, or the process by which one could be transformed into the other, so replicating Nāgārjuna's insight. The Madhyamaka was also open to the risk of nihilistic interpretations in which *śūnyatā* was taken to imply nonexistence. Hindu philosophers regularly attacked Nāgārjuna's teachings on these grounds, and there is no doubt that the Madhyamaka is not an easy or straightforward doctrine to understand, for all of its rigorous clarity.

Yogācāra philosophy provided an account of the relationship between ordinary or conventional reality and the relational level at which Nāgārjuna's account was pitched. It also developed a technical vocabulary that was of help in comprehending the experiences of yogic practice in pursuit of that insight. If the Madhyamaka is a statement of the ultimate goal, insofar as it can be described in words, the Yogācāra philosophy is more concerned with making the path to that goal intelligible. In this way there is a certain natural complementarity between the two.[5] Subsequent philosophical developments in India generally took the form of elaborations or syntheses of these two schools.

It would be inappropriate to trace these subsequent developments in detail, although they were of considerable significance for the Tibetans. Some basic themes of the Yogācāra however will be discussed briefly.

The two most important components of the Yogācāra philosophy for the later tradition were probably the 'three natures' theory of reality and the famous concept of the 'store-consciousness' or *ālayavijñāna*. The 'three natures' theory is a kind of expansion of the 'two truths' theory, which is associated with the Mahāyāna in general and the Madhyamaka in particular. The 'two truths' theory contrasts the illusory nature of our ordinary perception of reality (*saṃvṛtisatya*, conventional or deceptive truth) with the ultimate or absolute truth of reality as perceived by the Enlightened Buddha *(paramārthasatya)*. According to the new Yogācāra scheme, all phenomena have three 'natures' or characteristics *(svabhāva, lakṣaṇa)*. The *parikalpita*, or mentally constructed nature, corresponds to the names and labels that are applied to the phenomenon. The *paratantra*, or dependent nature, corresponds to the phenomenon seen as defined in a structure of dependence on other phenomena, while the *parinispanna*, or perfected nature, corresponds to the absolute truth of the Buddha's perception.

The scheme allows for an analysis of the creation of ordinary understandings of the world as a relationship between the names and designations of *parikalpita* and the provisional entities, existing in a network of mutual dependence, of *paratantra*. At the same time it avoids specifying 'absolute truth' in terms of this relationship. The *parinispanna* is something else again, not to be limited by the terms of this analysis.

The *ālayavijñāna* or 'store-consciousness' is again part of an analysis of ordinary consciousness. Here there are eight components, the five sense-perceptions, mental perception, the 'defiled mind,' and an underlying awareness, the *ālayavijñāna* or store-consciousness, which supplies the images and concepts through which the other seven forms of consciousness operate.[6] As with all Buddhist philosophical schemes, the eight forms of consciousness are significant primarily as an aid to practice. Thus the practitioner learns to withdraw the awareness from the five sense-perceptions and the mind-perception to the defiled mind that underlies them, and beyond to the store-consciousness that underlies the defiled mind. Then, to quote the late German lama Anagarika Govinda, "the waves on the surface of this ocean-like universal consciousness, which contains the treasures of all that has been and can be experienced, will be smoothed and converted into a shining mirror, 'in which the images of all forms *(rūpa)*' are reflected undistorted, in pristine purity" (Govinda 1969:83).

We can easily recognize here another description of the shamanic vision. This particular kind of language, along with the Yogācāra emphasis on consciousness or 'mind' *(citta,* Tibetan *sem)* was to be taken up particularly by those Tibetan traditions, such as the Nyingmapa, who were closest to the 'shamanic' aspects of the Tibetan tradition.

We will examine briefly one further philosophical development that is associated in a general sense with the Yogācāras. This is the concept of the *tathāgatagarbha,* often translated as the 'Buddha-nature,' more precisely the 'seed' or 'essence' *(garbha)* of the Buddhas (*tathāgata* is a synonym for Buddha). It was held to be present within all living beings and all phenomena. This doctrine emerged in some of the Mahāyāna Sūtras, and was developed in what was perhaps the most important of the 'Five Teachings of Maitreya,' the *Uttaratantra,* also known as the *Ratnagotravibhāga* (Takasaki 1966). The *tathāgatagarbha* doctrine is significant here as representing a contrasting pole in the literary presentation of Buddhism to the Madhyamaka philosophy of Nāgārjuna.

The idea of *tathāgatagarbha* doctrine provided the basis for a different way of conceptualizing the process of Enlightenment, and one which was to be highly influential, especially within the Tantric schools. Rather than a progress along a path or way in which the yogin attained the requisite qualities through gradual purification, the *tathāgatagarbha* perspective saw the attainment of Buddhahood as the uncovering of a potential that was always there, of the revealing of the underlying structure of reality.

Like the Buddha in an ugly lotus flower,
Like honey surrounded by bees,
Like kernels of grains covered by the husk,
Like gold fallen into impurities,
Like a treasure under the ground,
Like a sprout grown from a small fruit,

Like an image of the Buddha wrapped in a tattered garment,
Like the kinghood in the womb of a poor woman,
And like a precious statue in the earthen mould;
In such a way, there abides this Essence
In the living beings obscured by occasional stains of defilements.

These famous nine images of the *Tathāgatagarbha Sūtra*, quoted and commented on at length in the *Uttaratantra*, represent an opposite approach to the attempt to define Buddhahood in rational terms. Each image points to an aspect of the concealing of the Buddha-nature by the various 'defilements' (Takasaki 1966:268–293).

Tathāgatagarbha theory contrasts strongly with Madhyamaka philosophy, even though it can be taken as a way of expressing the same underlying vision. The Madhyamaka description is entirely in negative terms. Only by destroying all of our mistaken beliefs concerning the universe and ourselves through rigorous logical argument is it possible to arrive at a more authentic vision. Understandably, the growth of Madhyamaka philosophy was to be associated with an efflorescence of the study of logic. A series of Buddhist philosophers, of whom the most famous are Diṅnāga and Dharmakīrti, developed logic, the analysis of perception, and the techniques of logical disputation to great heights of sophistication and complexity, and these subjects came to be seen as essential aspects of what was an increasingly academic and rational form of Buddhism.

Tathāgatagarbha theory is quite opposite in its approach. Rather than a rational description of the illusions of *saṃsāra*, we are offered a series of analogies, intended to help us to grasp the relationship between the view from the Enlightened state and the ordinary view of the world. This is a mode of approach much closer to the 'shamanic' end of the spectrum than is Madhyamaka philosophy, since for the practicing yogin what is significant is the state to be attained, and the detailed study of the process of ordinary reality is a distraction rather than an aid.

In Tibet, *tathāgatagarbha* theory was associated with the yogins and meditators, and regarded with suspicion by the later 'academic' tradition. Its leading proponents, the Jonangpa school, were proscribed and their *gompa* in central Tibet closed down in the seventeenth century, although the works of their greatest scholar, Tāranātha, were revived in the nineteenth century and are still studied. The positive assertion of Buddha-nature as a kind of 'substance' inherent in all reality was held to bring the Jonangpas dangerously close to the positions of the Hindu schools on the reality of the self *(ātman)*. This accusation was also leveled against the philosophical viewpoint of the Nyingmapa tradition for similar reasons.[7]

It is important to realize that what is at issue in these disputes is not merely a series of irrelevant doctrinal details. Doubtless at times these doctrinal points were excuses for or rationalizations of personal interest or political expediency, but for the most part, in Tibet at any rate, all parties took the language of the debates seriously, because they referred to real experiences that had real political and social implications in their own right.

In fact, the more sensitive and less polemical of the scholars of the later academic tradition, such as the great Tsongk'apa, or the famous eighteenth-century scholar T'ukwan Ch'ökyi Nyima, were willing to admit to the deep yogic realization of the Jonangpa scholars (Thurman 1984:60–61; Ruegg 1963:78). What they could not admit was that their description of the nature of Enlightenment was valid, because that attacked the very foundations of the compromise between academic and shamanic aspects of Buddhism on which the later academic (and particularly Gelugpa) tradition was to take its stand.

In these various conflicts, the body of philosophical thought that the Tibetans had taken over from India provided a vocabulary and a structure of argument, as well as certain basic presuppositions. The Tibetans, however, were not simply reworking Indian doctrinal disputes for their own sake. They were using what they had learned from Indian Buddhism to understand their own experiences and the practical implications of those experiences.

To return to India, *tathāgatagarbha* theory is a reminder that the rational and literate world of Madhyamaka philosophy was not the only side of Indian Buddhism. The rationality of the Madhyamaka was a reflection of the ordered and relatively peaceful society in which it arose. With the decline of that society, in later centuries, other forms of Buddhism came to the fore of which the *tathagatagarbha* theory gives a partial foretaste. The most significant of these developments, at least for the Tibetans, was the rise of Tantric Buddhism, the main subject of Chapter 22. The period of the rise of Tantric Buddhism was also, however, that of the growth of the great north Indian Buddhist universities, in which the rational and academic tradition of the Madhyamaka would reach its apogee, and from where it, too, would be transmitted to Tibet.

CULTURAL PATTERNS

Buddhist monasticism (I5a) became firmly established in the period of this chapter, with extensive state patronage. At the same time, the complexity of religious behavior within these communities and the lay Buddhist population is more evident (I7a,b,c) and is reflected in new philosophical developments (I6a2,3). The precise lineages are difficult to trace, but the variety of patterns is important, since it contributes to the complexity of the Buddhism that was eventually to be transferred to Tibet.

22

India: Tantra and the Buddhist Siddhas

The period covered by this chapter (A.D. 400–1200) includes the growth of the great monastic universities of north India (I5b), and the development of Tantric Buddhism (I4a1,2; I7d). Both were to have important consequences for the Tibetans. The first few centuries of this period were still a time of general prosperity, but the deterioration of long-distance trade, especially along the western routes, seems to have led to a progressive economic decline and to have accelerated the collapse of the larger subcontinental and regional powers. Afghanistan, the trading states along the Silk Route, and northeast India gradually came under the control of Islamic dynasties. At the end of this period, the Islamic armies overran first north India and then the Buddhist heartlands of present-day Bihar and Bengal. The coming of Islam destroyed the social matrix that had supported the efflorescence of Buddhist culture in north India. Even where non-Islamic states survived, Buddhist monasticism and its lay following dwindled and disappeared. Before Buddhism finally disappeared from India, however, it had taken root firmly within Tibet.

The Buddhism that became established in Tibet included ele-

TABLE 3.
Cultural Patterns in Chapter 22

Later Indian States, Fifth to Twelfth Centuries A.D.

- I1 'Tribal' shamanic practitioners
- I2 Vedic Brahman priests
  - I2a Tantric Brahman priests
- I3 Folk shamanic practitioners
- I4 Wandering ascetics
  - I4a Kāpālika yogins <I4, I1
    - I4a1 Early Buddhist siddhas (?Padmasambhava) <I4a
    - I4a2 Monastic-Siddha syntheses (Nāropa, Virūpa, Atiśa) <I4a1, I15b
- I5 Urban monastics; Buddhist and Jain
  - I5a Buddhist monastic
  - I5b Buddhist universities <I5a, I6a
  - I5c Hindu monasticism
- I6 Philosophy
  - I6a Buddhist
    - I6a1 Abhidharma
    - I6a2 Madhyamaka
    - I6a3 Yogācāra, Tathāgatagarbha
  - I6b Hindu
    - 16b1 Śaṅkara
- I7 Mahāyāna religious traditions
  - I7a Devotional tendencies
  - I7b Ritual and magical tendencies
  - I7c Yogic tendencies
  - I7d 'Mantrayāna' (Kriyā, Caryā Tantra) <I7c, I1
- I8 Bhakti (Hindu devotional) movement

ments of the old 'Hinayāna' traditions (I5a), such as the monastic ordination lineages that had continued to provide the framework within which Mahāyāna Buddhist religious practice, yoga, and ritual (I7) had developed. It also incorporated the philosophical and academic tradition of the north Indian Buddhist universities (I5b, I6a), many of whose teachers traveled to Tibet during the flourishing of those institutions or immediately after their destruction. Most importantly, perhaps, for the later development of Tibetan Buddhism, it included the lineages of Tantric practice (I4a1,2).

This chapter describes the growth of Tantra and of the monastic universities, and then looks in some detail at the siddhas, the Indian teachers from whom the Tibetans acquired their major Tantric lineages. The academic and siddha strains were in many ways opposed, but they were also intertwined, and by the eleventh and twelfth centuries these approaches were often combined in the same people. The two strains represent another version of the relationship between clerical and shamanic tendencies that we have already seen both in Tibet (Chapters 1, 2, 11–18) and in the earlier stages of Indian Buddhism (Chapters 20 and 21). We begin with a note on the growth of the monastic universities.

THE MONASTIC UNIVERSITIES OF NORTH INDIA (15B)

In the later Buddhist period, several large monastic 'universities' grew up in northeast India. Abhidharma, Madhyamaka, and Yogācāra philosophy, along with the study of logic and disputation *(pramāṇa)* and the monastic disciplinary code *(vinaya),* formed a major part of the academic curriculum in these institutions, which were staffed largely or entirely by ordained celibate monks. They can thus be seen as an outgrowth of the monastic communities (I5a), which had existed from the early days of Indian Buddhism.

Secular subjects, however, were also taught at these new institutions, and it appears that many of the students at these institutions were not themselves destined for monastic careers (see Dutt 1962:325–327). The Buddhist universities became, like the universities of medieval Europe, centers of learning attended by lay students as well as clerics. This, no doubt, contributed to their support by secular rulers, and by lay patrons in general.

The Tibetans refer to a standard classification of the curriculum at these institutions into five minor and five major subjects. The study of the five minor subjects (astrology, poetry, lexicon, metrics, drama) led to the status of minor *paṇḍita,* while the remaining five (medicine, fine arts, Sanskrit grammar, logic, and Buddhist philosophy) led to recognition as a major *paṇḍita.*

The first and most famous of these institutions was Nālandā, founded originally by one of the Gupta rulers, probably in the fifth century (Dutt 1962:329–331). Nālandā was in northeast India, in the old heartland of Buddhism, although the Guptas were, in fact, nominally Hindus, not Buddhists. From the late eighth century onwards, this region formed part of the Pāla state, and the Pāla kings, who were Buddhists, continued to patronize Nālandā. They also founded and supported a series of further monastic universities at Odantapuri, Vikramaśīla, Somapura, and Jagaddala. These institutions continued to function right up to the Muslim conquest, and some of their teachers found refuge in Tibet at that time.

Teaching, at any rate of the more specifically Buddhist subjects, was also a regular part of the activities of other Buddhist monasteries. The Tibetans of the eleventh and twelfth centuries regularly studied in Nepal, Kashmir, and Bodhgayā, although there do not seem to have been institutions in these places of the scale or academic nature of Nālandā and the four later Pāla foundations. The most significant Indian academic figures for the Tibetans were men associated with Nālandā and Vikramaśīla.

All this represented the literate, rational, thoroughly 'clerical' side of Buddhism in north India. Nālandā and its successors would not have seemed remote to a student from the Islamic universities of around the same time, or those founded a little later in medieval Europe. The Buddhist universities shared both the celibate and ecclesiastical atmosphere of these institutions, their importance as centers of learning to which students came from distances of hundreds or thousands of miles to study, and the significance of secular subjects on the curriculum.

The universities were also, however, to become centers of Tantric practice, a development to which we will return towards the end of the chapter, after looking at Indian Buddhist Tantra in some detail.

THE GROWTH OF TANTRA (I7d)

The development of Tantra in India is complex and far from fully understood. It took place not only among Buddhists, but also among Hindu and Jain practitioners. Indeed, much of the ritual performed by modern Hindus, including practices of both Brahman and folk-religion priests, can be described as Tantric.[1] I have indicated some of the strands involved in the table of cultural patterns (Table 3), where Tantra appears in orthodox (I2a) and unorthodox (I4a) Hindu forms and in various Buddhist forms (I7d, I4a1, I4a2). The historical relationship of these components is uncertain, as is their connection with 'tribal' and folk shamanic practitioners (I1, I3).[2] Much of both Tantric vocabulary and Tantric techniques nevertheless seems to have derived from 'tribal' or folk shamans (see Chapter 12 and below).

The Tantras are, as previously discussed (Chapters 1 and 12) primarily traditions of practice. Most of them have 'root texts,' however, which are written in *sūtra* form. Like the Sūtras, these texts were held to represent the teaching of the Buddha, although they were taught not by his historical form of Śākyamuni but through his Tantric aspect, called Vajradhara. These root texts, and presumably therefore the associated traditions of practice, go back in some cases well before the period of the siddhas, which dates from roughly A.D. 700 onwards. Thus the Guhyasamāja Tantra, one of the major Anuttarayoga Tantra cycles, may date from as early as the fourth century (Wayman 1973: 13–19).

The prevalence of visionary, yogic, and analogical procedures within the later Mahāyāna Sūtra tradition has already been noted, and there was probably no sharp break between the later Mahāyāna Sūtras and the early Tantras (for example, Martin 1987:191–192). There was, however, a real if gradual change. The archaeological evidence shows what Nancy Hock has referred to as "an explosion of the pantheon—a proliferation of Buddhas, bodhisattvas and goddesses" (Hock 1987:33), indicating that new kinds of visionary techniques were now being employed in which these new deities took a central role.

New Tantras continued to appear until the last stages of Indian Buddhism. One of the most important of all Tantras for the Tibetans, the Kālacakra Tantra, appeared in India not long before the final destruction of the Buddhist monasteries by the Islamic armies. The Kālacakra came according to tradition from the hidden land of Shambhala. Its root text contains references to the Muslims and the troubled political situation (see Bernbaum 1980; Mullin 1982a:115–156; Hoffmann 1969; Sopa et al. 1985; Dhargyey 1985; Dalai Lama and Hopkins 1985).

A large commentarial literature on the Tantras also developed in India, much of it the activity of the more academic and literary siddhas. These texts take up more than half of the Tengyur, the Tibetan canonical collection of Indian commentarial literature.

The Tantras themselves, and the commentarial and other writings of the siddhas, have received considerable attention from Western scholars. Leaving aside Kazi Dawa Samdup's early translation of a text from the Cakrasaṃvara corpus (Kazi Dawa Samdup 1919), translations of the root Tantras themselves (generally with extensive reference to the Indian commentaries) include Snellgrove's version of the *Hevajra Tantra* (1959) and Tadeusz Skorupski's of the *Sarvadurgatipariśodhana Tantra* (1983) along with partial translations of the *Caṇḍamahāroṣaṇa Tantra* by Christopher George (1974), the *Mahākāla Tantra* by William Stablein (1976b), the *Abhidhanottara Tantra* by Martin Kalff (1979), and the *Tārā Tantra* by Martin Willson (1986).[3] Other important studies of Indian Tantric material include Giuseppe Tucci's *Theory and Practice of the Maṇḍala* (1969), Alex Wayman's work on the Guhyasamāja Tantra (1980b) and his other writings on Tantra (many of them collected in Wayman 1973), Snellgrove's introduction to the Tattvasaṃgraha (1981) and his *Indo-Tibetan Buddhism* (1987), and the writings of Herbert V. Guenther (for example, 1969, 1973), Per Kvaerne (1975) and Shin'ichi Tsuda (1978, 1982).

Much of this material refers to what the Tibetans were later to classify as Yoga and particularly Anuttarayoga Tantra, the types that involve the transformation of the practitioner into the form of a Tantric deity during the ritual and, in the case of Anuttarayoga Tantra, the internal yoga practices of the subtle body (the *tsalung* practices, see Chapter 12).[4] If Wayman's fourth-century dating for the Guhyasamāja (Wayman 1980c:360) is right, Anuttarayoga goes back to the earliest days of Indian Tantra. It seems, however, only gradually to have become part of the practice of Indian Buddhist communities in general, while the Tantras which the Tibetans later classified as Kriyā and Caryā were adopted much sooner. In these Tantras, the deity seems to have been originally visualized outside the practitioner, although in the later Tibetan tradition the generation of self as Tantric god was extended to many of these as well.

Thus Nancy Hock argues on the basis of archaeological finds from the Buddhist monastery at Ratnagiri in Orissa, and from other similar sites, that a clear distinction should be made between what she labels (after Winternitz) 'Mantrayāna,' based on the Kriyā and Caryā Tantras, and 'Vajrayāna,' corresponding to the Yoga and Anuttarayoga material (Hock 1987:30–36). At Ratnagiri, the material from the seventh and eighth century belongs only to the 'Mantrayāna' (the Kriyā and Caryā classes). This material includes, for example, several large sculptures of Amoghapāśa, images of Aṣṭamahābhaya Tārā and Mahākaruṇa Lokeśvara, and triadic groups of Śākyamuni, Vajrapāṇi, and Avalokiteśvara, along with votive *stūpa* and *dhāraṇī.*

Yoga and Anuttarayoga Tantra material begins to appear only in the late ninth and tenth century, with temple sculptures corresponding to the Guhyasamāja Tantra, and a number of small images of Heruka and other Anuttarayoga figures (Hock 1987:169–173). Iconographic material varies considerably even between sites that are geographically close, such as the three Orissan monasteries of Ratnagiri, Udayagiri, and Lalitgiri (1987:174–175). This suggests varying local traditions of practice. As far as I know, however, Anuttarayoga material in the form of large-scale sculpture is all quite late in date. Most of the surviving Anuttarayoga material from India and Southeast Asia is in the form of small images, suggesting private shrines rather than large-scale temples.[5]

I implied in Chapters 2 and 12 that the Kriyā and Caryā Tantras, in which, at least originally, the deity was visualized externally, were less threatening in their social and political implications than the Yoga and especially the Anuttarayoga forms, in which the practitioner identifies with the deity. The Kriyā and Caryā ('Mantrayāna,' I7d) probably grew up as an extension of ritual, yogic, and devotional tendencies already present within the Mahāyāna. They would certainly have been the forms that could most easily be absorbed into the ritual life and practice of established monastic communities. If Hock's interpretation is correct, they were an important part of the ritual life of some of these communities by the eighth and ninth centuries. The Anuttarayoga Tantra practices, by contrast, seem to have remained outside the monastic context until very late. They remained the preserve of siddha-style practitioners (I4a1), who seem (see below) to have formed small cult-groups of wandering yogins and yoginis. It seems that it was only at the end of the period we are considering, in the tenth and eleventh centuries, that these practices were taken up openly within the monasteries and the large monastic universities that had by then grown up.

The nature of the surviving evidence of Anuttarayoga practice in India and Southeast Asia supports this picture. Small, portable images may imply that much of Anuttarayoga practice, particularly in monastic circles, remained private or secret, and some of the surviving stories of the siddhas point in the same direction. The Tibetans in later centuries had the ideal of the practitioner whose external practice was

Hinayāna (i.e., governed by the Prātimokṣa rules), whose internal practice was Mahāyāna (the *bodhicitta* motivation) and whose secret[6] practice was Vajrayāna. This is a pattern that seems to bear more relationship to the Indian and early Tibetan context than to that of modern Tibet.

We can therefore suppose that Buddhist Tantra developed in two parallel contexts. In the monastic context, and perhaps also that of settled urban and village lay communities of religious practitioners, ritual and yogic practices based on the external visualization of deities became more and more important, perhaps from the fourth and fifth centuries onwards (I7d). This corresponds to Hock's 'Mantrayāna' and to the Kriyā and Caryā Tantras of the later Tibetan tradition. In the other context, small cult-groups of wandering ascetics whose practices involved identification with deities and the *nāḍī-prāṇa* (Tibetan *tsa-lung*) techniques developed at around the same time (I4a1). This pattern drew in part on the already-established practices of tribal and folk shamans. It corresponds to the Yoga and Anuttarayoga Tantras and to Hock's 'Vajrayāna.' In appearance and external behavior, the members of these cult-groups would scarcely have been distinguishable from members of the non-Buddhist Kāpālika cults (see below), and the term Kāpālika was perhaps applied to and used by both.[7] Buddhist and non-Buddhist practitioners would have differed primarily in that the Buddhists oriented their practice around Buddhist deities and incorporated Buddhist imagery and symbolism, above all that of *bodhicitta,* within their practice.

A gradual synthesis between the Mantrayāna and Vajrayāna trends developed (I4a2), and was widely represented by the tenth and eleventh centuries. The differences between the two bodies of material were already lessening at this time, and were to become still weaker in Tibet, where identification with the deity would become common even within the Kriyā and Caryā Tantras, and the elaborate ritual of Kriyā and Caryā would be adapted to the Yoga and Anuttarayoga Tantra (see Chapter 12).

This picture of the development of Buddhist Tantra would help to explain the contrast between figures like Padmasambhava (the Guru Rimpoch'e of later Tibetan tradition) and Vimalamitra, who were responsible for the transmission of the Old Tantras to Tibet in the eighth century, and men such as Nāropa, Virūpa, and Atīśa, who were major sources for the New Tantra transmission two centuries later. The Old Tantra material seems to represent a stage of siddha practice where siddhas and monastic Buddhists collaborate, but where they still represent noticeably different paths. The New Tantra material is more academic and monastic in tone, and suggest that a considerable degree of rapprochement had taken place between the siddha groups and the monastic centers by this time. A key role in this rapprochement would have been played by figures associated, like Nāropa, Virūpa, and Atīśa, with the great monastic universities of north India.

This general picture of the growth of Tantra in India thus seems plausible. In the remainder of this chapter I shall examine the material on Buddhist Tantra in India and its social context in more detail, since this represents the starting point for its subsequent development in Tibet. As I suggested in Chapters 12 and 13, the context of Tantric practice in eighth- to twelfth-century India was probably very different from that of premodern Tibet. The development between the two provides much of the subject matter for the remaining chapters of this book. To trace this development, we need as clear a picture as possible of what Tantra was like in India in the eighth to twelfth centuries.

Arriving at an accurate picture is not a straightforward task. We have a variety of sources about Indian Buddhist Tantra in general, and about the siddhas and their activities in particular, but all present difficulties for interpretation. We begin with the root texts of the Tantras themselves, along with the commentarial writings, which have survived in Sanskrit or (more often) in Tibetan translation. Then we turn to the Buddhist traditions about the siddhas in works such as the *Caturaśītisiddhapravṛtti* ('Lives of the Eighty-Four Siddhas') and the various other, more or less legendary, stories of the siddhas included in the Tengyur or narrated by later Tibetan authors such as Tāranātha, along with references in Indian literature of the period to Buddhist siddhas and to their non-Buddhist counterparts, the Kāpālika yogins. Finally, we will look at the songs and other noncommentarial texts of the siddhas themselves.

THE TANTRIC TEXTS

The root texts of several of the Tantras have survived in Sanskrit, along with some of the commentarial literature and associated ritual texts. Much more exists in Tibetan translation, and a few of these works were also translated into Chinese. This material is, of course, of great value in reconstructing Indian Buddhist Tantra, but it is often far from easy to interpret unambiguously. In part, this is due to the habit of Tantric writers, including the siddhas, of making extensive use of symbolic or metaphorical language (*sandhābhāṣa*, see Bharati 1965:164–184; Wayman 1973:128–135; Elder 1976; Broido 1982).

As a consequence, it can be hard to tell what is literal and what is metaphorical. At times both meanings may be intended simultaneously: *bodhicitta* can be both the *bodhisattva*'s motivation of compassion towards all living beings and the seminal fluid whose control forms a central part of the internal processes of Tantric yoga (see Samuel 1989). Elsewhere, the use of language may be purely symbolic.

Some indication of the problems may be gained from a brief look at the opening verses of the *Hevajra*, which was to become a specialty of the Sakyapa order in Tibet and one of the most revered and respected of Tibetan Anuttarayoga Tantric lineages. This is not one of the earliest or most obscure of the root Tantric texts:

> Thus have I heard—at one time the Lord dwelt in bliss with the Vajrayoginī[8] who is the Body, Speech, and Mind of all the Buddhas. There the Lord pronounced these words: 'Greatly to be revered is this most secret of all secret things, this essence which is the Body, Speech, and Mind of all the Buddhas. O Vajragarbha, good, good indeed, thou Great Bodhisattva of great compassion. Do thou listen to this which is named Hevajra, the essence of Vajrasattva, Mahāsattva, and Mahāsamayasattva.' Vajragarbha replied: 'Why Vajrasattva, how so Mahāsattva and wherefore Samayasattva? May the Lord please explain.' The Lord replied:
>
> 'It is indivisible and so known as Vajra. A Being which is unity of three;
> Because of this device he's known as Vajrasattva (Adamantine Being).
> He is full of the flavours of great knowledge, and so he is called Mahāsattva (Great Being);
> From his continual creation of conventional forms, as Samayasattva (Convention Being) he's named.'
>
> Vajragarbha said: 'What is meant by this composite name of HE-VAJRA? What is proclaimed by the sound HE, and likewise what by VAJRA?'

The Lord replied:

> 'By HE is proclaimed great compassion, and wisdom by VAJRA. Do thou listen to this Tantra, the essence of Wisdom and Means, which is now proclaimed by me. Its proficiency is known to be manifold; it teaches the gazes, how to conjure forth and the language of secret signs, how to petrify, how to drive away, how to bewitch an army into rigidity. It is the means of producing and maintaining the yoginīs in accordance with the right method; it is proficient in knowledge, both absolute and relative in the matter of the due order of appearance of the divinities. But in the first place it is the one means of producing Heruka, and it is by such production that men are released, O Vajragarbha of great compassion. They are bound by the bonds of existence and released by knowledge of them. O wise one, you should conceive of existence in knowledge of its non-existence, and likewise you should conceive of Heruka in knowledge of his non-existence. Great knowledge abides in the body, free of all falsification, but although it pervades all things and exists in the body, it is not in the body that it arises. (Snellgrove 1959, vol. 1, 47–48)

This first chapter of the Hevajra continues with a listing of the thirty-two principal 'veins' *(nāḍī)* within the body and of the four principal psychic centers *(cakra)*, which in the Hevajra system are at navel, heart, throat and head. It ends:

> Caṇḍālī [Tib. *tummo*] blazes up at the navel.
> She burns the Five Buddhas.
> She burns Locanā and the others.
> HAṂ is burnt and the Moon melts. (Snellgrove 1959, vol. 1, 50)

At one level, it is clear enough what is being taught here. The classic Buddhist transcendence of appearances, phrased in Mahāyāna terms as the unity of Wisdom *(prajñā)* and Means *(upāya)*, is brought about by the internal processes of Tantric yoga, which we discussed in Chapter 12: the production of the deity Heruka and of the yoginīs and the arousing of energy in the central channel, which destroys the deities of the *maṇḍala* who represent the conventional world in its transfigured form.

There are, however, puzzling elements. Why should a Buddhist text teach "how to conjure forth and the language of secret signs, how to petrify, how to drive away, how to bewitch an army into rigidity"? The following chapter lists a whole series of mantras and rituals for producing rain, rending clouds, destroying an enemy army, gaining mastery of a young woman, and so forth (Snellgrove 1959, vol. 1, 51–54). What kind of people are performing this practice and in what kind of setting? They do not sound like the philosophers of Nālandā or Vikramaśīla:

> Free from learning and ceremony and any cause of shame, the yogin wanders, filled with great compassion in his possession of a nature that is common to all beings. He has passed beyond oblations, renunciation, and austerities, and is freed from *mantra* and meditation. Released from all the conventions [*samaya*] of meditation, the yogin performs the practice. (Snellgrove 1957, vol. 1, 65)

Such passages were, of course, well known to the 'crazy siddhas' and practitioners of *tulshug chödpa* in Tibet (Chapter 16). A subsequent chapter describes the coming together of yogins for Tantric feasts:

> One should set about this feasting in a cemetery or a mountain cave, in a resort of nonhuman beings or in a deserted place. One should arrange seats there, reckoned as nine, in the form of corpses or tiger skins or shrouds from a cemetery. The one who embodies Hevajra should be placed in the center of the yoginīs, whose places are known, as taught before, in the main directions and intermediate points. Then seated upon one's tiger skin, one should eat the 'spiced food' of the sacrament, enjoying it, and one should eat with eagerness the 'kingly rice.' (Snellgrove 1987:161)

According to Snellgrove the 'spiced food' is "a concoction of the flesh of a human being, a cow, an elephant, a horse and a dog" while the 'kingly rice' is "specially selected human flesh, that of a man who has been hanged, a warrior killed in battle or a man of irreproachable conduct who has returned seven times to a good human state" (1987:161).

Snellgrove assumes that these substances were really used in at least some Tantric circles. Elsewhere he has noted that the Tibetans today do not use them, and replace them by harmless substitutes where they are required for offerings to the fierce divinities: human flesh "is made of parched flour and butter, but sometimes modelled to show a human head and hands and feet. It is also coloured realistically" (Snellgrove 1957:246). As Snellgrove points out, modern Tibetan practitioners have little concern for or interest in the details of such matters, which are mainly significant in the context of offerings to fierce guardian deities (1957:246–247). But were the Tantric siddhas themselves, the revered founding figures of the Tibetan lineages, really in the habit of feasting on human flesh and other such delicacies?

The problems of interpretation here are made worse by the long period of time that elapsed between the probable composition of the earliest actual Tantras (perhaps fourth century A.D., see Wayman 1980b) and the commentaries by Indian siddhas (ninth to twelfth centuries), let alone the later Tibetan commentaries and the contemporary Tibetan lamas who represent the living tradition of interpretation of these texts. What may have been literal at an early period may have become metaphorical at a later period. It is also likely that the reverse happened, and that practices that were originally meant symbolically were misunderstood as literal and performed in that way.

We should recall here the critical place of food in defining Indian social structure in modern times. The entire caste hierarchy is articulated around the issue of who can share what food with whom (Dumont 1970). Assuming that some of this was already true at the time of the siddhas, the consumption, even symbolically, of polluting (and magically potent) foods in a group meal would have placed the practitioners firmly outside the social norms of ordinary society.

The same may have been true, to some degree, of the Tantric sexual practices. Sexual relations share with food a key role in defining Hindu caste distinctions. Where the female partners were actually, or at least symbolically, of untouchable caste, sexual contact with them reinforced the message of rejection of conventional standards. The sexual practices were nevertheless important less for this reason than, as we have already seen in Chapter 12, for their yogic significance. They were intimately connected with the internal manipulations of the subtle body through which Enlightenment was to be achieved. As in later years in Tibet, they were probably performed in both literal and symbolic forms during the long history of Indian Tantra. Symbolic interpretations are suggested by many of the siddha commentaries, but there is no reason to assume that the practices were entirely symbolic. They have been maintained in both Hindu Tantric and Tibetan Vajrayāna traditions, and cognate practices form an important part of Daoist yoga (see Samuel 1989).

What is perhaps questionable is the orgiastic atmosphere in which texts like that quoted above suggest that Tantric practices were carried out, the bizarre substances specified for use in Tantric ritual (including excrement and urine, blood and semen, as well as the 'spiced food' and 'kingly rice' mentioned above), and the ritual prescriptions for gaining power over others, killing and causing destruction magically, and the like. Perhaps most striking are the injunctions "to kill, to rob, to live with total sexual licence, to lie" (Snellgrove 1987:174), which are an obvious and deliberate reversal of conventional Buddhist morality.

There is evidence that some of this was taken literally at some times, though not necessarily among Buddhist Tantrics. Snellgrove cites the story of how the Chinese Buddhist pilgrim Xuanzang was nearly killed by devotees of Durgā in search of a suitable human victim (1987:162). It is clear from the texts cited by Snellgrove that Indian Buddhist authorities regarded such injunctions as to be interpreted in other than the literal sense. This was true of the subsequent Tibetan commentators as well, although the idea of the yogin going beyond ordinary human moral restrictions always has to be born in mind (see the 'crazy siddhas' of Chapter 16).

What emerges from the texts is a picture of wandering yogins and yoginīs, of initiations into the cult of particular Tantric lineages, which may or may not be more 'literal' than the later Tibetan versions, and of regular meetings for ritual feasts at the various Tantric sacred places *(pīṭha)* around India. Even these meetings may be largely metaphorical, because the identification of the Tantric *pīṭha* with locations within the body, and of pilgrimages to them with the internal processes of Tantric yoga, seems quite early (Tsuda 1978). The long period of time which we are considering also has to be remembered. Nāropa had a regular center (at Pullahari or Puṣpahari) where his students came to study with him, and it may be that by this time (tenth century) Tantra was practiced by settled groups as much or more than by wandering yogins.

THE STORIES OF THE SIDDHAS (14A, 14A1, 14A2)

Another source of information about Tantric practice in India are the legends and stories about the siddhas that have been preserved by the

Tibetans.[9] The Tibetans in later centuries developed a sophisticated historical tradition. Given that the monastic historians viewed lamas of the past through a hagiographic perspective, and that miraculous signs and powers were a part of the world they were describing, these chroniclers are, by and large, reliable in dealing with events and places in Tibet from the eleventh and twelfth centuries onwards, and usable with care even for the earlier royal period (seventh century onwards).

Unfortunately, their accounts of Indian Buddhism are far less authoritative, and it is clear that, at best, they were synthesizing and attempting to reconcile a mass of oral traditions and legendary material varying between the dubious and the outright fictional. Different sources give entirely different accounts of the lives of the same siddhas, and while men such as the seventeenth-century Tibetan scholar Tāranātha (Templeman 1981, 1983, 1989) probably recorded the material available to them as accurately as they could, their writings in no way provide the kind of solid factual base we have for the history of Buddhism in Tibet. At most we can derive an approximate picture of the relative dating of the siddhas from the guru-student relationships in the various sources. Unfortunately there seem to be no detailed accounts of the siddhas by Tibetan authors of their own time.[10]

This legendary material nevertheless does give us some insights that may be of value. One useful source of information is the *Caturaś-ītisiddhapravṛtti*, apparently a collection of legends told by the Indian scholar Abhayadatta to a Tibetan monk in the late eleventh or early twelfth century. This collection has been translated twice into English (Robinson 1979; Dowman 1985). It consists of short narratives of the lives of each individual from a standard list of 84 siddhas. While the accounts are legendary rather than historical, they are close in time to the later figures in the tradition, and suggest something of how these siddhas were seen by their followers.

The range of occupational and caste backgrounds that this work ascribes to the siddhas is itself revealing: fishermen, weavers, cobblers, birdcatchers, kings, beggars, and brahmins. They also include four women. We gain a picture here of the siddha teachers as unconventional and often shocking in their behavior and their techniques, disrespectful for the most part of scholarly knowledge, and enmeshed in a world of visions and magical power. In this and much else they resembled their Hindu counterparts, the Śaivite yogins (also called siddhas) of the Kāpālika, Kālāmukha, and Pāśupata traditions. As I have already suggested, there seems to have been considerable overlap between Hindu and Buddhist yogins.

References to Kāpālikas and similar Hindu ascetics are common in the non-Buddhist Indian literature from the sixth century onwards. They are not portrayed in a flattering light. These bizarre characters, half naked and adorned with human bone ornaments, carry cups made from human skulls (*kapāla*, hence Kāpālika). They frequent cremation grounds where they perform evil rituals of destructive magic. With their low-caste female associates, witches rather than spiritual companions, the Kāpālikas seem far indeed from the quiet cloisters of the Buddhist monastic universities and the calm rationality of Madhyamaka philosophy (Lorenzen 1972, 1989).

And yet the Tibetan texts such as the translation of the *Caturaśītisiddhapravṛtti* or the writings of Tāranatha describe the Buddhist siddhas as sharing most of the external features attributed to the Kāpālikas and their fellows, including the bone ornaments and skull-cups, the low-caste female companions, and the midnight rituals in cremation grounds. It is only the valuation that is different. Here it should be borne in mind that the Indian sources are, almost by definition, from circles that were urban and literate, and frequently Brahmanical as well. Their authors were not people who would have reason to speak well of these wandering rural shamans who, as we have seen, rejected Brahmanical knowledge as irrelevant to true liberation.

The situation is neatly illustrated by the Buddhist and Brahmanical versions of the *Vetālapañcaviṃśati*. This famous series of medieval Indian stories is unified by a frame-story, similar to the story of Sheherezade in the 1001 *Nights*. In the *Vetālapañcaviṃśati*'s frame-story, the stories that make up the collection are narrated to the great Indian monarch Vikramāditya by a spirit *(vetāla)* who possesses a corpse that Vikramāditya is attempting to take from a cremation ground. In the several Brahmanical versions of the collection, which have survived in India and Nepal, the king is acting (for reasons I shall not attempt to explain here) as the ritual assistant of a classic Kāpālika-style ascetic, a thoroughly evil character who in fact intends to sacrifice the king himself as part of the ritual. In the Buddhist versions, which exist in Tibetan and Mongolian, this villainous magician is replaced by the great siddha Nāgārjuna, whose intentions towards the king are of course entirely benign.[11]

Doubtless, as with the sadhus or wandering holy men of modern

India, there is some truth in both pictures. Only Śiva ultimately knows who is a true sadhu, and who is a sorcerer or a mere charlatan.[12] The Buddhist Tantric texts surviving in Sanskrit and in Tibetan translation include more than the occasional prescription for destructive magical ritual, as we have already seen in the case of the *Hevajra Tantra*. Presumably, if one made one's living as a wandering holy man with magical powers, such things had their uses. Taken as a whole, however, these texts leave no doubt that the prime purpose of Tantric practice is the attainment of the Buddhist Enlightenment.

The Buddhist Tantras are paralleled by similar traditions, also called Tantras, among the Hindus and Jains. Both Hindus and Jains, like Buddhists, have a list of 84 great siddhas. There are several versions of the Hindu list, and some of them include names also occurring in the Buddhist list (Lorenzen 1972). Some of the Tantric traditions, too, seem to have circulated freely between siddhas of all backgrounds. We know that Mahākāla was an important deity for the Kāpālika ascetics, and the Mahākāla Tantra preserved in two rather different versions by the Buddhist tradition contains hardly anything specifically Buddhist, to judge by translated excerpts.[13]

Texts like the Mahākāla Tantra include rituals aimed at healing and destructive purposes, alchemical procedures *(rasāyana)*, and the like, forming part of the stock in trade of wandering holy men of the time whether Hindu, Buddhist, or Jain in formal allegiance. All this is the sphere of the 'ordinary' or 'mundane siddhis' (Tib. *t'ünmong ngödrub*), and much of it was to be handed on to the Tibetans. Each Tibetan religious tradition has, for example, one or more traditional forms of Mahākāla (Gompo) who act as 'protectors' of the teachings and the *gompa*, and Tibetan temples always include a shrine for these protective deities, often in a separate room to the main shrine.

The really important Tantras, for the Tibetans and, also we may assume, for the Buddhist siddhas of India, were not these, but the Tantras concerning with the 'supreme siddhi' of the Buddhist Enlightenment. These lineages, such as the Guhyasamāja, Cakrasaṃvara, Hevajra, and Kālacakra Tantras, are specifically Buddhist. The texts generally include prescriptions for the lesser magical powers, but these are ancillary to the central process described within them, which is that of the attainment of Enlightenment. The first three of the lineages enumerated are the Tantras that occur in the *Caturaśītisiddha-*

pravṛtti (see Robinson 1979:285–288). Along with the Kālacakra Tantra, which appeared in India at a later date, they remained the most important for the Tibetans.[14]

The basic texts of these Tantras all survive in Sanskrit as well as Tibetan, as does some of the commentarial literature on them, and they were clearly the most significant Tantric traditions for the north Indian siddhas from whom the Tibetans obtained most of their New Tantric transmissions in the eleventh and twelfth centuries. They continue to be practiced by Newari hereditary Buddhist Tantric priests *(vajrācārya)* in Nepal as well as by Tibetans throughout ethnic Tibet.

We should note that the term 'siddha' itself allows both possibilities. A siddha is someone who has attained *siddhi,* magical accomplishment. Yet there are many different kinds of *siddhi.* For the Buddhist practitioner, Enlightenment is the highest *siddhi,* and the ultimate goal of siddha practice. The 'relative' *siddhi,* the ordinary magical powers, are from this point of view mere by-products, although they are certainly part of what a siddha is expected to attain.

From these sources we can begin to form a picture of the Buddhist Tantric siddhas in their historical and social context: wandering holy men and women from a variety of backgrounds who made a living by performing rituals and teaching. They were distinguished from non-Buddhist siddhas not by their mode of livelihood, or by the magical rituals that formed most of their traveling stock in trade, but by the fact that they also practiced one or another set of more elevated Tantric rituals focusing on the Bodhi Orientation, the cult of Enlightenment, such as those of the Cakrasaṃvara, Hevajra, or Guhyasamāja cycles. These are what the later Tibetan tradition referred to as Anuttarayoga Tantra. If our sources are reliable, occasionally such practitioners would have dealt with kings, princes, and wealthy landowners, but much of their clientele must have been lower in the social scale.

By the end of the siddha period (eleventh to twelfth centuries) some of these people, like Nāropa, had permanent centers where the teachings and rituals of the Enlightenment cult were transmitted and where students from faraway regions such as Tibet could come to study. Others still practiced a wandering life style or lived in wild and remote places. Yet others practiced Tantra while maintaining the outward appearance of a Buddhist monk of the clerical tradition: as the Tibetans later put it "externally Hinayāna, internally Mahāyāna, in secret Vajrayāna." By the time of Atīśa (early eleventh century) such combined Sūtra and Tantra practitioners seem to have become quite common (I4a2).

THE SONGS OF THE SIDDHAS

A final body of literature from the period is also worth examining, because it brings us closer than anything we have considered so far to the atmosphere of the siddha groups, and so to explaining the fascination their practices had for their Tibetan followers. These are the songs of the siddhas. They share some of the same problems of interpretation as the Tantras and the commentarial literature, but their content as a whole seems less ambiguous, perhaps because they are more homogeneous in their origins. The songs come from a relatively restricted group of siddhas who lived over at most a couple of centuries and most of whom are included in the standard list of 84 siddhas referred to above. David Templeman has suggested that we can distinguish three main types of song, known as *dohā*, *vajragīti*, and *caryā* songs (Templeman, in press).

Dohā are short songs expressing the siddha's realization, often in an enigmatic or paradoxical manner. They were intended, according to later Tibetan tradition, primarily as a means of teaching, while *vajragīti* were songs "sung and danced to in ritual performance at the *gaṇacakra*, feast-gatherings of yogins at which the Tantric understanding of the absolute reality of the senses [was] celebrated" (Templeman, in press). In practice, though, as Templeman notes, it is difficult to distinguish sharply between the two types of song on the basis of the examples that have come down to us.

Saraha and Kāṇha (Kṛṣṇācārya) were the best known composers of *dohā*. Three lengthy sequences of these songs are attributed to Saraha. One of these has been translated by Guenther (1973), along with two commentaries by a twelfth-century Nepalese writer and a fifteenth-century Tibetan (Karmapa) writer, and another is translated by Snellgrove (in Conze 1964). In this second sequence he dismisses Brahmins, yogin-ascetics, Jainas, and monastic Buddhists as all equally far from the path, before giving his own advice (in Templeman's translation):

One who has no compassion and
Lives in a state of 'voidness'
Can never reach the highest path.
If he but meditates solely upon compassion,
He will also not gain liberation from this state of *saṃsāra*.
Whoever is able to combine both states of compassion and voidness
Will no longer abide in either *saṃsāra* or *nirvāṇa*.

Oh ho! Get rid of all your deceits and perverted views.
Whatever is an attachment—simply fling it out!
If you mentally review things all will be seen to be deceit, perversion
or attachment—
No one will find things to be any different to that.

There is no religious view that does not aim at these things—
Reading texts, mental understanding, meditation and preaching the
essence of the teachings,
But mark this—one can only hear these things from the Guru's mouth.

The Guru's words enter the heart
And it is like seeing a treasure in the palm of your hand.
A spiritually ignorant person does not see his actual state of
naturalness,
And is therefore deceived. Thus says Saraha. (Templeman, in press)

The *caryā* songs originate from a group of siddhas who lived in what is now Bengal, and their songs frequently use imagery deriving from that part of India, not unlike the songs of the Bauls, religious mendicants who have preserved a version of the Tantric practices into modern times (for example, Bhattacharya 1969). The major collection of these songs is the *Caryāgīti*, which has survived not only in Tibetan but in a nearly complete version in a medieval Indian vernacular. There have been several translations of the complete collection of songs, the most notable being by Per Kvaerne (1977). Here is one of Kāṇha's *caryā* songs as translated by Templeman:

I have made the Triple Refuge my boat, a vessel with eight maidens.
My own body is of the nature of compassion and I have a wife whose
nature is emptiness.

I cross the ocean of existence as if in an illusion or a dream
And even in its midst I see no waves.

I have made the five Tathāgatas my ferrymen and
Kāṇha will thereby deliver himself from all delusions.

As for smell, touch and taste,
They are just as they appear to be—a sleepless dream.

The mind, as ferryman, is in the stern of the boat of emptiness,
And Kāṇha, the passenger, proceeds in its company towards the state of supreme bliss. (Templeman, in press)

Here, as in a song by Virūpa quoted below, everyday imagery is used to point to the nature of Tantric processes; the Five Tathāgata, for example, represent the purified elements of one's own body (Kvaerne 1977:127).

There are also short instructional texts in verse, which are similar in style to the siddha songs. An example of this genre is Tilopa's Mahāmudrā instruction to Nāropa, traditionally delivered alongside the river Ganges. Here a series of images conveys the utter transcendence of all concepts in the state of Mahāmudrā, which is the usual siddha term for the experience of Enlightenment:

Homage to the Vajra Ḍākinī!

Mahāmudrā cannot be taught. But most intelligent Nāropa,
Since you have undergone rigorous austerity,
With forbearance in suffering and with devotion to your Guru,
Blessed one, take this secret instruction to heart.

Is space anywhere supported? Upon what does it rest?
Like space, Mahāmudrā is dependent upon nothing;
Relax and settle in the continuum of unalloyed purity,
And, your bonds loosening, release is certain.

Gazing intently into the empty sky, vision ceases;
Likewise, when mind gazes into mind itself,
The train of discursive and conceptual thought ends
And supreme enlightenment is gained.

Like the morning mist that dissolves into thin air,
Going nowhere but ceasing to be,

> Waves of conceptualization, all the mind's creation, dissolve,
> When you behold your mind's true nature. (Dowman n.d.:2)

There is a freshness and vitality, even now, about the siddha material that helps to explain how it must have appealed to both the academicians and the common people of its time. The message itself is conventionally Buddhist, but the siddhas were undoubtedly serious about achieving realization rather than simply discussing it. Over and over in the siddha songs we see one element that was to be so important in Tibet: the crucial role of the guru, who can lead his or her disciple past the illusions of the rational mind and phenomenal thought to the true vision of reality.

For the future course of the siddha ideal within Tibet, however, one further development in India was to prove of great importance: the gradual infiltration of the Anuttarayoga practices of the siddhas into the monastic universities from which most of the Tibetans' teachers would come.

What was it that led the Buddhist academics to leave in increasing numbers their serene universities and to seek Enlightenment in the doubtful company of the siddhas? And why, after a period of Indian history that marks one of the high points of rationality and scholarship in all of human history, should there be a revival of shamanic modes of thought? To answer this question, it is perhaps worth looking in more detail at the social context within which these events were unfolding.

THE SOCIAL CONTEXT OF THE SIDDHAS

The Gupta empire in the fourth and fifth centuries was still a period of prosperity and peace. The close relationship between Hindu and Buddhist thought at this period, and the activities of Asaṅga and the Yogācāra philosophers, reflect this setting. During the following centuries the political situation gradually deteriorated, and doubtless with the general collapse of long-distance trade the economy also declined.

The Gupta empire had covered most of the Indian subcontinent. King Harṣa's short-lived state in the first half of the seventh century was of similar extent, but no subsequent polity was comparable in size until the Mogul empire 800 years later. During the Gupta period the centralized administration of the state was already beginning to break down into a quasi-feudal system in which local hereditary chieftains dominated regional politics. By the eighth century, India was split into a number of smaller states, and the new expansionist Islamic kingdoms were beginning to impinge to the West. In the south, the growth of devotional and monastic Hinduism was accelerating (I8, I5c), supported by the new Advaita philosophy of Śaṅkara (I6b1), and aggressively anti-Buddhist policies were becoming common.[15] The Buddhists could rely for support and tolerance only on the Pāla regime in Bihar and Bengal and on a few smaller local regimes such as those in Nepal and Kashmir.

A transformation in the ethos of society, in the nature of its dominant cultural patterns, was also taking place, with the growth of the Indian caste system as we know it today, and the increasing supremacy of Brahmanical law. It can be seen clearly in the changing attitudes to relations between the sexes, which were becoming less tolerant and open, more hierarchical and patriarchal.[16]

Hindu thought suggested that the time was a period of decline, a Kali Yuga. The Buddhists had their own version of the same idea, in the theory of the progressive deterioration of the Buddhist teachings, which was to follow the Buddha's passing into *nirvāṇa*. The signs of such deterioration would have been clear enough. The Dark Ages were coming, and the rational knowledge of the Buddhist philosophers must have seemed increasingly inadequate. The terrifying shadow of the *ḍākinī* that fell on Nāropa's books (see Chapter 12) was surely not unconnected to those other shadows across the peaceful contemplative life at Nālandā. Indeed, Nālandā itself was to be razed to the ground by a Muslim army, and most of its scholars and monks killed, although that final catastrophe was still a couple of centuries away when Nāropa left to seek his guru (Dutt 1962:347–348).[17]

The foregoing is speculative, but it may help recreate the atmosphere within which the siddha movement took place. Shamanic modes of thought (I1, I3, I4) had never disappeared in India. They would have been marginalized in a similar way, though doubtless to a lesser degree, to the situation in modern India where they are characteristic of folk religion at the village level and especially of the various 'tribal' peoples (to use the modern Indian jargon) who must at that time have been much more widespread than they remain today. The tribal peoples would have provided a natural resource for a return to shamanic modes of thinking and practice, especially in view of the long-standing Indian tradition of retreating to remote and wild areas for meditation. As I pointed out in Chapter 12, several major Tantric pilgrimage sites were in tribal areas, and elements of Tantric practice suggest shamanic origins, among them the central process of transformation into a deity, the *maṇḍala* structure, and possibly the frequent presence of animal-headed deities within the *maṇḍala* (see Chapter 12, and Samuel 1990).

It remains to consider the meaning of the Tantras, and particularly their social implications, for their Indian siddha practitioners.

THE SIDDHA IDEAL AND THE SOCIAL ORDER

The aim of Anuttarayoga Tantra practice can be described as the attainment of the status or spiritual level known as Vajradhara (Dorje-ch'ang in Tibetan). We have already met Vajradhara in Chapters 12 and 13 as the form in which the Buddha taught the Tantras. Vajradhara also stands, as here, for the status that is to be achieved through Tantric practice. A key aspect of 'becoming' Vajradhara is the attainment of the free and spontaneous state known as Mahāmudrā, and celebrated in the songs within which the Indian siddhas, and later their Tibetan followers, described their experiences in analogical language. We have already read some of these songs. Here is another one, by Virūpa:

> One barmaid goes into two houses:
> With yeast and water she ferments the wine.
> Distill the wine, strengthened with the spontaneous:
> It is by this one becomes immortal.
> Seeing the sign at the tenth door,
> The customer who has come keeps going by himself.
> The merchandise is on sale sixty-four hours a day.
> The customer who has entered does not come out.
> There is one small jar with a narrow neck:
> Virūpa says: 'Pour it in carefully.'[18]

The siddha who wrote this particular song, Virūpa, was the founder of what was to become the central teaching lineage of the Tibetan monastic order of the Sakyapa. His song in fact gives a precise description of the Completion Stage processes. The 'barmaid' is the goddess Nairātmyā ('Selfless Lady'), consort of Hevajra, Virūpa's main Tantric deity, while the two houses are the left and right psychic channels *(nāḍī)* along which the *prāṇa* flows.

The one authority whom Tantric practitioners had to accept was that of the guru who gave them initiation into Tantric practice. The Tantric guru or teacher was of central importance. Tantric practice could not be learned from the texts, but depended on the oral instructions of the guru, who was able to perceive the specific needs and problems of each student. In the later Tibetan *sādhana*, or Tantric liturgies, the guru (in Tibetan, lama) was, as we have seen, to become a central object of worship, and the Tantric deity is explicitly to be visualized as a form of one's principal teacher (*tsawé lama*, 'root lama').

The concept of guru, however, as we saw in Chapters 12 and 13, was more complex than this might indicate, since the guru relationship, like everything else, had ultimately to be experienced in nondichotomous terms. The external guru was an aspect of the guru principle, of the Tantric Buddha Vajradhara. The potential that Vajradhara represented had to be created within the yogins themselves. In this sense, the real guru was Vajradhara within the practitioner, just as the real Buddha was within every sentient being waiting to be uncovered. The external guru could only help to provoke this process (see Guenther 1977b:177–195).

While later Tibetan Buddhist writers, particularly of the Gelugpa tradition, generally insist that there is no difference between the conception of the Buddha in the Pāramitāyāna (the Sūtra teachings) and that in the Vajrayāna, there is little doubt that the growth of the Vajrayāna represented a shift in how the ideal of Buddha was viewed.[19] To achieve the status of Vajradhara and to become master (or mistress) of the shamanic vision of Mahāmudrā was also, as we have already seen, to attain command over the mundane siddhis. These this-worldly shamanic and magical powers were celebrated over and over again in the siddha biographies, and they evidently formed a central part of what a proper siddha was supposed to be.

These texts give the impression of having circulated as oral folklore among Tantric practitioners for some time before being committed to writing. The following anecdote comes from the best-known collection, the *Caturaśītisiddhapravṛtti* mentioned earlier in the chapter and dating from the late eleventh or early twelfth century:

> In the city of Kanasati, Virūpa bought wine from a tavern girl; she gave him a glass of wine and a plate of rice which he greatly enjoyed. He continued eating and drinking. For the space of two days and a night, he prevented the sun from moving and the king, amazed, exclaimed: 'Who is it who performs such a miracle?' In answer, the goddess of the sun appeared to the king in a dream and said, 'A yogin has pledged me as payment to a tavern girl.' The king and his subjects paid the price of the wine, which came to a million glasses, and Virūpa disappeared. (Robinson 1979:29)

As with the song about the barmaid, we may suspect some double meanings here. What is also notable about this story is the implicit comparison of Virūpa's Tantric power and the king's temporal power. Indeed, Abhayadatta's collection includes a number of examples of kings, princes, and princesses who abandoned their royal status to follow the life of a Tantric yogin. This is an ancient Buddhist theme, since Śākyamuni himself was supposed to have begun life as a prince, but it is here reinforced by the strong emphasis in these stories on the magical powers attained by the Tantric adept.

The contrast between shamanic and ordinary political power was not lost on the Tibetans. The story about the tavern and the sun standing still recurs in the Tibetan biographies of Guru Rimpoch'e (Padmasambhava), the Tantric guru *par excellence* for the oldest and most 'shamanic' Tibetan Buddhist tradition, the Nyingmapa (Douglas and Bays 1978, vol. 1, 292–293). I have already referred, in Chapter 2, to the account in these biographies of Padmasambhava's first meeting with the Tibetan king, in which the king, who expects Padmasambhava to prostrate to him, is forced instead to prostrate to the guru (Douglas and Bays 1978, vol. 2, 376–383).

There is no doubt of the Siddhas' rejection of conventional standards and conventional religious practice. In the 'People Dohas' by Saraha, who was one of the most famous of the Siddhas, Brahmins, Jains, Hinayāna and Mahāyāna Buddhists, and scholastic interpreters of the Tantras themselves are all dismissed as being far from the true way (Conze 1964:224–225). As songs like Virūpa's indicate, the Siddhas took delight in apparently shocking imagery. Altogether, it seems plausible to interpret the siddha movement as part of a shamanic reaction against the clerical and rationalized tradition of an India where rationalized society was gradually collapsing. What is equally important for the present study, however, is what the Siddha movement was to mean to the Tibetans.

To make more sense of what the Siddha ideal was to imply within Tibetan society it is worth taking a closer look at some of the implications of Tantric sexuality. This is a subject that has received some attention in recent years, but discussion is often confused, in part because of the real differences between Buddhist Tantra as practiced in Tibet and the Hindu Tantric tradition in India.[20]

The nature of Hindu Tantra follows from its having become accommodated over the centuries to existence within the bounds of a series of effective centralized and rationalized state structures. This accommodation has resulted in a bifurcation within Indian Tantric practice. Much Indian Tantra has moved towards the doctrinally orthodox and politically unobjectionable. This is the case for the most part with the Tantric traditions of Kashmiri and Tamil Śaivism. The magical and shamanic powers have lost their importance, the 'disreputable' sexual practices are avoided, and Tantric ritual has become little more than a supplement to the ordinary Brahmanic cult. Much the same, although perhaps to a lesser degree, appears to be true for Buddhist Tantra among the Newars of the Kathmandu Valley and in Japan, and for both Buddhist and Hindu Tantra in Bali.[21]

This is in Indian parlance the 'right-hand' tradition, and it is accompanied by a 'left-hand' and disreputable tradition of Tantra as concerned with magic, shamanic power, and dubious sexual practices. This also continued to exist until modern times, if on a relatively small scale. In recent times at least, this was an oppositional subculture, a kind of underground movement among those already disreputable through low social status, such as the Baul sect of Bengal (Dasgupta 1976:157–187; Bhattacharya 1969), although there have been occasional adherents among the ruling class, for whom it perhaps served as an escape from the dominance of Brahminic orthodoxy. This kind of Tantra was committed to the realm of 'reputation' in a society dominated by 'respectability,' while the right-hand path had assimilated itself to respectability (cf Chapter 11).

Neither the right-hand nor the left-hand tradition of India correspond to the situation in Tibet. As we will see, secular powers in Tibet tried at intervals to 'clean up' Tantra and make it controllable, but their success was limited, because their power was equally limited. As time went on, Tibetan secular regimes were led to ally themselves increasingly with the shamanic power of the Buddhist Tantric lamas, and to accept the claims of that power to exist in its own right.

As explained in Chapter 15, the Tantric aspect of Tibetan Buddhism allowed for the development of new Buddhist religious roles, absent in the more 'clerical' Theravādin countries. In Tibet, lay Tantric practice was to become relatively common, carried out both by householders and by yogins, male or female, who renounced lay life to travel between pilgrimage sites and hermitages, or to stay in prolonged retreat under the guidance of a lama. These yogins grew their hair long, and wore the white cotton cloth of the *repa* or some other nonmonastic garb, contrasting in both respects with the shaven-headed celibate monks with their red robes.

The most significant implication of the Tantric siddha model for Tibet was not, however, to be the growth of this tradition of nonmonastic yogins alongside the Buddhist monks. It was the development of a new ideal that combined and transcended these two patterns—that of the lama.

The relationship implied by the monk and yogin roles alone is not very different from the situation in premodern India, where respectable Brahmins (including right-hand Tantrics) and more or less (dis)reputable wandering holy men (including left-hand Tantrics) coexisted within the bounds of a centralized state. The followers of the right-hand path accepted the patronage and support of the state, and traded in their shamanic practices to become rationalized clerics. The adherents of the left-hand path preserved the shamanism, but were unable to rival the power of the state, and had to accept the low status and subordination to the clerics that went with their position. The lamas were to transcend the opposition; within a political system where they were actors in their own right, and not subordinate to any political or clerical authority, they represented a union of shamanic and rationalized techniques.

There are aspects of the Siddha movement in India that point towards this kind of role. The later siddhas certainly prefigured the integration of shamanic and rationalized approaches. The lama was, however, essentially a Tibetan development, and the next five chapters will trace how it occurred. It took several centuries, from the initial coming of Buddhism in the time of the early kings, through the small-scale hereditary village lamas of the ninth to eleventh centuries, the growth of large monasteries and of the 'reincarnate lama' system, and the syntheses of rationalized and shamanic, monastic and yogic approaches, developed by great lamas such as Tsongk'apa and Pema Karpo.

Here the sexual imagery of the Buddhist Tantras was to stand the Tibetans in good stead. The left-hand path of Hindu Tantra, a religion of the powerless, was to become a cult of shamanic power in the form of the female role, the *śakti*. This is not surprising; the male role in patriarchal India naturally became identified, as Śiva, Viṣṇu, or Kṛṣṇa, with the all-powerful ruler of the hierarchical state. The Tibetans kept the complementarity of male and female, *upāya* and *prajñā*, and used it to balance and synthesize the shamanic and rationalized approaches into a unique whole, in which the central Mahāyāna motivation of *bodhicitta* was firmly integrated.

THE RAPPROCHEMENT BETWEEN SIDDHAS AND CLERICAL BUDDHISTS (I4A2)

While the siddhas and the academic monks represent the contrasting shamanic and clerical aspects of Buddhism in India, the opposition between them was never an absolute one. Nāgārjuna, whom we met in the last chapter as the founder of Madhyamaka philosophy, was revered not only as a philosopher but as a practicing yogin.[22] Buddhist philosophy was always thought of as valuable not for its own sake but for the assistance it gave in attaining the Buddhist Enlightenment.

Given this fundamental orientation, it is unlikely that the academic tradition was ever entirely separate from yogic or shamanic practice. Nevertheless, the degree of mutual involvement between the two orientations clearly increased with the passage of time.

I have already sketched, at the beginning of this chapter, the probable course of this development, with the monastic pattern of the Kriyā and Caryā Tantras (I7d) and the siddha pattern of the Yoga and Anuttarayoga Tantras (I4a1) being at first relatively separate. If we can rely on the traditional Tibetan accounts of the establishment of Buddhism in Tibet in the late eighth century, the Tantric siddha (Padmasambhava, Vimalamitra) and the clerical scholar (Śāntarakṣita, Kamalaśīla) were still distinct roles. Despite the elaborate later accretions around the personality of Padmasambhava it seems that these men were all historical figures. Their contrasted backgrounds do not seem to have prevented them from establishing a working relationship. At any rate, the standard Tibetan account has the Tibetan ruler of the time inviting Padmasambhava to subdue the local deities of Tibet at Śāntarakṣita's recommendation (Douglas and Bays 1978:376–384; see Blondeau 1980).

By the tenth and eleventh centuries, the distinction between the patterns was less marked. We find individuals who combined both kinds of competence, and a movement towards syntheses of the two streams (I4a2). Several of the most famous siddhas, such as Nāropa, Virūpa, and Maitrigupta, had an academic background (Guenther 1963; Robinson 1979; Tatz 1987). These teachers either left their universities to study Tantra with the siddhas, as in Nāropa's case, or practiced in secret while maintaining their academic post, as with Virūpa. Atīśa (Dīpaṅkaraśrījñāna), who came to Tibet in 1042 after a distinguished academic career at Vikramaśīla, had likewise undergone a combined Tantric and academic training (Chattopadhyaya 1967; Eimer 1977, 1979, 1982). This development was to be of considerable significance for the Tibetans, who were in time to develop the combination of academic and Tantric training much further than ever happened in India itself.

CULTURAL PATTERNS

The major cultural patterns whose growth has been traced in this chapter, the monastic universities (I5b) and the various phases of the Tantras (I7d, I4a1, I4a2) were to be of central importance for the development of Buddhism in Tibet. The tension between the 'clerical' and 'shamanic' strains of Buddhism, as represented by the monastic universities and the Tantric siddhas, is already evident, as are attempts to reconcile the two (I4a2).

23

Tibet to A.D. 841

The origins and history of the Tibetan kingdom or empire have already been narrated briefly in Chapter 3. By about 625 A.D., King Songtsen Gampo of the Yarlung dynasty had come to power, moved his capital from Yarlung to Lhasa, and conquered the neighboring state of Shangshung. These events mark the beginning of real Tibetan history, both in terms of surviving literary and epigraphic records in Tibetan itself and in accounts of the Tibetans by the historians and analists of neighboring peoples. Songtsen Gampo was also the first specifically Buddhist king in Tibetan history.

Tibet, however, and particularly the Shangshung state, which seems to have been the dominant power on the Tibetan plateau for some centuries previously, must have had extensive contacts with neighboring societies before this time. Aspects of Tibetan religion, in particular the apparent origin of the terms *la* and *lha* in some unitary concept, point to a hypothetical stateless and shamanic situation (T1), but any such situation would have to be placed many centuries before the time of Songtsen Gampo, given the religious forms apparently present by his time (Spanien 1971; Haarh 1969).

TABLE 4.
Cultural Patterns in Chapter 23

Tibetans before the Seventh Century
T1 Religion of stateless period: *la* and *lha* undifferentiated
T2 Religion of proto-states: *la* and *lha* differentiated <T1
T3 Court religion of Shangshung, Yarlung regime ('after king Trigum') <?I2a, ?I4a, ?Iran, T2
T4 Folk religion of Shangshung, Yarlung regime <T2
Tibetan Empire, circa A.D. 625 to A.D. 841
T5 Court religion (*bön* and *shen* priests) <T3, ?I2a, ?I4a
T6 Buddhism
T6a Clerical Buddhism <I8, Central Asia, China
T6b Tantric and Ch'an tendencies <I4a1, I7c, China
T7 Folk religion <T4

The entire development would require at least two further phases prior to the time of Songtsen Gampo, and I have referred to these in Table 4 as the religion of proto-states (T2) and the court religions of Shangshung and of the Yarlung regime (T3). The transition between these two phases, in the case of the Yarlung dynasty, is marked in Tibetan historical accounts by the life of King Trigum Tsenpo, an event that is legendary rather than historical in nature.[1] In fact, Tibetan historical sources provide considerable material on the period up to the time of Songtsen Gampo, but very little of this material, which has been summarized in a magisterial fashion by Erik Haarh, can be taken as a literal historical record. The same is even more true of the Bönpo sources regarding the history of the Shangshung kingdom and its religion.

Nevertheless, as Haarh notes, the Tibetan historians use the life and death of King Trigum to mark an important transition in Tibetan religion, which he interprets to be the end of the dominance of the old shamanic religion and the introduction of a "new religion with new rites and a new spiritual content" (Haarh 1969:106). I call this the 'early court religion' (T3) and associate the transition with a growing differentiation between aristocratic and nonaristocratic families, and a growing movement towards state power. The future kings of central Tibet and rulers of the Tibetan Empire (the Yarlung dynasty) would at this time have been only one of a number of aristocratic lineages with regional power bases. Presumably, by this period, some degree of differentiation would have taken place between court religion and folk religion (T4).

With Songtsen Gampo, we enter the times for which we have reliable historical information. The Dunhuang texts, the materials preserved by later Tibetan historians, surviving inscriptions, and the accounts of Islamic and Chinese historians give a relatively firm basis for the sequence of historical events (Beckwith 1987a; Hoffmann 1990), although reconstructing the social and religious structure of the period (T5 to T7) is a more complex task.

For reasons already given in Chapter 1, I have avoided the use of the term Bön in referring to these various pre-Buddhist religious patterns.[2] The *bön* priests who formed part of the court religion at Lhasa (T5) were only one of a number of kinds of priest at this time. While it seems likely that the modern Bön religion has preserved a significant amount of early material, the question of reconstructing early Tibetan religion is essentially independent from that of studying contemporary Bönpo or, for that matter, Bön as it has been since the *terma* findings of the tenth century onwards and its organization as a Buddhist or quasi-Buddhist religious order.

THE ORIGINAL SHAMANIC RELIGION OF THE TIBETANS? (T1)

Reference has already been made, in Chapter 10, to the pair of terms *lha* ('deity') and *la* ('spirit-essence'), and the close relation that appears to exist between them. It would be natural to assume that these two modern concepts, *lha* and *la*, which are not clearly distinguished in the early texts, originated in a single concept. If so, an important clue to the nature of that concept is probably provided by the set of five *gowé lha nga*, the 'five guiding deities,' mentioned in Chapter 10. These gods are local and descent-group deities represented as born within an individual and as protecting that individual throughout life. The similarity between the *gowé lha* and the *la*, also located both within the individual and in external residences such as trees, lakes, and mountains, is striking (Stein 1957, 1972a).

The unitary concept of *la/lha*, if it existed, would have been strikingly similar to concepts found in other shamanic religions, such as the Australian Aborigines. Such concepts represent indigenous vocabularies for speaking about the sociocentric modal states within a shamanic cultural pattern (see Chapter 19 and Samuel 1990). Originally the spirit-essence or life-force within the individual would have been constituted by this set of forces active both within the individual and in the external world, where they were associated in a typical shamanic manner with specific places, primarily the local mountains and lakes. This picture of early Tibetan religion as shamanic is strengthened by Rolf Stein's study of the narratives in which folk-religion rituals are traced back to mythical events in a primal time entirely typical of shamanic thought (Stein 1971).

This picture is also reinforced by the importance of divination within Tibetan society, already apparent in the earliest documents (Spanien 1971b).[3] Shamanic religion is primarily concerned with acting in harmony with the powers that constitute both human beings and the universe they live within. It is these powers that the unitary *la-lha* concept might have symbolized in our postulated early Tibetan religion. At any particular time the situation, which is the pattern of influence of the powers, is favorable or auspicious for certain kinds of action, and unfavorable or inauspicious for others. The primary need is to uncover these patterns and to act in accordance with them. There is also the possibility of influencing the powers in one's own favor, and of increasing the auspiciousness (Tibetan *trashi*) of the situation towards one's intended actions. This was what rituals such as the widespread Tibetan practice of *sang*, the purification-ritual of the local deities, are concerned with.

An 'original' Tibetan religion of this kind would seem plausible in terms of later developments and of partial parallels among relatively stateless Tibeto-Burman societies elsewhere in the Himalayan regions (for example, Gurung, Tamang, or Lepcha). Such an original religion, though equivalent to the Bakhtinian 'ancient matrix' discussed by Mumford (1989:16ff), is not directly attested anywhere in the Himalayan region, and we should be cautious about assuming that it necessarily ever existed in a 'pure' or ideal-typical form. As I commented in Chapter 1 in relation to the 'ancient matrix,' it might be better to treat such a situation as logically rather than chronologically prior to Tibetan religion in the historical period. It provides a way of conceptualizing a cultural pattern that exists in Tibetan societies, being most directly and strongly represented in various forms of Tibetan folk religion (T4, T7).

The Buddhism that came to Tibet from India had already been

strongly influenced by South Asian forms of such shamanic conceptions. I have referred to the shamanic contribution to both early Buddhism (Chapter 20) and Buddhist Tantra (Chapter 22). These elements were to be taken up and reinforced by the Tibetans in later centuries, in large part because they fitted in with a perspective on the world that was already strongly present within indigenous Tibetan cultural patterns and modes of thought.

Traditionally, the first contact with Buddhism took place during the time of King Lhat'o T'ori (five generations before Songtsen Gampo), a reign that Haarh regards as marking "the dawn of historical time in Tibet" (1969:128). The first Buddhist temples are said to have been constructed at the time of Songtsen Gampo, through the encouragement of his Nepalese and Chinese wives. While the traditional life of Songtsen Gampo derives from much later *terma* sources, it is clear from inscriptions of the royal period that he was regarded as being responsible for the introduction of Buddhism into Tibet. It was only several generations later, in the late eighth century, however, that King Tr'isong Deutsen and his successors attempted to establish Buddhism as the Tibetan state religion, that extensive translation work was begun, the Old Tantric lineages introduced, and the first Tibetan monks ordained.

If the Buddhism that came from India to Tibet contained a complex mixture of shamanic and clerical elements, in Tibet it encountered a society that was by and large far more 'shamanic' than India but that had already moved a considerable distance in the direction of the centralized state and clerical religion. In its broad outlines, the interpretation suggested here is as follows. It is assumed that Tibet at this period was still largely 'shamanic' in its mode of operation, but that the Tibetan kings, initially shamanic-type leaders of a tribal confederacy, attempted to move towards a more hierarchical, 'clerical,' politically centralized system. The introduction of writing from India, of elements of bureaucratic organization from China, and the transformation of the pre-Buddhist court religion, associated with the *bön* and *shen* priests (T5), reflects this policy. Centralization was opposed by representatives of the old 'tribal' groupings and by factions at court that were linked to them.[4]

Buddhism came to Tibet from India, China, and Central Asia. In its clerical and rationalized form (T6a) it offered possibilities for the centralizing policy of the early kings, but in the form of the Tantras and other yogic orientations (T6b) it was also capable of being incorporated into the essentially shamanic religion of the majority of the population. With the collapse of the early kingdom, it was this shamanic and Tantric form of Buddhism that survived in Tibet until the renewed contact with India in the early eleventh century. In the remainder of the chapter, we will examine the religion of the early courts, and the initial stages of the arrival of Buddhism in more detail.

RELIGION IN THE EARLY COURTS (T3, T5)

If an actual differentiation between *lha* and *la* took place in historical time, it must have already have been well under way by the time of the transition associated with King Trigum. We might speculate as to the nature of the proto-state religion (T2) before the time of Trigum, which marks the beginning of the court religion proper.

The kings before Trigum were connected to the sky by a cord or rope *(mu)*. The term *mu* also refers to their heavenly home, and they are described as returning there each night. Each king went back to heaven finally when his son achieved his majority, so that these kings left no tombs. Trigum challenged the clan heads to a combat in which the *mu*-cord was broken and the king himself killed (Stein 1972a:48–49). Trigum and the following kings were interred in monumental tombs. Funerary ritual was one component of the new religion associated with Trigum and his successors.

The traditions concerning King Trigum are capable of a variety of interpretations. They seem to imply a transition between a primarily ritual king and one who forms part of a constitutional structure of power, although Haarh is doubtless correct when he notes that these traditions are too late and too inconsistent to allow us to draw any "conclusions as to the relationship between the royal and the sacerdotal power during the development of the [Yarlung] Dynasty" (1969:110). In the post-Trigum period, according to Giuseppe Tucci, the kings continued to be regarded as of divine descent. Power was exercised by a trinity of king, a ritual officiant called the *shennyen* (Tucci and Haarh translate this as 'head shaman') and the chief minister. To quote Haarh's summary:

> As *lhasé,* son of *lha,* the person of the king represented the continually reborn essence of the divine ancestor, who was reincarnated in each

> king at the age of maturity, thirteen years, and remained incarnated in him until his eldest son reached the same age of maturity and ascended the throne as the consecutive link of the ancestral reincarnation. (Haarh 1969:108)

The religion of the early courts such as Yarlung and Shangshung (T3) can be regarded as an adaptation of the shamanic 'ancient matrix' (T1) to the growth of centralized power and literacy. Logically, and probably also historically, the unified *la-lha* concept, representing the unified cultural patterns of a shamanic society (the modal states of Samuel 1990), gradually broke up as centralization took place and particular families and their associated *la* came to enjoy especially high status. The *la-lha* complexes gradually transformed into external gods *(lha)* as they came to be seen as outside the individual rather than both within and outside. Once externalized, their association with the ruling families came to be seen in terms of ancestry from particular mountain-gods (see Kirkland 1982). At the same time, the residue of the internal side of the *la-lha* concept developed into the concept of spirit-force or *la*.

In the texts, the ritual of these early courts is performed by priests called *bön* and *shen*. They seem to have borrowed many of their original techniques and concepts from neighboring literate societies such as Iran, Gilgit, and India. As contacts with these societies grew, knowledge of more sophisticated literate religion would have gradually filtered through to the Tibetan plateau. At that time Buddhism was at the height of its influence both in India and China, and along the Central Asian trade routes (see Guenther 1974b; Dargyay 1978; Klimburg-Salter 1982; Snellgrove 1987).

By the time of Songtsen Gampo, our information about court religion (T5) becomes considerably more solid. Court religion was undoubtedly closely tied up with the maintenance of the royal dynasty. The royal cult was centered around the mountain-gods who were held to be ancestors of the royal lineage. It has been studied in detail by Ariane Spanien (1971b), primarily on the basis of the manuscripts preserved at Dunhuang, a settlement on the trade routes through Central Asia that was controlled by the Tibetans for some time in the seventh and eighth centuries.

Alongside this specifically state ritual, however, Spanien's sources describe much that is close to the modern folk religion as described in

Chapter 10. The local deities, malevolent spirits and complex divinatory techniques of the modern folk religion can all be paralleled in the early texts. The religion of the time of the Tibetan empire retained strong elements of the shamanic 'ancient matrix' (T1) within its new rationalized structure.

The Tibetan court in the seventh to ninth centuries was still in the early stages of centralization and clerical religion, although later Tibetan Buddhist writers probably overstate the 'primitiveness' of pre-Buddhist Tibet.[5] Our information about its administration suggests a military alliance between relatively autonomous 'tribal' groups that only gradually accepted the predominance of the Yarlung dynasty. Powerful members of the ruling families of these tribes, often related to the king through marriage alliances as mother's brothers or *shang*, acted as chief minister at the Yarlung dynasty's court, which moved in the seventh century to a new site, Lhasa. These ministers played a leading role in the various political and religious intrigues of this period, which came to center around the conflict between the supporters of the *bön* and *shen* priests (T5) and the supporters of Buddhism (T6), and among the supporters of various schools of Buddhism (Richardson 1977a).

The process of political centralization was to be interrupted by the division and collapse of the early Tibetan empire after the killing of the anti-Buddhist king Langdarma. No subsequent Tibetan state was to rival the geographical extent of this early empire. The process of fragmentation that began with Langdarma's death was gradually countered from the thirteenth century onwards by a movement towards regional unification, focusing around the two central provinces of Ü and Tsang, but none of these successive regimes was able to maintain an effective administration for more than a couple of generations until the establishment of the Gelugpa monastic regime, with Mongol military backing, in A.D. 1642.

It is in this general political context of lack of centralized political power and continuous rivalry among local aristocratic families that Tibetan religion was gradually to develop into its modern form. As time went on, the *gompa* and other religious institutions themselves became part of the political process, lending their support to one side or another among the nobility, and becoming major estate-owners and political powers in their own right. Before turning to the early stages of this process, we shall look at some of the evidence for the nature of

Buddhism in Tibet before the collapse of the united Tibetan kingdom in A.D. 842.

BUDDHISM IN THE TIBETAN EMPIRE: INSCRIPTIONS AND DOCUMENTS (T6A)

Several inscriptions from the royal period survive, and give important indications of the contemporary attitude to Buddhism. They can best be regarded as a kind of compromise between the orientations of Indian clerical Buddhism (I5a) and those of the shamanic religion of Tibet (T5). They are in no way unorthodox as Buddhist doctrine goes, but the aspects of the teachings that they present give a picture of Buddhism less as an individual search for liberation and more as a shamanic technique for transforming the overall cultural pattern of the Tibetan population.

The well-known Karchung inscription, from the early ninth century (reign of King Sednaleg) is an example. Here the building of temples and other religious foundations by the Tibetan kings is a kind of ritual act bringing about future benefits:

> As for the practice of the religion of the Buddha in this way by successive generations, if it is never destroyed or abandoned, good beyond measure results; but if it is abandoned or destroyed, there come sins without number. . . . But from the time when the king, his sons, and grandsons are young until the time when they become rulers of the kingdom and thereafter, too, teachers of virtue from among the monks shall be appointed and by teaching religion, as much as can be absorbed into the mind, the gate of deliverance for all Tibet through the learning and practice of religion shall not be closed. (Richardson 1973:15–16)

Another, unfortunately fragmentary, text from Dunhuang gives a similar picture:

> [The early kings] received the doctrine and devoted themselves to it and caused it to spread among all creatures. . . . Such wise teachings are the Ocean in which the deeds of ruler and subjects are as Mount Sumeru. The tradition of such actions being long established, the bounds of the dominion increased and the land of Tibet was happy.

> Harvests were good, diseases of men and cattle rare. The sound qualities and right behaviour of the people increased; and, far from shunning the rites of gods and men, they revered them and, clinging even more strongly to those principles, they did not fail in proper respect and affection towards teachers and parents, brothers, sisters, and kinsmen, and to those who through age are in a position of honour. (Richardson 1977b:220–221)

The reference to the 'rites of gods and men,' *lhach'ö mich'ö*, suggests that the anti-Buddhist party had been arguing that the Buddhist teachings were opposed to these already prevailing practices. In later usage, *lhach'ö* refers to Buddhism itself, but at this time it would have meant either the cult of local deities in general, or the cult of the ancestral deities of the royal dynasty. *Mich'ö*, the 'rites,' 'practices,' or 'teachings' of men, is the whole body of myths, stories, proverbs, riddles, songs, and genealogical narratives that defined the proper relationships and behavior among people (Stein 1971:100, 191–199). In other words, *mich'ö* is the body of cultural items that defines the shamanic religion, and the text is stating that Buddhism led to an increase in the observance of these practices.

One of the most interesting documents from this early period is a narrative surviving in nine Dunhuang manuscripts and recently translated into French by Yoshiro Imaeda (Imaeda 1981). This 'Story of the Cycle of Birth and Death,' loosely modeled on the *Gaṇḍavyūha Sūtra*, again dates from around A.D. 800. It begins with the death of a 'god' *(lha)*. The god's son, Rinch'en, the central character in the story, then sets out to find a spiritual teacher who will show him how he can bring his father back to life, meet him, and bring peace and contentment to him.

Rinch'en's search ends when he meets the Buddha Śākyamuni, who explains that birth and death are the result of karma, and neither gods nor human beings within the triple world of *saṃsāra* can escape them. Only the Buddhist teachings and the performance of virtuous actions are of any use in the face of death. Through these, and through the Tantric practice of reciting the formula of Uṣṇīṣavijayā, one can avoid rebirth as a hell-being, *preta*, or animal and attain the higher realms.

As José Cabezón has noted, the 'death of a god' theme is an attack on the cult of the gods, who are portrayed as being in no way free from karma and death (Cabezón 1982). Only the Buddha has such freedom. A major theme of the work is the magical powers displayed by the Buddhist sages met by the hero on his journey, and by the Buddha himself, which as Cabezón observes would go down well in shamanic Tibet. Buddhism can protect one from gods and demons, and enable the acquisition of shamanic powers greater than that of any non-Buddhist shaman.

The Karchung inscription and the first Dunhuang manuscript seem to reflect the Tibetan side of the accommodation between Buddhism and shamanic religion. Buddhism was acceptable as a new, improved shamanic technique, which would maintain the good fortune and welfare of the country without threatening the established order laid down in the past. The 'Story of the Cycle of Birth and Death' is more in the line of Buddhist missionary propaganda. Its survival in several manuscripts may suggest that it was well received. According to the 'Story,' the old powers are not what they claim to be, and only Buddhism can help at the time of death. At the same time, the narrative implies that Buddhism is fully capable of competing on the ground of the old religion, in defending against gods and demons and conferring other 'magical' powers.

Shamanic religion generally does not give much attention to the problem of the fate of the individual after death. There is ritual, often very elaborate, to ensure a proper transition and to protect against the danger associated *with* death, but ideas concerning the after-death state are in most shamanic societies vague and little emphasized. Only the shaman, to the extent that he or she has already overcome death through the shamanic initiation, may be in some sense exempt from dying in the normal way. The special ritual deaths of the Dinka shamans or 'masters of the fishing spear,' which serve as a kind of denial of ordinary death, are an example (Lienhardt 1961:298–319; see Huntington and Metcalf 1980).

The myths in which the early Tibetan kings are described as ascending directly to heaven by the *mu*-cord attached to their heads suggest that they, like many rulers in only partially 'rationalized' states, were regarded as having shamanic powers, symbolized by the supreme power over death itself (Tucci 1955; Stein 1972a). This is a theme that will recur in the later history of Tibetan religion. We have already seen in Chapter 12 that the powers of the Tantric siddhas were closely connected with their mastery of the process of dying. The possession of such mastery by the Buddhist lamas of Tibet was to be of great significance, for example in the development of the *trulku* ('incarnate lama') concept.

In shamanic societies, death is often heavily ritualized, but the main concern is with fear of the spirits of the dead if they are not properly disposed of, rather than the individual survival of the deceased. The emphasis in funerary symbolism is with the preservation and continuity of the surviving community rather than with the dead themselves. The dead, if suitably qualified by their life, can become ancestral spirits such as those found in many African societies, exemplars of the cultural patterns who interfere in the affairs of the living mainly to keep them on the right track. Alternatively they can go into some vague reservoir of spirit-material, to be reborn as members of the group at a later time. They can, however, have a future as individuals only to the extent that the society has given the individual more importance than its fundamental premises can allow.

With the breakdown of the shamanic 'ancient matrix' through new, more individualistic, modes of thinking the survival of the individual after death becomes more of an issue.[6] It is a major theme in the 'Story of the Cycle of Birth and Death,' which suggests that such concerns were becoming prominent among eighth- and ninth-century Tibetans. One of the main functions of Buddhist monks in Tibetan society, as in other Buddhist societies, was to become the performance of funerary ritual.[7]

Further evidence of the importance of shamanic modes of thinking within Tibet at this time can be found in the vocabulary that was used to translate Buddhist concepts. Like the Chinese, but unlike the Buddhists of Sri Lanka and Southeast Asia, the Tibetans translated the Buddhist scriptures into their own language. Consequently, they had to find Tibetan equivalents for the Sanskrit terms for Buddhist philosophical concepts. These equivalents were fixed in the late eighth century, with the compilation of the great Sanskrit-Tibetan vocabulary, the *Mahāvyutpatti* (Sakaki 1962).

I have discussed some of these terms elsewhere, and suggested that *lama* and *sanggyé,* the Tibetan equivalents for 'guru' and 'Buddha,' two of the most central terms of the later Buddhist tradition, both have suggestive connections with key concepts, *la* and *sang,* of the pre-Buddhist shamanic order in Tibet (Samuel 1985:392).[8]

A third term is also worthy of some comment. *Tendrel* is the Tibetan equivalent for *pratītyasamutpāda,* the important early Buddhist concept referring to the relational nature of all phenomena. *Tendrel* is an abbreviation for *tenpar drelwar jungwa* or *gyurwa*, both literal enough translations of the Sanskrit ('arising in mutual connection'). The point is the range of additional meanings that *tendrel* has acquired in Tibetan usage. These center around the idea of 'omen,' especially in the sense of an indication that circumstances are auspicious for a particular action or development. The underlying concept is something like 'connections that are not visible on the surface.'

As I noted above, the concern with omens and divination is characteristic of the shamanic perspective. In the language of my previous book (Samuel 1990), the kind of connections involved are those where a particular set of 'modal states' is coming into manifestation. At one extreme, as in the story of Marpa and Milarepa cited later in this chapter, a whole new cultural pattern may be coming into being within the general social context. More typically, we are concerned with a shift of balance within the repertoire of patterns already prevailing. The *tendrel* is a sign of this, and an indication of the (normally positive) development that is to come. Dream events, apparently chance combinations of words in conversation, the behavior of animals and other natural phenomena can all supply *tendrel.*

OMENS, DIVINATION, AND *TENDREL*

The whole complex of ideas connected with *tendrel* is worth examining more closely, since it has a significant bearing on the whole issue of shamanic religion in Tibet. The importance of omens and divination in the folk religion was discussed at some length in Chapter 10, where I gave a series of examples from Kurt Schwalbe's description of the erection of a *stūpa.* The power to manipulate *tendrel* in one's favor is one of the accomplishments of the Tantric siddha, and may be specified as an objective of Tantric practice.

An example of what is meant by the manipulation of *tendrel* might be Marpa's behavior when first receiving his disciple Milarepa, as described in the well-known *namt'ar* or hagiography of Milarepa by the fifteenth-century yogin Tsangnyön Heruka (see Chapter 26). When Milarepa first arrives at Marpa's residence he meets a monk ploughing a field, who gives him beer and tells him to finish the ploughing.

When he encounters Marpa himself, he recognizes him as the monk he had met in the field. Later Milarepa offers Marpa an empty cooking pot. Marpa declares that the gift is auspicious *(tendrel sang)*[9] and takes it into his shrine room to offer it to his own lama, Nāropa. Marpa strikes the pot to make it ring, then fills it with melted butter. It is only much later, after Milarepa has undergone many severe trials and at last been given the Tantric teachings for which he longs, that Marpa explains the meaning of these actions. His going to meet Milarepa in the disguise of a laborer was a mark of respect for him.

> You drank all the beer I had given you. This beer and the work that you had finished signified that, in penetrating to the heart of the Doctrine, you will grasp the entire teaching. The copper pot you gave with the four handles signified the coming of my four great disciples. Its unblemished surface signified that your mind will become free from blemish and in your body you will have power over the bliss of the fire of *tummo* [see Chapter 12]. The empty pot symbolized the meagreness of your food during the time of your meditation in solitude. But in order to sow the seeds of your long life, of well-being for your many disciples, and of your filling your disciples with the sweetness of the teaching, I with my blessing filled the pot with butter from the altar lamps. I made it ring to signify your future renown. (Tsangnyön Heruka, *Milé Namt'ar*, Lhalungpa 1979:74)

One can see here the confluence between the Indian theory of karma and the Tibetan picture of the shamanic order of the universe. Good actions sow seeds within the karmic continuum *(saṃtāna)* of the individual, which will ripen into their results at a later stage. But in the less individualistic language of the shamanic perspective, it would be more appropriate to speak of the good action as either promoting a positive modal state within the total cultural pattern, or (as here) initiating a new positive cultural pattern. In either case, it renders the forces of the universe favorable to the performer, so that good consequences will naturally emerge.

This kind of perspective underlay the Karchung inscription and the first Dunhuang text as well. It did not contradict the Indian Buddhist understanding of *pratītyasamutpāda*. Instead it linked that understanding with what were already indigenous Tibetan ideas, and in the process laid the foundation for an eventual Tibetan understanding of *pratītyasamutpāda* that brought it back towards the Buddha's original shamanic vision.

In this connection it is worth noting that much of the vocabulary used to describe Tantric ritual remains very close to that evidenced in pre-Buddhist texts such as those studied by Ariane Spanien. In these texts offerings are made to the gods, who are pleased and bestow protection upon their clients. The same mode of discourse applies to the Tantric gods and to the personal lama when treated as a Tantric deity; offerings are made to them, they are visualized as being pleased, and they bestow waves of empowerment or blessing.[10]

The term for the waves of empowerment, *jinlab*, which translates Sanskrit *adhiṣṭhāna*, is literally 'wave of *jin*,' and *jin* is one of the attributes associated with the old Tibetan kings; its original meaning seems to have been the quality of invincibility in battle (Spanien 1971b:339; see also Karmay 1988a:2). Another attribute of the early kings, *tr'ul*, seems to have indicated a set of magical powers, particularly that of moving between earth and sky (Spanien 1971b:336–339). It comes from the same root as *trulpa*, used to refer to the magical powers of the Buddha. Another related term, *trulku*, Sanskrit *nirmāṇakāya*, is the normal term for an 'incarnate lama.' Continued study of the Dunhuang documents will doubtless throw much more light on the process by which the shamanic religion of Tibet was reinterpreted in Buddhist terms, but there is enough to make it clear that this process was a complex one, and to suggest that the new Buddhist terms must have carried over a considerable weight of pre-Buddhist associations.

It is important to realize that 'Buddhism' was not a single, coherent body of beliefs and practices that the Tibetans could simply take over from India or China. Buddhism, even within India alone, was a variety of different things. It included the straightforward moral teachings and devotional practices of lay Buddhism, the sophisticated scholastic and academic tradition of the monastic universities, and the shamanic training of the Tantric siddhas, and no doubt other components as well. The process of translation of terminology was in itself in part a construction of a specifically Tibetan understanding of Buddhism.

The key element in this Tibetan understanding would seem to be that Buddhism offered a more effective control over the order of the universe than was available from the older cults. This control was achieved in two ways:through the lama's Tantric ritual to control the deities and demons of the folk-religion, and through the moral teachings on virtuous and nonvirtuous actions. In addition, the growing concern with individual survival, doubtless fueled by the arrival of the Indian concept of a continuing cycle of rebirth, led to an interest in Buddhism as an answer to the problem of what happened to the individual at death. If the 'control of the universe' orientation led to a shamanic and collective approach to karma and causation, the 'survival after death' orientation led to a rationalizing, individual and protoclerical approach, based on the accounting of good and bad actions within the continuity of the individual's consciousness.

For the rulers of Tibet, there would have been both shamanic and clerical (or 'rationalized') understandings of Buddhism. Within the shamanic framework, the establishment of proper practices of behavior, as prescribed by Buddhism, would lead to the prosperity of society through the attainment of balance between the modal states making up the overall cultural pattern. Within the rationalized and individual framework, Buddhist morality could help secure the royal power, but only provided that the Buddhist shamans did not become a rival center of power in their own right. It is not being suggested that this second orientation could not have arisen within a shamanic society. The shamanic approach at most weakens the individual motivation by reinforcing the collective and sociocentric aspects of the cultural pattern (see Samuel 1990:93–99). Contact with the rationalized and centralized societies surrounding Tibet can, however, only have strengthened the individual and rationalizing orientation.

Tr'isong Detsen, king of Tibet in the late eighth century, is traditionally said to have decided between two forms of Buddhism, represented by Indian and Chinese teachers respectively, at a council held either at Lhasa or at the newly founded first Tibetan monastic *gompa* of Samyé. Tr'isong Detsen is said to have chosen in favor of the 'Indian' version, represented by Śāntarakṣita's disciple Kamalaśīla, and against the 'Chinese' version, represented by a teacher known as Hashang Mahāyāna. While descriptions of this event given by the later Tibetan historians have been open to question since Paul Demiéville's publication of a pro-Chinese account from Dunhuang (Demiéville 1954; see Snellgrove 1987:430–436), the incident was to be important for how the Tibetans would later understand their history, and it provides the earliest real evidence for the relationship between shamanic and rationalizing tendencies on the one hand, and political power on the other.

INDIAN AND CHINESE BUDDHISM: THE COUNCIL OF SAMYÉ

The standard Tibetan historical tradition, represented by writers such as Putön and Gö Lotsawa, associates the arrival of Buddhism in Tibet with the marriage alliances formed by King Songtsen Gampo with the Chinese and Nepalese courts in the early seventh century (for example, Putön, *Ch'öjung* = Obermiller 1932–1933, vol. 2, 184–185; Gö Lotsawa, *Debt'er Ngönpo* = Roerich 1976). Over the next century and a half, Buddhists both from China and from India and Nepal were active in Tibet, until the Tibetan king, Tr'isong Detsen, in the traditional account, decided in favor of the Indian form at a council held at the first Tibetan monastery of Samyé. Thereafter the Tibetan form of Buddhism followed the Indian pattern.

The Chinese Buddhism that was rejected is described in these texts as close to some forms of Ch'an (corresponding to Japanese Zen) in that it counseled the irrelevance of the gradual approach to Buddhahood and of moral observance. Instead it taught a sudden awakening of the Enlightened state through the absence of mental activity. Since Tr'isong Detsen became regarded as an emanation of the bodhisattva Mañjuśrī, a doctrine which will be discussed in Chapter 25, his decision was regarded by later authors as especially authoritative.

As Guenther, Dargyay, and others have noted, there are problems with this traditional historical account, arising from the orientation of the historians, who wanted to make Tibet before the arrival of Buddhism, and especially of what they regarded as the approved varieties of Indian Buddhism, appear 'uncouth and savage' (Guenther 1974b:81; Dargyay 1978; N. Norbu 1981). This standard history describes only one contact with Buddhism before the early seventh century, namely the miraculous appearance of a casket containing two Sūtras and a golden *stūpa* some five generations earlier, at the time of King Lhat'o T'ori. This is itself implausible, as Guenther notes, given that Tibet at this stage was virtually surrounded by Buddhist countries. What is of more concern here is that the picture of Tibetan Buddhism in the seventh and eighth centuries as consisting exclusively of an Indian and orthodox stream and a Chinese and quietist stream, the latter disappearing after the Council of Samyé, is much oversimplified.

In fact, there survive writings by the main Indian and Chinese speakers at the Samyé debate, Kamalaśīla and the Hashang Mahāyāna. When these are examined in the light of the later historical tradition it is clear that what that tradition represents is in many respects a retelling of the debate from the point of view of later apologists. These later writers identified themselves with the Indian parties, and accused their opponents of continuing the mistaken doctrines of the Chinese party.[11] Their attacks were aimed most generally at the Nyingmapa order, which claimed to go back to the time of the early kings. Sakya Pandita, however, accused various Kagyüdpa schools of committing the same errors. It seems that in actuality Hashang Mahāyāna's position may not have been unequivocally dismissed, and that his arguments were in any case more subtle than later Tibetan scholars were prepared to allow.[12]

The motives behind these later accounts will be considered when we turn to the period from which they came. We are left, however, with the question of what the debate of Samyé was about and why it resulted in a decision in favor of the Indian party, assuming that this much is historical fact.

As Guenther notes, the opposition between 'sudden' and 'gradual' accounts of Enlightenment is really a distinction between describing the view from the goal, and emphasizing the gradual approach to it (Guenther 1974b). We could rephrase this as a distinction between the perspective of the shaman, who is primarily interested in the state to be achieved, and the cleric, who is primarily concerned with providing a rationalized account of how it is achieved, and with preventing its misuse by insisting on a thorough moral training before it is attained.

Indian Buddhism itself includes both types of descriptions. Texts such as the *Abhidharmakośa* contain elaborate descriptions of the stages of path, while others such as the *Uttaratantra*, the principal text of the *tathāgatagarbha* theory, describe Buddhahood as potential to be uncovered within anyone or anything, and the Tantric siddhas often speak in similar terms. Both sides were also present in China, even among the Ch'an Buddhists. The various Ch'an schools of Chinese Buddhism in the eighth century, while sharing the Ch'an emphasis on meditation as the center of the path (the word Ch'an derives from the Sanskrit *dhyāna*, meditation), did not reject the need for the observance of Buddhist morality, and had a variety of positions on how this was related to the attainment of insight.

In Tibet, at this time, shamanic approaches to Buddhism (T6b) seem to have been represented by teachers deriving from both Chinese and Indian traditions, and to have included both Tantric and Ch'an-like elements. There are suggestions that teachers associated with the so-called Old Tantras, some at least of which date back to this period, did have connections with China, but they certainly had Indian connections as well (Guenther 1974b; Snellgrove 1987).

What would really seem to have been at issue at Samyé was not a struggle between Chinese and Indian Buddhism as such, but between a Buddhism that emphasized the moral teachings for the laity (T6a), and a Buddhism that emphasized the shamanic vision, and so stressed meditation, Tantric and otherwise, and the magical powers to be obtained from it (T6b). In this connection it is worth noting that the early kings appear to have controlled the translation and practice of Tantric texts quite strictly (Karmay 1980a:151, 1985, 1988a:4–6).

> [D]uring the royal period, Tantras were looked upon with suspicion and their spread subjected to restriction . . . The 'Religious Council' presided over by the abbot of Samyé was a very powerful and fastidious body which certainly tried to control the spread of Tantric teachings in the country. The other main task of this body was to maintain the monastic communities on the basis of the Vinaya as pure as possible. . . . In spite of the watchfulness of the 'Religious Council,' one would expect that certain people followed the Tantric teachings all the same . . . It became the dominant faith during the period following the collapse of the monastic institution and the central authority. (Karmay 1988a:6)

It is hardly surprising that the king would favor the moral varieties of Buddhism against the potentially antinomian, the 'tame' against the 'wild,' since the former reinforced his position and the latter threatened it. In supporting Kamalaśīla, Śāntarakṣita's student and a proponent of conventional Buddhist morality and the 'gradual path,' against a Chinese teacher whose position in these respects was at least somewhat less clear-cut, he was delivering a message about the kind of Buddhism compatible with a centralized state that was to be repeated in various forms, with varying degrees of success, by many later rulers of Tibet.

Tr'isong Deutsen, then, was indicating a preference for 'clerical' Buddhism (T6a) over 'shamanic' Buddhism (T6b). His decision was not a rejection of Tantric Buddhism itself, and it would seem that even those court circles who wanted a fully clerical and so controllable religion had accepted the need for some of the more shamanic aspects, if only as a temporary expedient. The later Tibetan tradition describes Tr'isong Deutsen as a Tantric adept and a disciple of Guru Rimpoch'e. Tr'isong Deutsen's verdict, however, did imply that those aspects of the shamanic tradition that might conflict with conventional morality were to be held severely in check. Shamanic religion had to be subordinated to the gradual path of moral and ethical discipline taught by Śāntarakṣita and Kamalaśīla, and deriving from the academic and clerical curriculum of the North Indian Buddhist universities.

Thus, in the eighth century, both clerical and shamanic Buddhist religious patterns were already present in Tibet. Their mutual reactions and relationships were to shape the future history of Tibet, in combination with the political circumstances that helped to shape them and which in turn they helped to shape.

The political circumstances immediately following the collapse of the early kingdom in A.D. 842 were, however, to be more propitious to shamanic than to clerical religion. The decline of clerical Buddhism at this time is traditionally attributed to the persecution by the last king, Langdarma, but it would probably have followed on the fall of the united Tibetan state in any case. The state's economic and material support for clerical Buddhist institutions such as Samyé must have vanished within a few years.

Buddhism, to the extent that it was to survive the next 150 years at all, did so in its most 'shamanic' forms. The clerical tradition would only be effectively reimplanted in Tibet in the eleventh century, through the sponsorship of a surviving offshoot of the royal dynasty in West Tibet and other lay patrons in central Tibet. These developments will be traced in the next chapter.

CULTURAL PATTERNS

The precise nature of Tibetan society and Tibetan religion at the time of the arrival of Buddhism is a matter for speculation. In an article some years ago (Samuel 1985), I argued for an initial 'shamanic' religion close to that of contemporary stateless, preliterate societies. In the present chapter, I have suggested that such a situation (T1) would have undergone considerable development by the time of the court and folk religion of the Shangshung state and its neighbors (T3, T4), the immediate predecessors of the first Tibetan empire.

'Shamanic' aspects are nevertheless clear in the documentary evidence from the first Tibetan empire (T5, T6) and would certainly have characterized the undocumented folk religion of its time (T7). Buddhism, both clerical and shamanic (T6a, T6b), entered into this general context and its initial adoption has to be understood in terms both of the general shamanic orientation of Tibetan society and the process of clericalization that began at the Shangshung court (T3) and developed further in the Tibetan empire after A.D. 625.

24

Tibet: The Local Hegemonic Period

During the ninth to fourteenth centuries, the various forms of Buddhism, both 'shamanic' and 'clerical,' became firmly established in Tibet, and began to assume the place in the social and political system that they were to occupy into modern times. With the collapse of the early kingdom, a pattern in which centers of local authority competed for some degree of wider influence was to hold sway. This is what Turrell Wylie referred to as the 'Local Hegemonic Period,' a label I have adopted above (Wylie 1963). The new Buddhist and Bön religious centers (T8, T9, T10) were, to begin with, under the patronage of these local aristocrats and big landowners. They rapidly became involved in the competition for political influence in their own right.

At the beginning of this period, however, there was hardly a monastic tradition worth speaking of in Tibet, and no religious centers with any significant political role. Buddhist monasticism in Tibet was initiated, according to the traditional account, with the ordination of seven Tibetans as monks at Samyé, but it only just survived the following two centuries. The fourteenth-century historian Putön tells how the monastic ordination was transmitted onwards through the

TABLE 5.
Cultural Patterns in Chapter 24

Local Hegemonic Period, A.D. 841 to A.D. < 1276

- T7 Folk religion
- T8 Old Tantric and *terma* complex
  - T8a Hereditary priest lineages
    - T8a1 Buddhist <T6b
    - T8a2 Bönpo <T6b, T5
- T9 Kadampa monks
- T10 New Tantric complex
  - T10a New Tantric priests and yogins (early Sakya masters, Marpa, Milarepa, Ky'ungpo Neljor, etc.) <I4a2
  - T10b Tibetan Monk-New Tantra syntheses; growth of clerical *gompa*
    - T10b1 Sakya synthesis (*Lamdré* system) <I4a2
    - T10b2 Kagyüdpa synthesis <T9, T10
  - T10c Chöd yogins <I4a2

ninth-century monk Gongpa Rabsel with the assistance of some Chinese monks, although he admits a few pages later that the details have been contested (Putön, *Ch'öjung* = Obermiller 1932–1933, vol. 2, 201–211; see Tucci 1980:17–19). Evidently the number of monks in Tibet in the ninth century came close to zero, although there is still a Tibetan tradition of monastic ordination that is traced back to Gongpa Rabsel, as well as a later one that goes back to the arrival of the 'Kashmiri Pandit,' Śākyaśrībhadra in 1204.

The form of Buddhism that survived and to some extent flourished (T8) was that closest to the 'shamanic' folk religion of Tibet. It was a form of Tantric Buddhism, continued by hereditary lineages of lay Tantric practitioners who provided ritual services to the surrounding population. It is with these hereditary Buddhist shamans, the ancestors of what was to become the Nyingmapa religious order (T8a1), and with their non-Buddhist counterparts in what was to become the Bönpo order (T8a2), that this chapter begins. It was only at the end of the period that the Buddhist academic and clerical tradition and Buddhist monasticism began to establish themselves effectively within Tibetan society.

Hereditary lineages of Bönpo followers, who claimed continuity from the pre-Buddhist religion, developed along with the early Buddhist hereditary shamanic lineages. The Bönpo in later centuries reckoned six main hereditary lineages, which became the basis of later Bönpo practice (for example, Karmay 1972:3–13). These lineages are traced back to Shench'en Luga, an early Bönpo teacher who, according to Karmay, played a central part in creating the organized religious order of Bön, and to his immediate disciples and contemporaries (Karmay 1975a:183–186; see also Smith 1970a:6 n. 13). Unfortunately, the dating of Shench'en Luga and of the early Bönpo teachers in general is uncertain, and the dates accepted in the earlier writings of Karmay, Snellgrove, and Kvaerne, based on the chronological table of Nyima Tendzin (compiled in 1842), now seem likely to be too early. According to this table, Shench'en Luga lived from 996 to 1035, but a recently studied and possibly more reliable chronological table, that of Ts'ultr'im Gyants'en (compiled in 1804), places him 120 years later, from 1116 to 1155 (Kvaerne 1990a).[1]

HEREDITARY SHAMANIC LINEAGES: THE ORIGINS OF NYINGMAPA AND BÖNPO (T8A1, T8A2)

In a 'shamanic' religious system, ritual knowledge and shamanic ability are frequently regarded as property to be handed down within the family or passed on to others only through payment and a protracted apprenticeship. There was already something of this attitude to the methods and procedures of the Tantras among the Indian siddhas, where the student had to undergo a long apprenticeship and often pay substantially for teaching and initiation. In Tibet, this seems by the tenth and eleventh centuries to have become a regular pattern. In historical texts such as Gö Lotsawa's 'Blue Annals' (*Debt'er Ngönpo* = Roerich 1976) and in the biographies of the early lamas there is frequent reference to hereditary lama families, and a regular assumption that the techniques would be handed on through the family (T8a).

The well-known eleventh-century yogin Milarepa, for example, is described as coming from one of these hereditary families (Tsangnyön Heruka, *Milé Namt'ar* = Lhalungpa 1979:13), though the last to practice the family business had been his great-grandfather, who settled in Gungt'ang where he "was called to the houses of people living there to read the sacred books, offer sacrificial effigies, protect them from hailstorms, and save children from evil spirits" (1979:14). Milarepa's own teacher Marpa did not have such a background, and

Marpa's efforts to set up a hereditary lineage were prevented by the death of his sons, but his disciple Ngog founded a family lineage, which by the fifteenth century had included eleven generations of teachers (Roerich 1976:406ff).

We have already met two of the most famous of these hereditary lineages in Chapters 3 and 4, the K'ön family of Sakya and the lama-princes of Dergé, both of whom claimed genealogies stretching back to the times of the early kings and to mountain-god ancestors (Cassinelli and Ekvall 1969; Amipa 1976; Chogay Trichen 1983; Kolmaš 1968). These two families were in later times to preside over large monastic *gompa* and wield great secular power, but there would have been nothing on this scale in the ninth and tenth centuries. The hereditary lineages of that time would have been much more modest in importance, perhaps resembling the hereditary lamas described by Snellgrove and Jest in areas such as the remote valley of Tarap (see Chapter 17). The most successful of these hereditary lamas would have gradually built up small communities of lay followers and disciples, who would not necessarily have taken *gelong* vows (T8a).

The rituals performed by these early Tibetan Buddhist practitioners were based on the 'Old' or Nyingma Tantras. As we saw in Chapter 12, a few later Tibetan scholars rejected these 'Old Tantric' lineages as dubious or inauthentic on the grounds that no Sanskrit texts relating to these Tantras had survived. Western authors have tended to echo these opinions, and have given much more scholarly attention to the texts of the 'New Tantra' lineages. The Tibetans received these from India in the eleventh and twelfth centuries, and many have Sanskrit originals and commentaries. As Gene Smith and David Snellgrove have both pointed out, however, there is good reason to believe that at least some of the 'Old Tantras' did have lost originals in Sanskrit and other languages, as their proponents claim, and that these are in fact Buddhist Tantric texts with many features in common with the 'New Tantra' tradition (Smith 1970a:68; Snellgrove 1987:458–459; Martin 1987:183).[2] For the Tibetans of that time and most Tibetans of subsequent times as well, the question of scholarly authenticity was irrelevant, since the authenticity of the practices was demonstrated if they worked, in other words if they brought about the desired transformations within the practitioners and within the external world.

The *kama* (i.e., orally transmitted) lineages of the Nyingma Tantras, which the Tibetans hold to have been passed on in continual succession from the time of the early kings, formed the basic ritual repertoire for the hereditary Buddhist Tantric practitioners of the ninth and tenth centuries. From the eleventh century onwards, a second class of lineages began to appear that was to become of great importance for the Nyingmapa tradition. These lineages, known as *terma*, were also held to date from the time of the early kings and are particularly associated with the great siddha Padmasambhava (Guru Rimpoch'e) who visited Tibet at the end of the eighth century A.D.

The *terma* lineages and their discoverers, the *tertön*, have already been discussed at some length in Chapter 16. Their origins of the *terma* represent a characteristically shamanic mode of revelation. The *terma* lineages were associated with texts and other objects said to have been written by Guru Rimpoch'e and his circle and hidden to await discovery at an appropriate time. The *tertön*, their discoverers, were held to be rebirths of actual disciples of Guru Rimpoch'e, who received the teachings directly from him in their previous lives. The Nyingmapa tradition in later times was thus made up of two components, the *kama* lineages, which were held to go back through a direct succession of teachers to the time of the early kings, and the *terma* lineages (see Chapters 12 and 16), which continued to be discovered at frequent intervals into the modern period.

Terma do not necessarily involve, in the Tibetan conception, the discovery of actual physical texts. This may occur in some cases *(sater, ch'uter)* but the whole *terma* concept has more to do with visionary and shamanic revelation than with the material discovery of hidden texts. The locations where the *terma* are found are often more symbolic than real and the texts are said to be written in obscure, ancient, or symbolic scripts. Frequently, too, the discovered object provides only a stimulus to the discovery of the actual *terma*, by recalling to the mind of the *tertön* the occasion on which Padmasambhava gave the original teaching. Many *terma*, especially in later times, are explicitly classified as *gongter*, 'treasures' hidden in the mind of the disciple, a term that does not imply any physical textual transmission. *Terma* lineages may also be supplemented through *dagnang*, 'pure vision,' a term referring to direct revelation from a Tantric deity.

The whole concept of *terma* revelation closely resembles that of the Mahāyāna Sūtras and the Tantras themselves, and, as in those cases, there is little doubt that many *terma* texts were visionary creations through which their discoverers were able to found new lineages of practice, or modify existing lineages. In either case they produced a version of the teachings more appropriate to the times and place in which they were living.

The first Buddhist *terma* were found by Sanggyé Lama (ca. 1000–1080) in Lowo Gekar (in the south of Mustang, in modern Nepal) in the early eleventh century (Dargyay 1978:92–93; D. Jackson 1976:42). The Bönpo also have *terma* (see Karmay 1975a:187–188), and it is possible that they may have originated the concept, although the previously accepted date of 913 for the first Bönpo *terma* is based upon Nyima Tendzin's chronological table, which no longer seems reliable (Kvaerne 1990a). The first major discovery of Bönpo texts was made by Shench'en Luga (see above) in 1017 according to Nyima Tendzin and 1137 according to Tsultr'im Gyants'en (see Karmay 1972:117ff, 1975a:187–188; Kvaerne 1990a). This single discovery constitutes the main part of the Bönpo canon. Bönpo *terma* all involved physical discoveries of texts but the Bönpo lamas also had a category of 'orally transmitted texts' or *nyengyüd,* which were discovered within the mental continuum of later lamas in a rather similar fashion to the Buddhist *gongter,* as well as other *nyengyüd* texts handed down through a series of named teachers (Karmay 1975a:188).

The Bönpo scriptures claim as their origin a teacher named Shenrab Miwo. This teacher's name means something like 'Supreme *shen*-priest.' He is held to have lived in the land of Tagsig, usually identified with Iran, well before the time of Śākyamuni. He is described as visiting Tibet and predicting the later spread of his teachings in that region.

Shenrab's biography is strongly influenced by the canonical accounts of the life of the Buddha Śākyamuni, although it may reflect genuine influences on early Bön from Iran or other places to the West (Karmay 1972, 1975a; Snellgrove 1967a; but see Kvaerne 1987). With the exception of a few texts held to have been continuously transmitted, all the works attributed to Shenrab are *terma* or 'rediscovered' *nyengyüd* (Kvaerne 1974).

Western research into Bön is only just beginning,[3] and it is becoming apparent that the Bönpo scriptures, despite the heavy Buddhist influence throughout, are much more than simple copies of Buddhist texts. There were evidently close links between Nyingmapa Buddhists and Bönpo teachers in the early period. Some discoverers of *terma* found both Bönpo and Nyingmapa texts. Thus, the well-known Buddhist *tertön* Dorje Lingpa (1346–1405) seems to have also been active as a Bönpo *tertön* under the name of Yungdrung Lingpa (Blondeau 1982–1983:130). There is even disagreement about whether such an important early figure as the monk Gongpa Rabsel was Bönpo or Buddhist (Karmay 1972:xxxvi, 107 n. 1).

THE BEGINNINGS OF DZOGCH'EN IN TIBET

The close connections between Nyingmapa and Bönpo teachers is evident from what was to become regarded as the special property of both orders, the Dzogch'en or 'Great Perfection' teachings. We have already briefly examined one short Dzogch'en text, Göddemchen's *Kunsang Mönlam*, in Chapter 1, and we will be looking at another in Chapter 27. The origins of Dzogch'en are obscure and perhaps go back to the mixture of Indian and Chinese shamanic currents in eighth-century Tibet (see Prats 1978; Hanson-Barber 1984, 1986; Karmay 1975b, 1985 and 1988a; Kvaerne 1983). While there are some Dzogch'en Tantras dating from the early period, Dzogch'en *terma* texts began to appear in both Nyingmapa and Bönpo circles from the eleventh century onwards, and soon became very numerous.[4] The close cooperation between some Nyingmapa and Bönpo lamas at these period seems to have declined in later centuries, although some east Tibetan Bönpo were involved in the Rimed movement in the nineteenth century (see Chapter 27).

Dzogch'en is the point of greatest conflict between the Nyingmapa-Bönpo group and the other religious orders. For Nyingmapa and Bönpo followers, the Dzogch'en lineages represent the highest teachings. Both orders, as we saw in Chapter 12, have classifications of the teachings into nine 'vehicles,' with Dzogch'en as the ninth and ultimate vehicle. The New Tantra traditions did not have a formal place for Dzogch'en, and reacted to it in various ways. The Sakyapa (see below) retained some Old Tantra practices, but the great thirteenth-century Sakyapa scholar Sakya Pandita (an early representative of T10) attacked Dzogch'en, along with various Kagyüdpa teachings, as invalid teachings affiliated to the Chinese doctrines that were rejected at the Samyé debate (R. Jackson 1982). Later Sakyapa lamas took a more tolerant attitude, and the nineteenth-century Sakyapa lama Jamyang Ky'entsé Ongpo was one of the leaders of the Rimed movement, within which Dzogch'en had a central place. The Kagyüdpa, who were, on the whole, more yogic and less scholastic in their general orientation than the Sakyapa, were sympathetic towards Dzogch'en from the beginning, and important Kagyüdpa lamas such as Karma Pakshi (1204–1283), Tsele Nats'og Rangdröl (b. 1608), and Karma Ch'agmed (1613–1678) developed a syncretic orientation based on the equivalence of Mahāmudrā (Ch'agch'en) and Dzogch'en (Kapstein 1985:370; Blondeau 1983–1984:133–138). By the mid-twentieth century, most Sakyapa and Kagyüdpa lamas were at least in part products of the nineteenth-century Rimed movement, in which Dzogch'en and Old Tantra lineages were included on an equal footing to the New Tantra material. The strongest opposition to Dzogch'en and to the Nyingmapa teachings in general was to come from the more purist and clerical elements among the Gelugpa, although the 5th Dalai Lama was a noted Dzogch'en practitioner, as well as a *tertön*, and some Gelugpa lamas have followed his example.

The discomfort of the more 'clerical' orders with Dzogch'en is in part connected with its tendency to use positive imagery to describe the state of Enlightenment. Here we return to the question of different conceptualizations of Enlightenment and their social and political implications, introduced in Chapter 21 in relation to Madhyamaka, Yogācāra, and *tathāgatagarbha* teachings. Essentially, Dzogch'en is a formless and nonconceptual system of meditation, conceived of, at least in the later Nyingmapa and Bönpo schemes, as the final stage of Tantric practice, and as going beyond the transformational techniques of Tantra itself to the goal of the Enlightened state. The Dzogch'en texts, however, postulate a primordial purity (*kadag, dödmé shi,* etc.) on the basis of which both Enlightenment and the deluded appearance of *saṃsāra* have arisen. These and other Dzogch'en terms can be interpreted as implying some kind of positive conceptualization of Enlightenment.

How much validity there really is in such an interpretation is difficult to judge. Terms such as *kadag* are used differently by different authors and do not necessarily mean the same through their entire history. There is no doubt about the positive phraseology in one fundamental Tantra of the Dzogch'en tradition, the *Kunched Gyelpo* or 'All-Performing King.' Karmay has compared the language of the *Kunched Gyelpo* with the *prakṛti* doctrine of the Hindu Sāṃkhya philosophy

(Karmay 1975b), but Lipman and Martin have both asserted the fundamentally Buddhist nature of the text (Lipman 1987; Martin 1987:199, 204 n. 81).

The 'All-Performing King' is a kind of personification of the underlying basis of Buddhahood. He is immanent in all phenomena and prior to all Buddhas, and his entourage, consisting of emanations of his own nature, constitutes the universe (Dargyay 1985a, 1985c). It seems plausible to view this text as another example of the tendency of the more shamanic members of the Buddhist tradition, those more concerned with attaining the shamanic vision than with defining its nature rationally and avoiding its misuse, to use positive phraseology to describe the Enlightened state.

The positive language of some Dzogch'en texts, and especially the personified role of the 'All-Performing King,' would have been particularly compatible with Bönpo thought, which included the concept of a supreme deity, perhaps taken from Indian or Iranian sources. The Bönpo supreme deity was called Kuntu Sangpo ('All-Good'), which was also the name of the Buddha-form by whom the Nyingma Tantras were revealed (see Chapter 1; Snellgrove 1961; Karmay 1975a).

In fact, Nyingmapa writers in general often placed more emphasis on the Yogācāra conceptualizations of the path than on the *via negativa* of the Madhyamaka, although this is by no means a universal rule. For example, Longch'en Rabjampa's *Ngelso Korsum* (translated by Herbert Guenther as *Kindly Bent to Ease Us*, Guenther 1975b), a text which, like most of Longch'en Rabjampa's writings, is grounded in the Dzogch'en perspective, is presented in terms of the Yogācāra account of *sem* or 'mind' (= Skt. *citta*). A contrasting case is Lama Ju Mip'am, the most important Nyingmapa scholar of the late nineteenth century and a prominent member of the Rimed movement (see Chapter 27), who argued for a Madhyamaka interpretation of the Nyingmapa teachings, in this respect opposing the tendency of other Rimed teachers such as the Kagyüdpa lama Jamgön Kongtrul to employ more positive *(shentong)* phraseology.

Another important idea in Dzogch'en, both Nyingmapa and Bönpo, was that of the 'rainbow body' or *jalü*, into which the physical body of the Dzogch'en siddha dissolves at death. There are similarities here to the idea found among the New Tantra circles of the Mahāmudrā adept disappearing into the sky *(k'achöd)* rather than physically dying. Both concepts have obvious linkages to the shamanic world view, and at least one later Tibetan scholar noted the similarity to the old Tibetan belief of the kings returning bodily to heaven, mentioned in Chapter 23.[5]

THE KINGS OF PURANG, ATĪŚA, AND THE KADAMPA ORDER (T9)

The royal lineages did not disappear entirely with the collapse of the kingdom, and several branches of the royal family survived in parts of west Tibet (see D. Jackson 1976, 1984; Petech 1977) and also in the east.[6] One of the west Tibetan branches, the kings of Purang, was to be responsible for the revival of the monastic and academic side of Buddhism in Tibet in the late tenth and early eleventh century.

I mentioned in Chapter 23 that the early kings controlled the translation and practice of Tantra strictly (see Karmay 1980a:151, 1980b, 1985:276). The kings of Purang seem to have shared their doubts about Tantra. At any rate they attempted to control the activities of the hereditary shamans who represented the Tantric tradition in their time. The following comes from a decree by the first of these pro-Buddhist kings, Yeshe Öd, who lived in the late tenth century and himself became a monk:

> Now as the good karma of living beings is exhausted and the law of the kings is impaired,
> False doctrines called Dzogch'en are flourishing in Tibet.
> Their views are false and wrong.
> Heretical Tantras, pretending to be Buddhist, are spread in Tibet . . .
> Village abbots, your tantrist way of practising,
> Will shock if the people of other countries hear of it.
> These practices of you who say 'we are Buddhists,'
> Show less compassion than a demon of action.
> More avaricious for meat than a hawk or a wolf.
> More lusty than a mere donkey or an ox . . .
> Those who wish to be Mahāyānist
> Must accumulate the two kinds of merit and abandon the notion of grasping and that which is to be grasped.
> Must practice the ten Pāramitā, alms giving, etc.,

Must achieve all the practices of a Bodhisattva.
Must accomplish the welfare of living beings through love and compassion.
If you practise religion in this way, then you will be Mahāyānist!
—Sent to the Tibetan tantrists by the king of Purang, the Lha Lama. (Karmay 1980a:154–155)

The kings of Purang seem to have been particularly opposed to the practices of *jorwa* ('union') and *drölwa* ('liberation'), associated with the Guhyagarbha (Sangwé Nyingpo) Tantra, one of the principal Old Tantras of the Mahāyoga class and a primary source for Dzogch'en itself (Karmay 1988a:10, 139ff; on the Guhyagarbha see also Martin 1987). Karmay interprets *jorwa* as Tantric practices involving sexual union, and *drölwa* as the sacrifice of animals and perhaps even of human beings. Guenther's work on the Guhyagarbha, which relies heavily on the writings of the fourteenth-century lama Longch'en Rabjampa and other later commentators, interprets *jorwa* and *drölwa* as primarily internal processes of "fusion . . . [w]ith the primal source" and "release" of the energy frozen within the rigidity of emotional structures (Guenther 1984:156–157). As in India, there may have been people who took what was meant symbolically in a literal sense. Yeshe Öd's reference to Dzogch'en is slightly ambiguous, since it could also be translated "False doctrines are flourishing in Tibet under the name of Dzogch'en," which would not condemn Dzogch'en itself (see Karmay 1975b:150–151). The general drift of his language is quite clear, however. Lamas were expected to behave in a disciplined and clerical manner, and the Pāramitāyāna (Sūtra) practices were to be the basis, not the Tantras.

To combat these alleged misinterpretations of the teachings, Yeshe Öd and his grand-nephew Changch'ub Öd sent a group of Tibetans to study in Kashmir. The best known of these is the 'great translator' Rinch'en Sangpo (see Snellgrove and Skorupski 1980:83–116). Later, Changch'ub Öd arranged for the great Indian scholar Atīśa (Dīpaṅkaraśrījñāna) to be invited to Tibet. It was through the activities of Atīśa that the clerical or monastic tradition of Buddhism was firmly established in Tibet.

Atīśa was, however, not simply a celibate monk practicing the Sūtra teachings. He was a representative of the combined Sūtra and

Tantra approach (I4a2) and a highly developed Tantric practitioner. In this he was perhaps a typical product of the Indian monastic universities of the early eleventh century. His initial training, according to the Tibetan accounts, was Tantric. Later he became a monk, but continued to study with Vajrayāna teachers, and for many years was a senior teacher at the Buddhist university of Vikramaśīla. He traveled widely and studied with many gurus, and is regarded as having brought together two major streams of the Mahāyāna teachings, that concerned with insight into reality *(prajñā)* and that concerned with the creation of *bodhicitta* (Roerich 1976:241–243; Ruegg 1981; Chattopadhyaya 1967; Eimer 1977, 1979, 1982; Thubten Kalsang 1983; Berzin 1972).

These two orientations correspond to *prajñā* and *upāya*, 'insight' and 'method,' the duality represented by the male and female deities of Tantric practice. The terms *prajñā* and *upāya* can be understood in terms of the Pāramitāyāna (non-Tantric) teachings, in which case *upāya* corresponds to the bodhisattva's development of the altruistic motivation of *bodhicitta* and of the first five of the six *pāramitā* or Perfections, but they attain their full meaning for the Tibetans in terms of the Tantras.

Consequently when the Tibetans describe Atīśa as bringing together these two complementary aspects, it is also implied that he brought together the Sūtra and Tantra teachings. As we have seen, Sūtra and Tantra had been separate in the early royal period (T6a, T6b) and the surviving tradition of monastic ordination seems to have remained distinct from the hereditary Tantric lamas of what would eventually become the Nyingmapa and Bönpo orders. This reflected both the early kings' preference for the Sūtra teachings and the nature of the early Tantric lineages introduced by Padmasambhava. In the meantime, however, the siddha movement in India itself had moved closer to the clerical norm of the universities, with men such as Virūpa and Nāropa combining clerical and siddha training, and respectable clerics such as Atīśa having a substantial Tantric component in their background and practice (see Chapter 22).

Atīśa's arrival thus opened up a new set of possibilities for Tibetan religion. His presence inaugurated a new cultural pattern within which Tibetan practitioners could attempt a synthesis of clerical and shamanic approaches. Further moves in the same direction would soon follow.

After spending some time in western Tibet, Atīśa moved to central Tibet where he spent the last twelve or so years of his life. Here he founded the monastic *gompa* of Nyet'ang, near Lhasa, with the aid of his wealthy lay follower Dromtön. This *gompa* was to be the center of a religious order, the Kadampa, of great importance in the later development of Tibetan religion (T9).

Dromtön is said to have dissuaded Atīśa from teaching Tantra openly (see Beyer 1973:12–13). Initially the Kadampa monks, who called themselves not lama but *geshé*, a term deriving from the Sanskrit *kalyānamitra* ('spiritual friend' in the sense of 'teacher'), seem to have concentrated primarily on the Pāramitā (non-Tantric) practices of moral observance and the development of bodhicitta. The practice of *lojong* ('mind training') was the central Kadampa practice for the cultivation of bodhicitta, and the following well-known Kadampa *lojong* text by the Geshé Langri T'angpa gives some idea of the general approach of these teachings, which were to be taken up by many later traditions. It expounds the central Kadampa practice of 'exchanging self and others':

> Being determined to accomplish the highest welfare for all beings who excel the wish-fulfilling gem, I shall constantly hold them dear.
>
> When accompanying anyone I shall view myself as the lowest of all and in the depth of my heart shall hold dearly others as supreme.
>
> Examining my continuum throughout all actions, as soon as an emotional affliction arises that endangers myself and others, by facing it I shall strictly avert it.
>
> When seeing a being of wicked nature who is forced by violent wrongs and sufferings, I shall hold dear this one so hard to find as though discovering a precious treasure.
>
> When others, out of jealousy, treat me badly with abuse, insults and the like, I shall accept their hard words and offer the other the victory.
>
> When someone whom I have assisted and in whom I have placed great hope inflicts me with extremely bad harm, I shall view him as my supreme spiritual friend.
>
> In short, I shall offer benefit and bliss to all mothers in this actual (life) and in the (future) continuum, and secretly I shall take upon myself all of the harms and sufferings of my mothers.

> Also, having not defiled all these by the stain of preconceptions of the eight (worldly) feelings and by perceiving all phenomena as illusory, free from attachment, I shall be released from bondage.
> (Langri T'angpa, *Lojong Tsig-gyed,* from Dalai Lama 1980)

We have already met the standard Tibetan meditation that is alluded to in the seventh verse, in which all living beings, human or other, are seen as having been one's mother in some past life, and so as deserving the same love and gratitude as one's actual mother in this life.

As time went on, the Kadampa came to occupy a similar place to the hereditary shamans of the Nyingmapa and Bönpo as performers of rituals for the lay population. The *Debt'er Ngönpo,* for example, describes an occasion where a lay patron and her husband wished to hold a religious assembly, and debated whether to invite a Nyingmapa lama, a Bönpo lama, or a (Kadampa) monk to preside over it. In the end they invited all three, and after some arguments the three built a joint temple, and took turns to protect the countryside from hail (Gö Lotsawa, *Debt'er Ngönpo* = Roerich 1976:112–113).

INITIAL MOVES TO A SYNTHESIS

The Tibetans who invited Atīśa may have wanted a fully rationalized and non-Tantric Buddhism. What Atīśa brought to Tibet, however, was a combination of the clerical and shamanic approaches. His activity was the first important step in the establishment of a Buddhist tradition that would combine both elements.

Atīśa's own attitude to Tantra and to Buddhist practice in general is laid down in a short and very influential work known as the *Bodhipathapradīpa* or 'Light of the Path to Enlightenment,' extant only in Tibetan (Wayman 1978:9–14; Sherburne 1983; Snellgrove 1987:481–484). This text lays out three stages of the Buddhist path, in terms of the kind of motivation characteristic of the person at each stage. The first kind of person is still interested in the pleasures of *saṃsāra;* the second avoids nonvirtuous actions and aims at his or her own liberation; the third, the bodhisattva, desires to relieve the sufferings of others.

The *bodhicitta* vow should only be taken after taking one of the Prātimokṣa vows (lay follower, novice, monk), of which the highest are those of the monk *(bhikṣu)*. The *bodhicitta* vow should be taken in front of a competent guru or a visualization of the protective deities. Given this foundation of morality, training then consists of a balanced combination of 'means' *(upāya*, here meaning the meditative concentrations, *samādhi)* and 'insight' *(prajñā*, study of the Madhyamaka logical arguments for *śūnyatā)*. The aim of this procedure is to bring discursive thought to an end.

The last few verses of the text states that the Tantras may be used to perfect the equipment for enlightenment, but forbids the second and third initiations (which involve actual or visualized sexual union) for those who have taken vows of celibacy. The wording has some ambiguity, however, and can be taken to imply that these practices are permissible for celibates who have a true understanding of *śūnyatā*. Atīśa's own commentary on the text seems to support this interpretation (see Sherburne 1983:176–179; Rabten 1978:61).

The general purport of the scheme is nevertheless clear. Tantric practice was to be undertaken only after a thorough preliminary training in the Sūtra practices, which would ensure the correct motivation *(bodhicitta)* and a correct understanding of *śūnyatā* or the true nature of reality. This scheme was accepted in its broad outlines by all Tibetan Buddhist traditions, although they were to differ about the stage at which the student was ready for Tantric practice.

It is difficult at this distance in time, and given the polemical nature of our sources, to know how far and in what ways Tantric practice had 'degenerated' in tenth- and eleventh-century Tibet. We have little real indication of Atīśa's own attitude towards the Buddhist shamans of the Nyingmapa and Bönpo traditions. Some of his Tibetan supporters were clearly opposed to them, but there are suggestions that Atīśa himself was more sympathetic.[7] At any rate, he never denied the usefulness or validity of the Tantric path. He only specified that those who undertook it should do so after adequate preliminary training, and in particular that they should have the right motivation *(bodhicitta)*. Atīśa himself remained a practicing Tantric yogin, with particular devotion to the goddess Tārā, whose cult he firmly established in Tibet (Beyer 1973; Willson 1986).

In considering what Atīśa's synthetic scheme, and Buddhist shamanism in particular, had to offer to the Tibetans of the eleventh century and later times, we need to recognize two major aspects: the desire for shamanic power, and the desire to see that power used responsibly. For those of us who live in societies where the powers of a shaman seem fantastic or illusory, it may take an effort of the imagination to see why these matters should have been so significant for Atīśa or for his Tibetan supporters. For the eleventh-century Tibetans, both the reality of shamanic power, and the need for it to be used on behalf of the community, were taken for granted. In their society, shamanic practices still played a central role in maintaining the well-being of the community. There is little doubt on this question, because the same remained true of Tibetan society into modern times, as described in Chapters 9 to 18.

In a society where shamans are common and culturally valued, the risk of self-interest and exploitative behavior on thc part of thc shaman is a real one. What the Buddhists had to offer was a training that was some kind of guarantee of the *bona fides* of the practitioner. It is here that we can see the significance of the Tibetan insistence on the development of the *bodhicitta* motivation and its cognitive counterpart, insight into the 'voidness' of the self and the phenomenal world, as a prelude to shamanic training. Ideally at least, it helped to guarantee that the power attained through Tantric training would be used for socially constructive ends.

In the centralized and rationalized states of South and Southeast Asia, shamanic power as such was a matter of less concern. Shamanic practices were tolerated at the village level, but they were in no position to threaten the authority of the state, and were subordinated to clerical and rational forms of religion such as were constituted by the monastic tradition of Theravāda Buddhism (see Chapter 2). There is little doubt that the kings of Purang, and powerful lay patrons like Dromtön, would have preferred to establish this kind of situation in Tibet, but they were never able to do so. Monasticism survived through support from the general population, and the general population was concerned with the use of shamanic power on behalf of individuals and of village and urban communities, not on its restriction as a potential threat to the relatively weak local rulers. In this situation it was perhaps inevitable that shamanism would survive by becoming Buddhist, and Buddhist monasticism would survive by becoming shamanic.

Monasticism nevertheless was to have a complex relationship to shamanism within Tibet. If Indian Tantric Buddhist theory implied that full shamanic ability was precluded by celibacy, the Tibetans, too, seem to have felt that the celibate career of the monk, however virtuous or desirable in its own right, was not entirely compatible with shamanic power. Monks in Tibet, as in other Buddhist countries, are involved with the acquisition of good karma, both in their own lives and through their support by others. The popular ideal of a Buddhist shaman was less the monk than the hermit-yogi, of whom the prototype is the eleventh-century teacher and poet Milarepa.

The gradual evolution of the concept of the Tantric lama as head of a monastic *gompa* of celibate monks but himself an accomplished Tantric practitioner (T10b), as in the case of the head lamas of the Sakyapa order, was to offer a partial solution to the question of the role of monasticism in tibet. This new cultural pattern was to grow up initially not among the Kadampa but among the new lineages of Tantric practice that became established in Tibet during the eleventh and twelfth centuries. It laid the basis for a further innovation that would be of critical importance, the idea of the reincarnate lama, and here the disciples of Gampopa, a lama who combined Kadampa and Tantric training, would play a central role.

THE GROWTH OF THE SAKYAPA, KAGYÜDPA, AND OTHER TRADITIONS (T10A, T10B)

With the renewal of contact with the Buddhists of India around A.D. 1000, Tibetans began once more to travel to India in search of Tantric teachers. The eleventh century was a period of great innovation in Tibetan religion, and it marked the beginning of a wide range of different lineages and traditions of teachings. In particular, it was the time of the great translators or *lotsawa*, who brought the New Tantras and their teaching lineages to Tibet.

Some of those who took up the New Tantras were already hereditary Buddhist lamas and were looking for new, perhaps more genuine or more effective, Tantric teachings. This, for example, was the case with the K'ön family lamas, who took over a cycle of teachings, the *lamdré* ('Path and Fruit,' see Ngorchen 1987), based on the Hevajra Tantra, which had been transmitted to Tibet by the translator Drogmi Lotsawa (993–1077).[8] These teachings ultimately went back to the siddha Virūpa, whose song was quoted in Chapter 22, and whom I have already mentioned several times as another example of the later Indian siddhas of mixed clerical and shamanic background.

The first K'ön family lama to adopt the *lamdré* teachings was Sach'en Kunga Nyingpo (1092–1158), the son of K'ön Könch'og Gyelpo (1034–1102) who had founded the *gompa* of Sakya in 1073. The Sakyapa lamas also continued up to modern times to practice some Old Tantra rituals, as did the hereditary lama family of Dergé in east Tibet who adopted the new Hevajra practices from them (Amipa 1976; Davidson 1981).

Sakya *gompa* became one of the major centers for the teaching of New Tantras and in time it became the head *gompa* of the Sakyapa order (T10b1). This order, as we saw in Chapter 3, remained under the leadership of the descendants of the K'ön family. In the case of several early Sakyapa head lamas (Sakya Tr'ich'en), the lama was a monk and was succeeded by the son of a married brother. In later times the Sakya Tr'ich'en has generally been married. The *gompa* of Sakya nevertheless became a major center for celibate monks and for the scholarly and academic tradition of Indian Buddhism that was now being transmitted to Tibet. Two other suborders, Ngorpa and Ts'arpa (named after their main *gompa*, dating from the early fifteenth and mid-sixteenth centuries), grew up at a later period.[9]

The best-known and most successful of all the new traditions was the Kagyüdpa (T10b2), inaugurated by the translator Marpa (1012?–1093, see Trungpa 1982:199–201 n.) and his Tibetan disciple Milarepa (1040–1123). This was ultimately to lead to a rather different pattern of monastic organization from the Sakyapa model. Marpa had studied with the siddha Nāropa and other Indian teachers, concentrating particularly on the Guhyasamāja and Cakrasaṃvara Tantras and on the various siddha teachings on Mahāmudrā (Stott 1985). The Kagyüdpa were thus initially much more concerned with yogic practice than with academic study, although in later years they were to have a strong scholarly tradition as well.

Marpa and his followers took over the siddhas' practice of composing short songs (Skt. *dohā*, Tibetan *gur*) to record their realization. These songs (a collection of which has been translated into English) demonstrate the school's emphasis on meditation; we have already examined one of them in Chapter 11 (Trungpa 1980).

Milarepa in particular was a prolific composer of *gur*. His songs are best known from three collections dating from the late fifteenth century (Tsangnyön Heruka's *Milé Namt'ar* = Bacot 1925; Evans-Wentz 1969; Lhalungpa 1979; *Milé Gurbum* = Chang 1977; Lhatsün Rinch'en Namgyel's *Sunggyün T'orbupaga* = Kunga and Cutillo 1978, 1986) and Marpa's in Tsangnyön Heruka's biography from the same period (*Marpé Namt'ar* = Bacot 1937; Trungpa 1982).[10] Songs like the following one (written in the meter of Tibetan epic poetry, see Samuel, in press b) represent a convincing reworking of the Indian *dohā* into a new and wholly Tibetan genre.

> Once while Jetsün [Milarepa] was staying in Pelma Gel cave he went begging at a large encampment. A young patroness paid respects and offered a small piece of butter. Remembering that he had already received his daily share of food, he said, 'I don't even have a container to hold this butter; keep it yourself.' The woman was impressed and asked him to stay for the day. He did so, sitting a ways off. A torrential rain fell, and she said to him, 'Oh my, let me pitch a tarp overhead.' Mila replied with this song:
>
> I bow at the feet of the jewel crowning my head,
> Holy fulfiller of all wants and needs [Marpa, his lama].
> Gracious woman blessed with offspring and wealth
> Managing an abundant treasury of gifts,
> Clothed in the woolen robe of merit—
> Listen here, faithful lady.
> If you don't know my name,
> I'm Milarepa of Gungt'ang Plain—
> A beggar wandering by myself.
> Moved by my suffering from cold wind and rain,
> You offered this help in true spirit of mercy.
> Such good intentions are indeed a great wonder.
> I've travelled the plains of six illusory realms
> Where a rain of misery fell without pause
> And the dark fog of delusion pressed close around me.
> I lacked the broad hat of right view,
> The raincoat of unfaltering faith,
> And the warm dry cave of good refuge.
> Swept by the river of desire and craving
> Swollen by driving rains of bad action,
> I was borne to the horizon of the ocean of misery,

Buffeted on waves of three lower realms,
And battered on rocks of unwholesome action.
In fear of such insufferable miseries
In future lives beyond number,
I pitched the white tent of right view
On the great plain of unfaltering faith.
I tied the tent ropes of meditative experience,
Drove in the tent pegs of unerring practice,
Erected the poles of resultant three bodies,
And hoisted the banner of pure behaviour.
I broadcast the holy dharma drumbeat to all directions,
And on the throne of manifold objective world
Imbibe the broth of all profound precepts.
On the great plateau of love and compassion
I herd the six realms' sheep from the edge
And gather the nectar of omniscient gnosis
Unobstructed toward all objects.
Blissful within, I don't entertain
The notion 'I'm suffering,'
When incessant rain is pouring outside.
Even on peaks of white snow mountains
Amidst swirling snow and sleet
Driven by new year's wintry winds
This cotton robe burns like fire.
(Lhatsün Rinch'en Namgyel, *Sunggyün T'orbupaga*, f. 116b6 onwards; Kunga and Cutillo 1978:55–57)[11]

The 'cotton robe' of the last line is the thin cotton garment worn by yogins of Milarepa's tradition in the harsh Tibetan climate, indicating their ability to generate inner heat through yogic processes.

The yogic and 'shamanic' aspects of Milarepa, at any rate as viewed by the later tradition, are even more obvious in other songs and stories. Milarepa is described, for example, as transforming himself into a snow-leopard (Tsangnyön Heruka, *Milé Gurbum* = Chang 1977, vol. 1, 25), as engaging in magical competitions with a Bönpo practitioner (*Milé Gurbum* = Chang 1977, vol. 1, 215–224) and with the Buddhist teacher P'adampa Sanggyé (*Milé Gurbum* = Chang 1977, vol. 2, 606–614; *Sunggyün T'orbupaga* = Kunga and Cutillo 1978:85–91) and as encountering, overcoming, and teaching the mountain goddesses of Tibet, with whom he performs the Tantric sexual practices (*Milé Gurbum* = Chang 1977, vol. 1, 296 to vol. 2, 361; see van Tuyl 1975).

Milarepa had a large number of disciples. Most of them were lay hermit-yogis, but one, Gampopa, was an ex-Kadampa monk. Gampopa is also known as Dagpo Lhaje, the 'doctor from Dagpo,' in reference to his origin and medical training. He will be discussed in more detail below, since his combination of Sūtra and Tantra teachings (T10b2) was to prove immensely influential, and many of his disciples were founders of important *gompa*. Over the next few centuries the growth of these *gompa*, which would eventually be major teaching centers of the Kagyüdpa order, was to overshadow the continuing hermit-yogin tradition. The Kagyüdpa *gompa* nevertheless contained yogins as well as celibate monks, and they provided a context in which the clerical and Tantric synthesis could develop further.

Other near-contemporaries of Milarepa included his relative Ky'ungpo Neljor, from a hereditary Bönpo family, who went to India and originated a set of practices very similar to Nāropa's Six Teachings and attributed to Nāropa's sister (or Tantric consort) Niguma. Ky'ungpo Neljor's historicity is perhaps open to question, since this tradition, the Shangpa Kagyüd, was kept secret until the thirteenth century. It was always strongly committed to visionary techniques. We have already met the Shangpa Kagyüd in Chapter 18 as one of Kalu Rinpoch'e's main lineages. It remained a tradition of hermit-yogins more than of monastic practitioners (Kapstein 1980; Gyatso 1980b; J. Hanson 1982; J. and M. Hanson 1985; Gö Lotsawa, *Debt'er Ngönpo* = Roerich 1976:728ff).

The *shiched* and *chöd* traditions (T10c), founded by the Indian siddha P'adampa Sanggyé and his Tibetan consort Machig Labdrön (see Allione 1984:141–204), also remained closely associated with the hermit-yogins, although *chöd* is sometimes performed in a monastic context. Both these teachers were active in the late eleventh and early twelfth centuries. We have already come across Machig Labdrön's system of *chöd,* with its strong shamanic overtones. It involves solitary meditation in areas held to be haunted by demons. The yogins visualize their bodies being cut up and given as offerings to Tantric deities, local gods and demons, whom they summon by calling on a human thighbone trumpet (Tucci 1980:87–93; Allione 1984:141–204; Evans-Wentz 1967:277–334; Gyatso 1985).

Machig was the only female lama to found a major teaching lineage, although women in Tibet have regularly taken up yogic practice. *Chöd* was taken up by most of the other major traditions as a supplementary practice, as well as having some followers outside Tibet; Machig is reputed to have remarked that while the other Buddhist traditions came from India to Tibet, hers was the only one to have been exported from Tibet back to India (Gyatso 1985). It is carried out under the protection of a goddess who is a form of Prajñāpāramitā, the female personification of insight.

At the same time as all of this activity concerning New Tantric and Sūtra practices, the discovery of *terma* texts was getting under way in the Old Tantric (Nyingmapa) and Bönpo lineages. These texts were to provide the basis for the gradual reorganization of the Nyingmapa and Bönpo traditions so as to be better able to compete with the large new monastic and yogic *gompa* that were growing up. These monastic centers, unlike those in India at that time, were based from the beginning on a combination of Sūtra and Tantra practices of the kind implied by Atīśa's *Bodhipathapradīpa*. We have already mentioned Gampopa, the originator of this new and highly successful cultural pattern. We now turn to examine his activity and his followers.

GAMPOPA AND THE KAGYÜDPA MONASTIC TRADITION (T10B2)

Gampopa's classic manual on the Path to Enlightenment, the *Dagpo T'argyen* or *Jewel Ornament of Liberation* (Guenther 1970), is a presentation of the Sūtra teachings in the tradition of the Kadampa order from which he came, as well as of classic Indian texts such as Nāgārjuna's *Suhṛllekha* (Kawamura 1975) and Śāntideva's *Bodhicaryāvatarā* (Matics 1970). In his discussion of *prajñā*, Gampopa presents the logical arguments of Madhyamaka as used by Atīśa's school, but then goes on to give a non-Tantric presentation of the Mahāmudrā practices of the siddhas, quoting Tilopa (Nāropa's teacher): "Place the mind free from strain, without any thoughts of existence or non-existence, accepting or rejecting. As Tilopa says: Don't think, don't contemplate, don't cognize; don't meditate, don't examine, leave [the mind] in its own place" (*Dagpo T'argyen*, f.143b = Guenther 1970:216).

This 'Sūtra Mahāmudrā' system, which involves non-Tantric meditation practices intended to attain the Mahāmudrā state, was to become an important teaching for the Kagyüdpa tradition and later for the Gelugpa also. It offered a way to attain the central vision of the Tantras without breaking monastic vows or engaging in the elaborate and difficult exercises of Tantric practice. It was, however, criticized by other schools as an inadequate substitute for the genuine Mahāmudrā state, which they claimed was only to be obtained by Tantric meditation. Tantric practice continued in the Kagyüdpa orders alongside this Sūtra Mahāmudrā system, but the new approach was to be taught widely (Berzin 1978; Takpo 1986; Tsele 1988).

Gampopa begins his work with a chapter on the *tathāgatagarbha* as the underlying motive for following the path. He is concerned throughout to emphasize that the Enlightened state is beyond any conceptualization we may have of it. The nature of Buddhahood is unborn and ineffable. The transcending awareness of the Buddha, according to Gampopa's teacher, Milarepa, is "beyond any predication such as existence or non-existence, eternalism or nihilism, and beyond the realm of intellect. Whatever name it is called does not alter its nature . . ." (Guenther 1970:261). Gampopa's position is a compromise between the shamanic perception of Enlightenment as beyond words but positive, and the academic analysis of it in purely negative terms. This makes sense, since historically he marks, as the Tibetans term it, a merging of the two streams of Sūtra and Mahāmudrā, and thus a compromise between clerical and shamanic forms of Buddhism in general.

Among Gampopa's disciples were several founders of major monastic *gompa*, each of which served as the center for a Kagyüdpa suborder in later days. The main initial Kagyüdpa centers were Densa T'il, head *gompa* of the P'agmo Drupa, founded in 1158 by Drogön P'agmo Drupa (d. 1170); Drigung, head *gompa* of the Drigung Kagyüdpa, founded in 1179 by Drigung Rinpoch'e (1143–1217); Ralung, the head *gompa* of the Drugpa Kagyüdpa, founded in 1180 by Lingrepa Pema Dorjé (1128–1188);[12] Taglung, head *gompa* of the Taglung Kagyüdpa, founded in 1180 by Taglung T'angpa Trashipel (1142–1210); and Ts'urp'u, head *gompa* of the Karma Kagyüdpa, founded in 1189 by Karmapa Düsum Ky'enpa (1110–1193). These *gompa* were to be the Sakyapa order's main rivals in the power struggles of the thirteenth century.[13]

The further history of all of these orders was in part to be shaped by one of the most intriguing and unusual aspects of Tibetan religious life: the growth of the concept of *trulku* (reincarnate lama), of the lama as an emanation of a Tantric deity, and as a rebirth of a previous lama. This concept developed over a period of some time, and much of Chapter 25 will be concerned with tracing its evolution and consequences.

CULTURAL PATTERNS

The form of Buddhism that survived in Tibet after the fall of the first Tibetan empire was transmitted by hereditary shamanic priests of both Buddhist and Bönpo traditions (T8a1, T8a2). By the time that clerical Buddhism began to be reestablished (T9), it had already achieved a degree of rapprochement with the shamanic Buddhism of the siddhas in India (see Chapter 22) and this process appears to have been taken considerably further in Tibet, where there was no major court center whose influence might shift the balance decisively in favor of clerical forms. The growth of the New Tantric complex (T10) in its various forms corresponds to a period of experimentation and innovation with Indian material leading to the development of specifically Tibetan variants of Buddhism. These in various degrees, combined clerical and shamanic elements.

25

Tibet: Mongol Overlordship

Most of the cultural patterns listed in Table 6 have already been given in Table 5, and some will recur in the succeeding chapters. This does not imply a lack of change during the period of this chapter. Some of these patterns (e.g., T10b) were beginning to take shape in the previous period, and grew to much larger proportions in the thirteenth and fourteenth centuries. Others, such as the hereditary Tantric priest pattern (T8a), changed significantly in content as a result of the continuing flow of *terma* material, which gradually came to dominate over the original *kama* lineages. Two new strains, which can be associated with the Tantric deities who came to symbolize them, Avalokiteśvara and Mañjuśrī, represent specifically Tibetan developments from earlier material. Finally, the growth of a new pattern of political alliances between lamas and secular rulers (T11) is typified by the activities of the leading lamas of the Drigung and Karma Kagyüdpa and by the Sakya Tr'ich'en, who became rulers of Tibet during the period of Mongol overlordship.

TABLE 6.
Cultural Patterns in Chapter 25

Thirteenth and Fourteenth Centuries

- T7 Folk religion
- T8 Old Tantric and *terma* complex
  - T8a Hereditary priest lineages
    - T8a1 Buddhist
    - T8a2 Bönpo
  - T8b Dzogch'en-based syntheses
    - T8b1 Buddhist <T8, T10
    - T8b2 Bönpo <T8, T10
- T9 Kadampa monks
- T10 New Tantric complex
  - T10a New Tantric priests and yogins (early Sakya masters, Marpa, Milarepa, Ky'ungpo Neljor, etc.)
  - T10b Tibetan Monk-New Tantra syntheses; growth of clerical *gompa*
    - T10b1 Sakya synthesis (*Lamdré* system)
    - T10b2 Kagyüdpa synthesis
    - T10b3,4 Shalupa, Jonangpa, etc.
  - T10c Chöd yogins
  - T10d Reincarnate lama <T10b
- T11 Buddhist-secular political alliances
  - T11a Ruler as emanation of Avalokiteśvara; cult of Avalokiteśvara <T5, T8, India
  - T11b Sakya lamas as emanations; hereditary lama as ruler (Sakya Tr'ich'en)
  - T11c Secular ruler with lama support (Neudong Gongma etc.)

THE CULT OF AVALOKITEŚVARA (T11A)

One of the most important of all *terma* texts is traditionally held to have been discovered in several sections from the mid-eleventh to early twelfth centuries by the siddha Ngödrub, the famous *tertön* Nyangrel Nyima Öser (1124 or 1136–1204) and others (Kapstein, in press). This is the *Mani Kabum*, a collection of texts concerning the early King Songtsen Gampo in which the king is described as the human emanation or incarnation of the Tantric deity (bodhisattva) Avalokiteśvara, and his two principal wives are described as forms of the deities Tārā and Bhṛkuṭī. The *Mani Kabum* also includes a body of ritual texts concerned with the cult of Avalokiteśvara in a form known as T'ugjé Ch'enpo, 'Great Compassion.' Avalokiteśvara throughout the *Mani Kabum* is regarded as a patron deity of Tibet. He is also the direct ancestor of the entire Tibetan people in the form of one of his earlier incarnations, a monkey-Bodhisattva who mated with the goddess Tārā in the form of a rock-demoness and fathered the six ancestors of the six Tibetan 'tribes' (see Chapters 9 and 11).

There is evidence that the cult of Avalokiteśvara, and the belief in his special relationship to the Tibetans, may predate the *Mani Kabum*. Matthew Kapstein cites a passage attributed to Machig Labdrön, the founder of the *chöd* practice, which refers to the cult of Avalokiteśvara and Tārā and describes them as being specially linked to the Tibetans (Kapstein, in press). Atīśa and various eleventh- and twelfth-century Tibetans were responsible for traditions of meditation on Avalokiteśvara.[1] It is possible that the idea that Songtsen Gampo was an emanation of Avalokiteśvara also predates this text. No references to it are so far known from before the mid-twelfth century, but several Southeast Asian Buddhist monarchs claimed bodhisattva status, and Avalokiteśvara, the 'Lord of the World' (Lokeśvara) and the 'Lord who Looks Down *(avalokita)*' upon the world with compassion from his mountain-palace of Potala would be an obvious candidate to replace the mountain-deities as ancestor and divine counterpart of the Tibetan ruler.

It is the *Mani Kabum*, however, that first presents Avalokiteśvara as an underlying theme throughout Tibetan history, and indeed as responsible for the very existence of Tibet and the rest of the known universe. The 'Great Chronicle' of the *Mani Kabum* describes Avalokiteśvara as a kind of creator god who emanates vast numbers of universes, each equipped with a Mount Meru, a Jambudvīpa (the 'Southern Continent' of human existence), a Tibet, a Songtsen Gampo and his wives in order to benefit living beings.

The *Mani Kabum* has many features typical of the Nyingmapa tradition in later centuries. It is much more concerned with the goal of Enlightenment than with any particular method of reaching it. It presents teachings from a whole series of different traditions, including Dzogch'en, Mahāmudrā, the progressive system of teaching *(lamrim)* associated with the Kadampa, and the nine successive vehicles of the Nyingmapa Tantra system, but describes these as "magical fragments of instruction" *(menngag tr'ulgi dumbu)*, each able to benefit a particular individual. Ultimately, the aim is not to realize any specific form of Avalokiteśvara, the Great Compassionate One, but to attain the Tantric unity of compassion and *śūnyatā*, which underlies all these manifestations (Kapstein, in press).

As a specific aspect of manifestation of Buddhahood, however, Avalokiteśvara, Chenresig in Tibetan, is a manifestation of compassion (Skt. *karuṇā*). As we saw in Chapter 12, the immediate purpose of meditation upon him and of the recitation of his mantra, *oṃ maṇi padme hūṃ*, is to develop within the meditator the compassion for all living beings which Chenresig symbolizes. The six syllables of the mantra correspond to the six 'realms' within which living beings suffer in *saṃsāra* (hells, hungry ghosts, animals, humans, demi-gods, and gods). They form the basis for a complete set of analogical associations in standard Tantric manner, so that through meditating on Avalokiteśvara one can indeed attain the unity and harmonious interplay of all potentialities, which is the goal of Buddhist activity (Govinda 1969: Karmapa n.d.).

BODHISATTVAS AND CULTURAL PATTERNS

It is worth a closer look at the whole idea of Avalokiteśvara, the embodiment of compassion, as an agent active in Tibetan history. I have argued elsewhere that the 'gods' and 'spirits' found in cultures with shamanic religious patterns may be understood as symbolic markers for the various patterns within a culture (modal states in Samuel 1990; see also Chapters 15 and 19). Thus, when 'deities' such as the *orisha* of West Africa are described as intervening in human affairs, this may be interpreted as an analogical description of a growth or change in the importance of particular cultural patterns.

The same argument can be applied to Avalokiteśvara and the other Tantric *yidam* who were described as manifesting themselves in Tibetan affairs. The 'deities' of Tantric Buddhism constitute a vocabulary for speaking about cultural patterns (see Samuel 1990). However such repertoires are never static. The appearance of new patterns and new relationships between patterns was a recurrent feature of Tibetan history. From this point of view, what Avalokiteśvara represents was a real force within Tibetan history, and the *Mani Kabum*, for all of its mythical language, was an interpretation of Tibetan history as structured around the growth and transformations of this particular cultural pattern. The *Mani Kabum* was also, of course, itself an event in the growth of the pattern it describes.

Avalokiteśvara's cult and mantra were to assume immense importance within Tibet. The *Mani Kabum* marked the emergence of a new set of cultural patterns (T11a) that opened up further radical possibilities for social, political, and intellectual developments. Consequently it is worth examining the meaning that the cult of Avalokiteśvara, along with the related cult of the goddess Tārā, was to assume in Tibet.

The cult of Avalokiteśvara undoubtedly bore some relationship to what in the Indian context would become known as *bhakti* (I8), a devotional cult focusing on a transcendent and all-powerful deity. *Bhakti*, as I mentioned in Chapter 21, had its Buddhist equivalents in India (I7a) and these were exported to the Far East, where Avalokiteśvara's Chinese form, Guanyin, became the object of a straightforward devotional cult.[2] Avalokiteśvara and Tārā in Tibet cannot be as simply pigeon-holed. Avalokiteśvara and Tārā remained Tantric deities, and while Tibetans often speak of Avalokiteśvara or Tārā in language that suggests an external entity intervening in human affairs, any attempt to define their role more closely indicates that the situation is more complex than this, as we saw in Chapter 13 in relation to the identity of Mañjuśrī and Tsongk'apa. Multiplicity of meanings is characteristic of Tibetan symbolism.

For the present, it is enough to observe that if the cultural pattern of Avalokiteśvara had manifested in human form in ancient times, it could do so again. The first lamas on behalf of whom such claims were to be made belonged to the Sakyapa and Kagyüdpa orders. It is not clear precisely when this first happened, although the Sakyapa doctrine was well advanced by the fourteenth century, when Gorampa Sönam Sengge refers to it.[3] The head lamas of the Karma Kagyüdpa order were involved in promoting the Avalokiteśvara cult from the thirteenth century onwards, and are nowadays regarded as emanations of Avalokiteśvara, but it is not certain when this doctrine first emerged.[4] It is not mentioned directly in the *Blue Annals*, written in 1478 (Gö Lotsawa, *Debt'er Ngönpo* = Roerich 1976).

The Sakyapa tell a story of how the Indian scholar Atīśa, who like all great lamas had the gift of prophecy, passed the future site of the monastery of Sakya on his journey to central Tibet:

> On the mountain's dark slope, a large mirror-like patch of white earth was visible. Near it, two black wild yaks stood grazing. Upon seeing them, Palden Atīśa turned to his companion disciples and made the prediction that in the future two emanations of Mahākāla, the vowed protector of the holy Buddhist Dharma, would appear in this place. The Guru then dismounted and made prostrations in the direction of the white disc, for on its circle he saw seven glowing images of the letter *dhīḥ*, the mantric symbol of the Bodhisattva Mañjuśrī. Shining radiantly there, too, were the letters *hrīḥ* and *hūṃ*, the symbols of Avalokiteśvara and Vajrapāṇi. The vision of these letters, Palden Atīśa explained, signified that seven emanations of Mañjuśrī and one each of Avalokiteśvara and Vajrapāṇi would also appear for the benefit of all beings. (Thutop and Ngawang 1968:i–ii)

This text identifies the bodhisattva-emanations with the early teachers of the Sakyapa ruling family, K'ön Könch'og Gyelpo, who founded the monastery some thirty years after Atīśa passed by its future location, and his immediate successors.

As the seven Mañjuśrī emanations suggest, the Sakyapa came to see themselves as representing particularly the activity of the bodhisattva Mañjuśrī, and in fact it was eventually claimed that all male members of the K'ön lineage were Mañjuśrī emanations. If Avalokiteśvara represents compassion *(karuṇā)*, Mañjuśrī is insight *(prajñā)*, and in particular the penetrating insight of Buddhist scholarship. His symbols are the sword of *prajñā*, which cuts through all dualistic illusions, and the book containing the Prajñāpāramitā teachings. It was indeed at Sakya that the academic and scholastic tradition of Indian Buddhism was to find its first secure home on Tibetan soil.

SAKYA PANDITA AND THE RISE OF THE SAKYAPA TO POWER (T11B)

The *gompa* that were founded in the eleventh and twelfth centuries grew rapidly, and they provided a location where the strictly academic tradition of the Indian universities could be recreated in Tibet. To begin with, this process was aided by Indian scholars such as the 'Kashmiri Paṇḍita' Śākyaśrībhadra who came to Tibet in 1204. The destruction of the Indian Buddhist universities in the Muslim invasions soon brought any initial dependence on Indian scholarship to an end, and Tibet began to produce its own scholars and systematizers of the teachings. The first major figure in this Tibetan scholastic tradition was Sakya Pandita (i.e., 'the scholar from Sakya'), Kunga Gyalts'en (1182–1251), the head lama of the old hereditary lama family of K'ön in the early thirteenth century.

Sakya Pandita was a monk. The K'ön lineage included several monks from around this time, although at least one brother always married to provide continuity to the family line. Sakya Pandita's particular specialty was logic and the theory of perception, and he wrote one of the standard Tibetan texts on these topics. He was a relatively prolific author for his time, although his works are short in comparison with the productions of lamas of later periods and take up only one volume of the *Sakya Kabum*, the collected works of the early Sakyapa lamas (*Sakya Kabum*, vol. 5). Many of his writings have a strong flavor of controversy and logical disputation. His usual targets are the Nyingmapa and the Kagyüdpa, both of whom he accuses of carrying on the rejected and morally suspect 'Chinese' tradition and of running the risk of omitting the necessary moral foundation of *bodhicitta* (Karmay 1975b; Jackson 1982; M. Tsering 1988).

Sakya Pandita wrote sometimes in prose, but often in a simple seven-syllable verse with a decidedly colloquial flavor. One of his best known works is a collection of moral maxims in verse, the *Legshed Rinpoché Ter* (Bosson 1969). His treatise on the three vows *(Domsum Rabyé)* was referred to in Chapter 11, and his summary of the Buddhist teachings *(T'ubpé Gongpa Rabsel)* has recently been translated into English (Wangyal and Cutillo 1988).[5] As the title 'Paṇḍita' indicates, with Kunga Gyalts'en the Tibetans felt they had a scholar on a par with the scholars of India. For all the respect with which the Indian texts were held, the Tibetans were willing to advance their own arguments and interpretations; Sakya Pandita for example, introduces several new terms in his work on logic to fill in apparent gaps in his Indian sources (Lati 1980; van der Kuyp 1985).

Sakya Pandita's great scholarship, as we have already seen, led to his being considered an emanation of Mañjuśrī, the celestial bodhisattva of insight. To quote the contemporary Sakyapa scholar Chogay Tr'ichen:

> the inspiration of Mañjuśrī had accompanied him in his 25 [previous] incarnations as a *paṇḍita*. In ultimate truth he was an incarnation of Mañjuśrī as had been prophesied by Tārā to the astrologer K'ach'e Panch'en. This was recognized as fact by the scholar Tsangnagpa when he saw the numerous marks on his body. In relative truth he studied the teachings in order to guide beings. Whatever the teaching he understood its meaning immediately and obtained a clear comprehension as to the status of all objects of knowledge. Since he viewed his lama as inseparable from Mañjuśrī he was able to realize all the internal and external signs. He received teachings from countless Indian, Nepalese, Kashmiri and Tibetan spiritual friends, becoming a vast reservoir of wisdom achieved through study, reflection and meditation, and master of all teachings. (Chogay 1983:17–18)

Sakya Pandita is depicted in paintings and sculpture with Mañjuśrī's emblems, the sword of *prajñā* and the book of Prajñāpāramitā, to indicate his emanation status. As has been already said in Chapter 15, the concept of *trulku* should not be taken as literally implying a physical rebirth of some celestial deity. As with many Tibetan Buddhist concepts, there are possibilities of naive and of more sophisticated interpretations. Here as always the doctrine of *upāyakauśalya*, of skill in means, can be used to justify encouraging a naive interpretation, and even a degree of political exploitation.

Sakya Pandita's greatest historical importance lay in the political arena. When the Mongols threatened Tibet with invasion, it was Sakya Pandita who was sent to intercede on behalf of Tibet with the Mongol prince Godan. As a consequence, the Sakyapa head lamas (Sakya Tr'ich'en) were to become the first religious rulers of Tibet, establishing a new and important cultural pattern (T11b).

The Mongols had first come into contact with the Tibetans at the time of the Mongol conquest of the largely Tibetan state of Xixia or Tangut (Tib. Minyag) in what is now northeast Tibet in 1227. There seem to have been a number of Mongol reconnaissance missions in the general area of Tibet at around that time, and in one of these, in 1239, two *gompa* were severely damaged and several hundred *trapa* killed. The Mongol commander in this region was Prince Godan, one of Chinggis Khan's grandsons, and the assembled notables of Tibet agreed to send Sakya Pandita to negotiate with him. Sakya at this time was one of several powerful monastic 'hegemonies,' to use Turrell Wylie's term (1963:279; see also Roerich 1973; Shakabpa 1967). Others included the Drigungpa and Taglungpa, both Kagyüdpa suborders, and there were also powerful secular families in many parts of Tibet, including the surviving branches of the royal family.

We can only speculate about the precise nature of the rise to power of the various *gompa* over the previous century or so. Lamas would frequently have served as mediators in local disputes as they still did in recent times in the less centralized areas of Tibet. *Gompa* were customarily granted land by local secular rulers, and this implied some degree of administrative power over those working on the land. In addition, as the *gompa* became wealthy, this would in itself give them some political leverage.

It is likely that many of the early lamas saw religious and political activity from the beginning as related to each other; Wylie has suggested that the well-known story of Milarepa building a series of towers for Marpa reflects such a political strategy, although our sources for this episode are considerably later (fifteenth century) and probably involve extensive literary reworking, at least in the case of Tsangnyön Heruka's *Milé Namt'ar* (Wylie 1963; see Smith 1969b). Wealth and power, if properly used, were not necessarily viewed as contrary to the Buddhist teachings, especially for lamas who were laymen rather than monks. By the thirteenth and fourteenth centuries some Tibetan monasteries were to become extremely wealthy, and their head lamas were to acquire an opulent and luxurious life style. This development would in its turn lead to a reaction.

At any rate, Sakya Pandita met Godan in 1247, and offered him Tibetan recognition of his overlordship. Sakya Pandita defended his action to the Tibetans in a letter in which he described resistance to the Mongols as pointless and noted that he and his two nephews, who had accompanied him, had made a good impression on the Khan. Sakya Pandita himself died in 1251, but the elder of these two nephews, P'agpa, was to become the ruler of Tibet under the Mongol overlordship of Khubilai Khan in 1276.

Later Tibetan historians place considerable importance on the relationship between P'agpa and Khubilai Khan, which is described as being not that of feudal vassal and lord, but of religious teacher and lay patron. P'agpa had initiated Khubilai into the practices of the Hevajra Tantra, and Khubilai had 'given' the thirteen provinces (*tr'ikor*, 'myriarchies' or areas containing 10,000 people) of Tibet to him as the offering to the spiritual preceptor made at a Tantric initiation. There is no doubt that Khubilai Khan became a patron of Buddhism, but the later historians with their emphasis on the lama/patron *(ch'ödyön)* relationship were also constructing a political theory to define the relationship between the later Chinese emperors and the Dalai Lamas, the head lamas of the Gelugpa order (Farquhar 1978). The Mongols regularly ruled through local administrators belonging to their subject nations, and they may have been prepared enough to let the Tibetans put their own construction upon the situation (Morgan 1982).

At any rate, the principle of a lama as head of state had been established in Tibetan political theory, and an important new cultural pattern was set into movement (T11b). The successive head lamas of the Sakyapa order were given the title of *di shi* or 'Imperial Preceptor,' and were the formal rulers of Tibet under the Mongols, although the actual administration was given to a layman from the Sakya household, entitled *pönch'en* (i.e., 'great *pönpo*,' see Chapter 8). Beneath the *pönch'en* were the various myriarchies, each with its administrator. These 'myriarchs' *(tr'ipön)* mostly seem to have been powerful local landowners.

The Sakya administration of Tibet was not a great success. The Sakya head lamas came to play an increasingly nominal role, while real control belonged to the *pönch'en* who was appointed by a Department of Tibetan Affairs in Khubilai Khan's government. The *pönch'en* seem to have been generally corrupt and incompetent, and few of them lasted very long. The Sakyapa exploited their political preeminence to settle old scores against the Drigungpa, their principal rival for influence. Drigung *gompa* was destroyed in 1290, but resentment against Sakya power was evidently growing. Sakya rule was eventually brought to an end in 1354 by Changch'ub Gyantsen (1302–1373), a myriarch and a member of the Lang family, who had close links with the Drigungpa and particularly with the P'agmodrupa, another Kagyüdpa suborder. Changch'ub Gyantsen himself became a monk in this order.

The Mongol (Yuan) regime in China had by this stage little choice but to recognize the new regime; the Yuan dynasty itself was to come to an end in 1368. The P'agmodrupa rulers are usually referred to as the Neudong Gongma, after their administrative center, Neudong, at the northern end of the old royal valley of Yarlung. They represent the other main cultural pattern according to which Tibetan states were to be constructed over the following centuries, that of the secular ruler with close links to one or more major monastic orders (T11c).

MAÑJUŚRĪ AND THE GROWTH OF THE ACADEMIC TRADITION

Sakya Pandita was one of the first major Tibetan figures of the academic and clerical approach, but he was to be followed by many others, and the production of scholarly texts soon became as significant a part of Buddhist life in Tibet as the practice of meditation. The 'graduated path' *(lamrim)* scheme of Atiśa's *Bodhipathapradīpa* was to be very influential, especially after being taken up by Tsongk'apa and the Gelugpa tradition (see Chapter 26), but it was by no means the only scheme of this kind. The *lamdré* ('Path and Result') system of the Sakyapa tradition, originally deriving from the Indian siddha Virūpa, also provided an overall framework for Sūtra and Tantra teachings (Ngorchen 1987; Amipa 1976; Chogay Trichen 1983).

At the same time, the work of editing and classifying the Indian texts in translation continued. It was essentially completed in the fourteenth century by Putön (Putön Rinch'en Drubpa, 1290–1364, see Ruegg 1966), the founder and abbot of the monastery of Shalu and the author of the history of Buddhism *(Ch'öjung)* referred to in previous chapters, which includes a catalog of the Indian Buddhist texts.[6] Putön, like many of these academic teachers, was by no means opposed to Tantra. His biography expounds at length upon his attainment in Tantric meditation, and indeed it would have been difficult for him to make much sense of the Tantric sections of the canon without some practical background in this area.

Putön's relatively clerical position however emerges in his opposition to the Jonangpa tradition, who developed a famous 'positive' *(shentong)* interpretation of *śūnyatā* and of the *tathāgatagarbha* theory on the basis of the Kālacakra Tantra. Putön, like the Jonangpa lamas, was deeply involved with the Kālacakra tradition, and wrote on *tathāgatagarbha*, but he upheld the orthodox Madhyamaka position against the Jonangpa lamas, maintaining that *tathāgatagarbha* could not be conceived of as some kind of entity within the consciousness-stream of an unenlightened being (Ruegg 1966:152 n. 1, 1973).

In taking this position, Putön was upholding the rationalized approach of the Madhyamaka against the Jonangpa lamas' attempts to use the Sūtras to express the shamanic insight, whatever the relationship between vision and scholarship in his own life. Here he was a true forerunner of Tsongk'apa, who was also centrally concerned to hold that Tantric vision could and must be consistent with Madhyamaka philosophy.

It was Putön who established the contents of and edited the two canonical collections of Buddhist scriptures, the Kangyur, which contains the Sūtras, Tantras, and Vinaya, and the Tengyur, which consists of Indian commentarial works. These were to be widely distributed in printed editions from the seventeenth century onwards, but served more as objects of devotion and as scholarly resources than as books for everyday study and teaching.

Sakya and Shalu were the major centers of the academic tradition in fourteenth-century Tibet, and Tsongk'apa, who was to produce the definitive Tibetan synthesis of the teachings, visited both monasteries and studied with both Sakyapa and Shalupa lamas. The Sakyapa curriculum was based on a selection of Indian classics supplemented by the works of Sakya Pandita and other Sakyapa scholars, and the subjects covered (Pāramitā, Pramāṇa or logic, Vinaya, Abhidharma, and Madhyamaka) were to be those taught in the colleges of the new Gelugpa tradition, which Tsongk'apa's disciples were to establish.

All this scholarly activity had its impact on the Nyingmapa schools. Longch'en Rabjampa (1308–1363), generally regarded as the greatest scholar of the Nyingmapa tradition, and like Sakya Pandita reckoned to be an emanation of Mañjuśrī (see Uhlig 1981:97), was a younger contemporary of Putön. Longch'en Rabjampa was responsible for ordering the Dzogch'en teachings into a consistent system as well as bringing them into relationship with the New Tantra tradition with which he was also well acquainted. Several of his works have been translated into English.[7]

Longch'en Rabjampa, appropriately enough for the greatest proponent of the Nyingmapa school, had a troubled relationship with the Neudong ruler Changch'ub Gyantsen. The conflict between them was apparently provoked by his attempt to mediate in a revolt against Changch'ub Gyantsen and it led to Longch'en Rabjampa's exile for some years in Bhutan. He was eventually reconciled with Changch'ub Gyantsen, but the episode forms a contrast with the partiality of Changch'ub Gyantsen's successors towards Tsongk'apa and his much more clerical approach (Guenther 1975b). The work of Longch'en Rabjampa and of his scholarly successors, along with the continuing production of *terma* texts, would eventually provide the basis for the growth of the Nyingmapa monastic tradition in the seventeenth century (see Chapter 27). Until that period, however, the Nyingmapa tradition remained on a relatively small scale, while the Sakyapa, Kagyüdpa and Gelugpa *gompa* became powerful and wealthy institutions, deeply involved in the political struggles of the period (see Smith 1968a, 1969b).

The Kagyüdpa order in particular provided the context for the growth of another major new cultural pattern in Tibetan religion, the system of reincarnate lamas, which first arose towards the end of the period of Mongol overlordship.

THE KAGYÜDPA AND THE SYSTEM OF REINCARNATION (T10D)

We have already met the idea of the lama as an emanation of a celestial bodhisattva (Tantric deity) in the case of the Sakya Pandita and other senior Sakya lamas (T11b). This is only one aspect of what was to become the fully developed doctrine of the *trulku,* usually known in English as 'incarnate' or 'reincarnate lama' (T10d). The other main component is the recognition and appointment of lamas on the basis of them being rebirths of previous lamas (see also Chapter 15).

The Tibetan system of selecting lamas according to the principle of rebirth is well known and has been described by many authors. Only the basic principles will be indicated here. When a lama who is the head of a monastery or occupies an important monastic office is about to die he is normally expected to predict his rebirth and give some details of where it is to take place and in what family. On the basis of these indications and various divinatory procedures, the officials of the monastery go to find the child two or three years after the lama's death. The child is supposed to show certain signs, such as partial memory of his previous life.[8]

In the case of important posts such as that of Dalai Lama there may be several claimants, and these are tested to find which is genuine, although it is also possible for several distinct rebirths of one individual to be recognized. Once the child has been identified, he is brought back to the monastery for training and is eventually installed in the place of the previous lama, whose property and household he now owns.

The oldest of these chains of successive rebirths (*kutr'eng*, 'rosary of bodies') goes back to the twelfth century, its first member being Gampopa's disciple Düsum Ky'enpa who is reckoned as the first of the Gyalwa Karmapa series. The most recent lama in this series, the 16th, died in 1981. The official identification of the rebirth, by then seven years old, was made in June 1992.[9] Other important rebirth-series include the Dalai Lamas and Panch'en Rimpoch'e, the two highest *trulku* of the Gelugpa orders, but there were several hundreds, if not thousands, of such *trulku* in Tibet and Mongolia by the twentieth century. The most important of these lamas are generally also considered to be emanations of *saṃbhogakāya* deities; Avalokiteśvara, for example, in the case of the Dalai Lamas and Gyalwa Karmapa, and Amitābha in the case of the Panch'en Rimpoch'e.

The concept of *trulku* as rebirth seems to have first arisen in the Kagyüdpa order, and to be connected with the theory of controlling rebirths, which forms part of the 'Six Teachings of Naropa' *(Naro Ch'ödrug)*, a special property of that order.[10] In fact, although Düsum Ky'enpa (1110–1193) is recognized as the first of the Gyalwa Karmapa series, it would seem that the theory and procedure developed gradually in various Kagyüdpa suborders in the course of the thirteenth and fourteenth centuries. The fifteenth-century historian Gö Lotsawa, who was himself a Karma Kagyüdpa, carefully avoids describing Karma Pakshi, the second of the series (1204–1283), as a rebirth of Düsum Ky'enpa although he places him in the appropriate position in the sequence of rebirths (*Debt'er Ngönpo* = Roerich 1976:485–487). There was in fact a ten-year gap intervening between the two, which is much longer than the usual practice in later times. The normal period between rebirths is up to 49 days, although there are various ways of explaining a longer period, such as an intermediate birth.

Gö Lotsawa however does describe the 3d Gyalwa Karmapa, Rangjung Dorjé (1284–1339), as the rebirth of Karma Pakshi, and Rangjung Dorjé seems to have regarded himself as such. Rangjung Dorjé, in the late 1280s, would thus seem to have been one of the first cases of the formal recognition of a child as a rebirth of a lama (Roerich 1976:487–488).[11] Turrell Wylie has suggested that the innovation would make good sense in terms of the political circumstances of that time. Sakyapa power was declining, and the Karmapa were their principal competitors for influence at the Mongol court, where Karma Pakshi had made a great impression (Wylie 1978). The system obviously also provided a way of securing a recognized successor to a celibate monk while avoiding the Sakyapa system of a hereditary lineage of whom some members were celibate monks and others laymen.

The system of recognizing rebirths spread to other *gompa* during the fourteenth and fifteenth centuries, and it developed various further complexities, such as the idea of a single lama being reborn as two or more simultaneous rebirths (see Chapter 27). Its widespread use was probably fairly recent, since many reincarnation-series today only go back one or two centuries. By the mid-twentieth century, the only important *gompa* without reincarnate lamas as their abbots were a few of the older *gompa* such as Sakya and Mindröl Ling, who still followed the hereditary system, and several large Gelugpa institutions, including the three largest, Sera, Ganden, and Drepung, where the head lamas were appointed or elected (Sherpa 1977). There were still many small *gompa* with hereditary lamas, however, particularly in the Nyingmapa order.

THE MEANING OF THE REINCARNATE LAMA

In an intriguing recent book, *The Tibetan Symbolic World,* Robert Paul looks at the symbolic structure of Tibetan society as a series of attempted resolutions of the Oedipal conflict between senior and junior male generations. Paul observed that the *trulku* or reincarnate lama was the perfect resolution of this conflict, since he was his own predecessor. He was his own 'father,' so could take over his 'father's' (i.e., the previous lama's) position of authority without creating any problem of transition (Paul 1982b).

Paul's general emphasis on Oedipal processes and the adequacy of his psychoanalytically derived framework for an overall understanding of Tibet are issues I shall not address here. Paul's specific point about the 'rebirth' (as opposed to the 'emanation') aspects of the *trulku,* however, has some interesting features that are not dependent on his general theoretical framework.

Insofar as Paul's Oedipal framework deals with the succession of generations, it is concerned with the passage of time, and one of the most obvious features of the reincarnate lama system is its implicit denial of passing time. Ordinary human beings may come and go, but there will always be a Dalai Lama in the Potala and a Gyalwa Karmapa at Ts'urp'u. Now a central feature of the shamanic vision itself is also a kind of denial of time (see Samuel 1990:102–105). The shamanic vision involves an entry into a world that is, strictly speaking, outside time since it contains the frameworks that define time as we experience it.

From this point of view, the *trulku* is a kind of temporal projection or reification of the shamanic vision. This manifestation of the shamanic vision in a living person is an illusion, since the shamanic conquest of time is not really a denial of birth, illness, old age, and death. In another way, it is also a reality, because by skillful selection and training, and perhaps other procedures at present outside our full understanding, it may be possible for one lama to continue the activity, the cultural pattern, of his predecessor in some meaningful sense.

There was more to the situation than this, however. The reincarnate lama was also a political device. This is evident both from the initial context in which the system arose, and from its practice in premodern times. The presence of an reincarnate lama was a major strength for a *gompa* from the political and economic points of view, and the higher the ranking of the incarnation, in terms of depth of lineage, notable previous members, and the like, the more this was true.

Here as always we should beware of seeing the political and economic factors as 'primary' and the others as some kind of ideological obfuscation. A major point of this book is the need to avoid such inappropriate dichotomies between 'mental' and 'material' factors (see Samuel 1990). Paul's suggestion from psychoanalytic theory that the whole concept of reincarnate lama may have a deep basis in the psychic structure of humans as biological animals may help to emphasize this point, if it still needs driving home.

What human beings are, at any given point in time and in society, allows for certain kinds of possibilities; this is what the language of cultural patterns is intended to capture. The idea of *trulku* would not have arisen in eighteenth-century England, since the basic building blocks, in terms of cultural patterns and their associated conceptual material, were not available. If any such concept had arisen, it would have had no impact on society. The failure of William Blake's contemporaries to understand his very personal version of the shamanic vision is a case in point (see Samuel 1990:135).

In fourteenth-century Tibet, the concept of *trulku* and the system of recognizing reincarnations could and did arise, as a natural extension and unfolding of possibilities already present within the cultural patterns active in Tibet at that time. The *trulku* cultural pattern arose, as it had to, from the very beginning as a unity of thought and action, of 'spiritual,' 'political,' and 'economic' implications. There never was, nor could be, any separation between them.

The *trulku* cultural pattern (T10d) provided the linchpin for the reconciliation of the monk and shaman-yogin ideals. A lama could be a monk, and still have shamanic powers, since these could have been acquired in a previous life when he was a noncelibate yogin. Merely to be a reincarnate lama implied that the lama had such abilities, since he had been able to control his rebirth. With the reincarnate lama system there arose a new social role, that of the child trained from an early age to be leader of a monastic *gompa* and performer of Tantric ritual, but that role was itself, as our framework implies, part of a wider system of relationships and modes of behavior.

The reincarnate lama pattern allowed the monastic *gompa* to take a more central role in the provision of shamanic services to the Tibetan population, and it likewise strengthened their position in the political system. The secular rulers of Tibet in the fourteenth to seventeenth centuries tended to favor the new system over the old hereditary-lama *gompa*. While they were in no position to eliminate the older pattern, even had they wished to do so, their preference for monastic *gompa* with reincarnate lamas would have been reflected by more land-grants and donations, so leading to a greater rate of growth for the new pattern.

The new incarnate-lama *gompa* also provided a secure context for the further growth of the academic and scholastic aspects of Buddhism. The classic synthesis of 'shamanic' and 'clerical' currents in Tibet, the Gelugpa school founded by Tsongk'apa in the early fifteenth century, was not initially based upon the *trulku* system, but it rapidly adopted it. In this form it was to dominate Tibetan politics from the seventeenth to twentieth centuries, under the leadership of its two most senior reincarnate lamas, the Dalai Lama and the Panch'en Rimpoch'e. The growth of the Gelugpa order will form the main focus of Chapter 26.

CULTURAL PATTERNS

The period described in this chapter was characterized by further specifically Tibetan developments, including that well-known Tibetan institution, the reincarnate lama (T10d). Particularly noteworthy are the various forms of accommodation between secular and religious power (T11a, T11b, T11c). This is an area in which Tibetan societies have continued to demonstrate remarkable creativity and inventiveness into modern times. The involvement of external power in the form of the Mongols was a feature that would also recur in later periods.

26

Tibet: Gelugpa Synthesis and Shamanic Reaction

During the period discussed in this chapter, Tibetan religion continued its evolution towards the contrasting patterns of 'clerical' and 'shamanic' discussed in Parts One and Two of this book. This evolution went hand in hand with the growth of the new kind of centralized regimes (T11), based on alliances between religious and secular power, whose emergence was noted in Chapter 25. The shamanic pattern within Tibetan religion was in many respects formed by the fourteenth century, although subsequent developments within Tibetan religion, above all the Nyingmapa revival and the Rimed movement in the eighteenth and nineteenth centuries, would have an impact in these areas, too. Political centralization and the interwoven growth of the more clerical form of Buddhism was still, however, in its early stages.

Within Tibet, as I have repeatedly emphasized, speaking of a clerical form of Buddhism does not imply the pattern of 'clerical dominance,' of a centralized state with a state Saṃgha, found in the Theravādin countries. 'Clerical' in Tibet is always a relative term, and what we really have is a series of syntheses between shamanic and clerical patterns that can be regarded as more or less clerical. The Gelugpa

TABLE 7.
Cultural Patterns in Chapter 26

A.D. 1358 to 1642

- T7 Folk religion
- T8 Old Tantric and *terma* complex
  - T8a Hereditary priest lineages
    - T8a1 Buddhist
    - T8a2 Bönpo
  - T8b Dzogch'en-based syntheses
    - T8b1 Buddhist
    - T8b2 Bönpo
- T10 New Tantric complex
  - T10a New Tantric priests and yogins (early Sakya masters, Marpa, Milarepa, Ky'ungpo Neljor, etc.)
    - T10a1 Shamanic reaction: the Mad Yogins <T10a
  - T10b Tibetan Monk-New Tantra syntheses; growth of clerical *gompa*
    - T10b1 Sakya synthesis (*lamdré* system)
    - T10b2 Kagyüdpa synthesis
    - T10b3,4 . . . Shalupa, Jonangpa etc.
  - T10c Chöd yogins
  - T10d Reincarnate lama
  - T10e Gelugpa synthesis: large clerical *gompa* <T10b, T9
- T11 Buddhist-secular political alliances
  - T11a Ruler as emanation of Avalokiteśvara; cult of Avalokiteśvara
  - T11c Secular ruler with lama support (Neudong Gongma, Rimpung and Tsangpa rulers)

synthesis of clerical and shamanic elements, created by the great fourteenth-century lama Tsongk'apa and his followers, was one of the most important, and politically the most successful, of these syntheses, and it is the primary subject of the present chapter. To understand the background to this development, we turn first to consider the nature and extent of centralized power in Tibet at the beginning of this period.

POLITICAL FACTORS: CIRCA 1350 to 1642

The Sakyapa lamas had nominally ruled all of Tibet as representatives of the Mongol empire, although the rapidity with which Sakyapa rule disintegrated demonstrated that local centers of power persisted and indeed had never more than temporarily accepted the Sakya-Mongol regime. Changch'ub Gyantsen and his successors, known as the Neudong Gongma from their capital, or as the P'agmodrupa from the Kagyüdpa suborder with whom they were associated, took over from the Sakyapa as nominal rulers of Tibet. However the Neudong regime had effective power over little more than the two central provinces of Ü and Tsang and even this was to decline rapidly after Changch'ub Gyantsen's death in 1364 (Tucci 1949).

This was to set the pattern for the next three hundred years of Tibetan history. A succession of 'strong men' were effective rulers over one or another central Tibetan province for a few decades each. After their deaths, the dynasties they founded rapidly collapsed, as regional powers established their independence and the central administration rapidly became nominal. The second of these hegemonies, that of Rimpung, was based in Tsang and never established effective control over Ü. Neither did the dynasty of Tsangpa kings (Depa Tsangpa or Desid Tsangpa) at Shigatsé, which followed it from the mid-sixteenth century. The Tsangpa rulers patronized the Karmapa religious order (one of the largest Kagyüdpa suborders) while Ü became increasingly dominated by the Gelugpa.

It seemed as if no regime was capable of effectively governing more than one of the two central provinces directly, and that the other province routinely became a center of opposition to the ruling regime. The conflict between Ü and Tsang culminated in 1639–1642, when Gushri Khan, a Mongol chieftain and supporter of the 5th Dalai Lama, established Gelugpa rule over both Ü and Tsang, as well as over the larger part of K'am (eastern Tibet) and Ngari (western Tibet). This takes us onto the subject matter of Chapter 27, though it is worth noting here that the Gelugpa regime would soon lose direct control of K'am, and that the conflict between Ü and Tsang continued in an altered form.

All this suggests that the degree of effective state power, for the fourteenth to seventeenth centuries at any rate, was only slightly greater than that of the period before the rule of the Mongols and the Sakyapa. One can perhaps account for this by a mixture of economic and geographical factors (see also Samuel 1982). Communications in Tibet were slow and difficult. The economic surplus, such as it was, probably derived mostly from trade along the international routes from

China to India, Nepal, and Kashmir, but this trade was highly subject to fluctuation as a result of external political factors.

It would have needed a large standing army and a highly effective administration to maintain a centralized government by force in such circumstances, and there was no standing army in Tibet until the twentieth century (Rahul 1969). Administration, even during the period of Gelugpa rule (1642–1959), was a continual process of compromise between central and local leadership, and while a more or less regular flow of tax and tribute to the center was maintained, it was never enough to allow the center to extend its power more effectively. Lhasa, the largest Tibetan city, had a population of around 20,000 to 30,000 in premodern times.

I do not mean to suggest that Tibetan history can be explained in terms of ecological or economic determinism. Tibetan cultural patterns allowed for certain kinds of usage of the material situation. Had the productive surplus been directed to armies and military technology rather than to building *gompa* and printing books, Tibetan societies would have been very different. It seems likely, nonetheless, that no power internal to Tibetan society would have been capable of providing steady and effective centralized government. Nor did the Tibetans need any such style of government.

Major shifts in the balance of power within this system generally resulted from the involvement of external military forces, whether Mongol or Chinese, but since neither Mongols nor Chinese were able or prepared to maintain a large permanent garrison in Tibet until the 1950s, these incursions created a temporary reshuffling of the elements but left the underlying situation much as it was.

Even the establishment of Gelugpa rule in 1642 (with Mongol support) was only a partial change to the system. The Chinese incursions of the eighteenth century were to bring about more substantial transformations, but central weakness and regional rivalry continued to limit the scope of any effective centralized government in Tibet.

What these various foreign involvements do seem to have achieved was the gradual weakening of the old local aristocracy in relation to the growing power of the monasteries. As with the Mongols in the thirteenth century, later Mongols and Chinese generally favored monastic over secular powers in their attempts to manipulate the Tibetan situation for their own ends.

The situation outside central Tibet was much the same. The remainder of Tibet was divided into a patchwork of 'states,' some of them consisting of little more than a couple of valleys, while the larger ones were engaged in constant struggles to maintain some kind of centralized control over local power bases within their territory. Most of these states were to consist of some kind of compromise or alliance between secular and monastic power.

It is against this general background that further developments within Tibetan religion need to be viewed, and it is to these that we now turn.

SHAMANIC AND CLERICAL TRADITIONS IN THE LATE FOURTEENTH CENTURY

Chapter 25 traced the development of various currents within Tibetan Buddhism up to the mid-fourteenth century. Buddhism in Tibet by this stage was composed of a whole series of different traditions, shamanic and clerical, yogic and monastic, Old and New Tantra, with each major monastery, each new cycle of *terma* texts, and each teaching lineage introducing features of its own.

For the shamanic tradition this diversity of approaches was not a real problem. They could simply be regarded, as in the *Mani Kabum*, as "magical fragments of instruction," differing only because they were each partial and therefore limited approaches to the truth of the shamanic vision (Kapstein, in press). Similar perspectives can be found in many writings of the Nyingmapa tradition and of those influenced by them, such as the 2d Gyalwa Karmapa, Karma Pakshi, who was quite prepared to concede that non-Buddhist teachings, too, might have partial validity (Kapstein 1985).

The so-called Tibetan Book of the Great Liberation *(Rigpa Ngotröd)* is indicative of the approach within the shamanic tradition. This text forms part of a *terma* cycle (the *Karling Shitr'o*) discovered by the fifteenth-century *tertön* Karma Lingpa (1356–1405), and it presents the view of the Dzogch'en teachings, which we have already encountered in the previous two chapters. As I have noted, Dzogch'en was closely associated with the shamanic side of Tibetan religion.

The *Rigpa Ngotröd* was first translated by two of Evans-Wentz's Tibetan associates (Evans-Wentz 1968) and has recently been re-edited and retranslated into German (Back 1987) and English (Reynolds 1989). For this *terma* text, the terminologies of the various traditions are simply pointers, equivalent in meaning and referring to something beyond definition by any of them:

> As for this sparkling awareness which is called 'mind,'
> Even though one says that it exists, it does not actually exist . . .
> With respect to its having a name, the various names that are applied to it are inconceivable (in their numbers).
> Some call it 'the nature of the mind' or 'mind itself.'
> Some Tīrthikas call it by the name *ātman* or 'the Self.'
> The Śrāvakas call it the doctrine of *anātman* or 'the absence of a self.'
> The Cittamātrins call it by the name *citta* or 'the mind.'
> Some call it the *prajñāpāramitā* or 'the Perfection of Wisdom.'
> Some call it the name *tathāgatagarbha* or 'the embryo of Buddhahood.'
> Some call it by the name *Mahāmudrā* or 'the Great Symbol.'
> Some call it by the name 'the Unique Sphere' [*t'igle nyagchig*].
> Some call it by the name *dharmadhātu* or 'the dimension of Reality.'
> Some call it by the name *ālaya* or 'the basis of everything.'
> And some simply call it by the name 'ordinary awareness' [*t'amal shepa*].
> (Reynolds 1989:11–12)

In so far as the language used by the *Rigpa Ngotröd* resembles that of any of the classical Indian Buddhist philosophical positions, it is that of the Cittamātra: "There exist no phenomena other than what arises from the mind" (Reynolds 1989:15). However, the similarity, as with Longch'en Rabjampa's use of Cittamātra concepts, is misleading, since Cittamātra is used primarily as a language within which the transcendence of philosophical positions (including Cittamātra) can be stated.

For those who were attempting to continue the academic and clerical tradition of Indian Buddhism, and to establish a rationalized synthesis of the teachings as the basis of a graduated monastic curriculum, such approaches would have seemed dangerously wild and undisciplined. While they could not deny that Buddhahood was beyond all verbal formulations, they were certainly not prepared to concede that all such verbal formulations were equivalent. Their job was to compare, to classify, to relate to each other, to exclude the unauthentic, and finally to create a unified body of teachings that would incorporate all the important elements in a balanced whole.

This opposition between two approaches, one eclectic and syncretistic, the other purist and sectarian, can be traced throughout the history of Buddhism in Tibet, and it can be correlated with a tendency to more or less shamanic orientations. The opposition is not a rigid one. One could be a purist, academic monk, such as Putön or Tsongk'apa, and still be deeply involved in Tantric practice. For such people, however, their personal shamanic realization tended to act as a confirmation of the validity of the tradition they upheld and so of the falsity of others.

There were also lamas of high status and great scholarly accomplishment in the monastic system who were much closer to the yogic tradition. These lamas, such as Pema Karpo, Tāranātha, and several of the Gyalwa Karmapas, were mostly outside the Kadampa-Gelugpa orders. As we shall see below, they provided a means by which the latest yogic developments could be integrated into the monastic system, given the prestige of a major religious order and spread throughout Tibet.

Gene Smith has suggested that there are regional differences in these orientations, with tolerant and eclectic attitudes characteristic of the south (Lhodrag, Lhok'a) and east (K'am, Amdo). In the center and (at least in the earlier period) the west, conflict was more the usual pattern. Initially, this was primarily Buddhism against Bön, but as the Bön traditions were gradually suppressed, the Nyingmapa (Old Tantra) followers became the primary target for the "puritanical intellectuals of the New Tantric transmissions" (Smith 1970a:6).

This geographical pattern resembles the distribution of political centralization, with the more centralized and hierarchical areas being the areas of greater conflict between academic (New Tantra) and shamanic (and largely Old Tantra) approaches. This makes sense, since it is in the more hierarchical areas that one would expect support from the ruling strata for a monastic and clerical religion and opposition to a shamanic religion more associated with the broad masses of the population. I mentioned in Chapter 1 the *terma* biographies of Guru Rimpoch'e (Padmasambhava), typical products of the Nyingmapa and shamanic tradition during the thirteenth and fourteenth centuries, where the Tibetan king is described as being forced to acknowledge the power of the miracle-working shaman-yogi Guru Rimpoch'e and to prostrate before him (Douglas and Bays 1978). The point could hardly have been lost on the lay and clerical rulers of Tibet.

The monastic orders nevertheless continued to grow throughout the period of the present chapter, and they continued to form political alliances with the various secular powers. The Sakyas did not play a significant political role after the collapse of Sakyapa rule at the start of the period. The most significant monastic orders in political terms were two Kagyüdpa suborders, the Karmapa and the Drugpa, and, from the 1420s onwards, the new order of the Gelugpa. Other smaller orders, such as the Shalupa, Jonangpa and the various Nyingmapa traditions, were less directly involved in these large-scale political intrigues.

The position of the Drugpa in central Tibet was greatly weakened by a dispute over recognizing the rebirth of their head lama at the end of the sixteenth century, and the competition for power and patronage continued between the Karmapa and the Gelugpa, who were eventually to become the dominant power in central Tibet in 1642. We now turn to examine the nature of the Gelugpa synthesis of shamanic and clerical religion (T10e), which was to prove so effective.

TSONGK'APA AND THE GELUGPA SYNTHESIS (T10E)

Tsongk'apa was born in 1357 in Amdo, at a site later commemorated by the *gompa* of Kumbum. He studied extensively with teachers of most of the main *gompa* and traditions of his time. At the age of 33, despite the advice of his principal teacher, Remdapa, he gave up his academic studies to concentrate on yogic practice. Over the next eleven years he received a series of revelations from Mañjuśrī, mediated by the shamanic lama Umapa. Finally, in 1398, Tsongk'apa attained what he regarded as conclusive insight into the nature of reality, following a dream in which he was blessed by the great Indian scholar Buddhapālita (see Thurman 1984:65–85). He became an active teacher, and he and his disciples founded the *gompa* of Ganden, Sera, Drepung, and Trashi Lhunpo, the central institutions of the new Gelugpa order.

An earlier generation of scholars described Tsongk'apa (1357–1419) as a kind of Tibetan Luther, on the grounds of his reformation of the monastic order, his alleged opposition to Tantric practice, and possibly his insistence on the validity of the 'original' (i.e., Indian) texts over the Nyingmapa tradition. That Tsongk'apa placed a renewed (and perhaps for Tibet altogether new) emphasis on the status of ordained monk as the basis of Buddhist practice is certainly true, and even authors such as Gö Lotsawa, who had no particular reason to favor the Gelugpa, admitted to Tsongk'apa's significance in this respect (Roerich 1976:1076–1078). At the same time, the great growth of the Gelugpa monastic order was more the work of Tsongk'apa's followers than of Tsongk'apa himself, and its final access to power took place in the seventeenth century, not the fifteenth.

It is tempting on a superficial reading to see Tsongk'apa exclusively as a proponent of 'clerical' and academic forms of Buddhism over shamanic and Tantric forms. In fact, as the reference above to his visionary career may suggest, this would be to misread the situation considerably. Tsongk'apa was throughout his life deeply involved in Tantric practice, and much of the inspiration for his activity came from his various visions of Tantric deities, above all from Mañjuśrī of whom he was later considered an emanation. His central perception of the inseparability of transcending insight and karmic causality was certainly a personal version of the shamanic vision.[1]

Tsongk'apa did, however, treat full Tantric practice as a difficult and dangerous exercise, to be taken by advanced students only, after an extensive course of study in the Sūtra teachings and above all after the student had both developed the *bodhicitta* motivation and acquired some intellectual understanding of *śūnyatā*. In this he was following in the footsteps of Atīśa, and indeed the Gelugpa are sometimes known as the 'New Kadampa' and regarded themselves as above all a continuation of Atīśa's work.

Perhaps the most useful perspective on Tsongk'apa is to regard him as the creator of the most influential of all Tibetan syntheses between Sūtra and Tantra practice (see Thurman 1985). In this respect he can be seen as one of many lamas who were working towards similar ends, rather than as a unique and exceptional figure. The specific features of Tsongk'apa's synthesis nevertheless were of importance in understanding why it was to become more successful than its competitors.

Tsongk'apa's summary of the overall structure of the Sūtra teachings is given in the *Lamrim Ch'enmo* or 'Large Version of the Gradual Path,' a work that develops the 'three levels of motivation' scheme of Atīśa's *Bodhipathapradīpa* into a comprehensive framework for the teachings. Tsongk'apa himself produced two shorter adaptations of this work, and later Gelugpa authors have written several further versions.[2] It is worth giving a brief summary of the structure of the whole *lamrim* scheme.

The *lamrim* teachings begin with a lengthy discussion of the need for devotion and obedience to the teacher, who is to be regarded as an emanation of the Buddha, and continue with the sufferings of the lower realms of *saṃsāra* and the need to take refuge in the Buddha, his teachings, and the community of his followers.

Here we are at the first level of motivation, or first type of person. At this stage the student is still trapped within the delusions of *saṃsāra*, and the highest goal in sight is rebirth as a god or superior human being. "When . . . you see the doings of this world as being like a drunkard dancing on the edge of a precipice, and without ever being attached to this life, your mind is always, day and night, steadily concerned with your future life, the state of mind of the lowest type of person has arisen" (Yeshe Gyents'en, *Sergi Yangshun*, f.5, see Guenther 1971:82).

This is the level I referred to in Parts One and Two as that of the Karma Orientation. It corresponds to the kind of practice that Melford Spiro, speaking of Burma, called 'Kammatic Buddhism' (Spiro 1971). It is noteworthy that while Spiro considers 'Kammatic Buddhism' to be a decline from the original teachings of the Buddha, Tsongk'apa and the Tibetan tradition in general treat it as an integral foundation for Buddhist practice.

At the next level, the teachings are to do with the suffering inherent even within the higher states of rebirth (men, demi-gods, and gods), and the aim is to bring about complete renunciation of *saṃsāra*. We are held within *saṃsāra* by the action of the *kleśa*, mental and moral defilements or obscurations, which must be eradicated to prevent the further accumulation of karma and so permit escape. The way to do this is through the triple training of moral discipline, mental concentration, and discriminating insight *(śīla, samādhi, prajñā)*, but rather than practice these with the motivation of the second type of person, the student is enjoined to progress to the third and highest level, that of the bodhisattva.

The teachings for the bodhisattva begin with the methods of meditation for arousing the *bodhicitta* motivation and the teachings on the *bodhicitta* vows. They continue with the six 'perfections' *(pāramitā)* that are the classical description of the bodhisattva's practice. The last two, *dhyāna* and *prajñā,* are explained at length in terms of the two aspects of meditation, which we first met in Chapter 20, *śamatha* and *vipaśyanā*. *Śamatha* is here explained as the development of calmness of mind and one-pointed attention, and *vipaśyanā* as the point-by-point contemplation of the logical arguments of the teachings, culminating in those for the voidness of the self and all phenomena (Berzin 1972:555–641; Wayman 1978). The *lamrim* scheme ends with the discussion of these two modes of meditation.

Tsongk'apa also wrote a synthetic treatment of the Tantras, the *Ngagrim Ch'enmo* (partially translated in Hopkins 1977, 1981), as well as several large commentaries on specific Tantras.[3] He was concerned primarily with the Vajrabhairava, Guhyasamāja, and Cakrasaṃvara Tantras, and these have continued to be the Tantric traditions most followed by the Gelugpa order.

In his treatment of Tantra, Tsongk'apa emphasizes the necessity of treating all Tantra, even those of the lower three classes, as being primarily concerned with the attainment of Enlightenment. He also stresses that the philosophical viewpoint of the Tantras must be taken as that of the Prāsaṅgika subschool of Madhyamaka, which claims to work purely in terms of logical argument, without making any assumptions about the nature of reality. In this way he rules out any tendencies, such as that of the Jonangpa, to hypostatize the state of Enlightenment in positive terms.

In Chapter 1, I quoted most of a short verse work by Tsongk'apa, the 'Three Main Points of the Path.' It gives something of the character of the Gelugpa teachings, with their emphasis on moral renunciation of secular life, the development of the bodhisattva motivation, and the 'correct' understanding of *pratītyasamutpāda* and of Madhyamaka philosophy. Tsongk'apa's argument on the last point is particularly characteristic of both him and the Gelugpa tradition as a whole, and worth commenting on further here. It is concerned with the understanding that 'dependent origination' *(pratītyasamutpāda,* Tib. *tendrel)* and *śūnyatā* are mutually equivalent.

> Your understandings of independent origination in the world of
> appearance
> And of *śūnyatā* free from all assertions, these two,
> As long as they appear to be separate,
> You have still not understood the Sage's [Śākyamuni's] thought.

> When at the same time, not having set them up separately,
> Through that very seeing of independent origination
> All habitual views of objects as certainly known are destroyed
> Then the study of views has been completed.

We have met *pratītyasamutpāda* several times in the previous chapters. For the Mahāyāna, it is the arising of all phenomena in mutual dependence, conditioned by each other, so that nothing within or outside the individual can be said to have true independent existence. As such, it is more or less synonymous with *prajñā*, insight, and with *śūnyatā* or 'voidness,' which is the perception of things being without real independent existence.

Tsongk'apa's particular insight, and the teaching of the Gelugpa order, emphasized the identity of karma and causation in the 'world of appearances' with *śūnyatā*, the absence of real independent existence, at the level of ultimate reality. Thus the 'conventional level' of truth *(saṃvṛtisatya)* and the 'absolute level' *(paramārthasatya)* have to be understood not merely as equivalent but as identical. This is the basis of a critique of the Nyingmapa tradition, and of the other orders to the extent that they can be associated with the alleged faults of the Nyingmapa position. Tsongk'apa insists that *śūnyatā* is in no sense a different or transcendent reality to the reality of the ordinary world, when the latter is seen in terms of karma, impermanence, and nonself (for example, Williams 1980).

The Nyingmapa and Jonangpa traditions were prepared to offer a positive analogical description of the state to be achieved, in the hope that the description might help in the achievement. Ultimately, the Nyingmapa lamas would agree with Tsongk'apa and his Gelugpa successors that Enlightenment is inexpressible, and that any imagery is deceptive. For Tsongk'apa, the risk of self-deception was such that any such device had to be avoided. Instead, the rationalizing philosophy of the Madhyamaka was to ensure that the Tantric yogin, secure in his prior intellectual understanding of voidness, would risk neither the extreme of nihilism nor that of the belief in the real permanent existence of entities. To quote Robert Thurman, perhaps the leading Western authority on the work of Tsongk'apa:

> . . . reason, through its proof of emptiness by the reason of relativity, leads directly and inexorably, without any gap or leap, to the confrontation with the ultimate truth of truthlessness. Philosophy is thus vindicated as a complete path of liberation and transformation; the con-

> clusively reasonable mind is esteemed as completely capable of transcending the unreasonable prejudiced mentality trapped in the vicious circle of inconclusive rationalization. One should therefore resist the temptation to discard critical reason and relapse into experiential confirmation of mundane intuition, habitually conditioned by prejudice, and hold out until critical wisdom experientially becomes the reliable and liberating intuition of reality. (Thurman 1984:171)

This might be a safer approach, but it was also a more difficult one, and its consequence was to make the gate for the trainee Buddhist shaman very narrow indeed. The message is clear: Tantric practice is dangerous and it should be left to the great lama-meditators with their decades of prior discipline and academic training. All schools agree that there are risks with Tantric practice, but most are more willing to take them than the Gelugpa. The Gelugpa system was to produce a small minority of intensively trained scholastics and a smaller elite of Tantric adepts, while the vast majority fell out at some point early in the academic training.

As for the Tantric sexual practices, while Tsongk'apa and his successors were not prepared to deny their validity, they argued that they were better avoided. In the section on *karmamudrā* practice in his commentary on the 'Six Teachings of Nāropa' *(Naro Ch'ödrug)*, Tsongk'apa gives a long and intimidating list of qualifications that the male and female partners would need to have, warns that anyone practicing without these qualifications is certain to be reborn in hell, and omits any actual description of the practices (*Sablam Naro Ch'ödrug* 108b–109a). As I mentioned in Chapter 15, Tsongk'apa himself was said to have avoided these practices, in case his followers imitated him without proper preparation (Cozort 1986:92).

This can be correlated with the greater Gelugpa emphasis on celibacy and monastic discipline (which pertain to the conventional level), and the generally clerical nature of the Gelugpa tradition in comparison with the others, which have always had a greater investment in nonmonastic practice. It was no surprise that the Gelugpa approach appealed to secular authority from its earliest days. The Neudong Gongma, the P'agmodrupa rulers of central Tibet, despite their formal Kagyüdpa allegiance, were patrons of Tsongk'apa and his followers, and the order rapidly established a number of large monastic centers.

The three central points of the short Tsongk'apa text cited in Chapter 1 were indeed the essentials of the Sūtra path as taught by the Gelugpa and for them they were a necessary preliminary to any Tantric practice:

1. Ascetic withdrawal from life, primarily through monasticism;

2. The development of *bodhicitta* and compassion for all beings;

3. The transformation of one's present view of the world into a radically different mode of seeing things in which phenomena are mutually dependent, void of independent reality, conditioned by each other, and so no longer potential objects of attachment or repulsion.

In fact, no Tibetan Buddhist school would have objected to these points as such. The differences were questions of emphasis rather than substance. What might be regarded as characteristically Gelugpa is the great emphasis on withdrawal—specifically *monastic* withdrawal—and also the stress on epistemology and on the philosophical understanding of the nature of perception, knowledge, and 'reality.'

The Gelugpa placed more emphasis than any of the other orders on the necessity of thorough philosophical preparation and on the intellectual understanding of *śūnyatā* as a prerequisite for Tantric practice. It was in the large Gelugpa teaching monasteries that the scholastic tradition of eighth- to twelfth-century India, with its emphasis on logic and formal disputation, was to find its true home in Tibet. While such topics are studied in other orders, it is generally recognized that they are a Gelugpa specialty.

Tsongk'apa's ideas were put into effect in the Gelugpa monastic *gompa*, which began to grow up in central and eastern Tibet from the early fifteenth century onwards. In time, some of these were to become larger than any previous Tibetan *gompa;* Sera, Ganden, and Drepung, the three principal monastic *gompa* near Lhasa, each had several thousand monks, as did Trashi Lhunpo in west-central Tibet, Kumbum at Tsongk'apa's birthplace in northeast Tibet, and Labrang near the Chinese border. These great *gompa* were centers to which monks would come for study from all over Tibet, each containing several 'colleges' *(trats'ang)* and numerous hostels for students from different parts of Tibet. A network of smaller monastic *gompa*, with maybe several hundred monks each, spread throughout the entire Tibetan region, many of them dependencies of one or another of the major central or east Tibetan *gompa*. The only areas without Gelugpa monasteries were Bhutan, Sikkim, and Dergé,[4] which were explicitly non-Gelugpa states, and some stateless areas such as northern Nepal and Lahul.

The basic curriculum of the new Gelugpa monastic colleges followed closely that of the Sakyapa, although as time went on the material was studied increasingly from the textbooks and digests of Gelugpa authors. The five major subjects, with their principal Indian texts, were as follows:

1. Pramāṇa (logic and theory of perception, along with the techniques of formal disputation), using the *Pramāṇavārttika* of Dharmakīrti as principal text;

2. Pāramitā (i.e., the Mahāyāna Sūtra teachings in general), using the *Abhisamayālaṃkāra*, one of the five texts traditionally revealed by Maitreya to Asaṅga;

3. Madhyamaka philosophy, based on the *Madhyamakāvatāra* of Candrakīrti;

4. Vinaya (monastic discipline), based on the *Vinayasutra* of Guṇaprabha;

5. Abhidharma philosophy, using the *Abhidharmakośa* of Vasubandhu.

Tsongk'apa himself wrote extensive commentaries on the *Abhisamayālaṃkāra* and the *Madhyamakāvatāra;* part of the latter is available in English translation (Hopkins 1980). His disciples and followers created a large commentarial literature, with each major college having its own school-texts for the various topics of the Gelugpa curriculum. Good descriptions of the Gelugpa curriculum in modern times have been given in autobiographical accounts by Gelugpa teachers (for example, Rabten 1980; Dhargyey 1978:1–9; Rato 1977; see also Lati 1980). As we saw in Chapter 18, the full training could take from seventeen to twenty years for the academic degree of *geshé,* followed by another eight or nine years for the higher status of *geshé lharampa*.

The Gelugpa system in practice meant large institutions full of monks *(trapa),* most of whom remained at a fairly elementary stage in the academic curriculum, and a relatively small elite who persisted through the system to its higher ranks. The appointed heads of the largest monastic *gompa* and their colleges all came from this small elite, as did the members of the two exclusive colleges for Tantric practice in Lhasa. Even *trulku* (reincarnate lamas) had to go through this thorough academic training, although in their case it could be reduced in length (see Chapter 18).

The two Lhasa Tantric colleges were not the only places where Tantra was practiced in the Gelugpa systems. All the large teaching *gompa* had Tantric colleges, and most monks received some basic training in Tantric ritual and procedures, if only to the extent necessary to keep the ritual observances of the *gompa* functioning. The emphasis, however, throughout the Gelugpa tradition was not on the Tantric colleges but on the colleges of dialectics and philosophy *(pramāṇa).* The Gelugpa undoubtedly had their quota of serious Tantric meditators, but the system was organized so as to restrict such practice to a small and highly trained minority.

Since there remained a basic difference between a monk, however learned, and a lama believed to be capable of conducting effective Tantric ritual in his own right, this created a fairly rigid distinction in the Gelugpa monastic *gompa* between the two types of monk, with in some cases a third class of nonacademic monks developing. The possibility of working through the system to the highest offices remained, although in practice many of these high-level positions were filled by *trulku* who had gone through the appropriate training (Sherpa 1977; see also Chapter 18).

In this the Gelugpa pattern contrasted with the large teaching *gompa* of the other orders (Kagyüdpa, Sakyapa, and to a lesser extent Nyingmapa and Bön), which predated them. In these monasteries it was possible and normal to specialize in Tantric meditation from an early stage, and most of them continued to train noncelibate yogis as well as monks.

The Gelugpa order rapidly realized the political significance of the large bodies of *trapa* in its *gompa,* and many monasteries were built in strategically important places. In later years, the numbers in these institutions were sometimes kept up by compulsory recruitment in the form of an obligation on the local community to supply fixed numbers of *trapa* to the local monastery. The creation of a sound base for the Dharma required people, not just money. In a predominantly Nyingmapa and Kagyüdpa area like Dingri, as we have seen (Chapter 17), these obligations could be perceived by the lay population as highly onerous, although in many areas voluntary recruitment may have been adequate to keep up the numbers (Aziz 1978:234–237).

The place of the shamanic vision within the developed Gelugpa system may not be obvious, although in fact it was to keep resurfacing. The Gelugpa had an authentic yogic tradition of their own (see Willis 1985), of which the 5th and 7th Dalai Lamas were prominent examples (Mullin 1982b; Karmay 1988b). It is nevertheless hardly surprising that the development of these large monastic institutions was to provoke a reaction from the shamanic side of Tibetan religion.

THE SHAMANIC TRADITION, FOURTEENTH TO SIXTEENTH CENTURIES (T8, T10B, T10C)

The period of the growth of the great monastic *gompa* was also a time of intense activity among the hermits and lay yogis of the Nyingmapa, Kagyüdpa, and Bönpo traditions. The discovery of *terma* continued. In the Nyingmapa tradition, these largely centered on Guru Rimpoch'e (Padmasambhava). Nyangrel Nyima Oser, the twelfth-century *tertön* who found part of the *Mani Kabum*, also found a biography of Guru Rimpoch'e (Kapstein, in press; Blondeau 1980). A whole series of similar historical texts dealing with Guru Rimpoch'e's life and the surrounding events appeared in the fourteenth century onwards. The most important of these are the *Kat'ang Denga* and the *Sheldragma* version of the *Pema Kat'ang*, both discovered by Orgyen Lingpa (1329–1367).[5]

The *Sijid*, the longest version of the biography of Shenrap, legendary founder of the *Bön* religion, probably also appeared towards the end of the fourteenth century, when it was dictated in a vision to the Bönpo lama, Loden Nyingpo.[6] It was in part based on two earlier biographies that may date back to the tenth and eleventh centuries (Karmay 1975a; Snellgrove 1967a; Kvaerne 1986).

Most of the *terma* material related, however, to ritual and meditation rather than to hagiography, and a particular 'discovery' often included a whole series of texts related through the same central deities and mandala. A well-known example is the cycle of 'Tranquil and Fierce Deities' *(shitr'o)*, discovered in the early fifteenth century by Karma Lingpa (*Karling Shitr'o*, see Snellgrove 1957; Govinda 1969;

Reynolds 1989). This included the most familiar version of the so-called Tibetan Book of the Dead (*Bardo T'ödröl* = Evans-Wentz 1960; Fremantle and Trungpa 1975). The *Bardo T'ödröl* became widely used as a liturgy at the time of death, but it was closely related to the teachings of the 'Six Teachings of Naropa' *(Naro Ch'ödrug)* on the intermediate state between death and rebirth, and like them could be used as part of Tantric meditation. The 'Tibetan Book of the Great Liberation' *(Rigpa Ngotröd),* from which I quoted earlier in this chapter, comes from the same cycle of texts, although, unlike the *Bardo T'ödröl,* it does not use the *maṇḍala* of the *shitr'o* deities, and is more in the nature of a short statement of the underlying vision behind the cycle (Evans-Wentz 1968; Back 1987; Reynolds 1989).

Other well-known cycles of this kind include the fourteenth-century *Jangter* ('Northern *terma*'), of which the *Kunsang Mönlam* discussed in Chapter 1 forms a part, the *Namch'ö,* discussed in Chapter 16, and the *Könch'og Chindü* ('Union of the Precious Ones'), discovered in the seventeenth century by Letr'ö Lingpa (Jats'ön Nyingpo). In the *Könch'og Chindü,* Guru Rimpoch'e (Padmasambhava) is explicitly treated as a Tantric deity with eight physical manifestations, two of them being Śākyamuni and the Padmasambhava who visited Tibet in the eighth century (Snellgrove 1957; Smith 1970a:13; Dargyay 1978).

The large number of separate cycles of revelations determined the specific nature of the Nyingmapa tradition in relation to the other Buddhist traditions. There was no single coherent body of teachings such as was held in common by the Sakyapa, Gelugpa, or even the divergent branches of the Kagyüdpa tradition. The Nyingmapa had no large *gompa* until the seventeenth century, so the solid institutional basis that these orders had was also lacking.

Instead, the various *terma* cycles must have waxed and waned in popularity in accordance with the fate of the small local Nyingmapa centers that employed one or another, and with their relevance to the needs of the time. Each major cycle was a complete body of teachings in its own right, along with a series of ritual texts appropriate for various occasions.

At the same time such a situation meant that the Nyingmapa could be, and had to be, far more responsive to the needs of their clientele among the villages and pastoral encampments than the other orders, who more often relied on patronage from large local landowners and regional powers.

One can exaggerate this distinction. The four fifteenth- to seventeenth-century lamas in the outlying district of Dolpo (see Chapter 17), whose biographies Snellgrove has translated, were equally reliant on the support of the lay population. Yet these lamas went to central Tibet to study at Ngor Ewam, a *gompa* deriving from the Sakyapa tradition with all the academic content for which that tradition was renowned (Snellgrove 1967b; for Ngor Ewam, see Davidson 1981). In more recent times, Dolpo gradually switched to the Nyingmapa traditions, though this may be a reflection of the recent activities of Nyingmapa lamas here as in Sherpa country; the equally remote district of Lahul remained Drugpa Kagyüdpa in its practice (see Chapter 17).

One aspect of the Nyingmapa tradition that reflected with particular clarity its responsiveness to the needs of ordinary Tibetans in the face of the political and moral uncertainty of much of Tibetan history was the belief in 'hidden valleys' or *beyül,* places set aside by Guru Rimpoch'e as refuges to be discovered at an appropriate time in a rather similar way to the discovery of the *terma* texts. Sikkim, in which many Tibetans found refuge at the time of the wars of the early seventeenth century, was supposed to have been such a *beyül,* as was the district of Pemaköd at the bend of the Brahmaputra River in southeast Tibet. There are still legends among Tibetan populations all along the Himalayas about such places, as well as *terma*-style guidebooks that explain how to find them and narrate their marvelous properties. Some of these *beyül* were quiet refuges set aside for meditation, but others, like Sikkim and Pemaköd, were places where lay people could settle to escape political turmoil (see Bernbaum 1980; Reinhard 1978; Aris 1975).

The nearest equivalent to such a belief in the New Tantric traditions was the hidden realm of Shambhala, situated apparently somewhere to the north of Tibet. This was the traditional place of origin of the Kālacakra Tantra. The Kālacakra Tantra appeared during the last days of Indian Buddhism, and contains clear references to the threat of Muslim invasion. Shambhala was believed to be ruled by a succession of wise Buddhist kings, the last of whom would emerge at some future date to liberate the world from its oppressive and evil rulers. The Kālacakra Tantra had a great popular appeal, and the Dalai Lama's initiations for this Tantra in recent years have attracted vast numbers of participants. There are descriptions of how to travel to Shambhala, but these are more in the nature of shamanic visionary journeys than travels to any material place (Bernbaum 1980).

Another visionary and folk-hero who demonstrated the close links between the Buddhist shamanic tradition and the common people of Tibet was T'angtong Gyelpo (1385–1510; Gyatso 1980b, 1980c). T'angtong Gyelpo discovered several *terma*, but his links are more with the Shangpa Kagyüdpa than with the Nyingmapa. This small Kagyüdpa tradition, which claimed to go back to Ky'ungpo Neljor and to the teachings of Niguma, Nāropa's sister or consort, rather than to Marpa and Nāropa, was one of a number of Kagyüdpa yogic traditions that continued to exist quietly alongside the large monastic *gompa* of the Karmapa, Drugpa, and Drigungpa.

We have already discussed the short and influential *sādhana* on Avalokiteśvara by T'angtong Gyelpo, which was to play a major role in the growth of the popular cult of Avalokiteśvara (Gyatso 1980a; Karmapa n.d.). Two other aspects of T'angtong Gyelpo's activity were his building of iron bridges all around Tibet, and his institution of theatrical performances of Buddhist legends. These were the *ache lhamo* plays that continued to be widely performed into modern times (Schuh 1976; Snyder 1979).

Bridge-building is not as unusual an activity for a Tibetan lama as it might seem at first sight. The biographies of many Tibetan lamas recount their role in promoting public works of various kinds, mediating disputes, setting aside game-reserves to protect animals, and the like, and these were evidently part of the role of the lama, especially in a small village *gompa* rather than a large monastic center.

THE MAD YOGINS: A SHAMANIC CRITIQUE OF CLERICALIZATION

In the fifteenth century, the shamanic side of Tibetan religion produced several figures who posed a direct challenge to the growing clerical orthodoxy. These were the mad lamas *(lama nyönpa)* or crazy yogins, to whom reference was made in Chapter 16. The best known were the Mad Yogin of Tsang, Tsangnyön Heruka (1452–1507), already mentioned as the author of the *Milé Namt'ar* and *Milé Gurbum*, and Drugpa Kunleg (1455–1529), whose apparently scurrilous activities were to become a common subject of Tibetan folk stories.

These 'crazy yogins' were not without precedent. The unconventional behavior of many of the Tantric siddhas has already been referred to, and Milarepa provided a Tibetan prototype. More generally, all these figures can be related to the 'trickster' aspect of the shamanic role (see Samuel 1990:118–119). Thus Milarepa, as I mentioned in Chapter 24, is described in Tsangnyön's works and other sources as transforming himself into a snow-leopard and into a clump of flowers, consorting with the local mountain-goddesses, prophesying the future, engaging in magical competitions with a Bönpo shaman, and generally displaying shamanic abilities. His constant ridiculing of the pretensions of respectable society, and of the Kadampa clergy in particular, also suggests the 'trickster' aspect of his role.

Tsangnyön came from a village lama family. At the age of eighteen he had a vision that sent him off on a journey to meet his guru, under the guidance of whom he undertook the Kagyüdpa yogic practices in solitary retreat. He then spent some time at the Sakyapa college at Gyantsé, but eventually decided that the monastic life would not lead him to Enlightenment. He began behaving oddly, laughing and chattering without cause, and left the college after insulting and ridiculing the visiting Prince of Gyantsé.

For the rest of his life, he traveled around the Himalayas, collecting disciples, being supported by sundry lay patrons, and meditating in mountain caves and other remote places, especially those where Milarepa was reputed to have stayed. During these years he wrote his three well-known biographical works, the *Milé Namt'ar* ('Life of Milarepa,' Bacot 1925; Evans-Wentz 1969; Lhalungpa 1979) and *Milé Gurbum* ('Collected Songs of Milarepa,' Chang 1977), completed in 1488, and the *Marpé Namt'ar* ('Life of Marpa,' Bacot 1937; Trungpa 1982), completed in about 1505. He also wrote other works, primarily on the Kagyüd oral tradition of the Tantras (Smith 1969b).

Tsangnyön's writings on Milarepa and Marpa were based in part on earlier works such as Karmapa Rangjung Dorjé's collection of Milarepa songs (the *Dzödnagma*), and the songs of both of these early Kagyüdpa lamas had evidently been in oral circulation for centuries. The narrative framework within which Tsangnyön set the songs, however, reflected the author's own attitudes and perspective. These works were the vehicle for a critique of the practices of the contemporary monastic tradition. Tsangnyön himself had taken a female consort and lived the life of a hermit-yogi, not a monk. In the *Gurbum*, he describes Milarepa as performing the sexual practices of the Anuttarayoga Tantra with the Himalayan mountain-goddesses, who were among the most powerful of the old folk-religion deities (*Milé Gurbum* 394–399 = Chang 1977, vol. 2, 357–360). Tsangnyön and his circle did not trace their lineage of teachings back to Gampopa, Milarepa's foremost monastic disciple and the founder of the Kagyüdpa monastic tradition. Instead, they claimed to continue the oral tradition *(nyen-gyüd)* of Rech'ungpa, Milarepa's foremost lay yogi disciple.

Tsangnyön clearly aligned himself with the shamanic tradition not the academic one. Perhaps in view of the many wealthy lines of reincarnate lamas that existed in his time, he is reported as refusing to allow himself to be recognized as a reincarnation of Tilopa (Nāropa's guru), although later historians describe him as a rebirth of Milarepa himself or of Marpa:

> When Ch'öje Yamchilwa announced that he had had a dream to the effect that Tsangnyön was the incarnation of Tilopa, Tsangnyön replied: 'That may indeed be your vision. I am (indeed) one who upholds the tradition of Tilopa. I have no idea whether I am an incarnation or not.' (Smith 1969b:5)

In Tsangnyön's *Milé Namt'ar* a similar incident occurs, in which one of Milarepa's disciples asks if he is an incarnation:

> The Master replied: 'I never heard whose incarnation I am. Maybe I am the incarnation of a being from the three lower realms, but if you see me as Buddha you will receive his blessing by virtue of your faith. Although this belief that I am an incarnation springs from your devotion to me, actually there is no greater impediment to your practice. It is a distortion of the true Dharma. The fault lies in not recognizing the true nature of the achievement of great yogins. The Dharma is so effective that even a great sinner like myself has reached a stage not far from Enlightenment due to my belief in karma, my subsequent renunciation of the aims of worldly life, and due especially to my single-minded devotion to meditation.' (Lhalungpa 1979:144–145)

It is reasonable to interpret passages such as this as indicating Tsangnyön's opposition to the rigid hierarchy of great incarnate lamas and ordinary monks that was developing in his time. Anyone could achieve Enlightenment in a single life, even someone like Milarepa who had acquired terrible karma through his use of destructive shamanic power. Another aspect of Tsangnyön's approach was a distinction between the 'gradual' and 'sudden' path, which harked back to the debate of Samyé and the whole question of the need for progressive training. Tsangnyön held that a sufficiently able candidate could be introduced directly to Mahāmudrā (for example, Trungpa 1982:62).

The clerical figures in Tsangnyön's writings, who were mostly early Kadampa monks, were at best well-meaning fools and at worst thoroughly evil characters such as the Geshé Tsagp'uwa who poisons Milarepa out of jealousy (Lhalungpa 1979:153–169 = *Milé Namt'ar* 251–277). Their academic knowledge is meaningless next to the yogi's realization (*Gurbum* 412–448 = Chang 1977, vol. 2, 375–395).

Gampopa himself, as one of Milarepa's two leading disciples and the founder of the Kagyüdpa monastic tradition, is of course not presented in such a negative manner. Milarepa nevertheless has to go to some trouble, in Tsangnyön's account, to free Gampopa from the obstacles of his pride, his attachment to the monastic rules, and his tendency to overintellectualize and overrate his meditation experiences (*Milé Gurbum* 535–598 = Chang 1977, vol. 2, 463–496 = Trungpa 1980:217ff).

Rech'ungpa, Milarepa's principal yogi-disciple and the origin of Tsangnyön's teaching lineage, receives much more attention than Gampopa in Tsangnyön's writings. His attainments are described at length. His main faults are self-will, a desire for fame, and occasional neglect of his guru's instructions. In one instance he insists on traveling to central Tibet, where he becomes attached to a noblewoman whom he has taken as a Tantric consort. Milarepa extricates him from this situation, and explains that this practice can only be performed at the right time and under the right conditions, whatever Rech'ungpa's level of attainment. The lady also repents and becomes a yoginī (*Milé Gurbum* 698–729, 766–81 = Chang 1977, vol. 2, 584–605, 637–648).

Milarepa himself has faults in his early days, although the career in destructive magic that he has to expiate with such suffering is undertaken at his mother's request and in order to revenge her injuries (*Milé Namt'ar*, Lhalungpa 1979:22–35). The path of the Tantric yogin can overcome even the blackest karma and lead one to Buddhahood in a single lifetime. While Tsangnyön advocates the shamanic over the academic tradition, he has little respect for the village shamans with their rituals to control the weather and cure petty ailments. Their techniques may work, as does Milarepa's destruction of his wicked uncle's household, but what is really important is the attainment of Enlightenment.

Milarepa already seems to have been a popular figure in folklore by Tsangnyön's time, but the *Namt'ar* and *Gurbum* gave an immense boost to his popularity, and are still among the best-known works in Tibetan literature. Tsangnyön's students continued his literary activities. One of them, Lhatsün Rinch'en Namgyel, wrote the life of Nāropa referred to in earlier chapters (*Nāropé Namt'ar*, Guenther 1963) as well as a supplementary collection of Milarepa songs (*Sunggyün T'orbupaga*, Kunga and Cutillo 1978, 1986; see Smith 1969b:26–27).

Gene Smith has commented on the *nyönpa* or 'crazy yogins':

> the evidence is fairly conclusive that the *nyönpa* phenomenon was, at least partly, a reaction against the hereditary lineages with their great prestige and wealth. It was an attempt to reinvest the Kagyüdpa tradition with some of its former religious fervor, the incandescent spirituality of the early yogis. The chief symbol of this movement was Milarepa who had never been a monk, the mystic poet who had founded no monastery or school, a saint who remained a legend. (Smith 1969b:3)

The Kagyüdpa in fact accepted much of Tsangnyön's critique, if at the same time perhaps defusing its radical potential by incorporating it into the monastic and academic context. The 8th Gyalwa Karmapa, Mikyöd Dorjé (1507–1554), compiled a selection of songs by Marpa, Milarepa, and other Kagyüdpa lamas for liturgical use, borrowing heavily from Tsangnyön's work (*Kagyüd Gurts'o*, Trungpa 1980). Mikyöd Dorjé was a scholar and a prolific author. His work and that of other sixteenth-century scholar-lamas outside the Gelugpa tradition, such as Pema Karpo (1527–1592) and Tāranātha (1575–?), can be seen as a further attempt to integrate the shamanic tradition that had reemerged with the Mad Yogins and other nonmonastic practitioners with the rational, academic approach to Buddhism. In so doing they were aiming at a synthesis that gave a much more central place from the earliest stages to Tantra and the shamanic vision than had the synthesis developed by Tsongk'apa.

It is perhaps significant that Mikyöd Dorjé placed great importance on the *shentong* concept, the idea of Buddhahood as a positive potentiality, which was to provide the pretext for proscribing the Jonangpa order (see Karma Thinley 1980:93). Mikyöd Dorjé, along with other Kagyüdpa lamas since the thirteenth century, was also closely involved with Dzogch'en and the Nyingmapa tradition (Karma Thinley 1980).

Pema Karpo, the head incarnate lama of the Drugpa Kagyüdpa order, was another prolific writer in the scholarly tradition, whose relation to the yogic tradition is illustrated by his commentary, meditation-guide, and other writings on the 'Six Teachings of Naropa' (*Ch'ödrug Düpé Sindri*, Evans-Wentz 1967:155–252; *Sep'ö Tr'id, Sep'ö Shungdrel*, see Broido 1980, 1984, 1985a, 1985b). The last major figure of the Jonangpa tradition, Tāranātha, was similarly involved with the Shangpa Kagyüdpa's 'Six Teachings of Niguma' *(Nigu Ch'ödrug Tr'idyig, Nigu Ch'ödrug Shungtr'id)*. All this academic commentary on the yogic traditions helped to prepare the way for the achievement of the nineteenth-century Rimed or 'nonsectarian' movement.[7]

Drugpa Kunleg, the other figure among the 'Crazy Yogins' of this period to be mentioned here, has quite a different place in Tibetan culture from Tsangnyön Heruka. Drugpa Kunleg wrote no books, although his songs and exploits were narrated in several *namt'ar*. Like Milarepa, he became a popular figure in folklore. The stories about him center on his outrageous sexual exploits—all of course the genuine activity of a fully enlightened Buddha—and on his ridiculing of respectable monastic Buddhism. There are three *namt'ar* or biographies of Drugpa Kunleg available in Western translation, one each in French (Stein 1972b; see Jamyang Namgyal 1973), English (Dowman and Paljor 1980), and German (Kretschmar 1981). The French translation is made from the standard Tibetan *namt'ar*, while the English and German translations represent two somewhat different versions of a modern Bhutanese text, less clerical in style than the standard *namt'ar* and emphasizing the outrageous nature of Drugpa Kunleg's behavior (see Aris 1987).

One of the milder stories in the Dowman version tells how Drugpa Kunleg visits the Academy of Palk'or Stūpa where he watches the monks debating. His attention is held by a beautiful woman sitting on the edge of the stūpa and when a monk rebukes him for not prostrating to the stūpa, he prostrates to the woman instead, with appropriate verses. The monks are scandalized, but he reminds them that women in the Tantric teachings have the nature of wisdom, and that when they entered the *maṇḍala* they symbolically passed between a woman's thighs. Why should he distinguish between the girl and the *stūpa* as objects of refuge? In response to their further protests he sings a song using imagery straight from Tibetan folk-poetry:

Proud Kongpo stallion, matchless in style and elegance,
Black Tibetan horse, lifting high its white socks,
Both racing together on the wide open plains—
Aku's Stableboy bear witness—
See which is first to pass the flag!

Bengali peacock, matchless in fine feathered display,
Tibetan vulture, bird-lord with the wide wings,
Circling high in the empty sky—
Snow Mountain Heights bear witness—
See which bird has the bird's eye view!

Blue cuckoo in the tree's upper branches, matchless in song,
Red breasted house cock with deafening cokorico,
Both aroused by the season, stretching their lungs—
Old Man of the World bear witness—
See who tells the time correctly!

Ferocious mountain snow lioness, matchless in pride and paw-power,
Striped Indian tiger in the Sengdeng jungle, savage in anger,
Both in the Sengdeng jungle aroused to pitch of cunning fury—
Gomchens [meditators] and nuns bear witness—
See who truly rules the jungle!

Palden Stūpa abbots and professors of the robe, matchless Panditas,
And I, Drugpa Kunleg of Ralung, relaxing in the stream of events,
All examining our moral performance—
Incontestable Truth bear witness—
See who finally gains Buddhahood![8]

CULTURAL PATTERNS

A series of syntheses between clerical and shamanic Buddhism (T8b1, T8b2, T10b1, T10b2, etc.) developed during this period, giving increasing weight to monasticism and the clerical dimension. The Gelugpa tradition (T10e), originating in the early fifteenth century, was the most successful and influential of these. The growth of clerical Buddhism and the power of the big monastic establishments led to a shamanic reaction that stressed its foundation in the shamanic practice of the New Tantras (T10a1).

27

Tibet: Gelugpa Power and the Rimed Synthesis

THE GELUGPA REGIME, SEVENTEENTH TO NINETEENTH CENTURIES (T10d, T11d)

Drugpa Kunleg may well have been far closer to Buddhahood than the scholars of Palden Stūpa, but the clerical lamas whom he satirized in his verses were to become more and more dominant in terms of worldly power. Tsongk'apa had been patronized by the Neudong Gongma, the successors of Changch'ub Gyantsen, the fourteenth-century ruler of central Tibet, despite their formal Kagyüdpa affiliation. The Neudong administration, which was located in Ü, the eastern province of central Tibet, continued to favor the Gelugpa in the sixteenth and seventeenth centuries. During this period, power over the western province of Tsang and much of central Tibet had fallen into the hands of the Rimpung family, originally ministers of the Neudong Gongma, and of their successors, the kings of Tsang or Desid Tsangpa, whose capital was at Samdrubtsé (the modern Shigatsé). While these Tsangpa rulers favored the Karmapa (Karma Kagyüdpa) order, Gelugpa influence gradually grew in Ü, and particularly around

TABLE 8.
Cultural Patterns in Chapter 27

A.D. 1642 to 1950

- T7 Folk religion
- T8 Old Tantric and *terma* complex
  - T8a Hereditary priest lineages
    - T8a1 Buddhist
    - T8a2 Bönpo
  - T8b Dzogch'en-based syntheses
    - T8b1 Buddhist
    - T8b2 Bönpo
  - T8c New *terma*; Rimed synthesis <T8b, T10a
- T10 New Tantric complex
  - T10a Continuing yogic tradition
  - T10b Tibetan Monk-New Tantra syntheses; growth of clerical *gompa*
    - T10b1 Sakya synthesis
    - T10b2 Kagyüdpa synthesis
  - T10c Chöd yogins
  - T10d Reincarnate lama
  - T10e Gelugpa synthesis: large clerical *gompa*
    - T10e1 Clerical conservatism (P'awongk'a Rimpoch'e)
- T11 Buddhist-secular political alliances
  - T11c Secular ruler with lama support
  - T11d Reincarnate lama as ruler and emanation of Tantric deity (5th Dalai Lama, 1st Shabdrung Rimpoch'e) <T11a, T11b
  - T11e Moves to centralization (13th Dalai Lama)

Lhasa, which remained under the control of the Neudong administration. The political rivalry between Ü and Tsang gradually acquired a religious dimension as well, and was further complicated when Mongol tribes to the north and east of the Tibetan region became drawn into Tibetan politics.

The formal head of the Gelugpa order was the abbot of the Ganden monastic center, the Ganden Tr'ipa or titular successor of Tsongk'apa, but it was the Dalai Lamas, reincarnations of one of Tsongk'apa's younger disciples, Gendün Drub (1391–1474), who rapidly became the most influential figures in the order. These lamas were recognized as emanations of Avalokiteśvara, and eventually as rebirths of those previous Avalokiteśvara emanations, the monkey-ancestor of the Tibetans and the early Tibetan kings.

The third of these lamas visited the Tumat or Tümed Mongols in 1577–1578. He converted Altan Khan, the leader of this Mongol tribe, to Buddhism, and received the Mongolian title of 'Dalai' (= Ocean) from him. After his death a few years later, his rebirth, known as the 4th Dalai Lama, was discovered in the family of Altan Khan's grandson. The Karmapa were also building up their own contacts with the Mongols. The various intrigues and alliances culminated in fighting between Mongol and Tibetan supporters of the two monastic orders, and eventually the defeat and death of the last of the pro-Karmapa princes of Shigatsé. In 1642 the 5th Dalai Lama (1617–1682) was installed in the palace of Shigatsé as temporal and spiritual ruler of Tibet, with a lay regent *(desid)* responsible for the political administration. Gushri Khan, the Mongol ally of the Gelugpa, had the title of King of Tibet (Pödki Gyelpo).

The 5th Dalai Lama came from an aristocratic family attached to the Neudong court (Karmay 1988b:6). It is unclear how deeply he was implicated in the military intervention of the Mongols. A modern pro-Gelugpa historian presents evidence that he tried to avoid the fighting (Shakabpa 1967:106–110; see also Karmay 1988b:8–9, 29–30). In fact, it would seem that some such outcome was sooner or later inevitable.

The 5th Dalai Lama moved back to Lhasa, which was to be the new capital. His palace, the Potala (named after the mountain-residence of Avalokiteśvara), was built at Lhasa over the ruins of a palace that had belonged to the seventh-century King Songtsen Gampo whose rebirth the Dalai Lamas claimed to be. Like Changch'ub Gyantsen in the fourteenth century, the 'Great 5th,' who was a distinguished scholar and historian, was to make a conscious attempt to revive the old Tibetan royal style.

Gushri Khan's conquests included most of K'am as well as central Tibet. Direct Gelugpa control over K'am did not last, but the network of large Gelugpa *gompa,* which was set up at this time, was to have a continuing influence on K'am politics, as were the pro-Gelugpa secular rulers who were placed in power or had their position confirmed by the new regime (see Chapter 4). In central Tibet, the Lhasa administration was to have constant problems over its relationship with the Panch'en Rimpoch'e's administration, which was located at the *gompa* of Trashi Lhunpo at Shigatsé, the former capital of Tsang. All this was some way ahead, however, in the lifetime of the 5th Dalai Lama, who presided over a larger Tibetan state than had existed since the time of Changch'ub Gyantsen.

In 1649–1651 the 5th Dalai Lama paid a visit to China, where the Manchus had recently come to power. While Tibetan lamas had regularly visited China during the Ming period and been received with respect by the Chinese emperors, none of the Ming rulers had intervened militarily in Tibet or taken a particularly close interest in Tibetan affairs (Wylie 1980a; Sperling 1980). The situation with the Manchus was quite different. When the Dalai Lama reached Beijing there was an exchange of titles and gifts, and the establishment of a relationship that the Tibetan participants, at least, viewed as a renewal of the priest-lay patron relationship between the Sakyapa lamas and the Mongol emperors of China (see Ahmad 1970; Petech 1973a; Grupper 1984).

The 5th Dalai Lama was not a narrow-minded proponent of Gelugpa doctrinal supremacy. His own family had close ties with the Nyingmapa, Jonangpa, and Kagyüdpa, and he had studied Nyingmapa and Dzogch'en teachings, as had his teacher, the 1st Panch'en Rimpoch'e (see below). Consequently, the Dalai Lama's government was not necessarily opposed to the practice of other religious traditions within its new domains. Relationships with the other orders seem to have been determined by a mixture of political and religious considerations.

Thus the Drugpa Kagyüdpa had split into a northern (Tibetan) and southern (Bhutanese) branch over the issue of rival claimants to the reincarnation of its head lama, Pema Karpo. One claimant was supported by the Desid Tsangpa, while the other, who belonged to the hereditary lineage of the Drugpa order's founder, Tsangpa Gyaré, fled to Bhutan in 1616. This lama, later known as Shabdrung Ngawang Namgyel (1594–1651?), became the head of a monastic state in Bhutan similar to that which the Gelugpa established in central Tibet (Smith 1968a; Aris 1979; Rahul 1971). The conflict between the Gelugpa regime and the Bhutanese government gave good political reasons for maintaining friendly relations with the Tibetan branch of the Drugpa (Smith 1968a, 1970a:17).

The Karma Kagyüdpa and Jonangpa had been closely associated with the Shigatsé princes, the Gelugpa's main rivals for power in central Tibet, and they were treated less leniently by the new Gelugpa regime, as were the Bönpo. The Jonangpa order was closed down altogether, its head *gompa* converted into a Gelugpa institution, and its printing blocks placed under seal, where they remained until the mid-nineteenth century when the Rimed lamas managed to gain access to them (see Smith 1970a:17, 34–35, 1971:2). Despite this, some Jonangpa *gompa* survived in east Tibet, and the Karmapa continued their interest in the Jonangpa's *shentong* teachings (Ruegg 1963; Wylie 1962:104, 189 n. 691; Smith 1968b:8).

Several Karmapa *gompa* were also converted into Gelugpa institutions, though some of these were in fact Gelugpa *gompa* that had been taken over by the Karmapa during the conflicts of the previous century. A number of Bönpo *gompa* were also closed down or converted, and the Bönpo generally were to have a difficult time during the period of Gelugpa dominance (Karmay 1975a:186). The Karmapa, however, after the initial period of persecution, were to become on relatively good terms with the Lhasa regime, while the Sakyapa and Nyingmapa were also for the most part left alone (Smith 1970a: 16–22).

The 5th Dalai Lama was particularly partial to the Nyingmapa and was deeply involved with Dzogch'en and Old Tantra practice. He is reckoned by the Dzogch'en as a Dzogch'en master (N. Norbu 1986b:41–42), and his teacher, the 1st Panch'en Rimpoch'e (1567–1662), also had interests in Dzogch'en and syncretic sympathies (Karmay 1988a:144–146). As a consequence of the 5th Dalai Lama's Nyingmapa sympathies, a number of Old Tantra rituals thus came into the Gelugpa repertoire, especially at the Dalai Lama's own *gompa*, Namgyel Trats'ang, at the Potala.

Parenthetically, it is worth noting that all the non-Nyingmapa Buddhist schools adopted some Old Tantra rituals. The Sakyapa had in fact retained some Old Tantra practices, in particular the Vajrakilaya cycle, from the time preceding their adoption of the New Tantras,[1] whereas the various Kagyüdpa suborders all adopted some of them. There was a certain complementarity between these practices and the New Tantra traditions because while the Kagyüdpa, Sakyapa, and Gelugpa regarded the New Tantras as providing the best techniques for attaining Enlightenment, they considered Old Tantra practices, such as the Vajrakilaya, as particularly powerful in terms of the pragmatic sphere.

The tripartite system of government, headed by Dalai Lama, Tibetan regent, and Mongol chieftain, worked well enough during the later years of the 5th Dalai Lama's reign. He was a strong and effective ruler and soon established himself as the dominant power in the system. After his death, however, it was to prove dangerously vulnerable, especially during the period when the Dalai Lama was too young to rule in his own right.

The precise details of these political intrigues are not too important for our purposes (see Ahmad 1970; Petech 1973a, 1973b; Shakabpa 1967; Dhondup 1984). The death of the 5th Dalai Lama (in 1682) was concealed for fifteen years by his regent, Sangyé Gyats'o. Eventually the truth got out, and Sangyé Gyats'o installed the 6th Dalai Lama, who had been brought up in secrecy. The 6th Dalai Lama proved unwilling to take on the life of a celibate monk. He became renowned for his adventures with the young women of Lhasa, refused to take the full monastic vows of a *gelong* and eventually renounced his *gets'ul* (novice) vows. His behavior provided an excuse for Lhazang Khan, Gushri Khan's grandson and inheritor of his rights in the Tibetan situation, to intervene and depose the Dalai Lama, who died soon afterwards on his way to China in 1706. Not long before his death he wrote the last of the sixty or so short poems, in the folk-poetry meter of four six-syllable lines, which have made him part of the Tibetan poetic tradition (see Dhondup 1981; Tatz 1981; Houston 1982; Sorensen 1990):

> White crane,
> Lend me your wings.
> I won't fly far,
> After circling Lit'ang, I'll return.

Lit'ang is the place in east Tibet, several hundred miles away, where his reincarnation, the 7th Dalai Lama, was to be found (see Sorensen 1990:251–254).

For the next half-century, the political situation continued to be disordered and violent, both in central Tibet and in Bhutan. There were two who claimed to be the 7th Dalai Lama, one, from Lit'ang, supported by the Manchus and the other supported by Lhazang Khan. Another Mongol tribe, the Dzungars, attacked and plundered Lhasa and killed Lhazang Khan, as well as destroying the two most important Nyingmapa *gompa,* Dorjé Drag and Mindröl Ling. The Manchu regime in China sent an army to Tibet, which was defeated, and another, which succeeded in expelling the Dzungars, with Tibetan assistance, in 1720. The Manchu candidate was installed as 7th Dalai Lama, and the *desid* or regent was replaced by a council of four (later five) ministers.

Meanwhile, in Bhutan, the death of the first ruler of the Bhutanese religious state, Shabdrung Ngawang Namgyel, apparently in 1651, had been concealed, as was to happen in the case of the 5th Dalai Lama. It was not formally made public until 1705, and Bhutan in the meantime was governed by a succession of lay regents *(desid).* Following a series of disputes over the identity of the reincarnation of Shabdrung Ngawang Namgyel, a compromise solution was reached according to which three claimants were all regarded as simultaneous rebirths of the dead lama, generated by his body, speech, and mind respectively. The body incarnation (the son of a king of Sikkim) played no further role in Bhutanese politics, but the speech incarnation *(sungtr'ul,* from *sung-ki trulku)* and the mind incarnation *(t'ugtr'ul)* each formed the origin of a series of further rebirths. The *t'ugtr'ul* (or 'Dharmarāja') lamas were the religious heads of the Bhutanese state, and continued to rule with the aid of a lay (or sometimes monastic) regent, the Drugpa Desid (Aris 1979:258–261). This system of multiple reincarnations was widely adopted in the nineteenth and twentieth centuries, especially among the non-Gelugpa orders.

In central Tibet, after disagreements within the council of ministers and the arrival of another Manchu army, one of the ministers, P'olhané, emerged as the effective power in central Tibet in 1728. He remained so until his death in 1747. Phohané had, however, to accept the presence of a Chinese garrison and two Manchu officials. These officials, the Ambans, were stationed in Lhasa until the fall of the Manchu dynasty in 1911, although the amount of power they had varied greatly, depending in particular on how prepared or able the Chinese government was to intervene militarily in Tibet. Manchu armies came to Tibet on two further occasions, in 1751 and again in 1788–1792 on the occasion of a Gurkha invasion from Nepal.

The 7th Dalai Lama (wisely, considering what was happening around him) was almost entirely uninvolved in politics. He was an accomplished yogin and devoted to his religious duties (see Mullin 1982b:19–21, 166–180). A collection of his songs, which are on entirely orthodox religious themes, and often quite moving, has been translated (*Nyengur*, Mullin 1982b).

> Jetsün Lama, king of all Buddha families,
> Wishing tree possessing four kāyas,
> Cloud raining the millions of siddhis,
> I offer you my spiritual aspirations.
>
> When the parched grass of negative karma
> Tosses in the scorching winds of attachment,
> The flames of misery rise higher and higher;
> O Lama, light rain that pacifies.
>
> On the desolate plateau fenced by attachment,
> Barren of the waters of calm, clear Dharma,
> The heat of anger blazes ever on:
> O Lama, thick white cloud that cools.
>
> Help me to understand bliss and wisdom united:
> To see all forms as the Guru's body,
> To hear all sounds as the Guru's chant,
> And to know all thoughts as his vajramind.
>
> Direct a rain of your auspicious blessings
> In a steady flow to the life-drop at my heart,
> Quickly to open the laughing lotus
> Of my every temporary and ultimate fulfillment.
> (Mullin 1982b:91–92 = *Nyengur* 447–450)

Following the Gurkha episode in 1788–1792, which was blamed on intrigues involving the 10th Shamarpa, brother of the recently deceased 3d Panch'en Rimpoch'e, the Manchu government of China attempted to take control of the finding of reincarnations of high lamas. The Qianlong emperor (1735–1796) supplied a golden vase, and the Ambans were required to supervise the choice of suitable candidates and the use of the vase to select a slip of paper bearing the name of one of them. The Qianlong emperor's ruling that the Dalai Lama and Panch'en Rimpoch'e should not be selected from members of aristocratic families was generally observed, but the golden vase seems only occasionally to have been used. It was abandoned entirely with the decrease of Manchu influence in Tibet in the course of the nineteenth century, during which the Chinese presence was restricted to the small garrison at Lhasa (Shakabpa 1967:172–174, 176; Lessing 1942:60–61).

The 7th Dalai Lama had died in 1757. The 8th (1758–1804) followed his example and had little involvement in politics, while the 9th to 12th all died young. The Lhasa administration was headed throughout almost all of the nineteenth century by a regent, who was normally chosen from among the reincarnate lamas of four Gelugpa *gompa* at Lhasa. The history of central Tibetan politics for this period is mostly the history of intrigues between rivals for the regency, with the three major Gelugpa monastic centers of Ganden, Sera, and Drepung taking sides one way or the other (see Goldstein 1968, 1973, 1989).

Meanwhile the situation was equally disordered in eastern Tibet, where a remarkable religious movement was gradually taking shape.

THE NYINGMAPA REVIVAL AND THE RIMED MOVEMENT (T8C)

Four of the six main centers of the Nyingmapa order in Tibet were founded between 1656 and 1685 (Kat'og,[2] Pelyul, Mindröl Ling, and Dzogch'en). Despite the destruction of Mindröl Ling and of the earlier *gompa* of Dorjé Drag in the Dzungar troubles of 1717–1720, the Nyingmapa movement continued to grow during the eighteenth century. Mindröl Ling and Dorjé Drag were rebuilt, and the sixth major center, Shech'en, was founded in 1734. The Nyingmapa tradition, which until the seventeenth century had been essentially a decentralized affair of small *gompa* and hermitages, now had monastic centers, which while never reaching the size of the largest Gelugpa and Kagyüdpa *gompa*, were able to maintain a fully respectable academic and clerical tradition (see Smith 1969a; Khandro 1988; Eimer and P. Tsering 1978, 1982).

This development was doubtless assisted by the positive attitudes that the 5th Dalai Lama and P'olhané, the ruler of central Tibet in the early eighteenth century, had towards the Nyingmapa, although in point of fact four of the six *gompa* were in the state of Dergé in K'am outside the area of direct Gelugpa influence. The Nyingmapa revival in the seventeenth and eighteenth centuries also reflected innovations within the Nyingmapa tradition itself, including new and influential collections of *terma* such as the 'Union of the Precious Ones' *(Könch'og Chindü)* and 'Sky Dharma' (*Namch'ö*, see Chapter 16), both discovered in the early seventeenth century. Each of the new centers specialized in one or two of the *terma* cycles. There was also an upsurge in scholarly and academic activity (Smith 1969a:6–9).

The most famous of these scholars, Jigmed Lingpa (1730–1798), was also a *tertön* who received extensive teachings, while in a visionary state, from the great fourteenth-century Nyingmapa scholar Longch'en Rabjampa (Dargyay 1978:186–190; Goodman 1983). Like Longch'en Rabjampa, Jigmed Lingpa was especially involved with the philosophy and practices of Dzogch'en. The cycle of revelations known as the *Longch'en Nyingt'ig*, which Jigmed Lingpa received from Longch'en Rabjampa, became the basis of the main Dzogch'en teaching lineages in more recent times.

A short text from the *Longch'en Nyingt'ig* cycle, the *Nedsum Shanjed* ('Analysis of the Three Points'), presents some of the differentiating points between the Dzogch'en position and the other Tibetan religious traditions. It has been translated and discussed by Guenther (1977a:142–147). Here I summarize the text, using Tibetan terminology rather than either Guenther's occasionally idiosyncratic renderings ('decisive existence' for *ch'öku* = Dharmakāya), or the Sanskrit equivalents. As Guenther has rightly noted, key terms such as *rigpa* cannot necessarily be equated in Dzogch'en discourse to the formal Sanskrit equivalents (e.g., *vidyā*) implied in the Indian-derived discourse of most Tibetan Buddhist philosophy.

The first of the three points is the distinction between *kunshi* (Skt. *ālaya-vijñāna*) and *ch'öku* (Skt. Dharmakāya), the Enlightened mode of being. *Kunshi* is the lowest underlying state of consciousness in the 'eight levels of consciousness' scheme of the Yogācāra. Jigmed Lingpa, like Longch'en Rabjampa (Thondup 1989:210–212) is concerned to distinguish it clearly from *ch'öku*. *Kunshi*, according to the *Nedsum Shanjed*, is like muddy water. *Ch'öku* is like water when the mud, which represents the obscuration of mental processes, has settled. Mind *(sem*, Skt. *citta)* for the Dzogch'en tradition is not some kind of container within which thoughts take place but a continuing screen of concepts that obscures the true nature of reality. Awareness of *kunshi* comes about through treating ultimate being as an object, and it is compared to the formation of ice on water. It is generally mistaken, since the real objective is to rest in the purity of *ch'öku*. The implication is that followers of traditions other than Dzogch'en may run the risk of inappropriate reification of ultimate being, and so become stuck at the level of the awareness of *kunshi*, mistaking it for the ultimate goal.

The second point of the *Nedsum Shanjed* takes up the distinction between *sem*[3] and the open and all-encompassing awareness (Tib. *rigpa*),[4] which is a key concept of Dzogch'en thought. *Sem* is like the wind, *rigpa* like the sky through which it blows. *Sem* is a response to the passing images of perceived objects, while *rigpa* is an all-embracing background against which anything can appear (see Thondup 1989:212–213).

Finally Jigmed Lingpa contrasts *shiné* (Skt. *śamatha*) and *lhagt'ong* (Skt. *vipaśyanā*), the two forms of meditation that we met in early Buddhism, and which Tsongk'apa uses as central terms in his *Lamrim Ch'enmo*. *Shiné* "is like a man who is not in the possession of all of his faculties." It is an absorption of the attention in a single objective reference, while *lhagt'ong*, "like a man having the five senses in full," remains fully with the reality of what is.

While Jigmed Lingpa's three points imply a critique of various Kagyüdpa, Sakyapa, and Gelugpa trends, they also demonstrate the Dzogch'en concern with the positive, open, and creative aspects of the Enlightened state. The aim here is not so much intellectual definition as analogical suggestion. Jigmed Lingpa works through images rather than logical argument. This, he is saying, is what the shamanic vision feels like: the decisive clarity of pure water, the openness of space within which any event is met by a free and open response, the full possession of one's faculties. To become attached to intellectual models of the experience or meditational states encountered in the course of trying to achieve it is to mistake the path for the goal, whereas the real aim is to turn the goal into the path.

Several other texts from the *Longch'en Nyingt'ig* are available in English.[5] Jigmed Lingpa's version of Dzogch'en proved immensely influential, and laid the foundations for the Rimed movement, which has dominated the non-Gelugpa traditions since the mid-nineteenth century. Rimed and Gelugpa, as I have pointed out several times in this book, represent the two major syntheses between shamanic and clerical elements within premodern (and contemporary) Tibetan Buddhist practice. Of the two, the Gelugpa synthesis is the more clerical, Rimed the more shamanic.

Before moving to examine Rimed itself, we can note two features of Jigmed Lingpa's Dzogch'en teachings that were carried over into Rimed: the emphasis on the self-discipline of the yogic path, rather than the external discipline of the monastic career; and the emphasis on the openness and purity of the Enlightened state, beyond all limitations of logical thought or of conventional ideas. The first feature harked back to the 'crazy siddhas' of the fifteenth and sixteenth centuries (Chapter 26), while the second enabled Dzogch'en to be treated as a kind of ultimate teaching, towards which all of the various Sūtra and Tantra traditions were pointing. The convergence between Mahāmudrā (Chagch'en) and Dzogch'en, pioneered in the thirteenth century by Karma Pakshi (Chapter 24), and greatly developed in the seventeenth century by lamas such as Tsele Nats'og Rangdröl (b. 1608, see Blondeau 1983–1984) and Karma Ch'agmed (1613–1678, see Schwieger 1978) helped to bring the Old Tantra-Dzogch'en and New Tantra streams together. Karma Ch'agmed, also known by the Sanskrit version of his name, Rāgāsya, was closely involved in the founding of Pelyül *gompa,* which from the beginning was built around elements of both Kagyüdpa and Nyingmapa traditions (Khandro 1988; see Chapter 16). Other eastern Tibetan *gompa* developed similar eclectic approaches in the eighteenth and early nineteenth centuries.[6]

Jigmed Lingpa lived in central Tibet, but his fame rapidly spread to the east, particularly to the kingdom of Dergé, where his collected works were printed around 1790–1798 (Goodman 1983:85–86, 98–99). The principal heirs to his tradition were also in east Tibet. The two main transmitters of the *Longch'en Nyingt'ig* teachings were the 1st Dodrub Ch'en Rimpoch'e, Jigmed Tr'inlé Öser (1745–1821), the spiritual preceptor of the Queen of Dergé, and Jigmed Gyalwé Nyugu, both of them active in east Tibet. Jigmed Lingpa's three recognized rebirths, Do Ky'entse (1800?–1859?), Jamyang Ky'entsé Ongpo (1820–1892), and Dza Peltrul (1808–1887), were all key figures in the further transmission of the *Longch'en Nyingt'ig* (Goodman 1983; Thondup 1984). They were all also involved in various ways in what was to become the Rimed[7] movement, and Jamyang Ky'entsé Ongpo was one of its originators (see Dargyay 1978:197–209; Smith 1970a).

Jamyang Ky'entsé Ongpo was a Sakyapa lama, although closely associated with Nyingmapa and Dzogch'en traditions. Other central lamas in the early years of Rimed were Jamyang Ky'entsé Ongpo's close associate Jamgön Kongtrul Lodrö T'ayé (1813–1899, see Smith 1970a), who was a Karmapa lama of Bönpo background, their friend Shalu Losel Tenkyong, who was instrumental in releasing the Jonangpa texts from the ban they had been placed under by the Gelugpas in central Tibet (Smith 1970a:34–35, 1971), Dzogch'en Gyelsé Shen-p'en T'ayé (b. 1800?, see Goodman 1983:104–105), and the famous *tertön*, Ch'oggyur Lingpa (Ch'oggyur Dech'en Shigpo Lingpa, 1829–1870; Dargyay 1978:190–197; Tobgyal 1988). Ky'entsé Ongpo and Kongtrul were also *tertön*, and these three *tertön* were considered to be rebirths of close disciples and associates of Guru Rimpoch'e: thus Kongtrul had been Vairocana, and Ch'oggyur Lingpa had been Murug Tsenpo, son of King Tr'isong Deutsen, while Ky'entsé Ongpo was a rebirth of Vimalamitra, of Tr'isong Deutsen, and of the king's grandson Gyelsé Lharje (Dargyay 1978:190, 192; Blondeau 1985:155–156).

Tibetan Buddhism today outside the Gelugpa order is largely a product of the Rimed movement. Jamyang Ky'entse and Jamgön Kongtrul each had several recognized rebirths (Smith 1970a:73–76), and these lamas along with other Rimed followers dominated the great non-Gelugpa teaching *gompa* of east Tibet by the early twentieth century. Their names turn up over and over again in the biographies of contemporary lamas outside the Gelugpa order (see Chapter 18; Karma Thinley 1980; Tarthang 1977b), and the collections of texts they authored, such as the *Rinch'en Terdzöd, Damngag Dzöd, Gyudé Kuntü*, and *Drubt'ab Kuntü* (Smith 1970a:2, 62–67) have gone into standard usage.

The importance of Rimed is therefore evident enough, and I have already suggested several times that Rimed and Gelugpa can be considered as the two major and contrasting syntheses of clerical and shamanic elements within premodern Tibetan religion. The Rimed movement and the Gelugpa order were nevertheless very different kinds of phenomenon. Rimed was not a school with a definite doctrinal position. Jamgön Kongtrul, for example, was a strong proponent of the Jonangpa *shentong* theory, the 'positive' interpretation of *śūnyatā*, which had been revived by the eighteenth-century Kagyüdpa scholar Situ Panch'en (see Smith 1968b:8, 1970a:34–35). Kongtrul saw *shentong* as a unifying concept underlying the various religious traditions of Tibet (Smith 1970a:69). By contrast, however, Ju Mip'am (1846–1914), an important Nyingmapa scholar and Rimed lama of the next generation (Dowman 1973; Goodman 1981; Lipman 1981), rejected *shentong* and maintained the validity of the Prāsaṅgika-Madhyamaka philosophy, although with some differences from Tsongk'apa and his followers. Rimed today does not constitute an organized monastic order with its own *gompa*. The lamas who carry the Rimed tradition today continue to come from Sakyapa, Nyingmapa, and Kagyüdpa *gompa,* and to continue the specific lineages and practices of their own *gompa* as well as the general Rimed practices.

The term *rimed* is sometimes translated as 'eclectic'; Seyfort Ruegg has suggested that this is an inadequate rendering. "In fact this *rimed* movement was not exactly eclectic but universalistic (and encyclopedic), *rimed (pa)* (the antonym of *risu ch'edpa*) meaning unbounded, all-embracing, unlimited, and also impartial" (Ruegg 1989:310). It can be seen why Dzogch'en appealed to the Rimed masters; its emphasis on an unlimited, all-embracing Enlightened state within which all partial teachings could find their goal provided the basis for their synthetic orientation.

There were other unifying themes to Rimed. The epithets Jamyang and Jamgön indicate that Jamyang Ky'entsé Ongpo and Jamgön Kongtrul Lodrö T'ayé were considered to be emanations of Mañjuśrī. So were several other Rimed masters, including Ch'oggyur Lingpa and Ju Mip'am. As this cluster of Mañjuśrī emanations implies, Rimed involved a renewal of the academic and intellectual tradition within the non-Gelugpa schools.

The Gelugpa academic tradition of this time had become, for the most part, a fairly arid business. There were still Gelugpa scholars whose work displayed originality and insight, but many of the authors of the seventeenth to nineteenth centuries did little more than write commentaries, summaries, and textbooks based closely on the works of Tsongk'apa and his immediate followers. The emphasis on logical argument and disputation, as against Tantric meditation and direct experience, militated against much originality. The scholastic manuals *(yigch'a)* of the various monastic colleges provided catalogues of positions and refutations that could simply be memorized and applied in disputation without any real understanding of the underlying experience (for example, Sopa and Hopkins 1976; Lati 1980).

The Rimed lamas returned to the Indian originals, and their students were expected to study these directly, with the aid of interlinear annotations and expansions (Smith 1970a:26).[8] The aim was more to understand the meaning of the arguments than to label and name incorrect positions, and by returning to the originals the whole body of controversy that had emerged over the centuries through the Tibetan exegesis of these texts could be bypassed.

Rimed was however by no means simply an academic movement. It also had a strongly popular side. Dza Peltrul, one of Jigmed Lingpa's three rebirths, was a wandering yogin after the pattern of the fifteenth-century 'crazy yogins' and wrote a summary of the Buddhist path in colloquial and easily comprehensible language, the *Kunsang Lamé Shel-lung,* which became a popular religious classic (Bruyat 1987; Kazi 1989). Dza Peltrul's work is formally a book of instruction *(tr'idyig)* for the *Longch'en Nyingt'ig* preliminary practices *(ngöndro)* (Thondup 1982; Dilgo Khyentse 1988). It concludes with a section on the *p'owa* techniques for guiding the consciousness at the time of death. These, originally part of the Kagyüdpa 'Six Teachings of Nāropa,' became widely taught to lay people (Brauen 1985). Dza Peltrul is also known for short verse works such as the 'Propitious Speech from the Beginning, Middle and End' (Thinley Norbu 1984) and the 'Letter to Abushri' (Trungpa 1972:15–19), which present the essence of the Rimed and Dzogch'en teachings in a concise and popular way. The 'Propitious Speech' sums up the entire path in terms of the most basic and universal of all Tibetan religious acts, the recitation of the six syllables of Avalokiteśvara's mantra, *oṃ maṇi padme hūṃ:*

> Limitless phenomena are delusion, never the truth.
> *Saṃsāra* and *nirvāṇa* are just conceptions, nowhere real.
> If it is known that arising thoughts are self-liberated, this accomplishes perfectly the stages of the path.
> By this pith of liberation, recite the six syllables.
>
> Awareness and great void, inseparable, is continuous Dharmakāya.
> Without contriving, remaining in unending mind, luminosity self-arises.
> Spontaneously without effort, traverse the path by this sole method and accomplish Dharma.
> Just leave awareness fresh and recite the six syllables.
>
> With calm, stillness-mind cut following moving thoughts.
> With moving thoughts watch on the calm, stillness-mind.
> There is no difference between stillness and movement, so sustain fresh ordinary mind.
> Remaining in this sole experience, recite the six syllables.
> (Thinley Norbu 1984:27)

Another way in which Rimed lamas appealed to a popular audience was in their use of folk material, in particular the east Tibetan epic of King Gesar of Ling. Do Ky'entse, who wrote a book of Dzogch'en teachings in the style and language of the epic, is one of the earliest examples of this tendency, but it was Ju Mip'am's interest in the Gesar epic that made it into a major Rimed preoccupation. Mip'am wrote numerous works centered around the Tibetan epic hero, including a *guruyoga* text using the style and diction of epic poetry, a series of rituals focusing on Gesar as a long-life deity, a text for Gesar arrow-divination, and song-texts to accompany a series of folk dances inspired by the epic (the *Lingdro*, Lerner 1983). Three of the principal episodes of the epic were edited and printed under his supervision (Stein 1956). Several subsequent Rimed-influenced lamas such as the 8th K'amtrul Rimpoch'e, Döngyüd Nyima (1929–1980), and Kalu Rimpoch'é (see Chapter 18) composed new episodes for the epic (Helffer 1977:565; Samuel, in press a).

The Gesar epic has close links to the shamanic aspects of folk-religion, and Gesar himself is a trickster-shaman figure with many similarities to Padmasambhava. Visionary procedures continue to be involved in the creation of new episodes of the epic (Samuel, in press a, in press b; Yang 1989, 1990). The adoption of the epic by Rimed teachers again suggests the extent to which their position was open to the shamanic aspects of Tibetan religion and society. So does the importance of visionary techniques for the central Rimed figures. As I mentioned above, several of the original group of Rimed lamas were also *tertön*, and there have been many more *tertön* among subsequent Rimed lamas.[9]

If this suggests that the Rimed lamas were less universally committed to the clerical path of monastic renunciation than their contemporaries among the Gelugpas, then this was undoubtedly true, in that the ideal Rimed practitioner was as likely to be an unordained yogin as a celibate monk. Many important Rimed masters were not celibate monks, and several senior reincarnate lamas who were influenced by the Rimed movement took female consorts or *sangyum*, among them the 15th Gyalwa Karmapa, K'aky'ab Dorjé (1871–1922, Karma Thinley 1980:127) and the 10th Drugch'en, Jigmed Mip'am Ch'öwang (1884–1930). There were also many celibate monks among the Rimed movement, however, and as time went on they probably became more common. The essence of Rimed teaching was not to reject one path (e.g., monasticism) in favor of another (such as that of the lay yogin) but to maintain all paths as possible options that might be suitable for particular students. Thus, Śākya Śrī (1854–1919), an important Rimed lama of the early twentieth century, and incidentally a married yogin, many of whose descendants became important lamas in their own right, was equally noted for his mastery of the Mahāmudrā teachings and of the Dzogch'en teachings. He taught Mahāmudrā to some students, and Dzogch'en to others, depending on the individual student's needs and capacities.

Consequently, a central aspect of Rimed was the bringing together and transmitting of the numerous diverse traditions of Tantric yogic practice that had developed in Tibet over the preceding ten centuries. Jamyang Ky'entse and Jamgön Kongtrul appear to have combed east Tibet in search of the initiations and oral instructions of these lineages, both the famous and the obscure, and Kongtrul and his assistants assembled them in a series of great collections, the 'Kagyüd Tantra Treasury' *(Kagyüd Ngagdzöd),* the 'Jewel Treasury of *terma*' *(Rinch'en Terdzöd),* the 'Treasury of Oral Instructions' (*Damngag Dzöd,* covering Nyingmapa, Kadampa, Gelugpa, Kagyüdpa, Shangpa, Sakyapa, and Jonangpa teachings, as well as obscure minor traditions), and the 'Collection of Sādhanas' *(Drubt'ab Kuntü),* which brings together ritual texts from all the major traditions (Smith 1970a).

Once these works were assembled and the empowerments brought together in a single person, they could then be passed on as a whole. Empowerments of, for example, the entire *Rinch'en Terdzöd* (in sixty volumes!), allowing the receiver to perform any of the hundreds of practices within, were to become regular events (see Chapter 18). In this way, the Rimed masters opened up the entire wealth of methods and practices which had been accumulated over the centuries.

Clearly, the Rimed lamas did not regard these practices and teachings as exclusive alternatives, but as a body of partial descriptions and approaches, each of which might help to provoke the central insight of the shamanic vision. Rather than presenting a unique method for attainment, they made as many different methods as possible available, in a way that was quite unprecedented within Tibetan Buddhism.

All the Rimed lamas I have mentioned so far were Buddhist, but the Bönpo of east Tibet also became involved in the Rimed movement. Jamgön Kongtr'ul's own background was Bönpo, and he and

Jamyang Ky'entsé were particularly open to the Bönpo tradition (Blondeau 1979–1980, 1980–1981, 1984–1985, 1985, 1985–1986). The most significant figure on the Bönpo side was Shardza Trashi Gyantsen (1859–1935), author of a history of Bön, which has been edited and translated in part by Samten Karmay (Karmay 1972; see also Smith 1970a:35–36). The relationship between the 'new Bön' *(bön sar)* of east Tibet, associated with the Rimed movement, and inclining to Buddhist-Bön syncretism, and the more conservative 'old Bön' *(bön nying)* of central Tibet, which had become steadily more monastic and academic in tone (for example, see Skorupski 1981; Cech 1984, 1987), has some parallels to that between Rimed generally and the Gelugpa, although relations between the followers of the two orientations remained close.

The Rimed lamas were probably aware that in creating their vast compilations of both well-known and obscure lineages they were preserving traditions that might otherwise soon vanish in a rapidly changing world. The Tibetans have never been ignorant of the outside world. The continual contact with China and India through trading journeys could hardly have allowed them to be. The Rimed lamas, living in east Tibet, close to the Chinese borders, during the latter half of the nineteenth century, could hardly have avoided becoming fairly well informed about the Western impact on China.[10]

At the same time, events in east Tibet itself were far from peaceful. Dergé, the center of the Rimed activities, was occupied and the great Karmapa teaching *gompa* of Palpung was threatened with closure during the Nyarong troubles of 1863–1865. These events began when the Nyarong prince Gompo Namgyel embarked on a campaign of conquest that was to engulf much of east Tibet and lead to the arrival of an army from Lhasa and the increase of Gelugpa power in the region (Smith 1970a; T. Tsering 1985; Goodman 1985:60–61, 64).

We can see Rimed as a new attempt at a synthesis of academic and shamanic aspects of Tibetan religion that maintained the academic tradition but retained a much more central place for the shamanic vision than the Gelugpa synthesis allowed. At the same time, as its name indicated, it helped to break down the sectarian divisions that had developed over the centuries between the different traditions, each progressively entrenched within its own institutional monastic base.

If Rimed is considered as a synthesis, it is so in a quite different manner from the Gelugpa position. Tsongk'apa and his successors sought to narrow down, to define, to bring together in a single set of teachings all that was essential within Tibetan Buddhism. Even the various New Tantric traditions were to be reduced as far as possible to a common framework (see Lessing and Wayman 1968; Beyer 1973:111–143; Hopkins 1977, 1981; Cozort 1986). The Rimed approach was quite the opposite. All methods were to be gathered together and made available. Any one might contain the liberating potential appropriate to one or another student. Nor, as we have already seen, did the Rimed movement have any common philosophical standpoint.

The Rimed movement began in K'am, politically a patchwork of small secular and monastic states and of areas with little or no centralized authority, over which the Chinese amban at Xining and the Dalai Lama's government at Lhasa made vague claims of suzerainty (see Chapter 4). It is not surprising that the approach here leaned more to the shamanic and popular, while in central Tibet it leaned more to the academic and clerical. Rimed had little direct influence on the Gelugpa in central Tibet. Indeed, the Gelugpa tradition during the twentieth century was to become more centralized, hierarchical, and academic, paralleling the 13th Dalai Lama's efforts to increase the centralized power of the Lhasa regime.

THE TWENTIETH CENTURY (T10E1, T11E)

We come now to the premodern period, described in Parts One and Two of this book, a period in which the religious scene was dominated by the two contrasting approaches of Rimed and Gelugpa. The political events of the twentieth century in Tibet are relatively well known and have already been dealt with in part in Chapters 3–6. They will only be summarized in brief here (see Goldstein 1989). The 13th Dalai Lama (1876–1933) was the first Dalai Lama for many years to reach maturity and become an effective ruler in his own right (Bell 1946; Rahul 1969; Shakabpa 1967; Dhondup 1986). Before he could do so he had to survive the British military expedition to Tibet in 1903–1904 and the Chinese attempt to reestablish control in 1910–1911. The

Chinese threat was temporarily brought to an end by the overthrow of the Manchu regime in 1911, although fighting continued in K'am until 1918 and intermittently during the 1920s (Chapter 4).

During the 1920s, the 13th Dalai Lama's government introduced the various measures designed to modernize and centralize the Tibetan administration and the Gelugpa monastic system, which I referred to in Chapter 3. They included the creation of a standing army, the sending of young Tibetans to study at British schools, the attempted introduction of Western-style education within Tibet, and much greater control over the system of monastic degrees leading to senior Gelugpa administrative positions.

One can see in all these moves a desire on the part of the 13th Dalai Lama and his government to transform Tibet into an effective centralized state. It is known that the 13th Dalai Lama was deeply concerned about the possible future of Tibet after his death (Michael 1982:171–175; Dhondup 1986). The measures he introduced, however, had only partial success during his life and were largely to collapse after his death in 1933. As Melvyn Goldstein has observed, the Lhasa government was made up of representatives of monastic and aristocratic estates, and it was hardly to be expected that they would go very far against their own interests by strengthening the Lhasa government against those estates (Goldstein 1973). The new taxes that were introduced to pay for the standing army were particularly resented, and led to a conflict with the Panch'en Rimpoch'e, who fled to China, where he and subsequently his rebirth, the 7th (or 10th) Panch'en Rimpoch'e (1938–1989), were to play a significant role in China's Tibet policy (Mehra 1976). Meanwhile, the greater part of K'am and all of Amdo remained outside the control of the Lhasa administration, under the various combinations of local autonomy and nominal Chinese rule described in Chapters 4 and 5.

The Lhasa government was consequently ill-prepared to offer effective resistance in 1950, when the Chinese Communist regime decided to incorporate Tibet within the newly reunified Chinese state. The Dalai Lama's government was forced to accept the so-called 17-point agreement, which effectively brought Tibet into the Chinese People's Republic and led to the stationing of Chinese armed forces in Tibet. The Chinese regime rapidly proved unwelcome to the Tibetans. Resistance to the Chinese began in east Tibet, which had been placed under direct Chinese rule, and spread to central Tibet in

1959, leading to the flight of the 14th Dalai Lama and some 70,000 refugees to India and Nepal.

The Dalai Lama settled at Dharamsala in northern India, which has remained the center of the Tibetan administration in exile. Most of the refugees still live in India or Nepal, either in the northern hill-towns or in large agricultural settlements in south and northeast India. Many lamas and monks were among the refugees, and the major teaching *gompa* of the Gelugpa and other traditions have been reconstituted in exile.

The new monastic centers in India and Nepal have helped promote a revival of monasticism in the border areas, as well as opening up a new field of activity for Tibetan lamas in Europe and North America (see Chapter 18 for several examples). Further discussion of the state of the Tibetans and of Tibetan religion today is reserved to the Epilogue. The history of the Gelugpa order in Tibet until 1950 however requires some comment here.

At a time when the non-Gelugpa traditions were moving towards a nonsectarian approach that accepted the coexistence of different doctrinal positions, the Gelugpa order was moving in the opposite direction. As I have already suggested, the 13th Dalai Lama's efforts to transform Tibet into a modern centralized state were accompanied by similar moves to centralize the Gelugpa order under the control of the Dalai Lama's government (see Chapter 3).

The dominant Gelugpa figure of this period, apart from the 13th Dalai Lama himself, was his near contemporary, the 1st P'awongk'a Rimpoch'e (1878–1943). P'awongk'a Rimpoch'e was by all accounts a brilliant scholar and accomplished Tantric meditator, who is remembered with devotion by his disciples (see Rato 1977; Berzin 1972). He is remembered with less favor by the Nyingmapa order in K'am where, as the Dalai Lama's representative, his attitude was one of sectarian intolerance towards the non-Gelugpa orders and the Nyingmapa in particular (see Beyer 1973:239).

P'awongk'a Rimpoch'e was not an originator of new teachings or approaches. His significance for the Gelugpa was as a transmitter and codifier of the Gelugpa tradition. He stood for a strict and pure continuation of the tradition of Tsongk'apa as it had developed in the great Gelugpa monasteries of central and east Tibet.

P'awongk'a thus stood in a complex relationship to the 13th Dalai Lama, and in fact the two men were not personally close. The 13th

Dalai Lama, like the Great 5th, was interested in the Nyingmapa and Dzogch'en traditions, and received teachings from Rimed lamas such as Tertön Sogyal (also known as Lerab Lingpa; see Smith 1969a:17 n. 59; Mullin 1988:37). His own orientation seems to have been open-minded and eclectic, and he was not identified with P'awongk'a's conservative and traditionalist faction. Nevertheless, P'awongk'a was in some respects the logical expression in the religious sphere of the transformation that the 13th Dalai Lama was trying to bring about. Had the Lhasa government ever succeeded in turning Tibet into an effective centralized state, the Gelugpa might have continued to move in this direction and might have gradually eliminated the other Tibetan religious traditions in favor of a well-controlled academic and clerical version of Tibetan Buddhism.

In fact, P'awongk'a's influence was strongest after his death and that of the 13th Dalai Lama, and particularly after the forced resignation of the regent Reting (Ratreng) Rimpoch'e in 1941 and his replacement by Tagtrag Rimpoch'e, who had been a close associate of P'awongk'a and shared his conservative orientation (Goldstein 1989:353–363). It was at this time that P'awongk'a's students gradually moved into the dominant position that they have held within the Gelugpa order into the 1970s and 1980s. It is perhaps significant that the closest to a 'crazy yogin' in the modern Gelugpa tradition, the great scholar and historian Gendün Ch'öp'el (c. 1895–1951), met his unhappy fate at the hands of the Lhasa authorities during Tagtrag's regency. He was imprisoned in 1947 on charges of spying for the Chinese but there is little doubt that his unacceptable religious and political views (respectively Rimed and socialist) and his unconventional lifestyle were the real problems. He was released in 1950 when the 14th Dalai Lama took office, but died soon after (Norboo 1977; Dhondup 1978; Stoddard 1985a, 1985b).[11]

GELUGPA AND RIMED: TWO APPROACHES WITHIN TIBETAN BUDDHISM

Gelugpa and Rimed as they exist today are two different approaches to the question of how to reconcile the two polarities I have sketched within Tibetan religious life, the academic, scholarly, monastic, and clerical polarity, and the yogic, shamanic, and visionary polarity. They represent two different ways in which Tibetans frame their own traditions. For the Gelugpa, the most significant and valuable of the teachings have been organized through the work of Tsongk'apa and his successors into a linear, structured single path. For Rimed, the activities of the visionary teachers of India and Tibet have opened up many possibilities, all of them pointing towards an ultimate goal that goes beyond any verbal formulation, and the lamas and yogis of the present are both guardians and recreators of this complex heritage. Gelugpa and Rimed both contain shamanic and clerical elements, but the Rimed approach is weighted towards the shamanic side, and the Gelugpa approach towards the clerical.

To recapitulate some of the contrasts between the two approaches, I shall briefly examine two texts, one by P'awongk'a Rimpoch'e and the other by Jigmed Lingpa. The P'awongk'a text is one widely used among the Gelugpa today, his *T'undrug Lamé Neljor* ('Six-Session Guru Yoga,' Sherpa and Berzin 1981). This text is frequently given as a daily (or rather six times daily) recitation in conjunction with Gelugpa Tantric empowerments. While it is not strictly speaking a Tantric *ngöndro,* it has a similar role as an introductory Tantric practice to Jigmed Lingpa's *Longch'en Nyingt'ig Ngöndro* (Thondup 1982), one of the best-known Rimed *ngöndro* texts.[12]

P'awongk'a's text makes an interesting contrast with Jigmed Lingpa's. There are some differences resulting from the need in Jigmed Lingpa's case to incorporate the standard *ngöndro* sequence, and from the somewhat greater length of Jigmed Lingpa's text, but many of the basic constituents are the same. Both practices include the taking of refuge, the arousing of *bodhicitta,* the *maṇḍala* offering, along with the purificatory practice of Vajrasattva and the visualization of the lama as Tantric deity (these two combined into a single sequence by P'awongk'a) and the final dedication of merit.

There are also some differences: P'awongk'a's practice, for example, includes a detailed listing of the bodhicitta and Tantric vows (Sherpa and Berzin 1981:72–73, b6 to b11), while Jigmed Lingpa's practice includes an extended visualization of receiving the four empowerments (Thondup 1982:22–25, section 9). These make some sense in terms of the clerical-shamanic contrast. The Gelugpa student is constantly reminded of the need for discipline, whereas the Rimed student is directed towards the attainment of shamanic powers.

Jigmed Lingpa's text also includes a short *chöd* visualization (Thondup 1982:13–14, section 6). *Chöd* is, as we recall, a characteristic yogic and shamanic practice.

What is noticeable when equivalent sequences in the two texts are placed side by side is that the Gelugpa text stays at the level of the student's relationship to the visualized guru whereas the Rimed text constantly points to subtler meanings. These subtler meanings, which derive from Jigmed Lingpa's Dzogch'en perspective, underlie and eventually undercut the conventional reality at which the ordinary relationship between lama and student takes place. Compare P'a-wongk'a's refuge (actually a standard formula)

> I go for refuge, until I am enlightened
> To the Buddhas, the Dharma and the Highest Assembly.
> (Sherpa and Berzin 1981:71)

with Jigmed Lingpa's:

> To the actual three rare and supreme Jewels, those Gone to Bliss and the Three Roots [Guru, *yidam, ḍākinī*],
> To the awakening mind—the nature of the psychic system, energy winds and essential nucleus,
> And to the *maṇḍala* of the essence, nature and compassion,
> I go for refuge until the attainment of the quintessence of awakening.
> (Thondup 1982:9)

Here Jigmed Lingpa's text points beyond the conventional Three Jewels (Buddha, Dharma, Saṃgha), to the internal energy-structure *(tsalung)* of the body that is utilized in Tantric yoga, and further to the ultimate Dzogch'en refuge in the true nature of reality, in 'things as they really are,' defined by the three attributes of essence, nature, and compassion *(ngowo, rangshin, t'ugje)*.

The same is true of the *maṇḍala* offerings in the two texts.[13] P'a-wongk'a's offering is at the level of 'conventional truth':

> The body, speech and mind of myself and others,
> Our wealth as well as our virtues amassed in the past, present and the future,
> An excellent jewelled *maṇḍala* together with a mass of Samantabhadra's offerings—

I envision these all and present them to you,
O my Guru, my Yidam and the Three Precious Gems.
Accepting these in your compassion, bestow on me waves of blessings.
(Sherpa and Berzin 1981:72)

The *maṇḍala* offering in Jigmed Lingpa's text, by contrast, is made successively at three levels corresponding to the three *kāya*, first the material level *(nirmāṇakāya):*

A billion universes encompassing the three-thousand worlds
Filled with the wealth of gods and men and the seven precious jewels,
I offer in its entirety together with my body and possessions
That I may attain the state of a Dharma-ruler of the universe.
(Thondup 1982:12)

The *saṃbhogakāya* level, that of the Tantric deities, follows:

By offering the ultimately blissful, beautifully arrayed pure realm of Akaniṣṭha,
With assemblies of the five Buddha families endowed with the five certainties,
And inconceivable billowing clouds of offerings comprising the sensory objects,
May I enjoy the Buddhafield of the perfect body of enjoyment [*saṃbhogakāya*].
(Thondup 1982:12–13)

At the third level, that of the *dharmakāya,* we are once again in the ultimate realm of the natural purity of reality:

By offering utterly pure phenomenal appearances, the perfect body of the vase of immortality (eternal youth),
Embellished by unimpeded compassion, and the play of Reality Itself,
Together with the utterly pure apprehension of perfect form and energy,
May I delight in the Buddha field of the perfect body of truth [*dharmakāya*].
(Thondup 1982:13)

Examples could be multiplied from these and other texts, but the general contrast in emphasis should be clear enough. The Gelugpa ideal was the ordained monk, member of a large and reputable institution, properly respectful of the hierarchy within which he had a place, gradually purifying his consciousness and his behavior in imitation of the incarnate lama-monks who headed the system. The Rimed teachers were not antimonastic. Many of them were themselves monks. Nor did they reject the idea of purification. Nevertheless they sought constantly to remind their students that 'purification' was only a relative concept and that 'Enlightenment' involved a move beyond the order and certainty of the monastic life or indeed of any fixed pattern of existence.

All this goes along with the Gelugpa insistence on the single path defined by the works of Tsongk'apa, and the Rimed tolerance of a multiplicity of paths leading to the state in which there is only the awareness *(rigpa)* of the true nature of reality in its ultimate purity and perfection. In practice, the situation is more complex. One can certainly find signs of sectarian intolerance among the Gelugpa today, among whom the students of P'awongk'a Rimpoch'e are as dominant as the Rimed-educated lamas are among the Kagyüdpa and Nyingmapa. One can also, though, find sectarian feeling among the non-Gelugpa orders, and open-minded and tolerant lamas among the Gelugpa. The present Dalai Lama in particular is a leading example of such an attitude of tolerance and nonsectarianism, and has done much to maintain good relations among the various traditions of Tibetan religion in exile.

In other words, any generalization is an oversimplification. The overall contrast between Gelugpa and Rimed nevertheless does have considerable truth in it, both in regard to the attitudes of individual lamas, and in the way in which the lamas have adapted to Western and Indian society. The Gelugpa tend to be academics and purists, for whom mastery of the scholastic curriculum is a *sine qua non* for Tantric practice, while the other orders, especially the Kagyüdpa and Nyingmapa, place much more stress on meditation and the Tantric preliminary practices from an early stage.

Politically, too, Gelugpa and Rimed are associated with different approaches; the hierarchical structure exemplified in the great monasteries built by the Gelugpas, and the transcendence of any hierarchy except for the purely spiritual authority of the Dzogch'en master or Mahāmudrā guru at the higher stages of the Rimed path. As I have pointed out elsewhere (Samuel 1990), the shamanic approach is most at home in a stateless society, while the clerical is normally supported by and supportive of state power. The Rimed lamas in Dergé and elsewhere undoubtedly took advantage of state patronage for purposes such as the building of their *gompa* and retreat centers and the publication of their texts, but they never approached the degree of centralization and bureaucratic structure found in the large Gelugpa *gompa* of central Tibet, with their close integration with the developing structures of state power.

Thus Buddhism in Tibet, on the basis of the materials it took from India, and the creative innovations of Tibetan lamas through the centuries, developed two principal synthetic positions. In contrasting these positions, it has to be recognized that they have many features in common. Both accept the importance of monasticism, of philosophical and academic study, and of Tantric practice. Both accept the reincarnate lama system and the existence of an elite group of lamas who are the main teachers of Tantra and performers of shamanic ritual. Both treat the authority of the lama as essential. The difference in the social and political role of the *gompa* between the two is of degree, not of kind. All this is not surprising; they grew up in the same society, and incorporated many of the same cultural patterns and elements.

The Gelugpa synthesis, however, became more and more closely tied to the political supremacy of the Gelugpa order in central Tibet, while the Rimed approach, with its main centers in less centralized areas, retained a less hierarchical and more open view of Buddhist practice. The Gelugpa model was based on the large *gompa* of celibate monks, while Rimed kept a place alongside these large monastic *gompa* for the smaller centers of hereditary lamas, *serky'im*, and nonmonastic yogis. Each represents a development at once social, political, intellectual, and religious, and has to be understood in terms of such a unity. In the last chapter, I shall discuss some of the underlying processes behind these developments, and discuss their implications for the understanding of Tibetan societies and for anthropology more generally.

CULTURAL PATTERNS

During the period covered by this chapter Gelugpa monasticism achieved state power in central Tibet in alliance with local aristocrats and Mongol converts, while a similar Drugpa Kagyüdpa state took shape in Bhutan (T11d). Elsewhere, petty states governed by secular rulers with the support of lamas (T11c) alternated with more stateless regions. The Manchu dynasty of China, unlike the preceding Ming dynasty, intervened directly in Tibetan politics on several occasions, and succeeded in establishing temporary dominance over the Lhasa regime, although its influence decreased during the nineteenth century and disappeared after 1911.

The revival of the shamanic tradition noted in the previous chapter continued, and the Rimed synthesis (T8c) developed under its influence from the mid-nineteenth century onwards. In the twentieth century, Gelugpa and Rimed are the two major versions of Tibetan Buddhism, and the polarity between them represents the present-day form of the continuing polarity between clerical and shamanic aspects.

28

Conclusion

Chapters 20 to 27 have traced the course of the historical sequence (two converging historical sequences, if one takes India and Tibet separately) that led to the two major syntheses, Gelugpa and Rimed, of premodern and contemporary Tibetan religion, with their contrasting clerical and shamanic orientations. I have emphasized that this developmental process has to be understood as a total phenomenon. The term 'cultural pattern' in Chapters 20 to 27 refers to such a total phenomenon (the 'modal states' of Samuel 1990).

What was transforming in this process was not just the religious forms of a people, but their total orientation towards social relations and to life in general. It is also important that at any given time Tibetan societies contained several differing and even conflicting cultural patterns, and that these were distributed in complex patterns across the geographical and social space occupied by Tibetan societies.

To trace these developments in their full depth and complexity would be a more ambitious task than I have undertaken here. I have concentrated here on religious and political forms, as our best and most easily accessible information is available in this area. I have given less weight to the transformations in social structure or in emotional and cognitive patterns that were equally part of these developments. Other transformations, in technology, or in the techniques of using the human body, have scarcely been mentioned, but cannot be regarded as secondary.

I will return in a few pages to the question of how one may analyze such a process of total transformation. First, let us consider some of the more general issues raised by the analysis in its present form.

WHY BUDDHISM IN TIBET?

I start with a deceptively simple question: why Buddhism in Tibet at all? Western scholarship and Tibetan chronicles tell us that Buddhism came from India and, to a much lesser extent, China, but this does not explain why the Tibetans adopted it. The highland peoples of Southeast and South Asia, such as the Karen, Lisu, or Lahu in Thailand, the Naxi, Lisu, and Yi in Yunnan, or the Tamang and Gurung in Nepal, though exposed to Buddhism, have adopted it to a limited degree, as part of a largely non-Buddhist religious system, or not at all. By comparison, Tibetan society is pervaded by Buddhist thought, Buddhist concepts, and Buddhist practices. As I pointed out in Chapter 2, Buddhism in Tibet encompasses more of the religious activity of the population than in Thailand or Burma, or, for that matter, anywhere else in the Buddhist world.

A sociological answer might point to a number of factors, including the existence of states, if of limited extent and control, in Tibet, and the long-distance trade routes and consequent mobility, which meant that Tibetans were exposed to a much wider range of social contexts than any of the hill-peoples I have mentioned. In Chapter 20, I suggest that Buddhism in India, from the sixth century B.C. onwards, was, in large part, a response to the breakdown of small-scale traditional Indian societies at that time. Tibetans, too, live in a large and variable world, and the 'universalistic' religion of Buddhism supplies many of the cultural resources they need. These factors, however, point towards a second question to which, in fact, Chapters 20 to 27 are largely designed to answer: why did Buddhism take on the specific form it did in Tibet?

A Tibetan response to these questions ('why Buddhism in Tibet?'

and 'why did Buddhism take its specific form in Tibet?') would probably be phrased quite differently. A lama, at least, would be likely to answer 'because of the compassionate activity of Avalokiteśvara (Chenresig) and other great bodhisattvas.' As I suggested in Chapter 25, this is not as unscientific an answer as a Western scholar might at first suppose. If we consider Avalokiteśvara not as some kind of supernatural entity but as a label for a transformative mechanism acting through the lives of the Tibetan people, then Avalokiteśvara (and Mañjuśri, Tārā, and other Tantric deities) correspond to analyzable historical processes. We might proceed to note that the activity of Avalokiteśvara, in Tibetan thought, took a variety of forms. Among these were the initial fathering of the Tibetan population, and the introduction of agriculture. More significant in the present context, Avalokiteśvara was active through the early Tibetan kings who sponsored the introduction of Buddhism, and through powerful reincarnate lamas such as the Dalai Lama, the Gyalwa Karmapa, and Gyalwang Drugch'en. He was also active through his emanation Padmasambhava, and so through the 'shamanic' tradition of the *terma* revelations for whom Padmasamhava is the central figure. This points to two aspects of the development of Buddhism in Tibet. Buddhism was encouraged from above, by the rulers of Tibet who acted as its patrons, and it was adopted from below, by the common people of Tibet whose spiritual and religious needs it met. We can look at these two aspects separately.

I begin with the relationship between Buddhism and state patronage in Tibetan societies. If we look at the early stages of Buddhism in Tibet (Chapter 23), we see elements of a process common to many other Asian states from the time of the Emperor Aśoka onwards. The adoption of Buddhism was at least in part a matter of state policy, and was closely linked to the adoption of other cultural, political, and administrative forms. Buddhist temples and monasteries were part of the panoply of state power, and were expected to aid in maintaining that state power. This would seem to have been true of the Tibetan kings of the seventh and eighth centuries A.D., as of the rulers of the Indianizing states of Southeast Asia and elsewhere. The introduction of the pre-Buddhist court religion of the Shangshung and other Tibetan courts (T3 in Table 4) was probably an earlier stage of the same process.

The inner logic of this process was towards the achievement of a fully 'clericalized' form of Buddhism, such as largely happened in the Theravādin states of Southeast Asia. The events leading to the collapse of the Tibetan state in A.D.841, and particularly those of the following Local Hegemonic period (Chapter 24) nevertheless demonstrated the fragility of state power within Tibetan societies, and the consequent weakness of Buddhism insofar as it existed primarily as a branch of state power. Buddhism survived and flourished in Tibetan societies because it established itself outside the context of state sponsorship, as a part of Tibetan village communities. The weakness of state power meant that there was a lack of any authority able to enforce the process of clericalization, and Buddhism became, especially in its earlier phases in Tibet, a primarily shamanic religion.

When we turn to the adoption of Buddhism by the common people of Tibet, we see a different, and in the long run, more significant, aspect of its adoption. The folk religion (Chapters 9 and 10) was concerned with power; with defense against the dangerous powers of the physical and social environment, and with the utilization of the beneficial powers of the Buddhist clergy (primarily the lamas) for the good of the community. So, in effect, was the cult of Enlightenment, at any rate as pursued through the Tantras (Chapters 12 to 14). Power here was the power of the personal religious teacher, the *tsawé lama*, and of the Buddhist Tantric deities who were accessed through him. Ultimately this power was internalized within the practitioner and became available to help others.

It was primarily in the context of death that an alternative mode of thought became prominent, that of the inevitability of karma and of karmically determined rebirth (Chapter 11). If this was taken straightforwardly then Tantric power was useless to help at the time of death. Only virtue or good deeds *(södnam)* could help. Tantric methods were developed, however, to direct the consciousness at the time of death, both through the dying person's volition and through that of a lama in attendance.

From this point of view, the place of 'clerical' Buddhism within Tibetan societies seems to have been limited, and we may wonder why the Sūtra teachings and celibate monasticism should have existed at all in Tibet, let alone have become as pervasive a part of the system as they did. There is more to be said on this topic, however. For one thing, Tantric power in Tibet as elsewhere within the Indic cultural area was linked to austerity, asceticism, and the rejection of ordinary life. As I have suggested, this dying to ordinary life is perhaps a prerequisite of shamanic power in any society. Celibacy was not, for Tibetans, an essential part of this rejection of ordinary life and, as we have seen, an absolute commitment to celibacy was held to be a bar to the ultimate shamanic power associated with Enlightenment itself. The life of a celibate monk, however, was still an important step towards Enlightenment.

Celibacy and the observance of the Vinaya, the Buddhist monastic disciplinary code, were also an indication to possible disciples, and particularly to potential sponsors and lay patrons, that practitioners were not concerned with their own material success or with the acquisition of power over other people. I suggested in Chapter 2 that the rulers of centralized states in all Buddhist countries tended to insist on a well-ordered and celibate monastic community *(saṃgha)* for their own protection. Outside Tibet they largely succeeded in establishing control over the *saṃgha* and in containing and marginalizing shamanic modes of practice.

In Chapters 23 to 27 we have seen numerous attempts by Tibetan rulers or foreign powers in Tibet to do the same. Thus the early Tibetan kings restricted the Tantras and promoted Sūtra-style moral teachings, as did their successors in Western Tibet in the tenth and eleventh centuries. The Mongol leader Gushri Khan brought the Gelugpa order with its emphasis on celibate monasticism to supremacy. His successor Lhazang Khan intervened to remove the 6th Dalai Lama. The Manchu Qianlong emperor attempted to keep the appointment of reincarnate lamas out of noble families and to centralize it under representatives of the Imperial bureaucracy. Most recently, the 13th Dalai Lama centralized the structure of the Gelugpa order, and P'awongk'a Rimpoch'e, as the Gelugpa agent in K'am, attempted forcible conversions of *gompa* of the more shamanic Nyingmapa tradition.

What is conspicuous about these and other examples is the limited degree to which they succeeded. State power within Tibetan societies, whether internal (as with the early kings and the Dalai Lamas) or external (as with the various Mongol and Manchu powers who intervened in Tibetan affairs) failed to reduce the shamanic side of Tibetan Buddhism to the marginal role it had in other Buddhist societies, because no centralized regime ever had the ability or the will to enforce such policies within Tibetan societies over a prolonged period.

Nevertheless they must have aided the growth of the clerical side of Buddhism.

Ordinary Tibetans, too, were interested in the morality and holiness of the lamas to whom they turned for aid. Shamanic power is two-edged; there are few societies where white magic is not accompanied by its black and antisocial counterpart. This was doubtless one reason for the incorporation of the ethical dimension of *bodhicitta,* the desire to achieve Enlightenment specifically in order to save all other beings from their suffering in *saṃsāra,* at the center of the Tantric process (see Samuel 1989). It also helps to explain the respect and devotion towards celibate Tantric lamas among ordinary lay Tibetans. Given a noncelibate lama renowned for his power and a monk without much repute in Tantric practice, Tibetans would often choose the first to perform a ritual. Many leading figures among lamas in the premodern period, however, were both monks and Tantric masters.

This was one of the key advantages of the reincarnate lama concept. The reincarnate lama could be totally selfless (he had, with a few exceptions, no wife or family) and yet he could continue to act within the world and to return in successive generations. Indeed the mere fact that he had voluntarily accepted human rebirth implied his selflessness. Tibetans were by no means naïve about reincarnate lamas, but the idiom nevertheless inclined them to respect them. So did the presence of a substantial and well-disciplined following of celibate monks about any lama, reincarnate or not. In terms of the 'taming' metaphor of Chapter 11, it was an indication of the lama's ability to 'tame,' and so of his personal strength and power.

The monastic life also had its attractions from the point of view of individual practitioners *(ch'öpa).* It was a withdrawal from the karmic consequences of ordinary life in *saṃsāra* and a recognized step onwards in the spiritual path. It provided time to pursue one's personal spiritual practice and access to teachers and to training in that pursuit. Tibetans, in other words, became celibate practitioners because they regarded the goal of Enlightenment, so highly valued within their society, as personally important within their own lives, and saw celibacy as an important aid to pursuing Enlightenment.

This is not to deny that there could also be more material factors. Joining a celibate *gompa* could, for some people, have provided the main opportunity of acquiring an education beyond the elementary level. For others, it might simply have been more congenial than the sometimes harsh life of a Tibetan villager or nomad. From the point of view of parents (or siblings), a monk in the family could provide connections and access to resources otherwise unavailable, and perhaps relieve pressure on a family's limited land and other resources.[1] Becoming a monk, or having one's child become a monk, was a choice that earned respect and prestige among one's community. These are pragmatic advantages, and it is evident that Tibetans were often well aware of them.

Thus, monasticism became established within Tibetan societies, and we have seen how even the most shamanic orders, the Nyingmapa and Bönpo, developed a substantial celibate monastic tradition alongside the tradition of hereditary married lamas and lay yogic practice. Monasticism was clerical insofar as it was defined by a regulated life and a formal ethical code. It also provided the essential context within Tibet for the continuation and growth of other aspects of the clerical tradition of Buddhism: scholarship and literacy, philosophical and historical knowledge, the production of books, of images, and paintings. Elsewhere, as in the Nepal Valley, the arts and some degree of scholarship survived without celibate monasticism. In Tibet, with its far harsher climate and lower and less dependable agricultural surplus, it is hard to imagine how much of the sophisticated culture of Buddhist India would have survived, let alone prospered as it did, without the monasteries. We can thus see some of the logic of the Tibetan system as it finally emerged in the premodern period.

The Tibetan version of Buddhism was based, undoubtedly, on Indian Buddhist traditions, along with an admixture of Chinese teachings that are still difficult to evaluate properly (Guenther 1974b; Lai and Lancaster 1983). Yet these elements became in Tibet something qualitatively different, in many respects, from what they had been in India. The Tibetans achieved a succession of syntheses between religious orientations and modes of practice that were initially quite different from each other. This process had begun in India in the persons of siddhas such as Nāropa and Virūpa with a strong academic background and academic teachers such as Atiśa who were also trained in Tantra (Chapters 22 and 24). It went very much further in Tibet. It was accompanied by and in many ways inseparable from the growth of centralized power. Tibetan Buddhism in the period after the collapse of the early kingdom was, in various times and places, both an aid to political centralization and a brake on its progress, which was in any case limited by geographical and technological factors. Another part of this development was the gradual incorporation and 'Tibetanization' of originally non-Tibetan and mostly politically stateless groups. I have already suggested that this was connected with the continuing vitality of the shamanic aspects of Tibetan religion (Chapter 8) and I shall comment further on it below.

Each new synthesis between shamanic and clerical aspects offered a new series of roles and of relationships between roles. Each synthesis presented a series of what the anthropologist Victor Turner has called 'root paradigms' (Turner 1974), of possibilities for human behavior, culturally sanctioned opportunities to be, depending on your point of view, lived out or exploited. I have described these groups of roles and relationships here as 'cultural patterns.' They are grounded in the patterns of use of the minds and bodies of human beings, and they have an onward momentum that leads in its turn to further changes and developments (see Samuel 1990).

Shamanism is, among other things, a technique for manipulating and discovering these cultural patterns. In the shamanic Buddhism of Tibet they may be captured and propagated by the *tertön* or other visionary lama in a new form of a traditional deity, a new meditational cycle or yogic technique, a new philosophical school inspired by divine revelation (as in the case of Tsongk'apa), or an innovation such as the reincarnate lama system. In Chapters 20 to 27, I attempted to highlight the points at which such major innovations occurred, to point out their implications for the further development of the system, and to indicate how they maintained an onward momentum that led to the two major syntheses of shamanic and clerical Buddhism with which Chapter 27 ended, Gelugpa and Rimed.

TIBETANIZATION AND SHAMANIC BUDDHISM

Another aspect of the development of Tibetan Buddhism was its missionary and expansionist activity. This was a central part of the process that I referred to in Chapter 8 as 'Tibetanization,' the gradual adoption by an originally non-Tibetan (but usually Tibeto-Burman speaking) population of Tibetan cultural practices. Among the examples we have come across are the early absorption of the Shangshung and

Dardic populations in the west, the 'Tibetanization' of Hor and Mongolian groups in K'am and Amdo, the 'Tibetanization' of populations to the southeast (Gyelrong) and south (Naxi, Lisu) of Tibet, and of the Mön people, including the Bhutanese population, and the adoption by Tamang, Gurung, and other Nepalese peoples of Tibetan lamas and other cultural items.

This is a substantial list but not a complete one. In particular almost the entire history of eastern and northeastern Tibet can be seen in terms of the absorption of various non-Tibetan groups, many of whom, such as the Asha, Sumpa, and Minyag (also known as Tangut or Xixia), have vanished but for surviving names of places and lineages. As we have seen, the early phases of western Tibetan history followed much the same pattern.

In making sense of Tibetan religion, it is worth bearing in mind its involvement in this onward dynamic, which has undergone reverses (as with the Mongol and Chinese arrival in northeast Tibet, or the Muslim impact in the far west) but has never really stopped. The significance of lamas from recently Tibetanized areas such as Gyelrong in the last couple of centuries has been quite striking, both for the Gelugpa and particularly for the Rimed school.

The adoption of Buddhism was a critical part of the process of 'Tibetanization.' In Chapter 11 we saw how the same word in Tibetan, *dulwa*, implied taming, civilizing, bringing under cultivation, and conversion to Buddhism. For the Tibetans, spreading the Buddhist Dharma was a highly valued cultural goal; however, in constantly bringing new populations within the orbit of Buddhism, the Tibetans were also helping to shape the nature of Tibetan Buddhism itself.

Alexander Macdonald has discussed processes of 'Hinduization' (or 'Sanskritization') and 'Tibetanization' throughout the Himalayas in an important recent paper (1987b). As he points out, these processes in the Himalayan context have received little attention from anthropologists or historians so far. They have generally been seen in terms of the expansion of agriculturally based states located in the valleys into stateless hill areas, in the course of which the hill population gradually accepts the religion (Hindu or Buddhist) that constitutes the state's ideological support.

Macdonald agrees that states of any consequence have been located in valleys. He points out, however, that the hill peoples had their own local chiefs who had no need of Hindu or Buddhist ideologies of state, citing Philippe Sagant's study of Limbu society before the triumph of the Hindu state (Sagant 1981):

> That chiefs can have, can acquire charisma and 'clout' through the intelligent manipulation of subjects, livestock, land and labour without having recourse to either Hindu or Buddhist ideology will seem obvious to all of Sagant's readers. Political, economic and religious charisma are not separated out at this level. Authority and power are not qualities, in this context, which are either religious or political; they are both, and their manipulation is moral, in local eyes. (Macdonald 1987b:7)

He goes on to suggest that the Hindu or Buddhist states of Nepal (i.e., the Gorkha regime), Ladakh, central Tibet, or Bhutan could not have arisen through the voluntary adoption by such chiefs and their subjects of a Hindu or Buddhist ideology of state. Instead these polities were, "in their formative periods, characterized by domination achieved through violence" (1987b:7).

The role of violence in the creation and maintenance of these states is undeniable. I have discussed several examples in the Tibetan context, of which the most notable was the emergence of the Gelugpa regime through Mongol military assistance at the end of a long period of conflict between contending religious orders (see, for example, Wylie 1980a). Such factors undoubtedly help to explain the initial Tibetanization of Shangshung in the seventh century onwards and they still operated in the eighteenth century when the Manchu emperor supplied the forces to destroy three Bön states in the Gyelrong area of K'am and to convert a local monastery to the Gelugpa order (Martin n.d.). Nor was the exploitation of such factors confined to the Gelugpa (see Aris 1979 on seventeenth- and eighteenth-century Bhutan).

Yet organized violence alone does not explain the continuing processes of adoption of Buddhist ritual throughout these regions or its survival in Tibet itself where this kind of military backing was by no means always available. Nor does it explain why local chiefs in Bhutan or central Tibet or pastoral tribes in Amdo should choose to give their support to the lamas.

These local chiefs, in the earlier period in central Tibet and into recent times in areas like K'am or Bhutan, were very much of the kind described by Sagant and Macdonald. These men, the classic 'big men' of stateless societies around the world, manipulated their resources in terms of subjects and land and built up alliances with neighboring chiefs in an attempt to achieve greater power and status. What is striking is that from an early stage, Buddhist lamas and *gompa* became a vital factor in the construction of their alliances.

The distinction between clerical and shamanic Buddhism seems to me a key factor here. Clerical Buddhism in its ideal-typical form is a state religion encouraged and supported by the rulers and government of a centralized state whose existence it legitimatizes. There is little reason why the people of a decentralized society should adopt such ideas. If anything, they are oriented towards defending their society against the state (see Clastres 1977; Samuel 1990; Samuel, in press d).

Shamanic Buddhism is a form of religion adapted to such a social context. Its similarities to shamanic religion in small-scale preliterate societies is not at all accidental, although Tibetans had widespread literacy and were by no means parochial or isolated. I have pointed out elsewhere how a similar 'literate' shamanic religion arose in parts of the Islamic world where there was an analogous lack of centralized state power (Samuel 1982).

The state monopoly of power involves the rulers of the state specifying, or at least attempting to specify, the basic patterns of society. Centralized regimes typically have law codes and ethically oriented clerical religions based on a single dominant deity or divine figure who exemplifies their ideal pattern. In the absence of this specification of the bases of social life, the patterns of society and of religion take a different form (see Samuel 1990). In place of one supreme, officially endorsed deity, one typically finds a variety of such figures, each with their own slightly different mode of living. The manipulation of power in such a society involves the manipulation of these individual forces (or powers) just as much as the manipulation of labor-power and of land. This is the essence of shamanism (see Samuel 1990), and it is what the shamans (the lamas, in the Tibetan case) provide for their clientele. My suggestion is that Tantric Buddhism was adopted by stateless populations throughout the Himalayas and in Tibet in large part because it was believed to provide a superior set of techniques for manipulating these powers.

Shamans and diviners in shamanic societies are not simply concerned with manipulating powers. They are also entrusted by society with maintaining the balance between the powers. Judith Gleason puts this well in her book on the cult of the goddess Oyá in another and very different shamanic society, the Yoruba:

> [T]he diviners . . . are concerned not only with getting people who ought to be worshipping her to do so, but with keeping Oyá herself in line as well. The Yoruba oracle, known as Ifa, is a sort of regulatory agency created to foster a balance of forces in society, the universe, and the human soul. The worshippers of a particular god or goddess, by contrast, shamelessly extol his or her powers. They would, if they could, seduce the world to their own, their god's, own brand of madness. (Gleason 1987:2)

We can glimpse this kind of world in action in the Tibetan epic, which moves almost entirely within the shamanic world-view. Each character invokes his or her patron deities at the start of his or her song. The lama, and above all Gesar, the central figure in the epic, are left to ensure that the appropriate balance of powers within society and in the souls of human beings is maintained. In the context of the epic this is guaranteed by the role of the highest Buddhist patron deities, in particular Padmasambhava as the prototype shaman and the representative of Avalokiteśvara (see Samuel, in press b, in press d).

The role of the Tantric deities here reminds us that shamanic Buddhism was not just a variant form of shamanism dressed up in Buddhist vocabulary. The Buddhists were using shamanic procedures for their own purposes. In fact, as I argued in Chapter 20, and as Mircea Eliade suggested many years ago, Hindu and Buddhist yoga were in their origins a form of shamanism, and the possibility of reviving the shamanic aspects of these traditions never entirely disappeared. Buddhism from its early days involved a kind of transcendentalizing of shamanic processes, and the shamanic role of Tibetan lamas did not necessarily exclude a concern with Mahāyāna Buddhism's ultimate aim of the achievement of Enlightenment for oneself and others. For the lamas it could be seen as a skillful means *(upāyakauśalya)* to bring their followers towards Enlightenment, just as the ethical provisions and subtle philosophical understandings of clerical Buddhism were other kinds of skillful means appropriate to other circumstances.

SOME THEORETICAL ISSUES

In Chapters 20 to 27, I traced the major changes and transitions in Tibetan religion from the early days through to the modern period. I have tried to show that we cannot meaningfully separate innovations at the level of 'consciousness' from those at the material level within this overall process of development.

This is true for the social analysis of any society, but it is rarely put into practice. The Weberian tradition in sociology attempted to deal with the relationship of consciousness and society in terms of what Weber called 'elective affinities' *(Wahlverwandschaften).* Changes in consciousness and changes at the material level could harmonize with each other and reinforce each other as with his classic example of the Protestant ethic and the growth of capitalism.

Since Weber's time, the impact of the major transformations in the natural sciences between 1890 and 1930 has led to the gradual collapse of empiricist epistemologies. Westerners are, by necessity, beginning to accept what the Buddhists always asserted: that the world cannot be separated from the human beings who observe it and interact with it. One consequence is that it no longer makes sense to see, for example, the Protestant ethic and the growth of capitalism as two essentially separate but mutually reinforcing processes. They were part of a single process that was taking place both in the minds of individuals and in the development of new financial institutions and political forms.

The social sciences are only beginning to respond to this new situation. One might say, very broadly, that for both social anthropology and sociology in the last two or three decades there have been two major families of approaches. One, typified by symbolic anthropology, Lévi-Straussian structuralism, some varieties of psychological anthropology, and social interactionism in sociology, attempted to integrate human consciousness with reality but failed to produce an adequate account of large-scale social processes. The other dealt with large-scale social processes by one or another form of materialist reduction. Examples include most so-called Marxist approaches in sociology and anthropology (which had little to do with Marx beyond a few borrowed concepts), Marvin Harris's 'cultural materialism,' and various approaches derived from evolutionary biology such as Edward Wilson's 'sociobiology.'

Devising a mode of analysis that copes with transformations operating simultaneously in 'consciousness' and 'reality' is not an easy process. Perhaps the most promising approach in recent years has been Gregory Bateson's 'ecology of mind' (Bateson 1973). Nevertheless, neither Bateson nor his followers have produced a convincing account of how the 'ecology of mind' operates over time within a given society. This would, I take it, involve describing how modes of consciousness (incorporating intellect, emotion, and behavior) develop and affect each other, within the total context that is defined by the collectivity of such modes as well as by the material aspects of the environment as perceived through them.

The last eight chapters of this book could be described as a sketch of the transformations of the 'ecology of mind' in Tibet since the seventh century (with a backwards look at the earlier 'ecology' of Buddhism in India). I am very aware that the operative word is 'sketch.' In particular, the relationship between the transformations in consciousness and those in the perceived world have been dealt with only implicitly. In addition, many vital factors have been dealt with only sketchily, for example the role of trade and of technology within Tibetan history (Samuel 1982). In a land where wheels were well known but not used for transport and where an economic surplus was likely to be recycled into building a new image, *stūpa* or *gompa*, it hardly needs adding that neither trade nor technology can be seen as purely material factors.

The theoretical issues involved in such an analysis are not insuperable, although there have been few attempts as yet at dealing with them. I have presented my own views on these issues at length elsewhere in the form of a theoretical framework, the 'multi-modal framework' (Samuel 1990). In the present book, the framework is present mainly in an implicit form but it underlies much of what I have to say about shamanic and clerical approaches and cultural patterns.

A central point of the 'multi-modal framework' is the necessity of including changes in consciousness as factors within the total ecological picture. Innovations such as hereditary shamans adopting Buddhist Tantric techniques, the *Mani Kabum* with its concept of Avalokiteśvara being active in human affairs, the first recognitions of heads of *gompa* as rebirth of previous heads, or Tsongk'apa's specific version of the unity of the two truths were not simply new items of doctrine or ideology. They changed the nature of the reality that Tibetans experienced and within which they acted. Each new cultural pattern provided possibilities that led in turn to further patterns arising. Elsewhere, I have compared this to Thomas Kuhn's model of scientific paradigms and scientific revolutions, but what is important to appreciate is that the patterns are not just intellectual products but shapings or patternings of the way human beings operate (see Samuel 1990).

Looking back on the previous chapters we can see a series of major innovations, of which I have just listed a few, leading to an overall transformation of the Tibetan social field over the centuries in the direction of a synthesis of clerical and shamanic procedures. Retrospectively, such a synthesis may seem an understandable development in an environment where a strongly centralized form of government was probably impossible with premodern technology. The forms that Buddhism eventually took in Sri Lanka and Southeast Asia were not viable in Tibet. The power of centralized government that led to the gradual elimination of Mahāyāna and Vajrayāna Buddhism in those countries and to the institution of a heavily clerical and state-controlled monastic Sangha were far weaker in Tibet. Consequently, forms of Buddhism that vanished elsewhere survived and prospered in the Tibetan environment.

They did so by adapting to that environment or, more precisely, by being gradually adapted to it as they were integrated into the ongoing existence of the Tibetan population. The Tibetan *gompa* may have had prototypes in the forest hermitages of the Indian siddhas, in the monastic communities of Nepal or Kashmir or in the great clerical universities of north India, but as they became an established part of Tibetan society they became something different from any of their prototypes.

That process of change and adaptation continued throughout Tibetan history. I hope that one thing this book has demonstrated is how Tibetan societies, still occasionally used as a by-word for the static and conservative, were in fact in a process of continual flux and transformation. Scarcely a century passed without a major transformation in the nature of Tibetan religion and in its integration within Tibet's varied social forms. The Tibetan region in the immediately premodern period was the scene for two major processes of this kind, the increasing clericalization and rationalization of the Gelugpa regime under the 13th Dalai Lama and the revival of yogic or shamanic practice in both lay and monastic contexts promoted throughout Tibet by lamas of the Rimed schools.

Ideally, the account I have given in this book would be complemented, as I pointed out at the beginning of this chapter, by equally detailed accounts of transformations in technology, in bodily practices, and in the underlying structures of emotion and world-view. We are some way from achieving either, although I refer the reader to two works I have already mentioned, Robert Paul's psychoanalytic reading of the underlying structures of Tibetan (primarily Sherpa) society (Paul 1982b), and Sherry Ortner's attempt to demonstrate the presence of an underlying cultural schema through several centuries of Sherpa history (Ortner 1989a). Neither seem to me to cope with the problems of long-term transformation in cultural patterns, but both provide useful suggestions on the nature of what is being transformed.[2]

CLERICAL AND SHAMANIC: A FINAL COMMENT

The contrasting terms, clerical and shamanic, which I first introduced in Chapter 1, have played a central part in this book. I return to them here at its conclusion.

A convenient starting point is Peter Wilson's distinction between the unilinear scale of 'respectability,' which I associated with the clerical pattern, and the multivalued field of 'reputation,' which I linked with the shamanic pattern (see Chapter 11). Consider this distinction in relation to the variable and multifaceted figure of the lama. For all of the rational structure provided by Buddhist philosophers, the very multiplicity of possible roles and positions within the Tibetan system tended to place it in the camp of 'reputation.' There was no single hierarchy along which Tibetan religious specialists can be placed, even in the Gelugpa order, which was the most 'rationalized' and which excluded for the most part the various noncelibate options.

Thus, being a *trulku* (reincarnate lama) with a long and important lineage going back to famous Indian and Tibetan teachers certainly conferred prestige on an individual lama. So did being awarded a *geshé lharampa* degree by the Dalai Lama, or receiving the empowerments and the right to transmit important and valued Tantric lineages from respected teachers. Ultimately, though, Tibetans made judgments more on the personal qualities of particular lamas than on their formal qualifications.

Such an attitude was explicitly encouraged by Tibetan tradition. It is stated that one should examine a lama carefully before accepting him as one's Tantric guru, and even that it is good to try out many different lamas before reaching a decision. The multiplicity of Tantric lineages and other teachings reinforced this perspective, because the sheer variety of possible alternatives meant that the lama was essential in a way that a teacher in the more unilinear Theravādin system was not.

It was the lama's role to choose which practice was appropriate for a given student. The idea was not that certain teachings were better than others in any absolute sense, although some, such as the various Mahāmudrā traditions and the Nyingmapa and Bön teachings of Dzogch'en were regarded as more 'direct' and closer to the ultimate truth of the Dharma. The different teachings were thought of as appropriate to various students at different stages of their development and with differing personal needs and imbalances. Only the lama, who like the Buddha, had the ability *(upāyakauśalya)* to teach each individual in accordance with his or her needs, could see what a particular student required. This was true for the Sūtra teachings, and it was true with far greater force for the Tantra teachings, where the different Tantric lineages with their various *yidam* (tutelary deities) were specifically regarded as appropriate for different problems and imbalances within the particular individual.

Thus, the whole Tibetan system had a degree of fluidity, openness, and choice, which contrasts markedly with the Theravādin Buddhist societies to the south. Tibet was not part of the purely shamanic world of competing cult-groups found in, for example, parts of sub-Saharan Africa, but it was far from the official state-sponsored Buddhism of Sri Lanka or Thailand.

Theravādin societies, too, of course, have magic-working monks whose home is the shamanic world of reputation, and their importance at the level of popular religious attitudes is very evident in such matters as, for example, the Thai cult of amulets (Tambiah 1984). In Theravādin countries, however, these practices have a kind of 'unofficial' status, tolerated by the Buddhist hierarchy but hardly approved by it. In Tibet such attitudes and orientations pervaded the whole system.

Lamas constantly presented their students with systematic presentations of the teachings within which any particular practice has its place, and we came across some of these schemes in the course of our historical account (for example, the Sakyapa *lamdré* system and the Gelugpa *lamrim* teachings). There was, however, no overarching system within which all practices could be subsumed. All that they really have in common, apart from the *bodhicitta* motivation, which ideally underlies their practice, was their convergence on the indescribable and indefinable state of Buddhahood itself. In the last instance, the multiplicity of lamas, teachings, and Tantric lineages means that individual Tibetans who decided, as most Tibetans do at some stage or another in their lives, to 'practice the Dharma' have to rely on their own judgment of the possibilities available, and the judgment of the lama they chose as their personal teachers, rather than on any external criterion of what was a good or bad teacher or teaching.

This was true even of the monks who, I have argued, represented the most clerical and disciplined part of the Tibetan religious world. In Chapter 11, I quoted David Snellgrove's description of the Sherpa *gompa* of Jiwong in the 1950s, which spoke of the monks' "strong sense of personal responsibility and their wide freedom of action" (Snellgrove 1957:220). This is the positive converse to Sherry Ortner's view of Sherpa society as individualistic and atomistic (Ortner 1978a:18ff, 157–162). Few who know the Tibetans would disagree with Snellgrove's assessment.

The rituals performed by the lamas, when considered in Buddhist rather than folk-religion terms, were part of this pattern of multiple choices and shamanic power. They did not fit into any single linear scheme of progress to Enlightenment. The rituals themselves, at whatever level they are taken, were 'symbolic' not 'rational' devices, and the superabundance of such rituals in Tibet can be contrasted with the much more limited range of ritual performed by monks in Theravādin countries. Nor do such rituals as Theravādin Buddhist monks perform have anything like the complexity and sheer symbolic and aesthetic exuberance of Tibetan rituals.

Tibetan society and Tibetan religion nevertheless contained a continuum of practices from (to use the terms of Chapter 11) the 'wildest' and most shamanic to the 'tamest' and most clerical. At one ('tame') extreme could be found the process of training in the vast Gelugpa monasteries of central Tibet, with their heavy emphasis on monastic discipline as the foundation of the path, and their scholastic curriculum lasting up to twenty years preceding serious Tantric practice. At the other ('wild') extreme, the wandering yogi of the Nyingmapa or Kagyüdpa traditions might travel from teacher to teacher or meditate in solitude for many years, following his or her own path towards Enlightenment with the external guru providing constant inspiration but only intermittent guidance.

There is little doubt that secular authority in Tibet as elsewhere has preferred the 'tame' to the 'wild,' disciplined and celibate monks to autonomous Tantric practitioners, but the weakness of secular authority through most of Tibetan history has meant that the nonmonastic tradition survived and, in some measure, prospered.

As we have seen, even the Gelugpa tradition accepted that the attainment of Enlightenment in the Vajrayāna was incompatible with the strict maintenance of the Vinaya (see Lessing and Wayman 1968:37–39). Monastic discipline, for Tibetans, was something one took on, ideally at least, as part of a training that would eventually lead one beyond the need for such discipline. The ultimate objective of the Vajrayāna was not to be disciplined but to be beyond discipline, however far such an objective might have been from the daily reality of life as a junior monk in a large Tibetan monastery.

It is this ultimate objective that opened the way for a reconciliation between the centralized and stateless poles of Tibetan society. Whatever tradition they belonged to, all practitioners aimed at eventually achieving the transcendent freedom from all dualities and restrictions, which was implied by Buddhahood. Thus the lama was not just the 'tamer,' but a figure who in his own person reconciled the opposition between 'wild' and 'tame.' Symbolically, we find lama-figures in Tibetan thought who emphasized the 'tame' end of this opposition (Atiśa, Tsongk'apa, the 7th Dalai Lama) and others who emphasized the 'wild' aspects (Milarepa, Tsangnyön, Drugpa Kunleg, the 6th Dalai Lama).

Perhaps the prototypical symbolic representation of the 'wild' lama was someone who is often thought of more as a secular or political figure, the epic hero King Gesar (see Samuel, in press b, in press d). Gesar was an image of a kind of free and creative activity that went well beyond the bounds of the centralized and hierarchical state (see Tarthang 1978). Gesar was also preeminently a 'tamer,' both of demons and hostile forces in general, and of men. As I have suggested elsewhere, Gesar was only to a limited degree a figure of centralized authority. He was much more a figure of shamanic power, as his close links to Padmasambhava also indicate; a lama more than a king.

It may indeed be argued that in the epic, as ideally within the 'untamed' regions of east Tibet where Gesar's activity was centered, the role of shamanic power was not to create a state, but to maintain freedom from the state. Gesar's wars were wars of defense against hostile powers who desired to subdue and defeat the people of Ling (i.e., the Tibetans). Frequently these powers were identified as explicitly anti-Buddhist *(mutegpa* or *bön)* in their religious allegiance (see Samuel, in press b). While hostile powers tended in the epic to be assimilated to the nomadic model, their fortresses *(dzong)* were potential centers of state power, and their defeat by Gesar represented a successful struggle against the state.

Here we can refer to the work of theorists such as Pierre Clastres, Gilles Deleuze and Félix Guattari on mechanisms that inhibit or contest the growth of state power. Buddhism in the Theravādin countries became part of a state ideology, supportive of the power of the centralized state which in turn provided it with material support. Karma and merit *(södnam)* have some of these associations within Tibet but the other, 'wilder,' aspects of Tibetan value systems may be taken as reflecting a rejection of such ideology (see Clastres 1977; Deleuze and Guattari 1987).

It is perhaps not going too far to assimilate the Tibetan Vajrayāna as exemplified by figures such as Gesar or Tsangnyön to Deleuze and Guattari's concept of a 'nomadic science,' outside and intrinsically opposed to the official knowledge and to the structures of power of the state (Deleuze 1985; Deleuze and Guattari 1987). Nomadic science, as Deleuze and Guattari note (1987:362), is constantly subject to appropriation and transformation by State science, a process all too familiar in the history of Buddhism as in that of other religious traditions. Whether because of the special circumstances of Tibet's political and economic history, or for some other reason, that appropriation remained far from complete in Tibet.

Perhaps it would be more true to say that the nomadic science of the Vajrayāna, already appropriated by state institutions in India by the eleventh and twelfth centuries, was reclaimed by the 'civilized shamans' of Tibet as a weapon against the incipient state. At any rate, the Vajrayāna came to present to the Tibetans a way of being, and a form of social and political activity, capable of flowing around and beyond any kind of hierarchical structure. In a world where life is increasingly dominated by bureaucratic control, that ideal may continue to have an appeal to Tibetans and to other peoples.

Epilogue

The Tibetans and Tibetan Religion Today

Contemporary politics is not the subject of this book. However, the present situation of the Tibetan people requires at least some mention. Since 1959 the Tibetan population of the People's Republic of China (PRC), divided artificially between the Tibet Autonomous Region (TAR) and parts of four Chinese provinces (see Map 2 and Chapters 3–6), has undergone a period of forcible subordination to the modern Chinese state. During much of this period Tibetan religious and cultural institutions were actively suppressed, and Tibetans opposed to Chinese rule were imprisoned or killed. In the 1980s, under a more liberal Chinese policy, restrictions on Tibetan religion, language, and literature have been partially relaxed, and there has been an enthusiastic revival of Tibetan culture and of Tibetan religious institutions. This has been accompanied by the growth of a Tibetan nationalism that is unlikely ever willingly to accept Tibetan incorporation within a Chinese state.

The Chinese case for Tibet being a part of China has been canvassed and debated at length by other writers, and I have little to add to it here. Seen historically, it is weak; about as plausible as, say, a hypothetical claim by the Republic of India to Burma, on the grounds that the British rulers of India also ruled Burma for a while (a parallel to Mongol and Manchu rule over Tibet), and considerably weaker than a British claim to the Republic of Ireland or a Japanese claim to Korea. Chinese claims that Tibetans are one of the nationalities that make up the Chinese people are no more than linguistic sleight-of-hand. The Tibetans do not even have a word for this supposed Chinese people that includes Tibet. The Tibetan words for China and Chinese, *gyanag* and *gyemi*, unambiguously refer to Han-speaking plains peoples, excluding the Tibetans, Mongolians, and Turkic peoples. (This is why these words have been replaced in contemporary usage within the PRC by the borrowed Chinese word *zhongguo*.) The strength of the Chinese position is that they are in military occupation of Tibet, and that few national governments are prepared to compromise relations with the government of the world's most populous state in order to defend Tibetan autonomy.

It is clear from this book that Tibetans are very different from Han Chinese along many dimensions and that, whatever the formal political relationships among Tibetans, Mongols, and Manchus over the past centuries, Tibetans have never been incorporated into a Chinese state. I have argued that Tibetans in the premodern period were only to a limited degree incorporated into state structures of any kind. Tibetan communities were, to a large degree, autonomous and self-governing. What has often been presented as an atavistic desire by Tibetans to return to an allegedly feudal regime under the rule of the so-called God-King of Lhasa should be better seen as an unwillingness by Tibetans to be subordinated to any state regime, and especially one as unsympathetic to and as uncomprehending of Tibetan modes of thought and Tibetan institutions as the Chinese rulers of Tibet have so far proved.

It is also clear from Chapters 4 and 5 that the Tibetan 'problem' cannot be confined to the 1.8 million Tibetans who live in the Tibet Autonomous Region but also involves the 2.1 million Tibetans who live in what are formally parts of Qinghai, Gansu, Sichuan, and Yunnan provinces. With the exception of some areas along the eastern borders and parts of Amdo (Qinghai), where there are substantial populations of Han Chinese, Hui, and other minorities, these Tibetans live in regions that are entirely Tibetan in cultural terms and have been so for many centuries. They were no more effectively incorporated into the Chinese state in the past than were the people of central Tibet, and their claims to independence are as strong as those of the population of the Tibet Autonomous Region.

In practice, there may be little choice for the Tibetans in the foreseeable future except to settle for some degree of autonomy within the Chinese People's Republic, and little choice for any sensible Chinese government except to allow substantial autonomy to its Tibetan population. With the increasing penetration of the Chinese People's Republic, as of all modern states, by the world economic system, with all that that penetration implies for the autonomy of the Chinese and other governments, it may well be that within a few decades it will not make much difference whether Tibet is nominally independent or formally part of China. What is important is that Tibetans are able to participate fully in determining their own future and in determining the system under which they choose to live.

The future of Tibetan Buddhism today is difficult to foresee. Its social context has changed drastically from the premodern period. In the Tibetan regions of the Chinese People's Republic a large-scale religious revival is under way and many of the *gompa* destroyed during the Cultural Revolution are being reconstructed. The continuity of teaching and practice, however, has been largely broken and another change in Chinese policy could destroy much of what has been rebuilt. The nature of the revived Buddhism still remains to be seen.

Among the refugees, in Bhutan, and in the culturally Tibetan regions of India and Nepal, most of the major teaching lineages have survived, but potential students are exposed to a world that has little place for such an apparently archaic and irrelevant set of procedures as Tantric meditation. The overall body of cultural patterns that Tibetan Buddhism formed part of has largely disappeared, and it seems likely that the Vajrayāna will have to undergo drastic transformation if it is to find a viable and continuing place among future generations of Tibetans either in or outside the PRC.

There is a third context in which Tibetan Buddhism is active today besides Chinese-controlled Tibet and the Tibetans outside China. By now, tens of thousands of Westerners have had direct exposure to the teachings of the lamas. Thousands have done some Tantric practice and hundreds have undertaken traditional three-year retreats or been ordained within the Tibetan traditions. The numbers involved are growing steadily, if with little publicity, and the eventual consequences for what is increasingly a world cultural system may be significant. It is evident, however, that any survival of Tibetan forms of Buddhism outside the Tibetan community will again involve their radical transformation.

I have tried in this book to portray the traditional context of Tibetan religious practice as a whole and to sketch the processes through which it evolved. I hope anthropologists will appreciate this demonstration that the mystique of old Tibet was not without some foundation in reality. The book may be useful also to students of Buddhist societies and to Westerners interested in the Tibetan teachings. Tibet was a society that combined the literacy and rationality that we associate with centralized states with the subtle exploitation of shamanic processes more familiar from stateless and tribal peoples. As our own world moves past the certainties of the nation-state system into an uncharted future, we may still find that we have something to learn from Tibet's experience.

Appendix 1

The Monastic Population of Tibet

Writers on Tibet have traditionally assumed that very high proportions of the male population (25 percent or more) were celibate monks, but the evidence for these assertions is weak (see Andersson 1981). It is worth examining the figures for some of the areas discussed in Chapter 17. I shall mainly be concerned with the centralized agricultural areas.

Dingri. Barbara Aziz estimates that the twenty-seven *gompa* of Dingri contained "about nine hundred men and women by the middle of this century" (Aziz 1978:205). These included the two large centers of Dzarong, with five hundred, and Shelkar Ch'ödé, with three hundred. Aziz does not state what the male-female breakdown is, although Shelkar Ch'ödé would have been all male. Nor is it clear whether all of the community at Dzarong were celibate *ch'öpa;* however, we might assume a maximum of around 750 to 800 *trapa*. Aziz estimates the total population of Dingri as around 12,000 (1978:7, 51), perhaps on the low side since the Tibetan population of Tingri county, an only slightly larger unit, is today around 37,500 (Li 1987, map 33), not counting the 2,000 or so refugees in Nepal. Aziz's figures therefore amount to 750 to 800 out of 6,000 men, or 12½ percent to 13 percent of the male population at the outside. Another 850 men (14 percent of the male population) were *serky'im* or part-time religious practitioners or married *ch'öpa* (205).

Claes Corlin has given some figures for monasteries in the nearby region of Kyirong, and they would amount to around 750 *trapa* for a total population of 8,000 (Corlin 1975; the 1982 Chinese census figure for the modern county is around 7,500). Assuming that they all came from the local region, this would be about 19 percent of the male population; however, 650 of these 750 *trapa* are at the Gelugpa *gompa* of 'Samdeling' (i.e., Trashi Samten Ling), and it now seems unlikely that this figure is correct. Dieter Schuh, in his recent study of the archives of Samten Ling *gompa,* includes a list of the *trapa* for around 1956, which includes only 59 names, and this covers three associated *gompa* as well as the main *gompa* of Samten Ling (Schuh 1988:51). There may be some reason why not all *gompa* members were included on the list, but Corlin's figure is evidently too high.[1] Schuh notes that, on the basis of his archival material, 7.6 percent of the total population (i.e., men and women) of the villages attached to the *gompa*'s estate are *trapa*. Since no *ani* are mentioned, this amounts to about 15 percent of the male population on the estate. He suggests that this should be regarded as an upper limit for the monastic proportion of the Tibetan population (1988:50–53).

Sakya. Cassinelli and Ekvall estimate the population of the two monasteries of the Sakya capital, North and South Monasteries, as around 200 and 300 respectively (1969:289). Around 75 of the South Monastery *trapa* were from outside the Sakya territory proper, most of them from K'am (1969:297). Most of the rest were recruited through the monk levy system, as were almost all the North Monastery *trapa*. There were about another 500 *trapa* in the various *gompa* outside the capital, of whom 200 were at Ch'ök'or Lhunpo. Cassinelli and Ekvall state that "probably two-thirds" of the *trapa* at this *gompa*, who were all volunteers, came from outside Sakya proper. They list thirteen other *gompa* with a total of 284 *trapa* of whom 58 are described as "retired" (1969:400ff). Cassinelli and Ekvall estimate the total population of Sakya proper as about 16,000 (1969:33). The figure given in the last census for the modern county (Sagya) is 35,000, but this covers a considerably larger area (Li 1987, map 33). This gives a total of about

1,000 *trapa* for a male population of 8,000, or 12½ percent; however, around 75 *trapa* at South Monastery and around two-thirds of the *trapa* at Ch'ök'or Lhunpo were from outside the territory of Sakya proper and so should not be counted. This would take the number of locally recruited *trapa* down to 790 or just under 10 percent. (There is no indication of the origins of the 200 *trapa* at North Monastery, so I assume these are local.) Presumably, few Sakya men would have gone to *gompa* elsewhere.

Cassinelli and Ekvall give figures for female religious practitioners as well. There were 110 women at two *ani gompa* near the capital, Sasang and Rinch'en Gang, mostly recruited through the levy system, and 183 (of whom five were 'retired') at seven other *gompa* outside the capital. This would be around 3.75 percent of the female population, assuming they were all recruited locally; however, Cassinelli and Ekvall note that many of the *ani* spent around half their time working away from the *gompa* (1969:405).

Ladakh. As I mentioned in Chapter 17, Singh's figures for 'lamas' attached to the Ladakh monasteries seem high. In addition it is unclear whether all of these are actually celibate *trapa.* Given these reservations we can use Singh's figures as an indication of the proportion of celibate *trapa* in Ladakh. He estimates 2,905 'lamas' attached to the thirteen principal *gompa* and serving a total of 57,083 people (Singh 1977:368–369). Assuming half the population is male, and that all the lamas are male (see 1977:362, n. 9), this amounts to just over 10 percent of the male population.

Dergé. Kessler's figures, referred to in Chapter 17, amount to 7,235 in a total population that he estimates at 100,000 to 150,000. The figures for the monastic population may be exaggerated, but it is also likely that a number of smaller *gompa* were excluded. The total population seems reasonable in view of the 1982 figures (see Chapter 4). In any case, this amounts to 10 to 15 percent of the male population. There do not seem to be any specifically female *gompa* in Kessler's list.[2]

Hor States. Kessler suggests a population of 50,000 for the Hor states as a whole circa 1900 (1984:24), which is probably too low (see Chapter 4). His figures for the monastic population amount to 9,400, which, if accurate, would amount to 38 percent of the male population. As noted in Chapter 17, Teichman's figures for the large Gelugpa *gompa* are much lower and point to a total of 4,000 to 5,000 at most (16 percent to 20 percent of 50,000).[3]

The most reliable sources here (Dingri, Sakya, and Ladakh) give *trapa* as around 10 percent to 12 percent of the male population, although in each case these figures may be on the high side.

I have less information on remote agricultural areas. Jest's figures for Tarap in Dolpo refer to three villages with a total of 464 people living in 110 households. Thirty of these households contain lay *ch'öpa* (including seven who are Bön), amounting to 40 to 43 men (three only joined in at major rituals). There is one hereditary lama (Kagar Rimpoche) and one *trapa*, a hermit from K'am. In other words, around 17 percent to 19 percent of the male population are part-time practitioners (Jest 1976:310–314).

Melvyn Goldstein gives a similar picture for Limi in northwest Nepal, a community consisting of three villages and 791 people with a mixed agricultural and pastoralist mode of subsistence. There are three Drigungpa *gompa* with fifty 'monks' but it is clear from Goldstein's account that these are lay *ch'öpa* or *serky'im*, not celibate *trapa:* "The monks are recruited in the form of a tax and live together in the monastery for about three months during the winter. Monks are not celibate and do not wear robes when not in the monastery or performing rituals." This amounts to 12½ percent of the local population (Goldstein 1974:261, 266).

For the region of Shorung (Solo), one of the main Sherpa areas in Nepal, we have the figures of Oppitz and Funke for the late 1960s. Oppitz gives the total population as 11,680, apparently excluding post-1959 refugees (1968). According to Funke (1969) there were nine celibate *gompa* in Shorung at this time with around 140 *trapa* and 40 *ani* (2.4 percent of the male population and 0.7 percent of the female population). He also lists nine important village temples with 32 (hereditary) lay 'lamas.' These are the only lay *ch'öpa* mentioned, but it appears that many Sherpa have some religious knowledge and participate in occasional rituals.

For Lahul, the only figures I have are Harcourt and Lyall's from

1870 (Harcourt 1972), which give 1,100 lay *ch'öpa* out of a population of 6,300, or around 35 percent. The 71 'nuns' would amount to 2¼ percent of the female population.

I have not given any figures for pastoral areas since none having any degree of reliability are available.

The figures for celibate *trapa*, even in the centralized agricultural areas, are considerably lower than those usually quoted in the literature. We should perhaps take into account the very large Gelugpa *gompa* outside the areas considered above. The 31,000 *trapa* at Sera, Ganden, and Drepung came from all over Tibet, and there were several other very large *gompa* (e.g., Ch'amdo, the large Kandzé *gompa*, Kumbum, Labrang) that would have recruited from a very wide area. If we allow for 50,000 *trapa* in this category and a total Tibetan population (excluding Bhutan, which was outside this system of recruitment) of around 4 million, or 2 million males, this might add another 2½ percent overall to the celibate proportion of the male population. Much of this recruitment, however, would have come from areas, unlike Dingri, Sakya, or Ladakh, without large celibate *gompa* of their own. In addition, many of the *trapa* at these large Gelugpa *gompa* would in fact have come from the heavily populated agricultural areas close at hand.

There undoubtedly were areas in premodern Tibet where there were high local concentrations of celibate *trapa*. Spiti, for example, was one of these (see Chapter 17). Here monasticism may have been a local result of population pressure, though there are again the possibilities of a monk levy on villages outside Spiti and of voluntary recruitment from outside the Spiti region. Generally, though, for premodern Tibet as a whole, the proportion of the male population who were celibate *ch'öpa* (i.e., *trapa* or 'monks') would seem to have been in the region of 10 percent to 12 percent in the centralized agricultural areas, and considerably lower elsewhere. In some areas, at least 15 percent or 20 percent may have been lay *ch'öpa*. The proportion of women in both categories was much lower.

Notes

CHAPTER 1

1. I generally use Sanskrit for terms such as this, which are common to the wider Buddhist literature, so as not to obscure comparisons with other Buddhist societies. The languages of the Theravādin Buddhist countries borrowed Pali and Sanskrit words for Buddhist terminology; Tibetan, like Chinese, translates them.

2. On Bönpo, see below. Tibetan terms are given in phonetic transcription. Their correct Tibetan spelling, where ascertainable, is given in parentheses according to the Wylie system (Wylie 1959) in the Guide to Tibetan Spelling or (for book titles) References.

3. See Aziz (1976a), Stablein (1976b), and also Eliade (1958, 1970) on the general connection between yoga and shamanism.

4. Future lives are in the Tibetan Buddhist conception part of this world, not of the alternative mode of existence that the Tantric deities represent. They are part of the illusory or provisional truth *(saṃvṛtisatya)*. As in other Buddhist societies, death and rebirth are major concerns of Buddhism in Tibet.

5. Also spelled Bon, P'ön, etc. In the passages from Hoffmann I have reg-

ularized his spelling conventions to correspond to my own. This is done generally throughout the book except where it might cause confusion.

6. Although Hoffmann's two examples, both modern, are of spirit-mediumship, not soul-flight (1979:26–27).

7. Hoffmann's 'Systematized Bön' is equivalent in some respects to the modern religious order of Bön, but it implies more connection with the religion of the early Tibetan court than may be justifiable.

8. On this order, see Snellgrove 1961, 1967a; Karmay 1975a; and Kvaerne 1976b.

9. *T'ogmé sangyé* in Tibetan, often Sanskritized as 'Adi-Buddha' by Western scholars.

10. The Sanskrit term *saṃbhogakāya* originates in the Mahāyāna schools of India (Conze 1962:233–234) and was developed into the Trikāya or 'three body' doctrine of Buddhahood. *Saṃbhogakāya* deities are clearly distinguished in Buddhist theory from the various gods living in this world and in the heavens, who are karma-bound 'sentient beings' like humans or animals. For Tibetan lay people the boundary may be more hazy, especially since the same generic term *lha* 'god' = Skt. *deva* can be applied in both cases. See Chapters 9, 10, and 13.

11. Since Kuntu Sangpo is a symbol of the underlying unity from which all *saṃbhogakāya* forms derive, he is often described as a symbol of the *dharmakāya* rather than *saṃbhogakāya*. In the present context, as a deity to be evoked and identified with, he is nevertheless, as Dowman implies above, a *saṃbhogakāya* form.

12. Tibetan Buddhists group the Tantras in four graded classes (six for the Nyingmapa) culminating in the Anuttarayoga Tantra (or, for the Nyingmapa, the Anuyoga followed by the non-Tantric teachings of Dzogch'en).

13. On Tsongk'apa, see Chapter 26, and Kaschewsky (1971) and Thurman (1982, 1984, 1985). For a detailed commentary on the *Lamtso Namsum*, see Tharchin (1990).

14. 'Sentient beings' is Buddhist English corresponding to Tibetan *semchen*. It includes all beings who have consciousness *(sem)*, including humans, animals, gods, demi-gods, hungry ghosts, and hell-beings.

15. The reference is to a standard meditation for generating *bodhicitta* in which all sentient beings are thought of as having been our mothers in one or another previous lifetime, so that all are deserving of our compassion.

16. The Sanskrit term *bodhisattva* has a range of meanings that will become clearer in the course of the book.

17. Some purist Gelugpa scholars and lamas may reject Nyingmapa *terma* such as those of Göddemchen, and, as we will see in later chapters, there is a certain amount of interschool polemics. In practice, however, most Tibetans, monastic and lay, treat the texts of all schools as worthy of respect.

18. As also in clerical or shamanic Bön terms. For Bön accounts see Francke (1924), Snellgrove (1967a), Karmay (1972), and Martin (1986). Of these, the text translated in Karmay (1972), which is by a twentieth-century Bön lama with Rimed affiliations, is the most 'clerical.'

CHAPTER 2

1. I shall speak in this book of Bodhi-oriented and Karma-oriented Buddhism in preference to Nibbanic and Kammatic, the terms introduced by Melford Spiro (Spiro 1971). Apart from the inappropriateness of Pali-derived terms in a Tibetan context, Nibbanic suggests an orientation towards *nirvāṇa,* whereas Enlightenment for the Tibetans is explicitly beyond the duality of *saṃsāra* and *nirvāṇa.* The contrast intended is nevertheless similar to that drawn by Spiro.

2. Mandelbaum's article contrasts 'transcendental' and 'pragmatic' aspects of religion. Here, both Bodhi and Karma orientations may be classed as transcendental, although the Bodhi Orientation also has pragmatic implications. This is true in Theravādin societies as well (see Southwold 1983; Tambiah 1984).

3. Spiro himself separates these kinds of activity off into two further 'varieties' of Buddhism, apotropaic and esoteric. Here, again, his classification tends to conceal essential interrelations. As Tambiah has shown for Thailand, and the present work demonstrates for Tibet, the esoteric and apotropaic aspects of Buddhist practice are intimately linked with what I have called the Bodhi Orientation.

4. Technically, the defining characteristic of Tantric practice in Tibet is that it derives from a lineage of practice specifically defined as Tantric. Less formally, we can regard the orientation of the practice towards *saṃbhogakāya* deities as a diagnostic mark of Tantra.

5. In practice, monks may be astrologers or exorcists, monks often sacralize amulets and perform other protective functions, and lay exorcists and other practitioners may use Buddhist texts and sacred objects as part of their operating technique. This is, in part, what leads Tambiah to speak of a 'tantric' pole to Thai Buddhism. The relationship between these practices and the 'official' role of the Buddhist clergy is nevertheless quite different in character, and much less direct, than in Tibetan Buddhism.

6. Reincarnate lamas is a conventional and not entirely satisfactory English term. The concepts involved will be examined in detail in Chapters 15 and 25.

7. I deliberately use the Tibetan term *gompa* rather than 'monastery' throughout this book. 'Monastery' inevitably evokes a community of celi-

bate monks for a Western reader. This was only one of several kinds of *gompa* (see Chapter 17).

8. I use the slightly clumsy term 'series' rather than 'lineage' to avoid confusion with genealogical lineages and particularly with lineages of the teachings.

9. See Samuel (1982), and Chapters 3 to 8. A recent account of Tibet that adopts a 'centralized' model is Michael (1982). It does so by ignoring almost all of the literature on Tibetan political systems (see in particular Carrasco 1959; Cassinelli and Ekvall 1969; Goldstein 1973).

10. Guenther 1975, vol. 1, 158, translating the *Ngelso Korsum* of the fourteenth-century Nyingmapa scholar Longch'en Rabjampa (74ii et seq.). The fifteenth-century Gelugpa author K'edrubje cites this tradition but rejects it on the grounds that one contemplates oneself as a god in all four Tantras (Lessing and Wayman 1968:162–167).

CHAPTER 3

1. The plural form 'societies' is nevertheless not intended to imply that these various societies were rigidly bounded from each other. On the contrary, they formed in most respects a continuous social field.

2. Some commentators, notably Melvyn Goldstein (1991), refer to the Dalai Lama's regime as 'Tibet,' thus implying that most of K'am (Chapter 4) and Amdo (Chapter 5) were not part of Tibet. Goldstein uses the term 'ethnic Tibet' for this wider region. The distinction between the Dalai Lama's regime and other Tibetan political entities is an important one, but referring to the former as 'Tibet' is confusing and risks conveying the misleading implication (explicit in Goldstein 1991:9) that the Tibetan regions of K'am east of the Dri River (Yangtze) and of Amdo should legitimately be regarded as part of China.

3. This is not to suggest that these sources have yet been fully exploited, either in this work or by other writers. This is far from the case. Work with Tibetan literary sources, in particular, is in its early stages as far as social and political history is concerned, despite the pioneering work of scholars such as Turrell Wylie and Luciano Petech.

4. It is difficult to know what degree of reliability to attach to the census. The figures in the *Atlas* are internally consistent, for the most part, but doctoring for political purposes can hardly be ruled out. The low numbers of Han Chinese implied for most areas of Tibet are surprising.

5. Counting the Tibetan population of Sichuan and Yunnan along with the Qamdo prefecture of the TAR. This is an approximate figure, since parts of Yushu prefecture in Qinghai and of Nagqu prefecture in the TAR

were traditionally regarded as belonging to K'am, while Amdo included parts of the Aba prefecture of Sichuan.

6. Including the Tibetan population of Qinghai and Gansu provinces.

7. See similar ambiguities about ethnic identity in Burma and Thailand (Leach 1970; Moerman 1965; Lehman 1967). Lehman argues, rightly in my opinion, that ethnic identity should be seen as formally rolelike, rather than as a permanent attribute. Individuals in these regions can often shift between majority and minority ethnic identities.

8. The head of the Gelugpa order is the abbot of Tsongk'apa's monastery of Ganden (the Ganden Tr'i Rimpoche). The post is filled by a process of election and appointment, and its occupant is not necessarily a reincarnate lama (Sherpa et al. 1977).

9. Franz Michael, in disagreement with most other authorities, gives 60,000 for the population of Lhasa at the beginning of the twentieth century (1982:122). Like many of his population figures this is surely too high. The population for the greatly expanded modern city was only 105,866 in the 1982 census. Around half of these were Han Chinese (see Li 1987:30, 94–207). Martin Brauen, presumably following Heinrich Harrer, gives 30,000 for Lhasa in 1950 and 12,000 for Shigatsé (1974:197).

10. Rockhill cites the Chinese regulations governing the office of Amban, which give them very extensive powers (Rockhill 1891:291–295). Rockhill, who had not been to Tibet, appears to take these regulations at face value, but it seems clear that by his time they were a dead letter for the most part. For the Ambans' participation in the selection of the Dalai Lama, which rapidly became nominal, see Shakabpa 1967:172, 174–175, 176, 183, 192. They retained considerable privileges and according to Sarat Chandra Das, who visited central Tibet twice between 1879 and 1883, they were then still feared by the common people for their exactions (1904:236–241).

11. The Tibetan word *dzong* is still used for the *xian* or counties, the lowest unit in the Chinese administrative system.

12. According to Michael, there were provincial headquarters at four locations in central Tibet: (1) at Shigatsé (with two governors, one monk, one layman), (2) at Neudong in the Yarlung Valley, (3) at Yatung in the Dromo Valley, and (4) at Nagch'uk'a in the Changt'ang, where the two officials, a monk and a layman, were raised to Chiky'ab status in the 1940s. Ngari (Western Tibet) had two regional administrators of lower rank known as *garpön*. Michael lists two *chiky'ab* in eastern Tibet, one for K'am (at Ch'amdo, see Chapter 4), actually of *kalön* rank from 1913 onwards, and one for Hor. The powers of these officials and the degree of control they had over *dzongpön* within their provinces varied considerably (Michael 1982).

13. Fosco Maraini, who went along on Giuseppe Tucci's visit to central Tibet in 1948, claimed that the posts were so profitable that they were sold

to the highest bidder (1951:146). He gives no evidence for this statement, and other elements in his account seem exaggerated.

14. In the 1950s there were six *yabshi* families, i.e., families within which a Dalai Lama had been born, and five *depön* families (Prince Peter 1954). An interesting recent source on the politics of high-status *gerpa* families is the autobiography of Dorje Yudon Yuthok (Yuthok 1990).

15. The fact that they were also the heads of an order (the Sakyapa) other than the Dalai Lama's Gelugpa order was in no way an obstacle. This indicates how mistaken it is to see the Tibetan religious orders in terms of religious sectarianism. In fact, the basis of the K'ön family's repute for magical power seems to have been the Old Tantra rituals inherited from before the foundation of the Sakya tradition proper, so that in sectarian terms we would have a Sakyapa family performing Nyingmapa rituals for a Gelugpa patron!

16. Other authors might prefer to avoid this loaded terminology and speak of peasants who were defaulting on tax obligations to their estates; see Chapter 6.

17. Although one might expect Drayab, as a Gelugpa monastic estate without Sakya's historical status as former rulers over Tibet, to have less autonomy than Sakya in relation to Lhasa.

18. Goldstein (1968:26) lists eight *dzong* that had been given over to the Tashi Lhunpo estate to administer permanently.

19. The term Ganden P'odrang for the Lhasa government is actually a reference to the household of the Dalai Lamas at Drepung monastery, although they have resided in the Potala since the mid-seventeenth century.

20. Goldstein comments that "Before that time the Shigatsé District Commissioner had been a fifth rank lay official, but when friction with [Trashi Lhunpo] occurred it was embarrassing for the Central Government to have its officials outranked by a subordinate unit and therefore have to show deference. They therefore instituted the Tsang Province unit and filled it with a fourth rank official" (1968:37–38).

21. Despite Michael, who writes that "the political conflict originated not because of a conflict over territorial jurisdiction or power and authority, but because of a conflict over the privilege of tax exemption and the question of revenue" (1982:114). The prime importance of 'power and authority' in traditional Tibet was to secure revenue and corvée labor.

CHAPTER 4

1. Alternative terms of a more literary nature exist for these regions, Domed ('Lower Region') and Dotöd ('Upper Region'), but these terms are

not consistently applied. Thus the recent three-volume Tibetan-Chinese dictionary defines Dotöd as an alternative name for the Hainan and Golog prefectures (Tshe-brtan Zhabs-drung 1986:1383). Domed is explained as (1) another name for Qamdo prefecture, and (2) equivalent to Yermo T'ang, i.e., the region to the southwest of Lake Kokonor and to the south of the Ma River (Huang-Ho). The second meaning would seem to make Dotöd and Domed into subdivisions of Amdo. Paltul (n.d.) divides the whole region of K'am and Amdo into Dotöd and Domed but, while the greater part of K'am counts as Domed, the Nyingmapa *gompa* of Shech'en and Dzogch'en are counted as being in Dotöd. Lama Tsenpo (Wylie 1962) seems to use Dok'am and Med Dok'am as synonyms and to include part of Amdo within them.

2. For other descriptions of Jyekundo, see Rockhill 1891:203–208; Duncan 1952:198–200.

3. According to Rockhill, speaking of the 1880s, there were three permanent military garrisons on the road from Kangding to Lhasa, at Nyagch'uk'a, Lit'ang, and Ba (Bat'ang), and three more, which had at that time only recently been established, on the road from Kangding to Jyekundo, at Dailing (Kata), Dawu, and Kandzé. The garrisons were unarmed and had "absolutely no authority over the native chiefs" (1891:221–222).

4. According to Tashi Tsering, this Beri was not the Beri that later formed one of the five Hor states, but a place near Ky'ungpo (pers. comm.).

5. For example, Parmee 1972:18–25, 127. Three of Parmee's four K'amba informants attempted to reconcile this story with that of Avalokiteśvara's monkey-emanation, on whom see Parts Two and Three. The other, who came from Lingts'ang, stated it directly: "All K'ambas [are] descended from Gesar" (1972:18). Parmee's interpreter may have influenced his informants in the direction of the Gesar story; they are suspiciously consistent on the four kingdoms Gesar defeated. Also see the Sherpa genealogy given in Funke 1978:22, which begins with Gesar; the Sherpas originated in K'am.

6. According to Maria Phylactou, several places in Ladakh are associated with Gesar. Ladakhi marriages are explicitly said to be modeled on the marriage of Gesar (Phylactou 1989, pers. comm.). According to the 'Chronicle of the Ladakhi Kings' *(Ladag Gyelrab)*, the first Ladakhi kings were descended from Gesar (Petech 1977:16–17; see also Haarh 1969).

7. There were in fact few major *gompa* of any tradition that dated from before this period in K'am east of the Dri River (Upper Yangtze), though there were several to the west, including early Kagyüdpa centers in Pagshöd and in Mark'am, both dating from the twelfth century, and the Gelugpa *gompa* at Ch'amdo (1437). The Nyingmapa center of Kat'og dated from 1159 or 1164 and was just to the east of the Dri River but had largely fallen into

decay by the fifteenth and sixteenth centuries (Smith 1969a:6). The religious pattern in most of K'am until the seventeenth century was probably one of small hereditary-lama *gompa* of the Nyingmapa and Bön traditions (see Chapter 17).

8. There are two short and mainly demographic studies from the 1940s (Li 1947; Chen 1949). Their reliability seems dubious, which is perhaps not surprising in view of the conditions just described (see Appendix, nn. 2, 3). More recently, there have been brief contributions on Dergé (Thargyal 1988) and Gyelt'ang (Corlin 1978, 1980).

9. These figures are for the total population. Comparison with the distribution map for Tibetan nationality (Li 1987, map 33) nevertheless indicate that the population is almost entirely Tibetan except where indicated in my text.

10. Michael (1982:91–93) gives the misleading impression that K'am as a whole was under administrative control from Lhasa. He provides a long list of the local units under the Governor at Ch'amdo, some of which I refer to in the text. His information should be treated with considerable caution.

11. Tashi Tsering (pers. comm.). Franz Michael would seem to be incorrect when he refers to the *gompa* as Gelugpa, and describes Riwoch'e as governed by a monk official appointed from Lhasa (Michael 1982:89–90). Presumably the *chidzöd* or his local equivalent was appointed subject to Lhasa's confirmation, as at Dragyab.

12. Tashi Tsering (pers. comm.).

13. For descriptions, see Sermey Ribur Tulku 1988:5–12; Duncan 1952:125–130.

14. According to Teichman, Gonjo was a dependency of Mark'am, under a *depa* (1922:176). Anak Dorje Namgyal, who belongs to one of the nine ruling *(pönpo)* families of Gonjo, is not aware of the existence of a *depa* (pers. comm., August 1990), so this may be an error or reflect an earlier state of affairs. According to Franz Michael, the region consisted entirely of Lhasa government land and was alternately administered by a monk and a lay official (1982:91).

15. The nomenclature is slightly confusing. The upper parts of the region of Powo were under Lhasa control, while the lower parts constituted the Kanam Depa's state. Rockhill, Teichman, and other early visitors generally refer to the state as Pomed (= 'lower Powo'), while contemporary Tibetans generally refer to it as Powo. I use Poyul for the entire region and Powo for the state.

16. Tashi Tsering (pers. comm., July 1990). A Tibetan history of Nangch'en has been published by Karma Thinley (1965).

17. Tashi Tsering (pers. comm., July 1990).

18. Anak Dorje Namgyel (pers. comm., August 1990). The Anak family

in modern times had three *pön* positions, while the K'angsar family had two, so that there were only nine *pön* families for the twelve offices.

CHAPTER 5

1. The 1982 census listed 159,632 Tu and 69,135 Salar.

2. Not to be confused with the Sherpas of Nepal or the Zangskar in Ladakh.

3. The term Minyag is also applied to the Chagla region of K'am, see Kessler 1984, map 27.

4. The Tibetan population of Qinghai in the 1982 census was around 750,500 with a further 305,000 in Gansu (Li 1987). These figures include the Jyekundo-Nangch'en area (Yushu Tibetan A.P.), which belongs in K'am rather than Amdo and they exclude the Aba Tibetan A.P., parts of which belonged to Amdo. An article in *Beijing Review* 31(42), Oct. 17–23, 1988, gives a more recent figure of 810,000 for the Tibetan population of Qinghai.

5. There is a certain amount of inconsistency in nomenclature in Ekvall, Rock, and other writers on the region, which probably reflects a lack of consistency 'on the ground.' *Ts'o* is perhaps primarily a political term. *Gyüd* is a more general term for 'descent group' or 'lineage.' I have no information about the nature of kinship and descent groups among these populations.

6. The exchange between T'ukwan Ch'ökyi Nyima and his teacher Sumpa K'enpo (who, despite his origins, took the central Tibetan position) is perhaps symptomatic (Kapstein 1989). It was Amdo, too, that produced Gendün Ch'öp'el, the most unorthodox of all modern Gelugpa scholars (see Chapter 27).

CHAPTER 6

1. The exception was those parts of Ngari that lay within the Dalai Lama's state, and the area of Tawang to the east of Bhutan (Aris 1980:9).

2. The term Mönpa was also used to refer to the non-Tibetan population of Bhutan, and Mön to refer to Bhutan itself (though it does not seem to have this implication in the Gesar epic). There may be a relationship with the Mon populations in Southeast Asia; there were Mon states in what is now northern Thailand up to the twelfth century. Further west, in Ladakh and Baltistan (see below), the same ethnonym, Mön, is used to refer to a low status but thoroughly Tibetanized blacksmith and musician caste.

3. Tibetans were aware that the Lopa were a mixture of populations, see Aris 1980:15, 18, where Lo K'akar K'anag K'atr'a ('White-Mouthed, Black-

Mouthed, and Striped-Mouthed Lopa') is used to refer to "the whole medley of tribal groups in Arunachal Pradesh who live to the east of the Mönpa," and Aris 1979:142.

4. A more recent and detailed account is given by Imaeda and Pommaret 1990.

5. The ruling clans of eastern Bhutan up to the seventeenth century traced their ancestry to a member of the Tibetan royal family, a Prince Tsangma, eldest son of King Tr'idé Songtsen (also called Sednaleg, ruled c. 800–815), who was supposedly exiled to Bhutan (Aris 1979:83–114). Other aristocratic clans still extant in central Bhutan (the *dung* families) have similar myths claiming descent from other members of the Tibetan royal family or from a sky-god descended to earth, a common pattern for Tibetan genealogies (Aris 1979:114–145).

6. Not counting Rolwaling, which has a Sherpa population of 200 according to Sacherer (1974). There are now also substantial Sherpa populations in the Kathmandu Valley and in the Darjeeling- Kalimpong area.

7. For other research on religion among non-Tibetan highland populations in Nepal, see Fürer- Haimendorf (1974), Hitchcock and Jones (1976), Macdonald (1987a), Toffin (1987), Bouillier and Toffin (1989).

8. Traditionally, Ngari would have also included the western parts of present-day Xigazê prefecture, such as the regions of Dingri and Kyirong (see Map 3), but these areas with their large agricultural populations are best considered, as we have done, as part of central Tibet (see Surkhang 1984:20, 28 n. 2).

9. An earlier study by one of the Moravian missionaries (Ribbach 1986) includes useful comparative material.

CHAPTER 7

1. A term that, as Aziz points out, also includes traders *(ts'ongpa)* in trading centers such as the main Dingri town.

2. The large proportion of *serky'im* in the Dingri region doubtless reflected the important Nyingmapa and Kagyüdpa pilgrimage centers located there. *Serky'im* were, however, found throughout Tibetan society (see Chapters 15 to 17).

3. Goldstein argues implausibly, that the question of 'serfdom' has no bearing on Tibetan political claims, since the Chinese tolerated the estate system from 1951 to 1959 (Goldstein 1986:109 n. 2). In Goldstein and Beall's recent account of Tibetan nomads (1990), while still retaining the nomenclature of 'serfdom,' they emphasize the autonomy of these pastoral 'serfs' in relation to their daily lives.

4. Ortner's hypothesis as to how the office of *pönpo (pembu)* developed out of land ownership is not entirely convincing (Ortner 1989a:40–41). It would seem more likely that it originated at the same time as the tax obligations to the Nepalese government. Revenue-collection was also the primary function of *dzongpön* and similar officials in Tibet, so that *pönpo* would be a natural term for a tax collector.

5. These were the Sapön or 'Headmen' and the Shik'a or 'District Officers.'

6. Sherry Ortner emphasizes the separateness and independence of Sherpa households, and the difficulty involved in achieving even a minimum of social cooperation, in her film *The Sherpas of Nepal* (in the Granada *Disappearing World* series) as well as in Ortner 1978a. Sherpa households were perhaps more independent than households in central Tibet or in some of the other Tibetan communities in Nepal. Sherpas tended to build their houses at some distance from each other instead of in compact villages.

7. We should also bear in mind the existence of slavery in some of the far western groups, such as the Nyinba (Levine 1980).

8. In Ladakhi dialect, unlike central Tibetan and many Eastern dialects, the final 's' is sounded.

9. The *phaspun* group in Zanskar consists according to Dargyay of the male members of a *ruspa* along with their wives (1988:127). This seems compatible with Brauen's account for Ladakh although Brauen does not mention *ruspa* at all (1980a, 1980b). In Ladakh, according to Brauen, a *magpa* husband joined his wife's *phaspun,* and presumably this happened in Zanskar, too. The concept of *rüpa* is also significant in the northern part of K'am, judging from my enquiries in Jyekundo in August 1991, and possibly through much of eastern Tibet. I know of no substantial research, however, on K'amba kinship as yet.

10. The first two examples refer to actual events, while the third is fictional. Ekvall's novels (1954a, 1981) may be treated as an ethnographic source, with appropriate caution. Ekvall approvingly quotes a review that describes *Tents Against the Sky* as "of indifferent quality as fiction but most excellent ethnography" (1968:99) and states in the introduction to *The Lama Knows* that the book is "basically a record of phenomenal happenings, and tells of actual persons and their deeds—some real and some ascribed," going on to give his sources for the events in the novel (1981:xiii–xvi). In fact the novels, along with the autobiographical account *Tibetan Skylines* (1952), are a useful complement to the abstract generalizations of Ekvall's strictly anthropological writings (for example, 1939, 1964a, 1964b, 1968).

11. This point is of significance in relation to the argument in Chapter 2 about the state and the 'domestication' of the Saṃgha in Theravādin societies, and the weakness of such a relationship within Tibet.

CHAPTER 8

1. Two more examples of some interest are the term *dé*, which Lama Tsenpo uses as an all-purpose label for any kind of community, whether agricultural or pastoral, in the *Dzamling Gyeshed* (Wylie 1962) and the gradual expansion and modification by which the four *rü* and the six-tribe and eighteen-tribe schemes were adapted to non-Tibetan peoples undergoing Tibetanization (Smith 1969c:22–24 n. 52).

2. Even in the twentieth century when a particularly strong Lhasa administration forced a showdown with these two regions over revenue they encountered heavy fighting in one case and provoked the Panch'en Rimpoch'e's flight to China in the other.

3. There has been some discussion of the relevance of trade routes to the spread of Buddhism in Tibet, for example, von Schroeder (1981) and Klimburg-Salter (1982).

4. Robert Paul's analysis (1982b) of Tibetan symbolism in terms of a succession-scenario derived from Freud's treatment of the Oedipus myth reveals much of the psychological background to these processes of continuity and succession. He rightly notes the significance of the incarnate lama as a solution to the psychological problem of succession (see Chapter 25).

5. The temple-as-microcosm has Indian parallels too, but the point here concerns the way in which it fits into Tibetan modes of thought.

CHAPTER 9

1. From the mantra *oṃ maṇi padme hūṃ* commonly inscribed on them.

2. In a recent paper on two east Tibetan pilgrimage sites (1990a), Larry Epstein has made an similar contrast between 'ontic' and 'epistemic' modes of experiencing space and place. Of the two sites, one (Murdo in Gyelrong) can be seen as more ontic (shamanic, in my terms) and the other (Dragkar in Amdo) as more epistemic (clerical).

3. On the relation between *drib* and karma, see Lichter and Epstein (1983) and Schicklgruber (1989).

4. Interview with Namk'a Drimed Rimpoch'e, Chandragiri, 3 August 1990, transcribed with assistance from Tashi Tsering.

5. Information from Drugu Choegyal Rimpoch'e, Tashijong, July 1989.

6. Although deities such as Gompo (Mahākāla) may be in origin forms of Śiva, who is a heavenly deity in this classification (see Snellgrove 1957), they are mostly classed as Tantric deities. Śiva himself (Lhach'en Wangch'ug Ch'enmo) is sometimes employed as a protective deity in *gompa* ritual, but is conceptually distinct from the forms of Mahākāla.

7. Interview with Namk'a Drimed Rimpoch'e, 3 August 1990, translated with assistance from Tashi Tsering.

CHAPTER 10

1. For example, Burmese 'animism' as described in Spiro (1967), the *abangan* complex in Geertz's description of Javanese religion (1964).

2. Rather than by the classic shamanic journey of Siberia as described by Eliade (1970), although there are traces of that in the *delog* literature that consist of narratives of persons who have 'died' and returned to life (see Chapter 16). Tantric practice itself, as argued in this book, is closer to the classical shamanic pattern of conscious and controlled travel to other realms than to a spirit-possession or spirit-mediumship approach.

3. Berzin 1972:183–184. The story comes from the *Lamrim Sindri Namdröl Lagchang* by the 3d Trijang Rimpoch'e.

4. For the Bönpo, these vows would not be those imposed by Guru Rimpoch'e, but those that the gods had sworn to Shenrab Miwo on the occasion of his much earlier visit to Tibet (see Chapter 9).

5. Interview with Anak Dorje Namgyel, August 1990.

6. Interview with Namk'a Drimed Rimpoch'e, Chandragiri, 8 August 1990, transcribed with assistance from Tashi Tsering.

7. Interview with Anak Dorje Namgyal, Chandragiri, August 1990.

8. Thubten Norbu does not actually state that the incense was offered to Kyeri, but he mentions the mountain immediately after.

9. Presumably = *kangso*, a general term for propitiation rituals, see Kohn (1988:57–58).

10. This may reflect the importance of the *nāga* cult for the Newars (Singh Nepali 1965) and elsewhere in Nepal. See also Ortner (1978b).

11. For 'folk-religion' rituals see, for example, Tucci (1980:176–186) on the *dö*, *yé*, *lüd*, and *to* rituals. Many of these are also performed in the *gompa*. On the *ch'am* and related *gompa* rituals see Chapter 14.

12. Misfortune is, however, not necessarily attributed only to local deities. Other concepts such as the four or five individual energy components of Tibetan astrology can also be significant (see Cornu 1990:93–95; Karmay 1990). These elements are *sog* (vitality, life-energy), *lü* (body), *wangt'ang* (personal power) and *lungta* (good fortune), to which may be added also *la* (soul, life-force).

13. This prayer is by the nineteenth-century Nyingmapa and Rimed lama Ju Mip'am, and similar prayers exist in other Tibetan traditions. Schwalbe mentions recitations of the prayer at pp. 9, 24, 27, 30, 46, and 54.

14. According to Aziz, the four *lhak'a* in D'ingri were all women

(1978:253n). Also see Diemberger and Schicklgruber (1984) on female spirit-mediums (called *k'androma*) among Tibetans in eastern Nepal.

15. For detailed descriptions of Buddhist and Bönpo versions of the closely related *lalu* ritual, see Karmay (1987).

16. A juniper wood seal for this purpose with the syllable *dhīḥ* was distributed on the 13th Dalai Lama's orders to various districts of Tibet along with a small text on child care (Sangay 1984a:9).

CHAPTER 11

1. For example, Hanson 1977:29–49; Khetsun Sangbo 1982:45–100; Kalu 1986:31–37.

2. The situation in Far Eastern societies such as China is a little more complex because of the significance of the ancestors as spirit-guardians of the living in these societies.

3. This point, as we shall see later, was a particular specialty of the Gelugpa tradition, being at the center of Tsongk'apa's own revelations.

4. Dharma here = 'teachings of the Buddha,' Saṃgha = monastic community.

5. The main Tibetan discussion of the Three Vows is Sakya Pandita's *Domsum Rabyé,* a work that has been commented on and argued with by several later writers of various traditions (for commentaries see David Jackson 1983:12–23). The *Domsum Rabyé* has recently been studied by J. R. Rhoton (1985).

6. The taking of Refuge itself is more complex for the Tibetans, because of the much expanded conception of the Saṃgha, and because of the mediating role of the lama and Tantric deities. A typical Tibetan 'refuge visualization' may involve several hundred deities, lamas, and other symbolic elements.

7. And still to a large extent is, despite the rapid growth in meditation centers for laymen in countries like Burma and Thailand.

8. As opposed, that is, to attaining Enlightenment immediately after death in the *bardo* state that intervenes before a subsequent rebirth. See Chapter 12.

9. Maria Phylactou discusses the performance of this ritual *(yanguk)* in Ladakh, where it is done each year after harvest (1989:197–198) and also when a woman leaves her natal household to be married: "In this instance it is performed primarily so that household wealth is not diminished, so that the departing daughter does not take all the fortunes of her natal house with her" (1989:252). A more detailed description of *yanguk* in Ladakh is given by Sophie Day (1989:148–166).

10. 'Reputation'-like scales did of course exist in societies like Thailand (see Mulder 1985), linking up with the emphasis on power and success in the shamanic and 'Tantric' sides of Thai Buddhism. What we are considering here is a question of relative importance of different value scales.

11. An interesting point of comparison between the Tantric lama's role in taming disciples and taming local deities is the role of the oath *(damts'ig* = Skt. *samaya)* in both cases (see Dowman 1984:227–228 and Guenther 1971:99 n. 1 on *samaya*).

12. For other comments about the symbolism of these stories, see Gyatso (1987) and Marko (1988).

CHAPTER 12

1. The main exception is Beyer (1973).

2. These were held to have been revealed to the Indian teacher Asaṅga by the future Buddha Maitreya, and are of great importance in the Tibetan scholastic tradition.

3. The Theravādins would be a Hinayāna school in the Tibetan classification, but the Tibetan characterization of the Hinayāna does not represent the Theravādin understanding of their own practices. For the Theravādins, neither Mahāyāna Sūtras nor Tantras are the authentic word of the Buddha. The Tibetan characterization of the Hinayāna position, while doubtless originating in polemics between Indian Buddhist schools many centuries ago, serves for Tibetans not as a critique of Theravādin Buddhism, which they scarcely knew of until quite recently, but as an indication of a possible level of practice within the Tibetan system.

4. This Tantric form of the Buddha, called Dorjé Ch'ang (Skt. Vajradhara) or, in the case of the Old Tantras and *terma,* Kuntu Sangpo (Skt. Samantabhadra), was distinct from the historical Buddha Śākyamuni, in particular in not being limited to any specific time or place of manifestation.

5. I would like to thank Janet Gyatso for clarifying this important point for me. See also Decleer (1978) who cites the Tibetan saying, *pecha ch'ö ma red,* 'books are not Dharma,' and Kawamura (1984).

6. The term *men-ngag* (Skt. *upadeśa*) refers to advice and instructions deriving from past practitioners in the teachings. Such advice may be orally transmitted, but it may also be in written form.

7. While it was possible and quite common for an individual to study with lamas from several different orders, especially outside the Gelugpa tradition, and so to collect a variety of Tantric lineages, it was normal to have one 'root lama' *(tsawé lama)* in a particular tradition around whom one's practice was centered.

8. The main exceptions are the Sūtra Mahāmudrā system (see Chapter 24) and the Dzogch'en teachings. In practice, most Sūtra Mahāmudrā practitioners had at least some experience of Tantra as well, and Dzogch'en yogis had extensive prior experience of Tantra.

9. In fact, the question of whether the Tantras involve a philosophical position distinct from that of the Sūtras is a complex one to which various answers have been given by Tibetan scholars.

10. The Old Tantra lineages included some Tantras, such as the Guhyasamāja, which are extant in Sanskrit and were transmitted again from India at the time of the New Tantra transmissions. An important group of Old Tantras also appears to exist in Chinese translation (Martin 1987:183, citing Eastman 1981).

11. Bönpo chronology is currently under dispute, so the question of historical priority is unclear (see Kvaerne 1990 and Chapter 24).

12. On Putön's classification see Lessing and Wayman (1968), Wayman (1973:234–239). David Stott comments (pers. comm.) that an earlier version of the same scheme was given in the *Gyüddé Chi Namshag* of Södnam Tsemo.

13. The text has been translated into English at least twice, in Gyatso (1980a) and Karmapa (n.d.), which is a commentary on the practice by the 15th Karmapa. My summary is based on these two sources. For the background to the text, see Gyatso (1981).

14. 'Dedication of merit' is the conventional but not entirely appropriate translation of *ngowa*. See Blondeau (1987–1988:76) and Schwieger (1978:24–27).

15. Thus the 1st Dalai Lama comments with reference to the Kālacakra Tantra that certain aspects of the *nāḍī* and *cakra* have to be visualized differently in this Tantra from other Tantras (Mullin 1982a:132–133). See also Cozort (1986:115–133).

16. Chogyal Trichen Rinpoch'e has commented that the two are equivalent (David Stott, pers. comm.).

17. The Nāropa practices are described by Tsongk'apa (*Sablam Nārö Ch'ödrug*, translated in Muses 1961), Pema Karpo (*Ch'ödrug Düpé Sindri*, translated in Evans-Wentz 1967:155–252), and Rinch'en Namgyel (*Nāropé Namt'ar*, translated by Guenther 1963). The last is the most satisfactory description so far available in English. The 2d Dalai Lama's account of the Six Yogas of Niguma has been translated by Glenn Mullin (1985).

18. Dzogch'en practitioners, traditionally less concerned with building up a monastic following, are more likely to be described as entering the Rainbow Body *(jalü)* at death. This is the traditional Dzogch'en technique for attaining Enlightenment through dissolving into the five elements (see N. Norbu 1986b:124–128, 156–157).

CHAPTER 13

1. Snellgrove translates *abhiṣeka* as 'consecration' and *adhiṣṭhāna* as 'empowerment' on the grounds that the latter is the actual conveyance of blessing to the student (1987:634). This is correct, but I have maintained 'empowerment' for *wang* (= *abhiṣeka*) since the central part of the *wang* for Tibetans is not the formal consecration but the associated blessing.

2. These illustrations are taken from Geshé Ngawang Dhargyey's lectures at the Library of Tibetan Works and Archives, Dharamsala, in 1972.

3. David Stott points out that this kind of language can even be used of a lama and his subsequent rebirth; Karmapa Mikyöd Dorjé (1507–1554) is described as seeing visions of his predecessor Düsum Ky'enpa (1110–1193) (pers. comm.).

4. See also the *Gurupañcāśikā*, the standard Indian text on devotion to the Tantric teacher. It was attributed to Aśvaghoṣa (Aśvaghoṣa 1975; see also Lessing and Wayman 1968:272–273).

5. See Norbu and Turnbull (1969:271–277) and Norbu and Ekvall (1969), which is a translation of a Tibetan play arguing for a particular view of the Dalai Lama–Panch'en Rimpoch'e relationship through a story about the two in a previous rebirth. The Jātaka stories of the previous lives of the historical Buddha, with their identification of Śākyamuni, Devadatta, Ānanda, and the others playing out similar relationships in succeeding rebirths may have provided the model for this idea of repeating karmic relationships. This continuing relationship contrasts with what can be expected in the normal course of *saṃsāra*, where relationships will not be carried on in the same way through succeeding lives. A well-known Tibetan story (Berzin 1972:288–289) tells of a girl eating a fish (her former father), fondling her child (her murderer reborn), and beating a dog (her mother reborn) to stop it from eating the fish (its husband in a previous life)! The lama-student relationship is specifically claimed to be an exception to this general condition of *saṃsāra*.

6. Geshé Ngawang Dhargyey, lectures at LTWA, 1972. The story is told slightly differently in Marpa's biography, where Nāropa says to Marpa "Even if he had plenty of gold, it wouldn't be sufficient [for me to take him as my student]. He needs merit, and *letr'o* [karmic influence]" (Bacot 1937:15, 80).

7. 457iv–458ii = Guenther 1963:107. See also Guenther 1977b:188.

CHAPTER 14

1. It will be remembered that the relationship between guru and student is carried on from one lifetime to the next. Since it involves the student's

spiritual progress towards Enlightenment, it is specifically exempted from the rule by which *saṃsāric* relationships do not recur in future lifetimes.

2. For one such *sādhana,* focusing on White Tārā, see Mullin (1983:95–104).

3. For Tr'ulshig Rimpoch'e, see Kohn (1988:239–240). For the Tengboche Rimpoche, see Zangbu and Klatzel (1988:38), where the empowerment is referred to as a *ter whong,* presumably an error for *torwang.* The ritual is depicted, along with the accompanying *ch'am,* in Richard Kohn's film *Lord of the Dance: Destroyer of Illusion.*

4. This rice-*maṇḍala* (Tib. *mendel*) is an offering of the universe symbolically represented as a metal plate upon which rice, semiprecious stones, etc., are arranged to correspond to Mount Meru, the four continents, and so on (see Hanson 1977:92–105). It should not be confused with the Tantric *maṇḍala* (Tib. *ky'ilk'or*), which is a structured arrangement of Tantric deities visualized in Tantric meditation and symbolically represented by a two-dimensional painting or structure of colored sand or occasionally by a three-dimensional structure.

5. That is the Tantric *maṇḍala* (Tib. *ky'ilk'or*), the assembly of deities, not the rice-offering *maṇḍala.*

6. Among the more detailed descriptions are those of the *ch'am* associated with Mani Rimdu among the Sherpa (Fürer-Haimendorf 1964:220; Jerstad 1969:137–139; Paul 1982b; Zangbu and Klatzel 1988; Kite and Childs 1988; much the best account is in Kohn 1988), the Gelugpa *ch'am* at Kumbum in Amdo (Filchner 1933) and Spituk in Ladakh (Marko, in press), and the Drugpa Kagyüdpa *ch'am* at Hemis in Ladakh (Helffer 1980). More general accounts may be found in Stein (1957) (see also Stein 1972a:189–191 and Nebesky-Wojkowitz 1976).

7. This is not to suggest that these 'incidental' sequences are lacking in cultural meaning for the spectators. See Robert Paul's analysis of the Sherpa monastic dances for suggestions, from a Freudian perspective, of their relationship to central cultural themes (Paul 1982b). The *ch'am* are above all, however, magical rituals in which the lamas destroy the powers of evil. The frequent association of these dances with the story of the murder of King Langdarma is closely linked to this central meaning.

8. See Paul (1982b), who interprets the murder of Langdarma as a crucial mythical statement of the position of Buddhism in Sherpa and Tibetan society.

CHAPTER 15

1. Though it should be noted that these rebirths are said to have taken place in secret during the nineteenth century, and no official rebirth was rec-

ognized between the 10th Shamarpa who died in 1792 and the 11th who was born around 1880 (Douglas and White 1976). The present (13th) Shamarpa, born in 1952, was one of the four lamas entrusted with administering the Karmapa suborder after the death of the 16th Gyalwa Karmapa, the head of the suborder, in 1981.

2. A note on nomenclature: I use the term 'order' rather than 'sect' for Gelugpa, Nyingmapa, etc., although it possibly conveys too structured an impression, especially for the more heterogeneous and informal Nyingmapa and Bönpo. 'Tradition' is a more general term than order, and refers to practices not necessarily confined to a single order. 'Lineage' refers to the continuity from teacher to student of a particular practice; each order may contain hundreds of individual lineages connected with specific practices.

3. These statements refer to overall differences in emphasis. As Leonard van der Kuijp rightly notes, the orders have been too easily taken as distinct and concrete entities. Even the Gelugpa cannot be assumed to present a uniform front in relation to any particular issue (van der Kuijp 1985:33–35).

4. The suffixes -pa, -po in many of these terms are used to form a personal noun or adjective from the root syllables, thus a Gelugpa is a member of the Gelug order, a Nyingmapa of the Nyingma order, and so on. Western scholars have mostly included these suffixes in the names of the order, as I do here.

5. Krystyna Cech (pers. comm.).

6. The large-scale growth of lay meditation centers in the Theravādin countries is a very recent phenomenon (see Tambiah 1976; Kornfield 1977).

7. See Atiśa's comments in his *Bodhipathapradīpa*, which appear to be a compromise between the anti-Tantric views of his lay patrons and his own pro-Tantric position (Snellgrove 1987:481–483, and see Chapter 24).

8. The exceptional case of Reting (Ratreng) Rimpoch'e, a high Gelugpa lama who was Regent of Tibet during the early years of the 14th Dalai Lama, indicates how far tolerance could go. In this case, the Regent was forced to resign, in part because his noncelibate status made it impossible for him to administer vows of celibacy to the Dalai Lama (see Goldstein 1989).

9. Elisabeth Stutchbury (pers. comm.).

10. In some contexts, Amitābha may be treated as a Dharmakāya figure (for example, Blondeau 1977–1978:78–79). The relationships between the *kāya* are more significant than the assignment of a particular figure to one or another *kāya*, which may vary.

11. For example, Berzin 1972. Contrast the Shangpa theory as given in the Shangpa *namt'ar* of Vajradhara (J. Hanson 1982; J. and M. Hanson 1985).

12. Though not in the case of the Dalai Lama or Panch'en Rimpoch'e,

subsequent to the Manchu regime's prohibition on these lamas being found in aristocratic families (see Chapter 27).

13. David Stott, pers. comm. Some early Sakya head lamas were believed to be emanations of Vajrapāṇi or Avalokiteśvara (see Thutop and Ngawang 1968; Amipa 1976).

14. In Theravādin countries, *upāsaka* vows are taken by laymen and they do not imply becoming part of a monastic establishment. In Tibetan society, laymen may take *upāsaka* vows, either for a short period of time (as at the full moon ceremony, *sojong,* Skt. *upoṣadha,* or on a retreat, *nyungné*), or for more extended periods. The *upāsaka* vows are, however, also taken in Tibet as the regular first stage of a monastic career. The same is true for *upāsīka* vows for women.

15. The term appears as *thawa* in Fürer-Haimendorf's writings on the Sherpa.

16. There is in fact some controversy about whether the Tibetans preserved a valid ordination lineage for *bhikṣuni.* The ordination lineage survived in the Far East, and some Western women who had received the Tibetan *gets'ulma* ordination have recently taken the Chinese *bhikṣunī* vows, with the aim of reviving the Tibetan *gelongma* ordination. See *Vajradhatu Sun* (Boulder, Colorado) 4(2):21–22 (Dec. 1981–Jan. 1982).

17. See in particular Berzin 1972, Sherpa et al. 1977.

CHAPTER 16

1. Perhaps this reflects a lesser degree of 'encapsulation' of the local folk-shamanic complex by clerical Buddhism (see Samuel 1990), as one might expect among Tibetan pastoralists. Visionary Gesar bards are also primarily of pastoralist *(drogpa)* origins.

2. Samdrub (a *babdrung* from east Tibet), pers. comm., Chengdu, November 1990.

3. The "practice of taking every experience in the great equal taste" *(ronyom ch'enpö tulshug chödpa)* is discussed later in the chapter.

4. As I have emphasized elsewhere (Chapter 1) Tibet had its rational and clerical side, including historians whose concern for linear rational time is reminiscent of Western modes of linear rationality. This is one strand, however, and a relatively minor one, within Tibetan religious consciousness. Even men such as Sumpa K'enpo and T'uken Ch'ökyi Nyima, or the great historian Gö Lotsawa, author of the 'Blue Annals' (*Debt'er Ngönpo,* Roerich 1976), were scarcely living in the same world as modern Western rationalist scholars.

5. Meaning he produced the results and experiences appropriate for the teachings.

6. The Nyingmapa also had many *dagnang,* and *gongter* may be revealed as a result of a *dagnang* involving Guru Rimpoch'e, so the line between the two types of visionary experience is not a rigid one.

7. Interview of 12 August 1990, transcribed with assistance from Tashi Tsering.

8. Lecture at Blackheath, Australia, January 1988.

9. Interviews with Namk'a Drimed Rimpoch'e, Chandragiri, 31 July and 12 August, 1990, and with Andzin Rimpoch'e, 12 August, transcribed with the assistance of Tashi Tsering. See also Trungpa 1971.

CHAPTER 17

1. Examples include Tr'ulshig Rimpoch'e in Shorung and Khumbu (see below) and Ch'ogling Rimpoch'e in Gyasumdo (see Mumford 1989). This latter lama was the 3d Neten Ch'ogling Rimpoch'e, reincarnation of the Neten Ch'ogling discussed in Chapter 16 (see Tobgyal 1988:53–59).

2. 'Zatul Rinpoche' in Ortner 1989a.

3. Dzarong *gompa* is often referred to in literature on the Sherpas as Rongphu or Rumbu (for example, Ortner 1989a:131). On this *gompa,* see also Macdonald (1973).

4. Ortner's 'Tushi Rinpoche' (1989a:189).

5. Information from Gegen Ky'entse of Manali, who is one of Tsibri Tr'ipön's disciples (Elisabeth Stutchbury, pers. comm.).

6. There is also some information about Sikkim (Nakane 1966; Gorer 1939), which was a small state whose hereditary rulers were affiliated with the Nyingmapa tradition, but the complex ethnic situation in Sikkim, where most of the population is now not Tibetan, makes it difficult to compare directly with the areas we have been considering.

7. Although Kessler's reliance on Gelugpa sources may give an exaggerated impression of this. For a Kagyüdpa view of the Kandzé region, see Kalu (1985:69–70). There was serious conflict between Gelugpa and non-Gelugpa *gompa* and their secular patrons in this region, leading to actual fighting in the 1930s and to intervention by the Chinese authorities (see Duncan 1952 and Chapter 4).

8. Some of his index numbers refer to more than one *gompa,* for example, p. 183 no. 2 and p. 184 no. 10.

9. One hundred, according to Teichman (1922:231).

10. See Jackson (1978:218 n. 86), correcting Snellgrove's dates (Snellgrove 1967b).

11. There is considerable confusion about when Sangwa Dorjé lived and Ortner's narrative, though plausible, is based on oral history and speculative reconstruction. She suggests that the Sherpas arrived in Khumbu in the mid-sixteenth century and that Sangwa Dorjé lived a century later, founding the *gompa* at Pangboche in 1667 (1989a:26, 47). By contrast, a history based on oral sources compiled by Sangyé Tenzin, the abbot of Serlo *gompa* in Shorung, and by Alexander Macdonald, places Sangwa Dorjé in the previous century, and makes him one of two lamas who arrived from K'am with the original immigrants (Macdonald 1980b:140; see Ortner 1989a:49, 209 n. 8, 210 n. 9). Neither account is consistent with Ortner's statement (1989a:49, see also 210 n. 10) that Sangwa Dorjé was a student of the famous *tertön* Ratna Lingpa (or 'Rena Lingpa,' 1403–1478, see Dargyay 1978:146), but then the Tengboche lama, whose dating is closer to Ortner's, states that Sangwa Dorje's teacher was the fifth in a teacher-disciple succession from Ratna Lingpa rather than Ratna Lingpa himself (Zangbu and Klatzel 1988:12).

12. Although one Sherpa incarnate lama, Lama Zopa, the rebirth of a hermit from Thami, received a Gelugpa training from Dungkar *gompa* in Tibet and subsequently studied with the late refugee teacher Lama T'ubten Yeshe. He has been primarily active in teaching Westerners, and is now the head of Lama Yeshe's organization, the Foundation for the Preservation of the Mahayana Tradition. See *Wisdom* (Magazine of the FPMT), no. 2 (1984), pp. 52–53.

13. Snellgrove has described some of the Spiti *gompa* (1957). Handa's survey of *gompa* in Himachal Pradesh summarizes information from many sources, including the author's own research, on *gompa* in Spiti and also in Lahul and Kinnaur, but is often inaccurate (Handa 1987).

14. According to Harcourt. Pedro Carrasco gives figures of 3,024 and 3,014 (1959:34, 160), apparently derived from the same census. I have not been able to consult the census itself.

15. This *gompa*, Peen or Pin, was an intriguing community some of whose members, the so-called *buzhen*, traveled around performing dances and religious plays (Khosla 1956:134–136; Chopra 1964:46). Like the Ach'e Lhamo troupes in central Tibet they traced their lineage back to the famous fifteenth-century holy man T'angtong Gyelpo (on whom see Gyatso 1980a, 1980b, 1981).

16. Information from Kirti Tsenshab Rimpoch'e (pers. comm., Dharamsala, July 1989) and from the *Debt'er Gyats'o* (*karchag* to vol. 3, p. 6).

CHAPTER 18

1. According to the April 1991 edition of *Vajrayana News* (Sydney), Geshé Rabten's rebirth has been identified in India and will be enthroned in mid–1991.

2. Candrakīrti's *Madhyamakāvatāra*, Dharmakīrti's *Pramāṇavārttika*, Maitreya's *Abhisamayālaṃkāra*, Vasubandhu's *Abhidharmakośa*, and Guṇaprabha's *Vinayasūtra*.

3. I follow his spelling. The name would be Ratöd Kyongla Ngawang Lobsang in the transcription used in this book.

4. Not to be confused with the Nyingmapa gompa of Kat'og in Dergé state.

5. The Sharpa Ch'öjé or abbot of Shartsé Tr'ats'ang at Ganden is appointed from the most senior retired abbot of Gyüdtöd, and the abbot of the other Ganden college (Changtsé) from the most senior retired Gyüdmed abbot. The position of Ganden Tr'ipa or abbot of Ganden, titular head of the Gelugpa order, alternates between Sharpa Ch'öjé and Changtsé Ch'öjé and is held for seven years (Berzin 1972:415–420; Sherpa et al. 1977).

6. Or the second, according to Berzin 1972.

7. On the *chöd* practice, typical of traveling yogins, see Gyatso (1985) and Chapter 20. According to Namkhai Norbu Rimpoche, Tromo Geshe also practiced Dzogch'en extensively (transcript of talk by Namkhai Norbu in California, 17 July 1982).

8. The shamanic emphasis of Tromo Geshe Rimpoch'e's career does not imply that he was particularly sympathetic to the non-Gelugpa orders. He was closely associated with the Dorjé Shugden cult (see Kapstein 1989), and a story in Tr'ichang Rimpoch'e's *Gyalch'en Töd-drel*, a commentary on P'awongk'a Rimpoch'e's verses in praise of Shugden, describes an incident in which he employed Shugden rituals against a Bönpo community (138i; reference from Tashi Tsering).

9. Surmang consisted of two large gompas, Namgyel Tsé and Düdtsi T'il, dating from the late fourteenth century and a number of smaller centers (see Trungpa 1971:32ff; Roerich 1976:510–512). Trungpa states that Namgyal Tsé had 1,000 *trapa* (600 *gelong*, 300 *gets'ul*, and 100 *genyen*); Düdtsi T'il had 300 *trapa*, of whom 170 were *gelong* (1971:41, 36).

10. It was common, especially among the Nyingmapa, to recognize several rebirths of the same lama. Frequently these were three in number, corresponding to body, speech and mind; or five, with the addition of *yönten* (ability, accomplishment) and *tr'inlé* (activity).

11. *Dharma Gate* 1(1):8 (January 1991).

12. See note 10. Kalu Rinpoche was recognized informally as an activity emanation of Kongtrul, but this did not involve his formal enthronement as

a rebirth. There were also five or six formally recognized rebirths of Kongtrul (Smith 1970a:76).

13. While the other Kagyüdpa traditions (collectively known as the Marpa Kagyüdpa) trace their lineage through Milarepa and Marpa to the Indian *siddha* Nāropa, the Shangpa Kagyüd trace theirs through the Tibetan teacher Ky'ungpo Neljor to the Indian women teachers or *ḍākinī* Sukhasiddhi and Niguma (Nāropa's sister or consort). Unlike the Marpa Kagyüdpa, the Shangpa teachings never became the basis of a religious order in Tibet, being passed down by yogic teachers within and outside the established orders. They were a specialty of the Jonangpa lama Tāranātha and were revived by Jamgön Kongtrul (see Kapstein 1980; Hanson 1982). They contain a set of Six Doctrines (or Teachings) of Niguma parallel to the better-known Six Doctrines of Nāropa (for a description by the 2d Dalai Lama, see Mullin 1985:92–151).

14. Though Tromo Geshé Rimpoch'e also spent many years in solitary meditation after completing his *geshé* degree.

15. The autobiography of this teacher was published in Gangtok in 1975 (Jetsün Loch'en Rimpoch'e, *Namt'ar*).

16. Tashi Tsering has pointed out (pers. comm., August 1991) that there were nevertheless women lamas with a more academic orientation, among them Mindröl Ling Jetsün Mingyur Paldrön, who was the daughter of the *tertön* Terdag Lingpa, and was responsible for the rebuilding of Mindröl Ling *gompa* after its destruction by the Dzungars in the early eighteenth century, and several of the successive female reincarnations of Dorjé P'amo at Samding *gompa*, which was the main center of the Bodong tradition.

17. Though it also occurs in relation to a man (Nāropa), in Lhatsün Rinch'en Namgyel's *Naropé Namt'ar* (Guenther 1963).

18. Anak Dorje Namgyel (pers. comm.), Chandragiri, August 1990.

19. See Norbu 1986b:157.

20. Interview with Anak Dorje Namgyel, Chandragiri, August 1990.

CHAPTER 19

1. In the Sherpa case, for example, these other factors might include the growth of the economic surplus that seems to have played a significant part in enabling Sherpa monasticism, and the impact of the active new celibate *gompa* at Dzarong.

CHAPTER 20

1. For general accounts of Indian history at this period see Rapson (1962) and Thapar (1966).

2. Some general references on early Buddhism are Conze (1962), Ling (1973) (who argues strongly for a sociocentric interpretation of the Buddha's teachings), and Bareau (1955).

3. See in particular Haarh 1969; Spanien and Imaeda 1979; Richardson 1985; Bogoslovskij 1972.

4. For an interesting recent account, see Parpola 1988.

5. I avoid the term preliterate, since the Indus Valley states had some degree of literacy.

6. This is not intended as a general endorsement of the Great and Little Tradition model for Asian societies. The reciprocal relationship between urban and rural contexts, with the literate tradition based in the urban center and an 'encapsulated' shamanism in the villages, seems characteristic of Indian society. It appears less applicable to Southeast Asian states and hardly at all to Tibetan societies.

7. The single label I2 is not meant to imply that there was a single type of practitioner in the stateless period. There may well have been some form of the priest-shaman distinction. I assume, however, that both roles were supported by the same body of modes of thought, feeling, and activity, and it is to this that the label I2 refers. At a later (Tantric) period, 'tribal' shamanism (I4) seems to have become a major resource for Indian ascetics. Whether this was so at the time of Śākyamuni, I do not know. For that matter, the distinction between 'Vedic' (I1, I2) and 'tribal' (I3, I4) should probably be regarded with caution for this early period.

8. Thus it is possible for Trevor Ling (1973) to argue on the basis of the early Sūtras that Buddhism was primarily sociocentric in its intention. This seems to me to give meditation technique *(samādhi)* and insight into the nature of reality *(prajñā)* far too low a place in the early Buddhist system, but it helps to counter those who dismiss the Buddhist tradition in its early stages as primarily world-renouncing.

9. The Theravādin tradition is nevertheless, of course, a later interpretation of these early Sūtras, as are all contemporary Buddhist schools.

10. On the modern Theravādin understanding of *śamatha* and *vipaśyanā*, see, for example, Nyanaponika (1969) and Kornfield (1977). For the Tibetan equivalents *(shiné, lhagt'ong)*, see Wayman (1978, Gelugpa tradition), Guenther (1977a:146, Nyingmapa tradition), and Chapters 26 and 27.

11. For a classic (but definitely Hinducentric) formulation of the equivalence of Buddhist and Hindu languages, see Murti (1970).

12. The recent revival of meditation as a lay and largely middle class practice in Theravādin countries, through teachers such as Mahasi Sayadaw and U Ba Khen, incidentally emphasizes the *vipaśyanā*, 'insight,' side to the virtual exclusion of *śamatha*. *Śamatha* is still associated with the acquisition of magical and shamanic powers, and for modern Thais and Burmese represents the side of Buddhism least compatible with contemporary society. *Vi-*

paśyanā can be seen as a source of rational insight consistent with the presentation of Buddhism as a rational, scientific tradition (Kornfield 1977). In Tibet, by contrast, the balance between *vipaśyanā* and *śamatha* remained central in Tantric Buddhist practice, even for the most 'clerical' and 'rationalized' forms of Tibetan religious practice.

CHAPTER 21

1. For general sources on Mahāyāna Buddhism and philosophy, see Conze (1962, 1980), Warder (1970), Robinson and Johnson (1977), and for Madhyamaka philosophy in particular, Ruegg (1981).

2. For Tibetan teachings on the generation of *bodhicitta*, see, for example, Berzin (1972) and Mullin (1982a:60–75).

3. On Madhyamaka, see Ruegg (1981) and Murti (1970). Conze is the main Western authority on the Prajñāpāramitā Sūtras; see especially 1960, 1970, 1975.

4. For other translations, see Stcherbatsky (n.d.:111–113) and Inada (1970:39–40).

5. My account here is based in part on Willis's discussion (1979:13–19).

6. In the terms of the multimodal framework (Samuel 1990), one could say that the store-consciousness is where the modal states are stored.

7. On the Jonangpa, see Ruegg (1963). Ruegg has written extensively on the *tathāgatagarbha* concept in Tibet (see 1969, 1973). For parallel criticisms of the Nyingmapa, see Guenther (1977a).

CHAPTER 22

1. This is in part a matter of definition, since Tantric can be used as a general term for non-Vedic practices (see Bharati 1976).

2. Influences from entirely outside the Indian cultural area were probably also present, as indicated by Indian references to Cīna or Mahācīna and Tibetan references to China (Old Tantra) and Shambhala (Kālacakra).

3. There is also a recent German translation of the *Guhyasamāja Tantra* (Gäng 1988) and an English version of the seventh chapter of the same tantra (Fremantle 1990). I have not had an opportunity to study either as yet.

4. The principal text of the Caryā class, the *Mahāvairocanābhisaṃbodhi Tantra* (or *Sūtra*) has recently been translated by Chikyo Yamamoto (1990). See also Lessing and Wayman (1968:204–207).

5. For examples see Uhlig (1981, nos. 28 to 37).

6. Though 'secret' here *(sangwa)* in modern Tibetan usage implies less that the practice is hidden from others than that it is carried out at the most subtle of internal levels.

7. Thus Kāṇha describes himself as a Kāpālika in his songs (Kvaerne 1977:113, 150), although the reference should perhaps not be taken at face-value.

8. Snellgrove's translation is slightly bowdlerized: the text actually says "dwelt within the *bhaga* [sexual organ] of the Vajrayoginī . . ."

9. It should be noted that several of the best-known Tibetan accounts of the siddhas, particularly such as the *Nāropé Namt'ar* (Guenther 1963) and the *Marpé Namt'ar* (Trungpa 1982), are literary reworkings from the end of the fifteenth century (see Chapter 26). While they include earlier material, they need to be treated with caution as sources about Indian Tantric practice. The works of Tāranātha, while also late, show fewer signs of literary reworking and are probably closer to the Indian sources (Templeman 1981, 1983, 1989).

10. The biography of Ch'ag Lotsawa Ch'öje Pel, who visited India in 1234–1237, gives a picture of Nepal and of northeastern India (modern Bihar and Bengal) immediately after the Muslim conquests and the destruction of the major Buddhist centers. Unfortunately, it gives little information about the siddha circles themselves (Roerich 1959).

11. For the Indian versions, see Riccardi (1971); for the Tibetan version, Macdonald (1967). Although the Tibetan version does not correspond to any surviving text in an Indian language, it may well go back to sources as old or older than the Indian versions, see Macdonald (1967:16–17).

12. A saying quoted in the autobiography of a contemporary Hindu Tantric yogin of German origin, Agehananda Bharati (1980).

13. For Mahākāla in the Hindu tradition, see Lorenzen (1972); in the Buddhist tradition, see Stablein (1976a, 1976b). An interesting Tibetan legend concerning the bringing of the Mahākāla cult to Tibet is recounted in Snellgrove and Skorupski (1980, vol. 2, 99–100), and also in Helffer (1976) and Canzio (1981).

14. The dominance of these Tantras in the Tibetan tradition is indicated by the preponderance of texts related to them in the Tibetan Buddhist canon and the writings of the Tibetan scholars themselves. The major religious orders (Gelugpa, Kagyüdpa, Sakyapa) each specialized in one or more of these Tantras. The Nyingmapa, as explained in Chapters 12 and 13, emphasized another group of texts, the so-called Old Tantras.

15. See Glenn Yocum's account of a Hindu-Buddhist confrontation in South India (Yocum 1980).

16. Archer 1966. On the general historical context, see Rapson (1962) and Thapar (1966).

17. On the chronology of the Tantras see Y. Matsunaga (1977), Wayman (1973, 1980b).

18. Translation from the journal *Virupa* 3(2), Spring 1976. See also Kvaerne (1977:81–82).

19. From the Vajrayana point of view, the Pāramitāyāna by itself is not sufficient to attain Buddhahood. See Lessing and Wayman (1968:24–39).

20. As Bharati notes (1976), almost any Hindu ritual that is not Vedic can in a sense be described as Tantric. Here, however, we are concerned specifically with the Indian traditions deriving from the Hindu equivalents to the Buddhist Tantric siddhas.

21. See Samuel (1982) for references on Newars and Balinese.

22. For example, Mahāyāna Sūtras were said to have been revealed to him by the *nāga*. This side of Nāgārjuna's activities is one reason why the Tibetans (presumably following the later Indian tradition) had less trouble than modern scholars in identifying Nāgārjuna the philosopher with Nāgārjuna the Tantric siddha (see Warder 1970:374, 488; Snellgrove 1987:286 n. 281).

CHAPTER 23

1. According to the various lists of Tibetan kings, it took place some 25 generations before Songtsen Gampo (Haarh 1969:40).

2. In terms of the tripartite division used by Buddhist authors such as Putön, T'ukwan Ch'öki Nyima, or Pawo Tsuglag, T2 corresponds to the 'original Bön' *(döl bön* or *jöl bön)*, and T3 and T5 to 'deviating' or 'irrational' Bön (*ky'ar bön*, *talog bön*, or *dur bön;* Haarh 1969:105–106). Some authors also refer to *yungdrung bön*, 'Swastika Bön,' a term that can perhaps be taken as corresponding to the non-Buddhist religion of the imperial period (T5). The third stage of Bön *(gyur bön)* corresponds to the modern Bön religion, and lies outside the period of this chapter. According to the Bön historians themselves, both the 'Bön of Cause' *(gyui bön)* and the 'Bön of Effect' (*drebui bön*, corresponding to the Bodhi Orientation and to Tantra) existed prior to King Trigum (T2), but the persecution of Bön at the time of King Trigum led to the disappearance of the Bön of Effect so that only parts of the Bön of Cause existed during the subsequent period (T3 and T5). The Bön of Effect reappeared through the discovery of *terma* texts from the tenth century onwards (Karmay 1972; T8a2 in Chapter 24). The reader may appreciate by now why it is better to avoid using the term Bön to refer to early Tibetan religion.

3. Amy Heller has produced a useful analytic summary of this lengthy and complex article (Heller 1986).

4. The term 'tribe' (Tibetan *rü*, 'bone') is used loosely, since it is not too certain precisely what these groups were, anthropologically speaking. See Stein 1959b. There was an ideology of descent from a common ancestor; there also seem to have been particular families with dominant status within

a 'tribe.' The relationship between the 'tribes' of this period and the various lineage and household structures in the premodern period (see Chapters 3–8) is complex and not fully understood.

5. As Namkhai Norbu has recently argued (1981).

6. Haarh suggests that this was also a major concern of the religion of the *bön* and *shen* priests. I am less sure about his suggestion that they were responsible for introducing the cult of the gods or *lha* (Haarh 1969:111–112).

7. See Chapter 11. For parallels in other Buddhist societies, see Welch (1967, China), Tambiah (1970, Northeast Thailand), and Spiro (1971, Burma).

8. *Sang* is a common folk-religion term. As noted in Samuel (1985), the root *sang*, 'to cleanse' or 'to purify,' is found in the term for the central purificatory ritual of the Tibetan folk-religion *(sang)*. *Sang* also occurs in a variety of contexts and divine names (such as *masang* as a type of deity, *masang kyebu* as a title of the epic hero Gesar, and the Bön deity Sangpo Bumtr'i. *Sang* in the Old Bön language apparently had the general meaning of 'sky' or 'heaven' (Stein 1959b:59–60). The inner purification of the Buddha was thus made to parallel the purifying action of shamanic ritual and to incorporate the power of the pre-Buddhist deities. The compilers of the *Mahāvyutpatti*, while they comment at some length on the range of meanings of the Sanskrit terminology, unfortunately tend to take the Tibetan side of the process for granted. For their comments on *buddha*, see Simonsson (1957:265–266) and Wayman (1955:257 n. 27).

9. This is a phonemically distinct root from the *sang* = cleansed, purified, discussed above. In the Wylie transcription, the words are *(b)sang(s)* and *bzang*. In the Lhasa dialect on which my transcription is based, the distinction is realized as a tonal contrast.

10. Spanien 1971b:299; Beyer 1973. See Edgerton on *adhiṣṭhāna*, (1972:15–16, 12–13); he makes it 'to empower,' from 'to assume mastery of,' *adhitiṣṭhati*.

11. See Roger Jackson 1982. For other discussions of the debate see Demiéville (1952), Wayman (1977), Tatz (1978), Houston (1980).

12. One Tibetan account, the *Samten Migdrön* of Nub Sanggyé Yeshé, possibly a contemporary of Hashang Mahāyāna, gives a more sympathetic interpretation of the Chinese position, and has recently been studied in some detail by Samten Karmay (1988a:90ff, 99ff).

CHAPTER 24

1. On the problems of early Bönpo chronology, see also Blondeau (1982–1983:129–30, 1984–1985:107–108).

2. On the Nyingma Tantras, see Guenther (1974b, 1975b), Karmay (1975b), Dargyay (1978), and Thondup (1984).

3. For a survey of research so far, see Kvaerne (1990b).

4. On Dzogch'en in Bön, see in particular Kvaerne (1983) and Karmay (1988a). On Dzogch'en in Buddhism, see Tucci (1980), Namkhai Norbu (1986b), Lipman (1987), Norbu and Lipman (1987), and Karmay (1975b, 1985, 1988a).

5. On *jalü* see Robinson (1979), Dowman (1984), Namkhai Norbu (1986b). For the early Tibetan kings, see Haarh (1969), Karmay (1975b:155), and Kirkland (1982).

6. Eastern Tibetan lineages claiming descent from the old royal family included the Lhagyari family, who retained an important position among the central Tibetan aristocracy into the twentieth century, and the kings of Powo in K'am (the Kanam Depa). Gene Smith lists several others (1969c:8 n. 9).

7. Thus he is described as recognizing the Nyingma yogin and scholar Ngülch'u Dharmabhadra as a reincarnation of his own guru Kṛṣṇācārya (David Stott, pers. comm.).

8. See Chogay Trichen 1983:13, Roerich 1976:205–209. The dates for Drogmi are given in Ngorchen (1987:xiv). According to Tucci (1980:250), he died in 1074.

9. On the Ngorpa see Davidson 1981.

10. By the time that these collections were compiled (see Smith 1969b), the songs had undergone some centuries of oral transmission. Variant versions of some songs can be found in other sources (for example, Tsongk'apa's *Sablam Naro Ch'ödrug,* translated in Muses 1961), and there is an earlier collection by the 3d Karmapa, Rangjung Dorje *(Dzödnagma).* (This text is included in the PL480 collection, although I have not as yet had an opportunity to examine it.) It is difficult to judge how many of these songs were actually the work of Milarepa, but if some are apocryphal, they are presumably similar in style to the authentic material.

11. I have removed Kunga and Cutillo's paragraph and verse divisions, which are not in the original Tibetan.

12. The head lamas of the Drugpa Kagyüdpa transferred their seat to Sang-ngag Ch'öling in Tsari in the sixteenth century (Smith 1968a:3).

13. A useful survey of Kagyüdpa lineages and suborders is given by Gene Smith in his introduction to the Barapa version of the *Kagyüd Sertr'eng* (1970b:1–8). On the Karmapa, Richardson (1958–1959) is still of use.

CHAPTER 25

1. On the early history of the cult of Avalokiteśvara in Tibet, and especially its links to the figure of Padmasambhava, see also Blondeau (1977–1978, 1978–1979).

2. Guanyin is female, not male, combining attributes of Avalokiteśvara and Tārā from the Tibetan point of view, but historically she derives from Avalokiteśvara.

3. See his commentary on the *Domsum Rabyé,* in which he refers to the leading early K'ön lamas as emanations *(namtr'ul)* of Avalokiteśvara, Mañjuśrī, and Vajrapāṇi *(Sakya Kabum* 14:121–1–3). It is said that Sach'en Kunga Nyingpo's own lama Namk'aupa was the first to prophesy that all male members of the K'ön lineage would be Mañjuśrī emanations (David Stott, pers. comm.).

4. Kapstein, in press. According to Karma Ch'agmed, the first eight Gyalwa Karmapa were the eight emanations of Guru Rimpoch'e as well as being emanations of Avalokiteśvara.

5. David Jackson (1983) gives a useful bibliography of commentarial literature on the principal writings of Sakya Pandita. On the *Domsum Rabyé,* see Rhoton (1985).

6. Not included in Obermiller's translation (1932–1933).

7. See Berzin (1979), Guenther (1975b, 1975c), Lipman (1977, 1980, 1987), Chokhorling (1978), and Thondup (1989).

8. Descriptions of the process of finding *trulku* include Trungpa (1971), Govinda (1974), etc. Matthias Hermanns has some interesting comments on the relationship between actual events and official story in the case of the finding of the 14th Dalai Lama (1970, vol. 3, 123ff).

9. For the Gyalwa Karmapa incarnations, see Douglas and White (1976) and Karma Thinley (1980). On the 17th Karmapa, see *Tibetan Review,* August 1992.

10. See Guenther (1963:82–85). Gö Lotsawa's account in the *Debt'er Ngönpo* makes explicit reference to these practices (= Roerich 1976:493–494). The Sakyapa *lamdré* teachings also included control over the process of rebirth (David Stott, pers. comm.).

11. Leonard van der Kuijp has recently pointed out that references to *trulku* of the Drugpa Kagyüdpa lama Gödts'angpa and to *trulku* of some early Ts'elpa Kagyüdpa lamas appear to predate the recognition of Rangjung Dorjé as a rebirth of Karma Pakshi (van der Kuijp 1989).

CHAPTER 26

1. See the poem he wrote after his crucial vision, translated in Wangyal (1973:175–186). Of course the idea itself had Indian precedents, see Ruegg (1981) and also Eckel (1987).

2. The last section of the *Lamrim Ch'enmo* has been translated into English in Wayman (1978). For translations of the shorter of the two adaptations *(Lamrim Düdön),* see Berzin (1972), Lhalungpa (1968), and Wangyal

(1973). Of later *lamrim* texts, that by the 3d Dalai Lama has been translated by Glenn Mullin (1978). Guenther has translated a text by Yeshe Gyents'en (1713–1793), tutor to the 8th Dalai Lama, which is mostly based on the *lamrim* scheme for its first (Pāramitāyāna) section (1971:77–103; *Sergi Yangshun*). There is also an English version of the entire *lamrim* teachings based on an oral presentation by a contemporary Gelugpa lama, Ngawang Thargyay (Berzin 1972).

3. A survey of the Tantras by Tsongk'apa's leading disciple K'edrubjé (Lessing and Wayman 1968) has also been translated into English.

4. There were some Gelugpa *gompa* in the north of Dergé state (see Chapter 17).

5. Blondeau 1980. The *Sheldragma* text, an extensive verse biography of Padmasambhava, was published in a French translation by Gustave-Charles Toussaint in 1933 (see Bischoff 1979:409–410) and has recently been translated into English (Douglas and Bays 1978). An abridged translation of a related prose biography was published in 1954 by W. Y. Evans-Wentz (Evans-Wentz 1968). Two sections of the *Kat'ang Denga* are available in Western translations or summaries (Laufer 1911; Blondeau 1971).

6. For Loden Nyingpo's dates, see Kvaerne (1990a:159).

7. Rimed collections such as the *Damngag Dzöd* quote Pema Karpo, Tāranātha, and their contemporaries heavily.

8. Dowman and Paljor 1980:78–79. For the Tibetan text and a (somewhat more literal) German translation, see Kretschmar (1981:30–32, 91–92).

CHAPTER 27

1. For the story of how they came to keep the Vajrakilaya cycle, as told in the *Ngor Ch'öjung,* see Davidson (1981:79–80).

2. Kat'og was originally founded in the late twelfth century but had fallen into decay. It was refounded in 1656 (Smith 1969a:6, n. 15).

3. 'Mentation' in Guenther's translation.

4. The usual Sanskrit equivalent of *rigpa* is *vidyā,* but the meaning of the term in Dzogch'en thought represents an indigenous Tibetan development, and does not correspond to the usage of *vidyā* in Sanskrit. Guenther translates *rigpa* in this text by 'value awareness.'

5. They include two more short philosophical texts (*Yeshe Longi Gyüd,* Guenther 1977a:115–130; *Sengge Ngaro,* Trungpa 1972:21–26) and the widely used *chöd* and *ngöndro* (Tantric preliminary) practices (*K'andro Gegyang* = Evans-Wentz 1967:301–334; *Longch'en Nyingt'ig Ngöndro,* Thondup 1982; see Khetsun Sangbo 1982; Dilgo Khyentse 1988; and below).

6. For example, Rip'a *gompa* in the north of Pagshöd, founded in the early

nineteenth century, and based on a combination of Kagyüdpa and Tagshampa (Nyingmapa) teachings (Andzin and Namk'a Drimed Rimpoch'e, Chandragiri, pers. comm., August 1990).

7. For Rimed in general, see Smith (1970a). Translations of Rimed texts, apart from those referred to in subsequent notes, include three short texts by Kongtrul (McLeod 1974; Trungpa 1980:81–90; Trungpa 1981:7–17), a guide to the pilgrimage sites of central Tibet by Jamyang Ky'entsé Ongpo (Ferrari 1958), and several short works by Ju Mip'am (Dowman 1973; Guenther 1972; *Crystal Mirror* 2 (1973):40–43, 3 (1974):3–6, 41–44, *Gesar* 4(1) (Winter 1977):5–8). A short history of Buddhism by the twentieth-century Rimed lama, Jamyang Ky'entse Ch'öki Lodrö, has been edited and translated by Michael Aris (1977).

8. For an example see Ju Mip'am's commentary on Nāgārjuna's *Suhṛllekha* (Kawamura 1975).

9. The *terma* produced by these lamas, particularly by Choggyur Lingpa and his slightly younger contemporary, Dudjom Lingpa (1835–1903), are often referred to as *ter sar*, 'New *Terma*.'

10. See the geographical work translated in part by Wylie (1962). Dan Martin has translated some of the comments on Europe in this text, along with others by T'ukwan Ch'ökyi Nyima (Martin 1990:127–130).

11. Ruegg suggests in the course of a review of Stoddard's recent book that it was his *nyönpa* tendencies that were responsible for getting him into trouble (Ruegg 1989).

12. This text as we now have it was arranged from the writings of Jigmed Lingpa by his disciple the 1st Dodrub Ch'en (Goodman 1983:130–131).

13. These (see notes to Chapter 14) are *mendel*, offerings of the universe, symbolized by a plate of rice and other substances, to the visualized guru and not to be confused with the Tantric *maṇḍala* of deities or with the '*maṇḍala* of essence, nature, and compassion,' which is a kind of metaphorical extension of the Tantric *maṇḍala*.

CHAPTER 28

1. While celibate practitioners are generally provided with material support by lay members of their family, for example in the form of the produce of land that is reserved for them and cultivated for them, many *gompa* have substantial resources of their own. In addition, celibate practitioners reduce strain on limited resources by not marrying and having children. This is probably particularly relevant in the case of female practitioners.

2. Other writings by Ortner and Paul that bear on these issues include Ortner (1978c, 1989b) and Paul (1982a, 1984, 1990).

APPENDIX 1

1. Schuh's list is described as a "name-list of the sangha," *gendün nam kyi ts'ent'o* (Schuh 1988:93). It begins with the abbot and four other officials, followed by 39 *gelong* and 15 *gets'ul*. This is a high proportion of *gelong* and it might be that younger *gets'ul* and *genyen* are not included.

2. There are also some figures for Dergé state given by Li An-Che (Li 1947). They apparently refer to the 1930s. The area in question is unclear, but may correspond approximately to the modern county of Dêgê (Tibetan population around 52,500). It is certainly much less than the old state of Dergé, as described in Kessler's study. The population figures given by Li (5,592 men and 5,580 women) are nevertheless very low, and must reflect the loss of population to areas under Tibetan control, extensive underreporting, or both. His figures for the monastic population (2,488 men and 88 females) sound more realistic but may also be on the low side. The area he studied contained several major *gompa* including Lhundrub Teng in Dergé town, Pelpung, Dzogch'en, and probably Shech'en. Li gives the monastic population of Dzogch'en as 257 (Li 1947:287), which may be compared to Teichman's 1,000 (1922:237), Paltul's 850 (n.d.:79), and Kessler's 800. In addition, these *gompa* would have recruited many of their *trapa* from outside the region. Altogether, the proportion of celibate *trapa* given by Li's figures (44 percent of the male population) probably has little meaning.

3. The figures given in Chen Han-seng's study of nine agricultural villages in the Hor states region in 1940 are, like Li An-che's for Dergé, of dubious reliability (Chen 1949). The total population of the nine villages consisted of 1,701 people in 548 households. According to Chen there were 111 'lamas' of whom 87 were male and 24 female. The number of *gompa* is unclear. Chen notes that only 23 of the lamas return home frequently to assist in their households, which suggests that most or all of them were celibate *trapa* or *ani*. The figures amount to about 10 percent of the male and 3 percent of the female population. Chen quotes Chinese figures suggesting that there had been a considerably higher proportion of *trapa* in the past (Chen 1949:126–127).

Guide to Tibetan Spelling

The transcription used for Tibetan words and names in this book is an eclectic one, based on a simplified version of the Lhasa dialect. In several cases I have kept more familiar forms (for example, Bön, Dingri) to avoid confusing nonspecialists. I have also normally retained people's preferred romanization of their own names (for example, Rato Khyongla). The following guide indicates the actual spelling in standard written Tibetan, where this is known to me, using the Wylie system (Wylie 1959). Dialect terms (for example, Sherpa, Ladakhi) are indicated as such. For their pronunciation, I have followed the ethnographic sources. Equivalents in standard written Tibetan are given where available. Pinyin terms are indicated (P) and Tibetan equivalents given. I have also given some Sanskrit equivalents for Tibetan terms (S).

Aba [P, n. of prefecture = *Ngawa*] rnga ba
ache lhamo a lce lha mo
Adzom Drugpa a 'dzom 'brug pa
Adzom Gar a 'dzom mgar
Ak'u Tönpa a khu ston pa
Akar T'egpa a dkar theg pa
Alchi [Ladakh] a lci

Ali [place in *Mön*] a li
Ali [P, n. of prefecture = *Ngari*] mnga' ris
Amdo a mdo
Amgön a mgon [= *Nyarong Gompo Namgyel*]
ani a ni
Ap'o Rimpoch'e a pho rin po che
Asha 'a zha
Awo go chö [Amdo] a bu rgod khyod
Ayu Khandro a yo mkha' 'gro

babdrung 'babs sgrung
Baiyü [P, n. of county = *Pelyül*] dpal yul
Bakula Rimpoch'e ba ku la rin po che
Bamiba sba mi sba
Banbar [P, n. of county = *Pelbar*] dpal 'bar
bangdzöd lha bang mdzod lha
Barapa 'ba ra pa
Barbung [K'am = *Pelpung*] dpal spungs
bardo bar do
Barkam [P, n. of county = *Bark'am*] 'bar khams
Barled bar slad
barshug bar bzhugs
Bat'ang 'ba' thang *or* 'ba'
Baxoi [P, n. of county = *Pagshöd*] dpag shod
beda [Ladakh] bhe da *or* be dha
Bengen ?ban rgan
bera [Dolpo] be ra
Beri be ri
beyül sbas yul
Bhutan [Anglo-Indian] 'brug yul
Bomi [P, n. of county = *Pomed*] spo mes
bön, Bön bon
bön nying bon rnying
bön sar bon gsar
bön-nyid bon nyid
bönpo, Bönpo bon po
Bönri bon ri
Bumt'ang 'bum thang
buzhen [Spiti] sp. unknown

Ch'ag Lotsawa Ch'öje Pel chag lo tsa ba chos rje dpal
Chagla lcags la
Ch'agna Dorjé phyag na rdo rje [= S Vajrapāṇi]
chagöd bya rgod
ch'agch'en phyag chen [= S mahāmudrā]
Chakgama [Amdo] sp. unknown
ch'am 'cham
Ch'amdo chab mdo
Champa Tendar byams pa bstan dar
Champa P'unts'og byams pa phun tshogs
Chandüd lcags mdud
ch'ang chang
Changch'ub Dorjé byang chub rdo rje
Changch'ub Gyantsen byang chub rgyal mtshan
Changch'ub Öd byang chub 'od
changch'ub sem byang chub sems [= S bodhicitta]
Changkya Qutuqtu [Mong] lcang skya ho thog thu, hu thug thu
changsem = *changch'ub sem*
Changt'ang byang thang
Changter byang gter
Ch'angtr'eng phyag phreng
Changtsé Ch'öjé byang rtse chos rje
Changtsé Trats'ang byang rtse grwa tshang
chayig bca' yig
Chemre [Ladakh] lce 'bre
Chenresig spyan ras gzigs [= S Avalokiteśvara]

ch'idé phyi sde
Chidzöd spyi mdzod
Chiky'ab spyi khyab
chin byin
chinlab byin rlabs
chinten ?byin rten
ch'ö chos [= S dharma]
chöd gcod
chödpa gcod pa
Ch'oggyur Lingpa mchog 'gyur (bde chen zhig po) gling pa
Ch'ogling = *Ch'oggyur Lingpa*
ch'ogmi phyogs mi
Chogtse lcog rtse
Ch'ögyam Trungpa Rimpoch'e chos (kyi) rgya m(tsho) drung pa rin po che
Ch'ögyel chos (kyi) rgyal (po) [= S Dharmarāja]
Ch'öje Yamchilwa chos rje g.yam spyil ba
Ch'öki Lodrö chos kyi blo gros
Ch'ök'or Lhunpo chos 'khor lhun po
ch'öku chos sku [= S Dharmakāya]
ch'ökyong chos skyong
chomo jo mo
chomoling [Ladakhi = *ani gompa*] jo mo gling
Choni [Amdo] co ne
ch'önyid chos nyid [= S dharmatā]
ch'öpa chos pa
ch'orten mchod rten [= S stūpa]
ch'ospun [Ladakh] chos spun
ch'öyön mchod yon
ch'uter chu gter
chuts'o [Ladakh] bcu tsho
Cona [P, n. of county = *Ts'ona*] mtsho sna

dabdob ldab ldob
Dailing [P, n. of place = *Kata*]
dag ky'edki dulcha shogchig bdag khyed kyi gdul byar shog cig
dagnang dag snang
Dagpo dwags po
Dagpo Lhaje [= Gampopa] dwags po lha rje
Dalai Lama tā la'i bla ma *or* rgyal dbang rin po che
damts'ig dam tshig [S = samaya]
damts'ig sempa dam ts'ig sems dpa' [= S samayasattva]
Danba [P, n. of county] rong brag
Daocheng [P, n. of county] 'dab pa
Dargyé dar rgyas
Darjeeling rdo rje gling
Dartsemdo dar rtse mdo [= P Kangding]
Dashi da bzhi
Dawu [P, n. of county] rta'u
dé sde
Dech'en Ch'ök'or bde chen chos 'khor
Dech'en K'andro bde chen mkha' 'gro
Dêgê [P, n. of county = Derge] sde dge
delog 'das log
Dêngqên [P, n. of county] steng chen
Denma 'dan ma
Densa T'il gdan sa mthil
depa sde pa
Depa Shung sde pa gzhung
Depa Tsangpa sde pa gtsang pa
Depön sde dpon
Dêqên [P, n. of county and prefecture = *Dech'en*] bde chen
Derge sde dge
Derge Gönch'en sde dge dgon chen
desid sde srid
Devuche [Sherpa] sp. unknown
Dewachen bde ba can [= S Sukhāvatī]
Dezhung Rimpoch'e sp. unknown
digpa sdig pa

Dilgo Ky'entse Rimpoch'e dis mgo *or* dil mgo mkhyen brtse rin po che
Dingri ding ri
dö mdos
Do Ky'entse mdo mkhyen brtse
Dochi mdo (smad) spyi (khyab)
dödmé shi gdod ma'i gzhi
Dodrub Ch'en rdo grub chen
Dodrub Ch'en Rimpoch'e rdo grub chen rin po che
Dok'am mdo khams
döl bön rdol bon
Dolpo dol po
Domed mdo smad
dompa sdom pa [= S saṃvara]
dön geg gdon bgegs
döndam denpa don dam bden pa [= S paramārthasatya]
Döngyüd Nyima don brgyud nyi ma
dorjé rdo rje [= S vajra]
Dorjé Ch'ang rdo rje 'chang [= S Vajradhara]
Dorjé Drag rdo rje brag
Dorjé Dragtsen ?rdo rje brag btsan
Dorjé Lingpa rdo rje gling pa
dorjé lobpön rdo rje slob dpon [= S vajrācārya]
Dorjé Neljorma rdo rje rnal 'byor ma [= S Vajrayoginī]
Dorjé Ngangkar rdo rje ngang dkar
Dorjé P'agmo rdo rje phag mo [= S Vajravārāhī]
Dorjé Sempa rdo rje sems dpa' [= S Vajrasattva]
Dorjé Shugden rdo rje shugs ldan
Doshang La sp. unknown
Dotöd mdo stod
drablha dgra lha *or* sgra bla
Dragkar brag dkar
Dragshed drag gshed
Dragyab brag g.yab
Dragyab Chamgön brag g.yab skyabs mgon
Dragyam [Dolpo] brag gyam *or* brag kyem
drandul nyenkyong dgra 'dul gnyen skyong
Drangk'ar brang mkhar
Dranggo brag mgo
Draur Beu gra 'ur be hu
Drayab [= *Dragyab*]
drebui bön 'bras bu'i bon
Drenjong 'bras ljongs [= Sikkim]
Dreo bre'o *or* tre'o
Drepung 'bras spungs
dri 'bri, 'bri mo
Dri River 'bri chu [= Yangtze]
drib sgrib
Drigung 'bri gung
Drigungpa 'bri gung pa
Drigung Chamgön 'bri gung skyabs mgon
Drigung Ch'ets'ang ?'bri gung che tshang [= *Drigung Chamgön*]
Drigung Ch'ungts'ang ?'bri gung chung tshang
Drogmi 'brog mi
Drogön P'agmo Drupa 'gro mgon phag mo gru pa
drogpa 'brog pa
dröl sgrol
Drölma Lhak'ang sgrol ma lha khang
Drölma sgrol ma [= S Tārā]
Dromo gro mo
Dromtön 'brom ston
Drönch'en mgron chen
drong 'brong
drongpa grong pa
drowa ngé dulcha yin 'gro ba nga yi gdul bya yin
drubch'en grub (thob) chen (po) [= S mahāsiddha]

drubnyön grub smyon
drubt'ab sgrub thabs [= S sādhana]
drubt'ob grub thob [= S siddha]
Drug [place in Pema Köd] ?'brug
Drug Desid 'brug sde srid
Drugmo 'brug mo
Drugnyön 'brug smyon [= *Drugpa Kunleg*]
Drugpa 'brug pa
Drugpa Kagyüdpa 'brug pa bka' brgyud pa
Drugpa Kunlek 'brug pa kun legs
Drugu gru gu
Drugyül 'brug yul [= Bhutan]
düd bdud
düdch'ung dud chung
Düdtsi T'il (or *Til?*) bdud rtsi ?mthil
dük'or dus (kyi) 'khor (lo) [= S Kālacakra]
dulcha gdul bya
dulkyong 'dul skyong, discipline and protection
Dulnagpa Palden Sangpo 'dul nag pa dpal ldan bzang po
dulwa 'dul ba [= S Vinaya]
dulwé rigpa gdul ba'i rigs pa
dung gdung
dunggyüd gdung brgyud
Dungkar dung dkar
dungma dung ma
dur bön dur bon
Düsum Ky'enpa dus gsum mkhyen pa
Dza Peltrul rdza dpal sprul
Dza River rdza chu [= Mekong]
Dza Samdrup rdza bsam 'grub
Dza Tengch'en rdza steng chen
Dzach'uk'a rdza chu kha
Dzambuling 'dzam bu gling [= S Jambudvīpa]
Dzarong rdza rong [also called *Rongphu*]
dzasa dza sag
Dzatr'ul Rimpoch'e rdza sprul rin po che
Dzogch'en rdzogs chen
dzogrim rdzogs rim [= S saṃpanna-krama]
dzong rdzong
Dzongkha [Bhutanese] rdzong skad
Dzongpön rdzong dpon
Dzongsar rdzong gsar

Eyül e yul

Gak'og sga khog
Galing dga' gling
Gampopa sgam po pa
Ganan [P, n. of prefecture] kan lho [South Gansu]
Ganden dga' ldan
Ganden P'odrang dga' ldan pho brang
Ganden Shedrub Ling dga' ldan bshad sgrub gling [= *Sechu*]
Ganden Trashi Ky'il dga' ldan bkra shis 'khyil [= *Gurdu*]
Ganden Tr'i Rimpoch'e dga' ldan khri rin po che
Ganden Tr'ipa dga' ldan khri pa [= *Ganden Tr'i Rimpoch'e*]
gang sgang
gangdrug rongshi sgang drug rong bzhi
Ganggar sgang sgar
Gangteng sgang steng
ganyé dga' gnyen *or* dga' nye
Gapa sga pa
Gar 'gar *or* mgar
gara [Ladakh] mgar ba
Garab Dorjé dga' rab rdo rje
garpa sp. unknown
garpön sgar dpon
Garzê [P, n. of town, county and prefecture = *Kandzé*] dkar mdzes

gau ga'u
gegen dge rgan
Gegen Ky'entsé dge rgan mkhyen brtse
Geje dge rgyas
gekö dge bskos
gelong dge slong [= S bhikṣu]
gelongma dge slong ma [= S bhikṣuṇī]
Gelugpa dge lugs pa
Gendün Ch'öp'el dge 'dun chos 'phel
Gendün Drub dge 'dun grub
gendün nam kyi ts'ent'o dge 'dun rnams kyi mtshan tho
genpo rgan po
genyen dge bsnyen [= S upāsaka]
Genyen Ch'enpo dge bsnyen chen po
genyenma dge bsnyen ma [= S upāsīkā]
gerpa sger pa
Gesar ge sar
geshé dge (ba'i) bshes (gnyen) [= S kalyāṇamitra]
geshé lharampa dge bshes lha rams pa
Geshé Ngawang Dhargyey dge bshes ngag dbang dar rgyas
Geshé Rabten ?dge bshes rab gtan
gets'ul dge tshul [= S śramaṇera]
gets'ulma dge tshul ma [=S śramaṇerikā]
Gö Lotsawa 'gos lo tsa ba
göd rgod
Göddemchen rgod ldem can
Gödts'angpa rgod tshang pa
Golog mgo log *or* 'go log
Gomang sgo mang
gompa dgon pa
Gompo mgon po [= S Mahākāla]
Gompo Dorjé mgon po rdo rje
Gompo Namgyel mgon po rnam rgyal
Gongpa Rabsel dgongs pa rab gsal
gongter dgongs gter
Gonjo go 'jo
Gonsar Rimpoch'e ?dgon gsar rin po che
Gönsar dgon gsar
Gorampa Sönam Senggé go rams pa bsod nams seng ge
gowa 'go ba
gowé lha 'go ba'i lha
gowé lha nga 'go ba'i lha lnga
Gulu sp. unknown
Gungt'ang gung thang
gur mgur
Gurdu [Amdo] kirti dgon [= *Ganden Trashi Ky'il*]
Guru Loden Ch'ogsed gu ru blo ldan mchog sred
Guru Rimpoch'e gu ru rin po che [= S Padmasambhava]
Gushri Khan [Mong] gu shrir khāng
Gyadé gya sde
Gyagar [= India] rgya gar
gyami [= Chinese] rgya mi
Gyanag [= China] rgya nag
Gyantsé rgyal rtse
Gyasumdo ?rgya gsum mdo
Gyêgu [P, n. of town = *Jyekundo*] khyer dgun mdo
gyel lön sum rgyal blon gsum
gyelling rgya gling
gyelpo rgyal po
Gyelrong rgyal rong
Gyelt'ang rgyal thang
gyeltr'en rgyal phran
gyelts'ab rgyal tshab
Gyelts'abjé rgyal tshab rje
Gyelwa Karmapa rgyal ba karma pa
Gyelwang Karmapa rgyal dbang karmapa [= *Gyalwa Karmapa*]
Gyelwang Drugch'en rgyal dbang 'brug chen
gyüd (1) rgyud [= S Tantra, saṃtāna]; (2) brgyud [lineage, etc.]

Gyüdch'en Sangyé Gyats'o rgyud chen sangs rgyas rgya mtsho
Gyüdmed Trats'ang rgyud smad grwa tshang
gyüdpa rgyud pa
Gyüdtöd Trats'ang rgyud stod grwa tshang
gyui bön rgyu'i bon
gyulü sgyu lus
gyur bön bsgyur bon

Haibei [P, n. of prefecture] mtsho byang [Kokonor North]
Haidong [P, n. of prefecture] mtsho shar [Kokonor East]
Hainan [P, n. of prefecture] mtsho lho [Kokonor South]
Haixi [P, n. of prefecture] mtsho nub [Kokonor West]
Heishui [P, n. of county] khro chu
Hemis [Ladakh] he mis
Hemis Shugpachen [Ladakh] he mis shug pa can
Hepo has po (ri)
Hikim [Spiti] sp. unknown
Hongyuan [P, n. of county] hung yon
Hor hor [generic term for populations of Turkic origin]
Hor Pönk'ag Nga hor dpon khag lnga
Huangnan [P, n. of prefecture] rma lho [South Yellow River]

jalü 'ja' lus
Jamgön Kongtrul Lodrö T'ayé 'jam mgon kong sprul blo gros mtha' yas
Jampa K'edrub ?byams pa mkhas grub
Jampel Shenp'en 'jam dpal gzhan phan
Jampel Yang 'jam dpal dbyangs
Jamyang Ky'entsé Ongpo 'jam dbyangs mkhyen brtse'i dbang po
Jamyang Shepa 'jam dbyangs bzhad pa
Jang 'jang [= Naxi]
Jats'ön Nyingpo 'Ja' mtshon snying po
jetsün rje btsun
Jetsün Lochen Rimpoch'e rje btsun blo chen rin po che
Jetsündampa Qutuqtu [Mong] rje btsun dam pa ho thog thu
Jigmed Gyalwé Nyugu 'jigs med rgyal ba'i myu gu
Jigmed Lingpa 'jigs med gling pa
Jigmed Mip'am Ch'öwang 'jigs med mi pham chos dbang
Jigmed Tr'inlé Öser 'jigs med phrin las 'od zer
jigten 'jig rten
jigtenlé depé lha 'jig rten las 'das pa'i lha
jigtenpé ch'ökyong 'jig rten pa'i chos skyong
jigtenpé lha 'jig rten pa'i lha
Jinchuan [P, n. of county] chu chen
Jiwong [Sherpa] spyi dbang
Jok'ang jo khang
jöl bön 'jol bon
Jomda [P, n. of county] 'jo mda'
Jonangpa jo nang pa
jor(wa) sbyor (ba)
Ju Mip'am 'ju mi pham
Junbesi dgon pa gzhung
Jyekundo khyer dgun mdo

K'ach'e kha che
K'ach'e Panch'en kha che paṇ chen
kached nang bka' bcad gnang
k'achöd mkha' spyod
kadag ka dag
Kadampa bka' gdams pa
Kag bkag *or* skags

Kagyüd Sertr'eng bka' brgyud gser phreng
Kagyüdpa bka' brgyud pa *or* (esp. *Drugpa*) dkar brgyud pa
K'aky'ab Dorjé mkha' khyab rdo rje
Kalimpong bka' blong spungs
Kalön bka' blon
K'am khams
kama bka' ma
K'amba khams pa
K'amtr'ul Rimpoch'e khams sprul rin po che
Kanam Depa ka (g)nam sde pa
K'andro K'achi Wangmo ?mkha' 'gro mkha' spyod dbang mo
k'androma mkha' 'gro ma [= S ḍākinī]
Kandzé dkar mdzes
kang sung [Sherpa] ?bskang gso
Kangding [P, n. of town and county = Dartsemdo] dar rtse mdo
K'angsar khang gsar
kangso bskang gso
k'angts'en khang tshan
Kangyur bka' 'gyur
karam sp. unknown
karchag dkar chag
Karchung skar cung
Kardang mkhar dang
Karma Ch'agmed karma chags med
Karma Geru ?karma sger ru
Karma Pakshi karma pakṣi
Karmapa karma pa
Karsha dkar zha [= Lahaul]
Kashag bka' shag
Kata [place in K'am] sp. unknown
kat'ag bka' gtags
Kat'og kaḥ thog
K'edrubjé mkhas grub rje
K'embalung mkhan pa lung
k'enpo mkhan po
khamendeu [Sherpa] sp. unknown
Khongshe [Nyarong tribe] sp. unknown
Khumbu [Sherpa] sp. unknown
Khumjung [Sherpa] sp. unknown
Kirti Rimpoch'e kirti rin po che
Kirti Tsenshab Rimpoch'e kirti mtshan zhabs rin po che
K'ön 'khon
Könch'og dkon mchog
Könch'og Chindü dkon mchog spyi 'dus
Könch'og Gyelpo dkon mchog rgyal po
Könch'og Sum dkon mchog gsum [Buddha, Dharma, Saṃgha]
Könch'og Tenpa Rapgyé dkon mchog bstan pa rab rgyas
Kongkaling [K'am] gangs dkar gling
Kongpo kong po
Kongtrul kong sprul [= *Jamgön Kongtrul*]
k'orlo 'khor lo [= S cakra]
Kroskyab [Gyelrong] khro skyab
kula sku bla
kulwa bskul ba
Kumbum (Chamba Ling) sku 'bum byams pa gling
Künched Gyelpo kun byed rgyal po
Kündeling kun bde gling
kündzob denpa kun rdzob bden pa [= S saṃvṛti satya]
Künga Gyalts'en kun dga' rgyal mtshan
Künsang Sherab kun bzang shes rab
Künsang Mönlam kun (tu) bzang (po'i) smon lam
Künsang Ch'öling kun bzang chos gling
künshi kun gzhi
Küntu Sangpo kun tu bzang po [= S Samantabhadra]
kurim sku rim
Kutang sp. unknown

kutr'eng sku 'phreng
kyang rkyang
Kyab skyabs
ky'ar bön 'khyar bon
kye kye so so . . . lha gyello lha gyello kye kye svo svo lha rgyal lo lha rgyal lo
kye ma kye ma
kyedrim bskyed rim [= S utpattik-rama]
Ky'entsé mkhyen brtse [= Jamyang Ky'entsé Ongpo]
Kyerok [Sherpa] sp. unknown
Kyi [Spiti] skyi *or* dkyil
Kyid River skyid chu
ky'ilk'or dkyil 'khor [= S maṇḍala]
ky'imlha khyim lha [= *ph'uglha*]
Kyirong skyid rong
kyorpön skyor dpon
Ky'ungpo Neljor khyung po rnal 'byor

la bla
labrang bla brang
Labrang (Trashi Ky'il) bla brang bkra shis 'khyil
Ladakh la dwags
Lagyab Lhojang sp. unknown
Lahul gar zha
lak'ug bla khug *or* bla 'gugs
lalu bla bslu
lama bla ma
lama nyönpa bla ma smyon pa
Lama Tsenpo bla ma btsan po (smin grol no mon han)
lama umdzed bla ma dbu mdzad
Lama Yeshé see *T'ubten Yeshé*
Lamayuru [Ladakh] (bla ma) g.yung drung
lamdré lam 'bras
lamé neljor bla ma'i rnal 'byor [= S guruyoga]
lamrim lam rim
Lang [n. of family] rlangs; [= ox] glang
Lang Darma glang dar ma
Langkor glang skor
Langri T'angpa glang ri thang pa
laptsé la rtse *or* lha rdzas
lashing bla shing
lats'é bla tshe
Leh [Ladakh] sles
Lengkashi [K'am] sp. unknown
Lerab Lingpa las rab gling pa
letr'ö las 'phro
Letr'ö Lingpa las 'phro gling pa
lha lha
lha min lha min, lha ma yin
lhach'ö mich'ö lha chos mi chos
lhadro lha sgro
lhagt'ong lhag mthong [= S vipaśy-anā]
Lhagyari lha rgya ri
lhak'a lha kha
Lhalung lha lung
lhapa lha pa
Lhasa lha sa
lhasé lha sras
lhasin tamdrag lha srin dam bsgrags
lhasin degyed lha srin sde brgyad
lhat'o lha tho
Lhat'o T'ori lha tho tho ri
Lhat'og lha thog
Lhatsün Künsang Namgyel lha btsun kun bzang rnam rgyal
Lhatsün Rinch'en Namgyel lha btsun rin chen rnam rgyal
Lhodrag lho brag
Lhok'a lho kha
Lhorong [P, n. of county] lho rong
Lhündrub Teng lhun grub stengs
Ligmi lig myi
Likir [Ladakh] li kyir *or* klu dkyil
Ling gling
lingam ling gam

lingdro gling bro
Lingrepa Pema Dorjé gling ras pa padma rdo rje
Lingts'ang gling tshang
Lit'ang li thang
Lixian [P, n. of county] li zhan
Lo K'akar K'anag K'atr'a klo kha dkar kha nag kha khra
lobpön slob dpon
Lobsang Ch'ökyi Gyantsen blo bzang chos kyi rgyal mtshan
Lobsang Tenpé Gyants'en blo bzang bstan pa'i rgyal mtshan
Loden Nyingpo blo ldan snying po
Lodrö T'ayé blo gros mtha' yas
lojong blo sbyong
Longch'en Nyingt'ig klong chen snying thig
Longch'en Rabjampa klong chen rab 'byams pa
longchödku longs spyod sku [= S saṃbhogakāya]
Longsel Sangwa Nyingchüd klong gsal gsang ba snying bcud
Lopa klo pa *or* lho pa
Losel Ling blo gsal gling
lotsawa lo tsā ba
Lowo Gekar glo bo dge skar
lu klu [= S nāga]
lü lus [body]
lüd glud [ransom-substitute]
Luhuo [P, n. of county = *Drango*] brag 'go
lung (1) lung [textual transmission]; (2) rlung [= S prāṇa]
lungta rlung rta
Luoba [P, n. of ethnic group = *Lopa*] klo pa *or* lho pa

ma rung ma rung
ma ma
Ma River rma chu [Yellow River]
Machig ma gcig = *Machig Labdrön*
Machig Labdrön ma gcig lab sgron
magpa mag pa
Mainling [P, n. of county] sman gling
mamo ma mo
Mangyal Lhasey Trulku sp. unknown
Mani Kabum ma ṇi bka' 'bum
Mani Rimdu [Sherpa] ma ṇi ril sgrub
mani-walls, -wheels maṇi-*Maowen* [P, n. of county] ma'o wun
Mark'am dmar khams
Mark'am Gart'og smar khams sgar thog
Mark'am T'eji dmar khams tha'i ji
Marpa (Ch'ökyi Lodrö) mar pa chos kyi blo gros
masang ma sang
masang kyebu ma sangs skyes bu
Masur ma zur
Matro [Ladakh] ma spro
Med Dok'am smad mdo khams
Mêdog [P, n. of county] me tog
Menba [P, n. of ethnic group = *Mönpa*] mon pa
mendel maṇḍala
men-ngag man ngag
men-ngag tr'ulgi dumbu man ngag 'phrul gyi dum bu
Meru Sarpa rme ru gsar pa
mibog mi bogs
migöd mi rgod
Mikyöd Dorjé mi bskyod rdo rje
Milarepa mi la ras pa
Mili smi li *or* mu li
Mindröl Ling smin grol gling
Mindröl Ling Jetsün Mingyur Paldrön smin grol ling rje btsun mi 'gyur dpal sgron
mindung [Sherpa] mig mthong
Mingyur Dorjé mi 'gyur rdo rje
Minyag mi nyag
miser mi ser

mo mo
molha mo lha
mon [Ladakh] mon
Mön, *Mönpa* mon, mon pa
mu dmu
Murdu mur rdo
Murug Tsenpo mu rug btsan po
Mustang [Nepali] blo smon thang
mutegpa mu stegs pa

Nagch'uk'a nag chu kha
Nagqu [P, n. of county and prefecture] nag chu
Nalendra na len dra
Namch'ö gnam chos
Namgyel Trats'ang rnam ryal grwa tshang
Namgyel Tsé rnam rgyal rtse
Namk'aupa nam mkha'u pa
Namri Lonts'en or *Namri Songtsen* gnam ri slon mtshan/sron btsan
namshé rnam shes [= S vijñāna]
namt'ar rnam thar
namtr'ul rnam 'phrul
Nangch'en nang chen
nangdé nang sde
Nangqên [P, n. of county = Nangch'en] nang chen
nangso nang gso
Naro Ch'ödrug nā ro chos drug
Nech'ung gnas chung
neljor rnal 'byor [= S yoga]
neljorma rnal 'byor ma [= S yoginī]
neljorpa rnal 'byor pa [= S yogin]
Neten Ch'ogling gnas brtan mchog gling
Neudong sneu gdong
Neudong Gongma sne'u gdong gong ma
ngag sungma sngags srung ma
ngagpa sngags pa
Ngalong [Bhutan] sp. unknown
Ngari mnga' ris
Ngawa rnga ba
Ngawang Kelsang ngag dbang skal bzang
Ngawang Lobsang ngag dbang blo bzang
Ngawang Namgyel ngag dbang rnam rgyal
Ngawang Tenzin Norbu ngag dbang bstan 'dzin nor bu
Ngedön Drubpé Dorjé nges don sgrub pa'i rdo rje
Ngog rngogs
Ngolok = *Golog*
ngöndro sngon 'gro
Ngorpa ngor pa
ngowa bsngo ba
ngowo ngo bo
Ngül River dngul chu [= Salween]
Ngülch'u Dharmabhadra dngul chu dharmabhadra
Ngura [Amdo] sp. unknown
nödchüd snod bcud
nödjin gnod sbyin
Norbu Lingka nor bu gling kha
Norbu Dun-kun Drubpa sp. unknown
norpa [Sherpa] sp. unknown
Nup-ri [N.Nepal] ?nub ri
nüpa nus pa
Nyag River nyag chu [= Yalung]
Nyagch'uk'a nyag chu kha
Nyagla Pema Düddul nyag bla padma bdud 'dul
Nyagla Gar nyag bla mgar
Nyamé [Nyarong] ?nyag smad
Nyangral Nyima Öser nyang ral nyi ma 'od zer
Nyarag nya rag
Nyarong nyag rong
Nyarong Gompo Namgyel nyag rong mgon po rnam rgyal
Nyatö [Nyarong] ?nyag stod

Nyelam gnya' nang
nyen gnyan
Nyench'en T'anglha gnyan chen thang lha
nyengyüd snyan rgyud
Nye-shang sp. unknown
Nyet'ang snye thang
Nyima Tenzin nyi ma bstan 'dzin
Nyingchi [P, n. of town and county] nying khri
nyingma rnying ma
Nyingmapa rnying ma pa
Nyingsang (La) snying sangs la
Nyö Lotsawa gnyos lo tsā ba
nyönpa smyon pa
nyungné smyung gnas

Orgyen Lingpa o rgyan gling pa
Orgyen Wangch'ug o rgyan dbang phyug
Ösel Tendzin 'od gsal bstan 'dzin

P'adampa Sanggyé pha dam pa sangs rgyas
P'agmo Drupa phag mo gru pa
P'agpa 'phags pa
P'agpa Lha 'phags pa lha
Pagshöd dpag shod
Panch'en Rimpoch'e paṇ chen rin po che
pandita ch'enpo paṇḍita chen po
Pangboche spang po che
Paro Ponlop [Bhutan] spa gro dpon slob
p'aspun [Ladakh] pha spun
pawo dpa' bo
Pawo Tsuglag dpa' bo gtsug lag
P'awongk'a Rimpoch'e pha bong kha rin po che
pecha ch'ö ma red dpe cha chos ma red
Peen [Spiti] spyin
Pehar pe har
Pelden dpal ldan
Pelden Lhamo dpal ldan lha mo [= S Śrīdevī]
Pelgyi Dorjé dpal gyi rdo rje
Pelk'or dpal 'khor
Pelpung [= *Barbung*] dpal spungs
Pelyül dpal yul
pem [Sherpa] ?dpa' mo
Pema Ch'ögyel = *Tsibri Pema Ch'ögyel*
Pema Garwang padma gar dbang
Pema Karpo padma dkar po
Pema Köd padma bkod
Pema Lingpa padma gling pa
Pema Sel padma gsal
pembu [Sherpa = *pönpo*] dpon po
Phala [P?] sp. unknown
Phiyang [Ladakh] spyi dbang *or* sgang sngon
Pöd bod
Pödki Gyelpo bod kyi rgyal po
Podong bo dong
p'olha pho lha
p'olha k'ar pho lha mkhar
P'olhané pho lha nas
Pomed spo smad
pön (= *pönpo*) dpon (po)
pönch'en dpon chen
pönpo dpon po
Potala po ta la
p'owa 'pho ba
Powo spo bo
Poyül spo yul
pu bu
p'uglha phug lha
Pungmo spung mo
Purang pu 'rangs
Putön (Rinch'en Drubpa) bu ston rin chen grub pa

Qamdo [P, n. of town, county and prefecture = *Chamdo*] chab mdo

rabchung rab byung
Ralung rwa lung
Ramoch'e ra mo che
Rangchönpa rang byon pa
Rangchung Dorjé rang byung rdo rje
rangshin rang bzhin
Ratak Trulku sp. unknown
Rato = *Ratöd*
Rato Khyongla ra stod skyong la
Ratöd ra stod
Ratreng Rimpoch'e rwa sgreng rin po che
Rdzakdumba [Amdo] sp. unknown
Remdapa red mda' pa
repa ras pa
Reting Rimpoch'e = *Ratreng Rimpoch'e*
Ridzong [Ladakh] ri rdzong
rigdzin rig 'dzin [= S vidyādhara]
Rigdzin Jats'ön Nyingpo = *Jats'ön Nyingpo*
rigpa rig pa
Rimed ris med
Rimijung [Sherpa] sp. unknown
Rimpoch'e rin po che
Rimpung rin spungs
Rimpungpa rin spungs pa
Rinch'en rin chen
Rinch'en Drubpa rin chen grub pa
Rinch'en Gang rin chen sgang
Rinch'en Sangpo rin chen bzang po
Rinch'en Terdzöd rin chen gter mdzod
Ringmo [Dolpo] ring mo
risu ch'edpa ris su chad pa
Riwoch'e rin po che *or* ri bo che
Riwoqê [P, n. of county = *Riwoch'e*] ri bo che
rolang ro langs [= S vetāla]
Rölpé Dorjé Rimpoch'e rol pa'i rdo rje rin po che
rong rong
rongpa rong pa
Rongphu = *Dzarong*
ronyom ch'enpö tulshug chödpa ro snyom chen po'i brtul zhugs spyod pa
rü rus
rukor ru skor
ruspa [Ladakh] rus pa

sa (1) sa [earth]; (2) gza' [planetary deity]
sabdag sa bdag
Sach'en Kunga Nyingpo sa chen kun dga' snying po
Sagya [P, n. of county = Sakya] sa skya
Sakya sa skya
Sakya Pandita sa skya paṇḍita
Sakya Tr'ich'en sa skya khri chen
Sakya Tr'idzin sa skya khri 'dzin
Sakyapa sa skya pa
Samada sa mda'
samadrog sa ma 'brog
Samding bsam lding
Samdrubtsé bsam 'grub rtse [= *Shigatsé*]
Samling bsam gling
Samtsa [Amdo] sp. unknown
Samyé bsam yas
sangts'en gsang mtshan
sang (1) bsangs [ritual]; (2) (b)sang(s) [to purify]; (3) srang [currency unit]
Sangen sa ngan
sanggyé sangs rgyas [= S Buddha]
Sanggyé Lama sangs rgyas bla ma
sang-ngag gsang sngags
Sang-ngag Ch'öling gsang sngags chos gling
Sangpo Bumtr'i sangs po 'bum khri
Sangskar [Amdo] zangs skar
sangwa gsang ba
Sangwa Dorjé gsang ba rdo rje

Sangyé Gyats'o sangs rgyas rgya mtsho
Sangyé Tenzin sangs rgyas bstan 'dzin
sangyum gsang yum
sapön bza' dpon
sarma gsar ma
Sasang sa bzang
Sat'am sa tham [= Lijiang]
sater sa gter
Sawang Ösel Rangdrol sa dbang 'od gsal rang grol
Sechu [Amdo] gser khri
Sednaleg sad na legs
Segyüd sre rgyud
sem sems [= S citta]
semchen sems can
Senggé Namgyel seng ge rnam rgyal
Sera se ra
Sera Ché se ra byas
Serkong Rimpoch'e gser kong rin po che
serky'im ser khyim
Serlo ser log
Sêrtar [P, n. of county = *Sert'ar*] gser thar
Sert'ar gser thar
Sertr'i gser khri
Serwa [Sherpa] sp. unknown
Sêrxü [P, n. of county] ser shul
Shabdrung Rimpoch'e zhabs drung rin po che
shabped zhabs pad
Shalu zha lu
Shalupa zha lu pa
Shamarpa zhwa dmar pa
Shambhala shambhala
Shami [Amdo] sp. unknown
shanag zhwa nag
Shanagpa zhwa nag pa [= Gyalwang Karmapa]
shang zhang
Shang Rimpoch'e sp. unknown
shanglha zhang lha
Shangpa shangs pa
Shangshung zhang zhung
Shannan [P, n. of prefecture = *Lhok'a*] lho kha
Shardza Trashi Gyantsen shar rdza bkra shis rgyal mtshan
Shardza Rimpoch'e shar rdza rin po che [= *Shardza Trashi Gyantsen*]
Sharlung Genyen Chenpo shar lung dge bsnyen chen po
Sharpa Ch'öjé shar pa chos rje
Shartsé Tr'ats'ang shar rtse grwa tshang
Sharwa [Amdo] shar pa
Shech'en zhe chen
Shelkar shel dkar
Shelkar Ch'ödé shel dkar chos sde
shen gshen
Shench'en Luga gshen chen klu dga'
shen-nyen gshen gnyan
Shenrab (Miwo) gshen rab (mi bo)
shentong gzhan stong
Sherdukpen [Arunachal Pradesh] sp. unknown
Sherpa [Sherpa] shar pa
Shey shel
shi gyé wang drag zhi rgyas dbang drag
Shibch'og zhib phyogs
shibdag gzhi bdag
shiched zhi byed
Shidé Trats'ang bzhi sde grwa tshang
Shigatsé gzhis dkar rtse
Shigatsé Chidzong gzhis ka rtse spyi rdzong
shik'a gzhis kha
Shimdrok [Amdo] sp. unknown
shimi gzhi mi
shiné zhi gnas [= S śamatha]
shingpa zhing pa
shitr'o zhi khro

sho zho
Shorung sp. unknown
shrindi [Sherpa] srin bdud
Shugseb shug gseb
shung gzhung
shung-gyugpa gzhung rgyugs pa
si gzi
Sidpé K'orlo srid pa'i 'khor lo
Sikkim [Anglo-Indian] 'bras ljongs
sinmo srin mo
Situ Panch'en si tu paṇ chen
Situ Rimpoch'e si tu rin po che
södnam bsod nams [= S puṇya]
Södnam Tsemo bsod nams rtse mo
sog srog
soglha srog lha
Sogpo Arig sog po a rigs
sojong gso sbyong [= S upoṣadha]
Solu [Nepali] = *Shorung*
Songpan [P, n. of county] zung chu
Songtsen Gampo srong btsan sgam po
sot'ar so (sor) thar (pa) [= S Prātimokṣa]
Spiti spyi ti *or* spi ti
Spituk [Ladakh] dpe thub
Stagna [Ladakh] stag sna
Stok [Ladakh] sp. unknown
Sumpa sum pa
Sumpa K'enpo sum pa mkhan po
sungma srung ma
Surmang zur mang
Surra Rakye zur ra rwa skyes

t'ablam thabs lam
t'ablha thab lha
Taglung stag lung
Taglungpa stag lung pa
Tagsig stag gzig
Tagtrag Rimpoch'e stag brag rin po che
Tagts'ang Lhamo stag tshang lha mo
Tagts'ang Repa stag tshang ras pa
T'ak [Thakkali] thag
talog bön lta log bon
t'amal shepa tha mal shes pa
Tambai [Gyelrong] ?dam pa
Tanggyüd btang rgyud
T'anglha thang lha
T'angpa Trashi Pel thang pa bkra shis dpal
T'angtong Gyelpo thang stong rgyal po
Tankar [Amdo] stong 'khor
Tap'o [Spiti] ta pho
Tāranātha Tāranātha *or* Tārānātha
Tarap [Dolpo] rta rabs
Tart'ang dar thang
Tawang rta dbang
t'egpa theg pa [= S yāna]
ten rten
tendrel rten 'brel [= S pratītyasamutpāda]
tendrel sang rten 'brel bzang
tendrel t'ab rten 'brel thabs
Tengboche [Sherpa] steng po che
Tengyé Ling bstan rgyas gling
Tengyur bstan 'gyur
Tenpa Ts'ering bstan pa tshe ring
tenpar drelwar jungwa/gyurwa rten par 'brel bar 'byung ba/'gyur ba
terma gter ma
tersar gter gsar
tertön gter ston
Tertön Sogyel gter ston bsod rgyal
Thami [Sherpa] sp. unknown
Tianzhu [P, n. of county] then kru'u
t'igle nyagchig thig le nyag gcig
Tiktse [Ladakhi] khrig rtse
to gto
Töd Ngari stod mnga' ris
Togden Rangrig rtogs ldan rang rig
t'ogel thod rgal
t'ogmé sangyé thog ma'i sangs rgyas [= S adibuddha]
torma gtor ma

tra pra
Tragt'og [Ladakh] brag stag
Trakshindo [Sherpa] sp. unknown
tr'amenma phra men ma
trangsong drang srong [= S ṛṣi and Bön equiv. to *gelong*]
trapa grwa pa
trashi bkra shis
Trashi Jong bkra shis ljongs
Trashi Lhunpo bkra shis lhun po
Trashi Lhap'ug bkra shis lha phug
Trashi Namgyel bkra shis rnam rgyal
Trashi Öser bkra shis 'od zer
Trashi Samten Ling bkra shis bsam gtan gling
trats'ang grwa tshang
tr'egchöd khregs gcod
Trehor tre hor
tr'elpa khral pa
tr'elpo khral po
Tr'ichang Rinpoch'e khri byang rin po che
tr'ich'en khri chen
Tr'ich'en Gyantsen Sengge khri chen rgyal mtshan seng ge
tr'id khrid
Tr'idé Songtsen khri lde srong btsan
Tr'idpön Pema Ch'ögyel khrid dpon padma chos rgyal
tr'idyig khrid yig
Trigum Tsenpo gri gum btsan po
tr'ikor khri skor
Tr'impön khrims dpon
tr'inlé 'phrin las
tr'ipön khri dpon
Tr'isong Deutsen khri srong lde'u btsan
Tromo Geshé Rimpoch'e gro mo dge bshes rin po che
Trongsar Ponlop [Bhutan] krong sar dpon slob
tr'ul 'phrul
tr'ulk'or 'khrul 'khor [= S yantra]
trulku 23 sprul sku [= S nirmāṇakāya]
trulpa sprul pa
Tr'ulshig Rimpoch'e 'khrul zhig rin po che
Trungch'en drung chen
Trungpa Trulku drung pa sprul sku
trungyig drung yig
tsa rtsa [= S nāḍī]
Tsagp'uwa rtsag phu ba
tsalung rtsa rlung
ts'am mtshams
Tsang gtsang
Tsang River gtsang chu [= Brahmaputra]
Tsangdrupa sp. unknown
Tsangla sp. unknown
Tsangma gtsang ma
Tsangnagpa sp. unknown
Tsangnyön Heruka gtsang smyon he ru ka
Tsangpa gtsang pa
Tsangpa Gyaré gtsang pa rgya ras
Tsari rtsa ri
Ts'arka tshar ka
Ts'arpa tshar pa
tsawé lama rtsa ba'i bla ma
ts'edzé tshe rdzas
Tsele Natsog Rangdrol rtse le sna tshogs rang grol
Ts'elpa tshal pa
Ts'emön Ling tshe smon gling
tsen btsan
ts'ennyid mtshan nyid
tsenpo btsan po
Ts'ering Ch'öp'el tshe ring chos 'phel
ts'ewang tshe dbang
Tsharuma [Amdo] sp. unknown
Tsibri rtsibs ri

Tsibri Tr'idpön Pema Ch'ögyel rtsibs ri khrid dpon padma chos rgyal
tsidpo rtsid po
ts'o (1) tsho [tribe]; (2) mtsho [lake]
Ts'o Ngönpo mtsho sngon po [Kokonor]
ts'og tshogs
Ts'ona mtsho sna
Tsongk'apa tsong kha pa
ts'ongpa tshong pa
Tsuglagk'ang gtsug lag khang (= *Jok'ang*)
Ts'ultr'im Gyants'en tshul khrims rgyal mtshan
Ts'urp'u mtshur phu
T'ubten Ch'öling thub bstan chos gling
T'ubten Yeshé thub bstan ye shes
t'ugjé thugs rje
T'ugjé Ch'enpo thugs rje chen po [form of Avalokiteśvara]
T'ugjé Ch'enpo Drowa Kündröl thugs rje chen po 'gro ba kun sgrol
T'ukwan Ch'ökyi Nyima thu'u bkwan chos kyi nyi ma
tulshug(i) chödpa brtul zhugs (gyi) spyod pa
tummo gtum mo [= S Caṇḍālī]
t'ünmong ngödrub thun mong dngos grub
tungshag ltung bshags

Ü dbus
Umapa dbu ma pa
Ü-Tsang dbus gtsang

wang dbang [= *wangkur*]
wangkur dbang bskur [= S abhiṣeka]
wangt'ang dbang thang
wanlog [Amdo] ban log
Wasze [Gyelrong] wa si
Weixi [P, n. of county] 'ba' lung
Wenchuan [P, n. of county] wun khron
wo go [Amdo] bu rgod
wo ga ma [Amdo] bu rgod ma
Wogzhi [Gyelrong] 'a gzhi
Womi Ts'o [Sherpa] 'o ma'i mtsho
Wulu [Nyarong] sp. unknown

Xiangcheng [P, n. of county = *Ch'angtr'eng*] phyag phreng
Xiaojin [P, n. of county] btsan lha
Xigazê [P, n. of town, county and prefecture = *Shigatsé*] gzhis ka rtse
Xining [P, n. of city] zi ling
Xinlong [P, n. of county = *Nyarong*] nyag rong

Yabshi yab gzhis
Yajiang [P, n. of county = *Nyagch'uk'a*] nyag chu kha
yangsid yang srid
yanguk [Ladakh] g.yang 'gugs
Yarlha Shampo yar lha sham po
Yarlung yar lung *or* klungs
yawa ya ba
yé yas
Yedzu Lhadrag Karpo ye brdzu lha brag dkar po
Yendum [K'am] byams mdun
yer-chang [Sherpa] dbyar chang
Yermo T'ang g.yer mo thang
Yeshé Gyents'en ye shes rgyal mtshan
Yeshé Ö ye she 'od
yeshé sempa ye shes sems dpa' [= S jñānasattva]
yeshepa = *yeshé sempa*
yeshepé ch'ökyong ye shes pa'i chos skyong
Yets'er g.yas mtsher
yidam yi dam [= S iṣṭadevatā]

Yidtr'ogma yid 'phrog ma
yigch'a yig cha
yogpo g.yog po
yönten yon tan
yug yug
yüllha yul lha
yungdrung bön g.yung drung bon
Yungdrung Lingpa g.yung drung gling pa
Yushu [P, n. of county and prefecture] yus hru'u
Yut'og g.yu thog
Zamtang [P, n. of county] dzam thang
Zayü [P, n. of county] rdza yul
Zhag'yab [P, n. of county = *Dragyab*] brag g.yab
Zhongdian [P, n. of county] rgyal thang
Zhung [Sherpa] (dgon pa) gzhung = *Junbesi*
Ziggag [Gyelrong] sp. unknown
Zongchung Rimpoch'e sp. unknown
Zopa sp. unknown

References

TIBETAN LANGUAGE

This list of references has two purposes: (1) to give the Tibetan titles in Wylie transcription of works mentioned in the main text; (2) where appropriate, to give references to text editions used. *Terma* are listed under name of *tertön*. Recent Tibetan works in book or article form are included in the Western bibliography.

Collections containing works by several authors

Damngag Dzöd: gdams ngag mdzod.
Text: *Gdams ṅag mdzod: A Treasury of Instructions and Techniques for Spiritual Realization.* Compiled by 'Jam-mgon Koṅ-sprul Blo-gros-mtha'-yas. Reproduced from a xylographic print from the Dpal-spuṅs blocks. 12 vols. N. Lungtok and N. Gyaltsan, Delhi, 1971.

Drubt'ab Kuntü: sgrub thabs kun btus

Gyudé Kuntü: rgyd sde kun btus

Kagyüd Gurts'o: bka' brgyud mgur mtsho
Text: mChog gi dngos grub mngon du byed pa'i myur lam bka' brgyud bla ma rnams kyi rdo rje'i mgur dbyangs ye shes char 'bebs rang grol lhun grub bde chen rab 'bar nges 'don rgya mtsho'i snying po zhes bya ba. Blockprint, Rumtek.

Kagyüd Ngagdzöd: bka' brgyud sngags mdzod

K'atön Chetü: kha ton gces btus
Text: *Buddhist Prayers and Devotional Pieces from Tibet.* Reproduced from rare Eastern Tibetan prints and manuscripts for the use of the faithful by Sherab Gyaltsen Lama. Gangtok, 1981.

Rinchen Terdzöd: rin chen gter mdzod

Sheldön Chetü: zhal 'don gces btus
Text: *bla ma'i rnal 'byor dang| yi dam khag gi bdag bskyed sogs zhal 'don gces btus 'khyer bde.* Dharamsala, n.d.

Sakya Kabum: sa skya bka' 'bum
Text: *The Complete Works of the Great Masters of the Sa sKya Sect of the Tibetan Buddhism.* Toyo Bunko, Tokyo 1968. (Bibliotheca Tibetica, I.)

Tokyo Tripitaka:
Text: *The Tibetan Tripitaka (Peking Edition).* Tokyo, Suzuki Research Foundation, 1962.

Collections and single works by individual authors

Atīśa *Changch'ub Lamdrön:* byang chub lam sgron
Text: *Tokyo Tripitaka* 103:20–21.

Dalai Lama, 6th [tā la'i bla ma drug pa tshangs dbyangs rgya mtsho] *Songs:* mgul glu *or* gsung mgur
Text in Sorensen 1990

Dalai Lama, 7th [tā la'i bla ma bdun pa blo bzang bskal bzang rgya mtsho] *Nyengur* (blo sbyong dang 'brel ba'i gdams pa dang) snyan mgur (gyi rim pa phyogs gcig tu bkod pa don ldan tshangs pa'i sgra dbyangs zhes bya ba)
Text in *The Collected Works (Gsuṅ 'bum) of the Seventh Dalai Lama Blo-bzaṅ-bskal-bzaṅ-rgya-mtsho.* Reproduced from a set of prints from the 1945 'Bras-spuns blocks from the library of the Ven. Dhardo Rimpoche by Lama Dodrup Sangye. Gangtok, 1975, 1:397–502.

Dodrub Ch'en, 3d [rdo grub chen 'jigs med bstan pa'i nyi ma] *Letr'o Tergyüd Namshed* las 'phro gter brgyud (kyi) rnam bshad (nyung gsal ngo mtshar rgya mtsho zhes bya ba)

Text in 3d Dodrub Ch'en's *Gsung 'bum*. Gangtok, 1975, 4:377–447.

Draggönpa Könch'og Tenpé Rabgyé [brag dgon pa dkon mchog bstan pa'i rab rgyas] *Debt'er Gyats'o* deb ther rgya mtsho (yul mdo smad kyi ljongs su thub bstan rin po che ji ltr dar ba'i tshul gsal bar brjod pa deb ther rgya mtsho zhes bya ba)

Text: Dkon-mčhog bstan-pa rab-rgyas *Histoire du Bouddhisme dans l'Amdo*. Introduction par Yon-tan rgya-mcho. Centre de Recherches d'Histoire et de Philologie de la IVᵉ Section de l'École Pratique des Hautes Études. Paris, n.d.

Gampopa [sgam po pa bsod nams rin chen, dwags po lha rje] *T'arpa Rimpoch'é Gyen* thar pa rin po che'i rgyan

Text: *dam chos yid bzhin nor bu thar pa rin po che'i rgyan zhes bya ba*. Modern blockprint from Rumtek.

Gendün Rinch'en [dge bshes brag phug dge 'dun rin chen]. *Namt'ar* of Drugpa Kunleg. 'gro ba'i mgon po chos rje kun dga' legs pa'i rnam thar rgya mtsho'i snying po mthong ba don ldan.

Text: Kretschmar 1981 (see Aris 1987:145 n. 23).

Gö Lotsawa ['gos lo tsha ba gzhon nu dpal] *Debt'er Ngönpo* deb ther sngon po

Text: 'gos lo tsa ba gzhon nu dpal. *Deb ther sngon po*. Si khron mi rigs dpe skrun khang. 2 vols., 1984.

Göddemchen [rgod ldem can]. *Changter* [*terma* cycle] byang gter

———. *Künsang Mönlam*. kun (tu) bzang (po'i) smon lam.

Text in *K'atön Chetü* [A6]

Gorampa Södnam Sengge [go ram pa bsod nams seng ge] *Domsum Rabyé Namshed* sdom pa gsum (gyi) rab (tu) dbye (ba)'i rnam bshad (rgyal ba'i gsung rab kyi dgongs pa gsal ba)

Text in *Sakya Kabum* [A9] 14:119–199.

Jats'ön Nyingpo *Konch'og Chidü* [*terma* cycle] dkon mchog spyi 'dus

Jetsün Loch'en Rimpoch'e [rje btsun blo chen rin po che] *Namt'ar:* rnam thar

Text: *Gaṅs śug ma ṇi lo chen rig 'dzin chos ñid bzaṅ mo'i rnam par thar pa rnam mkhyen bde ster.* The autobiographical reminissences of the famed religious master and reembodiment of Kloṅ-chen-pa Śug-gseb Rje-btsun Rig-'dzin-chos-ñid-bzaṅ-mo. Reproduced from a tracing of a print fom the Central Tibetan blocks by Sonam Topgay Kazi. Gangtok, 1975.

Jigmed Lingpa ['jigs med gling pa] *K'andro Gadgyang:* (klong chen snying gi thig le las: gcod yul) mkha' 'gro'i gad rgyangs

Text in *Longch'en Nyingt'ig* 3:53–67.

———. *Longch'en Nyingt'ig* [*terma* cycle] klong chen snying thig

Text: *kloṅ chen sñiṅ thig:* Treasured Rñiṅ-ma-pa precepts and rituals received in a vision of Kloṅ-chen-pa Dri-med-'od-zer by 'Jigs-med-gliṅ-pa Rang-byuṅ-rdo-rje Mkhyen-brtse'i-'od-zer. Reproduced from prints from the A-'dzom Chos-sgar blocks by Ngawang Sopa. 3 vols., New Delhi, 1973.

———. *Longch'en Nyingt'ig Ngöndro:* (rDzogs pa chen po) klong chen snying thig (gi) sngon 'gro('i ngag 'don khrigs su bsdebs pa rnam mkhyen lam bzang zhes bya ba).

Text in Thondup 1982.

———. *Nedsum Shanched:* (rdzogs pa chen po klong chen snying gi thig le las: rdzogs pa chen po'i) gnad gsum shan 'byed.

Text in *Longch'en Nyingt'ig* 3:116–120.

———. *Senggé Ngaro:* (snying tig sgom pa'i bya bral gyi| gol shor tshar gcod) seng ge'i nga ro.

Text in *Longch'en Nyingt'ig* 3:547–565.

———. *Yeshé Long-gi Gyüd:* (klong chen snying gi thig le las: rdzogs pa chen po kun tu bzang po) ye shes klong gi rgyud.

Text in *Longch'en Nyingt'ig* 3:73–95.

K'amtrül Rimpoch'e, 3d [Khams sprul Rin po che Ngag dbang kun dga' bstan dzin] *Drugpé Ngöndro:* 'brug pa'i sngon 'gro

Text: *phyag chen sngon 'gro'i bsgom rim gsal 'debs ngag 'don rgyas spel dngos gzhi'i rtsa tho dang bcas pa zab don rgya mtsho'i lam tshang.* Ms. copy.

Karma Lingpa [karma gling pa] *Bardo T'ödröl* bar do thos grol

Text: *Zab chos zhi khro dgongs pa rang grol las: bar do'i thos grol = The Tibetan Book of the Dead* by the Great Acharya Shri Sing-ha. E. Kalsang, Varanasi, 1969.

———. *Karling Shitr'o* [*terma* cycle] kar gling zhi khro

———. *Rigpa Ngötröd:* [Zab chos zhi khro dgongs pa rang grol las:] rig pa ngo sprod [gcer mthong rang grol].

Text in Back 1987 and Reynolds 1989.

Karmapa, 3d (Rangjung Dorjé) [Karma pa Rang 'byung rdo rje] *Dzödnagma* mdzod nag ma.

Text: *rnal 'byor gyi dbang phyug mi la bzhad pa'i rdo rje'i gsung mgur mdzod nag ma. The Life and Songs of Realization of Mi la ras pa (bzhad pa'i rdo rje)* edited and arranged by the 3d Black Hat Karmapa Rang byung rdo rje. 2 vols., Dalhousie, Damchoe Sangpo, 1978.

Lama Tsenpo [bla ma btsan po] *Dzamling Gyeshed* ['dzam gling rgyas bshad]
Partial text in Wylie 1982.

Langri T'angpa [glang ri thang pa] *Lojong Ts'iggyed* blo sbyong tshig brgyad
Text in *Sheldön Chetü* [A8]:519–522.

Lhatsün Rinch'en Namgyel [lha btsun rin chen rnam rgyal] *Naropé Namt'ar:* (paṇ chen) nā ro pa'i rnam thar (ngo mtshar rmad 'byung)
Text in *The Songs of Esoteric Experience (mgur) of Raṅ-rig-ras-chen*, edited by his disciple Nas-luṅ-pa Ṅag-dbaṅ-rdo rje together with two other Dkar-brgyud-pa devotional works from the Monastery of Gsaṅ-sṅags chos- gliṅ. New Delhi, 1976, 333–467.

———. *Sung-gyün T'orbupaga:* (rJe btsun mi la ras pa'i rdo rje mgur drug sogs) gsung rgyun thor bu pa 'ga'.
Text: Microfilm of blockprint in India Office Library, London (MS Lhasa I87 = IOL Neg. 2047).

Loden Nyingpo [blo ldan snying po] *Sijid* ('dus pa rin po che dri ma med pa) gzi brjid (rab tu 'bar ba'i mdo)
Excerpts in Snellgrove 1967a.

Longchen Rabjampa [klong chen rab 'byams pa] *Ngelso Korsum* ngal gso skor gsum
Text in *Ṅal gso skor gsum, Raṅ grol skor gsum, and Sṅags kyi spyi don. Structured Presentations of Nyingmapa Dzogchen Theory and Practice by Kloṅ-chen-pa Dri-med-'od-zer.* Reproduced from a set of prints from the A-'dzom 'Brug-pa Chos-sgar blocks by Dodrup Chen Rimpoche. Gangtok, 1973. (PL 480 I(Sik)-Tib 73–903533 = IASWR microfiche LMpj 011,822.)

Mingyur Dorjé [mi 'gyur rdo rje] *Namch'ö* (*terma* cycle) gnam chos
Collection des tresors revelés par Gnam-čhos Mi-'gyur-rdo-je. Publié conjointement par S.S. Dilgo Khyentsey Rinpoche, Monastère de Paro Kyichu, Bhoutan et Ven. Pema Norbu Rinpoche, "Nyingmapa Monastery," Bylakuppe, Mysore, Inde sous les auspices de l'École Française d'Éxtreme-Orient, Paris, 1983.

Mip'am Rimpoch'e ['ju mi pham rin po che] *Kyebu Ch'enpo Lamé Neljor* (rig pa 'gyur med ye shes kyi) skyes bu chen po'i bla ma'i rnal 'byor (byin rlabs myur 'jug ces bya ba)
Text in Mip'am, *Sungbum* 5:651–654.

———. *Lingdro* gling 'bro

———. *Sungbum:* gsung 'bum
Text: *Collected Writings of 'Jam-mgon 'Ju Mi-pham-rgya-mtsho* Comprising a collection of the works of the scholar-saint selected for their rarity

from recently unpublished xylographic prints and manuscripts from the libraries of Dudjom Rinpoche, Luding Khen Rinpoche, and other religious teachers and laymen by Sonam Topgay Kazi. Gangtok, 1976.
———. *Trashi Gyedpa:* ('phags pa) bkra shis brgyad pa('i tshigs su bcad pa) Text: *'phags pa bkra sis brgyad pa'i tshigs su bcad pa by Mi-pham-rgya-mtsho* Printed from the blocks preserved at the Hemis Rgod-tshaṅ Hermitage, Chemre 1968. Blockprint.

Nyangral Nyima Özer [Nyang ral Nyi ma 'od zer] (and others) *Mani Kabum* ma ṇi bka' 'bum

Orgyen Lingpa [o rgyan gling pa] *Kat'ang Denga* bka' thang sde lnga
———. *Lhadré Kat'ang* lha 'dre'i bka' thang
———. *Pema Kat'ang (Sheldragma):* padma bka' thang (Shel brag ma)

Pawongk'a Rimpoch'é *T'ündrug Lamé Neljor:* Thun drug bla ma'i rnal 'byor by *Pha bong kha Rin po che.*
Text in *Sheldön Chetü* [A8]:13–36.

Peltrul Rimpoch'é [rdza dpal sprul rin po che] *Kunsang Lamé Shellung* (rdzogs pa chen po klong chen snying tig gi sngon 'gro'i khrid yig) kun bzang bla ma'i zhal lung (zhes bya ba)
Text: modern blockprint.

Pema Karpo ['brug chen padma dkar po] *Ch'ödrug Düpé Sindri* chos drug bsdus pa'i zin bris
Text in Pema Karpo *Sungbum* 22 (za):265–301.

———. *Sep'ö Shungdrel:* (jo bo na ro pa'i khyad chos) bsre 'pho'i gzhung 'grel (rdo rje 'chang gi dgongs pa gsal bar byed pa)
Text in Pema Karpo *Sungbum* 23 ('a):320–640.
———. *Sep'ö Tr'id* (jo bo na ro pa'i khyad chos) bsre 'pho'i khrid (rdo rje'i theg par bgrod pa'i shing rta chen po)
Text in Pema Karpo *Sungbum* 22 (za):7–263.
———. *Sungbum:* gsung 'bum
Text: *Collected Works (gsun-'bum) of Kun-mkhyen Padma-dkar-po* Reproduced photographically from prints from the 1920–1928 Gnam 'Brug Se-ba Byan-chub-glin blocks. Kargyud Sungrab Nyamso Khang, Darjeeling, 1974.

Putön [bu ston rin chen grub] *Ch'öjung* (bde bar gshegs pa'i bstan pa'i gsal byed) chos (kyi) 'byung (gnas gsung rab rin po che'i mdzod ces bya ba)
Text: *Bu-ston's History of Buddhism.* Tibetan text edited by Prof. Dr. Lokesh Chandra. International Academy of Indian Culture, New Delhi, 1971.

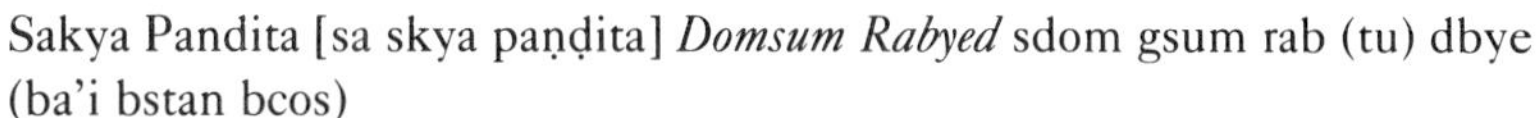

Sakya Pandita [sa skya paṇḍita] *Domsum Rabyed* sdom gsum rab (tu) dbye (ba'i bstan bcos)

Text in *Sakya Kabum* [A9] 5:297–320.

———. *Legshed Rimpoch'é Ter* legs (par) bshad (pa'i) rin po che'i gter

———. *T'ubpé Gongpa Rabsel* thub pa'i dgongs pa rab (tu) gsal (ba)

Shardza Rimpoch'e [shar rdza rin po che grub dbag bkra shis rgual mtshan] *Legshed Rimpoch'é Dzöd* legs bshad rin po che'i mdzod (dpyod ldan dga' ba'i char)

Excerpts in Karmay 1972.

Sönam Tsemo [bsod nams rtse mo] *Gyüdé Chi Namshag* rgyud sde spyi rnam bzhag

T'angtong Gyelpo [thang stong rgyal po] *Drodön K'aky'abma* 'gro don mkha' khyab ma

Text: Ms. copy.

Tāranātha [tāranātha] *Nigu Ch'ödrug Shungtr'id* (zab lam) ni gu chos drug (gi) gzhung khrid (ma mo'i lhan thabs)

Text in *Damngag Dzöd* [A1] 8:434–466.

———. *Nigu Ch'ödrug Tr'idyig* (zab lam) ni gu chos drug (gi) khrid yig (zab don thang mar brdal ba zhes bya ba bklags chog ma)

Text in *Damngag Dzöd* [A1] 8:333–433.

Trijang Rimpoch'e [yongs 'dzin khri byang rin po che] *Gyalch'en Töddrel* rgyal chen bstod 'grel

Text: *dge ldan bstan pa bsrung ba'i lha mchog sprul pa'i chos rgyal chen po rdo rje shugs ldan rtsal gyi gsang gsum rmad du byung ba'i rtogs pa brjod pa'i gtam du bya ba dam can rgya mtsho dgyes pa'i rol mo zhes bya ba.* In Trich'ang Rimpoch'e, *gSung 'bum*, vol. *ca.* Gurudeva Lama, New Delhi, 1975.

———. *Lamrim Sindri Namdröl Lagchang* lam rim zin bris rnam grol lag bcangs

Tsangnyön Heruka [gtsang smyon he ru ka] *Marpé Namt'ar* mar pa'i rnam thar

Text: *sgra bsgyur mar pa lo tsha'i rnam par thar pa mthong ba don yod. The Biography of Marpa the Translator by the Yogi Khrag-'Thung rGyal-po.* E. Kalsang, Varanasi, 1970.

———. *Milé Gurbum* mi la'i mgur 'bum

Text: *rje btsun mi la ras pa'i rnam thar rgyas par phye pa mgur 'bum. Complete Biography of Milarepa by the Yogi Rupa'i Gyan-chen.* Lobsang Tsultim, Sarnath, Varanasi, 1971.

———. *Milé Namt'ar* mi la'i rnam thar

Text: *rnal 'byor gyi dbang phyug chen po rje btsun mi la ras pa'i rnam thar thar pa dang thams cad mkhyen pa'i lam ston zhes bya ba. The Biography of Milarepa by the Yogi Rupa'i Gyan- chen.* Kalsang Lhundup, Varanasi, 1976.

Tsongk'apa [rje tsong kha pa blo bzang grags pa] *Lamrim Ch'enmo* lam rim chen mo

———. *Lamrim Düdön* lam rim bsdus don [= byang chub lam gyi rim pa'i nyams len gyi rnam gzhag mdor bsdus]

———. *Lamtso Namsum* lam (gyi) gtso (bo) rnam gsum
Text in *Sheldön Chetü* [A8]:513–518.

———. *Ngagrim Ch'enmo* sngags rim chen mo

———. *Sablam Narö Ch'ödrug* zab lam na ro'i chos drug (gi sgo nas 'khrid pa'i rim pa yid ches gsum ldan)
Text in *Tokyo Tripitaka* 160:208 to 161:13.

Yeshé Gyents'en [ye shes rgyal mtshan] *Sergyi Yangshün* gser gyi yang zhun
Text: mdo sngags gnyis ka'i lam gyi snying po'i gnad bstan pa gser gyi yang zhun zhes bya ba by *Ye shes rgyal mtshan* (1713–1793), tutor to the 8th Dalai Lama. In Guenther 1966.

Yut'og Lhundrub Trashi [g.Yu thog lhun grub bkra shis] *Yut'og Namt'ar* (rje btsun) g.yu thog (yon tan mgon po rnying ma'i) rnam (par) thar (pa bka' rgya ma gzi brjid rin po che'i gter mdzod ces bya ba).
Text in *G.yu thog gsar rnying gi rnam thar.* Mi rigs dpe skrun khang, 1982.

Authors unknown

Ladag Gyelrab la dwags rgyal rabs
Text in Francke 1926.

T'ugje Ch'enpo Drowa Kundröl thugs rje chen po 'gro ba kun sgrol [*terma* cycle]

WESTERN LANGUAGES

Abbreviations

AOH	Acta Orientalia (Budapest)
BEFEO	Bulletin d'École Française d'Extrême-Orient
CAJ	Central Asiatic Journal (Wiesbaden)
CNRS	Centre National de la Recherche Scientifique

HJAS	Harvard Journal of Asiatic Studies
HR	History of Religions
IAIC	International Academy of Indian Culture
IATS	International Association for Tibetan Studies
IsMEO	Istituto Italiano per il Medio ed Estremo Oriente
J.	Journal
JA	Journal Asiatique
JAOS	Journal of the American Oriental Society
JAS	Journal of Asian Studies
JIABS	Journal of International Association of Buddhist Studies
JRAS	Journal of the Royal Asiatic Society
JRCAS	Journal of the Royal Central Asiatic Society (London)
JTS	Journal of the Tibet Society (Bloomington)
LTWA	Library of Tibetan Works and Archives
RCAJ	Royal Central Asiatic Journal (formerly JRCAS)
SER	Serie Orientale Roma
SP	Śata-Piṭaka Series
SUNY	State University of New York
TJ	Tibet Journal
TR	Tibetan Review
ZAS	Zentralasiatische Studien

Four-syllable Tibetan names (e.g., Yonten Gyatso, Tshe-brtan Zhabs-drung) are alphabetized according to the second pair of syllables (Gyatso, Zhabs-drung). Where there is a title (other than Geshé, Lama, Rimpoch'e) the name is alphabetized under the title. Recent works in the Tibetan language are included in this bibliography, except for those in *dpe cha* form, which are included in the Tibetan bibliography.

Ahmad, Zahiruddin. 1970. *Sino-Tibetan Relations in the Seventeenth Century.* Roma, IsMEO. (SER 40).

Alley, Rewi. 1940. The Sungpan Valley Awakens. *Asia* (January 1940): 17–21.

Allione, Tsultrim. 1984. *Women of Wisdom.* London, Routledge and Kegan Paul.

Ames, M. M. 1964. Magical Animism and Buddhism. A Structural Analysis of the Sinhalese Religious System. In *Religion in South Asia,* edited by E. B. Harper, pp. 21–52. Seattle, University of Washington Press.

———. 1966. Ritual Prestations and the Structure of the Sinhalese Pantheon. In *Anthropological Studies in Theravada Buddhism,* edited by Manning Nash, pp. 27–50. Yale University, Southeast Asia Studies.

Amipa, Sherap Gyaltsen. 1976. *A Waterdrop from the Glorious Sea. A Concise Account of the Advent of Buddhism in General and the Teachings of the Sakyapa Tradition in Particular.* Rikon, Tibetan Institute.

Andersson, Jan. 1981. Tibetans: A Dwindling Population. *TR* 16(10) (Oct. 1981):6–13.

Anon. 1989. *Answers from the Lotus Born to the Questions of Nyang Wen Tingzin Zangpo.* Great Perfection, New Zealand.

Archer, W. G. 1966. Preface. In *The Koka Shastra. Being the Ratirahasya of Kokkoka,* translated by Alex Comfort, pp. 7–38. London, Tandem Books.

Ardussi, John, and Lawrence Epstein. 1978. The Saintly Madman in Tibet. In *Himalayan Anthropology: The Indo-Tibetan Interface,* edited by James F. Fisher, pp. 327–338. The Hague, Mouton.

Aris, Michael. 1975. Report on the University of California Expedition to Kutang and Nubri in N. Nepal. *Contributions to Nepalese Studies* 2(2) (June 1975):45–87.

———. 1977. Jamyang Khyentse's Brief Discourse on the Essence of All the Ways. *Kailash* 5(3):205–228.

———. 1979. *Bhutan. The Early History of a Himalayan Kingdom.* Warminster, Aris and Phillips.

———. 1980. Notes on the History of the Mon-yul Corridor. In *Tibetan Studies in Honour of Hugh Richardson. Proceedings of the International Seminar on Tibetan Studies, Oxford* 1979, edited by Michael Aris and Aung San Suu Kyi, pp. 9–20. Warminster, Aris and Phillips [= Proceedings of 2d Seminar of IATS.]

———. 1987. The Boneless Tongue: Alternative Voices from Bhutan. *Past and Present* 115 (May 1987):131–164.

———. 1988. *Hidden Treasures and Secret Lives. A Study of Pemalingpa (*1450–1521*) and the Sixth Dalai Lama (*1683–1706*).* Shimla, Indian Institute of Advanced Study and Delhi, Motilal Banarsidass.

Aris, Michael, and Aung San Suu Kyi (eds.). 1980. *Tibetan Studies in Honour of Hugh Richardson. Proceedings of the International Seminar on Tibetan Studies, Oxford* 1979. Warminster, Aris and Phillips. [= *Proceedings* of 2nd Seminar of IATS.]

Aśvaghoṣa. 1975. *Fifty Verses of Guru-Devotion.* Dharamsala, HP, LTWA.

Aufschnaiter, Peter. 1976. Lands and Places of Milarepa. *East and West* n.s. 26:175–189.

Aziz, Barbara N. 1974. Some Notions about Descent and Residence in Tibetan Society. In *Contributions to the Anthropology of Nepal,* edited by Christoph von Fürer- Haimendorf, pp. 23–39. Warminster, Aris and Phillips.

———. 1976a. Reincarnation Reconsidered: Or the Reincarnate Lama as Shaman. In *Spirit Possession in the Nepal Himalayas,* edited by John T.

Hitchcock and Rex L. Jones, pp. 343–360. Warminster, Aris and Phillips.

———. 1976b. Ani Chodon: Portrait of a Buddhist Nun. *Loka* (Journal of the Naropa Institute):43–46.

———. 1977. Views from the Monastery Kitchen. *Anima* 4(1):66–77. [Also in *Kailash* 4(2).]

———. 1978. *Tibetan Frontier Families*. New Delhi, Vikas.

———. 1980. The Work of Pha-dam-pa Sangs-rgyas as Revealed in Ding-ri Folklore. In *Tibetan Studies in Honour of Hugh Richardson. Proceedings of the International Seminar on Tibetan Studies, Oxford* 1979, edited by Michael Aris and Aung San Suu Kyi, pp. 21–29. Warminster, Aris and Phillips. [= *Proceedings* of 2nd Seminar of IATS.]

———. 1981. Jural Friends and Buddhist Teachers. In *Culture and Morality: Essays in Honour of Christoph von Fürer-Haimendorf*, edited by Adrian C. Mayer, pp. 1–22. Delhi, Oxford University Press.

———1985. On Translating Oral Traditions: Ceremonial Wedding Poetry from Dingri. In *Soundings in Tibetan Civilization*, edited by Barbara Aziz and Matthew Kapstein, pp. 115–132. New Delhi, Manohar. [*Proceedings* of 3d Seminar of IATS.]

———. 1987. Moving Towards a Sociology of Tibet. *TJ* 12(4):72–86.

———. 1988. Women in Tibetan Society and Tibetology. In *Tibetan Studies. Proceedings of the 4th Seminar of the International Association for Tibetan studies. Schloss Hohenkammer, Munich* 1985, edited by Helga Uebach and Jampa L. Panglung, pp. 25–34. Kommission für Zentralasiatische Studien, Bayerische Akademie der Wissenschaften.

Back, Dieter Michael. 1987. *Rig pa ṅo sprod gcer mthoṅ raṅ grol. Die Erkenntnislehre des Bar do thos-grol*. Wiesbaden, Otto Harrassowitz. (Freiburger Beiträge zur Indologie 18.)

Bacot, Jacques. 1925. *Le Poète Tibétain Milarepa*. Paris.

———. 1937. *La Vie de Marpa le 'Traducteur.'* Paris, Librairie Orientalists Paul Geuthner.

Bareau, André. 1955. *Les Sectes Bouddhiques du Petit Véhicule*. Saigon, École Française d'Extrême-Orient.

Batchelor, Stephen. 1987. *The Tibet Guide*. London, Wisdom.

Bateson, Gregory. 1973. *Steps to an Ecology of Mind*. Frogmore, Paladin.

Beckwith, Christopher I. 1977. Tibet and the Early Medieval *Florissance* in Eurasia. *CAJ* 21(2):89–104.

———. 1987a. *The Tibetan Empire in Central Asia*. Princeton University Press.

———. (ed). 1987b. *Silver on Lapis: Tibetan Literary Culture and History*. Bloomington, Indiana University Press.

Bell, Sir Charles. 1924. *Tibet, Past and Present*. Oxford.

———. 1928. *The People of Tibet.* Oxford.

———. 1946. *Portrait of a Dalai Lama.* London, Collins.

Benson, Herbert, et al. 1982. Body Temperature Changes during the Practice of gTum-mo Yoga. *Nature* 295 (21 January 1982):234–236.

Benedict, Ruth. 1935. *Patterns of Culture.* London, Routledge and Kegan Paul.

Berglie, Per-Arne. 1976. Preliminary Remarks on some Tibetan 'Spirit-mediums' in Nepal. *Kailash* 4(1):87–108.

———. 1980. Mount Targo and Lake Dangra: A Contribution to the Religious Geography of Tibet. In *Tibetan Studies in Honour of Hugh Richardson. Proceedings of the International Seminar on Tibetan Studies, Oxford* 1979, edited by Michael Aris and Aung San Suu Kyi, pp. 39ff. Warminster, Aris and Phillips. [= *Proceedings* of 2nd Seminar of IATS.]

———. 1982. Spirit-Possession in Theory and Practice—Séances with Tibetan Spirit-mediums in Nepal. In *Religious Ecstasy,* edited by Nils G. Holm, pp. 151–166. Stockholm, Almqvist and Wiksell. (Scripta Instituti Donneriani Aboensis 11.)

———. 1983. *Gudarna stiger ned. Rituell besatthet hos sherpas och tibetaner.* Stockholm University, Religionshistoriska institutionen. (Stockholm Dissertations in Comparative Religion 2.)

———. 1989. Tibetan Spirit-mediumship: Change and Continuity. Some Observations from a Revisit to Nepal. Paper given at the 5th Seminar of the IATS, Narita, August 27 to September 2, 1989.

Bernbaum, Edwin. 1980. *The Way to Shambhala.* Garden City, New York, Anchor Press.

Berzin, Alexander. 1972. *Lam.rim.man.ngag. A Standard Intermediate Level Textbook of the Graded Course to Enlightenment.* Typescript. [Pp. 1–436 only = Ph.D. dissertation, Harvard University 1972.]

———1978. *The Mahāmudrā Eliminating the Darkness of Ignorance. By the Ninth Karmapa Wang-ch'ug Dor-je.* Dharamsala, HP, LTWA.

———. 1979. *The Four-Themed Precious Garland. An Introduction to Dzog-ch'en, by Long-ch'en Rab-jam-pa.* Dharamsala, HP, LTWA.

Beyer, Stephan. 1973. *The Cult of Tara. Magic and Ritual in Tibet.* Berkeley, University of California Press.

———. 1974. *The Buddhist Experience. Sources and Interpretations.* Encino, California, Dickenson.

Bharati, Agehananda. 1965. *The Tantric Tradition.* London, Rider.

———. 1976. Making Sense Out of Tantrism and Tantrics. *Loka* 2:52–55.

———. 1980. *The Ochre Robe.* 2d edition. Santa Barbara, Ross-Erikson.

Bhattacharya, Deben. 1969. *The Mirror of the Sky. Songs of the Bauls from Bengal.* London, Allen and Unwin.

Bischoff, Friedrich A. 1979. Le'u Titles and Epitome of 'Le Dict de Padma.' *ZAS* 13:409–430.

Blofeld, John. 1972. *The Wheel of Life. The Autobiography of a Western Buddhist.* London, Rider.

Blondeau, Anne-Marie (= Large-Blondeau.) 1960. Les Pèlerinages Tibétains. *Les Pélerinages*, pp. 199–245. (Sources Orientales 3.) Paris, Editions du Seuil.

———. 1971. Le *Lha 'dre bka'-thaṅ.* In *Études Tibétaines Dédiées à la Mémoire de Marcelle Lalou*, edited by Ariane D. Spanien, pp. 29–126. Paris, Adrien Masonneuve. (Librairie d'Amérique et d'Orient.)

———. 1977–1978. Religions Tibétaines. *Annuaire. (Résumé des conférences et travaux). École Pratique des Hautes Études. Ve section. Sciences religieuses* 86:77–88.

———. 1978–1979. Religions Tibétaines. *Annuaire. (Résumé des conférences et travaux). École Pratique des Hautes Études. Ve section. Sciences religieuses* 87:99–106.

———. 1979–1980. Religions Tibétaines. *Annuaire. (Résumé des conférences et travaux). École Pratique des Hautes Études. Ve section. Sciences religieuses* 88:121–124.

———. 1980. Analysis of the Biographies of Padmasambhava according to Tibetan Tradition: Classification of Sources. In *Tibetan Studies in Honour of Hugh Richardson. Proceedings of the International Seminar on Tibetan Studies, Oxford* 1979, edited by Michael Aris and Aung San Suu Kyi, pp. 45–52. Warminster, Aris and Phillips. [= *Proceedings* of 2nd Seminar of IATS.]

———. 1980–1981. Religions Tibétaines. *Annuaire. (Résumé des conférences et travaux). École Pratique des Hautes Études. Ve section. Sciences religieuses* 89:163–169.

———. 1982–1983. Religions Tibétaines. *Annuaire. (Résumé des conférences et travaux). École Pratique des Hautes Études. Ve section. Sciences religieuses* 91:123–131.

———. 1983–1984. Religions Tibétaines. *Annuaire. (Résumé des conférences et travaux). École Pratique des Hautes Études. Ve section. Sciences religieuses* 92:133–138.

———. 1984–1985. Religions Tibétaines. *Annuaire. (Résumé des conférences et travaux). École Pratique des Hautes Études. Ve section. Sciences religieuses* 93:107–114.

———. 1985–1986. Religions Tibétaines. *Annuaire. (Résumé des conférences et travaux). École Pratique des Hautes Études. Ve section. Sciences religieuses* 94:145–154.

———. 1985. 'mKhyen-brce'i dbaṅ-po: La Biographie de Padmasambhava Selon la Tradition du bsGrags-pa Bon, et ses Sources. In *Orientalia Iose-*

phi Tucci Memoriae Dicata, vol. 1, pp. 111–158, edited by G. Gnoli and L. Lanciotti. Roma, IsMEO. (SER 56[1–3].)

———. 1987–1988. Religions Tibétaines. *Annuaire. (Résumé des conférences et travaux). École Pratique des Hautes Études. V^e section. Sciences religieuses* 96:74–81.

Bogoslovskij, V. A. 1972. *Essai sur l'Histoire du Peuple Tibétain ou la Naissance d'une Société de Classes*. Paris, Librairie C. Klincksieck.

Bosson, James E. 1969. *A Treasury of Aphoristic Jewels. The Subhāṣitaratnanidhi of Sa skya Paṇḍita*. Bloomington, Indiana University and The Hague, Mouton. (Indiana University Uralic and Altaic Series 92.)

Bouillier, Véronique, and Gérard Toffin. 1989. *Prêtrise, Pouvoirs et Autorité en Himalaya*. Éditions de l'École des Hautes Études en Sciences Sociales. (Collection Puruṣārtha 12.)

Brauen, Martin. 1974. *Heinrich Harrers Impressionen aus Tibet*. Völkerkundemuseum der Universität Zürich.

———. 1980a. The *pha-spun* of Ladakh. In *Tibetan Studies in Honour of Hugh Richardson. Proceedings of the International Seminar on Tibetan Studies, Oxford* 1979, edited by Michael Aris and Aung San Suu Kyi, pp. 53–58. Warminster, Aris and Phillips. [= *Proceedings* of 2nd Seminar of IATS.]

———. 1980b. *Feste in Ladakh*. Graz, Akademische Druck- u. Verlaganstalt.

———. 1982. Death Customs in Ladakh. *Kailash* 9(4):319–332.

———. (= Brauen-Dolma). 1985. Millenarianism in Tibetan Religion. In *Soundings in Tibetan Civilization*, edited by Barbara N. Aziz and Matthew Kapstein, pp. 245–257. New Delhi, Manohar. [Proceedings of 3d Seminar of IATS.]

Brauen, Martin, and Per Kvaerne (eds). 1978a. *Tibetan Studies Presented at the Seminar of Young Tibetologists, Zurich, June 26-July 1, 1977*. Völkerkundemuseum der Universität Zürich. [= *Proceedings* of 1st Seminar of IATS.]

———. 1978b. A Tibetan Death Ceremony. *Temenos* 14:9–24.

Bray, John. 1988. *A Bibliography of Ladakh*, by John Bray with Nawang Tsering Shakspo. Warminster, Aris and Phillips.

Broido, Michael M. 1980. The Term *dngos-po'i gnas-lugs* as Used in Padma dKar-po's *gZhung-'grel*. In *Tibetan Studies in Honour of Hugh Richardson. Proceedings of the International Seminar on Tibetan Studies, Oxford* 1979, edited by Michael Aris and Aung San Suu Kyi, pp. 59–66. Warminster, Aris and Phillips. [= *Proceedings* of 2nd Seminar of IATS.]

———. 1982. Does Tibetan Hermeneutics Throw Any Light on Sandhābhāṣa? *JTS* 2:5–40.

———. 1984. Padma Dkar-po on Tantra as Ground, Path and Goal. *JTS* 4:5–46.

———. 1985a. Padma Dkar-po on Integration as Ground, Path and Goal. *JTS* 5:5–54.

———. 1985b. Padma dKar-po on the Two *Satyas*. *JIABS* 8(2):7–59.

Bruyat, Christian. 1987. *Patrul Rimpoche: Le Chemin de la Grande Perfection*. Éditions Padmakara.

Burman, Bina Roy. 1976. Thirteenth Dalai Lama's Plan for Modernization of Tibet. *TR* 11–12 (Dec):12–14.

Cabezón, José. 1982. Review of Imaeda 1981. *JIABS* 5(2):118n.121.

Calkowski, Marcia S. 1986. Power, Charisma and Ritual Curing in a Tibetan Community in India. Ph.D. dissertation, Anthropology, University of British Columbia.

———. 1990. Contesting Hierarchy: On the Praxis of Competition in Tibetan Society. Paper for the International Seminar on Anthropology of Tibet and the Himalayas, September 21–28, 1990, Völkerkundemuseum der Universität Zürich.

Cantwell, Catherine M. 1985. A Tibetan Buddhist Ritual in a Refugee Monastery. *TJ* 10:14–29.

Canzio, Ricardo O. 1981. Ceremonias Tibetanas: El Culto de los Guardianes de la Doctrina. *Estudios de Asia y Africa* 16(2):273–286.

Carrasco, Pedro. 1959. *Land and Polity in Tibet*. Seattle, American Ethnological Society.

Cassinelli, C. W., and Robert B. Ekvall. 1969. *A Tibetan Principality. The Political System of Sa sKya*. Ithaca, Cornell University Press.

Cech, Krystyna. 1984. *The History, Teaching and Practice of Dialectics according to the Bon Tradition*. P. O. Ochghat, via Solan, H. P., Yungdrung Bon Monastic Center.

———. 1987. The Social and Religious Identity of the Tibetan Bonpos with Special Reference to a North-west Himalayan Refugee Settlement. Ph.D. dissertation, Oxford 1987.

Chakrabarty, P. B. 1980. Light of Buddhism in Sikkim. *TR* 15(10) (Oct): 17–19.

Chang, Garma Chen-chi. 1961. Life in a Tibetan Vajrayana Monastery. In *Buddhism*, edited by Richard Gard, pp. 196–202. London, Prentice-Hall.

———. 1977. *The Hundred Thousand Songs of Milarepa*. Boulder and London, Shambhala. 2 vols.

Chang, Kun, and Betty Shefts. 1964. *A Manual of Spoken Tibetan (Lhasa Dialect)*. With the help of Nawang Nornang and Lhadon Karsip. Seattle, University of Washington Press.

Chapman, F. Spencer. 1938. *Lhasa. The Holy City*. London, Chatto and Windus.

Chattopadhyaya, Alaka. 1967. *Atisa and Tibet.* Calcutta, Indian Studies Past and Present.

Chen Han-seng. 1949. *Frontier Land Systems in Southernmost China.* New York, Institute of Pacific Relations.

Chime Radha Rinpoche, Lama. 1981. Tibet. In *Oracles and Divination,* edited by M. Loewe and C. Blacker, pp. 3–37. Boulder, Shambhala.

Chogay Trichen Rinpoche [Thubten Legshay Gyatsho]. 1979. *Gateway to the Temple. Manual of Tibetan Monastic Customs, Art, Building and Celebrations.* Translated by David Paul Jackson. Kathmandu, Ratna Pustak Bhandar.

———. 1983. *The History of the Sakya Tradition. A Feast for the Minds of the Fortunate.* Bristol, Ganesha Press.

Chokhorling, Orgyan Kunsang. 1978. Trente Conseils données du Cocur par Gyalwa Longchenpa. *Kailash* 6(2):115–126.

Chophel, Norbu. 1983. *Folk Culture of Tibet.* Dharamsala, HP, LTWA.

Chopra, Pran. 1964. *On an Indian Border.* Bombay, Asia Publishing House.

Clarke, Graham. 1977. The Merchants of Mugu. *RCAJ* 8:299–305.

———. 1980a. Lama and Tamang in Yolmo. In *Tibetan Studies in Honour of Hugh Richardson. Proceedings of the International Seminar on Tibetan Studies, Oxford* 1979, edited by Michael Aris and Aung San Suu Kyi, pp. 79–86. Warminster, Aris and Phillips. [= *Proceedings* of 2nd Seminar of IATS.]

———. 1980b. A Helambu History. *J. Nepal Research Centre (Humanities)* 4:1–38.

Clastres, Pierre. 1977. *Society against the State.* New York, Urizen.

Comfort, Alex. 1979. *I and That. Notes on the Biology of Religion.* New York, Crown.

Conze, Edward. 1960. *The Prajñāpāramitā Literature.* The Hague, Mouton. (Indo-Iranian Monographs 6.)

———. 1962. *Buddhist Thought in India.* London, Allen and Unwin.

———. 1964. *Buddhist Texts Through the Ages.* New York, Harper and Row.

———. 1970. *Buddhist Wisdom Books.* London, Allen and Unwin.

———. 1975. *The Large Sutra on Perfect Wisdom with the Divisions of the Abhisamayālaṃkāra.* Berkeley, University of California Press.

———. 1980. *A Short History of Buddhism.* London, Allen and Unwin.

Corlin, Claes. 1975. *The Nation in Your Mind. Continuity and Change among Tibetan Refugees in Nepal.* Gøteborg, University of Gøteborg Press.

———. 1978. A Tibetan Enclave in Yunnan: Land, Kinship, and Inheritance in Gyethang. In *Tibetan Studies Presented at the Seminar of Young Tibetologists, Zurich, June 26–July 1, 1977,* edited by Martin Brauen and Per Kvaerne, pp. 75–89. Völkerkundemuseum der Universität Zürich. [= *Proceedings* of 1st Seminar of IATS.]

———. 1980. The Symbolism of the House in rGyal-thang. In *Tibetan Studies in Honour of Hugh Richardson. Proceedings of the International Seminar on Tibetan Studies, Oxford* 1979, edited by Michael Aris and Aung San Suu Kyi, pp. 87–92. Warminster, Aris and Phillips. [= *Proceedings* of 2nd Seminar of IATS.].

Cornu, Philippe. 1990. *L'astrologie Tibétaine.* Collection Présences.

Cowell, E. 1952. *The Jataka.* London, Luzac.

Cox, Thomas. 1987. Tibetan Nomads before the Chinese Invasion. *Himalayan Research Bulletin* 7(2–3):11–12.

Cozort, Daniel. 1986. *Highest Yoga Tantra. An Introduction to the Esoteric Buddhism of Tibet.* Ithaca, Snow Lion.

Dagyab, Loden Sherap. 1980. Die Verwaltung des Bezirkes Brag-g.yab (= Dagyab, Osttibet) durch die Brag-g.yab skyabs-mgon. In W. Franke and W. Heissig (ed), *Heilen und Schenken. Festschrift für Günther Klinge zum 70. Geburtstag,* edited by W. Franke and W. Heissig, pp. 12–21. Wiesbaden.

Dalai Lama, H. H. the 14th. 1980. Training the Mind. *Tibet News Review (UK)* 1(1):12–17.

Dalai Lama, H. H. the 14th, and Jeffrey Hopkins, 1985. *The Kalachakra Tantra. Rite of Initiation for the Stage of Generation.* London, Wisdom.

Dargyay, Eva K. 1978. *The Rise of Esoteric Buddhism in Tibet.* New York, Samuel Weiser.

———. 1981. A gTer-ston Belonging to the dGe-lugs-pa School. *TJ* 6(1): 24–30.

———. 1982. *Tibetan Village Communities. Structure and Change.* New Delhi, Vikas.

———. 1985a. The White and Red Rong-btsan of Matho Monastery. *JTS* 5:55–66.

———. 1985b. The Concept of a 'Creator God' in Tantric Buddhism. *JIABS* 8(1):31–47.

———. 1985c. A Rñiṅ-ma Text: The *Kun-byed rgyal po'i mdo.* In *Soundings in Tibetan Civilization,* edited by Barbara Aziz and Matthew Kapstein, pp. 283–293. New Delhi, Manohar. [*Proceedings* of 3d Seminar of IATS.]

———. 1986. Merit-making and Ritual Aspects in the Life of Sanskar. In *Karma and Rebirth. Post-Classical Developments,* edited by Ronald W. Neufeldt. Albany, SUNY Press.

———. 1988. Buddhism in Adaptation: Ancestor Gods and Their Tantric Counterparts in the Religious Life of Zanskar. *HR* 28:123–134.

Das, Sarat Chandra. 1904. *Journey to Lhasa and Central Tibet.* London, John Murray.

Dasgupta, Shashibhushan. 1976. *Obscure Religious Cults.* 3d edition. Calcutta, Firma K. L. Mukhopadhyay.

Datta, Subhash Chandra. 1970. A Short Geographical Account of Lahaul. *Geographical Review of India* 32(4):205–222.

David-Neel, Alexandra. 1971. *Magic and Mystery in Tibet.* London, Corgi.

Davidson, Ronald M. 1981. The Nor-pa Tradition. *Wind Horse (Proceedings of the North American Tibetological Society)* 1:79–98.

Day, Sophie. 1986. Abbot, Oracle and Witch in Ladakh. Paper for LSE seminar.

———. 1987. Ordering Spirits: The Initiation of Village Oracles in Ladakh. Typescript.

———. 1989. Embodying Spirits: Village Oracles and Possession Ritual in Ladakh, North India. Ph.D. dissertation, London School of Economics and Political Science.

Decleer, Hubert. 1978. The Working of Sādhana: Vajrabhairava. In *Tibetan Studies Presented at the Seminar of Young Tibetologists, Zurich, June* 26-*July* 1, 1977, edited by Martin Brauen and Per Kvaerne, pp. 113–124. Völkerkundemuseum der Universitát Zürich. [= *Proceedings* of 1st Seminar of IATS.]

Deleuze, Gilles. 1985. Nomad Thought. In *The New Nietzsche,* edited by David B. Allison, pp. 142–149. Cambridge, Massachussetts, MIT Press.

Deleuze, Gilles, and Félix Guattari. 1987. *A Thousand Plateaus.* Minneapolis, University of Minnesota Press.

Demiéville, P. 1952. *Le Concile de Lhasa.* Paris.

Dendaletche, Claude, and Patrick Kaplanian (eds.) 1985. *Ladakh, Himalaya Occidental: Ethnologie, Écologie.* Pau, Centre Pyrenéen de Biologie et Anthropologie des Montagnes. (*Acta Biologica Montana* 5.)

Desani, G. V. 1973. Mostly Concerning Kama and Her Immortal Lord. *Indian Horizons* 32:1–44.

Ven. Dezhung Rinpoche. 1977. The Biography of Kalu Rinpoche. In *Mahakala: The Awakened Energy of Compassion. A Tantric Invocation by Kalu Rinpoche.* San Francisco, Kagyu Droden Kunchab.

Dhargyey, Geshe Ngawang. 1978. *Tibetan Tradition of Mental Development.* 3d edition. Dharamsala, HP, LTWA.

———. 1985. *A Commentary on the Kalacakra Tantra.* Dharamsala, HP, LTWA.

Dhonden, Dr. Yeshi. 1986. *Health through Balance. An Introduction to Tibetan Medicine,* edited and translated by Jeffrey Hopkins. Ithaca, New York, Snow Lion.

Dhondup, K. 1978. Gedun Chophel: The Man Behind the Legend. *TR* 13(10) (Oct):10–18.

———. 1981. *Songs of the Sixth Dalai Lama*. Dharamsala, HP, LTWA.

———. 1984. *The Water-Horse and Other Years. A History of 17th and 18th Century Tibet*. Dharamsala, HP, LTWA.

———. 1986. *The Water-Bird and Other Years. A History of the 13th Dalai Lama and After.* New Delhi, Rangwang Publishers.

Diemberger, Hildegard. 1989. Lovanga [Lo 'bangs pa?] Lama and Lhaven [Lha bon]: Historical Background, Syncretism and Social Relevance of Religious Traditions among the Khumbo (East Nepal). Paper given at the 5th Seminar of the IATS, Narita, August 27 to September 2, 1989.

———. 1990. Beyul Khenbalung (sBas yul mKhan pa lung)—The Hidden Valley of the Artemisia. Paper for the International Seminar on Anthropology of Tibet and the Himalayas, Völkerkundemuseum der Universität Zürich, September 21–28, 1990.

Diemberger, Hildegard, and Christian Schicklgruber. 1984. Household Social Structure and Economy in a Tibetan Village. Paper given at the Bicentenary Csoma de Körös Symposium, Visegrád-Budapest, Hungary, September 13–19, 1984.

———. 1988. Preliminary Report on Use of Architecture among the Khumbo. In *Tibetan Studies. Proceedings of the 4th Seminar of the International Association for Tibetan studies. Schloss Hohenkammer, Munich* 1985, edited by Helga Uebach and Jampa L. Panglung, pp. 99–110. Kommission für Zentralasiatische Studien, Bayerische Akademie der Wissenschaften.

Dilgo Khyentse, H. H. 1988. *The Wish-Fulfilling Jewel: The Practice of Guru Yoga according to the Longchen Nyingthig Tradition*. Boston, Shambhala.

Diringer, David. 1965. *Writing*. London, Thames and Hudson.

Dollfus, Pascale. 1989. *Lieu de Neige et de Genévriers: Organisation Sociale et Religieuse des Communautés Bouddhistes du Ladakh*. Paris, Éditions du CNRS.

Don-grub, Rgya-mtsho. 1989. An Account of the History of Spo-smad Kagnam Sde-pa. *Tibet Studies* (Lhasa) 1:83–89.

Dorje, Rinjing. 1975. *Tales of Uncle Tompa. The Legendary Rascal of Tibet*. San Rafael, California, Dorje Ling.

Douglas, Kenneth, and Gwendolyn Bays (trans.). 1978. *The Life and Liberation of Padmasambhava*. Emeryville, California, Dharma.

Douglas, Nik, and Meryl White. 1976. *Karmapa: The Black Hat Lama of Tibet*. London, Luzac.

Dowman, Keith. 1973. *Calm and Clear.* Emeryville, California, Dharma.

———. 1981. *The Aspiration of Kuntuzangpo*. Kathmandu, Diamond Sow.

———. 1984. *Sky Dancer. The Secret Life and Songs of the Lady Yeshe Tsogyel.* London, Routledge and Kegan Paul.

———. 1985. *Masters of Mahamudra. Songs and Histories of the Eighty-Four Buddhist Siddhas.* Albany, State University of New York Press.

———. 1988. *The Power-Places of Central Tibet. The Pilgrim's Guide.* London, Routledge and Kegan Paul.

———. n.d. *Tilopa's Mahamudra Instruction to Naropa in Twenty-Eight Verses and Tilopa's Dohakosha Translated from the Tibetan.* Kathmandu, Diamond Sow.

Dowman, Keith, and Sonam Paljor. 1980. *The Divine Madman. The Sublime Life and Songs of Drukpa Kunley.* London, Rider.

Downs, James F., and Robert B. Ekvall. 1965. Animals and Social Types in the Exploitation of the Tibetan Plateau. In *Man, Culture, and Animals. The Role of Animals in Human Ecological Adjustment,* edited by Anthony Leeds and Andrew P. Vayda, pp. 169–184. Washington, D.C., American Association for the Advancement of Science.

Draper, John. in press. 'Lama Knows': Religion and Power in Sherpa Society. In *Tantra and Popular Religion in Tibet,* edited by Geoffrey Samuel. New Delhi, Aditya Prakashan.

Driessens, Georges. 1990. *Tsongkhapa Losang Drakpa. Le Grand Livre de la Progression vers l'Eveil. Tome premier, traduction française de G.D.* Jujurieux, Éditions Dharma.

Dumont, Louis. 1970. *Homo Hierarchicus. An Essay on the Caste System.* Chicago, University of Chicago Press.

Duncan, Marion H. 1952. *The Yangtze and the Yak.* Alexandria, Virginia.

———. 1964. *Customs and Superstitions of Tibetans.* London, Mitre Press.

Dutt, Sukumar. 1962. *Buddhist Monks and Monasteries of India.* London, Allen and Unwin.

Dzemay Rinpoche. 1982. A Short Biography of Trijang Rinpoche. *TJ* 7 (1–2):3–46.

Eastman, Kenneth W. 1981. The Eighteen Tantras of the Tattvasaṃgraha/Māyājāla. *Transactions of the International Congress of Orientalists in Japan.* Tōhō Gakkai (Tokyo) 26:95–96.

Eckel, Malcolm David. 1987. *Jñānagarbha's Commentary on the Distinction between the Two Truths. An Eighth Century Handbook of Madhyamaka Philosophy.* Albany, SUNY Press.

Edgerton, F. 1972. *Buddhist Hybrid Sanskrit Grammar and Dictionary, vol.* 2 *(Dictionary).* Reprint. Delhi, Motilal Banarsidass.

Eimer, Helmut. 1977. *Berichte über das Leben des Atiśa (Dīpaṃkaraśrījñāna). Eine Untersuchung der Quellen.* Wiesbaden, Otto Harrasowitz. (Asiatische Forschungen 51.)

———. 1979. *Rnam thar rgyas pa. Materialen zu einer Biographie des Atiśa (Dīpaṃkaraśrījñāna).* Wiesbaden, Otto Harrasowitz. (Asiatische Forschungen, 67.)

———. 1982. The Development of the Biographical Tradition Concerning Atiśa (Dīpaṃkaraśrījñāna). *JTS* 2:41–52.

Eimer, Helmut, and Pema Tsering. 1978. Äbte und Lehrer von Kaḥ thog. Eine erste Übersicht zur Geschichte eines Rñing-ma-pa-Klosters in Derge (Khams). *ZAS* 13:457–510.

———. 1982. A List of Abbots of Kaḥ-thog Monastery according to Handwritten Notes by the Late Katok Ontul. *JTS* 1:11–14.

Ekvall, Robert B. 1939. *Cultural Relations on the Kansu-Tibetan Border.* University of Chicago Press.

———. 1952. *Tibetan Skylines.* New York, Farrar, Straus and Young.

———. 1954a. *Tents Against the Sky.* London, Victor Gollancz.

———. 1954b. Mi sTong: The Tibetan Custom of Life Indemnity. *Sociologus* (n.s.) 4:136–145

———. 1956. Some Differences in Tibetan Land Tenure and Utilization. *Sinologica* 4:39–48.

———. 1960. Three Categories of Inmates within Tibetan Monasteries. *CAJ* 5:206–220.

———. 1963. Some Aspects of Divination in Tibetan Society. *Ethnology* 2(1):31–39.

———. 1964a. Peace and War among Tibetan Nomads. *American Anthropologist* 66:1119–1148.

———. 1964b. *Religious Observances in Tibet. Patterns and Function.* University of Chicago Press.

———. 1968. *Fields on the Hoof: Nexus of Tibetan Nomadic Pastoralism.* New York, Holt, Rinehart and Winston.

———. 1981. *The Lama Knows.* Novato, California, Chandler and Sharp.

Elder, George R. 1976. Problems of Language in Buddhist Tantra. *HR* 15(3):231–250.

Eliade, Mircea. 1958. *Yoga: Immortality and Freedom.* New York, Pantheon.

———. 1970. *Shamanism: Archaic Techniques of Ecstasy.* London, Routledge and Kegan Paul.

Ellingson, Ter. 1990. Tibetan Monastic Constitutions: The *bca'-yig.* In *Reflections on Tibetan Culture. Essays in Memory of Turrell V. Wylie,* edited by Lawrence Epstein and Richard F. Sherburne, pp. 205–230. Lewiston, Queenston, Lampeter, Edwin Mellen Press. (Studies in Asian Thought and Religion 12.)

Epstein, Lawrence. 1982. On the History and Psychology of the 'Das-log.' *TJ* 7(4):20–85.

———. 1990a. Ganja and Murdo: Prolegomenon to the Social Construction of Space at Two Eastern Tibetan Pilgrimage Sites. Paper for the International Seminar on Anthropology of Tibet and the Himalayas, Völkerkundemuseum der Universität Zürich, September 21–28, 1990.

———. 1990b. A Comparative View of Tibetan and Western Near-Death

Experiences. In *Reflections on Tibetan Culture. Essays in Memory of Turrell V. Wylie*, edited by Lawrence Epstein and Richard F. Sherburne, pp. 315–328. Lewiston, Queenston, Lampeter, Edwin Mellen Press. (Studies in Asian Thought and Religion 12.)

Epstein, Mark, and Sonam Topgay. 1982. Mind and Mental Disorders in Tibetan Medicine. *ReVision* 5(1):67–79.

Evans-Wentz, W. Y. 1960. *The Tibetan Book of the Dead.* 3d edition. London, Oxford University Press.

———. 1967. *Tibetan Yoga and Secret Doctrines.* 2d edition. London, Oxford University Press.

———. 1968. *The Tibetan Book of the Great Liberation.* London, Oxford University Press.

———. 1969. *Tibet's Great Yogi Milarepa: A Biography from the Tibetan according to the late Lama Kazi Dawa-Samdup's English Rendering.* 2d edition. London, Oxford University Press.

Faegre, Torvald. 1979. *Tents: Architecture of the Nomads.* London, John Murray.

Fairbank, J. K., and S. Y. Têng. 1941–1942. On the Ch'ing Tributary System. *HJAS* 6:135ff.

Fantin, Mario. 1976. *Mani-Rimdu, Nepal: The Buddhist Dance-Drama of Tengboche.* New Delhi, English Book Store.

Farquhar, David M. 1978. Emperor as Bodhisattva in the Governance of the Ch'ing Empire. *HJAS* 38:5–34.

Ferrari, Alfonsa. 1958. *Mk'yen Brtse's Guide to the Holy Places of Central Tibet.* Roma, IsMEO. (SER 16.)

Filchner, Wilhelm. 1933. *Kumbum Dschamba Ling. Das Kloster der hunderttausend Bilder Maitreyas. Ein Ausschnitt aus Leben und Lehre des heutigen Lamaismus.* Leipzig, in Kommission bei F.A. Brockhaus.

Francke, A. H. 1924. gZer myig: A Book of the Tibetan Bonpos. *Asia Major* 1. [Continued in *Asia Major* 3 (1926), 4 (1927), 7 (1930), n.s. 1 (1949).]

———. 1926. *Antiquities of Indian Tibet. Part 2: The Chronicles of Ladakh and Minor Chronicles.* Calcutta, Archaeological Survey of India.

Fremantle, Francesca. 1990. Chapter Seven of the Guhyasamaja Tantra. In *Indo-Tibetan Studies. Papers in Honour and Appreciation of Professor David L. Snellgrove's Contribution to Indo-Tibetan Studies,* edited by Tadeusz Skorupski, pp. 101–114. Tring, Institute of Buddhist Studies.

Fremantle, Francesca, and Chögyam Trungpa. 1975. *The Tibetan Book of the Dead.* Berkeley and London, Shambhala.

Frey, Kathleen. 1983. Studies in Bhutanese History Dealing with the Structural Organization of the Bhutanese Theocracy. *TR* 18(5) (May 1983):15–22.

Friedl, Wolfgang. 1983. *Gesellschaft, Wirtschaft und materielle Kultur in Zanskar (Ladak).* St. Augustin, VGH Wissenschaftsverlag.

Funke, Friedrich W. 1969. *Religiöses Leben der Sherpa.* Innsbruck and München, Universitätsverlag Wagner. (Khumbu Himal 9.)

———. 1978. *Die Sherpa und ihre Nachbarvölker im Himalaya.* Franfurt am Main, Wolfgang Krüger.

Fürer-Haimendorf, Christoph von. 1962. Moral Concepts in Three Himalayan Societies. In *Indian Anthropology,* edited by T. N. Madan and Gopala Śarana, pp. 279–309. Bombay.

———. 1964. *The Sherpas of Nepal: Buddhist Highlanders.* London, John Murray.

———. 1966a. Caste Concepts and Status Distinctions in Buddhist Communities of Western Nepal. In *Caste and Kin in Nepal, India and Ceylon: Anthropological Studies in Hindu-Buddhist Contact Zones,* edited by Christoph von Fürer-Haimendorf, pp. 140–160. London, Asia Publishing House.

———. (ed). 1966b. *Caste and Kin in Nepal, India and Ceylon: Anthropological Studies in Hindu-Buddhist Contact Zones.* London, Asia Publishing House.

———. 1967. *Morals and Merit.* London, Weidenfeld and Nicolson.

———. (ed). 1974. *Contributions to the Anthropology of Nepal.* Warminster, Aris and Phillips.

———. 1975. *Himalayan Traders: Life in Highland Nepal.* London, John Murray.

———. 1976. A Nunnery in Nepal. *Kailash* 4(2):121–154.

———. 1982. *Tribes of India.* Berkeley, University of California Press.

———. 1983. Bhotia Highlanders of Nar and Phu. *Kailash* 10(1–2):63–118.

———. 1984. *The Sherpas Transformed: Social Change in a Buddhist Society of Nepal.* New Delhi, Sterling.

Gäng, Peter. 1988. *Das Tantra der verborgenen Vereinigung. Guhyasamāja-Tantra. Aus dem Sanskrit übersetzt und herausgegeben von P.G..* Eugen Diederichs.

Geertz, Clifford. 1964. *The Religions of Java.* Glencoe, Illinois, Free Press.

George, Christopher S. 1974. *The Caṇḍamahāroṣaṇa Tantra. A Critical Edition and English Translation. Chapters* 1–8. American Oriental Society, New Haven. (American Oriental Series 56.)

Gill, Manohar Singh. 1972. *Himalayan Wonderland: Travels in Lahaul-Spiti.* New Delhi, Vikas.

Gleason, Judith. 1987. *Oya: In Praise of the Goddess.* Boston, Shambhala.

Goldstein, Melvyn C. 1964. Study of the *ldab ldob. CAJ* 9:123–141.

———. 1968. An Anthropological Study of the Tibetan Political System. Ph.D. dissertation, University of Washington, Seattle.

———. 1971a. Serfdom and Mobility: An Examination of the Institution of 'Human Lease' in Traditional Tibetan Society. *JAS* 30(3):521–534.

———. 1971b. Stratification, Polyandry and Family Structure in Central Tibet. *Southwestern J. of Anthropology* 27(1):64–74.

———. 1971c. Taxation and the Structure of a Tibetan Village. *CAJ* 15:1–27.

———. 1971d. The Balance between Centralization and Decentralization in the Traditional Tibetan Political System. *CAJ* 15:170–182.

———. 1973. The Circulation of Estates in Tibet: Reincarnation, Land and Politics. *JAS* 32:445–455.

———. 1974. Tibetan Speaking Agro-Pastoralists of Limi. *Objets et Mondes* 14(4):259–267.

———. 1975. A Report on Limi Panchayat, Humla District, Karnali Zone. *Contributions to Nepalese Studies* 12(2):89–101.

———. 1977a. Culture, Population, Ecology and Development: A View from N. W. Nepal. *Himalaya: Écologie—Ethnologie*, pp. 481–489. Paris, CNRS.

———. 1977b. Population, Social Structure and Strategic Behaviour: An Essay on Polyandry, Fertility and Change in Limi Panchayat. *Contributions to Nepalese Studies* 4(2):47–61.

———. 1982. Lhasa Street Songs: Political and Social Satire in Traditional Tibet. *TJ* 7(1–2):56–66.

———. 1986. Reexamining Choice, Dependency and Command in the Tibetan Social System: 'Tax Appendages' and other Landless Serfs. *TJ* 11(4):79–112.

———. 1987. Anthropological Fieldwork in Tibet: Studying Nomadic Pastoralism on the Changtang. *Himalayan Research Bulletin* 7(1):1–4.

———. 1988. On the Nature of Tibetan Peasantry. *TJ* 13(1):61–65.

———. 1989. *A History of Modern Tibet, 1913–1951: The Demise of the Lamaist State.* Berkeley, University of California Press.

———. 1991. The Dragon and the Snow Lion: The Tibet Question in the 20th Century. *TR* 26(4):9–26.

Goldstein, Melvyn C., and Cynthia M. Beall. 1986. Studying Nomads on the Tibetan Plateau. *China Exchange News* 14(4) (December):2–7.

———. 1989. The Impact of China's Reform Policy on the Nomads of Western Tibet. *Asian Survey* 29(6) (June):619–641.

———. 1990. *Nomads of Western Tibet: The Survival of a Way of Life.* London, Serindia Publications.

Goldstein, Melvyn C., and Paljor Tsarong. 1985. Tibetan Buddhist Monasticism: Social, Psychological and Cultural Implications. *TJ* 10(1):14–31.

Gombo, Ugen. 1985. Belief in Karma and its Social Ramifications in Samsara. In *Soundings in Tibetan Civilization*, edited by Barbara Aziz and Matthew Kapstein, pp. 233–244. New Delhi, Manohar. [*Proceedings* of 3d Seminar of IATS.]

Gombrich, R. F. 1971. *Precept and Practice: Traditional Buddhism in the Rural Highlands of Ceylon*. Oxford, Clarendon Press.

Goodman, Steven D. 1981. Mi-Pham rgya-mtsho: An Account of His Life, the Printing of his Works, and the Structure of His Treatise Entitled *mKhas-pa'i tshul la 'jug-pa'i sgo. Wind Horse (Proceedings of the North American Tibetological Society)* 1:58–78.

———. 1983. The *kLong-chen snying-thig:* An Eighteenth Century Tibetan Revelation. Ph.D. dissertation, University of Saskatchewan.

Goody, Jack. 1977. *The Domestication of the Savage Mind.* Cambridge University Press.

Gorer, Geoffrey. 1939. *Himalayan Village: An Account of the Lepchas of Sikkim.* London, Michael Joseph.

Goullart, Peter. 1957. *Forgotten Kingdom.* London, Readers Union and John Murray.

———. 1959. *Princes of the Black Bone: Life in the Tibetan Borderland.* London, John Murray. [U.S. edition is entitled *Land of the Lamas.*]

Govinda, Lama Anagarika. 1969. *Foundations of Tibetan Mysticism.* London, Rider.

———. 1974. *The Way of the White Clouds.* London, Rider.

———. 1977. H. V. Guenther as Interpreter of the Tantric View of Life. In *Buddhist Thought and Asian Civilization: Essays in Honor of Herbert V. Guenther on His Sixtieth Birthday,* edited by Leslie S. Kawamura and Keith Scott, pp. 39–46. Emeryville, California, Dharma Publishing.

Gregory, J. W., and C. J. Gregory. 1923. *To the Alps of Chinese Tibet.* London.

Grimshaw, Anna. 1983. Rizong: A Monastic Community in Ladakh. Ph.D. dissertation, Cambridge University.

Grupper, Samuel M. 1984 Manchu Patronage and Tibetan Buddhism during the First Half of the Ch'ing Dynasty. *JTS* 4:47–76.

Guenther, Herbert V. 1963. *The Life and Teaching of Nāropa.* Oxford, Clarendon Press.

———. 1966. *Tibetan Buddhism without Mystification.* Leiden, E. J. Brill. [Reprinted without Tibetan texts as Guenther 1971.]

———. 1969. *Yuganaddha: The Tantric View of Life.* 2d edition. Benares, Chowkhamba Sanskrit Series.

———. 1970. *The Jewel Ornament of Liberation.* London, Rider.

———. 1971. *Treasures on the Tibetan Middle Way.* Berkeley, Shambhala.

———. 1972. *Buddhist Philosophy in Theory and Practice.* Harmondsworth, Penguin Books.

———. 1973. *The Royal Song of Saraha*. Berkeley, Shambhala.

———. 1974a. *Philosophy and Psychology in the Abhidharma*. 2d edition. Berkeley, Shambhala.

———. 1974b. Early Forms of Tibetan Buddhism. *Crystal Mirror* 3:80–92.

———. 1975a. Mahāmudrā—the Method of Self-Actualization. *TJ* 1(1): 5–23.

———. 1975b. *Kindly Bent to Ease Us: The Trilogy of Finding Comfort and Ease*. 3 vols., Emeryville, California, Dharma.

———. 1975c. The Natural Freedom of Mind. *Crystal Mirror* 4:113–146.

———. 1977a. *Tibetan Buddhism in Western Perspective*. Emeryville, California, Dharma.

———. 1977b. The Spiritual Teacher in Tibet. In *Tibetan Buddhism in Western Perspective*, edited by Herbert V. Guenther, pp. 178–195. Emeryville, California, Dharma.

———. 1981. In Retrospect. *Wind Horse (Proceedings of the North American Tibetological Society)* 1:1–7.

———. 1984. *Matrix of Mystery: Scientific and Humanistic Aspects of rDzogs-chen Thought*. Boulder and London, Shambhala.

Guibaut, André. 1949. *Tibetan Venture: In the Country of the Ngolo-Setas*. London, John Murray.

Gurung, Nareshwar Jang. 1977. An Ethnographic Note on Nar-Phu Valley. *Kailash* 5(3):229–244.

Gyatso, Geshe Kelsang. 1980. *Meaningful to Behold: View, Meditation and Action in Mahayana Buddhism*. An Oral Commentary to Shantideva's *Bodhicaryavatara*. Conishead, Wisdom.

Gyatso, Janet. 1980a. *A Technique For Developing Enlightened Consciousness: A Traditional Buddhist Meditation on Avalokiteshvara by the Tibetan Saint Tangtong Gyalbo*. Buddhist Association of the United States.

———. 1980b. The Teachings of Thang-stong rGyal-po. In *Tibetan Studies in Honour of Hugh Richardson. Proceedings of the International Seminar on Tibetan Studies, Oxford* 1979, edited by Michael Aris and Aung San Suu Kyi, pp. 111–119. Warminster, Aris and Phillips. [= *Proceedings* of 2nd Seminar of IATS.]

———. 1980c. Literary Presentations of Visionary Buddhism as Typified in the Traditions Attributed to Thang-stong rGyal-po. Paper presented to the North American Tibetological Society meeting, Berkeley, August 1980.

———. 1981. The Literary Transmission of the Traditions of Thang-stong rGyal-po: A Study of Visionary Buddhism in Tibet. Ph.D. dissertation, Buddhist Studies, University of California at Berkeley.

———. 1985. The Development of the *gcod* Tradition. In *Soundings in Ti-*

betan Civilization, edited by Barbara Aziz and Matthew Kapstein, pp. 320–341. New Delhi, Manohar. [*Proceedings* of 3d Seminar of IATS.]
———. 1986. Signs, Memory and History: A Tantric Buddhist Theory of Scriptural Transmission. *JIABS* 9(2):7–35.
———. 1987. Down with the Demoness: Reflections on a Feminine Ground in Tibet. *TJ* 12(4):38–53.
Gyatso, Yonten. 1988. Le Monastère de Bla-braṅ bkra-šis 'khyil.' In *Tibetan Studies. Proceedings of the 4th Seminar of the International Association for Tibetan studies. Schloss Hohenkammer, Munich* 1985, edited by Helga Uebach and Jampa L. Panglung, pp. 559–566. Kommission für Zentralasiatische Studien, Bayerische Akademie der Wissenschaften.

Haarh, Erik. 1969. *The Yarlung Dynasty.* Copenhagen.
Handa, O. C. 1987. *Buddhist Monasteries in Himachal Pradesh.* New Delhi, Indus Publishing.
Hanna, Span. in press. Vast as the Sky: The Terma Tradition in Modern Tibet. In *Tantra and Popular Religion in Tibet,* edited by Geoffrey Samuel. New Delhi, Aditya Prakashan.
Hanson, Judith. 1977. *The Torch of Certainty by Jamgon Kongtrul.* Boulder, Shambhala.
———. (trans). 1982. Hagiography of Vajradhara by rMo-lcogs-pa; Hagiography of the Jñana-Dakini Niguma; A Story from the Life of the Jñana-Dakini Sukhasiddhi. Typescript.
Hanson, Judith, and Mervin V. Hanson. 1985. The Mediating Buddha. In *Soundings in Tibetan Civilization,* edited by Barbara Aziz and Matthew Kapstein, pp. 296–304. New Delhi, Manohar. [*Proceedings* of 3d Seminar of IATS.]
Hanson-Barber, A. W. 1984. The Life and Teachings of Vairocana. Ph.D. dissertation, University of Wisconsin at Madison.
———. 1986. The Identification of dGa' rab rdo rje. *JIABS* 9(2):55–63.
Harcourt, A. F. P. [1870] 1972. *The Himalayan Districts of Kooloo, Lahoul and Spiti.* Delhi, Vivek.
Harrer, Heinrich. 1955. *Seven Years in Tibet.* London, Reprint Society.
Harrison, Paul. 1987. Who Gets to Ride in the Great Vehicle? Self-Image and Identity among the Followers of the Early Mahayana. *JIABS* 10(1):67–90.
Heinze, Ruth-Inge. 1982. *Tham Khwan.* Singapore University Press.
———. 1988. *Trance and Healing in Southeast Asia Today.* Bangkok, White Lotus.
Heissig, Walther. 1980. *The Religions of Mongolia.* London, Routledge and Kegan Paul.

Helffer, Mireille. 1976. Traditions Musicales des Sa-Skya-pa Relatives au Culte de mGon-po. *JA* 264:357–404.

———. 1977 *Les Chants dans l'Épopée Tibétaine de Ge-sar d'après le Livre de la Course de Cheval: Version Chantée de Blo-bzan bstan-'jin*. Paris and Geneva, Librairie Droz.

———. 1980. The 'cham of Padmasambhava in the Monastery of Hemis. *World of Music* 22(1):107–124.

Heller, Amy. 1986. A propos de Mme Ariane Macdonald, 'Une Lecture des P. T. 1286.' *JTS* 6:73–78.

Hermanns, Matthias. 1949. *Die Nomaden von Tibet*. Wien, Verlag Herold.

———. 1970. *Schamanen-Pseudoschamanen, Erlöser und Heilbringer: Eine vergleichende Studie religiöser Urphänomene*. Teil 3: Erlöser und Heilbringer der Tibeter. Wiesbaden, Franz Steiner.

Hirschberg, Helga. 1980. *Ladakh: Das andere Tibet*. München, Geobuch.

Hitchcock, John T., and Rex L. Jones (eds). 1976. *Spirit Possession in the Nepal Himalayas*. Warminster, Aris and Phillips.

Hock, Nancy. 1987. Buddhist Ideology and the Sculpture of Ratnagiri, Seventh through Thirteenth Centuries. Ph.D. dissertation, University of California, Berkeley.

Hoffmann, Helmut. 1969. Kalacakra Studies I: Manichaeism, Christianity, and Islam in the Kalacakra Tantra. *CAJ* 13(1):52–72.

———. 1979. *The Religions of Tibet*. Westport, Connecticut, Greenwood Press.

———. 1990. Early and Medieval Tibet. In *The Cambridge History of Early Inner Asia*, edited by Dennis Sinor, pp. 371–399. Cambridge University Press.

Holmberg, David H. 1983. Shamanic Soundings:Femaleness in the Tamang Ritual Structure. *Signs* 9:40–58.

———. 1984. Ritual Paradoxes in Nepal: Comparative Perspectives on Tamang Religion. *JAS* 43:697–722.

———. 1989. *Order in Paradox: Myth, Ritual and Exchange among Nepal's Tamang*. Ithaca, New York, Cornell University Press.

Hooykaas, C. 1966. *Sūrya-sevana: The Way to God of a Balinese Śiva Priest*. Amsterdam, N.V. Noord-Hollandsche Uitgevers Maatschappij. (Verhandelingen der Koninklijke Nederlandse Akademie van Wetenschappen, Afd. Letterkunde, Nieuwe Reeks, Deel 72[3]).

———. 1973a. *Balinese Bauddha Brahmans*. Amsterdam, N.V. Noord-Hollandsche Uitgevers Maatschappij. (Verhandelingen der Koninklijke Nederlandse Akademie van Wetenschappen, Afd. Letterkunde, Nieuwe Reeks, Deel 80).

———. 1973b. *Religion in Bali*. Leiden, E. J. Brill. (Institute of Religious

Iconography, State University, Groningen, Iconography of Religions, 13[10].)

Hopkins, Jeffrey. 1977. *Tantra in Tibet: The Great Exposition of Secret Mantra by Tsong-ka-pa. Part One.* London, Allen and Unwin.

———. 1980. *Compassion in Tibetan Buddhism.* New York, Gabriel-Snow Lion.

———. 1981. *The Yoga of Tibet: The Great Exposition of Secret Mantra by Tsong-ka-pa, Parts Two and Three.* London, Allen and Unwin.

Houston, G. W. 1980. *Sources for a History of the bSam yas Debate.* St. Augustin, VGH Wissenschaftsverlag.

———. 1982. *Wings of the White Crane: Poems of Tshangs dbyangs rgya mtsho.* Delhi, Motilal Banarsidass.

Huber, Antoni M. 1989. A Pilgrimage to La-phyi: A Study of Sacred and Historical Geography in South-Western Tibet. M.A. dissertation, University of Canterbury, New Zealand.

———. in press. When What You See Is Not What You Get: Remarks on the Traditional Tibetan Presentation of Sacred Geography. In *Tantra and Popular Religion in Tibet,* edited by Geoffrey Samuel. New Delhi, Aditya Prakashan.

Hummel, Siegbert. 1960. Der magische Stein in Tibet. *International Archives of Ethnology* 49:224–240.

Humphrey, Caroline. 1985. Barter and Economic Disintegration. *Man* (n.s.) 20:48–72.

———. 1987. Fairness and Fertility: Moral Ideas in the Barter of the Lhomi of North-East Nepal. Typescript.

Huntington, Richard, and Peter Metcalf. 1980. *Celebrations of Death: The Anthropology of Mortuary Ritual.* Cambridge, University Press.

Imaeda, Yoshiro. 1981. *Histoire du Cycle de la Naissance et de la Mort: Étude d'un Text Tibétain de Touen-houang.* Geneva and Paris, Librairie Droz. (Centre de Recherches d'Histoire et de Philologie de la IVe Section de l'École pratique des Hautes Études, II. Hautes Études Orientales, 15.)

Imaeda, Y., and F. Pommaret. 1990. Note sur la Situation Liguistique du Bhoutan et Étude Préliminaire des Termes de Parenté. In *Indo-Tibetan Studies. Papers in Honour and Appreciation of Professor David L. Snellgrove's Contribution to Indo-Tibetan Studies,* edited by Tadeusz Skorupski, pp. 115–128. Tring, Institute of Buddhist Studies.

Inada, Kenneth K. 1970. *Nāgārjuna: A Translation of his Mūlamadhyamakakārikā with an Introductory Essay.* Tokyo, Hokuseido Press.

Jackson, Anthony. 1978. Tibetan Bön Rites in China: A Case of Cultural

Diffusion. In *Himalayan Anthropology: The Indo-Tibetan Interface,* edited by James F. Fisher, pp. 309–326. The Hague, Mouton.

———. 1979. *Na-khi Religion: An Analytical Appraisal of the Na-khi Ritual Texts.* The Hague, Mouton.

Jackson, David P. 1976. The Early History of Lo (Mustang) and Ngari. *Contributions to Nepalese Studies* 4(1):39–56.

———. 1978. Notes on the History of Serib, and Nearby Places in the Upper Kali Gandaki. *Kailash* 6(3):195–227.

———. 1983. Commentaries on the Writings of Sa-skya Paṇḍita: A Bibliographical Sketch. *TJ* 8(3):3–23.

———. 1984. *The Mollas of Mustang: Historical, Religious and Oratorical Traditions of the Nepalese-Tibetan Borderland.* Dharamsala, HP, LTWA.

Jackson, Roger. 1982. Sa skya paṇḍita's Account of the bSam yas Debate: History as Polemic. *JIABS* 5(2):89–99.

———. 1985. The Kalachakra in Context. In *The Wheel of Time: The Kalachakra in Context,* edited by Geshe Lhundub Sopa, Roger Jackson, and John Newman, pp. 1–50. Madison, Wisconsin, Deer Park Books.

Jäschke, H. A. [1881] 1968. *A Tibetan-English Dictionary with Special Reference to the Prevailing Dialects.* London, Routledge and Kegan Paul.

Jeffrey, J. H. 1974. *Khams or Eastern Tibet.* Ilfracombe, Devon, Arthur H. Stockwell.

Jerstad, L. G. 1969. *Mani Rimdu: Sherpa Dance-Drama.* Seattle and London, University of Washington Press.

Jest, Corneille. 1974. *Tarap: Une Vallée dans l'Himalaya.* Paris, Le Seuil.

———. 1976. *Dolpo: Communautés de Langue Tibétaine du Népal.* Paris, Éditions du CNRS.

———. 1978. Tibetan Communities of the High Valleys of Nepal: Life in an Exceptional Environment and Economy. In *Himalayan Anthropology: The Indo-Tibetan Interface,* edited by James F. Fisher, pp. 359–364. The Hague, Mouton.

———. 1985. *La Turquoise de Vie: Un Pèlerinage Tibétain.* Paris, Métailié.

Johnson, Russell, and Kerry Moran. 1989. *The Sacred Mountain of Tibet: On Pilgrimage to Kailas.* Rochester, Vermont, Park Street Press.

Kalff, Martin. 1979. Selected Chapters from the Abhidhānottara-Tantra: The Union of Male and Female Deities. Ph.D. dissertation, Philosophy, Columbia University.

Kalsang, Jampa, and Klaus Sagaster. 1971. Bericht über eine Reise zur Untersuchung des Phänomens der tibetischen Orakelpriester im Jahre 1970 in Indien. *ZAS* 5:225–246.

Kalu Rinpoche, H. E. 1985. *The Chariot for Traveling the Path to Freedom: The*

Life Story of Kalu Rinpoche. Translated by Kenneth I. McLeod. San Francisco, Kagyu Dharma.

———. 1986. *The Gem Ornament of Manifold Oral Instructions which Benefits Each and Everyone Appropriately.* San Francisco, KDK.

Kantowsky, Detlef, and Reinhard Sander. 1983. *Recent Research on Ladakh: History, Culture, Society, Ecology. Proceedings of a Conference held at the University of Konstanz, November* 1981. Köln, Weltforum Verlag.

Kapferer, Bruce. 1983. *A Celebration of Demons: Exorcism and the Aesthetics of Healing in Sri Lanka.* Bloomington, Indiana University Press.

Kaplanian, Patrick. 1981. *Les Ladakhi du Cachemire: Montagnards du Tibet Occidental.* Hachette (L'Homme Vivant).

———. 1985. Une Séance de la Lhamo de Sabu. In *Ladakh, Himalaya Occidental: Ethnologie, Écologie,* edited by Claude Dendaletche and Patrick Kaplanian, pp. 135–147. Pau, Centre Pyrenéen de Biologie et Anthropologie des Montagnes. (*Acta Biologica Montana* 5.)

Kapstein, Matthew. 1980. The Shangs-pa bKa'-brgyud: An Unknown Tradition of Tibetan Buddhism. In *Tibetan Studies in Honour of Hugh Richardson. Proceedings of the International Seminar on Tibetan Studies, Oxford* 1979, edited by Michael Aris and Aung San Suu Kyi, pp. 138–144. Warminster, Aris and Phillips. [= *Proceedings* of 2nd Seminar of IATS.]

———. 1985. Religious Syncretism in 13th Century Tibet: *The Limitless Ocean Cycle.* In *Soundings in Tibetan Civilization,* edited by Barbara Aziz and Matthew Kapstein, pp. 358–371. New Delhi, Manohar. [*Proceedings* of 3d Seminar of IATS.]

———Kapstein, Matthew. 1989. The Purificatory Gem and Its Cleansing: A Late Tibetan Polemical Discussion of Apocryphal Texts. *HR* 28(3): 217–244.

———. in press. Remarks on the Mani bKa'-bum and the Cult of Avalokitesvara in Tibet. In *Tibetan Buddhism: Reason and Revelation,* edited by Steven Goodman. Albany, SUNY Press.

Karan, Pradyumna Prasad. 1967. *Bhutan: A Physical and Cultural Geography.* Lexington, Kentucky University Press.

Karmapa, 15th. n.d. *A Continuous Rain to Benefit Beings.* Vancouver, B.C., Kagyu Kunkhyab Choling.

Karmay, Samten G. 1972. *The Treasury of Good Sayings: A Tibetan History of Bon.* London, Oxford University Press.

———. 1975a. A General Introduction to the History and Doctrines of Bon. *Memoirs of the Toyo Bunko* 33:171–218.

———. 1975b. A Discussion on the Doctrinal Position of rDzogs-chen from the 10th to the 13th Century. *JA* 263:147–155.

———. 1980a. The Ordinance of Lha Bla-ma Ye-shes-'od. In *Tibetan Studies in Honour of Hugh Richardson. Proceedings of the International Seminar on Tibetan Studies, Oxford* 1979, edited by Michael Aris and Aung San Suu Kyi, pp. 150–161. Warminster, Aris and Phillips. [= *Proceedings* of 2nd Seminar of IATS.]

———. 1980b. An Open Letter by Pho-brang Zhi-ba-'od to the Buddhists of Tibet. *TJ* 5(3):3–28.

———. 1985. The Rdzogs-chen in Its Earliest Text: A Manuscript from Tun-huang. In *Soundings in Tibetan Civilization,* edited by Barbara Aziz and Matthew Kapstein, pp. 272–282. New Delhi, Manohar. [*Proceedings* of 3d Seminar of IATS.]

———. 1986. L'Apparition du Petit Homme Tête-Noire. *JA* 274(1–2): 79–138.

———. 1987. L'âme et la Turquoise: Un Rituel Tibétain. In Rituels Himalayens, edited by Alexander W. Macdonald. Special issue of *L'Ethnographie* 83(100–101):97–130.

———. 1988a. *The Great Perfection (rDzogs Chen). A Philosophical and Meditative Teaching in Tibetan Buddhism.* Leiden, E. J. Brill.

———. 1988b. *Secret Visions of the Fifth Dalai Lama: the Gold Manuscript in the Fournier Collection.* London, Serindia.

———. 1990. The Wind-Horse and the Well-Being of Man. Paper for the International Seminar on Anthropology of Tibet and the Himalayas, Völkerkundemuseum der Universität Zürich, September 21–28, 1990.

Karsten, Joachim. 1980. Some Notes on the House of Lha rGya-ri. In *Tibetan Studies in Honour of Hugh Richardson. Proceedings of the International Seminar on Tibetan Studies, Oxford* 1979, edited by Michael Aris and Aung San Suu Kyi, pp. 153–168. Warminster, Aris and Phillips. [= *Proceedings* of 2nd Seminar of IATS.]

Kaschewsky, Rudolf. 1971. *Das Leben des Lamaistischer Heiligen Tsongkhapa Blo-bzaṅ-grags-pa (*1357–1419*) dargestellt und erläutert anhand seiner Vita "Quellort allen Glückes".* 2 vols. Wiesbaden, Otto Harrassowitz. (Asiatische Forchungen 32.)

———. 1973. Die Lehrworte des Pha-dam-pa. In *Serta Tibeto-Mongolica: Festschrift für Walther Heissig zum* 60. *Geburtstag am* 5.12.1973, edited by R. Kaschewsky, K. Sagaster, and M. Weiers, pp. 171–204. Wiesbaden, Otto Harrassowitz.

Kawamura, Leslie S. 1975. *Golden Zephyr.* Emeryville, California, Dharma.

———. 1984. Thus Have I Said-A Preliminary Study of the Tantra. In *Tibetan and Buddhist Studies Commemorating the* 200*th Anniversary of the Birth of Alexander Csoma de Körös,* edited by Louis Ligeti, pp. 363–376. Budapest, Akadémiai Kiadó, 2 vols.

Kessler, Peter. 1982. *Laufende Arbeiten zu einem Ethnohistorischen Atlas Tibets (EAT). Lieferung* 47.1*: rMi-li.* Rikon, Tibet-Instituts.

———. 1983. *Laufende Arbeiten zu einem Ethnohistorischen Atlas Tibets (EAT). Lieferung* 40.1*: Gling/sDe-dge.* Rikon, Tibet-Instituts.

———. 1984. *Laufende Arbeiten zu einem Ethnohistorischen Atlas Tibets (EAT). Lieferung* 41.1*: Die historische Landschaft TEHOR unter besonderer Berücksichtigung der frühen Geschichte Südosttibets (Khams).* Rikon, Tibet-Instituts.

Keyes, Charles F., and E. Valentine Daniel (eds). 1983. *Karma: An Anthropological Inquiry.* Berkeley, University of California Press.

Khamtrul Rinpoche [8th Khamtrul, Dongyud Nyima]. n.d. *Celebration of the Rite of the Unity of the Three Jewels in Padmasambhava and Padmasambhava's Birthday.* Kalimpong, Palphuntshog Chhokhorling Monastery.

Khandro, Sangye. 1988. *A Garland of Immortal Wish-fulfilling Trees: The Palyul Tradition of Nyingmapa By the Ven. Tsering Lama Jampal Zangpo.* Translated by Sangye Khandro. Ithaca, NY, Snow Lion.

Khetsun Sangbo Rinbochay. 1982. *Tantric Practice in Nying-ma.* London, Rider.

Khosla, G. D. 1956. *Himalayan Circuit.* London, Macmillan.

Kirkland, J. Russell. 1982. The Spirit of the Mountain: Myth and State in Pre-Buddhist Tibet. *HR* 21:257–271.

Kite, Bill, and Geoff Childs. 1988. *Myths, Mountains and Mandalas: Mani Rimdu and Tengboche Monastery Thru the Eyes of the Dancers.* Kathmandu, Tengboche Trust.

Klein, Anne. 1987. Primordial Purity and Everyday Life: Exalted Female Symbols and the Women of Tibet. In *Immaculate and Powerful: The Female in Sacred Image and Social Reality,* edited by Clarissa W. Atkinson, et al., pp. 111–138. London, Crucible.

Kler, P. Josef. 1957. Die Windpferdfahne oder das K'i-mori bei den Ordos Mongolen. *Oriens* 10:90–106.

Klimburg-Salter, D. E. 1982. *The Silk Route and the Diamond Path: Esoteric Art on the Trans-Himalayan Trade Routes.* Los Angeles, UCLA Arts Council.

Klinger, Ross E. 1980. The Tibetan Guru Refuge. *TJ* 5(4):9–19.

Kohn, Richard Jay. 1988. Mani Rimdu. Text and Tradition in a Tibetan Ritual. Ph.D. dissertation, University of Wisconsin, Madison.

Kolmaš, Josef. 1968. *A Genealogy of the Kings of Derge (Sde-dge'i rgyal-rabs).* Prague, Academia.

———. 1988. Dezhung Rinpoche's Summary and Continuation of the Sde-dge'i rgyal rabs. *AOH* 42(1):119–152.

Korn, V. E. 1960. The Consecration of a Priest. In *Bali: Studies in Life, Thought and Ritual,* edited by W. F. Wertheim et al., introduction by J. F. Swellengrebel, pp. 133–153. The Hague and Bandung, W. van Hoeve. (Selected Studies on Indonesia by Dutch Scholars 5.)

Kornfield, Jack. 1977. *Living Buddhist Masters.* Santa Cruz, Unity Press.

Kretschmar, Andreas. 1981. *'Brug pa kun legs: Das wundersame Lebens eines verrückten Heiligen*. St. Augustin, VGH Wissenschaftsverlag.

Lama Kunga Rimpoche, and Brian Cutillo. 1978. *Drinking the Mountain Stream: Further Stories and Songs of Milarepa, Yogin, Poet, and Teacher of Tibet*. New York, Lotsawa.

———. 1986. *Miraculous Journey: New Stories and Songs by Milarepa*. Lotsawa.

Kvaerne, Per. 1974. The Canon of the Tibetan Bonpos. *Indo-Iranian J.* 16:18–56, 96–144.

———. 1975. On the Concept of Sahaja in Indian Buddhist Tantric Literature. *Temenos* 11:88–135.

———. 1976. Who are the Bonpos? *TR* 11(9):30–33.

———. 1977. *An Anthology of Buddhist Tantric Songs*. Oslo, Universitetsforlaget. (Det Norske Videnskaps-Akademi. II.Hist.-Filos. Klasse. Skrifter. Ny Serie, 14.) [2d edition, Bangkok, White Orchid Press, 1986.]

———. 1983. 'The Great Perfection' in the Tradition of the Bonpos. In *Early Ch'an in China and Tibet*, edited by Whalen Lai and Lewis R. Lancaster, pp. 367–392. Berkeley Buddhist Studies Series.

———. 1986. Peintures Tibétaines de la Vie de sTon-pa-gçen-rab. *Arts Asiatiques* 41:36–81.

———. 1987. Dualism in Tibetan Cosmogonic Myths and the Question of Iranian Influence. In *Silver on Lapis: Tibetan Literary Culture and History*, edited by Christopher Beckwith, pp. 163–174. Bloomington, Indiana, The Tibet Society.

———. 1990a. A Bonpo bsTan-tsis from 1804. In *Indo-Tibetan Studies. Papers in Honour and Appreciation of Professor David L. Snellgrove's Contribution to Indo-Tibetan Studies*, edited by Tadeusz Skorupski, pp. 151–170. Tring, Institute of Buddhist Studies.

———. 1990b. The Bon Religion of Tibet: A Survey of Research. *NIAS Report* 1990, 143–153. Nordic Institute of Asian Studies.

Kychanov, E. I. 1978. Tibetans and Tibetan Culture in the Tangut State Hsi Hsia (982–1227). In *Proceedings of the Csoma de Kőrős Memorial Symposium held at Mátrafüred, Hungary, September* 24–30, 1976, pp. 205–212. Budapest, Akadémiai Kiadó.

Lai, Whalen, and Lewis R. Lancaster (eds). 1983. *Early Ch'an in China and Tibet*. Berkeley Buddhist Studies Series.

Lati Rinbochay. 1980. *Mind in Tibetan Buddhism*. Translated, edited and introduced by Elizabeth Napper. London, Rider.

Lati Rinbochay, and Jeffrey Hopkins. 1979. *Death, Intermediate State and Rebirth in Tibetan Buddhism*. Valois, New York, Gabriel/Snow Lion.

Lauf, Detlef I. 1977. *Secret Doctrines of the Tibetan Books of the Dead.* Boulder, Shambhala.

Laufer, Berthold. 1911. *Der Roman einer tibetischen Königin* [*bTsun-mo bka'-thang*]. Leipzig.

Leach, Edmund R. 1970. *Political Systems of Highland Burma.* London, Athlone Press.

LeBar, Frank M., Gerald C. Hickey, and John K. Musgrove. 1964. *Ethnic Groups of Mainland Southeast Asia.* New Haven, HRAF.

Lehman, F. K. 1967. Ethnic Categories in Burma and the Theory of Social Systems. In *Southeast Asian Tribes, Minorities and Nations,* edited by Peter Kunstadter, vol. 1, pp. 93–124. Princeton, New Jersey, Princeton University Press.

Lerner, Lin. 1983. Two Tibetan Ritual Dances: A Comparative Study. *TJ* 8(4):50–57.

Lessing, Ferdinand D. 1942. *Yung-ho-kung: An Iconography of the Lamaist Cathedral in Peking with Notes on Lamaist Mythology and Cult,* vol. 1. Stockholm. (Reports of the Sino-Swedish Expedition 8(1). Ethnography 1.)

———. 1951. Calling the Soul: A Lamaist Ritual. *Semitic and Oriental Studies* 11:263–284.

Lessing, Ferdinand D., and Alex Wayman (trans.) 1968. *Mkhas grub rje's Fundamentals of the Buddhist Tantras.* The Hague and Paris, Mouton. (Indo-Iranian Monographs 8.)

Levine, Nancy E. 1976. The Origins of sTod-pa: A Nyinba Clan Legend. *Contributions to Nepalese Studies* 4(1):57–75.

———. 1980. Opposition and Interdependence: Demographic and Economic Perspectives on Nyinba Slavery. In *Asian and African Systems of Slavery,* edited by James L. Watson, pp. 195–222. Oxford, Blackwell.

———. 1981a. The Theory of *Rü* Kinship, Descent and Status in a Tibetan Society. In *Asian Highland Societies in Anthropological Perspective,* edited by C. von Fürer-Haimendorf, pp. 52–78. New Delhi, Sterling.

———. 1981b. Law, Labor and the Economic Vulnerability of Women in Nyinba Society. *Kailash* 8(3–4):123–154.

———. 1981c. Perspectives on Love: Morality and Affect in Nyinba Interpersonal Relationships. In *Culture and Morality: Essays in Honour of Christoph von Fürer-Haimendorf,* edited by Adrian C. Mayer, pp. 106–125. Delhi, Oxford University Press.

———. 1982. Belief and Explanation in Nyinba Women's Witchcraft. *Man* 17:259–274.

———. 1987. Caste, State, and Ethnic Boundaries in Nepal. *JAS* 46(1): 71–88.

———. 1988. *The Dynamics of Polyandry. Kinship, Domesticity, and Population on the Tibetan Border.* Chicago, University of Chicago Press.

Lhalungpa, Lobsang P. 1968. Tsong-kha-pa's Song of Spiritual Experience [Lam rim bsdus don]. *Bulletin of Tibetology* 5(1).

———. 1979. *The Life of Milarepa: A New Translation from the Tibetan.* Frogmore, Granada.

Li An-che. 1947. Dege: A Study of Tibetan Population. *Southwestern J. of Anthropology* 3(4):279–293.

Li Chengrui (ed). 1987. *The Population Atlas of China.* Compiled and edited by the Population Census Office of the State Council of the People's Republic of China and the Institute of Geography of the Chinese Academy of Sciences. Hong Kong, Oxford University Press.

Lichter, David, and Lawrence Epstein. 1983. Irony in Tibetan Notions of the Good Life. In *Karma: An Anthropological Inquiry*, edited by Charles F. Keyes and E. Valentine Daniel, pp. 223–259. Berkeley, University of California Press.

Lienhardt, Godfrey. 1961. *Divinity and Experience: The Religion of the Dinka.* Oxford, Clarendon Press.

Ling, Trevor O. 1973. *The Buddha: Buddhist Civilization in India and Ceylon.* London, Temple Smith.

Ling Rinpoche. 1983. Autobiography. *TJ* 8(3):45–61.

Lipman, Kennard. 1977. How the Saṃsāra is Fabricated from the Ground of Being. *Crystal Mirror* 5:344–364.

———. 1980. The World as a Buddha Field: The Intelligent Universe. *Gesar* 6(3):6–9.

———. 1981. A Controversial Topic from Mi-pham's Analysis of Śāntarakṣita's *Madhyamakālaṃkāra. Wind Horse. (Proceedings of the North American Tibetological Society.)* 1:40–57.

———. 1987. *You Are the Eyes of the World* [*Longchenpa's Commentary on the Kun byed rgyal po*]. Lotsawa.

Lodro, Geshe Gedun. 1974. *Geschichte der Kloster-Universität Drepung mit einem Abriss der Geistesgeschichte Tibets. I. Teil: Tibetische Text.* Wiesbaden.

Lorenzen, David N. 1972. *The Kāpālikas and Kālāmukhas: Two Lost Śaivite Sects.* New Delhi, Thomson Press. (Australian National University, Centre of Oriental Studies. Oriental Monograph Series 12.)

———. 1989. New Data on the Kāpālikas. In *Criminal Gods and Demon Devotees: Essays on the Guardians of Popular Hinduism*, edited by Alf Hiltebeitel, pp. 231–238. Albany, SUNY Press.

Loseries, Andrea. 1990. Charnel-Ground Traditions in Tibet. Paper for the International Seminar on Anthropology of Tibet and the Himalayas, Völkerkundemuseum der Universität Zürich, September 21–28, 1990.

Macdonald, Alexander W. 1967. *Matériaux pour l'Étude de la Littérature Populaire Tibétaine, I. Édition et Traduction de Deux Manuscrits Tibétains des*

'*Histories du Cadavre*.' Paris, Presses Universitaires de France. (Annales du Musée Guimet, Bibliotheque d'Études 72.)

———. 1973. The Lama and the General. *Kailash* 1(3):225–236.

———. 1980a. The Writing of Buddhist History in the Sherpa Area of Nepal. In *Studies in History of Buddhism*, edited by A. K. Narian, pp. 121–131. Delhi.

———. 1980b. The Coming of Buddhism to the Sherpa Area of Nepal. *AOH* 34(1–3:139–146.

———. 1981. The Autobiography of a 20th Century Rnying-ma-pa Lama. *JIABS* 4(2):63–75.

———. 1986. Points de Vues sur Halase, un Lieu de Pèlerinage de l'Est du Népal. *La Nouvelle Revue Tibétaine* 13 (March):21–38.

———. 1987a. (editor). Rituels Himalayens. Special issue of *L'Ethnographie* 83(100–101).

———. 1987b. Remarks on the Manipulation of Power and Authority in the High Himalaya. *TJ* 12(1):3–16.

Macdonald, Ariane. See Spanien, Ariane.

Mandelbaum, David G. 1966. Transcendental and Pragmatic Aspects of Religion. *American Anthropologist* 68:1174–1191.

Manzardo, Andrew E. 1982. Impression Management and Economic Growth: The Case of the Thakalis of Dhaulagiri Zone. *Kailash* 9(1): 45–60.

Maraini, Fosco. 1951. *Secret Tibet*. London, Hutchinson.

March, Kathryn S. 1977. Of People and Naks: The Management and Meaning of High Altitude Herding among Contemporary Solu Sherpas. *Contributions to Nepalese Studies* 4(2):83–97.

———. 1987. Hospitality, Women, and the Efficacy of Beer. *Food and Foodways* 1:351–387.

Marko, Ana. 1985. Earth Spirits, or *kLu*, in Ladakh: Buddhist Monks and the Agricultural Cycle. Paper for the Australian Anthropological Society conference, Darwin, August 1985.

———. 1988. Civilising Woman the Demon: A Tibetan Myth of the State. Typescript.

———. in press. *Cham:* Ritual as Myth in a Ladakhi Gompa. In *Tantra and Popular Religion in Tibet*, edited by Geoffrey Samuel. New Delhi, Aditya Prakashan.

Marks, Thomas A. 1977a. Historical Observations on Buddhism in Bhutan. *TJ* 2(2):74–91.

———. 1977b. History and Religion in the Ladakhi Kingdom. *TJ* 2(2): 38–56.

Martin, Dan. 1985. Pearls from Bones—Relics, Chortens, Tertons and the Signs of Saintly Death in Tibet. Typescript (April 1985 version).

———. 1986. Human Body Good Thought (Mi Lus Bsam Legs) and the Revelation of the Secret Bonpo Mother Tantras. Master's thesis, Uralic and Altaic Studies, University of Indiana.

———. 1987. Illusion Web: Locating the *Guhyagarbha Tantra* in Buddhist Intellectual History. In *Silver on Lapis: Tibetan Literary Culture and History*, edited by Christopher I. Beckwith, pp. 175–220. Bloomington, Indiana, The Tibet Society.

———. 1990. Anthropology on the Boundary and the Boundary in Anthropology. *Human Studies* 13:119–145.

———. n.d. Bonpo Canons and Jesuit Cannons: On Some Sectarian Factors Involved in the Ch'ien-lung Emperor's Second Gold Stream Expedition of 1771–76 Based Primarily on Tibetan Sources. Typescript.

Matics, Marion L. 1970. *Entering the Path of Enlightenment: The Bodhicaryavatara of the Buddhist Poet Santideva*. New York, Macmillan.

Matsunaga, Daigan, and Alicia Matsunaga. 1974. The Concept of Upāya in Mahāyāna Buddhist Philosophy. *Japanese J. of Religious Studies* 1(1): 51–72.

Matsunaga, Yukei (ed). 1965. *Studies of Esoteric Buddhism and Tantrism in Commemoration of the 1150th Anniversary of the Founding of Koyasan*. Koyasan, Koyasan University Press.

Matsunaga, Yukei. 1977. A History of Tantric Buddhism in India with Reference to Chinese Translations. In *Buddhist Thought and Asian Civilization: Essays in Honor of Herbert V. Guenther on His Sixtieth Birthday*, edited by Leslie S. Kawamura and Keith Scott, pp. 167–181. Emeryville, California, Dharma Publishing.

Mayer, Adrian C. 1981. *Culture and Morality: Essays in Honour of Christoph von Fürer-Haimendorf*. Delhi, Oxford University Press.

McLeod, Ken. 1974. *A Direct Path to Enlightenment by 'Jam-mGon Kong-sPrul the Great*. Vancouver, B.C., Kagyu Kunkhyab Choling.

Mehra, Parshotam. 1976. *Tibetan Polity*, 1904–37*: The Conflict between the 13th Dalai Lama and the 9th Panchen*. Wiesbaden, Otto Harrassowitz. (Asiatische Forschungen 40.)

Mendelson, E. Michael. 1975. *Sangha and State in Burma: A Study of Monastic Sectarianism and Leadership*. Ithaca, New York, Cornell University Press.

Michael, Franz. 1982. *Rule by Incarnation: Tibetan Buddhism and Its Role in Society and State*. Boulder, Colorado, Westview Press.

———. 1986. Traditional Tibetan Polity and Its Potential for Modernization. *TJ* 11(4):70–78.

Migot, André. 1957. *Tibetan Marches*. Harmondsworth, Penguin.

Miller, Beatrice D. 1956. Ganye and Kidu: Two Formalized Systems of Mutual Aid among the Tibetans. *Southwestern J. of Anthropology* 12:157–170.

———. 1980. Views of Women's Roles in Buddhist Tibet. In *Studies in History of Buddhism*, edited by A. K. Narain, pp. 155–166. Delhi.

———. 1987. A Response to Goldstein's 'Reexamining Choice, Dependency and Command.' *TJ* 12(2):65–67.

Moerman, Michael. 1965. Ethnic Identification in a Complex Civilization: Who Are the Lue? *American Anthropologist* 67:1215–1230.

Morgan, D. O. 1982. Who Ran the Mongol Empire? *JRAS* 2:124–136.

Mulder, Neils. 1985. *Everyday Life in Thailand: An Interpretation*. 2d edition. Bangkok, Duang Kamol.

Mullin, Glenn H. 1978. *Essence of Refined Gold, by the Third Dalai Lama, with Related Texts by the Second and Seventh Dalai Lamas*. Translated by Glenn Mullin. Dharamasala, Tushita.

———. 1982a. *Bridging the Sutras and Tantras: A Collection of Ten Minor Works by Gyalwa Gendun Drub, the First Dalai Lama*. Ithaca, New York, Gabriel/Snow Lion.

———. 1982b. *Songs of Spiritual Change* [*by*] *Gyalwa Kalzang Gyats'o, the Seventh Dalai Lama*. Ithaca, New York, Gabriel/Snow Lion.

———. 1983. *Meditations on the Lower Tantras from the Collected Works of the Previous Dalai Lamas*. Dharamsala, LTWA.

———. 1985. *Selected Works of the Dalai Lama II*. Ithaca, Snow Lion.

———. 1987. *Death and Dying. The Tibetan Tradition*. London, Arkana.

———. 1988. *Path of the Bodhisattva Warrior: The Life and Teachings of the Thirteenth Dalai Lama*. Ithaca, New York, Snow Lion.

Mumford, Stan R. 1989. *Himalayan Dialogue: Tibetan Lamas and Gurung Shamans in Nepal*. Madison, University of Wisconsin Press.

Murti, T. R. V. 1970. *The Central Philosophy of Buddhism: A Study of the Madhyamika System*. 2d edition. London, Allen and Unwin.

Muses, Charles Arthur. 1961. *Esoteric Teachings of the Tibetan Tantra*. Lausanne, Aurora Press.

Nakane, Chie. 1966. A Plural Society in Sikkim. In *Caste and Kin in Nepal, India and Ceylon: Anthropological Studies in Hindu-Buddhist Contact Zones*, edited by Christoph von Fürer-Haimendorf, pp. 213–263. London, Asia Publishing House.

Namgyal, Jamyang. 1973. Review Article on Rolf A. Stein, *Vie et Chants de 'Brug-pa Kun- legs le Yogin*. *Kailash* 1(1):91–99.

Nebesky-Wojkowitz, René de. 1956. *Oracles and Demons of Tibet: The Cult and Iconography of the Tibetan Protective Deities*. The Hague, Mouton.

———. 1976. *Tibetan Religious Dances*. The Hague, Mouton.

Ngorchen Konchog Lhundrub. 1987. *The Beautiful Ornament of the Three Visions*. Singapore, Golden Vase.

Norboo, Samten. 1977. Life and Works of Gedun Chophel. *TR* 12(6):12–13, 16.

Norbu, Dawa. 1974. *Red Star over Tibet.* London, Collins.

Norbu, Jamyang. 1986. *Warriors of Tibet. The Story of Aten and the Khampas' Fight for the Freedom of Their Country.* London, Wisdom.

Norbu, Namkhai. 1966. Appendix II: p'o lha, p'ug lha, rluṅ rta. In *Tibetan Folk Songs,* 2d edition, edited by Giuseppe Tucci, pp. 155–194. Ascona, Artibus Asiae.

———. 1981. *The Necklace of gZi: A Cultural History of Tibet.* Dharamsala, Information Office of H. H. the Dalai Lama.

———. 1983. *A Journey into the Culture of Tibetan Nomads: Bod 'brog gi shes rigs.* Arcidosso, Shang-Shung Edizioni.

———. 1986a. *Talks in California, USA* 1979, 1980. Conway, Massachusetts, Tsegyelgar Dzogchen Community.

———. 1986b. *The Crystal and the Way of Light: Sūtra, Tantra and Dzogchen,* compiled and edited by John Shane. New York and London, Routledge and Kegan Paul.

———. 1986c. *The Little Song of 'Do as You Please.'* Arcidosso, Shang-Shung Edizioni.

———. 1988. 'Il canto dell'energia' di Nyag-bla Padma Bdud-'dul. In *Orientalia Iosephi Tucci Memoriae Dicata,* 3 vols. (1985–1988), edited by G. Gnoli and L. Lanciotti, vol. 3, pp. 1021–1028. Roma, IsMEO. (SER 56 1–3.)

———. 1990a. *Viaggio nella Cultura dei Nomadi Tibetani.* Merigar, Arcidosso, GR, Shang-Shung Edizioni.

———. 1990b. *Rigbai Kujyug. The Six Vajra Verses.* An oral commentary by Namkhai Norbu edited by Cheh-Ngee Goh. Singapore, Rinchen Editions.

Norbu, Namkhai, and Kennard Lipman. 1987. *Primordial Experience: An Introduction to rDzogs-chen Meditation.* Boston, Shambhala.

Norbu, Thinley. 1984. *The Practice of the Essence of the Sublime Heart Jewel. View, Meditation and Action. The Propitious Speech from the Beginning, Middle and End by Patrul Rinpoche translated by Thinley Norbu.* New York, Thinley Norbu.

Norbu, Thubten J. 1982. Festivals of Tibet. *J. Popular Culture* 16(1):126–134.

Norbu, Thubten J., and R. B. Ekvall. 1969. *gCung Po Don Yod: A Tibetan Play.* Bloomington, Indiana University Press for International Affairs Center.

Norbu, Thubten J., and H. Harrer. 1960. *Tibet is My Country.* London, Rupert Hart-Davis.

Norbu, Thubten J., and Colin Turnbull. 1969. *Tibet: Its History, Religion and People*. London, Chatto and Windus.

Nowak, Margaret. 1980. Change and Differentiation in Tibetan Sex Roles: The New Adult Generation in India. In *Tibetan Studies in Honour of Hugh Richardson. Proceedings of the International Seminar on Tibetan Studies, Oxford* 1979, edited by Michael Aris and Aung San Suu Kyi, pp. 219–225. Warminster, Aris and Phillips. [= Proceedings of 2d Seminar of IATS.]

Nyanaponika Thera. 1969. *The Heart of Buddhist Meditation*. London, Rider.

Obermiller, E. 1932–1933. *History of Buddhism (Chos-ḥbyung by Bu-ston)*. 2 vols. Heidelberg, in Kommission bei Otto Harrassowitz, Leipzig.

Obeyesekere, Gananath, 1966. The Buddhist Pantheon in Ceylon and Its Extensions. In *Anthropological Studies in Theravada Buddhism*, edited by Manning Nash, pp. 1–26. Yale University, Southeast Asia Studies.

———. 1977. Social Change and the Deities: Rise of the Kataragama Cult in Modern Sri Lanka. *Man* 12:377–396.

———. 1990. *The Work of Culture: Symbolic Transformation in Psychoanalysis and Anthropology*. Chicago University Press.

Olschak, Blanche C., and Geshé Thupten Wangyal. 1987. *Mystic Art of Ancient Tibet*. Boston and London, Shambhala.

Oppitz, Michael. 1968. *Geschichte und Sozialordnung der Sherpa*. Innsbruck and München, Universitätsverlag Wagner. (Khumbu Himal 8.)

———. 1974. Myths and Facts: Reconsidering Some Data Concerning the Clan History of the Sherpa. *Kailash* 2(1–2:121–132.

Orofino, Giacomella. 1990. *Sacred Tibetan Teachings on Death and Liberation*. Bridport, Prism and Garden City Park, New York, Unity.

Ortner, Sherry B. (= Sherry Ortner Paul). 1970. Food for Thought: A Key Symbol in Sherpa Culture. Ph.D. dissertation, University of Chicago.

———. 1973. Sherpa Purity. *American Anthropologist* 75:49ff.

———. 1978a. *Sherpas Through Their Rituals*. Cambridge University Press.

———. 1978b. The White-Black Ones: The Sherpa View of Human Nature. In *Himalayan Anthropology: The Indo-Tibetan Interface*, edited by James F. Fisher, pp. 263–286. The Hague, Mouton.

———. 1978c. The Decline of Sherpa Shamanism: On the Role of Meaning in History. Typescript.

———. 1989a. *High Religion: A Cultural and Political History of Sherpa Buddhism*. Princeton, New Jersey, Princeton University Press.

———. 1989b. Cultural Politics: Religious Activism and Ideological Transformation among 20th Century Sherpas. *Dialectical Anthropology* 14:197–211.

Pallis, Marco. 1974. *Peaks and Lamas*. London, Woburn Press.
Paltul Jampal Lodoe, Lama. n.d. *Record of Nyingmapa Monasteries in Tibet: Bod na bzhugs pa'i rnying ma'i dgon deb*. Dalhousie, HP, Indestructible Sacred Word Printing Press.
Parmee, Edward A. 1972. *Kham and Amdo of Tibet*. New Haven, Human Relations Area Files.
Parpola, Asko. 1988. The Coming of the Aryans to Iran and India and the Cultural and Ethnic Identity of the Dāsas. *Studia Orientalia (Helsinki)* 64:195–302.
Paul, Robert A. 1970. Sherpas and Their Religion. Ph.D. dissertation, University of Chicago.
———. 1976. Some Observations on Sherpa Shamanism. In *Spirit Possession in the Nepal Himalayas*, edited by John T. Hitchcock and Rex L. Jones, pp. 141–151. Warminster, Aris and Phillips.
———. 1979. Dumje: Paradox and Resolution in Sherpa Ritual Symbolism. *American Ethnologist* 6:274–304.
———. 1982a. Fire and Ice: The Psychology of a Sherpa Shaman. Typescript.
———. 1982b. *The Tibetan Symbolic World: Psychoanalytic Explorations*. Chicago, University of Chicago Press.
———. 1984. Recruitment to Monasticism among the Sherpas. Typescript.
———. 1990. Act and Intention in Sherpa Culture and Society. Typescript.
Petech, Luciano. [1950] 1973a. *China and Tibet in the Early Eighteenth Century: The History of the Establishment of the Chinese Protectorate in Tibet*. Westport, Connecticut, Hyperion Press. (T'oung Pao Monographs 1.)
———. 1973b. *Aristocracy and Government in Tibet (1728–1959)*. Roma, IsMEO. (SER 45.)
———. 1977. *The Kingdom of Ladakh: c.950–1842 A.D.* Roma, IsMEO. (SER 51.)
———. 1978. The *'Bri-guṅ-pa* Sect in Western Tibet and Ladakh. In *Proceedings of the Csoma de Körős Memorial Symposium Held at Mátrafüred, Hungary, 24–30 September 1976*, edited by Louis Ligeti, pp. 313–326. Budapest, Akadémiai Kiadó.
———. 1988. Yüan Organization of the Tibetan Border Areas. In *Tibetan Studies. Proceedings of the 4th Seminar of the International Association for Tibetan Studies. Schloss Hohenkammer—Munich 1985*, edited by Helga Uebach and Jampa L. Panglung, pp. 369–380. Kommission für Zentralasiatische Studien, Bayerische Akademie der Wissenschaften.
Peter, HRH Prince, of Greece and Denmark. 1952. The Moslems of Central Tibet. *JRCAS* 39(3–4):233–240.
———. 1954. *The Aristocracy of Central Tibet*. Kalimpong, G. Tharchin.
———. 1978a. Tibetan Oracles in Dharamsala. In *Proceedings of the Csoma de Körős Memorial Symposium Held at Mátrafüred, Hungary, 24–30 September*

1976, edited by Louis Ligeti, pp. 327–334. Budapest, Akadémiai Kiadó.

———. 1978b. Tibetan Oracles. In *Himalayan Anthropology: The Indo-Tibetan Interface,* edited by James F. Fisher, pp. 287–298. The Hague, Mouton.

———. 1979. Tibetan Oracles. *TJ* 4(2):51–56.

Phylactou, Maria. 1989. Household Organization and Marriage in Ladakh-Indian Himalaya. Ph.D. dissertation, London School of Economics and Political Science.

Pommaret, Françoise. 1989. *Les Revenants de l'Au-delà dans le Monde Tibétain.* Paris, Éditions du CNRS.

———. 1989. Les Revenants de l'Au-delà ('das-log): Sources Littéraires et Traditions Vivantes. Paper given at the 5th Seminar of IATS, Narita, August 27 to September 2, 1989.

Pott, P. H. 1965. Some Remarks on the 'Terrific Deities' in Tibetan 'Devil Dances.' In *Studies of Esoteric Buddhism and Tantrism in Commemoration of the* 1150*th Anniversary of the Founding of Koyasan,* edited by Yukei Matsunaga, pp. 269–278. Koyasan, Koyasan University Press.

Prats, Ramon. 1978. The Spiritual Lineage of the Dzogchen Tradition. In *Tibetan Studies Presented at the Seminar of Young Tibetologists, Zurich, June* 26*–July* 1, 1977, edited by Martin Brauen and Per Kvaerne, pp. 199–208. Völkerkundemuseum der Universität Zurich. [= *Proceedings* of 1st Seminar of IATS.]

Pye, Michael. 1978. *Skilful Means: A Concept in Mahayana Buddhism.* London, Duckworth.

Rabten, Geshe. 1978. A Guide to the 'Lamp for the Path.' In *Mahāyāna Texts on the Graded Path,* pp. 27–62. Dharamsala, HP, Dharmakaya.

———. 1980. *The Life and Teachings of Geshe Rabten: A Tibetan Lama's Search for Truth.* London, Allen and Unwin.

Rahul, Ram. 1969. *The Government and Politics of Tibet.* Delhi, Vikas.

———. 1971. *Modern Bhutan.* Delhi, Vikas.

Ramble, Charles. 1982. Status and Death: Mortuary Rites and Attitudes to the Body in a Tibetan Village. *Kailash* 9(4):333–360.

———. 1983. The Founding of a Tibetan Village: The Popular Transformation of History. *Kailash* 10(3–40):267–290.

———. 1985. The Lamas of Lubra: Tibetan Bonpo Householder Priests in Western Nepal. D.Phil. dissertation, Oxford.

Ramble, Charles A. E., and Michael Vinding. 1987. The Bem-chag Village Record and the Early History of Mustang District. *Kailash* 13(1–2): 5–48.

Ramesan, N. 1962. *Temples and Legends of Andhra Pradesh.* Bombay, Bharatiya Vidya Bhavan.

Rao, P. Raghunadha. 1978. *Sikkim: The Story of Its Integration with India.* New Delhi, Cosmo.

Rapson, E. J. 1962. *The Cambridge History of India: Volume* 1. Delhi, S. Chand.

Rato Khyongla Nawang Losang. 1977. *My Life and Lives: The Story of a Tibetan Incarnation.* New York, Dutton.

Rauber, Hanna. 1980. The Humli-Khyampas of Far Western Nepal: A Study in Ethnogenesis. *Contributions to Nepalese Studies* 8(1):57–82.

———. 1987a. Stages of Women's Life among Tibetan Nomadic Traders: The Humli- Khyampa of Far Western Nepal. *Ethnos* 1–2:200–228.

———. 1987b. Trade in Far West Nepal: The Economic Adaptation of the Peripatetic Humli-Khyampa. In *The Other Nomads,* edited by Aparna Rao, pp. 65–87. Vienna, Böhlau.

Rechung Rinpoche Jampal Kunzang, Ven. 1973. *Tibetan Medicine Illustrated in Original Texts.* London, Wellcome Institute of the History of Medicine.

Reinhard, Johan. 1978. Khembalung: The Hidden Valley. *Kailash* 6(1):5–36.

Reynolds, John Myrdhin. (= Vajranatha). 1988. The Nine Ways of Bon.' *Bönpo Bulletin* 1:1–3.

———. 1989. *Self-Liberation through Seeing with Naked Awareness.* Foreword by Namkhai Norbu. New York, Station Hill Press.

Reynolds, John Myrdhin (= Vajranatha), and Lynne Klapecki. 1978. *Tibetan Astrological Calendar and Almanac.* Boudha, Kathmandu, Kalachakra Publications.

Rhoton, J. R. 1985. A Study of the sDom-gSum of Sa Paṇ. Ph.D. dissertation, Columbia University.

Ribbach, S. H. 1986. *Culture and Society in Ladakh.* Translated from the German by John Bray. New Delhi, Ess Ess.

Riccardi, Theodore, Jr. 1971. *A Nepali Version of the Vetālapañcaviṃśati.* New Haven, American Oriental Soc. (American Oriental Series 54.)

Richardson, Hugh E. 1958–1959. The Karma.pa Sect: A Historical Note. *JRAS* 1958:139–164, 1959:1–18.

———. 1973. The sKar-cung Inscription. *JRAS* 1973(1):12–20.

———. 1977a. Ministers of the Tibetan Kingdom. *TJ* 2(1):10–27.

———. 1977b. 'The Dharma that Came Down from Heaven': A Tun-Huang Fragment. In *Buddhist Thought and Asian Civilization: Essays in Honor of Herbert V. Guenther on His Sixtieth Birthday,* edited by Leslie S. Kawamura and Keith Scott, pp. 219–230. Emeryville, California, Dharma Publishing.

———. [1962] 1984. *Tibet and Its History.* 2d edition, revised and updated. Boulder and London, Shambhala.

———. 1985. *A Corpus of Early Tibetan Inscriptions*. London, Royal Asiatic Society. [Incorporates Richardson 1973.]

———. 1986. *Adventures of a Tibetan Fighting Monk*, compiled by H. Richardson, edited by T. Skorupski. Bangkok, Tamarind Press.

Rijnhart, Susie C. 1901. *With the Tibetans in Tent and Temple*. Cincinnati, Foreign Christian Missionary Society.

Ringu Tulku. 1976. Zog-chen gon-pa. *TJ* 1(3–4):85–86.

Rizvi, Janet. 1983. *Ladakh: Crossroads of High Asia*. Delhi, Oxford University Press.

Robinson, James B. 1979. *Buddha's Lions: The Lives of the Eight-Four Siddhas*. Berkeley, Dharma.

Robinson, Richard H., and Willard L. Johnson. 1977. *The Buddhist Religion: A Historical Introduction*. 2d edition. Encino, California, Dickenson.

Rock, Joseph F. 1925. The Land of the Yellow Lama. *National Geographic* 47 (April):447–491.

———. 1926. Through the Great River Trenches of Asia. *National Geographic* 50(2) (August):133–186.

———. 1928. Life among the Lamas of Choni. *National Geographic* 54 (November):584–619.

———. 1931. Kongka Risumgongba, Holy Mountain of the Outlaws. *National Geographic* 60(1) (July):1–65.

———. 1935. Sungmas, the Living Oracles of the Tibetan Church. *National Geographic* 58 (October):475–486.

———. 1956. *The Amnye Ma-Chhen Range and Adjacent Regions: A Monographic Study*. Rome, IsMEO. (SER 12.)

Rockhill, William W. 1891. *The Land of the Lamas: Notes of a Journey through China, Mongolia and Tibet*. New York, Century.

———. 1894. *Diary of a Journey through Mongolia and Thibet in* 1891 *and* 1892. Washington, Smithsonian Institution.

Roerich, George N. (= Yu.N. Rerikh). 1959. *Biography of Dharmasvāmin (Chag lo-tsa-ba Chos-rje-dpal). A Tibetan Monk Pilgrim*. Patna, K. P. Jayaswal Research Institute.

———. 1973. Mongol-Tibetan Relations in the 13th and 14th Centuries. *Tibet Society Bulletin* 6:40–55.

———. 1976. *The Blue Annals*. 2d edition. Delhi, Motilal Banarsidass.

Rudolph, Susanne H. 1987. Presidential Address: State Formation in Asia—Prolegomenon to a Comparative Study. *JAS* 46(4):731–746.

Ruegg, D. Seyfort. 1963. The Jo naṅ pas: A School of Buddhist Ontologists According to the *Grub mtha' śel gyi me loṅ*. *JAOS* 83(1):73–91.

———. 1966. *The Life of Bu ston Rin po che with the Tibetan Text of the Bu ston rNam thar*. Roma, IsMEO. (SER 34.)

———. 1969. *La Théorie du Tathāgatagarbha et du Gotra. Études sur la Sotereologie et la Gnoseologie du Bouddhisme.* Paris, École Française d'Extrême-Orient. (École Française d'Extrême-Orient, Publications 70.)

———. 1973. *Le Traité du Tathāgatagarbha de Bu Ston Rin Chen Grub.* Paris, École Française d'Extrême-Orient.

———. 1981. *The Literature of the Madhyamaka School of Buddhist Philosophy in India.* Wiesbaden, Otto Harrassowitz. (*A History of Indian Literature* 7[1].)

———. 1989. A Tibetan's Odyssey: A Review Article. *JRAS* 2:304–311.

Russell, Jeremy. 1986. A Brief History of the Taglung Kagyu. *Chö-Yang* 1(1):120–127.

Sacherer, Janice M. 1974. Sherpas of the Rolwaling Valley: Human Adaptation to a Harsh Mountain Environment. *Objets et Mondes* 14(4):317–324.

———. 1977. The Sherpas of Rolwaling: A Hundred Years of Economic Change. *Himalaya: Écologie-Ethnologie,* pp. 289–294. Paris, CNRS.

Sagant, P. 1981. La Tête Haute: Maison, Rituel et Politique au Népal Oriental. In *L'Homme et la maison en Himalaya,* edited by G. Toffin, pp. 149–180. Éditions du CNRS.

Sakaki, R. (ed.) [1916] 1962. *Mahāvyutpatti.* Suzuki Research Foundation. (Reprint Series 1.)

Sakya, Jamyang, and Julie Emery. 1990. *Princess in the Land of Snows: The Life of Jamyang Sakya in Tibet.* Boston, Shambhala.

Samdup, Kazi Dawa. 1919. *Srichakrasambhara Tantra.* (Tantrik Texts 7.) London and Calcutta.

Samuel, Geoffrey. 1975. The Crystal Rosary: Insight and Method in an Anthropological Study of Tibetan Religion. Ph.D. dissertation, Social Anthropology, University of Cambridge.

———. 1982. Tibet as a Stateless Society and Some Islamic Parallels. *JAS* 41(2):215–229.

———. 1985. Early Buddhism in Tibet: Some Anthropological Perspectives. In *Soundings in Tibetan Civilization,* edited by Barbara Aziz and Matthew Kapstein, pp. 383–397. New Delhi, Manohar. [*Proceedings* of 3d Seminar of IATS.]

———. 1989. The Body in Buddhist and Hindu Tantra. *Religion* 19: 197–210.

———. 1990. *Mind, Body and Culture: Anthropology and the Biological Interface.* Cambridge University Press.

———. In press a. Gesar of Ling: The Origins and Meaning of the East Tibetan Epic. To be published in *Proceedings* of the 5th Seminar of the IATS, Narita, Japan, August 27 to September 2, 1989.

———. In press b. Music and Shamanic Power in the Gesar Epic. To be published in *Metaphor: A Musical Dimension*, edited by Jamie Kassler. Sydney, Currency Press.

———. In press c. (ed.) *Tantra and Popular Religion in Tibet*. New Delhi, Aditya Prakashan.

———. In press d. Gesar of Ling: Shamanic Power and Popular Religion. To be published in *Tantra and Popular Religion in Tibet*, edited by Geoffrey Samuel. New Delhi, Aditya Prakashan.

Sangay, Thubten. 1984a. Tibetan Traditions of Childbirth and Childcare. *Tibetan Medicine* 7:3–24.

———. 1984b. Tibetan Rituals of the Dead. *Tibetan Medicine* 7:30–40.

Sannella, Lee. 1981. *Kundalini-Psychosis or Transcendence?* San Francisco, H. S. Dakin.

Schenk, Amelie. 1990. Ladakhische Orakelheiler. Paper for the International Seminar on Anthropology of Tibet and the Himalayas, Völkerkundemuseum der Universität Zürich, September 21–28, 1990.

Schicklgruber, Christian. 1989. Grib: On the Significance of the Term in a Socio-Religious Context. Paper given at the 5th Seminar of the IATS, Narita, August 27 to September 2, 1989.

———. 1990. Remarks on the Kinship System of the Khumbo (NE Nepal). Paper for the International Seminar on Anthropology of Tibet and the Himalayas, Völkerkundemuseum der Universität Zürich, September 21–28, 1990.

Schrader, Heiko. 1987. Trading Patterns in the Nepal Himalayas: The Case of Walongchung Gola. *Internationales Asienforum* 18(3–4):253–278.

Schram, Louis M. J. 1954. *The Monguors of the Kansu-Tibetan Frontier: Their Origin, History, and Social Organization*. Philadelphia, American Philosophical Society. (*Transactions* n.s. 44(1).)

Schuh, Dieter. 1976. Der Schauspieler des tibetischen Lha-mo Theaters. *Zeitschrift für Asiatische Studien* 10:339–384.

———. 1983. Frühe Beziehungen zwischen dem ladakhischen Herrscherhaus und der südlichen 'Brug-pa Schule. *Archiv für Zentralasiatische Geschichtsforschung* 2:27–68.

———. (ed.). 1985. *Tibetische Handschriften und Blockdrucke. Teil* 9. Beschrieben von Peter Schwieger. Wiesbaden, Franz Steiner.

———. 1988. *Das Archiv des Klosters bKra-šis-bsam-gtan-glin von sKyid-gron*. Teil 1. Bonn, VGH Wissenschaftsverlag.

Schuttler, Anneliese, and Peter Schuttler. 1980. *Ladakh und Zanskar: Lamaistische Klosterkultur im Land zwischen Indien und Tibet*. Köln, DuMont.

Schwalbe, Kurt J. 1979. The Construction and Religious Meaning of the Buddhist Stūpa in Solo Khumbu, Nepal. Ph.D. dissertation, Graduate Theological Union, Berkeley.

Schwieger, Peter. 1978. *Ein tibetisches Wunschgebet um Wiedergeburt in der Suk-*

hāvatī. St. Augustin, VGH Wissenschaftsverlag. (Beiträge zur Zentralasienforschung 1.)
———. 1988. The Biographies of the Grand Lamas of Dagyab (Brag-g.yab) as a Contribution to the History of East Tibet. In *Tibetan Studies. Proceedings of the 4th Seminar of the International Association for Tibetan Studies. Schloss Hohenkammer—Munich* 1985, edited by Helga Uebach and Jampa L. Panglung, pp. 435–438. Kommission für Zentralasiatische Studien, Bayerische Akademie der Wissenschaften.
Schwieger, Peter, and Loden Sherap Dagyab. 1989. *Die ersten dGe-lugs-pa-Hierarchen von Brag-g.yab (1572–1692)*. Bonn, VGH Wissenschaftsverlag.
Sermey Ribur Tulku (Ser smad ri 'bur sprul sku). 1988. *dGe sdig las kyi myong ba. Deb dang po*. Dharamsala, Tibetan Cultural Printing Press
Shakabpa, W. D. 1967. *Tibet: A Political History*. New Haven, Yale University Press.
Shastri, Jampa Samten. 1987. Notes on the Lithang Edition of the Tibetan bKa'-'gyur. *Tibet Journal* 12(3):17–40.
Shelton, Flora Beal. 1912. *Sunshine and Shadow on the Tibetan Borderland*. Cincinnati, Foreign Christian Missionary Society.
Sherburne, Richard. 1983. *A Lamp for the Path and Commentary by Atīśa*. London, Allen and Unwin.
Sherpa Tulku. 1984. Kyabje Yongdzin Ling Dorjechang. *Wisdom* 2:38–40.
Sherpa Tulku, et al. 1977. The Structure of the Ge-lug Monastic Order. *TJ* 2(3):67–71.
Sherpa Tulku, and Alexander Berzin. 1981. The Full Six-Session Yoga. In *Kalachakra Initiation: Madison*, 1981. Madison, Deer Park.
Siiger, Halfdan. 1967. *The Lepchas: Culture and Religion of a Himalayan People*. Copenhagen, National Museum of Denmark.
———. 1976. Two Indigenous Peoples of the Hindukush-Himalayan Regions. *Temenos* 12:93–99.
Simonsson, Nils. 1957. *Indo-tibetische Studien: Die Methoden der tibetischer Übersetzer, untersucht im Hinblick auf die Bedeutung ihrer Übersetzungen für die Sanskritphilologie*. Uppsala, Almqvist and Wiksells.
Singh, H. 1977. Territorial Organization of Gompas in Ladakh. *Himalaya: Écologie- Ethnologie*, pp. 351–370. Paris, CNRS.
Singh Nepali, Gopal. 1965. *The Newars: An Ethno-Sociological Study of a Himalayan Community*. Bombay, United Asia Publications.
Skorupski, Tadeusz. 1981. Tibetan g-Yung Drung Monastery at Dolanji. *Kailash* 8(1–2):25–44.
———. 1982. The Cremation Ceremony according to the Byang-gter Tradition. *Kailash* 9(4):361–376.

———. 1983. *The Sarvadurgatipariśodhana Tantra, Elimination of All Evil Destinies.* Delhi, Motilal Banarsidass.

Skorupski, Tadeusz, and Krystyna Cech. 1984. Major Tibetan Life Cycle Events—Birth and Marriage Ceremonies. *Kailash* 11(1–2):5–32.

Smith, E. Gene. 1968a. Foreword. In *Tibetan Chronicle of Padma-dKar-po,* edited by Lokesh Chandra, pp. 1–8. New Delhi, IAIC. (SP 75.)

———. 1968b. Introduction. In *The Autobiography and Diaries of Si-tu Paṇ-chen,* editedby Lokesh Chandra, pp. 1–23. New Delhi, IAIC. (SP 77.)

———Smith, E. Gene. 1969a. Preface. In *The Autobiographical Reminiscences of Ngag- dBang-Dpal-bZang, Late Abbot of Kaḥ-Thog Monastery,* edited by Sonam Topgay Kazi, pp. 1–20. Gangtok, Sonam T. Kazi. (Ngagyur Nyingmay Sungrab 1.)

———. 1969b. Preface. In *The Life of the Saint of Gtsaṅ by Rgod-tshaṅ-ras-pa Sna-tshogs-raṅ-grol,* edited by Lokesh Chandra, pp. 1–37. New Delhi, IAIC. (SP 79.)

———. 1969c. Introduction. In *A 15th Century Tibetan Compendium of Knowledge,* edited by Lokesh Chandra, pp. 1–32. New Delhi, IAIC. (SP 78.)

———. 1970a. Introduction. In *Kongtrul's Encyclopaedia of Indo-Tibetan Culture, Parts* 1–3, edited by Lokesh Chandra, pp. 1–87. New Delhi, IAIC. (SP 80.)

———. 1970b. Introduction. In *dKar brgyud gser 'phreng. A Golden Rosary of Lives of Eminent Gurus,* compiled by Mon-rtse-pa Kun-dga'-dpal-ldan and edited by Kun- dga'-'brug-dpal, pp. 1–13. Leh, Sonam W. Tashigang. (Smanrtsis Shesrig Spendzod 3.)

———. 1971. Introduction. In *On the History of the Monastery of Zhwa-lu. Being the Texts of the Zhwa lu gdan rabs and the Autobiography of Zhwa-lu-Ri-sbug Sprul-sku Blo-gsal-bstan-skyong,* pp. 1–3. Leh, Sonam W. Tashigang. (Smanrtsis Shesrig Spendzod 9.)

Snellgrove, David L. 1957. *Buddhist Himalaya.* Oxford, Bruno Cassirer.

———. 1959. *The Hevajra Tantra: A Critical Study.* 2 vols. London, Oxford University Press. (London Oriental Series 6.)

———. 1961. *Himalayan Pilgrimage.* Oxford, Bruno Cassirer.

———. 1967a. *The Nine Ways of Bon: Excerpts from gZi brjid.* London, Oxford University Press. (London Oriental Series 18.)

———. 1967b. *Four Lamas of Dolpo.* 2 vols. Oxford, Bruno Cassirer.

———. 1979. Place of the Pilgrimage in Thag (Thakkola). *Kailash* 7(2): 73–170.

———. 1981. Introduction. In *Sarva-tathāgata-tattva-saṅgraha,* edited by Lokesh Chandra and David L. Snellgrove. New Delhi, IAIC. (SP 269.)

———. 1987. *Indo-Tibetan Buddhism: Indian Buddhists and Their Tibetan Successors.* 2 vols. Boston, Shambhala.

Snellgrove, David L., and Hugh E. Richardson. 1968. *A Cultural History of Tibet.* London, Weidenfeld and Nicolson.

Snellgrove, David L., and Tadeusz Skorupski. 1979. *The Cultural Heritage of Ladakh,* vol. 1. Warminster, Aris and Phillips.

———. 1980. *The Cultural Heritage of Ladakh,* vol. 2. Warminster, Aris and Phillips.

Snyder, Jeanette. 1979. A Preliminary Study of the Lha Mo. *Asian Music* 10(2):23–62.

Sopa, Geshe Lhundub, and Jeffrey Hopkins. 1976. *Practice and Theory of Tibetan Buddhism.* London, Rider.

Sopa, Geshe Lhundub, Roger Jackson, and John Newman. 1985. *The Wheel of Time: The Kalachakra in Context.* Madison, Wisconsin, Deer Park Books.

Sørensen, Per K. 1990. *Divinity Secularized. An Inquiry into the Nature and Form of the Songs Ascribed to the Sixth Dalai Lama.* Wien, Arbeitskreis für Tibetische und Buddhistische Studien, Universität Wien. (Wiener Studien zur Tibetologie und Buddhismuskunde 25.)

Southwold, Martin. 1983. *Buddhism in Life.* Manchester University Press.

Spanien (= Macdonald), Ariane D. (ed.). 1971a. *Études Tibétaines Dédiées à la Mémoire de Marcelle Lalou.* Paris, Adrien Maisonneuve. (Librairie d'Amérique et d'Orient.)

———. 1971b. Une Lecture des Pélliot Tibétain 1286, 1287, 1038, 1047, et 1290. Essai sur la Formation et l'Emploi des Mythes Politiques dans la Religion Royale de Sroṅ-bcan sgam-po. In *Études Tibétaines Dédiées à la Mémoire de Marcelle Lalou,* edited by Ariane Spanien, pp. 190–391. Paris, Adrien Maisonneuve. (Librairie d'Amérique et d'Orient.)

———. 1976. *Études tibétaines (Actes du XXIXe Congrès International des Orientalistes. Paris. Juillet* 1973*).* Paris.

Spanien, Ariane, and Yoshiro Imaeda. 1979. *Choix de Documents Tibétains Conservés à la Bibliothèque Nationale,* 2 vols. Paris, Bibliothèque Nationale.

Sperling, Elliot. 1976. The Chinese Venture in K'am, 1904–11, and the Role of Chao Erh-feng. *TJ* 1(2):10–36.

———. 1980. The 5th Karma-pa and Some Aspects of the Relationship between Tibet and the Early Ming. In *Tibetan Studies in Honour of Hugh Richardson. Proceedings of the International Seminar on Tibetan Studies, Oxford* 1979, edited by Michael Aris and Aung San Suu Kyi, pp. 280–289. Warminster, Aris and Phillips. [= Proceedings of 2d Seminar of IATS.]

Spiro, Melford E. 1967. *Burmese Supernaturalism: A Study in the Explanation and Reduction of Suffering.* Englewood Cliffs, New Jersey, Prentice-Hall. [Expanded edition, 1978, Philadelphia, Institute for the Study of Human Issues.]

———. 1971. *Buddhism and Society: A Great Tradition and its Burmese Vicissitudes*. London, Allen and Unwin.

Stablein, William G. 1976a. Mahākāla the Neo-Shaman: Master of the Ritual. In *Spirit Possession in the Nepal Himalayas*, edited by John T. Hitchcock and Rex L. Jones, pp. 361–375. Warminster, Aris and Phillips.

———. 1976b. The Mahākālatantra: A Theory of Ritual Blessings and Tantric Medicine. Ph.D. dissertation, Columbia University.

Stcherbatsky, T. n.d. *The Conception of Buddhist Nirvāṇa*. Revised and enlarged edition. Varanasi, Bharatiya Vidya Prakashan.

Stein, Rolf A. 1956 *L'Épopée Tibétaine de Gesar dans sa Version Lamaïque de Ling*. Paris, Presses Universitaires de France.

———. 1957. Le *Liṅga* des Danses Masquées Lamaïques et la Théorie des âmes. *Sino-Indian Studies* 5(3–4) *(Liebenthal Festschrift)*:200–234.

———. 1959a. *Recherches sur l'Épopée et le Barde du Tibet*. Paris, Presses Universitaires. (Bibliothèque de l'Institut des hautes Études Chinoises 13.)

———. 1959b. *Les Tribus Anciennes des Marches Sino-Tibétaines*. Paris. (Bibliothèque de l'Institut des Hautes Études Chinoises 15.)

———. 1971. Du Récit au Rituel dans les Manuscrits Tibétains du Touenhouang. In *Études Tibétaines Dédiées à la Mémoire de Marcelle Lalou*, edited by Ariane Spanien, pp. 479–547. Paris, Adrien Maisonneuve. (Librairie d'Amérique et d'Orient.)

———. 1972a. *Tibetan Civilization*. London, Faber.

———. 1972b. *Vie et Chants de 'Brug-pa Kun-legs le Yogin*. Paris, G.-P. Maisonneuve et Larose.

———. 1981. Introduction to the Gesar Epic. *TJ* 6:3–13.

———. 1985. Tibetica Antiqua III: A Propos du Mot *gcug-lag* et de la Religion Indigène. *BEFEO* 74:83–132.

———. 1988. Les Serments des Traités Sino-Tibétains (8e–9e Siècles). *T'oung Pao* 74(1–3):119–138.

Steinmann, Brigitte. 1987. *Les Tamang du Népal: Usages et Religion, Religion de l'Usage*. Paris, Éditions Recherche sur les Civilisations.

———. 1989. The Local Reinterpretation of a Nying ma pa Cycle among the Tamang of Nepal. Paper given at the 5th Seminar of the IATS, Narita, August 27 to September 2, 1989.

Stoddard, Heather (= Karmay). 1985a. *Le Mendiant de l'Amdo*. Paris, Société d'Ethnographie.

———. 1985b. dGe-'dun Chos-'phel: The Two Latest Versions of His Life Story. *TJ* 10(1):44–48.

Stott, David J. 1985. The History and Teachings of the Early Dwags-po bKa'-brgyud Tradition in India and Tibet. Ph.D. dissertation, Theology, University of Manchester.

Streng, Frederick J. 1967. *Emptiness: A Study in Religious Meaning.* Nashville, New York, Abingdon Press.
Strickland, Simon. 1983. The Gurung Priest as Bard. *Kailash* 10(3–4):227–266.
Stutchbury, Elisabeth. 1986. Rediscovering Western Tibet: Chopa of Karzha, Drukpa Kargyu Practitioners in the Western Himalaya. Typescript.
———. In press. The Making of a Gonpa: Norbu Rinpoche from Kardang. In *Tantra and Popular Religion in Tibet,* edited by Geoffrey Samuel. New Delhi, Aditya Prakashan.
Surkhang Wangchen Gelek. 1984. The Measurement of *lag 'don* Tax in Tibet. *TJ* 9:31–39.

Takasaki, Jikido. 1966. *A Study on the Ratnagotravibhāga (Uttaratantra).* Roma, IsMEO. (SER 33.)
Takpo Tashi Namgyal. 1986. *Mahamudra.* Translated by Lobsang Lhalungpa.
Tambiah, Stanley J. 1968. The Ideology of Merit and the Social Correlates of Buddhism in a Thai Village. In *Dialectic in Practical Religion,* edited by Edmund R. Leach, pp. 41–121. Cambridge, University Press.
———. 1970. *Buddhism and the Spirit Cults in North-East Thailand.* Cambridge, University Press.
———. 1976. *World Conqueror and World Renouncer: A Study of Buddhism and Polity in Thailand against a Historical Background.* Cambridge, University Press.
———. 1984. *The Buddhist Saints of the Forest and the Cult of Amulets: A Study in Charisma, Hagiography, Sectarianism and Millennial Buddhism* Cambridge, University Press.
———. 1985. *Culture, Thought, and Social Action: An Anthropological Perspective.* Harvard University Press.
Taring, Rinchen Dolma. 1986. *Daughter of Tibet.* London, Wisdom.
Taring, Zasak J. 1980. *Lhasa Tsug-Lag Khang gi Sata and Karchhag (The index and plan of Lhasa Cathedral in Tibet).* Dehra Dun, U. P., J. Taring.
———. 1984. *Map of Lhasa,* edited by Chie Nakane. Tokyo, Institute of Oriental Culture, University of Tokyo.
Tarthang Tulku. 1977a. *Time, Space, and Knowledge: A New Vision of Reality.*
———. 1977b. A History of the Buddhist Dharma. *Crystal Mirror* 5:3–330.
———. 1978. Gesar: Awareness through Myth. *Gesar* (Journal of the Nyingma Institute, Berkeley) 5(2):20–22.
Tatz, Mark. 1978. T'ang Dynasty Influences on the Early Spread of Buddhism in Tibet. *TJ* 3(2):3–32.
———. 1981. Songs of the Sixth Dalai Lama. *TJ* 6(4):13–31.

———. 1987. The Life of the Siddha-Philosopher Maitrigupta. *JAOS* 107(4):695–711.

Teichman, Eric. 1921. *Travels of a Consular Officer in North-West China.* Cambridge, University Press.

———. 1922. *Travels of a Consular Officer in Eastern Tibet.* Cambridge, University Press.

Templeman, David. 1981. Tāranātha the Historian. *TJ* 6(2):41–46.

———. 1983. *Tāranātha's bKa'.babs.bdun.ldan. The Seven Instruction Lineages by Jo.nang.Tāranātha.* Dharamsala, LTWA.

———. 1989. *Tāranātha's Life of Kṛṣṇācārya/Kāṇha.* Dharamsala, LTWA.

———. In press. Buddhist Tantric Song-Dohā, Vajragīti and Caryā Songs. In *Tantra and Popular Religion in Tibet,* edited by Geoffrey Samuel. New Delhi, Aditya Prakashan.

Terwiel, B. J. 1975. *Monks and Magic. An Analysis of Religious Ceremonies in Central Thailand.* Lund, Studentlitteratur. (Scandinavian Institute of Asian Studies Monograph Series 24.)

Tewari, Ramesh Chandra. 1987. Pre-Buddhist Elements in Himalayan Buddhism: The Institution of Oracles. *JIABS* 10(1):135–156.

Thapar, Romila. 1966. *A History of India,* vol. 1. Harmondsworth, Penguin.

Thar, Nyi-ma. 1989. On the Origin of the Tibetan Nationality. *Tibet Studies* (Lhasa) 2:193–201.

Tharchin, Geshe Lobsang. 1990. *Tsongkhapa: The Principal Teachings of Buddhism,* with a commentary by Pabongka Rinpoche, translated by Geshe Lobsang Tharchin with Michael Roach. Delhi, Classics India.

Thargyal, Rinzin. 1988. The Applicability of the Concept of Feudalism to Traditional Tibetan Society. In *Tibetan Studies. Proceedings of the 4th Seminar of the International Association for Tibetan Studies. Schloss Hohenkammer—Munich* 1985, edited by Helga Uebach and Jampa L. Panglung, pp. 391–396. Kommission für Zentralasiatische Studien, Bayerische Akademie der Wissenschaften.

Thinley, Karma (the 4th Karma Thinleypa). 1965. *Important Events and Places in the History of Nangchin Kham and E. Tibet.* Gangs ljongs mdo stod nang chen rgyal rabs dang 'brel ba'i lo rgyus phyogs bsdus ya rabs rna rgyan ces bya ba.

———. 1980. *The History of the Sixteen Karmapas of Tibet,* edited with an essay by David Stott. Boulder, Colorado, Prajñā Press.

Thondup, Ngawang. 1976. Rtze.slob.grwa-the Peak Academy of Tibet. In *Études Tibétaines,* edited by Ariane Spanien, pp. 75–89. (Actes du XXIXe Congrès International des Orientalistes. Paris. Juillet 1973).

Thondup [Rinpoche], Tulku. 1982. *The Dzog-chen Preliminary Practice of the Innermost Essence: The Long-chen Nying-thig Ngon-dro with Original Tibetan*

Root Text Composed by the Knowledge-Bearer Jig-me Ling-pa (1729–1798). Dharamsala, HP, LTWA.

———. 1984. *The Origin of Buddhism in Tibet: The Tantric Tradition of the Nyingmapa.* Marion, Massachusetts, Buddhayana.

———. 1986. *Hidden Teachings of Tibet: An Explanation of the Terma Tradition of the Nyingma School of Buddhism.* London, Wisdom.

———. 1987. *Buddhist Civilization in Tibet.* London, Routledge and Kegan Paul.

———. 1989. *Buddha Mind: An Anthology of Longchen Rabjam's Writings on Dzogpa Chenpo.* Ithaca, New York, Snow Lion.

Thubten Kalsang, Lama, et al. (trans.). 1983. *Atisha: A Biography of the Renowned Buddhist Sage.* Bangkok, Social Science Association Press.

Thurman, Robert A. F. 1982. *The Life and Teachings of Tsong Khapa.* Dharamsala, HP, LTWA.

———. 1984. *Tsong Khapa's Speech of Gold in the Essence of True Eloquence. Reason and Enlightenment in the Central Philosophy of Tibet,* translated with an introduction by R. A. F. Thurman. Princeton, New Jersey, Princeton University Press.

———. 1985. Tsoṅ-kha-pa's Integration of Sūtra and Tantra. In *Soundings in Tibetan Civilization,* edited by Barbara Aziz and Matthew Kapstein, pp. 372–383. New Delhi, Manohar. [*Proceedings* of 3d Seminar of IATS.]

Thutop Tulku and Ngawang Sonam Tenzin. 1968. *The Mañjuśrī Tradition and the Ženpa Židel (Parting from the Four Desires).* Dehra Dun, Sakya Centre.

Tobgyal, Orgyen. 1988. *The Life of Chokgyur Lingpa,* translated by Tulku Jigmey and Erik Pema Kunsang. 3d edition. Kathmandu, Rangjung Yeshe.

Toffin, Gérard (ed.). 1987. *Paysages et Divinités en Himalaya.* (Special issue of *Études Rurales* [107–108], Juillet–Décembre.)

Trippner, Josef. 1964. Die Salaren. *CAJ* 9:241–276.

Trungpa, Chögyam. 1971. *Born in Tibet.* Harmondsworth, Penguin.

———. 1972. *Mudra.* Berkeley and London, Shambhala.

———. 1978. Some Aspects of Pön. In *Himalayan Anthropology: The Indo-Tibetan Interface,* edited by James F. Fisher, pp. 299–308. The Hague, Mouton.

———. (trans.). 1980. *The Rain of Wisdom. Vajra Songs of the Kagyü Gurus,* translated by the Nalanda Translation Committee under the direction of Chögyam Trungpa. Boulder and London, Shambhala.

———. 1981. *Journey Without Goal: The Tantric Wisdom of the Buddha.* Boulder and London, Prajña Press.

———. 1982. *The Life of Marpa the Translator, by Tsang Nyön Heruka,* translated from the Tibetan by the Nalanda Translation Committee under the direction of Chögyam Trungpa. Boulder, Prajna.

Tsele Natsok Rangdrol. 1988. *Lamp of Mahamudra*, translated by Erik Pema Kunsang. Kathmandu, Rangjung Yeshe.

Tsering, Migmar. 1988. Sakya Pandita: Glimpses of His Three Major Works. *TJ* 13(1):12–19.

Tsering, Nawang. 1979. *Buddhism in Ladakh: A Study of the Life and Works of the 18th Century Ladakhi Saint Scholar.* New Delhi, Sterling.

———. 1985. A Survey of the Spread of Buddhadharma in Ladakh. In *Soundings in Tibetan Civilization*, edited by Barbara Aziz and Matthew Kapstein, pp. 157–164. New Delhi, Manohar. [*Proceedings* of 3d Seminar of IATS.]

Tsering, Pema. 1982. Epenkundliche und historische Ergebnisse einer Reise nach Tibet im Jahre 1980. *ZAS* 16:349–405.

Tsering, Tashi. 1985. Ñag-roṅ Mgon-po rnam-rgyal: A 19th Century Khams-pa Warrior. In *Soundings in Tibetan Civilization*, edited by Barbara Aziz and Matthew Kapstein, pp. 196–214. New Delhi, Manohar. [*Proceedings* of 3d Seminar of IATS.].

———. 1989. Preliminary Notes Towards the Reconstruction of the History and Genealogy of the Gling Tshang Dynasty of Kham. Paper given at the 5th Seminar of the IATS, Narita, August 27 to September 2, 1989.

Tsomo, Karma Lekshe. 1987. Tibetan Nuns and Nunneries. *TJ* 12(4):87–99.

Tsuda, Shin'ichi. 1978. A Critical Tantrism. *Memoirs of the Toyo Bunko* 36:167–231.

———. 1982. *'Vajrayoṣidbhageṣu Vijahāra':* Historical Survey from the Beginnings to the Culmination of Tantric Buddhism. In *Indological and Buddhist Studies: Volume in Honour of Prof. J. W. de Jong on his 60th Birthday*, edited by L. A. Hercus, pp. 595–616. Canberra, Australian National University, Faculty of Asian Studies.

Tucci, Giuseppe. 1949. *Tibetan Painted Scrolls.* 3 vols. Roma, Libreria dello Stato.

———. 1955. The Secret Characters [= Sacral Character] of the Kings of Ancient Tibet. *East and West* 6(2):197–205.

———. 1956. *To Lhasa and Beyond: Diary of the Expedition to Tibet in the Year MCMXLVIII.* Roma, Libreria dello Stato.

———. 1966. *Tibetan Folk Songs.* 2d edition. Ascona, Artibus Asiae.

———. 1967. *Tibet, Land of Snows.* London.

———. 1969. *The Theory and Practice of the Mandala.* London, Rider.

———. 1980. *The Religions of Tibet.* London, Routledge and Kegan Paul.

Turner, Victor W. 1974. *Dramas, Fields and Metaphors.* Ithaca, Cornell University Press.

Uhlig, Helmut. 1981. *Tantrische Kunst des Buddhismus*. Unter Mitarbeit von Heidi und Ulrich von Schroeder. Berlin, Safari bei Ullstein.

Uray, Geza. 1985. Vom römischen Kaiser bis zum König Ge-sar von Gliṅ. In *Fragen der mongolischen Heldendichtung: Teil III*, edited by Walther Heissig, pp. 530–548. Wiesbaden, Otto Harrassowitz. (Asiatische Forschungen 91.)

van der Kuijp, Leonard W. J. 1985. Miscellanea Apropos of the Philosophy of Mind in Tibet: Mind in Tibetan Buddhism. *TJ* 10(1):32–43.

———. 1989. U-rgyan Rin-chen-dpal and His Audiences with Qubilai and Shangda in 1292. Paper given at the 5th Seminar of IATS, Narita, August 27 to September 2, 1989.

van Sprengen, Wim. 1987. The Nyishangba of Manang: Geographical Perspectives on the Rise of a Nepalese Trading Community. *Kailash* 13(3–4).

van Tuyl, Charles D. 1975. The Tshe riṅ ma Account—an Old Document Incorporated into the Mi la ras pa'i mgur 'bum? *ZAS* 9:23–36.

Vinding, Michael. 1982. The Thakalis as Buddhists: A Closer Look at Their Death Ceremonies. *Kailash* 9(4):291–318.

von Schroeder, Ulrich. 1981. *Indo-Tibetan Bronzes*. Hong Kong, Visual Dharma.

Waddell, L. Austine. 1967. *The Buddhism of Tibet or Lamaism*. 2d edition. Cambridge, W. Heffer & Sons.

Wagner, Roy. 1978. *Lethal Speech: Daribi Myth as Symbolic Obviation*. Ithaca, Cornell University Press.

Walker, Deward E., Jr. 1987. Origins and Functions of Sacred Geography in American Indian Cultures of the Northern Rockies. Paper given to Harvard Workshop on Sacred Geography, Center for the Study of World Religions, Harvard University, May 1987.

Wangyal, Geshe. 1973. *The Door of Liberation*. New York, Maurice Girodias.

Wangyal, Geshe, and Brian Cutillo. 1988. *Sakya Pandita: Illuminations*. New York, Lotsawa.

Warder, A. K. 1970. *Indian Buddhism*. Delhi, Motilal Banarsidass.

Wayman, Alex. 1955. Notes on the Sanskrit Term *Jñana*. *JAOS* 75(4):253–268.

———. 1961. Totemic Beliefs in the Buddhist Tantras. *HR* 1(1):81–94.

———. 1971. Buddhist Dependent Origination. *HR* 10:185–203.

———. 1973. *The Buddhist Tantras: Light on Indo-Tibetan Esotericism*. New York, Samuel Weiser.

———. 1977. Doctrinal Disputes and the Debates of bSam yas. *CAJ* 21(2):139–144.

———. 1978. *Calming the Mind and Discerning the Real.* New York, Columbia University Press.

———. 1980a. Dependent Origination—the Indo-Tibetan Tradition. *J. Chinese Philosophy* 7:275–300.

———. 1980b. *Yoga of the Guhyasamājatantra: The Arcane Lore of Forty Verses.* New York, Samuel Weiser.

———. 1980c. Observations on the History and Influence of the Buddhist Tantra in India and Tibet. In *Studies in History of Buddhism,* edited by A. K. Narain, pp. 359–363. Delhi.

Weber, Max. 1966. *The Sociology of Religion.* London, Social Science Paperbacks in association with Methuen.

———. 1967. *The Religion of India.* Free Press Paperback edition. New York, Free Press.

Welch, Holmes. 1967. *The Practice of Chinese Buddhism.* Cambridge, Massachusetts, Harvard University Press.

Wijeyewardene, Gehan. 1986. *Place and Emotion in Northern Thai Ritual Behaviour.* Bangkok, Pandora.

Williams, Paul M. 1980. Tsong-kha-pa on *kun-rdzob bden-pa.* In *Tibetan Studies in Honour of Hugh Richardson. Proceedings of the International Seminar on Tibetan Studies, Oxford* 1979, edited by Michael Aris and Aung San Suu Kyi, pp. 325–334. Warminster, Aris and Phillips. [= Proceedings of 2d Seminar of IATS.]

Willis, Janice D. 1979. *On Knowing Reality: The Tattvārtha Chapter of Asaṅga's Bodhisattvabhūmi.* New York, Columbia University Press.

———. 1984. Tibetan A-nis: The Nun's Life in Tibet. *TJ* 9(4):14–32.

———. 1985. On the Nature of *rnam-thar:* Early Dge-lugs-pa *Siddha* Biographies. In *Soundings in Tibetan Civilization,* edited by Barbara Aziz and Matthew Kapstein, pp. 304–319. New Delhi, Manohar. [*Proceedings* of 3d Seminar of IATS.]

Willson, Martin. 1986. *In Praise of Tārā.* London, Wisdom.

Wilson, Peter J. 1973. *Crab Antics: The Social Anthropology of English-Speaking Negro Societies of the Caribbean.* New Haven and London, Yale University Press.

Wu Congzhong. 1989. The Deng People Developing from Blood Relationship to Territorial Relationship. *Tibet Studies* (Lhasa) 2:180–192.

Wylie, Turrell V. 1959. A Standard System of Tibetan Transcription. *HJAS* 22:261–276.

———. 1962. *The Geography of Tibet according to the 'Dzam-gLing-rGyas-bShad.* Roma, IsMEO. (SER 25.)

———. 1963. Mar.pa's Tower: Notes on Local Hegemons in Tibet. *HR* 3:278–291.

———. 1964. Ro-langs: The Tibetan Zombie. *HR* 4:69–80.

———. 1978. Reincarnation: A Political Innovation in Tibetan Buddhism. In *Proceedings of the Csoma de Kőrös Memorial Symposium Held at Mátrafüred, Hungary, 24–30 September 1976*, edited by Louis Ligeti, pp. 579–586. Budapest, Akadémiai Kiadó.

———. 1980a. Monastic Patronage in 15th-Century Tibet. *AOH* 34:319–328.

———. 1980b. Lama Tribute in the Ming Dynasty. In *Tibetan Studies in Honour of Hugh Richardson. Proceedings of the International Seminar on Tibetan Studies, Oxford 1979*, edited by Michael Aris and Aung San Suu Kyi, pp. 335–340. Warminster, Aris and Phillips. [= Proceedings of 2d Seminar of IATS.]

Yamamoto, Chikyo. 1990. *Mahāvairocana-Sūtra. Translated into English from the Chinese version of Śubhākarasiṁha and I-hsing (A.D. 725).* New Delhi, IAIC and Aditya Prakashan. (ŚP 359.)

Yang Enhong. 1989. On Artists Who Perform the Epic 'King Gesar.' Paper for the 1st International Symposium on Gesar Epic Studies, Chengdu, November 1–4, 1989.

———. 1990. The Forms of Chanting Gesar and the Bon Religion in Tibet. Paper for the International Seminar on Anthropology of Tibet and the Himalayas, Völkerkundemuseum der Universität Zürich, September 21–28, 1990.

Yocum, Glenn E. 1980. Buddhism through Hindu Eyes: Śaivas and Buddhists in Medieval Tamilnad. Paper for the 14th Congress of the International Association of the History of Religions, Winnipeg, August 1980.

Yuthok, Dorje Yudon. 1990. *House of the Turquoise Roof*, edited by Michael Harlin. Ithaca, New York, Snow Lion.

Zaehner, Robert C. 1977. *Hinduism.* Oxford University Press.

Zangbu, Ngawang Tenzin (Tengboche Lama), and Frances Klatzel. 1988. *Stories and Customs of the Sherpas.* Kathmandu, Khumbu Cultural Conservation Committee.

Zhabs-drung, Tshe-brtan. 1986. *Bod rgya tshig mdzod chen mo.* 3 vols. Beijing, Nationalities Publishing House.

Zvelebil, Kamil V. The Beginnings of *Bhakti* in South India. *Temenos* 13:222–257.

Index